Taking Stock

The Status of Criminological Theory

Advances in Criminological Theory
Volume 15

Edited by

Francis T. Cullen,
John Paul Wright
& Kristie R. Blevins

Transaction Publishers
New Brunswick (U.S.A.) and London (U.K.)

Second printing 2009

Copyright © 2008 by Transaction Publishers, New Brunswick, New Jersey.

Library of Congress Catalog Number: 2006040436
ISBN: 978-1-4128-0856-9
Printed in the United States of America

Library of Congress Cataloging-in-Publication Data

Taking stock: the status of criminological theory / Francis T. Cullen, John Paul
    Wright, Kristie R. Blevins, editors.
        p. cm. — (Advances in criminological theory; v. 15)
    Includes bibliographical references and indexes.
    ISBN 978-1-4128-0856-9 (alk. paper)
        1. Criminology.   I.   Cullen, Francis T.   II.   Wright, John Paul.   III.
Blevins,   Kristie R. IV.
        Series.

HV6018.T35   2006
364—dc22   2006040436

Contents

Part III. Theories of Power and Peace

Part IV. Life-Course Theories

Part V. Theories of Societal Reaction

Introduction:
Taking Stock of Criminological Theory

Francis T. Cullen, John Paul Wright, and Kristie R. Blevins

Criminology is experiencing unprecedented theoretical vitality. Traditional theories are reappearing in fresh forms that offer bold insights, while newer perspectives challenging old ways of thinking have emerged and garnered much notoriety. These theories earn their adherents because they are often elegantly stated, resonate with scholars' understanding of the world, and furnish an abundance of research "puzzles" to solve (Cole 1975). To be sure, this conceptual richness is not inevitable. In the early days of criminology, for example, the number of prominent theories was small—easily counted on a single hand. And two decades ago, scholars could accurately speak of the "demise of the criminological imagination" (Williams 1984). Even so, a variety of conditions have coalesced to encourage the discipline's theoretical diversity.

For one thing, there has been an increasing recognition that crime is a complex phenomenon that exists on different levels of analysis, manifests itself in various ways across the life course, is linked to forces inside and outside the individual, and is enmeshed in contexts extending from situational dynamics to socio-political, historical eras. Criminology also is becoming increasing interdisciplinary—not just in name but in practice. The immigration of scholars possessing special disciplinary knowledge and worldviews into criminology has infused the field with distinctive conceptual approaches. These scholars see crime from innovative angles that elaborate, if not change, the discourse about the causes of offending behavior. Ideology, as well, plays a role in ensuring that a comfortable theoretical consensus does not emerge. In particular, political sentiments are a source of the background assumptions that cause criminologists to self-select into theoretical camps whose perimeters they vigilantly defend (e.g., those who see crime as rooted in individual pathology versus unjust structural conditions).

Theoretical vibrancy certainly is preferable to a discipline mired in the conceptual doldrums (Collins 1986). But criminology risks an embarrassment of riches—of having too much of a good thing. As more and more plausible theories are authored, it becomes intellectually bewildering for the average criminologist—whether faculty member, student, or interested observer. It is possible, of course, to read and learn all the theories—to become "culturally literate" in this area by mastering a combination of primary sources and theory textbooks. The more stubborn challenge, however, is to be well informed as to which perspectives have empirical merit and thus deserve our allegiance. Such knowledge is confined only to the most ardent readers and organizers of the literature.

One barrier to seeing the forest through the trees of criminological theories is that we are notoriously inept at getting rid of perspectives that have scant empirical support. Convincing falsification is difficult because data sets generally are not complex enough to measure theories systematically and because it is typically impossible to test competing ideas through experimental designs (see, however, Cullen, Wright, Gendreau, and Andrews 2003). We also lack any firm rules as to what would constitute a theory being disproved to the point of abandonment. And no committee of criminologists has yet to be appointed with the mandate and power to render binding judgments on which theories should live and which should die!

In an imperfect disciplinary world, it is too much to anticipate a dramatic departure from this state of affairs. Even so, doing nothing strikes us as an unsatisfactory course to follow. Instead, we need a *middle-range* approach—one between leaving things as they are and a formal body to render judgments on each theory's viability. This middle-range approach might involve various strategies, but common to this enterprise would be the intent to *systematically organize theoretical knowledge—especially as it relates to each perspective's empirical status.*

Criminologists cannot be content simply to theorize or even to undertake individual studies that test the theories they set forth. An equally important task is to devote their efforts to *taking stock* of the theoretical research that is produced but otherwise remains poorly organized. As a discipline, we need to have a clear sense of where we are and where we should head. If not, then criminology risks being a field of study in which many ideas are developed and all are chosen—in which all theories have an equal claim to legitimacy and in which only the most highly specialized scholars can separate the theoretical wheat from the chaff.

Serious efforts to "take stock" of criminological theory exist but remain in short supply (for exceptions, see Akers and Sellers 2004; Burton and Cullen 1992; Kempf 1993; Pratt and Cullen 2000, 2005; Pratt, Sellers, Cullen, Winfree, and Madensen 2005; Thornberry and Krohn 2003). In this context, the current project was initiated as one effort to move criminology forward in the organization of its theoretical knowledge. The strategy was to entice scholars who had either authored a specific theory or had been prominent within a theoretical tradition to take stock of their respective perspectives. We were fortunate that, virtually without exception, the scholars who were contacted generously agreed to participate in the project. The resulting essays (with two exceptions) were first presented in seven Presidential Plenary Sessions that we organized for the 2004 meeting of the American Society of Criminology in Nashville, TN. With the support of Freda Adler and William S. Laufer, the general editors of the *Advances in Criminological Theory* series, the theorists prepared works for the ASC conference that they understood would eventually be published collectively in this volume.

The scholars have approached the task of taking stock of their theories in distinctive ways, in large part because the perspectives have different traditions and have been subjected to vastly different amounts and kinds of empirical scrutiny. Even so, the common purpose of each of the chapters is to inform fellow criminologists as to the status of the theory under consideration. It is thus intended that this collective effort in organizing criminological knowledge will clarify for readers both the accomplishments of, and challenges that await, the major theoretical perspectives of our discipline.

In developing this volume, difficult choices had to be made. First, in a discipline as diverse as criminology, it was not possible to include, under one cover, a review of every theory worthy of serious consideration. In making these decisions, we attempted to select a mixture of perspectives that reflected the wide *scope* of thinking in criminology. The end result has been a rich collection of works that explore both mainstream and critical perspectives, that span levels of analysis and periods in the life course, and that take as their starting points offenders and societal reaction to offenders.

Second, in organizing the volume, we made decisions on the *structure* of criminological theory—on which perspectives cohered into a common way of thinking and on how perspectives might be sequenced in terms of their development. This effort to provide a road map through criminological theory admittedly represents a social construction of reality—though, of course, we believe that it is defensible as a way to understand criminology's contemporary theoretical landscape. Other ways to envision criminology are undoubtedly possible, and we will leave it to motivated readers to explore these. In any case, consistent with our thinking, the current volume is organized into five parts, which we will discuss below.

The Core of Criminological Theory

For numerous decades, three theories have dominated American criminology: differential association/social learning theory, control theory, and anomie/strain theory (Agnew, 2001a: 117). These perspectives emerged and took hold of the field during the period that extended from the 1930s to the 1960s—what Laub (2004: 6) calls the "Golden Age of Theory." Together, the three paradigms comprise the "core of criminological theory." Three considerations underlie this designation.

First, these traditions have remained central to the field from the early days of American criminology, across the intervening decades, and into the present day (Kornhauser 1978). They are represented by contemporary versions, which are considered in Part I of this volume in the chapters authored by Akers and Jensen, Gottfredson, and Agnew. Second, the theories permeate other areas of criminological thinking. Thus, elements of these perspectives are often used in the formulation of newer theories (e.g., Braithwaite 1989; Colvin 2000; Sampson and Laub 1993) or are consolidated into "integrated" theories (e.g., Cloward and Ohlin 1960; Elliott, Ageton, and Canter 1979; Thornberry 1987). Third, although other perspectives are tested—and some are earning concentrated attention—these three theories have long generated a wealth of empirical studies (Akers and Sellers 2004; Burton and Cullen 1992; Kempf 1993; Pratt et al. 2005). Indeed, they are often portrayed as rival theories and have been tested against one another repeatedly (Hirschi 1969; Unnever, Cullen, and Agnew 2006).

Differential association/social learning theory and control theory trace their roots to a common ancestor: the Chicago School of criminology and, in particular, to the writings of Clifford Shaw and Henry McKay. Today, Shaw and McKay are mostly remembered for their analysis of the criminogenic effects of social disorganization and its antecedent structural conditions (e.g., poverty, heterogeneity, residential mobility, urbanism/density). In the contemporary literature, social disorganization is most often portrayed as the inability of a group to achieve its goals—such as social order—by effectively asserting informal controls. The linkage of crime to the *breakdown of control* is a common theme among early Chicago School theorists (Reckless 1961; Reiss 1951), and it is represented in various forms in current control theories.

As Kornhauser (1978; see also, Finestone 1976) recognized, however, Shaw and McKay did not limit their theorizing to the issue of control but offered a "mixed model" of delinquency. Drawing on the Chicago School's interest in culture conflict and on life-history research they conducted with delinquent boys (e.g., Shaw 1930; Shaw, McKay, and MacDonald 1938), Shaw and McKay also traced criminal participation to the delinquent traditions that arose in disorganized neighborhoods. These traditions were culturally transmitted, with younger youths learning criminal values and skills from older siblings and from youths in the community. Edwin Sutherland would later systematize these insights into his nine principles that constituted his theory of differential association.

The roots of strain theory extend to Robert Merton's (1938) "Social Structure and Anomie"—an essay of but ten pages that became perhaps the most cited work in the history of criminology (Cole 1975). Merton's theory was conceptualized at the macro-level, given that his primary concern was in explaining why rates of deviant behavior, including crime, were higher in the United States than in other nations and, within the U.S., higher in the lower social strata. He argued that the chief cultural goal of America—the universal prescription for all individuals to seek pecuniary success and social ascent—was malintegrated with a social structure that provided restricted, not universal, access to this goal. The result of this inconsistency was to exert pressure on the institutional norms that regulated acceptable or "institutional" means to attain success. As the norms attenuated due to this structural strain, "anomie" resulted and high rates of deviance ensued.

Although not often recognized, Merton's macro-level anomie theory is, in essence, a control theory: an explanation of why regulatory norms lose their power to "control" conduct. However, embedded with Merton's paradigm was a second theory that would ultimately gain more attention than his anomie perspective (Cullen 1984; Messner 1988). Although Merton was not interested in people's psychological states, it was implicit in his essay that individuals lacking opportunities would experience frustration when blocked from the cherished goal of material success. As his "typology of individual adaptations" suggested, many of these pressured people would adapt through deviant behavior. This individual-level theory would become known as "strain theory."

Hirschi (1969) was most responsible for reifying these theories into distinct, incompatible perspectives (see also, Kornhauser 1978). In *Causes of Delinquency*, he demarcated "three fundamental perspectives on delinquency and deviant behavior": strain theory, cultural deviance theory, and control theory (1969:3). In a concise and brilliant way, he proceeded to explain the central propositions of the theories and why the "reconciliation of their assumptions is very difficult" (p. 4). Hirschi then showed how, using self-report survey data, it was possible to measure the theoretical constructs and to test their relative empirical merits (Laub 2002). In this way—and in what constituted a major turning point in the discipline (Laub 2004)—Hirschi thus established the standard for theorizing in criminology: set forth a distinct theory and then test it against its rivals (see also, Hirschi 1989).

These three theories have shown remarkable durability—resisting all attempts to relegate them to the criminological dustbin. Central to their continued vitality, however, has been their capacity to be *evolving paradigms*. Thus, differential association theory has become more formalized as social learning theory (Akers 1998). Control theory has expanded from social bond theory (Hirschi 1969) to include self-control theory (Gottredson and Hirschi 1990). And strain theory—most at risk of being dismissed as empirically vacuous (Burton and Cullen 1992)—has been revitalized by "general strain theory" (Agnew 1992). In Part I of this volume, these three contemporary theories are assessed.

In chapter 1, Ronald Akers and Gary Jensen perform three important services. First, in a judicious review that attempts not to overstate the strength of social learning variables in extant studies, they nonetheless are able to show that their theory has achieved *consistent* empirical support across time periods, social contexts, varying measures of the theory's central explanatory variables, types of criminal and deviant behaviors, types of samples, and study designs (e.g., tested as a single theory or against rival theoretical approaches). This consistency lends credence to the conclusion that social learning processes are integral to criminal conduct (see also, Pratt et al. 2005).

Second, they caution against the tendency in the criminological literature to truncate social learning theory into the simple proposition that: *associating with peers—as measured by the number of delinquent friends one has—causes crime.* They remind us that social learning involves more than just differential association or even learned definitions; two less frequently studied learning mechanisms include differential reinforcement and imitation. They remind us as well that learning occurs in a variety of contexts, including the family. This latter observation is important because parental behavior in families, especially acts involving discipline, have been seen by criminologists as the province of control theory. They ask, "What is socialization and informal social control in the family if it is not social learning?" And they note that the "typical empirical measures of control theory variables such as family parental control, discipline, and management (parental sanctions) are transparently measures of differential social reinforcement (rewards and punishments) for conforming and nonconforming or disobedient behavior."

Third and perhaps most noteworthy, they outline an agenda for creating a distinctly *macro-level* social learning theory. Although Sutherland was not unmindful of macro-level issues, he devoted his thinking primarily to developing a systematic theory of why some individuals engage in criminal behavior and others do not. Thus, he developed propositions for his theory of differential association but not for a theory of social disorganization or, as he later termed it, differential social organization. Within criminology, Sutherland's legacy—for better or for worse—has been to define differential association theory and its successor, social learning theory, as a micro-level perspective. In chapter 1, however, Akers and Jensen suggest that social learning theory can be used to explain ecological variations in crime rates. In part, this might involve using the social learning perspective as a compositional theory, with crime rates reflecting the aggregation of individuals drawn into crime by learning processes. More interesting, however, is their claim that social learning concepts can be used to identify distinctly macro-level processes that can account not only for variations in crime rates across contexts but also for why rates of particular types of illegality might spike upward or downward. If their attempt to "macrotize" social learning theory proves successful, it might well provide new opportunities for theoretical and empirical research among macro-level criminologists.

In chapter 2, Michael Gottfredson provides an illuminating commentary on control perspectives, especially on Hirschi's (1969) social bond theory and, with Hirschi, on his own self-control theory (Gottfredson and Hirschi 1990). He argues that two distinguishing orientations inform control theories. First, scholars in this tradition have shown an abiding commitment to start with the prevailing empirical knowledge about crime and then to build their theories to explain these "foundational facts" (e.g., stability in individual differences in the propensity to offend; early delinquency predicts later delinquency; an inverse relationship between delinquency and ties to parents and doing well in school; versatility in offending; the interrelationship between participation in crime and other deviant behaviors). This strategy ensures that "a substantial empirical literature is consistent with" control theory, which gives this approach an advantage over rival perspectives that have not shown such initial fidelity to what is known about crime. It also helps to explain why control theories have long seen childhood as integral to crime causation and have argued that"childhood causes far outweigh in importance causes coming later in life."

Second, control theories embrace the assumptions that "people are all alike in that they tend to pursue self-interest" and that crime—and analogous deviant behaviors—are attractive to individuals because they supply immediate, easy gratification. Motivation to engage in wayward behavior thus is not problematic and, in fact, is seen as "relatively constant" across people. What is variable—and hence explains variation in criminal participation—is the degree to which self-interested individuals are restrained from the enticements crime offers. Such restraint or control is hypothesized to be produced by "the connections among individuals in society....these connections are referred to as the social bond—the glue connecting the individual to society."

In his essay, Gottfredson covers a range of topics (e.g., the debate with social learning theory over peer effects, the measurement of self-control). Even so, two theoretical clarifications offered by Gottfredson are particularly relevant and perhaps deserve special mention. First, he disclaims that his general theory of crime ever argued that self-control is the "sole cause of crime." Apart from self-control, crime is influenced by age, by opportunity, and by the gratifying nature of crime itself. Rather, Gottfredson and Hirschi only argued that self-control is the "most important individual-difference cause of crime." Admittedly, this is a bold enough assertion, since "as a general cause," self-control "should predict rate differences everywhere, for all crimes, delinquencies and related behaviors, for all times, among all groups and countries." His review of the extant literature is organized to show the empirical validity of this proposition.

Second, an odd omission in Gottfredson and Hirschi's (1990) *A General Theory of Crime* was the failure to discuss how self-control theory differs, or does not differ, from Hirschi's (1969) social bond theory, its direct intellectual predecessor. To an important extent, Gottfredson takes up this challenge and, in doing so, largely rejects those who see the theories as distinct, if not incompatible (Lilly, Cullen, and Ball 2002; Taylor 2001; Unnever et al., 2006). For Gottfredson, loving parents care enough to exert the effort to monitor and, if necessary, to sanction their children's behavior. This parenting style creates self-control. Here, however, Gottfredson adds the innovative insight that this self-control "is expressed by affection from the child to the parent and, by logical extension, to other socializing agents like schools and friends." In short, self-control makes attachment possible; it is the conduit through which social bonds from children to parents (and other conventional adults) are established and, by implication, are sustained. The connection is so close that social bonds and self-control become "very difficult to discriminate empirically." Still, questions remain. In particular, it is unclear whether social bonds have a unique causal effect or are merely another outcome of self-control. In the first case, social bonds would have a feedback effect, helping to restrain criminal impulses and possibly solidifying self-control. In the second case, any relationship between social bonds and crime would be spurious; both would be manifestations of self-control.

In developing "general strain theory"—now known by its popular acronym of "GST"—Robert Agnew (1992) has done more to rescue individual-level strain theory than any other scholar. He had the simple but consequential insight that the blockage of desired goals, such as economic success, was not the only source of strain. Beyond this type of pressure identified in the "classic" Mertonian tradition, he offered two other categories: the removal of valued stimuli ("losing something [people] value") and the presentation of noxious stimuli (being "treated in an aversive or negative manner by others"). Scholars soon realized that these strains could be operationalized in a myriad of ways—often with measures found in secondary data sets; the result was the publication of extensive research on GST (see also, Cole 1975). Agnew's paradigm included, as well, a second theoretical dimension. Building on the classic strain theory idea that strain does not inevitably lead to crime and thus that the adaptation to such pressures must be explained (Cullen 1984), Agnew identified a host of "conditioning" factors that make the response of criminal behavior, as opposed to conforming behavior, more or less likely. This feature to his theory has also generated a substantial body of research.

In chapter 3, Agnew reviews this research, showing how it has informed the evolution of GST over the past decade. At the conclusion of the essay, he sets forth a list of "the major propositions of GST as of 2005," which should be invaluable in directing future theory and research. Here, we call attention to three issues that represent significant advances to the original statement of the GST paradigm.

First, given the wide diversity of factors tested under GST as potential strains, Agnew has addressed the thorny task of sorting out which strains are, or are not, likely to be criminogenic. "Those strains most likely to cause crime" he proposes, "are seen as high in magnitude, are seen as unjust, are associated with low control, and create some pressure or incentive to engage in criminal coping" (see also, Agnew, 2001b). Second, a central feature of GST is the thesis that "negative emotions create pressure for corrective action, with crime being one possible response." Previous research has focused on the role of anger in fostering criminal adaptations. Agnew wishes to broaden this interest in emotions by examining a wider array of emotions (e.g., depression, anxiety, envy), the link between specific emotions and specific forms of crime, and the role of strain in generating emotional traits conducive to wayward conduct. Third, Agnew also encourages efforts to investigate how GST intersects with alternative criminological perspectives. He describes the "relationship between GST and other theories" as "quite intimate." As Agnew observes, "strain may reduce control, foster social learning of crime, and contribute to personality traits conducive to crime; these factors, in turn, may increase strain; and all of these factors may interact with one another in their effect on crime."

Macro-Level Theories

As noted, Hirschi's (1969) *Causes of Delinquency* reshaped the criminological enterprise by demonstrating the merits of rigorously defining theories and then of testing them using self-report data. An unanticipated consequence of this scholarly style was to encourage micro-level theory and, in particular, research. As a practical matter, criminologists could distribute surveys in a high school—completed by individual students—in a short period of time and, in turn, have a data set capable of yielding multiple publications. It was less clear how macro-level research on crime might be conducted. Accordingly, in the 1970s, research on this level of analysis stagnated.

Two classic research articles, however, were perhaps most responsible for revitalizing interest in macro-level studies of crime rates; in the subsequent years, over 200 empirical works would appear (Pratt and Cullen 2005). First, Blau and Blau (1982) combined FBI statistics and Census data to show that high rates of violent crime were a "cost" of racial and economic inequality in major metropolitan areas. This finding focused attention on how structural inequality is a salient root cause of crime rates both within the United States and, potentially, compared to other nations. Beyond this noteworthy finding, the Blau and Blau piece was an exemplar for how to conduct macro-level research: use information from Census (or similar) sources to develop measure of structural characteristics (e.g., inequality) and see how these factors predict rates of crime across ecological areas (e.g., SMSAs).

The same was true for a second work that appeared later in the decade. Aggregating the responses to the British Crime Survey of 10,905 respondents spread across 238 ecological units in England and Wales, Sampson and Groves (1989) were able to examine how area characteristics were associated with rates of crime victimization. Because individuals were surveyed about neighborhood informal controls, this approach allowed Sampson and Groves to measure directly the construct of social disorganization and to demonstrate that, consistent with Shaw and McKay's thesis, community disorganization mediated the impact of structural antecedents on crime rates. Once seen as a biased perspective for describing inner-city life as "disorganized," these results helped to provide an empirical basis for substantial interest in social disorganization theory (Lowenkamp, Cullen, and Pratt 2003).

In this context, Steven Messner and Richard Rosenfeld (1994) made a major theoretical breakthrough in advancing their "institutional-anomie theory"; we will use the acronym "IAT" to refer to this perspective. As noted, Merton's macro-level anomie theory had been largely ignored, as criminologists turned their attention to testing micro-level strain theory (Cullen 1984; Messner 1988). Messner and Rosenfeld, however, argued that criminology was impoverished by the neglect of this anomie theory and its understanding of crime as rooted in the U.S.'s cultural and social structures.

They agreed with Merton that the "American Dream"—the excessive emphasis on the universal acquisition of pecuniary success—fostered anomie by robbing institutional norms of their power and by creating a situation in which technical expediency, not moral standards, guided behavioral choices. Most salient, they expanded Merton's focus on the economy to include other major social institutions (i.e., family, education, polity, religion). Given the cultural emphasis on the American Dream, the economy assumes a dominant position, with other institutions subservient to economic goals. This institutional imbalance of power weakens the ability of America's non-economic institutions to exert control and supply support. The result is the emergence of conditions ripe for high rates of serious crime, which are often asserted to characterize the U.S.

Despite the difficulty of measuring key theoretical constructs across nations and within the United States, Messner and Rosenfeld's macro-sociological theory has generated a growing empirical literature. As shown in chapter 4 in Part II of the volume, the research has divided along two lines. First, studies of the *institutional dimension* of IAT have generally been supportive in showing that strong non-economic institutions tend either to moderate (tested through interaction terms) or mediate (tested through indirect relationships) the effects of the economy on crime rates. Second, research on the *cultural dimension* of IAT has been more mixed in whether the U.S. is "exceptional" in its emphasis on the desire for individual material wealth and on the values that reflect the dominance of economic institutions (e.g., support for free enterprise over government regulation of markets).

In chapter 5, Robert Sampson notes that "neighborhoods show remarkable continuities in patterns of criminal activity"—patterns characterized by the "non-random concentration of crime in certain neighborhoods." Many scholars have taken a "risk factor" approach to this problem, documenting the empirical correlates of higher versus lower rates of crime (Pratt and Cullen

2005). Although valuable, Sampson points out the need to interpret why these relationships remain by discerning "the underlying social mechanisms theoretically at work."

Given his classic study of Shaw and McKay's work discussed above (Sampson and Groves, 1989), we might have expected Sampson to use their disorganization perspective to tackle this theoretical task. But he does not. Although working within the Chicago School tradition, Sampson concludes that social disorganization theory is limited by the "idyllic notion" of the crime prevention powers of "'urban villages' characterized by dense social networks." As Snodgrass (1976) shows, the prime theorists in the Chicago School were raised in small, rural, midwestern communities—or "villages"—marked by close interpersonal ties and strong informal controls. It thus made sense for them to propose that crime and vice emerged in those areas within cities where "village life" had broken down under the pressure of the urban experience. By contrast, Sampson proposes that while dense social networks may play a role in limiting crime, twenty-first century America is characterized by "new urban realities." It is a social place where weak ties may matter as much as strong ties, where new forms of communications exist that do not require face-to-face interaction (e.g., internet), and where the capacity among neighbors to act in concert when a problem arises may be more important than having dinner with one another on a regular basis.

In this context, Sampson attempts to move beyond social disorganization theory by proposing, as a "key form of social organization," the concept of "collective efficacy" (see also, Sampson, Raudenbush, and Earls 1997). Collective efficacy consists of two intertwined dimensions: first, social cohesion, which involves "an emphasis on working trust and mutual support"; and, second, efficacy, which involves the "shared expectations for social control." Unlike social disorganization, which is a largely static social state, collective efficacy implies community differences in the more dynamic ability to act and be effective when specific problems arise. Thus, neighborhoods high on collective efficacy have the capacity for "agency"—that is, the ability to organize to confront problems, such as crime.

Collective efficacy is fostered by dense social networks but also has its roots in structural resources (e.g., high economic status, residential stability) and in organizational infrastructure or the "density of non-profit organizations." However, opening up a potentially important line of inquiry, Sampson also contends that collective efficacy—or the lack thereof—may have a feedback effect that either reinforces or attenuates the social and economic well-being of a neighborhood. In this way, levels of collective efficacy may be an important source of why some communities prosper over time while others experience a spiral of decay and decline (see also, Skogan 1990).

In *American Apartheid*, Massey and Denton (1993: 1) observe that during "the 1970s and 1980s a word disappeared from the American vocabulary....The word was segregation." They argue that though vaguely aware of racial patterns in housing, few citizens, policymakers, or scholars understand the degree of racial segregation experienced by African Americans or that "no group in the history of the United States has ever experienced the sustained high level of residential segregation that has been imposed on blacks in large American cities for the past fifty years" (p. 2). This apartheid-like situation "did not just happen" but rather was "manufactured by whites through a series of actions and purposeful institutional arrangements that continue today" (p. 2). Segregation is consequential because it concentrates, for lengthy periods of time, deprivation in black neighborhoods. Further, as Massey and Denton illuminate, the deleterious "effect of segregation on black well-being is structural, not individual. Residential segregation lies beyond the ability of any individual to change; it constrains black life chances irrespective of personal traits, individual motivation, or private achievements" (pp. 2-3).

With few exceptions, criminologists have been among those who have ignored racial segregation—an enduring and central fact of American life. There has been ongoing attention to racial economic inequality (Blau and Blau 1982; Pratt and Cullen 2005), but the specific role of racial *segregation* in producing this inequality and the concomitant criminogenic effects of racial isolation have received less consideration (see, however, Sampson and Wilson 1995). In chapter 5, Ruth Peterson, Lauren Krivo, and Christopher Browning seek to rectify this omission by bringing back into the discussion of inequality and crime the "forgotten factor" (Massey and Denton, 1993: 3) of racial segregation. Noting that social problems vary across communities, they assert that "segregation is a central structural force that sets the stage for differences in crime across groups." In fact, they continue, "its role as a source of criminal inequality has been undertheorized."

Taking up this challenge, Peterson, Krivo, and Browning identify three major ways in which racial segregation accounts for "spatial inequality" in crime rates across ecological areas. First, disadvantages that are tied to race (e.g., poverty, more single-parent families) now are corralled into definable communities. Above and beyond the impact conditions might have on individuals, this *concentration* of disadvantage has negative effects that would not exist if race did not define residence. Community-level processes emerge—such as the evolution and transmission of cultural traditions, weakened informal controls, out-migration of more advantaged residents, and the decline of the local economy—that foster high rates of crime and, in particular, of violence. Second, African American communities are placed further at risk by political and commercial decisions that lead to economic disinvestment and the use of black areas for dumps, highways, and stadium construction. The result is increased social isolation, instability that attenuates informal controls, and physical blight that undermines "defensible space." And third, segregated African American neighborhoods often do not exist as an island amidst a sea of white communities, but rather are clustered together. This phenomenon—what Peterson and her colleagues call "local segregation"—"means that communities are vulnerable to spillover from adjoining areas." Crime is thus amplified, not mitigated, by the concentration of disadvantage not only within but also around individual African American communities.

Theories of Power and Peace

Criminological theories can claim to be "new" to the extent that they illuminate a part of reality that previous theories have ignored or treated as though it were of secondary importance. The assertion is made that existing perspectives are incomplete, if not incorrect—that is, they distort reality—because they leave out a causal condition that is fundamental to crime. In the 1970s, a category of theories, which went by many names but might best be called "critical criminology," emerged that succeeded in offering such a fresh understanding of crime (Bohm 1982; Greenberg 1993; Taylor, Walton, and Young 1973, 1975). In its simplest terms, these perspectives shared the belief that "mainstream" theories had ignored the role that power, rooted in the prevailing political economy, plays in the creation of crime.

This view drew inspiration and then popularity from the social context of the times (Bohm 1982; Greenberg 1993; Lilly et al. 2002). As is well known, a series of major social events coalesced to unmask enduring barriers to equality and to question the legitimacy of the government: the Civil Rights Movement, the Women's movement, urban insurgency and riots, assassinations of public figures, the Vietnam War, Kent State and the suppression of protest, Watergate, revelations of corporate corruption, and a counter-cultural movement that challenged traditional structures of authority. Enmeshed in this context, scholars could not avoid probing how powerful interests controlled what was, or was not, called a crime; how race, class, and gender inequities were reproduced in the "extra-legal," discriminatory decisions of criminal justice officials; and how the wide gaps in economic wealth generated by unfettered capitalism fostered street crime by brutalizing the poor and, in contrast, white-collar crime by giving corporate and other powerful actors strong incentives to amorally pursue their interests with little regard for the consequences of their conduct. These scholars also wondered how traditional "core" theories could ignore the world around them—that is, could ignore the reality that race, class, and gender differences in power permeate virtually every aspect of life in the United States, including crime and its control.

Part III of this volume presents three chapters that are the contemporary descendants of this "new" or "critical" criminology. In chapter 7, Michael Lynch, Herman Schwendinger, and Julia Schwendinger note the distinctiveness of a radical perspective on the study of crime. They reject "reductionistic," traditional approaches to theory and method that portray crime as the sole product of individual experiences and/or pathology. Instead, reminiscent of the critique offered by C. Wright Mills (1942), they argue that individual action is situated within social structures and particular historical circumstances—salient causal forces that narrower theoretical efforts aimed at pathologizing offenders ignore. More specifically, a radical criminology calls attention to how an inequitable political economy stifles healthy human development, creates criminogenic conditions, and encourages efforts at social control that invariably reflect and reinforce existing structures of inequality.

In their discussion, Lynch and his colleagues not only alert readers to an array of past empirical research on radical criminology but also concretely illuminate the distinctiveness of a critical approach by focusing on "environmental harms." It is now well-established that exposure to environmental toxins—such as lead and pesticides—can negatively affect brain development that, in turn, imposes on children risk factors related to crime (e.g., impulsivity, learning disabilities) (see, e.g., Wright, Dietrich, and Ris 2004). A traditional analysis of this issue, however valuable, would likely stop at this point. But radical theory—concerned with issues of social justice and broader explanation—goes a step or two farther.

Thus, Lynch et al. show that weak governmental regulation of powerful interests permits, if not encourages, the release of toxins into the environment. More disquieting, they reveal that the placement of disposal facilities and other sources of pollutants in disadvantaged areas—in communities that lack the power to resist such incursions—means that minorities and lower-class children are differentially exposed to toxins that impede healthy human development and contribute to criminal involvement. This "environmental injustice" is further exacerbated by enforcement agencies either that allow toxins to be released with impunity or that apply only lax penalties when companies pollute in impoverished, as opposed to more affluent, communities.

Similarly, in a review of the past work of Herman and Julia Schwendinger that used innovative experiments with delinquents and non-delinquents, they contend that Sykes and Matza's (1957) theory of techniques of neutralizations lacks sufficient complexity and contextual foundation. They show that adolescent "discourse" on offending varies depending on whether it is expressed in private or public and that the "mode" of discourse might be switched depending on the audience (e.g., peers versus church group). This research also uncovered that the rationalizations of delinquents have a distinctive quality not predicted by Sykes and Matza—one that "overwhelmingly appealed to minimizing risks or other tactical considerations." Most salient, they suggest that "the general nature of discourses are determined by economic factors" in the sense that they reflect, for example, the "exchange principles common in market economies" and the ethic of exploitation that permeates the structures of inequality in the juveniles' local and larger environments. This approach thus "connects individual actions to group inclinations and cultures and to broader cultural institutions and economic structures that shaped each level of the underlying response." As they note, this is the hallmark of the "radical approach to crime."

As Jody Miller and Christopher Mullins observe in chapter 8, feminist scholars have worked for three decades to demonstrate the pitfalls of ignoring another structure of power in American society: gender inequality. An integral product of this hegemony of male privilege was that the role of gender in offending was traditionally neglected by criminologists, who were, of course, predominantly male. The result was that gender was not incorporated systematically into the core theories of the field. Female offenders typically were left unstudied and thus rendered invisible or, in those rare occasions when they were investigated, their criminality was attributed to their biology, sexuality, and/or failure to live up to stereotypical images of what it meant to be a "good" woman. Meanwhile, little attention was given to the role of gender—especially when intersecting with race and class disadvantage—in exposing women to dire, criminogenic circumstances, including economic marginality and victimization by men (e.g., sexual abuse when young, rape, domestic violence).

In chapter 8, Miller and Mullins show that feminist criminology—in large part a by-product of the Women's Movement and the gendering of the field of criminology by a generation of female scholars—has yielded a rich body of theory and research that seeks to place gender at the center of criminological inquiry. They elaborate the distinctive elements of a feminist approach to crime and control and explain how feminist scholarship within criminology is intimately influenced by "theoretical developments within a range of social science disciplines." Their analysis then, demarcates the main "contemporary directions in feminist criminology"—issues that are likely to shape discourse and investigation in the time ahead.

One of these enduring concerns is whether the causes of crime are gender specific or general. Because they invented by males, written about males, and originally tested mainly on males, feminist scholars see traditional or core theories as "men's theories" that do not capture the special circumstances inherent in women's criminality. As result, these scholars call for gender-specific theories that elucidate the ways in which gender-related experiences are fundamental to the criminal enterprise. By contrast, mainstream theorists argue that they have identified factors that are involved in all crime and thus that have the same—or "general"—effects across gender groups. Although different readings of the empirical evidence are possible, there appear to be substantial general effects in the causes of criminal involvement (Daigle 2005; Dowden and Andrews 1999; Moffitt, Caspi, Rutter, and Silva 2001).

These findings suggest that traditional approaches may have explanatory value that cannot be dismissed. Nonetheless, Miller and Mullins show that even if mainstream theories illuminate relevant causal factors, they remain incomplete explanations because they give short shrift to gender. For example, to show that differential association with antisocial peers increases crime does not mean that peer groups involve girls and boys in crime in precisely the same way. Traditional theories also focus on a limited number of variables and thus they overlook other factors—such as sexual victimization—that may foster distinct, "gendered pathways to lawbreaking." Miller and Mullins reveal as well that many facets of the criminal enterprise—for instance, roles played in burglary or whether intimate relationships contribute to the onset or desistance of offending—are finely shaped by patriarchy and institutional sexism. Moreover, in their review of "masculinities" and crime, they raise the question of how men's criminality can be adequately understood if their gender—their *maleness*—is simply taken for granted and not seen as integral to the personal identities, values and neutralizations, situational dynamics, life-styles, friendships, and decisions that are implicated in crime. In the end, criminal behavior reflects efforts to "do gender" because gender is not simply a "variable" in a causal model but something that constitutes the very fabric of who people are and the lives that are possible, or impossible, for them to lead.

In chapter 9, John Randolph Fuller and John Wozniak provide a tour across the origins, contents, and future prospects of peacemaking criminology. This approach has its roots in religious and secular bodies of thought that teach the enduring ethics and ultimately positive effects of pursuing "peace and harmony." Its foundation is built as well upon critical and feminist perspectives that unmask the suffering and harms caused by prevailing structures of inequality and that embrace social justice as a response to social problems, including crime and victimization. Fuller and Wozniak also provide two useful conceptual, visual schemes—one in the form of a pyramid and the other in the form of circles—as ways of grasping the core constructs that interrelate to constitute this perspective. Finally, in perhaps the most instructive part of the chapter, they outline a series of concepts and propositions that identify the core of peacemaking criminology and that supply researchers with clear-cut theses to test empirically. To our knowledge, this is the first attempt to translate the peacemaking paradigm to the larger criminological community through the conduit of systematic propositions.

As Fuller and Wozniak show, peacemaking criminology views crime as the failure to "do peace." In more peaceful social domains, there is an emphasis on the "Golden Rule" and on being "mindful" of others, especially when they are at risk of suffering. People seek personal transformation, a struggle that leads them to be mindful or compassionate—even in the face of adversity. As a result, they are predisposed to interconnect with one another and, in turn, to understand and challenge forms of dominance—whether racism, sexism, or class-bias—that are unfair and hurtful. In this context, responses to crime are not predicated on vengeance and the impulse to inflict pain—although these sentiments may be felt—but involve attempts to stay mindful and connected—

to discover non-violent ways to rectify the harm that was committed. By contrast, criminogenic contexts—such as contemporary America—expose individuals to cultures and practices of violence (e.g., violent values, weaponry, corporate punishment), to daily suffering that leaves human needs unmet and human dignity undermined, and to a criminal justice system that makes "war" rather than peace on crime.

Peacemaking criminology, observe Fuller and Wozniak, admittedly has a utopian twist to it—the kind of feel-good thinking that "sounds good but would never work." But on closer examination, its prescriptions for confronting crime arguably are pragmatic and consistent with existing criminological research on "what works" to reduce crime. First and foremost, the very word of "peace" powerfully calls into question the forms of repression that are now used with, at best, uncertain results in the ongoing "war on crime": get tough ideology that denies the dignity of offenders and justifies their exclusion from society, the over-use of prisons, rigid mandatory sentences that were passed for political expediency, and the embrace of capital punishment. As an alternative, the logic of peacemaking criminology would trumpet the merits of restorative justice and other forms of community justice, treatment programs for offenders, socially supportive early intervention for at-risk youths, programs in schools and neighborhoods to blunt the effects of social injustice, and efforts to ensure that the criminal justice system makes a firm commitment to doing justice and not doing harm. In the end, this approach offers the advice that creating a more peaceful world—whether in one's immediate social domain or in the larger society and its institutions—will result in less suffering and in less crime. Utopian?—perhaps, but this does not make the thesis incorrect or devoid of criminological wisdom.

Life-Course Theories

Although exceptions can be found (Glueck and Glueck 1950), American criminology has focused predominantly on why *juveniles* engage in delinquent behavior. Part of the reason for this adolescent-limited focus was empirical: the age-crime curve. As youths moved into the teenage years, it was discovered that participation in various forms of crime rises precipitously and begins to peak. To criminologists, this spike in criminal participation suggested that there was something special about this period of life that was especially criminogenic and thus deserving of investigation. Part of the reason for the focus on juveniles also was methodological. Again following Hirschi (1969), it was simply feasible to collect self-report data on kids who congregated on one place—a community's high school—and who were old enough to complete surveys. And part of the reason was the presence of prominent works—especially Cohen's (1955) *Delinquent Boys* and Cloward and Ohlin's (1960) *Delinquency and Opportunity*—that showed the innovative use of theory and called attention to the problem of youth subcultures and gangs, especially in urban areas.

Although never stated, the implicit assumption in these works that was *what went on in childhood—including infancy—was not very important*. In contrast to psychology where "child psychology" is a distinct specialization, criminologists ignored and under-theorized this period of life. For scholars, it was almost as though children arrived in adolescence in a malleable, if not unblemished, state, at which point society channeled them either into crime or away from crime. The theoretical debate thus hinged on what it was about the juvenile years that was specially crime-inducing. There was no sense that early childhood experiences might be critical in shaping later life chances or that crime, like other dimensions of the human experience, might be a *developmental process* with predictable pathways and or stages.

Among other factors, three key considerations served as "turning points" (Laub, 2004) that redirected scholars' attention toward childhood and, more broadly, toward the idea that crime should be viewed across the life course and potentially as a developmental process. First, in *A General Theory of Crime*, Gottfredson and Hirschi (1990) cited findings showing stability in antisocial conduct from childhood onward and attributed it to the failure of parents to instill self-control in the first years of life (by age eight or so). They offered the bold collateral thesis that correlates of crime found later in life and given causal weight by traditional theories—for example, school failure, disrupted relationships, unemployment—were spurious; these "causal variables" and crime were allegedly both accounted for by low self-control. Confronted in this way, criminologists no longer could ignore childhood and its impact on criminal involvement in adolescence and beyond. Second, at approximately the same time, important life-course theories of crime were proposed by Terrie Moffitt (1993) and by Robert Sampson and John Laub (1993). (We discuss these below.) They were greeted by receptive audiences who were anxious to hear a story about crime that challenged *A General Theory* and the idea that low self-control consigned children to a life of crime and social disability. And third, longitudinal data sets capable of addressing crime over the life course were discovered or became newly available. As downloading such information from the internet or disks became facile, the possibility for numerous criminologists to test life-course theories emerged, thus ensuring the perspective's continued vitality.

Given these developments, it seems certain that in the time ahead, the life-course perspective will be the major paradigm directing theory and research on crime (Benson 2002; Le Blanc and Loeber, 1998; see also, Piquero, Farrington, and Blumstein 2003). The range of theories reviewed in this volume are likely to be applied to life-course issues (e.g., how social learning, strain, or gender-specific experiences affect continuity and change in offending over people's lives). At the same, frameworks devised specifically as "life-course" or "developmental" theories—such as those presented in Part IV—will continue to exert a defining influence on criminological inquiry in this area.

They will be most instrumental in shaping theoretical discourse and in furnishing propositions that empirical research will investigate.

In chapter 10 in Part IV, Terrie Moffitt updates the status of her pathbreaking "developmental taxonomy" of offending. In her original essay, Moffitt (1993) proposed that offenders could be divided into two groups. One group, which she labeled as "adolescence-limited" ("AL's") largely obeys the age-crime curve. They show little sign of antisocial conduct in childhood, become involved in wayward behavior during the teenage years, and then desist from serious crime and deviance as they enter adulthood. The causes of their offending are social, rooted in attempts during adolescence to close the "maturity gap" and demonstrate autonomy from adults by breaking rules and mimicking precocious troublemakers. The second group, which she labeled as "life-course persistent" ("LCP's"), defies the age-crime curve. These individuals manifest antisocial conduct early in childhood, engage in high-rate criminal acts during the teenage years, and then persist in serious offending well into adulthood. This group is marked by strong individual differences that are reflected in antisocial personalities that foster offending and a range of social disabilities throughout life. The origins of their antisocial orientation starts with neuropsychological deficits (e.g., lower IQ, hyperactivity) that, in at-risk family and social environments, are responded to with harsh and erratic parenting, rejection at school, poor relations with prosocial peers, and a general knifing off of opportunities for healthy development. As cumulative disadvantage mounts, a life course of persistent offending is reinforced and opportunities for reform become limited.

In the growing literature on Moffitt's theory, there is controversy over whether distinct groups actually exist (some scholars see criminality as a continuum extending from high to low) and over whether there are only two groups (some scholars have identified several other offender categories). Drawing from research that either directly tests or is relevant to her theory's central propositions, Moffitt builds a strong case that her AL-LCP taxonomy explains a substantial amount of the variation in offending, with these groups having different predictors and behaving much as the theory hypothesizes. In her words, the "original theoretical taxonomy asserted that two prototypes, life- course persistent and adolescent-limited offenders, can account for the preponderance of the population's antisocial behavior. After more than ten years of research, this assertion appears to be correct."

Moffitt stops short of asserting that her theory explains everything, implying only that the AL-LCP taxonomy organizes much criminological knowledge and thus is a worthy candidate for further research. Thus, in a fair reading of the evidence, Moffitt admits that, contrary to her model, late onset offenders exist. She then shows, however, not only that this group is very small but also that its size is overestimated by research based on official data (i.e., arrests often lag several years behind the actual onset of crime as indicated by self-reports surveys). There is more support for the presence of a third group of "low-level chronics" who "offend persistently but at a low rate from childhood to adolescence or from adolescence to adulthood." There might also be a group that engages in childhood antisocial conduct, but that due to "off-putting personal characteristics" are excluded from "peer groups in which most delinquency happens." These "false positives"—those whose childhood profiles erroneously predict them to become LCP's—still lead dismal lives, likely suffering from "isolating personality disorders" that consign them to social and economic failure. Moffitt also takes pains to correct the assumption that her theory proposes that LCP's will engage in crime until old age robs them of their last breath. Agreeing that the "whole population may decrease its antisocial participation as it ages," her theory merely—but importantly—contends that as an age cohort moves into adulthood, "the life-course persistent individuals should remain at the top of the heap on antisocial behaviors."

In chapter 11, John Laub, Robert Sampson, and Gary Sweeten review the evolving life-course theory first set forth in *Crime in the Making* (Sampson and Laub 1993) and most recently updated in a significant way in *Shared Beginnings, Divergent Lives* (Laub and Sampson 2003). In its various versions, Sampson and Laub's life-course perspective builds directly on Hirschi's (1969) social bond theory in arguing, in their words, that the "organizing principle of the theory is that delinquency or crime is more likely to occur when an individual's bond to society is attenuated." Despite this intellectual link, their "age-graded theory of informal social control" presented in *Crime in the Making* moves far beyond Hirschi's more delimited model.

First, whereas Hirschi (1969: 243-244) believed that "structural determinants....do not explain much of the variance in delinquency," Sampson and Laub argue that these conditions have important effects on behavior that are mediated by social bonds. In particular, some social environments—such as urban areas marked by poverty and other structural disadvantages—lessen the ability of families to establish bonds and exercise controls. In short, *structure* impinges upon family *process*. Wayward behavior is the end result of this causal pathway (Sampson and Laub 1994). Second, although not explored by Hirschi, they observe that social bonds and delinquency have a reciprocal relationship: weak social bonds foster delinquency, while delinquency weakens social bonds. Over time, this ongoing connection helps to sustain individuals on a criminal life course and to explain continuity in offending.

Third and most important, Hirschi's conception of bonds was largely "static." Relying on cross-sectional self-report data from a study of junior high school and high school students, he focused on how, during the juvenile years, bonds to parents, schools, and peers inhibited delinquent involvement. By contrast, resurrecting the Gluecks' (1950) longitudinal data set that followed sample members to age thirty-two, Sampson and Laub examine how the nature of social bonds change as individuals age. In adulthood, the key domains are work and family—and, for some, military service and incarceration. Ties to these institutions matter because they are a source of informal social control. "Adult social bonds," Sampson, Laub, and Sweeten remind us, "have a direct negative effect on adult criminal behavior." As a result, social bonds across the life course account for continuity in offending (due to attenuated bonds) or change in offending (securing bonds can be a turning point away from a life in crime).

Notably, this conclusion is disputed by Hirschi and Gottfredson (1995), who see positive adult social bonds as a matter of self-selection and see any insulating effects as spurious. Self-control (or heterogeneity), not social control, accounts for criminal involvement and the quality of life across time. Beyond age effects, stability—not change—is modal once-offenders and non-offenders split onto divergent pathways in childhood. By contrast, Sampson et al. suggest that self-selection and social causation can occur simultaneously (see also, Sampson and Laub 1995). As they note, the "fact that individual differences influence choices one makes does not imply that social mechanisms emerging from these choices have no causal significance." Change throughout life is thus possible: "Although delinquents may be less likely to choose stable employment and marriage, sometimes they do make these choices and when strong social ties result, they are less likely to continue their criminal behavior."

In *Shared Beginnings, Divergent Lives*, Laub and Sampson extend the study of the Gluecks' sample of "500 delinquents" up until the age of seventy, collecting quantitative data and, on a subsample of fifty two men, qualitative (interview) data. This extraordinary methodological accomplishment—no other project has followed offenders this deep into the life course—yielded a number of theoretical insights, three of which we will highlight here. First, in a way distantly reminiscent of Hirschi's (1969) concept of "involvement," Laub and Sampson argue that offenders with ties to conventional institutions—work, family, the military—have "structured routine activities" that move them away from crime (see also, Felson 1986). Alternatively, those who persist in crime tend to have lives filled with free time and a lack of prosocial influences. As a result, they are more likely to encounter situations devoid of social control in which opportunities for offending are readily available.

Second and more provocatively, Laub and Sampson suggest that the decision to persist in, or desist from, offending is shaped by the exercise of "human agency." This strikes us as more of a "sensitizing concept" (Blumer 1969) than as a finely calibrated, easily measured variable. Regardless, "human agency" seeks to capture the reality that offenders have intentionality—whether to continue to break the law or to "go straight"—and that this agency or "will" to act potentially affects their decisions. Seen another way, this is an attempt by Laub and Sampson to introduce *variation in motivation* into control theory, whereas heretofore motivation had been treated as a constant by Hirschi and others. However, the motivation is not compelled but seemingly chosen or invoked by the offender; it can be either prosocial or antisocial in its direction; and it can be fleeting or more enduring. Human agency also is played out within a social context. Choices are "situated" in two senses: decisions are constrained by the options available, but also can affect what shape the options take. For example, an offender with the human agency to "go straight" might, on the one hand, be less likely to make this choice if a decent job is not available but might, on the other hand, strive diligently to overcome initial situational barriers and find employment because of the very fact that he (or she) is now specially motivated to do so.

Third, Laub, Sampson, and Sweeten in chapter 11 question whether continuity and change in adulthood—and ultimately virtually everyone's desistance from crime—can be explained by reference to predictors earlier in life. Between largely unpredictable purposeful human agency and the ongoing interaction between individuals and environment that produces "random developmental noise," what occurs as offenders age may be too variable to be tied to who these people were early in life. Within this observation is a criticism of theories that see life-course persistent offenders as falling into a neatly packaged category. In chapter 10, Moffitt responds to Laub and Sampson's critique by agreeing that there may be substantial heterogeneity in desistance from criminal careers that is unexplainable by early life factors. Still, Moffitt contends that consistent with her taxonomic theory, there is a distinct group of LCP's who "continue offending well beyond the age when most young men in their cohort populations desisted." This is a fascinating and important debate that will likely continue in the time ahead.

In chapter 12, David Farrington provides a systematic review of contemporary "developmental and life-course criminology (DLC)" theories—as he calls them. He "takes stock" of this theoretical landscape in four major ways (see also, Farrington 2005). First, in the beginning section of the chapter, he lists the key empirical and, in turn, theoretical issues that a DLC theory must tackle. Second, he identifies and provides a cogent summary of the eight major DLC theories. These theories are often tied to and informed by specific longitudinal studies (e.g., Sampson and Laub's theory to the Gluecks' Boston study; Farrington's theory to the Cambridge study in Delinquent Development). Third and perhaps most salient, he supplies a series of ten tables in which he illuminates how each of the eight DLC perspectives either differ or overlap theoretically and how these approaches address—or do not address—a range of empirical issues (e.g., the "key underlying construct" in each theory; the "factors that promote or inhibit offending" as people age; the importance accorded to life events later in life). Fourth, drawing from these discussions, Farrington then specifies fifteen questions or predictions that might be tested empirically (e.g., whether there are "discrete types of offenders"; the accuracy with which "childhood factors, compared to adult life events, predict desistance"). If undertaken, research on these issues would begin to sort out the relative merits of DLC theories, especially at those points where two or more theories make alternative predictions. Taken together, the components of Farrington's essay furnish an invaluable guide to the status and future prospects of DLC theories.

In addition, Farrington urges that research within DLC pay special attention to *within-individual changes over time*. This question is the hallmark of the DLC because the defining focus of this paradigm is tracing continuity and change in the offending of individuals over the life course. In this context, it is important to consider that *between-group differences* are not necessarily generalizable to what occurs within individuals. For example, as Farrington points out, offending is higher among youths who have antisocial peers versus those who have prosocial peers (a between-group difference); however, some research suggests that a change in delinquent peer relations over time is not followed subsequently by a change in offending (a within-individual difference). This issue is central to establishing the existence of causal processes, especially as a prelude for designing effective interventions. As Farrington observes, the "concept of cause implies that within-individual change in a causal factor is followed by within-individual change in an outcome, and ideas of prevention and treatment require within-individual change."

Theories of Societal Reaction

In the 1960s and into the 1970s, labeling theory emerged as the dominant paradigm for the study of crime and deviance (Cole 1975; Cullen and Cullen 1978). This perspective rejected the view, implicit in existing theories, that "deviance" was an inherent or intrinsic quality of socially disapproved acts. Instead, labeling theory argued that deviance, including crime, was "created" or "socially constructed"—that is, that deviance existed only when rules were developed that defined an act, such as drug use or corporate marketing of defective products, as wayward (see, e.g., Becker 1963; Erikson 1964; Kitsuse 1964). Even when rules exist, theorists argued, deviance remains problematic. Deviant labels are not applied to all rule-breakers: some escape detection and are considered "normal," whereas others, who have the misfortune of being caught, are now considered "deviant." This perspective appealed to a generation of scholars who were in the midst of a revolutionary social context—the 1960s—in which rules and authority were being questioned and in which countercultural lifestyles were becoming common.

Labeling theory's most provocative claim, however, was that "societal reaction" was the principal cause of stable wayward behavior. Rejecting traditional theories that attributed crime to individual differences or social circumstances, this perspective argued that "careers" in crime were caused by the very efforts meant to suppress the behavior. Societal reaction, especially formal social control by the criminal justice system, were seen to have a self-fulfilling prophecy—of having the unanticipated consequence of creating the very thing it meant to halt. Thus, once stigmatized as a "criminal" and brought within correctional agencies, the person was likely to internalize the identity as an "offender," to be denied employment as an "ex-con," to be rejected and have bonds to conventional society attenuated, and to associate more often with those who shared his or her disreputable status as a "criminal." For many scholars in this time period, this ironic approach—one which blamed the state for fostering crime through its repressive action—was appealing. As Hagan (1973) notes, it was a case of the "sociology of the interesting."

Again, labeling theorists proposed that this process of stigmatization and social exclusion would cause criminality that was nascent and unorganized—what Lemert (1951) called "primary deviance"—to evolve into criminality that was stable and organized—what Lemert called "secondary deviance." In so doing, these scholars anticipated the work of later life-course theorists who distinguished between the onset and persistence of criminal conduct. In essence, labeling theorists were depicting how societal reaction "knifed off" prosocial opportunities and contributed to the "cumulative disadvantage" of offenders. Labeled individuals thus were trapped in criminal roles and persisted in their offending. It is perhaps not surprising that contemporary life-course theories often include labeling processes—especially arrest and institutionalization—as factors that may increase persistent offending (see Farrington, chapter 12: Table 9).

As a number of critics pointed out, labeling theory had two potential empirical weaknesses (Cullen and Cullen 1978). First, it was apparent that many people become serious offenders before they are labeled by the criminal justice system. At worst, labeling theory had the causal ordering backwards. At best, the theory was only partially correct: among multiple causes of criminal behavior, labeling was only one factor that increased illegal involvement. Second, other scholars maintained that not only was labeling not criminogenic, but rather that it had its intended effect: *criminal justice sanctions reduced crime through deterrence.* As a result, researchers soon juxtaposed labeling and deterrence theory as two rival perspectives making diametrically opposed predictions on the consequences of state intervention (see, e.g., Thorsell and Klemke 1972; Tittle 1975). More recently, scholars have moved to a more mature stage in theoretical development, suggesting that the effects of sanctions will vary depending on the quality of the intervention and circumstances in the offender's life (Cullen and Cullen 1978; Palamara, Cullen, and Gersten 1986; Sherman 1993). What is needed, in short, is a systematic theory of the effects of the criminal sanction (Sherman 1993).

These issues provide the criminological context for the three essays that comprise Part V of this volume, each of which explores how societal reaction, and the criminal sanction in particular, influence offending. In chapter 13, Travis Pratt, Francis Cullen, Kristie Blevins, Leah Daigle, and Tamara Madensen take stock of deterrence theory through a meta-analysis of the extant empirical literature. Traditionally—and throughout this volume—scholars have assessed the merits of a theory by conducting a "narrative review" of works testing the perspective's core propositions (see, e.g., Akers and Sellers, 2004; Burton and Cullen 1992; Kempf 1993). In a narrative review, empirical tests are discussed one by one, and then conclusions are drawn as to the theory's strengths and weaknesses. Another strategy is to place studies in a table and to tally up whether the findings are statistically significant in the predicted direction. This is sometimes called a "ballot box" approach because, much like an election, a theory is declared a "winner" if the positive results exceed the negative results.

Narrative reviews have many of the strengths and weaknesses that characterize qualitative methodology. Thus, they supply a rich exploration of the details of individual studies that may allow for valuable understandings of the theory under review. This possibility is heightened when the reviewer has special expertise in the area and can furnish insights that a more standardized, confining method would render impossible. However, narrative reviews also are open to reviewer bias and selective interpretation, to being ill-equipped to make sense of a large number of studies, and to employing a methodology that makes replication virtually impossible. For this reason, investigators in the sciences and social sciences are increasingly relying on the technique of meta-analysis to quantitatively synthesize the existing empirical literature. Meta-analysis has its limitations, but it also enjoys the advantages of parsimony (it reports "effect sizes" for theoretical variables), of allowing for easier and more exacting theoretical comparisons (the effect sizes for variables from competing theories can be compared), of using quantitative methods to process large numbers of studies, of allowing for an assessment of how methodological factors condition theoretical findings, of being replicable, and of facilitating the cumulative growth of knowledge by providing a data set that can be added to continually. As a result, although qualitative narrative reviews have their value and should remain a strategy for organizing knowledge, a strong case can be made that the extant research on all theories of crime should be meta-analyzed (Pratt and Cullen 2000, 2005; Pratt et al. 2005).

In chapter 13, Pratt and his colleagues examine the research on deterrence theory by meta-analyzing studies of *perceived certainty and severity of punishment* (see also, Paternoster 1987). "Perceptual deterrence" studies became a widely used strategy for testing deterrence theory both for practical reasons (self-report surveys could be used to collect data) and for substantive reasons (whereas the objective risks of punishment might not be known, an individual's perception of these risks could be expected to affect the person's decision to offend). In all, Pratt and his colleagues were able to meta-analyze forty published studies that contained 200 effect size estimates for deterrence measures.

Overall, the results were not favorable to deterrence theory, in many ways replicating the results of Paternoster's (1987) earlier review. There was little support found for the impact of severity of legal punishment on offending. Although measures of certainty showed significant effects, the substantive impact of this factor was markedly reduced in studies that employed more sophisticated research designs (e.g., multivariate analyses, controls introduced for the "experiential effect," do not rely on convenience samples of college students). There was some evidence that deterrence variables have larger effects in studies of white-collar offenses (e.g., fraud, tax violations), and fairly consistent support for the conclusion that non-legal sanctions were inversely related to offending.

As Pratt and his colleagues point out, these findings have policy and theoretical implications. First, the modest to weak support for perceived deterrence variables reinforces other research that questions whether punitive legal sanctions have a meaningful impact on criminal involvement (see also, Cullen, Pratt, Miceli, and Moon 2002; Pratt and Cullen 2005). Policies that seek to effect reductions in crime through deterrence—especially through harsher sanctions that ignore other known predictors of crime—thus rest on a shaky empirical foundation. Second, at best, legal deterrence variables are likely to be only one of many factors that contribute to criminal behavior and are unlikely to be among the most important of these predictors. As Pratt and his colleagues suggest, a focus on non-legal sanctions and how they intersect with other criminogenic traits and circumstances (e.g., self-control, informal social control) might prove to be a more profitable avenue of exploration. Such theoretical integration would recognize that calculations on the costs of crime are made not by atomized individuals, but by people whose decisions are shaped by who they are and the context in which they are enmeshed.

In *Crime, Shame and Reintegration*, John Braithwaite (1989) provides important clues as to why deterrence, when based on pain-inflicting punitive policies, is not realized. Echoing the warnings of labeling theorists, Braithwaite details the criminogenic effects of efforts to raise the costs of crime by publicly degrading and socially excluding offenders. As predicted by labeling theory, such "disintegrative or stigmatizing shaming" only pushes individuals further into crime; societally, it produces high rates of crime. Unlike labeling theory, however, Braithwaite does not view social control, including state intervention, as invariably crime-engendering. In fact, he suggests that it would be irresponsible not to shame harmful behaviors—not to show that some acts are wrong and morally unacceptable. The key, however, is how to shame the wayward. In this regard, Braithwaite (1989: 55) proposes that criminal behavior will be reduced when wrongdoers are subject to "reintegrative shaming"—that is, to "expressions of community disapproval" that "are followed by gestures of reacceptance into the community of law-abiding citizens." Because traditional criminal justice courts and sanctions typically are stigmatizing,

Braithwaite (2002) has become a leading advocate of restorative justice. This approach emphasizes offenders' accepting responsibility for their actions, expressing remorse, and compensating victims for the harm they have committed in exchange for forgiveness and supportive acceptance back into the community.

In chapter 14, John Braithwaite, Eliza Ahmed, and Valerie Braithwaite take stock of the theoretical and empirical status of reintegrative shaming theory—a perspective now in existence for over a decade-and-a-half. Similar to other criminological theories, shaming theory is an evolving, not static, paradigm. In their review, Braithwaite and his colleagues assess a number of conceptual contributions that may further elucidate the processes through which shaming has positive rather than negative effects. These insights include the interaction of shame and guilt, the need to provide offenders with "redemption scripts" that allow them to redefine themselves as non-criminals, the importance of "shame acknowledgement" as opposed to "shame displacement," and the challenge of "pride management" and of praising offenders in healthy ways. These insights show that effective reintegrative shaming is a complex process that must attend to a variety of potential feelings, is influenced by offender capacities for emotional intelligence, and is contingent upon the community's skillful communication of messages about shame and redemption.

Braithwaite, Ahmed, and Braithwaite also furnish a judicious review of empirical investigations that either directly or indirectly test reintegrative shaming theory. Drawing on research evaluating restorative justice programs (criminal justice and school-bullying), assessments of parenting styles, self-report survey research, and qualitative studies of regulatory enforcement in industries, they reveal a pattern of results largely consistent with the predictions of shaming theory. Still, important issues remain to be addressed—not the least of which is whether shame and reintegration have separable main effects or, as the theory proposes, are interactive (i.e., stigmatizing shaming versus reintegrative shaming). Further, Braithwaite et al. caution that future research may prove vacuous if it attempts to measure the theory through the standard practice of simply adding a shaming scale to a survey instrument. The time has come, they observe, for "deep thought" about emerging conceptual issues and how, within the confines of empirical research designs, these complex issues can be meaningfully measured.

In chapter 15, Paul Gendreau, Paula Smith, and Sheila French also explore the conditions under which state intervention potentially creates or prevents criminal behavior. Guided by labeling theory and mistrustful of state power, criminologists in the late 1960s began to question whether correctional programs were effective in rehabilitating offenders (Cullen and Gilbert 1982). Their misgivings seemed to be confirmed when Robert Martinson (1974: 25) published his now-famous review of 231 evaluation studies in which he concluded that, "With few and isolated exceptions, the rehabilitative efforts that have been reported so far have had no appreciable effect on recidivism." Technical language aside, this statement was taken to mean that "nothing works" to reform offenders. This "doctrine" became part of a more general professional ideology among criminologists which insisted that, beyond broader social reform, nothing the government did would "work" to reduce crime (Cullen and Gendreau 2001).

Over the years, however, increasing evidence emerged—the most persuasive of which was supplied by meta-analyses—that correctional interventions were successful in reducing reoffending (Cullen 2002, 2005; Cullen and Gendreau 2000). A key finding was that there was considerable "heterogeneity" in treatment effects; that is, some programs were considerably more successful than others in blunting recidivism. But why was this the case? One conclusion soon emerged: across evaluation studies, punishment-oriented or deterrence-oriented interventions were found to be consistently ineffective (Cullen et al. 2002). But beyond this specific result, was it possible to discern what differentiated good from bad programs?

A group of Canadian psychologists, initially inspired by Donald Andrews, took up this challenge and developed a coherent "theory of effective correctional intervention" (Andrews and Bonta 2003; see also, Cullen 2002, 2005). This approach argued that based on certain principles, programs could be categorized as either "appropriate" or "inappropriate." Simply put, they proposed that appropriate programs reduce recidivism, whereas inappropriate ones do not. Active participants in this theoretical agenda, Gendreau, Smith, and French review these principles of effective treatment in chapter 15. This theory proposes that correctional interventions will "work" that target "criminogenic needs" for change (i.e., empirically established predictors of offending that are "dynamic" or changeable, such as antisocial attitudes), that use treatment modalities that are "responsive" to these needs (i.e., cognitive-behavioral programs), and that employ assessment instruments so as to focus the treatment on high-risk offenders. Importantly, Gendreau and his colleagues survey the extant empirical evidence and show that there is substantial support for this correctional theory.

In light of increasing calls for "evidence-based" corrections (Cullen and Gendreau 2000; Latessa, Cullen, and Gendreau 2002; MacKenzie 2000), it thus appears that this paradigm should play a large role in guiding future treatment interventions. Gendreau et al.'s chapter also serves to remind criminologists and policymakers that offenders are not intractably "wicked" and that we increasingly have the knowledge to design efficacious programs. In short, rehabilitation "works," and it should be reaffirmed as a core component of the correctional enterprise (Cullen 2005; Cullen and Gilbert 1982).

Taken together, the three chapters in Part V thus reveal that societal reaction in general, and criminal sanctions in particular, potentially have a significant causal role in offending and in persistent reoffending. There is an emerging consensus that harsh, mean-spirited punishment couched in "get tough" rhetoric is ineffective or even criminogenic. By contrast, sanctions are likely to prove effective (1) that avoid degradation and the infliction of gratuitous pain and (2) that challenge the way offenders think about those they harm, emphasize prosocial relationships, and provide a supportive context in which change can occur.

The Challenge of Taking Stock

Collectively, the contributors to this project have provided an invaluable service to the discipline. With the qualification that several noteworthy theories were omitted, this single volume represents a systematic compendium of what is known—and needs to be known—about the leading theoretical paradigms. This work should be an essential resource for those wishing to become culturally literate in the diverse field of criminological theory. The risk exists, however, that this joint effort to organize theoretical knowledge will be a one-time endeavor—a collaborative affair to be celebrated but one that has no enduring influence on the way we "do business" in criminology. If this were to occur, criminology would return to state of relative anarchy in which scholars are free to produce study after study but virtually nobody can say what they all mean. The challenge thus is to embed strategies for the organization of knowledge within the criminological enterprise. We will end with three suggestions.

First, as noted previously, we favor the use of meta-analysis to organize the empirical literature for every theory of crime (see, e.g., Pratt and Cullen 2000, 2005; Pratt et al. 2005). Ideally, these investigations would be undertaken on an ongoing basis and by researchers who are independent of one another. One goal would be to use this approach to compare the relative effects of the core variables of rival theories. Second, following David Farrington's approach in chapter 12 of this volume, there is a need to take stock *conceptually* of theories. Together, Farrington's tables are an example of how competing theories can be juxtaposed to one another on key criminological issues. This comparative analysis is a prelude for critical empirical tests that can show which theories' predictions have more merit. And third, we would encourage theorists to assume responsibility for taking stock of the empirical status of their perspective on an ongoing basis. Although this is a daunting task, it would ensure that someone is committed to organize the past and emergent knowledge on one's own intellectual property. If it became normative for scholars to synthesize research on their paradigms, taking stock volumes—like the present project—might become a regular feature of the criminological landscape.

References

Agnew, Robert. 1992. "Foundation for a General Strain Theory of Crime and Delinquency." *Criminology* 30: 47-87.

———. 2001a. *Juvenile Delinquency: Causes and Control.* Los Angeles: Roxbury.

———. 2001b. "Building on the Foundation of General Strain Theory: Specifying the Types of Strain Most Likely to Lead to Crime and Delinquency." *Journal of Research in Crime and Delinquency* 38: 319-361.

Akers, Ronald L. 1998. *Social Learning and Social Structure: A General Theory of Crime and Deviance.* Boston: Northeastern University Press.

Akers, Ronald L., and Christine S. Sellers. 2004. *Criminological Theories: Introduction, Evaluation, and Application,* 4th ed. Los Angeles: Roxbury.

Andrews, D. A., and James Bonta. 2003. *The Psychology of Criminal Conduct,* 3rd ed. Cincinnati: Anderson.

Becker, Howard S. 1963. *Outsiders: Studies in the Sociology of Deviance.* Glencoe, IL: The Free Press.

Benson, Michael L. 2002. *Crime and the Life Course: An Introduction.* Los Angeles: Roxbury.

Blau, Judith R., and Peter M. Blau. 1982. "The Cost of Inequality: Metropolitan Structure and Violent Crime." *American Sociological Review* 47: 114-29.

Blumer, Herbert. 1969. *Symbolic Interactionism: Perspectives and Method.* Englewood Cliffs, NJ: Prentice-Hall.

Bohm, Robert M. 1982. "Radical Criminology: An Explication." *Criminology* 19: 565-589.

Braithwaite, John. 1989. *Crime, Shame and Reintegration.* Cambridge: Cambridge University Press.

———. 2002. *Restorative Justice and Responsive Regulation.* New York: Oxford University Press.

Burton, Velmer S., Jr., and Francis T. Cullen. 1992. "The Empirical Status of Strain Theory." *Journal of Crime and Justice* 15 (No. 2): 1-30.

Cohen, Albert K. 1955. *Delinquent Boys: The Culture of the Gang.* New York: The Free Press.

Cloward, Richard A., and Lloyd E. Ohlin. 1960. *Delinquency and Opportunity: A Theory of Delinquent Gangs.* New York: The Free Press.

Cole, Stephen. 1975. "The Growth of Scientific Knowledge: Theories of Deviance as a Case Study." Pp. 175-220 in Lewis A. Coser (ed.), *The Idea of Social Structure: Papers in Honor of Robert K. Merton.* New York: Harcourt Brace Jovanovich.

Collins, Randall. 1986. "Is 1980s Sociology in the Doldrums?" *American Journal of Sociology* 91: 1336-1355.

Colvin, Mark. 2000. *Crime and Coercion: An Integrated Theory of Chronic Criminality.* New York: St. Martin's Press.

Cullen, Francis T. 1984. *Rethinking Crime and Deviance Theory: The Emergence of a Structuring Tradition.* Totowa, NJ: Rowman and Allenheld.

———. 2002. "Rehabilitation and Treatment Programs." Pp. 253-289 in James Q. Wilson and Joan Petersilia (eds.), *Crime: Public Policies for Crime Control,* 2nd ed. Oakland, CA: ICS Press.

———. 2005. "The Twelve People Who Saved Rehabilitation: How the Science of Criminology Made a Difference—The American Society of Criminology 2004 Presidential Address." *Criminology* 43: 1-42,

Cullen, Francis T., and John B. Cullen. 1978. *Toward a Paradigm of Labeling Theory.* Monograph Number 58, University of Nebraska Studies. Lincoln: University of Nebraska.

Cullen, Francis T., and Paul Gendreau. 2000. "Assessing Correctional Rehabilitation: Policy, Practice, and Prospects." Pp. 109-175 in Julie Horney (ed.), *Criminal Justice 2000: Vol. 3—Policies, Processes, and Decisions of the Criminal Justice System.* Washington, DC: U.S. Department of Justice, National Institute of Justice.

————.. 2001. "From Nothing Works to What Works: Changing Professional Ideology in the 21st Century." *The Prison Journal* 81: 313-338.

Cullen, Francis T., and Karen E. Gilbert. 1982. *Reaffirming Rehabilitation.* Cincinnati: Anderson.

Cullen, Francis T., Travis C. Pratt, Sharon Levrant Miceli, and Melissa M. Moon. 2002. "Dangerous Liaison? Rational Choice as the Basis for Correctional Intervention." Pp. 279-296 in Alex R. Piquero and Stephen G. Tibbetts (eds.), *Rational Choice and Criminal Behavior: Recent Research and Future Challenges.* New York: Taylor and Francis Books.

Cullen, Francis T., John Paul Wright, Paul Gendreau, and D. A. Andrews. 2003. "What Correctional Treatment Can Tell Us About Criminological Theory: Implications for Social Learning Theory." Pp. 339-362 in Ronald L. Akers and Gary F. Jensen (eds.), *Social Learning Theory and the Explanation of Crime: A Guide for the New Century—Advances in Criminological Theory, Vol. 11.* New Brunswick, NJ: Transaction.

Daigle, Leah E. 2005. *Gender, Risk Factors, and Juvenile Misconduct: Assessing the Specificity-Generality Debate.* Unpublished Ph.D. Dissertation, University of Cincinnati.

Dowden, Craig, and D. A. Andrews. 1999. "What Works of Female Offenders: A Meta-Analytic Review." *Crime and Delinquency* 45: 438-452.

Elliott, Delbert S., Suzanne S. Ageton, and Rachelle J. Canter. 1979. "An Integrated Theoretical Perspective on Delinquent Behavior." *Journal of Research on Crime and Delinquency* 16: 3-27.

Erikson, Kai T. 1964. "Notes on the Sociology of Deviance." Pp. 9-21 in Howard S. Becker (ed.), *The Other Side.* New York: The Free Press.

Farrington, David P., ed. 2005. *Integrated Developmental and Life-Course Theories of Offending—Advances in Criminological Theory, Vol. 14.* New Brunswick, NJ: Transaction.

Felson, Marcus. 1986. "Linking Criminal Choices, Routine Activities, Informal Control, and Criminal Outcomes." Pp. 119-128 in Derek B. Cornish and Ronald V. Clarke (eds.), *The Reasoning Criminal: Rational Choice Perspectives on Offending.* New York: Springer-Verlag.

Finestone, Harold. 1976. "The Delinquent and Society: The Shaw and McKay Tradition." Pp. 23-49 in James F. Short (ed.), *Delinquency, Crime, and Society.* Chicago: University of Chicago Press.

Glueck, Sheldon, and Eleanor Glueck. 1950. *Unraveling Juvenile Delinquency.* New York: Commonwealth Fund.

Gottfredson, Michael R., and Travis Hirschi. 1990. *A General Theory of Crime.* Stanford, CA: Stanford University Press.

Greenberg, David F., ed. 1993. *Crime and Capitalism: Readings in Marxist Criminology.* Expanded and updated ed. Philadelphia: Temple University Press.

Hagan, John L. 1973. "Labeling and Deviance: A Case Study in the 'Sociology of the Interesting.'" *Social Problems.* 20: 447-458.

Hirschi, Travis. 1969. *Causes of Delinquency.* Berkeley: University of California Press.

————. 1989. "Exploring Alternatives to Integrated Theory." Pp. 37-49 in Steven F. Messner, Marvin D. Krohn, and Allen E. Liska (eds.), *Theoretical Integration in the Study of Deviance and Crime: Problems and Prospects.* Albany: State University of New York Press.

Hirschi, Travis, and Michael R. Gottfredson. 1995. "Control Theory and the Life-Course Perspective." *Studies on Crime and Crime Prevention* 4: 131-142.

Kempf, Kimberly L. 1993. "The Empirical Status of Hirschi's Control Theory." Pp. 143-185 in Freda Adler and William S. Laufer (eds.), *New Directions in Criminological Century—Advances in Criminological Theory, Vol. 4*. New Brunswick, NJ: Transaction.

Kitsuse, John I. 1964. "Societal Reaction to Deviant Behavior: Problems of Theory and Method." Pp. 87-102 in Howard S. Becker (ed.), *The Other Side*. New York: The Free Press.

Kornhauser, Ruth Rosner. 1978. *Social Sources of Delinquency: An Appraisal of Analytic Models*. Chicago: University of Chicago Press.

Latessa, Edward J., Francis T. Cullen, and Paul Gendreau. 2002. "Beyond Correctional Quackery: Professionalism and the Possibility of Effective Treatment." *Federal Probation* 66 (September): 43-49.

Laub, John H. 2002. "Introduction: The Life and Work of Travis Hirschi." Pp. xi-xlix in John H. Laub (ed.), *The Craft of Criminology: Selected Papers*. New Brunswick, NJ: Transaction.

——. 2004. "The Life Course of Criminology in the United States: The American Society of Criminology 2003 Presidential Address." *Criminology* 42: 1-26.

Laub, John H., and Robert J. Sampson. 2003. *Shared Beginnings, Divergent Lives: Delinquent Boys to Age 70*. Cambridge, MA: Harvard University Press.

Le Blanc, Marc, and Rolf Loeber. 1998. "Developmental Criminology Updated." Pp. 115-198 in Michael Tonry (ed.), *Crime and Justice: A Review of Research, Vol. 23*. Chicago: University of Chicago Press.

Lemert, Edwin M. 1951. *Social Pathology*. New York: McGraw-Hill.

Lilly, J. Robert, Francis T. Cullen, and Richard A. Ball. 2002. *Criminological Theory: Context and Consequences*, 3rd ed. Thousand Oaks, CA: Sage.

Lowenkamp, Christopher T., Francis T. Cullen, and Travis C. Pratt. 2003. "Replicating Sampson and Groves's Test of Social Disorganization Theory: Revisiting a Criminological Classic." *Journal of Research in Crime and Delinquency* 40: 351-373.

MacKenzie, Doris. 2000. "Evidence-Based Corrections: Identifying What Works." *Crime and Delinquency* 46: 457-471.

Martinson, Robert. 1974. "What Works? Questions and Answers About Prison Reform." *The Public Interest* 35 (Spring): 22-54.

Massey, Douglas S., and Nancy A. Denton. 1993. *American Apartheid: Segregation and the Making of the Underclass*. Cambridge, MA: Harvard University Press.

Merton, Robert K. 1938. "Social Structure and Anomie." *American Sociological Review* 1: 894-904.

Messner, Steven F. 1988. "Merton's 'Social Structure and Anomie': The Road Not Taken." *Deviant Behavior* 9: 33-53.

Messner, Steven F., and Richard Rosenfeld. 1994. *Crime and the American Dream*. Belmont, CA: Wadsworth.

Mills, C. Wright. 1942. "The Professional Ideology of Social Pathologists." *American Journal of Sociology* 49: 165-180.

Moffitt, Terrie E. 1993. "Adolescence-Limited and Life-Course-Persistent Antisocial Behavior: A Developmental Taxonomy." *Psychological Review* 100: 674-701.

Moffitt, Terrie E., Avshalom Caspi, Michael Rutter, and Phil A. Silva. 2001. *Sex Differences in Antisocial Behaviour: Conduct Disorder, Delinquency, and Violence in the Dunedin Longitudinal Study*. Cambridge: Cambridge University Press.

Palamara, Frances, Francis T. Cullen, and Joanne C. Gersten. 1986. "The Effect of Police and Mental Health Intervention on Juvenile Deviance: Specifying Contingencies in the Impact of Formal Reaction." *Journal of Health and Social Behavior* 27: 90-105.

Paternoster, Raymond. 1987. "The Deterrent Effect of the Perceived Certainty and Severity of Punishment: A Review of the Evidence and Issues." *Justice Quarterly* 4: 173-217.

Piquero, Alex, David P. Farrington, and Alfred Blumstein. 2003. "The Criminal Career Paradigm." Pp. 359-506 in Michael Tonry (ed.), *Crime and Justice: A Review of Research, Vol. 23*. Chicago: University of Chicago Press.

Pratt, Travis C., and Francis T. Cullen 2000. "The Empirical Status of Gottfredson and Hirschi's General Theory of Crime: A Meta-Analysis." *Criminology* 38: 931-964.

————. 2005. "Assessing Macro-Level Predictors and Theories of Crime: A Meta-Analysis." Pp. 373-450 in Michael Tonry (ed.), *Crime and Justice: A Review of Research, Vol. 32*. Chicago: University of Chicago Press.

Pratt, Travis C., Christine S. Sellers, Francis T. Cullen, L. Thomas Winfree, Jr., and Tamara D. Madensen. 2005. "The Empirical Status of Social Learning Theory: A Meta-Analysis." Unpublished paper, Washington State University.

Reckless, Walter C. 1961. *The Crime Problem,* 3rd ed. New York: Appleton-Century-Crofts.

Reiss, Albert J. 1951. "Delinquency as a Failure of Personal and Social Controls." *American Sociological Review* 16: 196-207.

Sampson, Robert J., and W. Byron Groves. 1989. "Community Structure and Crime: Testing Social-Disorganization Theory." *American Journal of Sociology* 94: 774-802.

Sampson, Robert J., and John H. Laub. 1993. *Crime in the Making: Pathways and Turning Points Through Life*. Cambridge, MA: Harvard University Press.

————. 1994. "Urban Poverty and the Family Context Delinquency: A New Look at Structure and Process in a Classic Study." *Child Development* 65: 523-540.

————. 1995. "Understanding Variability in Lives Through Time: Contributions of Life Course Criminology." *Studies on Crime and Crime Prevention* 4: 143-158.

Sampson, Robert J., Stephen W. Raudenbush, and Felton Earls. 1997. "Neighborhood and Violent Crime: A Multilevel Study of Collective Efficacy." *Science* 277 (August 15): 916-924.

Sampson, Robert J., and William Julius Wilson. 1995. "Towards a Theory of Race, Crime, and Urban Inequality." Pp. 37-54 in John Hagan and Ruth D. Peterson (eds.), *Crime and Inequality*. Stanford, CA: Stanford University Press.

Shaw, Clifford R. 1930. *The Jack Roller: A Delinquent Boy's Own Story*. Chicago: University of Chicago Press.

Shaw, Clifford R., with the assistance of Henry D. McKay and James F. MacDonald. 1938. *Brothers in Crime*. Chicago: University of Chicago Press.

Sherman, Lawrence W. 1993. "Defiance, Deterrence, and Irrelevance: A Theory of the Criminal Sanction." *Journal of Research in Crime and Delinquency* 30: 445-473.

Skogan, Welsey K. 1990. *Disorder and Decline: Crime and the Spiral of Decay in American Neighborhoods*. Berkeley: University of California Press.

Snodgrass, Jon. 1976. "Clifford R. Shaw and Henry D. McKay: Chicago Criminologists." *British Journal of Criminology* 16: 1-19.

Sykes, Gresham M., and David Matza. 1957. "Techniques of Neutralization." *American Sociological Review* 22: 664-670.

Taylor, Claire. 2001. "The Relationship Between Social and Self-Control." *Theoretical Criminology* 5: 369-388.

Taylor, Ian, Paul Walton, and Jock Young. 1973. *The New Criminology: For a Social Theory of Deviance*. London: Routledge and Kegan Paul.

————, eds. 1975. *Critical Criminology*. London: Routledge and Kegan Paul.

Tittle, Charles R. 1975. "Deterrents or Labeling?" *Social Forces* 53: 399-410.

Thornberry, Terence P. 1987. "Toward an Interactional Theory of Delinquency." *Criminology* 25: 863-891.

Thorsell, Bernard A., and Lloyd W. Klemke. 1972. "The Labeling Process: Reinforcement and Deterrence? *Law and Society Review* 6: 393-403.

Thornberry, Terence P., and Marvin D. Krohn, eds. 2003. *Taking Stock of Delinquency: An Overview of Findings from Contemporary Longitudinal Studies*. New York: Kluwer Academic/Plenum.

Unnever, James D., Francis T. Cullen, and Robert Agnew. 2006. "Why Is 'Bad Parenting' Criminogenic? Implications from Rival Theories." *Juvenile Justice and Youth Violence* 4: 3-33.

Williams, Frank P., III. 1984. "The Demise of the Criminological Imagination: A Critique of Recent Criminology." *Justice Quarterly* 1: 91-116.

Wright, John Paul, Kim N. Dietrich, and M. Douglas Ris. 2004. "The Effect of Early Lead Exposure on Adult Criminal Behavior: Evidence from a 24-Year Longitudinal Study." Paper presented at the Annual Meeting of the American Society of Criminology, Nashville, TN.

Part I

The Core of Criminological Theory

1

The Empirical Status of Social Learning Theory of Crime and Deviance: The Past, Present, and Future

Ronald L. Akers and Gary F. Jensen

This paper has two goals. The first goal is to review the empirical research evidence on the validity of social learning theory as an explanation of criminal and deviant behavior. This is a topic about which we have written extensively, both separately and jointly, over a long period of time (see Akers 1973, 1985, 1998, Jensen 1972; Akers et al. 1979; Jensen and Rojek 1998; Akers and Jensen 2003; Jensen 2003; Akers and Sellers 2004). That previous work establishes that the theory fares very well in terms of all of the major criteria for sound theory, including logical consistency, scope, usefulness and, most importantly, strength of empirical support. Indeed, it is reasonable to propose that the theory has been tested in relation to a wider range of forms of deviance, in a wider range of settings and samples, in more different languages, and by more different people, has survived more "crucial tests" against other theories and is more strongly and consistently supported by empirical data than any other social psychological explanation of crime and deviance (see Akers 1998; Akers and Jensen 2003).

The second goal is to illuminate new directions for expanding, elaborating and testing the theory in the future. We will propose ways to build on the Social Structure and Social Learning (SSSL) model (Akers 1998) and our recent efforts in "taking social learning global" (Jensen and Akers 2003) toward an integrated theory that addresses issues that we believe have been ignored for too long. At the risk of over-reaching, we will attempt to stimulate attention, discourse and, perhaps, debate regarding extension of social learning theory by making a rather daring claim. We will assert that social learning theory can be elaborated to account for criminological and sociological regularities, making sense of events not only at the micro-level but also at higher levels of temporal and ecological aggregation, providing a better explanation than has been so far provided by other theories.

Overview of Social Learning Theory

Social learning is a general theory that offers an explanation of the acquisition, maintenance, and change in criminal and deviant behavior that embraces social, nonsocial, and cultural factors operating both to motivate and control criminal behavior and both to promote and undermine conformity. The basic proposition is that the same learning process in a context of social structure, interaction, and situation, produces both conforming and deviant behavior. That is, the theory is not, contrary to the misconception sometimes found in the literature, simply a theory of the acquisition of novel behavior, a theory of bad companions or a "cultural deviance" theory. It is not solely a "positivistic" theory of the causes of crime addressing only "why they do it" and incapable of explaining "why they do not" (Gottfredson and Hirschi 1990; see Akers 1996, 1998). Rather, the theory incorporates crime facilitating as well as protective and preventive factors. The probability of criminal or conforming behavior is a function of the balance of these influences on behavior, not only those operative in one's learning history, but also on those operating at a given time in a given situation and those predictive of future behavior (Akers 1998: 59).

The concepts, propositions and variables in social learning theory have been presented in published form in great detail over the past forty years, are well known in the classroom and widely cited in the literature (for example, Burgess and Akers 1966; Akers 1973, 1985, 1992, 1994, 1998; Akers et al. 1979; Akers and Jensen 2003; Akers and Sellers 2004). Therefore, we make the assumption that the reader will be somewhat familiar with the theory and, since our focus here is on the empirical status and future directions of the theory, the theory will not be presented in detail. Rather, our overview will concentrate on the four major explanatory concepts or dimensions of the theory—*differential association, definitions* (and other discriminative stimuli), *differential reinforcement, and imitation.*

Differential association refers to direct association and interaction with others who engage in certain kinds of behavior or express norms, values, and attitudes supportive of such behavior, as well as the indirect association and identification with more distant reference groups. The groups with which one is in differential association provide the major immediate and intermediate social contexts in which all the mechanisms of social learning operate. The most important of these groups are the primary ones of family and friends, but the concept of differential association also includes both direct and indirect interaction and exposure to secondary and reference groups as well as mass media, internet, computer games, and other "virtual groups" (Warr 2002). Those associations that occur earlier (priority), last longer and occupy more of one's time (duration), take place most often (frequency), and involve others with whom one has the more important or closer relationship (intensity) will have the greater effect on behavior. The theory hypothesizes that the more one's patterns of differential association are balanced in the direction of greater exposure to deviant behavior and attitudes, the greater the probability of that person engaging in deviant or criminal behavior.

Definitions are one's own orientations, rationalizations, justifications, excuses, and other attitudes that define the commission of an act as relatively more right or wrong, good or bad, desirable or undesirable, justified or unjustified, and appropriate or inappropriate. Definitions include those learned from socialization into general religious, moral, and other conventional values and norms that are favorable to conforming behavior and unfavorable to committing any deviant or criminal acts (or general beliefs or worldviews that support deviant acts). Specific definitions orient the person to particular acts or series of acts and to define given situations as providing opportunity or lack of opportunity for commission of crime. The greater the extent to which one has learned and endorses general or specific attitudes that either positively approve of, or provide justification (neutralizations) for, the commission of criminal or deviant behavior in situations discriminative for it, the greater the chances are that one will engage in that behavior. Cognitively, these definitions provide a mind-set that makes one more willing to commit the act when the opportunity is perceived. Behaviorally, they affect the commission of deviant or criminal behavior by acting as internal discriminative stimuli in conjunction with external discriminative stimuli (place, time, presence or absence of others, etc.) that provide cues or signals to the individual as to what kind of behavior s/he has the opportunity, or expectation, of exhibiting in that situation. Some of the definitions favorable to deviance are so intensely held as part of a learned belief system, for instance, the radical ideologies of militant groups implicated in terrorists acts, that they provide strong positive motivation for criminal acts (Akers and Silverman 2004). As another example, it appears that in Elijah Anderson's depiction, the "code of the street" (1999) may require that attacks on one's honor be responded to in ways that knowingly violate the law. For the most part, however, definitions favorable to crime and delinquency do not directly motivate action in this sense. Rather, they are conventional beliefs so weakly held that they fail to function as definitions unfavorable to crime or they are learned approving, justifying, or rationalizing attitudes that, however weakly or strongly endorsed, facilitate law violation in the right set of circumstances by providing approval, justification, or rationalization.

Differential reinforcement refers to the balance of anticipated or actual rewards and punishments that follow, or are consequences of, behavior. Whether individuals will refrain from, or commit, a crime at any given time (and whether they will continue, or desist, from doing so in the future) depends on the balance of past, present, and anticipated future rewards and punishments for their actions. The greater the value, frequency, and probability of reward for deviant behavior (balanced against the punishing consequences and rewards/punishment for alternative behavior), the greater the likelihood that it will occur and be repeated. Reinforcers and punishers can be nonsocial; for example, the direct physical effects of drugs and alcohol. However, the theory proposes that most of the learning in criminal and deviant behavior is the result of direct, and indirect, social interaction in which the words, responses, presence, and behavior of other persons directly reinforce behavior, provide the setting for reinforcement (discriminative stimuli), or serve as the conduit through which other social rewards and punishers are delivered or made available. The concept of social reinforcement (and punishment) includes the whole range of actual and anticipated, tangible and intangible, material and symbolic rewards valued in society or subgroups. Social rewards can be highly symbolic. In self-reinforcement the individual exercises self-control, reinforcing or punishing one's own behavior by taking the role of others, even when alone. The balance of reinforcement may motivate individuals to commit law violations or deviant acts even in the face of their own definitions unfavorable to those acts, but the acts are most probable when both the reinforcement balance, and the balance of one's own definitions, are in the same deviant direction.

Imitation refers to the engagement in behavior after the direct or indirect (e.g. in media depictions) observation of similar behavior by others. Whether or not the behavior modeled by others will be imitated is affected by the characteristics of the models, the behavior observed, and the observed consequences of the behavior (vicarious reinforcement) (Bandura 1977). The observation of salient models in primary groups and in the media affects both pro-social and deviant behavior (Donnerstein and Linz 1995). Imitation is more important in the initial acquisition and performance of novel behavior than in the maintenance or cessation of behavioral patterns once established, but it continues to have some effect in maintaining behavior.

These social learning concepts define sets of variables that are all part of the same underlying *process* that is operative in each individual's learning history (both learning from and influencing others), in the immediate situation in which an opportunity for a crime occurs, and in the larger *social structural* context (at both the meso-level and macro-level). The social learning process is dynamic and includes reciprocal and feedback effects. Reinforcement in operant conditioning is a response-stimulus-response process in which behavior produces consequences that, in turn, produce the probability of the behavior being repeated (Skinner 1959). Therefore, contrary to the way some have characterized the theory (Thornberry et al. 1994), reciprocal and sequential effects of social learning variables and deviant/conforming behavior are recognized, albeit with an emphasis on the effects of the learning variables on deviant behavior. The typical temporal sequence in the process by which persons come to the point of violating the law, or engaging in other deviant acts, is hypothesized to be one in which the balance of learned definitions, imitation of criminal or deviant models, and the anticipated balance of reinforcement produces the initial delinquent or deviant act. The facilitative effects of these variables continue in the repetition of acts, although imitation becomes less important than it was in the first commission of the act. After onset or initiation, the actual social and non-social reinforcers and punishers affect whether or not the acts will be repeated and at what level of frequency. Both the behavior and the definitions, favorable and unfavorable, are affected by the consequences of the initial acts. Whether a deviant act will be repeated in a situation that presents, or is perceived to present, the opportunity, depends on the learning history of the individual and the set of definitions, discriminative stimuli and reinforcement contingencies in that situation.

The theory does not hypothesize that definitions favorable to law violation only precede and are unaffected by the initiation of criminal acts. As noted, acts in violation of the law can occur even when defined as undesirable and, indeed, can occur in the absence of any thought given to right and wrong at the moment. Furthermore, definitions may be applied by the individual retroactively to excuse or justify an act already committed. To the extent such excuses successfully mitigate others' negative sanctions or one's self-punishment, however, they become cues for the repetition of deviant acts. At that point, they precede the future commission of the acts. Differential association with conforming and non-conforming others typically precedes the individual's committing the acts. As noted above, families are the principal primary groups included in the differential association process and it is obvious that association, reinforcement of conforming or deviant behavior, deviant or conforming modeling, and exposure to definitions favorable or unfavorable to deviance (socialization) occurs within the family (or family surrogate) prior to the onset of delinquency or law violations. While it is often the case that one has deviant acts or tendencies (as a function of previously learned patterns in the family) that makes him attractive to, and attracted to, deviant peer groups, associations are more typically formed initially around attractions, friendships, and circumstances, such as neighborhood proximity and family location and preferences, that have little to do directly with co-involvement in some deviant behavior. However, after the greater associations with those exhibiting deviant patterns have been established and the reinforcing or punishing consequences of the deviant behavior are experienced, both the continuation of old, and the seeking of new, associations (over which one has any choice) will, themselves, be affected. One may choose further interaction with others based, in part, on whether they, too, are involved in similar deviant or criminal behavior. But, the theory proposes that the sequence of events in which deviant associations and attractions precede the onset of delinquent behavior will occur more frequently than the sequence of events in which the onset of delinquency precedes the beginning of deviant associations. Further, after the deviant peer associations are taken up, they will continue to the extent that they are, on balance, more rewarding than alternatives, and any deviant behavior, or tendencies, will increase after the peer associations have been formed (Conger 1976). Whether the deviant patterns will be persistent and stable (or will desist) over time is a function of the continuity, or discontinuity, in the person's patterns of associations, definitions, and reinforcement.

Review of Research on Social Learning Variables

What Research Findings Are Relevant?

This review concentrates on research findings on social learning theory as developed by Ronald L. Akers. Akers' social learning theory was originally proposed as *differential association-reinforcement theory* in collaboration with Robert L. Burgess (Burgess and Akers 1966) as a behavioristic reformulation integrating Edwin H. Sutherland's (1947) differential association theory and behavioral psychology as a general theory of crime and deviance. It is well known that the designation of "social learning" may refer to any compatible cognitive-behavioral, or social-behavioral, approach in the social sciences and empirical evidence related to them could be included as relevant to the empirical status of social learning theory in criminology (Patterson et al. 1975, 1992; Bandura 1977; Jessor and Jessor 1977; White et al. 1991; Patterson and Chamberlain 1994; Patterson 1995).

There is a broad range of rehabilitation, prevention, treatment, and behavior modification programs operating in correctional, treatment, and community facilities and programs for juveniles and adults that are explicitly, or implicitly, predicated on the cognitive/behavioral principles in social learning theory. These programs have had greater success in treating, preventing, or correcting criminal and delinquent behavior than alternative approaches (see Pearson et al. 2002; Andrews and Bonta 2003; Cullen et al. 2003; Akers and Sellers 2004). But we do not include a review of the evaluation research on applications of social learning in such programs here. The outcomes of applied programs are valuable for directly assessing the usefulness of a theory, but can be used only indirectly to assess the truthfulness of a theory. Also, the empirical status of a theory can be indirectly assessed by examining the extent to which the theory fits, or makes sense of, the known empirical correlates and variations in crime and delinquency. But the empirical status of a theory is best evaluated by primary research findings on models, propositions, and variables derivable from the theory. It is this body of research to which our review here refers.

As is true for the empirical data on all major criminological theories, a great deal of the quantitative research relevant to social learning theory involves linear models based on the analysis of survey data. Even when the analyses allow identification of nonrecursive relationships using longitudinal data, such data cannot fully reproduce the behavioral process envisioned in social learning theory. For example, people may not recognize that their own behavior mimics the behavior of others, and survey methods may not capture subtle distinctions among types of learning mechanisms. A variety of distinct observational, quantitative, and qualitative methods may be necessary for empirically observing and isolating different learning mechanisms.

Nevertheless, quantitative models containing social learning variables are appropriate for assessing the empirical status of social learning theory (as well as other theories) because the principal independent variables in this process, and their operational measures, have been hypothesized as causally (in the probabilistic sense) linked to deviant behavior. If the theory is correct, then empirical findings on structural models, or multiple regression analyses of sets of variables derived from or consistent with the theory, that approximate or provide a snapshot of the underlying process, should be supported by the data when subjected to proper statistical analysis. It is reasonable to expect the theory to withstand empirical scrutiny with cross-sectional and longitudinal survey data even though such data do not fully reproduce the ongoing process. To the extent that such data do not conform to the expectations of the theory, then it reasonable to conclude the theory, and the underlying social learning process it hypothesizes, is not confirmed. In short, if the relationships are as predicted, then the theory is supported, if not, the theory is undermined. Likewise, the greater the magnitude of the observed relationships, the stronger the support for the theory. Similarly, weak relationships raise questions about the power of the theory, and relationships in the direction opposite from theoretical expectation disconfirm the theory.

Using the same type of data and empirical models for testing other theories (whether or not those other theories posit some underlying social process), allows direct comparisons of the effects of social learning variables with the effects of variables taken from other theories. Neither social learning theory nor any other theory of crime and deviance has been able to explain all instances or variation in such behavior, and none can withstand an absolute standard of necessary and sufficient causation with 100 percent of the variance explained. By that standard all current and past (and one should say future) theories fail. Rather, the standard is whether the presence of the explanatory variables increase or decrease the probability of the behavior occurring; and assessment of the empirical status of any theory should be based not only on how well the theory, or variables from the theory, do when tested alone, but also how well they do when compared to different, alternative or competing models.

A fair review of research on social learning variables and hypotheses derived from the theory, both on its own and in comparison with other theories, leads to the conclusion that social learning theory is supported by the preponderance of empirical evidence. There is a large body of research that includes one or more of the social learning concepts and variables of differential reinforcement, differential association, definitions, and modeling, mainly involving peer groups and the family, accounting for individual differences in criminal, delinquent, and deviant behavior. In empirical models, social learning variables (particularly differential association) nearly always have stronger net effects on criminal/deviant behavior than social psychological variables taken from other theories and remain controlling for a range of socio-demographic and structural variables. There are few findings in any of the research that are contradictory or inconsistent with the theory, and most of the research provides strong to moderate support for social learning hypotheses.

We view support for the theory, or lack of support for the theory, as coming from any research in which one or more of the social learning variables, separately, in combination or in an overall model with other variables, has been measured and related to dependent variables of criminal, delinquent, or deviant behavior. Most of the research findings we count as supportive of the theory are presented by the respective researchers as a direct or indirect test of social learning theory (by itself or in comparison or combination with other theories) or otherwise acknowledge that their research includes variables and hypotheses derived from or relevant to social learning (even when they make no claims to testing the theory). However, sometimes researchers include one or more empirical measures that have long been used as, or clearly can be seen to be, empirical operationalizations of social learning variables, but do not identify the variables as social learning as such, give other names to them, identify them with other theories, refer to social learning in crime or deviance without citation, or make no reference at all to social learning (for examples see Gwartney-Gibbs et al. 1987; Osgood et al. 1996; Bankston and Caldas 1996; Costello and Vowell 1999; Osgood and Anderson 2004).

For example, the lead article in a recent issue of *Criminology* (Osgood and Anderson 2004) applies "an individual-level routine activities perspective to explaining rates of delinquency" and concludes that: "Time spent in unstructured socializing with peers has both individual and contextual effects explaining a large share of variation in rates of delinquency across groups of adolescents who attend different schools." Unstructured socializing was measured by responses to a single item: "In an average week, how many hours do you spend hanging around with your current friends, not doing anything in particular, where no adults are present" (2004: 530). Because parental monitoring was found to affect unstructured socializing, they propose that it supports an integration of routine activity with social disorganization theory.

When the paper was presented at the ASC meetings prior to its publication in the journal, we (Akers and Jensen) expressed concerns that social learning was misclassified under "cultural or normative interpretation of the role of peer groups" and that no mention was made of the fact that the findings reported in the paper obviously fit social learning theory. The published paper did not address these concerns. Osgood and Anderson claim that their theory is distinct from cultural interpretations because they emphasize "contextual and situational influences rather than positing a causal role for peer culture valuing delinquency" (2004: 525). Their theory may be distinct from a theory that only posits a causal role for peer culture (whatever theory that may be), but it is not distinct from social learning. "Individual-level routine activities" theory then, appears to be a partial variant of individual-level social learning theory (partial because it does not include a measure of the behavior and attitudes of the peers with whom one is spending unstructured time). This example illustrates a tactic that is too often found in reporting research findings while ignoring or denying their relevance for social learning theory: mis-classify the theory and direct criticism at the category in which it is mis-classified. Anyone familiar with social learning theory knows that the theory is not in any way confined to the "causal role of peer culture." The theory clearly posits one normative learning mechanism and three non-normative mechanisms, including imitation, differential reinforcement, and differential association. What is involved in "unstructured socialization in peer groups" if not observation of peer behavioral models, exposure to peers' values, norms, and attitudes, and social interaction with peers in which behavior and attitudes are socially reinforced? The question measuring this unstructured socializing during time spent with peers free of adult surveillance is one type of measure of differential association and a setting in which imitation, social reinforcement, and sharing of attitudes and definitions occur as predicated by social learning theory. How do these social learning variables differ from "contextual and situational influences?" Contrary to Osgood and Anderson's claim, they do not. Moreover, while this measure of unsupervised peer association is not the most common measure (which is that respondents are asked to report proportions or numbers of peers engaged in particular behavior and/or holding particular attitudes), it is clearly closer to being an operationalization of the concept of differential peer association than any explanatory concept found in routine activities or social disorganization theory.

We believe it is reasonable to count empirical findings as supportive of the theory if the measures of the independent variables in the study are operationalization of social learning variables such as peer associations, parental modeling, prosocial and deviant attitudes, media imitation, and informal positive and negative social sanctions, whether or not the authors of the research specifically identify the variables as coming from social learning theory. For instance cross-sectional or longitudinal research in which some measure of number, frequency, or proportion of delinquent and non-delinquent peers, or some other indicator of differences in association with delinquent and non-delinquent peers, provides at least a partial test of social learning theory because it plainly includes measures of a key variable in the theory, namely, differential association. The same would be true of measures of differences in peer values, norms, or attitudes (definitions favorable and unfavorable).

This standard of relevance holds whether or not the authors reporting the research specifically identify the research as testing social learning theory and whether the variable is labeled by them as differential association, peer association, peer influence, deviant peer bonding, peer networks, gangs, peer attitudes, deviant peer pressure, unstructured peer socializing, or some other label. If the research finds a positive and significant relationship of that variable to a dependent variable of delinquency or deviance, then that can reasonably be seen as supportive of social learning theory. If no relationship or a negative relationship is found, then the findings can reasonably be seen as not supportive of the theory.

The same holds for all of the other major social learning variables. Research testing the relationship of the respondents' own balance of definitions favorable and unfavorable to their delinquent or deviant behavior is relevant to social learning theory whether the researchers call them neutralizations, techniques of neutralizations, attitudes, beliefs, justifications, or something else. Research finding that the balance of rewards and punishments, benefits and costs, positive and negative consequences, whether labeled as informal social control, reactions of peers or family, sanction threat, rational choice, or something else, is related to deviant behavior and supportive of the hypotheses in social learning theory regarding differential reinforcement. Research with measures of parental or peer modeling, media depictions, or other measures that can be seen as validly operationalizing imitation can also be seen as at least partially testing social learning theory.

A Half-Century of Supportive Research Findings

Although the first empirical tests of full models with all of the major social learning concepts measured and entered into the models came in the late 1970s (see Akers et al. 1979), published reports of research can be found for at least twenty years prior to that time in which one or more of the main variables incorporated into social learning theory are found to have the predicted relationship with delinquent and criminal behavior. Although Sutherland did not publish quantitative research specifically testing differential association theory, he viewed his classic qualitative study of professional theft (1937) as empirically supportive of differential association theory both in the sense that one learned the techniques of professional theft from other thieves, and in the sense that the criminal ideology of professional thieves constituted one form of "definitions favorable" to crime. Similarly, Cressey's (1953) classic study in the 1950s of apprehended embezzlers found that exposure to, and acceptance of, already existing definitions justifying or rationalizing violation of trust was the key part of the three-step process of embezzlement.

In each decade since the 1950s and continuing into the first decade of the twenty-first century, a sizeable number of journal articles, chapters, and books have been published reporting research findings that definitions, differential association, differential reinforcement, imitation, and other learning-relevant variables singly, or in some combination, have the relationship with delinquent or criminal behavior expected in social learning theory. The empirical relationships are not only statistically significant but usually of sufficient magnitude to conclude that the effects of variables identified as part of the social learning process are not trivial, but substantially account for variation in the dependent variables of criminal, delinquent, and deviant behavior. There is an abundance of such studies and we make no attempt here to list or cite all of them or to discuss them individually. We would assert that the volume of studies and the positive findings, with few negative findings, provides greater empirical support for social learning theory than for any other major social psychological theory of crime and deviance.

As is true for most of the research testing social psychological theories of crime and deviance, a considerable amount of social learning research has been done with samples of adolescents with the typical data collection technique being self-report surveys. The dependent variables in this research range from minor forms of adolescent deviance, to teenage use or abuse of alcohol, drugs and tobacco, to serious delinquent and criminal property and personal offenses. Some of the research has been conducted with adult samples with substance use and abuse or various types of criminal behavior as the dependent variable. The most commonly measured social learning variable is differential peer association (although it is sometimes given a different label such as "deviant peer bonding" or "delinquent opportunities"). This variable is typically measured by number or proportion of friends who are involved in delinquent or deviant behavior, but sometimes the modalities of associations (frequency, duration, intensity, and priority) are measured and sometimes the values, norms, or attitudes of the peers toward the behavior in question (the normative dimension) are measured. Learned definitions favorable and unfavorable, most often measured by respondents' endorsement or agreement with statements of positive/negative attitudes and beliefs or neutralizing definitions toward given deviant behavior, are also often found in this research as independent variables (again often given variable labels other than "definitions"). Measures of differential reinforcement are less frequently found in the research, but measures such as reports of peer reactions, parental sanctions, legal sanctions, or other actual or anticipated rewarding and punishing consequences of one's deviant behavior are found in the literature. Modeling or imitation is least often included in this research. Not surprisingly, when imitative effects are tested, it is most likely to be with adolescent or younger samples. It is sometimes measured directly, but is also inferred from parental behavior or from exposure to media portrayals.

The magnitude of the empirical relationships between these social learning variables and delinquent, criminal and deviant behavior reported in the literature is only sometimes weak. The typical finding is strong to moderate effects, differing somewhat by which social learning variable is considered, the type of deviance under study, how the variables are measured, or by the sample. The relationships have generally been stronger and more consistently found than for any other set of social psychological or sociodemographic variables included in the research and there has been very little negative or counter evidence reported in the literature.

Virtually all of the early self-report delinquency studies by Short (1957, 1958, 1960), Nye (1958), Voss (1964), and others who included measures of differential association (almost always differential peer association) found clear effects on delinquency in the expected direction. Even in the classic work by Travis Hirschi (1969) in which he presented and found clear empirical support for his social bonding theory, self-reported delinquency was more strongly related to differential peer association than any of the social bonding variables even though the measure of peer association used in Hirschi's study was, itself, a relatively indirect and weak measure (respondents' report of any close friends picked up by the police rather than respondents' reports of numbers or proportions of friends committing delinquent behavior or holding delinquent attitudes). Studies in the 1970s include Jensen (1972), Krohn (1974), Kandel (1974), Burkett and Jensen (1975), Conger (1976), Jessor and Jessor (1977) and others. Supportive research reported in the 1980s, include Minor (1980), Kandel and Adler (1982), Andrews (1980), Matsueda (1982), Dull (1983), Winfree and Griffiths (1983), Meier et al. (1984), Patterson and Dishion (1985), LaGrange and White (1985), Elliott et al. (1985), Massey and Krohn (1986), Dembo et al. (1986), Lanza-Kaduce and Klug (1986), White et al. (1986, 1987), Marcos et al. (1986), Kandel and Andrews (1987), Matsueda and Heimer (1987), Johnson, et al. 1987, Orcutt (1987), Burkett and Warren (1987), and Lopez et al. (1989),

Findings from research that are supportive of social learning continued to be reported in the 1990s such as by Sellers and Winfree (1990), Loeber et al. (1991), Kandel and Davies (1991), Agnew (1991; 1993; 1994), McGee (1992), Junger-Tas (1992), Warr and Stafford (1991), Rowe and Gulley (1992), Winfree et al. (1993, 1994a, 1994b), Lauritsen (1993), Warr (1993a; 1993b; 1996), Inciardi et al. (1993), Benda (1994), Burton et al. (1994), Elliott (1994), Simons et al. (1994), Dabney (1995), Conger and Simons (1995), Patterson, (1995), Snyder and Patterson (1995), Wood et al. (1995), Zhang and Messner (1995), Mihalic and Elliott (1997), Skinner and Fream (1997), Capaldi et al. (1997), Rowe and Farrington (1997), Esbensen and Deschenes (1998) and Warr (1998). This long line of research supportive of social learning theory has extended to the present time as shown by Kim and Goto (2000), Rogers (2001), Rebellon (2002), Ardelt and Day (2002), Warr (2002), Haynie (2002), Batton and Ogle

(2003), Sellers et al. (2003), Brezina and Piquero, (2003), Chappel and Piquero, (2004), Gordon et al. (2004), and McGloin et al. (2004).

The great preponderance of research conducted on social learning theory has found strong to moderate relationships in the theoretically expected direction between social learning variables and criminal, delinquent, and deviant behavior. When social learning theory is tested against other theories using the same data collected from the same samples, it is usually (but not always, see Hepburn 1977) found to account for more variance in the dependent variables or have greater support than the theories with which it is being compared (for instance, see Akers and Cochran 1985; Matsueda and Heimer 1987; White et al. 1986; Kandel and Davies 1991; McGee 1992; Benda 1994; Burton et al. 1994; Hwang and Akers 2003; Rebellon 2002). A recent meta-analysis reported support for the impact of social learning variables (differential association and definitions) but the effect of those variables were not stronger than effects of measures of Gottfredson and Hirschi's (1990) concept of self-control (Pratt and Cullen 2000). However, when social learning variables are included in integrated or combined models that incorporate variables from different theories in the same sample with the same data, it is the measures of social learning concepts that have the strongest main and net effects (Elliott et al. 1985; Kaplan et al. 1987; Thornberry et al. 1994; Kaplan 1996; Catalano et al. 1996, Huang et al. 2001; Jang 2002). Cross-cultural studies have found that social learning theory is not society or culture bound but is well supported by research in other societies (Kandel and Adler 1982; Lopez et al. 1989; Junger-Tas 1992; Bruinsma 1992; Zhang and Messner 1995; Kim and Koto 2000; Hwang and Akers 2003; Wang and Jensen 2003)

Research on Social Learning in the Family

Empirical findings on the impact of family variables (for instance, family relationships and parental disciplinary and supervisory practices) are rightly and fairly taken as evidence in support of versions of control theory because these measures were used by Hirschi (1969) as indicators of social bonds and Gottfredson and Hirschi (1990) stress the importance of early family socialization in the formation of self-control. But they are just as rightly and validly seen as evidence in support of social learning theory. Although the research of Gerald Patterson and his associates on family variables and processes in deviant behavior is often interpreted as being in the tradition of and supportive of control theories (Sampson and Laub 1993), it is worth remembering that all of this research has occurred under the aegis of the Oregon *Social Learning* Center (Patterson 1975; Patterson and Dishion 1985; Patterson et al. 1989; Patterson et al. 1991; Wiesner et al. 2003).

What is socialization and informal social control in the family if it is not social learning? The family is a key primary group with which one is differentially associated. The process of acquiring, persisting or modifying behavior in the family or family surrogate is a process of exposure to normative values and behavioral models and differential reinforcement. The typical empirical measures of control theory variables such as family parental control, discipline, and management (parental sanctions) are transparently measures of differential social reinforcement (rewards and punishment) for conforming and nonconforming or disobedient behavior. Informal social control in the family has long been conceptualized as part of the social learning process (learning of values and sanctioning of behavior) in producing conformity or deviance (Akers 1973, 1985). As Jacson Toby says, "Rewards and punishments are central to social control and are administered in all groups attempting to influence the behavior of members" (Toby 1974: 95).

The role of the family is usually as a conventional socializer. It provides conventional, anti-criminal definitions, conforming role models, and the reinforcement of conformity through parental discipline; it promotes the development of conformity and self-control. In the family, the balance of interactive and normative dimensions of differential association, behavioral models, and reinforcement of attitudes and behavior is typically in the pro-social, non-deviant direction. But delinquent and deviant behavior also has family origins (Fagan and Wexler 1987) and may be the outcome of internal family interaction (McCord 1991b). The acquisition and maintenance of deviant patterns may be directly affected by deviant parental models, ineffective and erratic parental supervision and discipline in the use of positive and negative sanctions and the endorsement of values and attitudes favorable to deviance. Patterson and his associates have shown that the operation of social learning mechanisms in parent-child interaction is a strong predictor of conforming/deviant behavior (Patterson 1975, 1995; Snyder and Patterson 1995; Wiesner et al. 2003). Ineffective disciplinary strategies by parents increase the chances that a child will learn behavior in the early years that is a precursor to his or her later delinquency. Children learn conforming responses when parents consistently make use of positive rewards for proper behavior and impose moderately negative consequences for misbehavior (Capaldi et al. 1997; Wells and Rankin 1988; Ardelt and Day 2002). In some cases, parents directly train their children to commit deviant behavior (Adler and Adler 1978), and in general, parental deviance and criminality are predictive of the children's future delinquency and crime (McCord 1991a). Youngsters with delinquent siblings (especially same-sex older siblings) in the family are more likely to be delinquent, even when parental and other family characteristics are taken into account, a combination of family and peer effects (Rowe and Gulley 1992; Lauritsen 1993; Rowe and Farrington 1997; Ardelt and Day 2002).

Research on Peers and Group Contexts

The family is the foundational primary group and plainly included in the concept of differential association, but beyond the family, the balance of associations, reinforcement, models, and definitions is affected by participation and identification with other primary and secondary groups. The most important of these (especially in the teenage years) is the peer group (especially same-sex but also opposite-sex peers). Pro-social tendencies learned in the family may be counteracted by, and any delinquent tendencies learned in the family may be exacerbated by, differential peer association (Simons et al. 1994; Lauritsen 1993). Too often social learning theory is mistakenly taken as only a theory of peer influence. It is not. However, there is no question that the mutual influences of peer behavior, associations, values, behavior, and reinforcement are central to social learning theory's explanation of acquisition, maintenance, and change in deviant behavior. No other general criminological theory has put as much focus on these peer factors and no other theory is as strongly supported by the findings on peer variables. Other than one's own prior deviant behavior, the best single predictor of the onset, continuance, or desistance of crime and delinquency is differential association with conforming and law-violating peers (Loeber and Dishion 1987; Loeber and Stouthamer-Loeber 1986; Loeber et al. 1991; Huizinga et al. 1991; Warr 2002). More frequent, longer-term and closer association with peers who do not support deviant behavior is strongly correlated with conformity, while greater association with peers who commit and approve of delinquency is predictive of one's own delinquent behavior. Virtually every study that includes a peer association variable finds it to be related to a range of delinquent behavior, alcohol and drug use and abuse, property and violent crime, and other forms of deviant behavior. This comes from research:

> "[u]sing alternative kinds of criminological data (self-reports, official records, perceptual data, etc.) on subjects and friends, alternative research designs and data on a wide variety of criminal offenses. Few, if any, empirical regularities in criminology have been documented as often or over as long a period as the association between delinquency and delinquent friends" (Warr 2002: 40).

It has long been known that one special context for the impact of differential peer association is delinquent gangs, and research continues to find the strong influence of gang affiliation, membership and participation on serious delinquency. Of course, learning delinquent behavior takes place before, and in the absence of, gang membership. Indeed, peer associations typically do not involve identifiable, specific groups that can be defined as "gangs." And it is most likely those who are already headed in a delinquent direction, or have participated in delinquent activity, who are also most attracted to, and become involved with, delinquent gangs. However, whatever the frequency and seriousness of one's previous delinquency, the research evidence is clear that the person joining a gang is very likely to develop an even higher level of delinquent involvement. While any level of association with delinquent peers increases the risk of delinquent conduct, gang membership produces more frequent, intense, and enduring association with delinquent friends, exposure to delinquent models and definitions, and reinforcement for delinquent behavior (see Winfree et al. 1994a, 1994b, Battin et al. 1998, Curry et al. 2002 and Liu 2003.) Both gang membership itself and gang-related, as well as non-gang related, delinquency are explained by the same set of social learning variables (attitudes, social reinforcers/punishers, and differential association) (Winfree et al. 1994a; Esbensen and Deschenes 1998). The processes specified in social learning theory are "nearly identical to those provided by qualitative gang research. Gang members reward certain behavior in their peers and punish others, employing goals and processes indistinguishable from those described by Akers" (Winfree et al. 1994a: 149).

Research on Sequence and Feedback Effects in the Social Learning Process

The sequence and reciprocal effects hypothesized in social learning theory have generally been supported (Kandel 1978; Andrews and Kandel 1979; Krohn et al. 1985; Sellers and Winfree 1990; Empey and Stafford 1991; Warr 1993b; Esbensen and Huizinga 1993; Thornberry et al. 1994; Menard and Elliott 1994; Winfree et al. 1994b; Akers and Lee 1996; Elliott and Menard 1996; Esbensen and Deschenes 1998; Battin et al. 1998).

> [T]he findings from several studies favor the process proposed by social learning theory. . . [that] a youngster associates differentially with peers who are deviant or tolerant of deviance, learns definitions favorable to delinquent behavior, is exposed to deviant models that reinforce delinquency, then initiates or increases involvement in that behavior which, then, is expected to influence further associations and definitions (Akers and Sellers 2004: 99).

Research Testing Social Learning Theory by Akers and Associates

Although occasional reference is made above to our own research, virtually all of the citations so far have been to that done by others. That research has consistently produced findings that are positive and supportive of the theory. Most of it includes only one or two social learning variables (most often peer association but also definitions), but some researchers have tested more or less full social learning models (for good examples see Winfree et al. 1994a; 1994b; Sellers et al. 2003). The research that is most likely to include all of the key social learning variables testing essentially full models of the theory has been done by Akers and associates. These studies, using primary data to test the empirical validity of social learning theory by itself and in comparison with other theories, have been reported in the literature in some detail (see Akers

1998; Akers and Sellers 2004) and are fairly well known. The dependent variables in this research have included adolescent deviance and *delinquency*; adolescent *alcohol and drug use and abuse* (Akers et al. 1979; Krohn et al. 1982, 1984; Lanza-Kaduce et al. 1984; Akers and Cochran 1985; Akers and Lee 1999; Hwang 2000; Hwang and Akers 2003) *teenage smoking* (Lauer et al. 1982; Krohn et al. 1985; Spear and Akers 1988; Akers 1992; Akers and Lee 1996), *elderly drinking and problem drinking* (Akers et al. 1989; Akers and La Greca 1991; Akers 1992), *rape and sexual coercion* among samples of college males (Boeringer et al. 1991; Boeringer 1992), *serious delinquency* (Jensen 2003), cross-national *homicide* rates (Jensen and Akers 2003), and *terrorist violence* (Silverman 2002; Akers and Silverman 2004). (See also additional studies by other researchers on *homicide, suicide and violence* in Batton and Ogle 2003; Sellers et al. 2003; Bellair et al. 2003.)

The social learning models tested in this research produce high levels of explained variance, much more than other theoretical models with which it is compared. The combined effects of the social learning variables produce explained variance of 31 to 68 percent of adolescent alcohol and drug use and abuse. Alternative social bonding and strain models explain much less (5 to 10 percent) of the variance. Similarly, the social learning model explained 54 percent of the variance cross-sectionally and 41 percent of the variance longitudinally in teenage cigarette smoking. The social learning model did not do well in predicting which of the initially abstinent youngsters in the study would begin smoking within the next two years (with only 3 percent explained variance). The model did a better, but still not a strong, job of predicting the onset of sustained smoking over a five-year period (15 percent explained variance). The findings on the sequencing and reciprocal effects of social learning variables and smoking behavior over the five-year period were as predicted by the theory. The onset, frequency, and quantity of elderly drinking is highly correlated with social learning variables (with empirical models accounting for 51 to 59 percent of the variance in drinking), and the theory also successfully accounts for problem drinking among the elderly (predicted probability of .683). The social learning variables explain the self-perceived likelihood of rape (54 percent explained variance) non-physical coercion of sex (22 percent explained variance), use of drugs or alcohol to induce unwanted sex (22 percent) and physically coerced rape (21 percent) by college men. Alternative theoretical models (social bonding, self-control, and relative deprivation) models account for 2 percent to 9 percent of the variance in these dependent variables.

Social Structure and Social Learning

Akers has proposed a Social Structure and Social Learning (SSSL) model that identifies four major dimensions of social structure (differential social organization, differential location in the social structure, differential social location, and social disorganization/conflict) and hypothesizes that social learning is the principal mediating process by which social structure has an effect on criminal and delinquent behavior. Thus, the SSSL model is a cross-level elaboration or integration that proposes that social structure has an indirect effect on criminal and conforming behavior through the social learning variables of differential association, differential reinforcement, definitions, and imitation. Social structural variables and factors are the primary macro-level and meso-level causes of crime, while the social learning variables reflect the primary proximate causes of criminal behavior mediating the relationship between social structure and the behavior of individuals that make up group, community, and societal crime rates (Akers 1998). This assertion is supported by much of the research already cited in which age, race, ethnicity, gender, social class, community and region, socio-demographic and community variables are inserted in empirical models. The findings typically are that the net effects of social learning variables remain in these models while the net effects of socio-demographic variables are reduced, typically to statistical non-significance. For instance, several studies have found that variations by age and life course are largely accounted for by family socialization, peer associations, and other social learning variables (Krohn et al. 1989; LaGrange and White 1985; Sampson and Laub 1993; Conger and Simons 1995; Bartusch et al. 1997; Junger-Tas 1992; Tittle and Ward 1993; Warr 1993b)

Tests of the SSSL model have produced positive findings for delinquency and substance use, elderly alcohol abuse, rape, violence, and binge drinking by college students (Lee 1998; Page 1998; Jensen 2003; Bellair et al. 2003; Lanza-Kaduce and Capece 2003; Lee et al. 2004). Also, Jensen and Akers (2003) found that social structural factors derivable from social learning principles accounted for 65 percent of the variance in homicide rates among eighty-two nations. These and other findings are consistent with what the SSSL model would predict (Warr 1998; Mears et al. 1998; Akers and Lee 1996; Rebellon 2002). Although research thus far is supportive, there has not yet been enough research conducted to confirm that social learning is the principal process mediating the relationship of social structure and crime as expected by SSSL. However, we would contend that social learning is the most applicable theory, and the most likely to be supported empirically, for specifying the variables and process mediating the effects of social structural factors on criminal and delinquent behavior. Moreover, we will argue that in the future, properly measured macro-level elaborations of social learning theory (building on the SSSL model) will prove empirically superior to alternatives.

The Future of Social Learning Theory: A Challenge to Criminology

As the review above shows, there is a long history of research on variables relevant to and derived from social learning theory of crime and deviance.

That previous research and the research done since the first full-model test was conducted twenty-five years ago (Akers et al. 1979), makes the case, at least arguably, that social learning theory has been subjected to more supportive empirical inquiry than virtually any other criminological theory in history. Articles on social learning theory are widely cited in the literature and included in reprinted and edited collections of readings in criminology. Also, it is among the list of leading criminological theories that are nearly always covered in the major textbooks for undergraduate and graduate courses in criminology, theories of crime, delinquency, and deviant behavior. There is little doubt of the place of the theory in criminology, and it will continue to be among the leading theories receiving prominent attention in the field, to be among the most tested theories, and to provide the basis for sound policy and practice. Yet, one still finds many times when the theory is ignored, misstated, or misapplied in the criminological literature and, on at least one occasion, social learning theory was initially left off the fairly long list of theories identified by the ASC Program Committee (in its call for papers) as the theories around which papers and sessions should be organized for the upcoming annual meetings.

It might be argued that the theory has fared so well that many criminologists now more or less take it for granted or are not interested in yet another test of its empirical validity. Of course, there is a premium placed on original theoretical contributions and it is easier to get excited about testing a "new" or iconoclastic theory than one that has generated such a large number of tests and applications. But the tendency to overlook the theory by some criminologists is probably more complicated than saturation and boredom, and there are other issues in the way the theory is sometimes treated in the literature. In the process of writing "Taking Social Learning Global," our chapter in *Social Learning and the Explanation of Crime* (Jensen and Akers 2003), we identified key instances where the relevance of the social learning theory is overlooked, downplayed, or misunderstood: 1) the continuing mistaken equating of social learning with "cultural deviance" theory (Messner and Rosenfeld 2001), 2) misleading crucial tests where social bonding theory is declared a victor over other theories even when the best model includes a direct effect of differential peer association, a key social learning variable (Costello and Vowell 1999), 3) studies that add peer group relationships to routine activities theory with no mention, or even a single citation, to social learning theory (Osgood et al. 1996), 4) critiques that misinterpret social learning theory as ignoring the importance of opportunity, fear of punishment, and conventional peers (Tittle and Paternoster 2000), and 5) the fact that the best-fitting models of international variations in homicide are more compatible with the logic of social learning theory than existing alternatives (Gartner 1990).

It was this last point about the underappreciated relevance of the logic of social learning theory and the SSSL model for accounting for macro, cross-cultural variations in crime that we addressed in the chapter on taking social learning global. We believe that the next phase in the development of the theory will be to build upon themes introduced in earlier and more recent presentations of the theory regarding explanation of meso and macro level variations in crime and deviance. An outline of features of a macro version of social learning theory is embodied in the original Burgess and Akers (1966) article and in Akers' first statement and later elaborations of social learning theory (1973, 1977, 1985).

> The general culture and structure of society and the particular groups, subcultures and social situations in which the individual participates provide learning environments in which the norms define what is approved and disapproved and the reactions of others (for example, in applying social sanctions) attach different reinforcing or punishing consequences to this behavior. In a sense, then, social structure is an arrangement of sets and schedules of reinforcement contingencies. (1977: 64)

This simple, straight-forward statement incorporates several distinctions that will prove to be important in specifying any macro-level version of the theory. General culture, social structure, subcultures, groups, and social situations are all mentioned as factors affecting learning environments, including "sets and schedules of reinforcement." Neither this short statement nor the later more elaborate formulation of the SSSL model (Akers 1998) was intended to exhaust the relevance of meso or macro level characteristics that affect learning environments, but clearly embodies fundamental considerations for making the transition from the micro to higher levels of sociological analysis.

One way to begin building a macro learning theory is to examine its fit with important distinctions in sociology and to consider regularities that can be explained by social learning theory at an aggregate level that are not explained, or perhaps not explained as well, by existing macro theories. Because prominent macro-level theorists pay so little attention to social learning theory, a central feature of its development is ignored. It is safe to say that few criminologists know the full origins of the theory's foundational principles and, indeed, when the first time the social learning label was featured in a prominent publication. This is because current social learning theory in criminology originally emerged, not only out of Sutherland's efforts, but also out of effort to integrate micro and macro ideas from the diverse fields of psychology and sociology specifically posited by Neal E. Miller and John Dollard at Yale University. In *Social Learning and Imitation* (1941: Preface) they proposed to "apply training in two different fields—psychology and social science—to the solution of social problems." They dedicated the book to a psychologist, Clark Leonard Hall, who was interested in imitation, and a sociologist, William Fielding Ogburn, who was a pioneer in the study of diffusion, contagion, and the transmission of cultural innovations.

Imitation, Contagion, and Auto-Correlation

The first regularity that can be addressed by social learning theory which has not, and likely cannot be, encompassed by existing sociological theory is *imitation* at any level of aggregation from micro to macro. For example, at the "macro" level there is considerable evidence that "crime causes crime" in that sudden upward movements (i.e. "surges," "epidemics," "waves," "outbreaks," etc.) involve a variety of imitative and/or reactive mechanisms. Moreover, to be considered a surge or a wave there has to be a downturn which means that self-limiting or *countervailing processes* have to be proposed to account for a return to the "normal" rate of crime. Of the major criminological theories that have been invoked to explain macro patterns of crime (anomie, social disorganization, routine opportunity, etc.) only SSSL theory can readily accommodate mechanisms (such as imitation, vengeance, retaliation and preparation for self-defense, etc.) that may account for escalating upward surges and mechanisms (such as satiation, exhaustion and institutional responses, etc.) that may limit surges. Theories designed to explain gradual shifts in level, variations among ecological units, and/or variations among individuals, do not incorporate explanatory mechanisms that can be applied to such short-term waves. All sociological theories are potentially relevant to identifying the underlying conditions that might start a surge, or might help explain why a population or sub-population was receptive to a surge, but we contend that only social learning directly incorporates mechanisms that can explain escalation and exhaustion.

Imitation and other learning processes are likely involved in what Jones and Jones (2000) explicate as "the contagious nature of antisocial behavior" operating both through *primary group interaction* and similarity in socio-demographic *location in the social structure*:

> One network [*cohesion*] consists of people who communicate with one another directly. The other network (*structural equivalence*) consists of people who occupy the same niche in society. . . . [T]eenagers identify with one another in specific contrast to adults and especially with teenagers who are demographically, socially or in their "proclivities," like themselves. Because the members of a teenage group also communicate directly with one another, a teenage group *exemplifies both kinds of network(ing)* and can function in both ways as a conduit of antisocial socialization (Jones and Jones 2000: 33, emphasis added).

It should be noted that criminologists' use of statistical tools to model and eliminate the effects of "outliers" and temporal and spatial "auto-correlation" is often an attempt to eliminate the confounding effects of contagion and imitation. Although viewed as a statistical necessity for various forms of statistical analysis, the underlying "problem" often involves self-reproducing and self-limiting phenomena, imitation and contagion, across territorial units and time. Imitation and contagion in macro level analysis are treated as part of a statistical problem eliminated through statistical adjustments and filtering (see Jensen 1997), or are introduced as an interesting issue with no specification of its more than fifty-year heritage in social learning theory (see Baller et al. 2001).

Conceptual Overlap with Organizational Theory

A second virtue of social learning theory is that its central principles or mechanisms are reproduced in contemporary literature in other areas of sociology. For example, any review of the literature on what is called institutional or organizational "isomorphism" will reveal the distinct mechanisms invoked to explain the standardization of features of organizations over time and space (DiMaggio 1983; DiMaggio and Powell 1983; Powell and DiMaggio 1991) parallel the learning mechanisms emphasized in social learning theory. Organizations operating in similar environments develop similar features, "isomorphism," through imitation, the development of shared normative frameworks, and coercion (e.g. state regulation). Among the major sociological theories of crime, only social learning encompasses all three sources of organizational conformity. Social learning theory includes imitation, normative learning, and coercive regulation as one type of formal schedule of threatened sanctions. The significance of general learning mechanisms at the macro level have become increasingly recognized in political scientists' attention to "organizational and societal learning" in international relations and conflicts. (see for instance the contributions by political scientists on Organizational & Societal Learning in Brown et al., 2006.)

Separable Effects of Structure and Culture

In addition to imitation, both contemporary organizational theory and social learning theory incorporate normative and, hence, cultural influences among the empirically separable determinants of patterned behavior whether in features of organizations or the behavior of groups and individuals. This feature reflects a central tenet of sociology. Structure and culture are interrelated but have separable effects on social order, disorder, stability, and change. This tenet has implications for criminological theory in that it does not propose only cultural values, norms and beliefs as the sole set of mediating variables (Matsueda 1982), but rather proposes both social and cultural mediating variables.

Messner and Rosenfeld (2001) raise this issue of positing only cultural variables in their criticism of cultural deviance theory. But they erroneously lump social learning theory together with cultural deviance theory. This point was brought up and institutional anomie theory was criticized for not being able to account for variation across societies as well as social learning principles (in the presentation of our paper at a 2004 ASC plenary session). Messner was in attendance and (in a statement from the floor) said that he was puzzled by, and disputed, this critique of institutional anomie theory. And in a private conversation with the senior author following that session, Messner repeated his conviction that the critique was not really correct. On the contrary, he asserted that he and Rosenfeld just assumed that social learning theory is quite compatible with, and indeed provides the primary mediating process for, institutional anomie theory. We agree with this and appreciate Messner's clarification. We may be missing something in our interpretation of Messner and Rosenfeld and stand ready to be corrected, but we do not find in their published works on institutional anomie a distinction between social learning theory and cultural deviance theory (of which they are very critical). They seem to view the two as the same theory. They make no statements about social learning as the underlying mediating micro process in the impact of institutional anomie on crime. Social learning theory includes both cultural and non-cultural learning mechanisms and, when that logic is extended to deal with macro-level issues, the theory would propose that both structural and cultural variables shape schedules of reinforcement and the strength and relative primacy of different institutional and group influences. Moreover, because social learning theory allows for imitation processes independently of differential reinforcement, differential association, definitions, and opportunity, it allows for "cultural" and other types of "lags" where forms of crime or rates of crime may be sustained.

The Primacy of Primary Relationships

A central tenet of sociology is that human motivation, and the expression of motivation are socially and culturally structured and learned primarily in interaction with other people. Of course, criminologists will recognize this statement as central to Sutherland's differential association theory and retained as a central part of social learning theory. When applied to criminological theory at the macro-level, we are directed to consider the relative primacy of different institutional and group influences. As just noted, among the main current sociological theories to address this issue topic is Messner and Rosenfield's (2001) "institutional-anomie" theory. This theory proposes that when primacy is accorded to a free market economy and the primacy of pecuniary values and goals for people in a society, other institutions, such as the family, are weakened. As a result of this weakening in the family institution, crime rates will be high in free market societies. In contrast, according to the theory, when state policies "decommodify" people and buffer them against market forces, other institutions, such as the family, will be strengthened and crime rates will be constrained.

We would ask, first, how such a pervasive and sustained learning of these widely shared pecuniary values can occur if the ultimate outcome is a weakening of those self-same institutions where such values are learned? Second, we are led to ask why those primary socializing institutions would emphasize goals that negate their primacy? Of course, such paradoxes disappear if we take the position that disputes both the perspective on values, and the arguments about decommodification. It can be proposed, from a structural-learning perspective that decommodification policies that diminish the market economy and increase dependence on the state actually weaken, rather than strengthen, dependence on primary socializing institutions such as the family. Third, it can be proposed that the dominant values emphasized in institutional anomie theory, according primacy to pecuniary values and goals, is a mischaracterization of American society and the "American Dream." It is when people are relatively free from primary socializing institutions that a higher value is accorded to the pursuit of money and pecuniary goals for their own sake. This is probably why governmental investments in decommodification among nations is associated with weaker, rather than stronger, primary institutions. Consistent with the view of the family as the primary institution for conventional socialization in social learning theory (and one should add in control theory), the pursuit of some form of "family" life can be proposed as the dominant goal or "value" in American culture. Indeed, debates about "family values" dominate "culture wars" in American society, and not just because some groups view the family as unimportant or secondary to other institutions; but, rather, "culture wars" in American society reflect the fact that the value placed on the family is widely shared. The culture conflict involves conceptions of what constitutes a "family" and the independence of the family from other religious and educational institutions (same sex marriage, adoption by homosexuals, home schooling, etc.).

Multiple Cultural Processes and Forms

The fact that social learning theory has not included a specific commitment to one or another version of the role of culture in the explanation of crime might be considered a weakness of the theory (see Jensen and Rojek 1998). One of the features of Hirschi's (1969) social bonding theory that appealed to sociologists was the fact that he addressed some meso or macro issues involving the role of culture and took a specific and testable position on the issue. He proposed that there is one dominant conventional cultural system in the United States defining crime as inappropriate conduct with no enduring subcultures or contra cultures positively defining crime as appropriate moral conduct. Because there is a single dominant culture, it was variable learning of the values, norms and beliefs of that one system that explained crime. Those who did not learn it, or were not taught it, had higher probabilities of committing crime than those who did. The presence of criminogenic subcultures and contra cultures, in which crime is a product of enduring or oppositional values, norms, or beliefs, was rejected as misrepresentative of the way cultural variables affect criminal behavior.

Hirschi's theory allowed for variable learning of the dominant, conventional culture introduced under the concept of "belief." In contrast, social learning theory did not incorporate a specific image of the manner in which culture was relevant to crime, although cultural phenomena such as values, norms and beliefs were clearly incorporated into the theory's concept of "definitions." In *Causes of Delinquency*, Hirschi (1969) argued that there were features of his theory that would emerge out of empirical investigation, and we might take that same approach in making the transition to a more macro learning theory.

Social learning theory does have stronger historical and theoretical links to some conceptions of culture than others, but could fit with a variety of conceptions. For one, a cultural system can be disorganized in the sense that there are conflicts among values, norms, and beliefs *within a widely shared, dominant culture* (Sykes and Matza 1957; Matza and Sykes 1961). This type of cultural disorganization can take the form of shared "subterranean" cultural perspectives that encourage crime or through "techniques of neutralization" learned in quite conventional contexts and reflected in legal codes as "extenuating circumstances." Thus, the culture shared by people in a society or locale can be "disorganized" in the sense that conflicting moral messages are built into the cultural system itself. Sykes and Matza (1957) recognized the clear connection of this view with differential association and explicitly portrayed them as types of "definitions favorable" to crime. A second way to introduce culture would be to advocate a view of society with a collection of socially differentiated groups with distinct subcultural perspectives that lead some of these groups into conflict with the law. This use of cultural concepts is another form of cultural disorganization, typically called cultural conflict or cultural deviance theory. There may be perfectly consistent messages conveyed within a given subculture, but they may conflict with the views of other subcultures.

A third use of cultural concepts involves the concept of contra cultures or oppositional subcultures that are constructed by people experiencing problems in the pursuit of success and respect (Cohen 1955; Jankowski 1991). Contra cultures do not begin as enduring subcultural traditions but are constructed by people sharing similar disadvantages. Their values, norms and beliefs reverse those of "conventional" society and status or respect is accorded based on criminal or deviant behavior. Sampson and Wilson (1995) reject the view that there are distinct subcultures of poverty where the norms espoused and internalized are in conflict with those embodied in law, but adopt a mild version of "contra cultures" in the form of "cultural adaptations to social isolation," a notion very similar to Kornhauser's concept of "structural values" (Kornhauser 1978). Variations in values, norms and beliefs that are "adaptations to constraints and opportunities" are considered distinct from the enduring traditions emphasized in cultural deviance theory.

Of course, in none of these contexts does social learning assume that socialization is complete or that knowledge of the culture, or sub-culture, is sufficient by itself to predict how each member of the group exposed to that culture will behave. Deviance can result from incomplete socialization in conventional norms and values as well as (as noted earlier) countervailing processes of reinforcement, imitation, and exposure to deviant definitions.

Hirschi hitched social control theory to one conception of culture and supported it with data from white male youths in the San Francisco Bay area in the mid-1960s. There has been little or no systematic survey research on the issue since that study, despite the fact that it was limited to white male students. Yet, it stands in major contrast to current theories about violence in the most disadvantaged, black neighborhoods. In *Code of the Street* (1999), Elijah Anderson reintroduces the notion of an oppositional subculture where self-respect requires a demonstration of toughness and maintenance of honor requires physical violence. Anderson's argument was based on ethnographic research among black males. There has been survey research on the strength of general conventional norms or values among adults (see Warner 2003), but there has been no thorough investigation using survey methods of the systematic distribution of such a "code" across neighborhoods or among youth or adults. Indeed, the most recent report of research based on Anderson's view of the code makes inferences from patterns of victimization, but acknowledges that there was no direct data in the study on such a set of normative orientations (Baumer et al. 2003).

Hence, at present, the concept of culture is introduced into theories of crime in quite diverse ways. At the micro-level, variable normative learning can take any of the forms discussed above—limited learning of conventional values, norms, and beliefs, successful learning of conflicting values, norms, and beliefs characterizing the dominant culture, subcultural learning of enduring values, norms, and beliefs, and contracultural construction and learning of "oppositional" values, norms, and beliefs. Akers (1998: 83) conceptualizes two continua of beliefs/definitions, one conventional/conforming and the other deviant/non-conforming, along which "individual beliefs and definitions can lie at any point" which could increase "the odds one will commit deviant acts, given opportunities or situations fitting the definitions and the anticipation of reward."

One direction for the "macrotization" of social learning theory would be to explore the possible relevance of the logic of the theory to generating hypotheses about the relative salience of different forms of cultural learning to the explanation of variation in crime and/or different forms of crime. For example, from a social learning perspective, the violent resolution of interpersonal conflicts could be argued to become "normative" in environments where institutional means of conflict resolution have been scarce, where relations with institutional authority have been strained, and/or where escape from violent situations is difficult. On the other hand, such behavior cannot become "too normative" or no viable social life could be sustained in such neighborhoods. Even the most "serious" gang members spend most of their time in quite normal activities and have a stake in maintaining some degree of stability in their territory. In fact, violent reactions to invasion or transgressions on territory are culturally acceptable among most groups in society and are not limited to subcultures. Moreover, because a perpetual and unlimited escalation of conflict would destroy a social system, the "code of the street" is likely to embody both cultural prescriptions and proscriptions on the situations and acceptable targets of violence. In short, "the code of the street" is likely to include rules that limit, as well as mandate, violence (definitions favorable and unfavorable to violence). For example, attacking an elderly woman for making a nasty comment is far less likely to be called for in the maintenance of respect and honor than being "dissed" by a peer. Similarly, attacking someone who is much smaller, younger, or physically able is less likely to be acceptable in the maintenance of honor than a similar response to someone of equal or greater size, age, or ability. Thus, for forms of violence directed at the maintenance of honor to be socially reinforced by those offended, or to develop into a subcultural or contracultural mandate within a subsystem, norms constraining such behavior must evolve. In short, "the code of the street" will be found to include normative rules of engagement that act as discriminative stimuli that regulate and moderate the escalation of violence in all social situations where some degree of normal social interaction is desired.

Another "macro" hypothesis that can be derived from the underlying logic of social learning is that the most common forms of criminal or delinquent activity will be those involving the most routine and ordinary learning processes. Indeed, Hirschi criticizes learning theory for assuming that people have to learn any specific technical knowledge or normative stance to engage in such activity as shoplifting. However, the relative prevalence of different types of offending does correlate highly with the relative normative "seriousness" accorded different forms of crime. Shoplifting violates fewer "normative" rules than purse snatching from an elderly lady. Robbing someone at gunpoint violates more normative rules than grabbing a bicycle from someone's driveway. Moreover, youth in racial or ethnic categories who feel they can shoplift and not be suspected by clerks and security personnel are more likely to do so than youth in racial or ethnic categories historically suspected by such employees. Shoplifting is most probable when youth have the opportunity to do so, can manage such activity without generating suspicion, and have either learned rationales or excuses for such activity or not learned to judge such activity as a violation of norms.

The more normative rules violated in the course of an offense, the lower the relative frequency of an offense. Hence, stealing through the direct threat of violence against an elderly woman violates more rules than grabbing money from the till at a convenience store and running away with it. Moreover, such regularities tend to reflect potential offenders' assessment of risk and the normative properties of the offense; that is, both moral evaluations and perceived risks or reinforcement balance exert an independent influence on the relative prevalence of different types of crime.

Countervailing Mechanisms

Both social disorganization/control theory and social learning theory assume that strong adult institutions inhibit crime and are likely to encourage law-abiding conduct. However, social learning theory introduces the possibility of conflicts among learning mechanisms that can explain the perpetuation of crime even when parents are depicted as endorsing law-abiding decisions among their children. Parents may attempt to teach their children not to smoke, but their own smoking behavior affects their children through processes of imitation and perceived vicarious reinforcement. Strong ties to such parents do not have the same inhibiting effect as strong ties to non-smoking parents. The same contingent impacts can be detected for other forms of drug use. While there is evidence that the presence of deviant parents is correlated with the deviance of their children, there is little evidence that strong bonds to deviant parents are criminogenic. The impact of such inconsistencies is to undermine the inhibiting influence of attachments to others and conventional socialization. "A child reared in a...family professing non-violent attitudes may, nonetheless, come to engage in, and justify, violence because he has witnessed abusive behavior in the home, has been the object of abuse himself or has otherwise learned violent behavior in spite of the nonviolent cultural norms to which he has been exposed" (Akers 1998: 103). In short, the inhibiting impact of attempts to teach norms prohibiting youthful deviance is weakened by other learning processes such as imitation and differential reinforcement that work in a contrary direction.

Were we to extend that logic to macro-level issues we would propose that some historical events or policies can have countervailing consequences through mechanisms that shift the schedules and balances of reinforcement in unexpected ways. For example, prohibitionist alcohol policies should have some effect on its price, the sanctions risked, and the situations where use occurs. Hence, prohibitionist laws and their enforcement should decrease alcohol consumption. Because alcohol use is a positive correlate of interpersonal violence, we might expect that homicide rates would be lowered through prohibition. Yet, the murder rate went up during most of the prohibitionist years despite the fact that consumption appears to have declined (See Jensen

2000). When such anomalies are found, the logic of social learning theory implies a consideration of countervailing mechanisms at the macro level. Prohibition may have lowered consumption but, at the same time, it increased competition over the illicit supply of alcohol and decreased the odds that people could invoke formal control mechanisms to deal with conflict in drinking situations. Prohibitionists policies structured the relative costs and rewards of the supply and situational use of alcohol in ways that reduced overall use while increasing violence associated with use. This statement is more consistent with social learning at the macro-level than it is with social disorganization, anomie, cultural deviance, or self-control theory.

Structural Correlates: Modeling and Occupational Structure

Akers (1998) notes the common criticism that social learning theory better applies to common forms of routine deviance than to serious forms of violence. However, that view is a product of the most common forms of survey research and not a limitation of the theory. In fact, Akers demonstrates that social learning theory better applies to the explanation of rape and sexual aggression than alternative theories. Jensen (2003) shows that social learning theory does the best job of explaining gender variations in delinquency regardless of seriousness or the use of official or self-report measures of offenses.

Bellair et al. (2003: 199) deal with this same issue, but "extend the literature by testing a social learning model of subcultural formation and violence among adolescents that has its roots in local labor market conditions and opportunity." They use a SSSL model to explain the "spatial concentration of violence among adolescents." Not only do they show that structural effects are explained or "mediated" by social learning mechanisms, but at the macro-level it is the prevalence of professional sector employment that is most intimately tied with such mechanisms. They argue that the structural distribution of violence reflects the "absence in the community of professional role models and a decline in employment opportunities" rather than the traditional measures of the concentration of disadvantage. Thus, not only are social learning mechanisms key mediators, but the macro-level condition that is most important is the presence, or lack thereof, of professional role models. In short, opportunities for "modeling" at the structural level are central to the explanation of the spacial distribution of violent crime.

Concluding Comments on Elaborating Social Learning Theory at the Macro Level

In "Taking Social Learning Global" (2003: 33), Jensen and Akers took the position that "the order of theories in terms of their ability to explain ecological and global variations is actually the same as their order in terms of ability to explain the prevalence and incidence of crime and delinquency based on self-reports collected from individuals." In this assessment of the state of social learning theory, we make what may strike many of our colleagues as an even more audacious claim: When the logic and concepts involved in social learning theory at lower levels of aggregation and analysis are extended to macro-level variations, they apply to a wider range of known patterns over time and space, fit with developments and arguments on other macro topics, and generate more complex and empirically valid models than any alternative sociological theory.

Such claims of consistency over micro-meso-macro levels may strike some criminologists as a contradiction of well-known warnings about the irrelevance of ecological correlations to claims about variations in prevalence and incidence using data from individuals. In an article in *Homicide Studies*, Chamlin et al. (2002: 55) cite Lieberson's critique (1985: 109) of mixed levels of analysis and reiterate the claim that "one cannot use theory designed to explain variations in outcomes at one level of analysis to explain variations in outcomes at another." However, this warning does not apply if data collected from individuals are aggregated at different levels and consistency across levels is demonstrated empirically; and it certainly does not apply to attempts to transform the concepts and causal logic of a theory focusing on learning mechanisms into a theory applicable to macro-level variations over time and space. Were we to take that warning too seriously there would be no point in assessing the ability of a theory to survive transitions across levels of analysis, to address variations over both time and space at different fractal scales nor to assess the implications of parallel theoretical developments in other sociological specialties. Social learning theory has worked so well at the level it was initially proposed that few will find it exciting to conduct yet another test again finding the theory is supported. Such tests, and extensions of the theory based on them, should, and will certainly continue; and the theory will also continue to have an important place in the field. However, we believe that interest in the theory in the future among sociologists and criminologists will also come to rest increasingly on the exploration of the macro and global issues raised, and claims for the theory asserted here. We look forward to that interest, even if it is garnered mainly to show that we are wrong in our claims for the applicability of the theory at all levels.

References

Adler, Patricia, and Peter Adler. 1978. "Tinydopers: A Case Study of Deviant Socialization." *Symbolic Interaction* 1: 90-105.

Agnew, Robert. 1991. "The Interactive Effect of Peer Variables on Delinquency." *Criminology* 29: 47-72.

————. 1993. "Why Do They Do It? An Examination of the Intervening Mechanisms Between 'Social Control' Variables and Delinquency." *Journal of Research of Crime and Delinquency* 30: 245-266.

————. 1994. "The Techniques of Neutralization and Violence." *Criminology* 32: 555-580.

Akers, Ronald L. 1973. *Deviant Behavior: A Social Learning Approach*. Belmont, CA: Wadsworth.

————. 1977. *Deviant Behavior: A Social Learning Approach*, 2nd ed. Belmont, CA: Wadsworth.

————. 1985. *Deviant Behavior: A Social Learning Approach,* 3rd ed. Belmont, CA: Wadsworth.

————. 1992. *Drugs, Alcohol, and Society: Social Structure, Process and Policy*. Belmont, CA: Wadsworth.

————. 1994. *Criminological Theories: Introduction and Evaluation*. Los Angeles: Roxbury Publishing.

————. 1996. "Is Differential Association/Social Learning Cultural Deviance?" *Criminology* 34: 229-248.

————. 1998. *Social Learning and Social Structure: A General Theory of Crime and Deviance*. Boston: Northeastern University Press.

Akers, Ronald L., and John K. Cochran. 1985 "Adolescent Marijuana Use: A Test of Three Theories of Deviant Behavior." *Deviant Behavior* 6: 323-346.

Akers, Ronald L., and Gary F. Jensen, eds. 2003. *Social Learning Theory and the Explanation of Crime: A Guide for the New Century. Advances in Criminological Theory, Vol. 11*. New Brunswick, NJ: Transaction Publishers.

Akers, Ronald L., Marvin D. Krohn, Lonn Lanza-Kaduce, and Marcia Radosevich. 1979. "Social Learning and Deviant Behavior: A Specific Test of a General Theory." *American Sociological Review* 44: 635-55.

Akers, Ronald L., and Anthony J. La Greca. 1991 "Alcohol Use Among the Elderly: Social Learning, Community Context, and Life Events." Pp. 242-262 in David J. Pittman and Helene Raskin White (eds.), *Society, Culture, and Drinking Patterns Re-examined*. New Brunswick, NJ: Rutgers Center of Alcohol Studies.

Akers, Ronald L., Anthony J. La Greca, John Cochran, and Christine Sellers. 1989. "Social Learning Theory and Alcohol Behavior Among the Elderly." *Sociological Quarterly* 30: 625-638.

Akers, Ronald L., and Gang Lee. 1996 "A Longitudinal Test of Social Learning Theory: Adolescent Smoking." *Journal of Drug Issues* 26: 317-343.

Akers, Ronald L., and Christine S. Sellers. 2004. *Criminological Theories: Introduction, Evaluation, and Application*, 4th ed. Los Angeles: Roxbury Publishing.

Akers, Ronald L., and Adam Silverman. 2004. "Toward a Social Learning Model of Violence and Terrorism." Pp.19-35 in Margaret A. Zahn, Henry H. Brownstein, and Shelly L. Jackson (eds.), *Violence: From Theory to Research*. Cincinnati: LexisNexis-Anderson Publishing.

Anderson, Elijah. 1999. *Code of the Street: Decency, Violence, and the Moral Life of the Inner City*. New York: W. W. Norton.

Andrews, D. A. 1980. "Some Experimental Investigations of the Principles of Differential Association through Deliberate Manipulations of the Structure of Service Systems." *American Sociological Review* 45: 448-62.

Andrews, D. A., and James Bonta. 2003. *The Psychology of Criminal Conduct*, 3rd ed. Cincinnati: Anderson Publishing.

Andrews, Kenneth H., and Denise B. Kandel. 1979. "Attitude and Behavior: A Specification of the Contingent Consistency Hypothesis." *American Sociological Review* 44: 298-310.

Ardelt, Monika, and Laurie Day. 2002. "Parents, Siblings, and Peers: Close Social Relationships and Adolescent Deviance." *Journal of Early Adolescence* 22: 310-349.

Baller, R.D., Anselin, L. Messner, S. F., Deane, G., and Hawkins, D. F. 2001. "Structural Covariates of U. S. County Homicide Rates: Incorporating Spatial Effects." *Criminology* 39: 561-590.

Bandura, Albert. 1977. *Social Learning Theory*. Englewood Cliffs, NJ: Prentice Hall.

Bankston, Carl L. III, and Stephen J. Caldas. 1996. "Adolescents and Deviance in a Vietnamese American Community," *Deviant Behavior* 17: 159-182.

Bartusch, Dawn Jeglum, Donald R. Lynam, Terrie A. Moffitt, and Phil A. Silva. 1997. "Is Age Important? Testing a General Versus a Developmental Theory of Antisocial Behavior." *Criminology* 35: 375-406.

Battin, Sara R., Karl G. Hill, Robert D. Abbott, Richard F. Catalano and J. David Hawkins 1998. "The Contribution of Gang Membership to Delinquency: Beyond Delinquent Friends." *Criminology* 36: 93-115.

Batton, Candice, and Robbin S. Ogle. 2003. "'Who's it Gonna Be–You or Me?': The Potential of Social Learning for Integrated Homicide-Suicide Theory." Pp. 85-108 in Ronald L. Akers and Gary F. Jensen (eds.), *Social Learning Theory and the Explanation of Crime: A Guide for the New Century. Advances in Criminological Theory, Vol. 11*. New Brunswick, NJ: Transaction Publishers.

Baumer, Eric P., Julie Horney, Richard Felson, and Janet Lauritsen. 2003. "Neighborhood Disadvantage and the Nature of Violence." *Criminology* 41: 39-72.

Bellair, Paul E., Vincent J. Roscigno, and Maria B. Velez. 2003. "Occupational Structure, Social Learning, and Adolescent Violence." Pp. 197-226 in Ronald L. Akers and Gary F. Jensen (eds.), *Social Learning Theory and the Explanation of Crime: A Guide for the New Century. Advances in Criminological Theory, Vol. 11*. New Brunswick, NJ: Transaction Publishers

Benda, Brent B. 1994 "Testing Competing Theoretical Concepts: Adolescent Alcohol Consumption." *Deviant Behavior* 15: 375-396.

Boeringer, Scot. 1992. *Sexual Coercion Among College Males: Assessing Three Theoretical Models of Coercive Sexual Behavior.* Unpublished Ph.D. Dissertation, University of Florida.

Boeringer, Scot, Constance L. Shehan, and Ronald L. Akers. 1991 "Social Contexts and Social Learning In Sexual Coercion and Aggression: Assessing the Contribution of Fraternity Membership." *Family Relations* 40: 558-64.

Brezina, Timothy, and Alex R. Piquero. 2003. "Exploring the Relationshiop between Social and Non-Social Reinforcement in the Context of Social Learning Theory." Pp. 265-288 in Ronald L. Akers and Gary F. Jensen (eds.), *Social Learning Theory and the Explanation of Crime: A Guide for the New Century. Advances in Criminological Theory, Vol. 11*. New Brunswick, NJ: Transaction Publishers

Brown, M. Leann, Michael Kenney, and Michael Zarkin (eds.). 2006. *Organizational Learning in the Global Context*. Aldershot, UK: Ashgate.

Bruinsma, Gerben. 1992. "Differential Association Theory Reconsidered: An Extension and its Empirical Test." *Journal of Quantitative Criminology* 8: 29-49.

Burgess, Robert L., and Ronald L. Akers. 1966. "A Differential Association-Reinforcement Theory of Criminal Behavior." *Social Problems* 14: 128-47.

Burkett, Steven, and Eric L. Jensen. 1975. "Conventional Ties, Peer Influence, and the Fear of Apprehension: A Study of Adolescent Marijuana Use." *Sociological Quarterly* 16: 522-33.

Burkett, Steven R., and Bruce O. Warren. 1987. "Religiosity, Peer Associations, and Adolescent Marijuana Use: A Panel Study of Underlying Causal Structures." *Criminology* 25: 109-131.

Burton, Velmer, Frank, Cullen, T. Evans, and R. Gregory Dunaway. 1994. "Reconsidering Strain Theory: Operationalization, Rival Theories, and Adult Criminality." *Journal of Quantitative Criminology* 10: 213-239.

Capaldi, D. M., P. Chamberlain, and G.R Patterson. 1997. "Ineffective Discipline and Conduct Problems in Males: Association, Late Adolescent Outcomes, and Prevention. *Aggression and Violent Behavior* 2: 343-353.

Catalano, Richard F., Rick Kosterman, and David J. Hawkins. 1996. "Modeling the Etiology of Adolescent Substance Use: A Test of the Social Development Model." *Journal of Drug Issues* 26: 429-455.

Chamlin, Mitchell B., John K. Cochran, and Christopher T. Lowenkamp. 2002. "A Longitudinal Analysis of the Welfare-Homicide Relationship: Testing Two (Non-reductionist) Macro-Level Theories." *Homicide Studies* 6: 39-60.

Chappell, Allison T., and Alex R. Piquero. 2004. "Applying Social Learning Theory to Police Misconduct." *Deviant Behavior* 25: 89-108.

Cohen, Albert K. 1955. *Delinquent Boys*. Glencoe, IL: Free Press.

Conger, Rand. 1976. "Social Control and Social Learning Models of Delinquency: A Synthesis." *Criminology* 14: 17-40.

Conger, Rand D., and Ronald L. Simons. 1995. "Life-Course Contingencies in the Development of Adolescent Antisocial Behavior: A Matching Law Approach." In Terence P. Thornberry (ed.), *Developmental Theories of Crime and Delinquency*. New Brunswick, NJ: Transaction Books.

Costello, Barbara J., and Paul R. Vowell. 1999." Testing Control Theory and Differential Association: A Reanalysis of the Richmond Youth Project Data." *Criminology* 37: 815-842

Cressey, Donald R. 1953. *Other People's Money*. Glencoe, IL: Free Press.

Cullen, Francis T., John Paul Wright, Paul Gendreau, and D. A. Andrews. 2003. "What Correctional Treatment can Tell us About Criminological Theory: Implications for Social Learning Theory." Pp. 339-362 in Ronald L. Akers and Gary F. Jensen (eds.), *Social Learning Theory and the Explanation of Crime: A Guide for the New Century. Advances in Criminological Theory, Vol. 11*. New Brunswick, NJ: Transaction Publishers.

Curry, G. David, Scott H. Decker, and Arlen Egley, Jr. 2002. "Gang Involvement and Delinquency in a Middle School Population." *Justice Quarterly* 19: 275-292

Dabney, Dean. 1995. "Neutralization and Deviance in the Workplace: Theft of Supplies and Medicines by Hospital Nurses." *Deviant Behavior* 16: 313-331.

Dembo, Richard, Gary Grandon, Lawrence La Voie, James Schmeidler, and William Burgos.1986. "Parents and Drugs Revisited: Some Further Evidence in Support of Social Learning Theory." *Criminology* 24: 85-104.

DiMaggio, Paul J. 1983. "State Expansion and Organization Fields." Pp. 147-161 in R. H. Hall and R. E. Quinn (eds.), *Organization Theory and Public Policy*. Beverly Hills, CA: Sage.

DiMaggio, Paul J., and Walter W. Powell. 1983. "The Iron Cage Revisited: Institutional Isomorphism and Collective Rationality in Organizational Fields." *American Sociological Review* 48: 147-160.

———. 1991. "The Iron Cage Revisited: Institutional Isomorphism and Collective Rationality in Organizational Field." In Paul J. Dimaggio and Walter W. Powell (eds.), *The New Institutionalism in Organizational Analysis*. Chicago: University of Chicago Press.

Donnerstein, Edward, and Daniel Linz. 1995. "The Media." Pp. 237-266 in James Q. Wilson and Joan Petersilia (eds.), *Crime*. Oakland, CA: ICS Press.

Dull, R. Thomas. 1983. "Friends' Use and Adult Drug and Drinking Behavior: A Further Test of Differential Association Theory." *Journal of Criminal Law and Criminology* 74: 1608-19.

Elliott, Delbert S. 1994. "Serious Violent Offenders: Onset, Developmental Course, and Termination." *Criminology* 32: 1-22.

Elliott, Delbert S., David Huizinga, and Suzanne S. Ageton. 1985. *Explaining Delinquency and Drug Use*. Beverly Hills, CA: Sage.

Elliott, Delbert S., and Scott Menard. 1996. "Delinquent Friends and Delinquent Behavior: Temporal and Developmental Patterns." In David Hawkins (ed.), *Current Theories of Crime and Deviance.* New York: Springer-Verlag.

Empey, LaMar T., and Mark Stafford. 1991. *American Delinquency: Its Meaning and Construction.* Belmont, CA: Wadsworth.

Esbensen, Finn Aage, and Elizabeth Piper Deschenes. 1998. "A Multisite Examination of Youth Gang Membership: Does Gender Matter?" *Criminology* 36: 799-827.

Esbensen, Finn Aage, and David Huizinga. 1993. "Gangs, Drugs, and Delinquency in a Survey of Urban Youth." *Criminology* 31: 565-590.

Fagan, Jeffrey, and Sandra Wexler. 1987. "Family Origins of Violent Delinquents." *Criminology* 24: 439-471.

Gartner, Rosemary. 1990. "The Victims of Homicide: A Temporal and Cross-National Comparison." *American Sociological Review* 55: 92-106.

Gordon, Rachel A., Benjamin B. Lahey, Eriko Kawai, Rolf Loeber, Magda Stouthamer-Loeber, and David P. Farrington. 2004. "Anti-Social Behavior and Youth Gang Membership: Selection and Socialization." *Criminology* 42: 55-87.

Gottfredson, Michael, and Travis Hirschi. 1990. *A General Theory of Crime.* Stanford, CA: Stanford University Press.

Gwartney-Gibbs, Patricia A., Jean Stockard, and Susanne Bohmer. 1987. "Learning Courtship Aggression: The Influence of Parents, Peers, and Personal Experience." *Family Relations* 36: 276-282.

Haynie, Dana L. 2002. "Friendship Networks and Delinquency: The Relative Nature of Peer Delinquency." *Journal of Quantitative Criminology* 18: 99-134.

Hepburn, John R. 1977. "Testing Alternative Models of Delinquent Causation." *Journal of Criminal Law and Criminology* 67: 450-461.

Hirschi, T. 1969. *Causes of Delinquency.* Berkeley, CA: University of California Press.

Huang, Bu, Rick Kosterman, Richard F. Catalano, J. David Hawkins, and Robert D. Abbott. 2001. "Modeling Mediation in the Etiology of Violent Behavior in Adolescence: A Test of the Social Development Model." *Criminology* 39: 75-108.

Huizinga, David, Finn-Aage Esbensen, and Anne Wylie Weither. 1991. "Are There Multiple Paths to Delinquency?" *Journal of Criminal Law and Criminology* 82: 83-118.

Hwang, Sunghyun. 2000. *Substance Use in a Sample of South Korean Adolescents: A Test of Alternative Theories.* Unpublished Ph.D. Dissertation, University of Florida.

Hwang, Sunghyun, and Ronald L. Akers. 2003. "Substance Use by Korean Adolescents: A Cross-Cultural Test of Social Learning, Social Bonding, and Self-Control Theories." Pp. 39-64 in Ronald L. Akers and Gary F. Jensen (eds.), *Social Learning Theory and the Explanation of Crime: A Guide for the New Century. Advances in Criminological Theory, Vol. 11.* New Brunswick, NJ: Transaction Publishers.

Inciardi, James A., Ruth Horowitz, and Anne E. Pottiger. 1993. *Street Kids, Street Drugs, Street Crime: An Examination of Drug Use and Serious Delinquency in Miami.* Belmont, CA: Wadsworth.

Jang, Sung Joon. 2002. "The Effects of Family, School, Peers, and Attitudes on Adolescents' Drug Use: Do They Vary with Age?" *Justice Quarterly* 19: 97-126.

Jankowski, M. S. 1991. *Islands in the Street: Gangs and American Urban Society.* Berkeley: University of California Press.

Jensen, Gary F. 1972 . "Parents, Peers, and Delinquent Action: A Test of the Differential Association Perspective." *American Journal of Sociology* 78: 63-72.

———. 1997. "Time and Social History: Problems of Atemporality in Historical Analysis with Illustrations from Research on Early Modern Witch Hunts." *Historical Methods* Winter: 46-58.

———. 2003 "Gender Variation in Delinquency: Self-Images, Beliefs, and Peers as Mediating Mechanisms." Pp. 151-178 in Ronald L. Akers and Gary F. Jensen (eds.), *Social Learning Theory and the Explanation of Crime: A Guide for the New Century. Advances in Criminological Theory, Vol. 11.* New Brunswick, NJ: Transaction Publishers.

Jensen, Gary F., and Ronald L. Akers. 2003. "Taking Social Learning Global: Micro-Macro Transitions in Criminological Theory." Pp. 9-38 in Ronald L. Akers and Gary F. Jensen (eds.), *Social Learning Theory and the Explanation of Crime: A Guide for the New Century. Advances in Criminological Theory, Vol. 11.* New Brunswick, NJ: Transaction Publishers.

Jensen, Gary F., and Dean G. Rojek. 1998. *Delinquency and Youth Crime,* 3rd ed. Prospect Heights, IL: Waveland Press.

Jessor, Richard, and Shirley L. Jessor. 1977. *Problem Behavior and Psychosocial Development.* New York: Academic Press.

Johnson, Richard E., Anastasios C. Marcos, and Stephen J. Bahr. 1987. "The Role of Peers in the Complex Etiology of Adolescent Drug Use." *Criminology* 25: 323-340.

Jones, Marshall, and Donald R. Jones. 2000. "The Contagious Nature of Antisocial Behavior." *Criminology* 38: 25-46

Junger-Tas, Josine. 1992. "An Empirical Test of Social Control Theory." *Journal of Quantitative Criminology* 8: 9-28.

Kandel, Denise B. 1974. "Interpersonal Influences on Adolescent Illegal Drug Use." Pp. 207-240 in Eric Josephson and Eleanor E. Carrol (eds.), *Drug Use: Epidemiological and Sociological Approaches.* New York: Wiley.

————. 1978. "Homophily, Selection, and Socialization in Adolescent Friendships." *American Journal of Sociology* 84: 427-36.

Kandel, Denise B., and Israel Adler. 1982. "Socialization into Marijuana Use Among French Adolescents: A Cross-Cultural Comparison with the United States." *Journal of Health and Social Behavior* 23: 295-309.

Kandel, Denise B., and Kenneth Andrews. 1987. "Processes of Adolescent Socialization by Parents and Peers." *International Journal of the Addictions* 22: 319-342.

Kandel, Denise, and Mark Davies. 1991. "Friendship Networks, Intimacy, and Illicit Drug Use in Young Adulthood: A Comparison of Two Competing Theories." *Criminology* 29: 441-469.

Kaplan, Howard B. 1996. "Empirical Validation of the Applicability of an Integrative Theory of Deviant Behavior to a Study of Drug Use." *Journal of Drug Issues* 26: 345-377.

Kaplan, Howard B., Richard J. Johnson, and C. A. Bailey. 1987. "Deviant Peers and Deviant Behavior: Further Elaboration of a Model." *Social Psychology Quarterly* 50: 277-284.

Kim, Tia E., and Sharon G. Koto. 2000. "Peer Delinquency and Parental Social Support as Predictors of Asian American Adolescent Delinquency." *Deviant Behavior* 21: 331-348.

Kornhauser, Ruth Rosner. 1978. *Social Sources of Delinquency: An Appraisal of Analytic Models.* Chicago: University of Chicago Press.

Krohn, Marvin D. 1974. "An Investigation of the Effect of Parental and Peer Associations on Marijuana Use: An Empirical Test of Differential Association Theory." Pp. 75-89 in Marc Riedel and Terence P. Thornberry (eds.), *Crime and Delinquency: Dimensions of Deviance.* New York: Praeger.

Krohn, Marvin D., Ronald L. Akers, Marcia J. Radosevich, and Lonn Lanza-Kaduce. 1982. "Norm Qualities and Adolescent Drinking and Drug Behavior." *Journal of Drug Issues* 12: 343-59.

Krohn, Marvin D., Lonn Lanza-Kaduce, and Ronald L. Akers. 1984. "Community Context and Theories of Deviant Behavior: An Examination of Social Learning and Social Bonding Theories." *Sociological Quarterly* 25: 353-71.

Krohn, Marvin D., William F. Skinner, James L. Massey, and Ronald L. Akers. 1985. "Social Learning Theory and Adolescent Cigarette Smoking: A Longitudinal Study." *Social Problems* 32: 455-473.

Krohn, Marvin D., William F. Skinner, Mary Zielinski, and Michelle Naughton. 1989. "Elaborating the Relationship Between Age and Adolescent Cigarette Smoking." *Deviant Behavior* 10: 105-129.

LaGrange, Randy L. and Helene Raskin White. 1985. "Age Differences in Delinquency: A Test of Theory." *Criminology* 23: 19-46.

Lanza-Kaduce, Lonn, Ronald L. Akers, Marvin D. Krohn, and Marcia Radosevich. 1984. "Cessation of Alcohol and Drug Use Among Adolescents: A Social Learning Model." *Deviant Behavior* 5: 79-96.

Lanza-Kaduce, Lonn, and Michael Capece. 2003. "Social Structure-Social Learning (SSSL) and Binge Drinking: A Specific Test of an Integrated General Theory." Pp. 179-196 in Ronald L. Akers and Gary F. Jensen (eds.), *Social Learning Theory and the Explanation of Crime: A Guide for the New Century. Advances in Criminological Theory, Vol. 11.* New Brunswick, NJ: Transaction Publishers.

Lanza-Kaduce, Lonn, and Mary Klug. 1986. "Learning to Cheat: The Interaction of Moral-Development and Social Learning Theories." *Deviant Behavior* 7: 243-259.

Lauer, Ronald M., Ronald L. Akers, James Massey, and William Clarke. 1982. "The Evaluation of Cigarette Smoking Among Adolescents: The Muscatine Study." *Preventive Medicine* 11: 417-428.

Lauritson, Janet L. 1993 "Sibling Resemblance in Juvenile Delinquency: Findings from the National Youth Survey." *Criminology* 31: 387-409.

Lieberson, Stanley. 1985. *Making It Count: Improvement of Social Research and Theory.* Berkeley: University of California Press.

Lee, Gang. 1998. *Social Structure and Social Learning in Adolescent Delinquency and Substance Use: A Test of the Mediating Process of Social Learning Theory.* Ph.D. Dissertation, University of Florida.

Lee Gang, Ronald L. Akers, and Marian Borg. 2004. "Social Learning and Structural Factors in Adolescent Substance Use." *Western Criminology Review* 5 [online] http://wcr.sonoma.edu/v5n1/lee.htm.

Liu, Ruth Xiaoru. 2003. "The Moderating Effects of Internal and Perceived External Sanction Threats on the Relationship Between Deviant Peer Associations and Criminal Offending." *Western Criminology Review* 4: 191-202

Loeber, Rolf, and Thomas J. Dishion. 1987. "Antisocial and Delinquent Youths: Methods for their Early Identification." Pp. 75-89 in J. D. Burchard and Sara Burchard (eds.), *Prevention of Delinquent Behavior.* Newbury Park, CA: Sage.

Loeber, Rolf, and Magda Stouthamer-Loeber. 1986. "Family Factors as Correlates and Predictors of Juvenile Conduct Problems and Delinquency." Pp. 29-149 in Michael Tonry and Norval Morris (eds.), *Crime and Justice, Vol. 7.* Chicago: University of Chicago Press.

Loeber, Rolf, Magda Stouthamer-Loeber, Welmoet Van Kammen, and David P. Farrington. 1991. "Initiation, Escalation, and Desistance in Juvenile Offending and their Correlates." *Journal of Criminal Law and Criminology* 82: 36-82.

Lopez, Jose Manuel Otero, Lourdes Miron Redondo, and Angeles Luengo Martin. 1989. "Influence of Family and Peer Group on the Use of Drugs by Adolescents." *International Journal of the Addictions* 24:1065-1082

Marcos, Anastasios, C., Stephen J. Bahr, and Richard E. Johnson. 1986. "Test of a Bonding/Association Theory of Adolescent Drug Use." *Social Forces* 65: 135-161.

Massey, James L., and Marvin D. Krohn. 1986. "A Longitudinal Examination of an Integrated Social Process Model of Deviant Behavior." *Social Forces* 65: 106-134.

Matsueda, Ross L. 1982. "Testing Control Theory and Differential Association." *American Sociological Review* 47: 489-504.

Matsueda, Ross L., and Karen Heimer. 1987. "Race, Family Structure, and Delinquency: A Test of Differential Association and Social Control Theories." *American Sociological Review* 52: 826-840.

Matza, David, and Gresham M. Sykes. 1961. "Juvenile Delinquency and Subterranean Values." *American Sociological Review* 26: 712-719.

McCord, Joan. 1991a. "The Cycle of Crime and Socialization Practices." *Journal of Criminal Law and Criminology* 82: 211-228.

———. 1991b. "Family Relationships, Juvenile Delinquency, and Adult Criminality." *Criminology* 29: 397-417.

McGee, Zina T. 1992. "Social Class Differences in Parental and Peer Influence on Adolescent Drug Use." *Deviant Behavior* 13: 349-372.

McGloin, Jean Marie, Travis C. Pratt, and Jeff Maahs. 2004. "Rethinking the IQ-Delinquency Relationship: A Longitudinal Analysis of Multiple Theoretical Models." *Justice Quarterly* 21: 603-631.

Mears, Daniel P., Matthew Ploeger, and Mark Warr. 1998. "Explaining the Gender Gap in Delinquency: Peer Influence and Moral Evaluations of Behavior." *Journal of Research in Crime and Delinquency* 35: 251-266.

Meier, Robert, Steven Burkett, and Carol Hickman. 1984. "Sanctions, Peers, and Deviance: Preliminary Models of a Social Control Process." *Sociological Quarterly* 25: 67-82.

Menard, Scott, and Delbert S. Elliott. 1994. "Delinquent Bonding, Moral Beliefs, and Illegal Behavior: A Three-Wave Panel Model." *Justice Quarterly* 11: 173-188.

Messner, Steven F., and Richard Rosenfeld. 2001. *Crime and the American Dream*, 3rd ed. Belmont, CA: Wadsworth.

Mihalic, Sharon Wofford, and Delbert Elliott. 1997. "If Violence Is Domestic, Does It Really Count?" *Journal of Family Violence* 12: 292-311.

Miller, N.E., and J. Dollard. 1941. *Social Learning and Imitation*. New Haven, CT: Yale University Press.

Minor, W. William. 1980 "The Neutralization of Criminal Offense." *Criminology* 18: 103-120.

Nye, F. Ivan. 1958. *Family Relationships and Delinquent Behavior*. New York: Wiley.

Orcutt, James D. 1987. "Differential Association and Marijuana Use: A Closer Look at Sutherland (with a Little Help from Becker)." *Criminology* 25: 341-358.

Osgood, Wayne D., and Amy L. Anderson. 2004. "Unstructured Socializing and Rates of Delinquency." *Criminology* 42: 519-549.

Osgood, Wayne D., Janet K. Wilson, Herald G. Bachman, Patricia M. O'Malley, and Lloyd D. Johnston. 1996. "Routine Activities and Individual Deviant Behavior." *American Sociological Review* 61: 635-655.

Page, Edwin R. 1998. *Family Structure and Juvenile Delinquency: The Mediating Role of Social Learning Variables*. Unpublished Ph. D. Dissertation, University of Florida.

Patterson, Gerald R. 1975. *Families: Applications of Social Learning to Family Life*. Champaign, IL: Research Press.

———. 1995. "Coercion as a Basis for Early Age of Onset for Arrest," Pp. 81-105 in Joan McCord (ed.), *Coercion and Punishment in Long-Term Perspectives*. Cambridge, MA:Cambridge University Press.

Patterson, Gerald R., D. Capaldi, and L. Bank. 1991. "The Development and Treatment of Childhood Aggression." Pp. 139-168 in D. Pepler and R. K. Rubin (eds.), *The Development and Treatment of Childhood Aggression*. Hillsdale, NJ: Erlbaum and Associates.

Patterson, Gerald R., and Patricia Chamberlain. 1994. "A Functional Analysis of Resistance During Parent Training Therapy." *Clinical Psychology: Science and Practice* 1: 53-70.

Patterson, Gerald D., B. D. Debaryshe, and E. Ramsey. 1989. "A Developmental Perspective on Antisocial Behavior." *American Psychologist* 44: 329-335

Patterson, Gerald R., and Thomas J. Dishion. 1985. "Contributions of Families and Peers to Delinquency." *Criminology* 23: 63-79.

Patterson, Gerald R., John B. Reid, and Thomas J. Dishion. 1992. *Antisocial Boys*. Eugene, OR: Castalia Publishing Co.

Patterson, Gerald R., J. B. Reid, R. Q. Jones, and R. E. Conger. 1975. *A Social Learning Approach to Family Intervention, Vol. 1*. Eugene, OR: Castalia Publishing Co.

Pearson, Frank S., Douglas S. Lipton, Charles M. Cleland, and Dorline S. Yee. 2002. "The Effects of Behavioral/Cognitive-Behavioral Programs on Recidivism." *Crime and Delinquency* 48: 476-496.

Powell, Walter W., and Paul J. DiMaggio, eds. 1991. *The New Institutionalism in Organizational Analysis*. Chicago: University of Chicago Press.

Pratt, Tavis C., and Francis T. Cullen. 2000. "The Empirical Status of Gottfredson and Hirschi's General Theory of Crime: A Meta-Analysis." *Criminology* 38: 931-964.

Rebellon, Cesar J. 2002. "Reconsidering the Broken Homes/Delinquency Relationship and Exploring its Mediating Mechanism(s)." *Criminology* 40: 103-136.

Rogers, Marcus K. 2001. *A Social Learning Theory and Moral Disengagement Analysis of Criminal Computer Behavior: An Exploratory Study*. Unpublished Ph.D. Dissertation, University of Manitoba.

Rowe, David C., and Bill L. Gulley. 1992. "Sibling Effects on Substance Use and Delinquency." *Criminology* 30: 217-233.

Rowe, David C., and David P. Farrington. 1997. "The Familial Transmission of Criminal Convictions." *Criminology* 35: 177-201.

Sampson, Robert J., and John H. Laub. 1993. *Crime in the Making: Pathways and Turning Points Through Life*. Cambridge, MA: Harvard University Press.

Sampson, Robert J., and William Julius Wilson. 1995. "Toward a Theory of Race, Crime, and Urban Inequality." Pp. 37-54 in John Hagan and Ruth D. Peterson (eds.) *Crime and Inequality*. Stanford, CA: Stanford University Press.

Sellers, Christine S., John K. Cochran, and L. Thomas Winfree, Jr. 2003. "Social Learning Theory and Courtship Violence: An Empirical Test." Pp. 109-128 in Ronald L. Akers and Gary F. Jensen (eds.), *Social Learning Theory and the Explanation of Crime: A Guide for the New Century. Advances in Criminological Theory, Vol. 11*. New Brunswick, NJ: Transaction Publishers.

Sellers, Christine S., and Thomas L. Winfree. 1990. "Differential Associations and Definitions: A Panel Study of Youthful Drinking Behavior." *International Journal of the Addictions* 25: 755-771.

Short, James F. 1957. "Differential Association and Delinquency." *Social Problems* 4: 233-239.

———. 1958. "Differential Association with Delinquent Friends and Delinquent Behavior." *Pacific Sociological Review* 1: 20-25.

———. 1960. "Differential Association as a Hypothesis: Problems Of Empirical Testing," *Social Problems* 8: 14-25.

Silverman, Adam L. 2002. *An Exploratory Analysis of an Interdisciplinary Theory of Terrorism*. Unpublished Ph.D. Dissertation, University of Florida.

Simons, R.L., C.I. Wu, R. Conger, and F.O. Lorenz. 1994. Two Routes to Delinquency: Differences between Early and Late Starters in the Impact of Parenting and Deviant Peers." *Criminology* 32: 247-275.

Skinner, B.F. 1959. *Cumulative Record*. New York: Appleton Century Crofts.

Skinner, William F., and A. M. Fream. "A Social Learning Theory Analysis of Computer Crime Among College Students." *Journal of Research in Crime and Delinquency* 34: 495-518.

Snyder, James J., and Gerald R. Patterson. 1995. "Individual Differences in Social Aggression: A Test of a Reinforcement Model of Socialization in the Natural Environment." *Behavior Therapy* 26: 371-391.

Spear, Sherilyn, and Ronald L. Akers. 1988. "Social Learning Variables and the Risk of Habitual Smoking Among Adolescents: The Muscatine Study." *American Journal of Preventive Medicine* 4: 336-348.

Sutherland, Edwin H. 1937. *The Professional Thief*. Chicago: University of Chicago Press.

————. 1947. *Principles of Criminology*, 4ᵗʰ ed. Philadelphia: J. B. Lippincott.

Sykes, Gresham, and David Matza. 1957. "Techniques of Neutralization: A Theory of Delinquency." *American Journal of Sociology* 22: 664-670.

Thornberry, Terence P., Alan J. Lizotte, Marvin D. Krohn, Margaret Farnworth and Sung Joon Jang. 1994. "Delinquent Peers, Beliefs, and Delinquent Behavior: A Longitudinal Test of Interactional Theory." *Criminology* 32: 47-84.

Tittle, Charles R., and Raymond Paternoster. 2000. *Social Deviance and Crime: An Organizational and Theoretical Approach*. Los Angeles, CA: Roxbury Publishing.

Tittle, Charles R., and David A. Ward. 1993. "The Interaction of Age with the Correlates and Causes of Crime." *Journal of Quantitative Criminology* 9: 3-53.

Toby, Jackson. 1974. "The Socialization and Control of Deviant Motivation." Pp. 85-100 in Daniel Glaser (ed.), *Handbook of Criminology*. Chicago: Rand McNally.

Voss, Harwin. 1964. "Differential Association and Reported Delinquent Behavior: A Replication." *Social Problems* 12: 78-85.

Wang, Shu-Neu, and Gary F. Jensen. 2003. "Explaining Delinquency in Taiwan: A Test of Social Learning Theory." Pp. 65-84 in Ronald L. Akers and Gary F. Jensen (eds.), *Social Learning Theory and the Explanation of Crime: A Guide for the New Century. Advances in Criminological Theory, Vol. 11*. New Brunswick, NJ: Transaction.

Warner, B. D. 2003. "The Role of Attenuated Culture in Social Disorganization Theory." *Criminology* 41: 73-98.

Warr, Mark. 1993a. "Age, Peers, and Delinquency." *Criminology* 31: 17-40.

————. 1993b. "Parents, Peers, and Delinquency." *Social Forces* 72: 247-264.

————. 1996. "Organization and Instigation in Delinquent Groups." *Criminology* 34: 11-38.

————. 1998. "Life-Course Transitions and Desistance from Crime." *Criminology* 36: 183-216.

————. 2002. *Companions in Crime: The Social Aspects of Criminal Conduct*. Cambridge: Cambridge University Press.

Warr, Mark, and Mark Stafford. 1991 "The Influence of Delinquent Peers: What they Think or What they Do?" *Criminology* 4: 851-866.

Wells, L. Edward, and Joseph H. Rankin. 1988. "Direct Parental Controls and Delinquency." *Criminology* 26: 263-286.

White, Helen Raskin, Marsha E. Bates, and Valerie Johnson. 1991. "Learning to Drink: Familial, Peer, and Media Influences." Pp. 177-197 in David J. Pittman and Helene Raskin White (eds.), *Society, Culture, and Drinking Patterns Reconsidered*. New Brunswick, NJ: Rutgers Center of Alcohol Studies.

White, Helene R., Valerie Johnson, and A. Horowitz. 1986. "An Application of Three Deviance Theories for Adolescent Substance Use." *International Journal of the Addictions* 21: 347-366.

White, Helene Raskin, Robert J. Pandina, and Randy L. LaGrange. 1987. "Longitu-dinal Predictors of Serious Substance Use and Delinquency." *Criminology* 25: 715-740.

Wiesner, Margit, Deborah M. Capaldi, and Gerald Patterson. 2003. "Development of Antisocial Behavior and Crime Across the Life-Span from Social Interactional Perspective: The Coercion Model." Pp. 317-338 in Ronald L. Akers and Gary F. Jensen (eds.), *Social Learning Theory and the Explanation of Crime: A Guide for the New Century. Advances in Criminological Theory, Vol. 11.* New Brunswick, NJ: Transaction Publishers.

Winfree, L. Thomas, and Curt T. Griffiths. 1983. "Social Learning and Marijuana Use: A Trend Study of Deviant Behavior in a Rural Middle School." *Rural Sociology* 48: 219-239.

Winfree, L. Thomas, Curt T. Griffiths, and Christine S. Sellers. 1989. "Social Learning Theory, Drug Use, and American Indian Youths: A Cross-Cultural Test." *Justice Quarterly* 6: 395-417.

Winfree, L. Thomas, Jr., G. Larry Mays, and Teresa Vigil-Backstrom. 1994b "Youth Gangs and Incarcerated Delinquents: Exploring the Ties Between Gang Member-ship, Delinquency, and Social Learning Theory." *Justice Quarterly* 11: 229-256.

Winfree, L. Thomas, Christine Sellers, and Dennis L. Clason. 1993. "Social Learning and Adolescent Deviance Abstention: Toward Understanding Reasons for Initiating, Quitting, and Avoiding Drugs." *Journal of Quantitative Criminology* 9: 101-125.

Winfree, L. Thomas, Jr., Teresa Vigil-Backstrom, and G. Larry Mays. 1994a. "Social Learning Theory, Self-Reported Delinquency, and Youth Gangs: A New Twist on a General Theory of Crime and Delinquency." *Youth and Society* 26: 147-177.

Wood, Peter, John K. Cohran, and Betty Pfefferbaum. 1995. "Sensation-seeking and Delinquent Substance Use: An Extension of Learning Theory." *Journal of Drug Issues* 25: 173-193.

Zhang, Lening, and Steven F. Messner. 1995. "Family Deviance and Delinquency in China." *Criminology* 33: 359-409.

2

The Empirical Status of Control Theory in Criminology

Michael R. Gottfredson

Modern control theories in criminology have their roots in systematic efforts to discover and then to explain the facts about crime (Hirschi 1969; Kornhauser 1978; Gottfredson and Hirschi 1990). Control theorists adhere to the normal science paradigm, including a critical focus on data collection, operationalization, and analysis. This stance has stimulated empirical research about many aspects of the theory itself—control theories are today among the most frequently researched and cited perspectives in criminology (Cohn, Farrington, and Wright 1998). Whatever else may be said about the empirical status of control theory in criminology, it most likely holds first place among modern theories for the generation of research. Vold et al. (2002: 194) go so far as to say "Control theories have more or less dominated criminology since Hirschi published his social control theory in 1969."

Few aspects of criminology are beyond the ken of control theories, including the definition of crime itself, methodology, the nature of criminal acts, the nature and scope of individual differences in delinquency and crime, cross-national criminology, and even public policy (Gottfredson and Hirschi 1990). The intended scope of the theory is so broad that a systematic review of its empirical status would be well beyond the allowable scope of this chapter. Consequently, some contemporary issues surfacing in the many serious efforts to test and explicate the theory will be identified and discussed in the hope of stimulating others to continue to consider the theory worthy of research attention.

Many of the key issues that have emerged involve the validity of the measures of control theory concepts. A review of the empirical status of control theory in criminology reminds us that criminology, as a behavioral science, allows only indirect measures of the most critical theoretical concepts. Measures of these concepts nearly always "pass through" the subject as well as the researcher; so, the facts rarely, if ever, speak for themselves. Theories also do not speak for themselves, of course, such that they must themselves be constantly questioned, studied, and debated, in interaction with the evolving empirical literature. It is hard to imagine how to understand the facts about crime and give them meaning other than from the point of view of a theory. Imagining how a theory, in its own terms, would construe the facts provides the distinctions among points of view that turn out to be the essence of much additional empirical work. Consequently, a review of the empirical status of any theory in criminology necessarily must involve critical appraisal of the meaning of variables employed in research, from the point of view of a theory.

Modern versions of control theory have developed by an active confrontation between theoretical assumptions and the commonly agreed upon facts or empirical generalizations about crime and delinquency. As a result, they tend to be consistent with the major empirical generalizations in criminology. For example, a large body of high quality empirical research about age and crime, about the connection between misconduct early in life and criminal behavior later in life, and the remarkable versatility in offending, forced the conclusion about the need to formulate a statement of control theory that explicitly attended to these facts (Hirschi and Gottfredson 1986), a version that ultimately developed the concept of self-control (Gottfredson and Hirschi 1990). It seemed plausible to us that the assumptions and concepts of control theory could be reconciled with these challenging data. Given the tendencies of substantive positivism (Hirschi and Gottfredson 1994), it was, in hindsight at least, inevitable that this reconciliation would be controversial. Some saw it as an abandonment of the sociological point of view, others as the adoption of a pessimistic view of human nature. In our view, self-control theory is neither; nor, as empirical literature now tells us (see below), is it an implicit rejection of the earlier social control theory upon which it is founded. And, when others have reviewed the subsequent research testing some aspects of the theory, they have generally concluded that there is substantial consistent support for the self-control theory thus developed (see, e.g., Pratt and Cullen 2000; Tittle et al. 2003; Vold et al. 2002; Vazonyi et al. 2004; Lanier and Henry 2004).

Varieties of Control Theories

Interpretation of the status of empirical research about control theory requires a brief discussion about the varieties of control theory and how different forms of control might be related for individuals and for groups. The root assumptions of control theories can find expression in many different ways, depending, for example, on the type of control thought to be critical, on conceptualizations of the nature of control themselves and on the perceived relations among types of control.

Control theories all assume that all people are alike in that they tend to pursue self-interest—they seek pleasure and try to avoid harm. Because most criminal and deviant acts satisfy human needs and desires, control theories assume relatively constant motivation for deviance. They further assume that individuals will engage in deviance if some form of restraint is not present. The connections among individuals in society are produced by these restraining factors—and at least in social control theories, these connections are referred to as the social bond—the glue connecting the individuals to society. Those who have weak bonds are more likely to engage in crime and delinquency than are those with strong bonds. Control theories are control theories because they stipulate one, and only one, collective interest which finds expression in values opposing the use of force and fraud to gain self-interest and related acts that subordinate the long-term interest of the group to self-interest. All control theories begin with these basic assumptions, which define control theory as a class of explanation and distinguish it from other perspectives about the causes of crime.

Because bonds are conceived of as variable, they may, conceptually, become established or extinguished at any point in time or even variously over time. Once established, the strength of the bonds may be relatively stable over time for individuals or groups (Gottfredson and Hirschi 1990), or may be thought of as highly variable over time or somewhat situationally dependent (Sampson and Laub 1995). If bond strength is thought to be variable after adolescence, then it might either increase or decrease in strength, although only the former has attracted the attention of theorists. Of course, there must be at least some level of "stability" in the bond for there to be any predict-ability from control theory concepts in the first place—the absence of such stability is probably more aptly the province of—and if empirically justified, support for—labeling theories.

In any event, control theories differ in the extent to which self-controls are relatively firmly established and in which social controls may continue to operate independently of self-control. And, again in principle, this could vary depending on the basis for the bond (e.g., legal sanctions may be effective late in life, but not during adolescence). When control theory focuses on explaining individual and group differences in crime and delinquency via bonds produced *primarily* by intimates (family, friends, teachers, etc.) the perspective has been referred to as social or self-control theory and such theory is the principal subject of this review. Several issues that have emerged from research efforts to test these versions of control theory will be the focus, issues that suggest the need for some theoretical analysis in the spirit of facilitating the research enterprise. We will first briefly comment on the current status of what may be called the "foundational facts" of control theory; the remainder to the paper will focus attention on several key conceptual matters generated by recent empirical studies of control theory.

Foundational Facts

As mentioned, modern control theories have been explicitly constructed with an appreciation of what the empirical literature depicts about crime and delinquency. This literature represents the foundation for these theories and, as such, the empirical status of control theory is tied ineluctably to the validity of these facts. For example:

> "...the fact that delinquents are less likely than nondelinquents to be closely tied to their parents is one of the best documented findings of delinquency research" (Hirschi 1969: 85).

> "Indicators of crime and deviance are consistently positively correlated among themselves" (Gottfredson and Hirschi 1990: 252).

> "The correlation between the delinquency of the subject and the delinquency of his or her friends is one of the strongest in the field" (Gottfredson and Hirschi 1990: 154).

> "Competent research regularly shows that the best predictor of crime is prior criminal behavior. In other words, research shows that differences between people in the likelihood that they will commit criminal acts persist over time" (Gottfredson and Hirschi 1990: 107).

> "School performance also strongly predicts involvement in delinquent and criminal activities. Those who do well in school are unlikely to get into trouble with the law" (Gottfredson and Hirschi 1990: 107).

An accounting of the empirical status of the theory should begin with an assessment of these "foundational facts." After all, if these facts are in doubt, critical tests of the distinctions among versions of the theory are not particularly important. It is thus of considerable moment to note that the empirical status of these facts has not been in serious dispute among empirically oriented criminologists for decades. It seems safe to conclude that recent research continues to validate them (see Vold et al. 2002; Farrington 2003; Hirschi and Gottfredson 1994, 2000). Although it is easy to overlook this consensus about the foundational facts, this consensus is a remarkable achievement. Because control theory has been built on these facts, it seems fair to conclude that a substantial empirical literature is consistent with the theory.

As indicated, self-control theory developed because of our interest in reconciling the assumptions of control theory with an additional set of empirical findings generated by a large number of studies. Age, versatility, and generality effects challenged traditional notions. How well have these facts fared subsequently? In our view, so well that they continue to force the adaptation of the theory we outlined (Hirschi and Gottfredson 1994; Britt and Gottfredson 2003).

The robust, general distribution of crime by age remains an overweening problem for social-psychological theories that claim to account for it; given the ubiquity of the relationship, it is best regarded as a direct cause of crime, delinquency and related behaviors. Post-hoc variability in the distribution of modest scope continues to be reported, particularly in age-restricted samples (e.g., for samples of individuals only in their teens) or for offense types for which age itself is a defining characteristic—some forms of employment crime are the best examples. But such variability does not challenge the principal empirical pattern that crime varies by age in predictable ways, regardless of the type of crime or characteristic of persons, so much so that it overwhelms psychological and sociological efforts at explanation. The summary of the relationship, for arguably the most important cohort of offenders ever studied, could not be more consistent with the arguments in Gottfredson and Hirschi, (1990):

> Hence …the classic age-crime pattern (Hirschi and Gottfredson 1983) is replicated even within a population that was selected for their serious, persistent delinquent activity….Aging out of crime is the norm—even the most serious delinquents desist. This conclusion holds, even if we impose a strict restriction on active offenders….Rather remarkably, then, the data….suggest that the age-crime decline in the general population is replicated, almost in identical (fractal?) fashion, for these active, serious offenders. (Sampson and Laub 2003: 565-569)

If the individual pattern is a fractal pattern of the aggregate, then, contrary to theories of Farrington (2003) and the criminal career tradition, empirical science strongly supports the control theory idea that the significant variability in individual rates of crime and delinquency is fashioned early in life. It is also an empirical finding that makes both the generality effect and the stability effect—as we have discussed them—axiomatic.

The correlation between early childhood problem behaviors and later misconduct continues to be reported regularly in a variety of disciplines. As recently summarized by Farrington (2003: 223), "...there is marked continuity in offending and antisocial behavior from childhood to teenage years and to adulthood [citations omitted]. This means there is relative stability of the ordering of people on some measure of antisocial behavior over time, and that people who commit relatively many offenses during one age range have a high probability of also committing relatively many offenses during another age range" (see also, Baumeister and Heatherton 1996).

The fact that "early delinquency predicts later delinquency" provides two critical elements to self-control theory that distinguish it from many (but by no means all) other perspectives—the period of early childhood is extremely critical in the causation of crime and delinquency and childhood causes far outweigh, in importance, causes coming later in life. Depending on the convention adopted to count, studies documenting this effect could easily number in the hundreds; in psychological research (e.g., Mischel et al. 1988), in basic criminology (e.g., Glueck and Glueck 1950; Hardwick 2002; Zhang et al. 2002), and in nearly all criminological recidivism studies.

Considered simultaneously, the age and stability facts imply that control theory envisions both "continuity and change"—the relative differences among people will tend to be similar, at least from late childhood on, and everyone will "grow out" of crime steadily after the teenage years. Every longitudinal study of delinquency and related problem behaviors seems to be consistent with these facts. The combination of these facts easily accounts for what appears to some to be a dilemma in criminology:"Adult antisocial behavior virtually *requires* childhood antisocial behavior [yet] most antisocial youths do *not* become antisocial adults" (Vold et al. 2002: 296, citing Robins 1978). The fact that nearly all adult offenders were delinquent as children, and most individuals who engage in delinquency as teens do not "persist" into adulthood, is a consequence of both stability and age effects, two continuous variables frequently made discrete in research studies with categories mistakenly cast as "types of people." The rowdy and self-interested behavior of many children becomes frequent enough and public enough to become "delinquency" during the teens, but, for most, it fades nearly as quickly as it arrives and they become "nondelinquents" (or, "adolescent-limited offenders") when their problem behavior generally follows the standard age curve. For a few, whose rowdy and self-interested behavior was marked in childhood, their teen "delinquency" is pronounced and, because they decline from this much higher rate, turn into what the life-course theories call "persisters"—even though it has been abundantly clear from the empirical research on recidivism for decades that they, too, decline with age. The general failure to find anything but very modest correlations distinguishing these "groups" in systematic empirical research easily fits the self-control interpretation that both "continuity" (of the relative differences) and change (due to age) are to be expected. Note also an important, highly consistent empirical finding—"change" overwhelmingly only goes one way in criminology—those with very low rates of delinquent and criminal activity as teens do not often become highly active offenders (even when the social bond might *appear* to break or whether, when relationships sour, jobs are lost, or the like).

Versatility continues to be reported, even though some modest "specialization" in crime-type can be discovered statistically in large samples of recidivists. Recent reviews confirm this fact; again, consider Farrington's recent summary (2003: 224) "...offending is versatile rather than specialized....the types of acts defined as offenses are elements of a larger syndrome of antisocial behavior, including heavy drinking, reckless driving, sexual promiscuity, bullying and truancy. Offenders tend to be versatile not only in committing several types of crimes, but also in committing several types of antisocial behavior." The body of empirical literature that has extended the versatility finding well beyond the traditional definitions of crime and delinquency to other problem and health behaviors is impressive. The importance of these studies—and the general pattern of versatility—are hard to overstate. They demonstrate a focus on a single crime type, or even on legal definitions of crime themselves, is inappropriate for a scientific criminology.

A few cites are illustrative. Messner et al. (2004) have recently shown that offenders in bias crimes cannot reasonably be thought to be "specialists" but rather engage in other, "non-bias" offenses as well; Sampson and Laub (2003) show the same thing in their most recent analysis of the life-offending of the Glueck samples (2004). Junger, Stroebe, and van der Laan (2001) have shown in a large sample of Dutch youth thirteen to twenty-four-years-old that self-reported delinquency is related strongly to soft drug use, alcohol use, and tobacco use. Delinquents had more somatic complaints and had a self-perceived poorer health status and more chronic health problems (see also, Donovan et al. 1991). Junger, Stroebe, and van der Laan (2001) show in a large nationwide survey of the Dutch population, pronounced relationships between criminal offending and personal victimization, property victimization, pedestrian and car accidents, and falls and tripping. "All in all, [the data] provide strong evidence for an interpretation that a constellation of problem behavious is experienced by certain individuals" (2001: 19).

Self-Control

Apart from these "foundational facts" upon which modern control theories have been based, a good deal of research has focused on self-control as a general cause of crime, delinquency, and analogous behaviors. We argued that self-control is the most important individual-difference cause of crime and delinquency (as opposed to aggression, self-esteem or psychopathy, for example). Sometimes our work is miscited to indicate that we argue that self-control is the sole cause of crime, an odd conclusion given our discussions of age, opportunity, and of the nature of criminal acts. Of course, to say self-control is a general cause of crime only makes sense within the context of the theoretical system being articulated (in our case, *The General Theory of Crime*). For one thing, a general cause of crime presupposes the definition of crime used in the theoretical system, a nontrivial matter but one that is ignored in some empirical tests. A scientific theory of crime requires a definition of crime; in self-control theory not all violations of the criminal law fall into the definition of crime used in the theory, (and thus some such acts are beyond the intended scope of the theory) and much noncriminal behavior is included.

In the context of the theory, however, the claims for self-control are quite strong. As a general cause, it should predict rate differences everywhere, for all crimes, delinquencies and related behaviors, for all times, among all groups and countries. In the context of the theoretical system within which it was developed, it should have direct effects and it should help interpret other major correlates of the dependent variable. A very large number of high quality empirical studies published since the theory was developed now, in the aggregate, provide very significant empirical support for these strong claims. Some illustrations of empirical support for some of these claims can be mentioned:

For All Groups

Vazsonyi et al. (2001) show self-control effects for males and females, in four different countries and in five different age groups. Vazsonyi (2003) shows similar results for African American and Caucasian adolescents. DeLisi (2001a, 2001b) shows self-control effects among offender samples; Baron (2003) for homeless youths for property crime, drug use, and violent crime. The list of empirical demonstrations of self-control effects in Tittle et al. (2003: 144) includes: "A relationship between low self-control and criminal or analogous behaviors has been documented for non-student adults [all citations omitted]...; college students; youth; males as well as females; those with and without official criminal backgrounds; and among people in various countries and places. In addition, many types of measures of self-control predict a variety of acts. At least some measures of self-control predict some misbehavior for cross-sectional and longitudinal samples as well as for experimental subjects."

For All Nations

A general cause should explain crime in different cultural settings. As Vazonyi et al. (2004: 190) put it, "...Gottfredson and Hirschi devote an entire chapter of their seminal book to culture and crime in which they carefully elaborate why self-control theory should apply across cultural settings both within countries as well as across countries. This may be one of their most daring theoretical propositions as it stands such a high probability of falsification." Vazonyi and colleagues then show common self-control effects for adolescent samples in the United States, Switzerland, Hungary, and Netherlands. Wright et al. (1999) show the relevance of self-control in New Zealand. Self-control has been used to explain differences among countries in crime rates (e.g., the relatively low crime rate in Japan (Komiya 1999), differences within Japan (Vazsonyi et al. 2004) and in Spain for a general antisocial behavior scale (Romero, Luengo, and Sobral 2001).

For All Crimes (As Defined)

A significant list of confirming studies is supplied by Perrone et al. (2004) [Burton et al. 1994; Burton et al. 1998; Burton et al. 1999; Deng and Zhang 1998; Gibbs and Giever 1995; Grasmick et al. 1993; Keane et al. 1993; Longshore 1998; Nagin and Paternoster 1993; Piquero and Tibbetts 1996; Polakowski 1994; Sellers 1999; Wood et al. 1993]. Vazonyi et al. (2001) show the effects for theft and assault, alcohol and drugs, vandalism and general deviance. Criminal justice system misconduct for active offenders (failure to appear, probation and parole arrests) is studied by DeLisi (2001a, b), serious delinquency by Junger and Tremblay (1999), intimate violence by Sellers (1999), crime by Brownfield and Sorenson (1993), Gibbs et al. (1998) and Polakowski (1994), occupational delinquency among juveniles by Wright and Cullen (2000), a wide variety of delinquent acts and drug use in French-speaking Canadian samples by LeBlanc and Girard (1997), general delinquency in a national probability sample of adolescents by DeLisi (2004), and general deviance by Gibbs et al. (1998, 2003).

For Analogous Behavior

There have been impressive demonstrations of the scope of versatility effects and of the connection between self-control and problem behaviors generally. An excellent example is Junger and Tremblay (1999) who provide evidence of the relation between accidents and delinquency, and the relation between self-control and problem behaviors. Their study followed a sizable group of boys from early childhood through adolescence. They discovered that the relation between accident involvement and general delinquency was significant (the likelihood of being involved in an accident was 50 percent greater for boys in the highest delinquency category than for boys in the lowest category). Their measures of self-control and social control both had significant, although modest, relations to accidents and to delinquency, an important set of findings particularly given the strong skew of the accident variable (see also Junger, West, and Timman 2001).

The connection between self-control and a wide variety of analogous acts is documented by Perrone et al. (2004) in a list including cheating, drugs, accidents, traffic risks, school truancy, misbehavior and dropping out; school problems by Nakhaie, Silverman and LaGrange, (2000); accidents by Keane et al. (1993); cheating by Cochran et al. (1998) and by Gibbs and Giever (1995); accommodation in romantic relationships by Finkel and Campbell (2001); drinking, drug use, and delinquency among adolescents by Zhang et al. (2002); grade point averages, self-esteem, binge eating, alcohol abuse, interpersonal relationships, and optimal emotional responses by Tangney et al. (2004); cigarette use, early unwed parenthood and early marriage by Martino et al. (2004); attention-deficit hyperactivity disorder and bullying by Unnever and Cornell (2003); counterproductive behavior at work by Marcus and Schuler (2003); risky sex, driving behavior, academic dishonesty, and gambling in college samples by Jones and Quisenberry (2004); and unemployment and homelessness by Baron (2003).

Across Time

As a general cause, self-control differences in the population should predict trends in crime rates. Although direct tests do not seem to have as yet been done, the structure of correlates predicting crime-rate trends are generally consistent with the expectations from control theory, especially family and age effects, even if not addressed by the research community in these terms (LaFree 1998; O'Brien 2003; Conklin 2003).

It seems fair to conclude that the empirical literature provides a very broad, empirical consensus about self-control as a general cause of crime, delinquency and problem behaviors.

Key Issues in Empirical Research on Control Theory

Parental Effects and Socialization: Self and Social Control.

Given the substantial empirical literature supporting the validity of both self and social control theories (see also, Dornbusch et al. 2001), the question arises of how to construe these interpretations together in light of this empirical work. Is evidence in support of one version evidence contrary to the other, as is sometimes asserted in textbooks in criminology? If self-control and social control are truly two different theories, rather than two interpretations of the control paradigm, then it should be possible to measure their central constructs in different ways.

Alternatively, consider how socialization of young people generates self-control (Gottfredson and Hirschi 1990; Hirschi and Gottfredson 2003): 1) Parental affection for the child establishes a long-term interest in the success of the child; 2) which enables a parenting style characterized by positive efforts to monitor conduct and appropriately sanction deviance; 3) which creates self-control; 4) which is expressed by affection from the child to the parent and, by logical extension, to other socializing institutions like schools and friends. Such a model implies that it is very likely that the social bonds among parents and children, and self-control in the child, will be very difficult to discriminate empirically and, under some circumstances, may amount to the same thing.

A study of the indicators used in research seems consistent with these expectations. Consider how the parental affection for the child, or attachment to the child, said by Gottfredson and Hirschi (1990) to be the threshold requirement for the creation of high levels of self-control in the child, might be measured in the earliest years. It seems likely that it could be operationalized by the physical and psychological presence of the parent in the child's immediate environment. Thus, parent abandonment and neglect would be sensible measures of low attachment, as would unloving forms of punishment such as physical abuse. And, the fact is that both neglect and abuse are correlated with later delinquency, consistent with the control expectation, (Maxfield and Widom 1996). Similar results are reported by Eckenrode et al., "Most of the maltreatment experienced by children in our study was neglect, and neglected children showed as many EO [early onset problem behaviors] as children experiencing physical or sexual abuse" (2001: 877).

Concern for the long-term welfare of the child might also be measured by the use of appropriate punishments for selfish behavior and, by indicators, of the subordination of the interests of the parent to the interests of the child. More refined measures, such as the amount of time and attention provided to the child by caregivers and the provision of health, and safety measures might also be useful. If so, then monitoring, sanctioning and care are, *at this stage of child development*, evidence of parental affection, a bond from parent to child. If a strong, capable bond is present from the parent to the child, self-control is much more likely to develop in the child than if it is not.

Taking the relationship further down the developmental path, how might parental affection for the child be measured during the teen years? Well, presumably by similar concepts—monitoring, care, sanctioning appropriately, and, by the subordination of the parent's interests to those of the child in ways that are clear to the child. Thus, knowing where the child goes and with whom, seem probable candidates. Efforts to force or encourage the child to attend to long-term obligations, such as school, health, and safety also seem good candidates to measure parental attachment. Thus, Junger and Tremblay (1999) measured supervision in their sample by asking respondents, "Do your parents know where you are when you are outside the house and do your parents know with whom you are with when you are outside the house?" In the logic just described, this also might be termed "parental affection" or "attachment."

With respect to self-control in the child, it may be measured relatively early in development, initially by studying behavior as reported by others, later by self-reports of attitudes and beliefs and by behavioral indicators. We can also study variation in the strength of the social bond in the child as measured by affection for parents, at least in early adolescence, attitudinally ("Do you want to be the kind of person your mother is?"). We could also, in principle, create behavioral measures of the same concept ("How often in the past year did you lie to your parents about where you were when you were out of the home in the evening?"). But note that each of these measures at this stage of development would, *prima fascia*, stand also as measures of self-control—children with higher self-control have a long-term concern for their parents and behave accordingly.

These measures of early parental attachment, which create self-control, are indistinguishable from measures of self-control in the child when applied later in life. If affection creates self-control, in large part through monitoring and appropriate sanctioning, then the child's affection for the parents, expressed as a desire to accommodate to their parents' wishes and expectations, is essentially an indicator of self-control. If this is so, then commonly used indicators of attachment to parents (and by extension to other social institutions such as schools and religions)—the social bond—is at the same time a good measure of self-control—also a social bond. It seems logical to say that common measures of self-control for adolescents are good proxies for attachment (both from the parent to child and child to parent).

Another way of saying all of this is: affectionate parents create self-control by establishing a reciprocal bond between parent and child. Once self-control is present, it may be witnessed by—and even described by—elements of the social bond. The likelihood of it developing in the first instance may be inferred from parental behaviors and attitudes. The key question is not self-versus-social control, but whether, and to what extent, the self-control/social control bond varies after childhood or early adolescence. Can the bond, once established, appreciably weaken? Does the bond appreciably strengthen as an adult due to changes in personal ties or relationships to employers?

It may be worth stressing here that caring or affection in child development seems to be the key to self-control—without it, there is not what might be called "child rearing with a long view." Curiously, sometimes it is suggested that control theory implies something else, that parental affection and a long-term interest in the success of the child may not be a critical component of the creation of self-control. But the evidence is clear:

> "Our model states that parental concern for the welfare or behavior of the child is a necessary condition for successful child-rearing" (Gottfredson and Hirschi 1990).

> "A major premise of the model outlined is that the parent, caretaker or guardian must care enough about the child or the child's behavior to devote the immense amounts of time and energy monitoring and discipline require....Interest in the outcome, whatever its source, tends to assure monitoring and discipline. It also severely limits the range of usable or acceptable sanctions" (Hirschi and Gottfredson 2003: 156-7).

Gibbs et al. (2003: 443) describe it well: "For their children to develop high levels of self-control, parents must regularly monitor them, recognize deviant behavior when it occurs and punish the behavior by noncorporal means. Self-control is associated with the consistent application of these principles during the early development of the child. Investment in the child, which often takes the form of an emotional attachment, is pivotal. It is a necessary but insufficient condition for the implementation of child rearing practices enhancing self-control."

Indicators have been used interchangeably for the concepts of self and social control. The item "Do your parents know where you are when you are away from home" is a standard indicator of social control (Hirschi 1969)—a measure of attachment to parents; it has also served, appropriately, as a measure of parental monitoring (Unnever et al. 2003) and a cause of self control. Unnever and colleagues report "...children who reported they were effectively parented were likely to report having more self-control (or, conversely, those who were ineffectively monitored and inconsistently punished had higher levels of low self-control)" (2003: 87). If both uses of the indicator are correct, then there is no conceptual difficulty in construing the empirical support for social control theory as support for self-control theory and *vice versa* (see Vitaro, Brendgen, and Tremblay [2000] for an empirical demonstration).

The above discussion of course presupposes that the empirical literature supports the idea of a strong parental effect for the establishment of self-control. What is the empirical status of the relationship? The family effect has been a staple of empirical criminology for decades (Loeber and Dishion 1983; Loeber and Strouthamer-Loeber 1986; Hirschi 1969; McCord and McCord 1959; Glueck and Glueck 1950). But what about evidence concerning how parental socialization works—does it indeed create self-control?

Wright and Cullen (2001; see also Burton et al. 1995) studied the connection between parenting behaviors and self-reported delinquency in the National Youth Survey data, documenting important effects for parenting: "Our empirical analysis found delinquency was reduced by child-parent attachment, household rules and parental supervision....Our research both reinforces and specifies the contention control is central to the etiology of delinquent involvement" (2001: 695). They sought to separate distinct elements of parental effects: what they call control and support. They measure "direct parental control" by items measuring supervision, expectations, and household rules; supervision by two items—how many of their child's close friends' mothers knew well and how often mothers know where their children were. "Support" is measured by how often both mothers and fathers miss important events or activities and a 15-item scale of mother and child responses to questions about how often the child is praised, shown affection and complimented, and by activities undertaken together. Interestingly, all of the items load on a single factor which explains delinquency: "From these data, it appears parents who are nurturing, reliable and closely attached to their youths and who provide guidance in the form of rules and supervision reduce the delinquency of their adolescents, even when the effects of delinquent peers and sources of parental heterogeneity are controlled" (2001: 693).

Feldman and Weinberger (1994) provide evidence that self-control and parental bonds are part and parcel of the same process, difficult to distinguish empirically, and probably develop much like we propose. In a carefully crafted study that provides multiple measures of self-restraint (from self, peers, teachers, and parents, etc.) and family influences, they sought to unravel the connections between parental effects, the development of self-restraint and delinquency, beginning when the boys were in the sixth grade and then again in the tenth. They found effects for parenting on self-restraint and, further, self-restraint on delinquency (both at time one and time two). The parenting effects on delinquency at times two could, however, be accounted for in their statistical model by self-restraint: "This pattern suggests effective parenting in childhood is associated with boys' acquisition of self-regulatory skills. In turn, these skills, as internal attributes, provide a mechanism for linking parental influences to adolescents' actions in nonfamilial contexts" (1994: 206). Parenting effects need not operate entirely through self-control, since supervision itself restricts the opportunity for some delinquency.

Perrone et al. (2004) use data from the first wave of the AddHealth study—a large, in-home interview study and a scale they invented that combined items measuring attention difficulties and interpersonal relations. Their measures of parental efficacy, what Gottfredson and Hirschi (1990) would call "recognizing problem behavior," predict delinquency.

If self-control and social control share indicators for children and for adolescents and are said to be caused by the same factors (largely parental and secondarily friend and school influences), then the old view in criminology that there are two types of control—internal and external—may well be incorrect and misleading. The correct view may be that although conceptually distinct, self and social controls cannot be separately measured during the critical formative years and even later they can be studied by identical indicators as well. In studies in which indicators of both self and social control are included in analysis, they increase predictability (Brannigan et al. 2002: 138) "...in our view, the juxtaposition of social control and self-control theories as mutually exclusive explanations of misconduct is not warranted on the evidence from [this study]" (see also, Nakhaie et al. 2000).

The critical empirical issues are, thus, not between self and social control interpretations of control theory, since they have become reconciled by their empirical treatments, but between these treatments and other versions of control theory. If so, then some important contemporary questions are: 1) whether and to what extent later changes in social controls affect the social bond, either due to increased attachments, self-control, or supervision; 2) whether and to what extent such bonds can compete with early bonds in influencing behavior over the life-course; and 3) whether and to what extent formal controls (like criminal penalties) can compete with self and social controls in influencing behavior over the life-course. As of now, empirical research seems to suggest:

1. The empirical support for social control theory is also best construed as empirical support for self-control theory, and *vice versa*;
2. Monitoring and affection of children and adolescents are part and parcel of the social bond necessary to create self-control. As such, measures of these parental attributes belong to both self-control and social control interpretations of control theory.
3. Care must be taken in the interpretation of evidence (unliquidated as it is) for increases in the social bond among adults late in life. Social control effects might be best construed as "monitoring" effects or reduced oppor-

tunity effects ("incapacitation effects?"), or social bonding effects. Because opportunities are required for crime, social institutions that restrict interaction with the times, places, and temptations for crime, such as some marriages and jobs, might reduce individual offending rates, even while self-control or bonding does not change appreciably.

Peer Effects

If parental effects are difficult to parse between versions of control theory, peer effects present no such difficulties. Both interpretations stipulate that the tendency to engage in delinquency and analogous behaviors is established prior to the adolescent years. Lower self-control and attenuated social bonds allow adolescents to migrate toward individuals and groups with similar attributes (and vice versa). Thus, control theory interprets the meaning of most measures of "friends' delinquency" quite differently than do social learning theorists (Gottfredson and Hirschi 1990; see the excellent discussion in Warr 2002). The empirical evidence now provides substantial support of the control theory point of view.

In this regard it is useful to consider the treatment of the peer variables in the meta-analyses literature. Such studies are important, both because of the systematic manner with which the empirical literature is addressed, and because they force analysts to make explicit decisions about the meaning of effect variables—whether they are for or against a particular theory. That is, explicitly in meta-analysis, variables commonly employed in the empirical literature must be "given" to one or another theory. Since this is explicit in meta-analysis, others can reconsider whether the allocation is in accord with the "theory's own view." One excellent recent study that discovered strong, consistent empirical support for self-control theory, also suggested that evidence for the continued existence of peer effects is more consistent with social learning theory (Pratt and Cullen 2000). But, it seems fair to ask, where do the peer variables, commonly used in delinquency research (especially "friends' delinquency) belong —to social learning theory or to control theory? Well, it all depends on the meaning of the indicators, a meaning that is in dispute.

The competition between control and social learning theories regarding peer effects can be briefly stated—for control theory, the variable "friends' delinquency" reflects selection effects (like people self-select to associate together) and measurement error (evidence of friends' delinquency comes from, and cannot be distinguished from, self delinquency). For social learning theory, the variable indicates learning and imitation as causes of self's delinquency.

Matsueda and Anderson (1998) in a critical study show the data provided by the National Youth Survey (the data most commonly used in this context) can best be interpreted in the control context:

> Consistent with control theories…we find that delinquent behavior exerts a large effect on delinquent peer associations. Moreover, the effect of delinquency on delinquent peers is larger than the effect of delinquent peers on delinquency (1998: 299).

Baron (2003) studied the relations among drug use, crime, homelessness, and deviant peers asking his subjects "How many of your current friends have been picked up by the police?" (none to all) and about deviant values "How wrong do you think it is to break the law?" He concludes: "Those with low self-control are more likely to have deviant peers and deviant values, to be unemployed for greater periods of time and to be homeless for greater periods of time controlling for age and gender. These results generally support Gottfredson and Hirschi's (1990) arguments that low self-control can lead to a flocking together with others who probably have low self-control, gravitation to the street where there is less social control and long periods of unemployment (2003: 414).

Zhang and Messner (2000) used data from the National Youth Survey to study the measurement bias hypothesis of Gottfredson and Hirschi (1990) that common measures of "peer influence" that use the respondent's reports of the delinquency of his or her "friends" are most likely a better measure of self delinquency than the influence of peers. They measure peer delinquency from parental reports of the delinquency of their children's friends –how many of them have been in trouble with authorities and have broken the law. They discover that, consistent with the speculation of control theory, the "…findings suggest that the measures of adolescent-reported peer delinquency overlap with the self-reported measures of adolescents' own delinquency to a considerable degree but are not fully redundant. These results are consistent with those of Matsueda and Anderson (1998)" (2000: 333). (Note that in this study the effect for time one delinquency is large whereas the effect for the parent's view of friend's delinquency is quite modest). Regnerus (2002) also casts doubt on the accuracy of self-reports about peer behavior, and in an important review of the drug and other problem behavior literatures, Kandel (1996) concludes "…that peer effects based on cross-sectional data and perceptions of peer behavior are overestimated at least by a factor of five" (1996: 289).

What, then, is the empirical status of control theory with respect to peer effects?

1. The evidence is consistent with the proposition that much of the variance in peer effects on delinquency is attributable to the selection effects of like individuals associating together; and
2. Most measures of peer delinquency, not to mention peer beliefs, contain too much measurement bias to allow inferences that are independent of the characteristics of the subjects being studied. As such, studies that do not seriously consider these issues are considerably missspecified and should not be counted as evidence in favor of social learning theory; and

3. The residual effect of peers not accounted for by selection or measurement bias is likely to represent the effects of attributing any delinquent acts committed by a member of a group to each member present and the benefits of group size on the opportunity for crime and delinquency; and, thus,
4. The best available research on the effects of peers on delinquency is consistent with control theory.

Prevention Experiments as Validity Studies for Control Theory

Control theory suggests the possibility of affecting the probability of delinquency by affecting parenting early in a child's development in ways consistent with the creation of self-control. Some experimental evidence from planned interventions in parenting seems consistent with these expectations and, thus, provides empirical support for the theory (see Greenwood 2002, for one summary of the research). Clarke and Campbell's (1998) review of early intervention programs that report positive effects and suggests that "Working with parents before the child enters kindergarten concerning ways to interact with, and manage, the child, may be essential for any effects on delinquency and youth crime....It is increasingly clear the most effective approach to the prevention of chronic problem behaviors requires early intervention before these behaviors emerge in late childhood and early adolescence [citations omitted]" (1998: 319). Eckenrode et al. (2001: 876, 886) reports that "There are many forms of family support and parent education programs aimed at reducing child abuse and neglect, but the interventions receiving the greatest attention in recent years have involved home visitation services to new parents [citations omitted]" and "These findings seem highly consistent with research suggesting neglected children are as likely to be involved with antisocial behavior, even violent offenses, as are physically abused children [citations omitted]." Olds et al. (1998: 73-4) argues that parenting differences may account for the prevention effect discovered in their famous nurse visitation experiments.

The Measurement of Self-Control

A lively and productive empirical literature has developed centered on the measurement of the concept of self-control. We are greatly encouraged by these early efforts, both because the results are so positive for the theory and because the research community deems the ideas worthy of their attention in the first place. Here we might highlight some potential issues for the next generation of measurement studies.

Measures of self-control need to be age-sensitive (i.e., self-control will be manifest differently for toddlers, teens, and adults). And, since self-control itself likely affects survey responses, behavioral measures, either respondent or informant based, are preferable to "attitudinal" survey responses. Of course, whether self-control is measured by self-reported tendencies or by actual behaviors, such measures will tend to correlate to the extent both contain some "true" variance. A benefit of the different available measurement studies for self-control theory has been highlighted by Pratt and Cullen (2000: 945): "The fact the effect size estimates for attitudinal and behavioral measures of self-control are similar, thus, undermines the criticism that support for Gottfredson and Hirschi's theory lies primarily on data biased by the use of tautological measures."

Intriguing, non-intrusive and reliable behavioral measures are possible, as shown by Junger, West, and Timman (2001). They studied the descriptions made by police on accident forms characterizing the riskiness of the driving behavior of persons involved in accidents. The relation of this measure to crime was striking: "Overall, the fact someone was involved in crime more than doubled the likelihood he or she would be involved in risky behavior in traffic" (2001: 448). Given method independence for their indicators, and given the "non-crime" measure of riskiness, there is, once again, little room for criticism of empirical tautology. And, as suggested above, they show that self-control (attitudinal risk seeking) and social control (attachment to school, belief) are correlated. Interesting behavioral measurements have also been undertaken by Keane, Maxim, and Teevan, (1993); by Brannigan, Gemmell, Pevalin, and Wade (2002); by DeLisi (2001); and by Junger and Tremblay (1999).

Since control theory assumes that characteristics of respondents, such as self-control, affect the validity of response to questionnaires (Piquero et al. 2004), it seems advisable to seek measures of self and social control that are assessed independently of the respondent. The same is true for measures of the dependent variables. This is not a fact to be celebrated, nor an excuse for lower validity; it simply inheres in the confluence of method and substance in the field and must be taken into account for valid inferences from such data. Currently popular techniques that ask respondents to estimate their own likelihood of offending in the future may be especially vulnerable. There is little reason to believe that responses to such inquires have the same validity across levels of self-control.

Marcus (2003) has been particularly critical of attitudinal measures. His argument that some elements of commonly used scales, such as risk-seeking and preferences for easy tasks and physical activities, are inconsistent with control theory because they refer to a motivational basis of behavioral choice rather than to constraints, seems to have merit. "In addition, attitudinal scales, by definition, are not based on a direct assessment of behavior from which the whole theory is deduced" (Marcus 2003: 675). He reports some success for his own behavioral scale.

Continued development of the measurement of control theory variables is important. Age-sensitive, behavioral measurement with sufficient numbers of indicators to increase reliability is needed. For adult samples, particular attention to the problem of separating self-control effects from what may be termed "external monitoring" or "supervision" or "restricted opportunity," would help resolve some theoretical matters about whether additional social bonding creates meaningful reductions in offending not already accounted for by age, self-control, and opportunity. Given the complexity of the statistical control needed for such analysis in non-experimental longitudinal studies, very large samples are likely to be required, although it may be nearly impossible to reduce the inherent ambiguity in these studies sufficient to avoid controversy about the results as a comparison of the conclusions of Hardwick (2002) and Sampson and Laub (1993) indicates.

Conclusions

There are many empirical aspects of control theory that we have not been able to review here, and many stimulating ideas that have emerged from consideration of its implications not discussed. Some recent intriguing examples deserve mention: Among offenders, the level of self-control may be related to the gains in property crime due to greater susceptibility to risky actions that inherently offer a greater benefit (Morselli and Tremblay 2004). Unnever, Cullen and Pratt (2003) show that the effects of ADHD on delinquency may be mediated through low self-control. Nagin and Pogarsky (2001) suggest that neglecting or devaluing the future is related to the efficacy of legally sanctioned threats (citing also Piquero and Tibbits 1996). Interesting work is being done on the collateral consequences of self-control (Evans et al. 1997). And low self-control may be related to feelings of unfairness in punishment (Piquero et al. 2004).

Control theory remains highly consistent with those facts about crime for which there is strong consensus in the empirical criminological community—the foundational facts, versatility, stability, and the age effect. Recent research suggests that the two major forms of control theory in criminology—self and social control—are not only compatible with each other, but also with the facts generated from research testing each of them. All in all, we see no reason to doubt the recent conclusions of scholars who have reviewed the research about crime causation:

Control theory "has the highest level of [empirical] support of all theories of crime causation" (Lanier and Henry 2004: 203).

"[With some caveats] the meta-analysis reported here furnishes fairly impressive empirical support for Gottfredson and Hirschi's theory...Taken together...these considerations suggest that future research omitting self-control from its empirical analyses risks being misspecified" (Pratt and Cullen 2000: 952).

"[Although critical of some aspects]...it is salient that self-control, as identified by Gottfredson and Hirschi, is a factor that should be incorporated into our understanding of crime causation. Its relationship to delinquent involvement is a "fact" for which extant theories must account" (Unnever et al. 2003: 492).

"Thus, the extant empirical research has clearly demonstrated that indicators of self-control are strongly associated with wayward behavior." (Perrone et al. 2004: 300).

If theories may be judged by how much research they stimulate, control theory is doing exceptionally well. If theories may be judged by their consistency with the facts, control theory is doing exceptionally well. And if theories may be judged by the frequency with which other perspectives seek to incorporate them, control theory is, perhaps, without peer.

References

Baron, S. 2003. "Self-control, Social Consequences and Criminal Behavior: Street Youth and the General Theory of Crime." *Journal of Research in Crime and Delinquency* 40: 403-25.

Baumeister, R., and T. Heatherton. 1996. "Self-regulation Failure: An Overview." *Psychological Inquiry* 7:1-15.

Brannigan, A., W. Gemmell, D. Pevalin, and T. Wade. 2002. "Self-Control and Social Control in Childhood Misconduct and Aggression: The Role of Family Structure, Hyperactivity, and Hostile Parenting." *Canadian Journal of Criminology* 44: 9-142.

Britt, C., and M. Gottfredson eds. 2003. *Control Theories of Crime and Delinquency. Advances in Criminological Research, Vol. 12.* New Brunswick, NJ: Transaction Publishers.

Brownfield, D., and S. Sorenson. 1993. "Self-Control and Juvenile Delinquency: Theoretical Issues and Empirical Assessment of Selected Elements of a General Theory of Crime." *Deviant Behavior* 14: 243:64.

Burton, V., F. Cullen, T. Evans, and R. Dunaway. 1994. "Reconsidering Strain Theory: Operationalization, Rival Theories, and Adult Criminality." *Journal of Quantitative Criminology* 10: 213-239.

Burton, V., F. Cullen, T. Evans, R. Dunaway, S. Kethineni, and G. Payne. 1995. "The Impact of Parental Controls on Delinquency." *Journal of Criminal Justice* 23: 111-126.

Burton, V., F. Cullen, T. Evans, L. Alarid, and R. Dunaway. 1998. "Gender, Self-Control, and Crime." *Journal of Research in Crime and Delinquency* 35: 123-147.

Burton, V., T. Evans, F. Cullen, K. Olivares, and R. Dunaway. 1999. "Age, Self-Control, and Adults' Offending Behaviors: A Research Note Assessing *A General Theory of Crime.*" *Journal of Criminal Justice* 27: 45-54.

Clarke, S., and F. Campbell. 1998. "Can Intervention Early Prevent Crime Later? The Abecedarian Project Compared with Other Programs." *Early Childhood Research Quarterly* 13: 319-343.

Cochran, J. Wood, P. Sellers. C., Wilkerson, W., and Chamlin, M. 1998. "Academic Dishonesty and Low Self-control: An Empirical Test of a General Theory of Crime. *Deviant Behavior:* 19: 227-255.

Cohn, E.D., D. Farrington, and R. Wright. 1998. *Evaluating Criminology and Criminal Justice.* Westport, CT: Greenwood Press.

Conklin, J. (2003). *Why Crime Rates Fell.* Boston: Allyn and Bacon.

DeLisi, M. 2001 "Designed to Fail: Self-Control and Involvement in the Criminal Justice System." *American Journal of Criminal Justice* 26: 131-148.

————. 2001. "It's All in the Record: Assessing Self-Control Theory With an Offender Sample." *Criminal Justice Review* 26: 116.

De Li, S. 2004. "The Impacts of Self-Control and Social Bonds on Juvenile Delinquency in a National Sample of Midadolescents." *Deviant Behavior* 25: 351-373.

Deng. X., and L. Zhang. 1998. "Self-Control as a Predictor of Shoplifting Behavior." *Journal of Crime and Justice* 23: 89-110.

Donovan, J., R. Jessor, and F. Costa. 1991. "Adolescent Health Behavior and Conventionality-Unconventionality: An Extension of Problem-Behavior Theory." *Health Psychology* 10:1:52-61.

Dornbusch, S., K. Erickson, J. Laird, and C. Wong. 2001. "The Relation of Family and School Attachment to Adolescent Deviance in Diverse Groups and Communities." *Journal of Adolescent Research* 16: 396-422.

Eckenrode, J., D. Zielinske, E. Smith, L. Marcynyszyn, C. Henderson, Jr., H. Kitzman, R. Cole, J. Powers, and D. Olds. 2001. "Child Maltreatment and the Early Onset of Problem Behaviors: Can a Program of Nurse Home Visitation Break the Link?" *Development and Psychopathology* 13: 873-890.

Evans, T. F., Cullen, V., Burton, R. Dunaway, and M. Benson. 1997. "The Social Consequences of Self-Control: Testing the General Theory of Crime." *Criminology* 35: 475-504.

Farrington, D. 2003. "Developmental and Life-Course Criminology: Key Theoretical and Empirical Issues—The 2002 Sutherland Award Address." *Criminology* 41: 221-255.

Feldman, S., and D. Weinberger. 1994. "Self-Restraint as a Mediator of Family Influences on Boys' Delinquent Behavior: A Longitudinal Study." *Child Development* 65: 195-211.

Finkel, E., and W. Campbell. 2001. "Self-Control and Accommodation in Close Relationships: An Interdependence Analysis." *Journal of Personality and Social Psychology* 81: 263-277.

Gibbs, J., and D. Giever. 1995. Self-Control and Its Manifestation Among University Students: An Empirical Test of Gottfredson and Hirschi's General Theory." *Justice Quarterly* 12: 231-255.

Gibbs, J., D. Giever, and G. Higgins. 2003. "A Test of Gottfredson and Hirschi's General Theory Using Structural Equation Modeling." *Criminal Justice and Behavior* 30: 441-458.

Gibbs, J. D. Giever, and J. Martin. 1998. "Parental-Management and Self-Control: An Empirical Test of Gottfredson and Hirschi's General Theory." *Journal of Research in Crime and Delinquency* 35: 42-72.

Glueck, S., and E. Glueck. 1950. *Unraveling Juvenile Delinquency*. Cambridge, MA: Harvard University Press.

Gottfredson, M., and T. Hirschi. 1990. *A General Theory of Crime*. Stanford, CA: Stanford University Press.

Grasmick, Harold G., Charles R. Tittle, and Robert J. Bursik, Jr. 1993. "Testing the Core Empirical Implications of Gottfredson and Hirschi's General Theory of Crime." *Journal of Research in Crime and Delinquency* 30: 5-29.

Greenwood, P. 2002. "Juvenile Crime and Juvenile Justice." Pp. 75-108 in J. Wilson and J. Petersilia (eds.), *Crime: Public Policies for Crime Control*. Oakland, CA: ICS Press.

Hardwick, K. 2002. *Unraveling 'Crime in the Making': Re-examining the Role of Informal Social Control in the Genesis and Stability of Delinquency and Crime*. Unpublished Ph.D. Dissertation, University of Calgary, Alberta.

Hirschi, T. 1969. *Causes of Delinquency*. Berkeley: University of California Press.

Hirschi, T., and M. Gottfredson 1983. "Age and the Explanation of Crime." *American Journal of Sociology* 89: 552-584.

———. 1986. "The Distinction Between Crime and Criminality." In T. Hartnagel and R. Silverman (eds.), *Critique and Explanation:Essays in Honor of Gwynn Nettler*. New Brunswick, NJ: Transaction Publishers.

———— , eds. 1994. *The Generality of Deviance*. New Brunswick, NJ: Transaction
    Publishers.
————. 2000. "In Defense of Self-Control." *Theoretical Criminology* 4: 55-69.
————. 2003. "Punishment of Children from the Point of View of Control Theory."
    Pp. 151-160 in C. Britt and M. Gottfredson, (eds.), *Control Theories of Crime
    and Delinquency. Advances in Criminological Theory, Vol 12*. New Brunswick,
    NJ: Transaction Publishers.
Jones, S., and N. Quisenberry. 2004. "The General Theory of Crime: How General Is
    It?" *Deviant Behavior* 25: 401-426.
Junger, M., P. van der Heijden, and C. Keane. 2001. "Interrelated Harms: Examining
    the Associations between Victimization, Accidents, and Criminal Behavior."
    Injury Control and Safety Promotion 8: 13-28.
Junger, M., W. Stroebe, and A. van der Laan. 2001. "Delinquency, Health Behaviour
    and Health." *British Journal of Health Psychology* 6: 103-120.
Junger, M., and R. Tremblay. 1999. "Self-Control, Accidents, and Crime." *Criminal
    Justice and Behavior* 26: 485-501
Junger, M., R. West, and R. Timman. 2001. "Crime and Risky Behavior in Traffic: An
    Example of Cross-Situational Consistency." *Journal of Research in Crime and
    Delinquency* 38 439-459.
Kandel, D. 1996. "The Parental and Peer Contexts of Adolescent Deviance: An Alge-
    bra of Interpersonal Influences." *Journal of Drug Issues* 26: 289-315.
Keane, C., P. Maxim, and J. Teevan. 1993. "Drinking and Driving, Self Control, and
    Gender: Testing and General theory of Crime." *Journal of Research in Crime and
    Delinquency* 30: 30-46.
Komiya, N. 1999. "A Cultural Study of the Low Crime Rate in Japan." *British Journal
    of Criminology* 39: 369-390.
Kornhauser, R. 1978. *Social Sources of Delinquency*. Chicago: University of Chicago
    Press.
LaFree, G., 1998. *Losing Legitimacy*. Boulder, CO: Westview Press.
Lanier, Mark and Stuart. Henry. 2004. *Essential Criminology*. Boulder:Westview
    Press.
LeBlanc, M., and S. Girard. 1997. "The Generality of Deviance: Replication Over Two
    Decades With a Canadian Sample of Adjudicated Boys." *Canadian Journal of
    Criminology* 39: 171-183.
Loeber, R., and T. Dishion.1983. "Early Predictors of Male Delinquency: A Review."
    Psychological Bulletin 94: 68-99.
Loeber, R., and M. Stouthamer-Loeber 1986. "Family Factors as Correlates and Pre-
    dictors of Juvenile Conduct Problems and Delinquency." Pp. 29-149 in M. Tonry
    and N. Morris (eds.), *Crime and Justice: An Annual Review of Research, Vol. 7*.
    Chicago: University of Chicago Press.
Longshore, D. 1998. "Self-Control and Criminal Opportunity: A Prospective Test of
    the General Theory of Crime." *Social Problems* 45: 102-113.
Marcus, B. 2003. "An Empirical Assessment of the Construct Validity of Two Alterna-
    tive Self-Control Measures." *Educational and Psychological Measurement*. 63:
    674-706.
Marcus, B., and H. Schuler. 2004. "Antecedents of Counterproductive Behavior at Work:
    A General Perspective." *Journal of Applied Psychology* 809: 647-0660.
Martino, S., R. Collins, and P. Ellickson. 2004. "Substance Use and Early Marriage."
    Journal of Marriage and Family 66: 244-257.
Matsueda, R., and K. Anderson. 1998. "The Dynamics of Delinquent Peers and Delin-
    quent Behavior." *Criminology* 36: 269-308.

Maxfield, M., and C. Widom. 1996. "A The Cycle of Violence: Revisited 6 Years Later." *Archives of Pediatric and Adolescent Medicine* 150: 390-395.

McCord, W., and J. McCord. 1959. *Origins of Crime*. New York: Columbia University Press.

Messner, S. S. McHugh, and R. Felson. 2004. "Distinctive Characteristics of Assaults Motivated by Bias." *Criminology* 42: 585-613.

Mischel, W., Y. Shoda, and P. Peake. 1988. "The Nature of Adolescent Competencies Predicted by Preschool Delay of Gratification." *Journal of Personality and Social Psychology* 54: 687-696.

Morselli, C., and P. Tremblay. 2004. "Criminal Achievement, Offender Networks, and the Benefits of Low Self-Control." *Criminology* 42: 773-804.

Nakaie, M., R. Silverman, and T. LaGrange. 2000. "Self-Control and Social Control: An Examination of Gender, Ethnicity, Class and Delinquency." *Canadian Journal of Sociology* 25: 35-39.

Nagin, D., and R. Paternoster. 1993. "Enduring Individual Differences and Rational Choice Theories of Crime." *Law and Society Review* 27:467-496.

Nagin, D., and G. Pogarsky. 2001. "Integrating Celerity, Impulsivity, and Extralegal Sanction Threat into a Model of General Deterrence: Theory and Evidence." *Criminology* 39: 865-893.

Olds, D., L. Pettitt, J. Robinson, C. Henderson, J. Eckenrode, H. Kitzman,B. Cole, and J. Powers. 1998. "Reducing Risks for Antisocial Behavior with a Program of Prenatal and Early Childhood Home Visitation." *Journal of Community Psychology* 26: 65-83.

O'Brien, R. (2003). "UCR Violent Crime Rates 1958-2000: Recorded and Offender-Generated Trends." *Social Science Research* 32: 499.

Perrone, D, C. Sullivan, T. Pratt, and S. Margaryan. 2004. "Parental Efficacy, Self-Control, and Delinquency: A Test of a General Theory of Crime on a Nationally Representative Sample of Youth." *International Journal of Offender Therapy and Comparative Criminology* 48: 298-312.

Piquero, A., and S. Tibbetts. 1996. "Specifying the Direct and Indirect Effects of Low Self-Control and Situational Factors in Offenders' Decision Making: Toward a More Complete Model of Rational Offending." *Justice Quarterly* 13: 481-510.

Piquero, A., Z. Gomez-Smith, and L. Langton. 2004. "Discerning Unfairness Where Others May Not: Low Self-Control and Unfair Sanction Perceptions." *Criminology* 42: 699-734.

Polakowski, Michael. 1994. "Linking Self- and Social Control with Deviance: Illuminating the Structure Underlying a General Theory of Crime and Its Relation to Deviant Activities." *Journal of Quantitative Criminology* 10: 41-78.

Pratt, T., and F. Cullen, F. 2000. "The Empirical Status of Gottfredson and Hirschi's General Theory of Crime: A Meta-Analysis." *Criminology* 38: 931-64.

Regnerus, M. 2002. "Friends' Influence on Adolescent Theft and Minor Delinquency: A Developmental Test of Peer-reported Effects." *Social Science Research* 31: 681-705.

Romero, E., M. Luengo, and J. Sobral. 2001. "Personality and Antisocial Behavior: Study of Temperamental Dimensions." *Personality and Individual Differences* 31: 329-348.

Sampson, R., and J. Laub. 1993. *Crime in the Making: Pathways and Turning Points Through Life*. Cambridge, MA: Harvard University Press.

———. 2003. "Life-Course Desisters? Trajectories of Crime? Among Delinquent Boys Followed to Age 70." *Criminology* 41: 555-592.

Sellers, C. 1999. "Self-Control and Intimate Violence: An Examination of the Scope and Specification of the General Theory of Crime." *Criminology* 37: 375-404.

Tangney, J., R. Baumeister, and A. Boone. 2004. "High Self-Control Predicts Good Adjustment, Less Pathology, Better Grades, and Interpersonal Success." *Journal of Personality* 72: 271-322.

Tittle, C., D. Ward, and H. Grasmick. 2003. "Gender, Age, and Crime/Deviance: A Challenge to Self-Control Theory." *Journal of Research in Crime and Delinquency* 40: 426-453.

Unnever, J., and D. Cornell. 2003. "Bullying, Self-Control, and ADHD." *Journal of Interpersonal Violence* 18: 129-147.

Unnever, J., F. Cullen and T. Pratt. 2003. "Parental Management, ADHD, and Delinquency Involvement: Reassessing Gottfredson and Hirschi's General Theory." *Justice Quarterly* 20: 471-500.

Vazsonyi, A., and J. Crosswhite. 2003. "A Test of Gottfredson and Hirschi's General Theory of Crime in African American Adolescents." *Journal of Research in Crime and Delinquency* 40: 1-26.

Vazsonyi, A., L. Pickering, L., M. Junger, and D. Hessing, D. 2001. "An Empirical Test of a General Theory of Crime: A Four-Nation Comparative Study of Self-Control and the Prediction of Deviance." *Journal of Research in Crime and Delinquency* 38: 91-131.

Vazonyi, A., J. Witteking, L. Belliston, and T. Van Loh. 2004. "Extending the General Theory of Crime to 'The East': Low Self-Control in Japanese Late Adolescents." *Journal of Quantitative Criminology* 20: 189-216.

Vitaro, F., M. Brendgen, and R. Tremblay. 2000. "Influence of Deviant Friends on Delinquency: Searching for Moderator Variables." *Journal of Abnormal Child Psychology* 28: 313-325.

Vold, G., T. Bernard, and J. Snipes. 2002. *Theoretical Criminology,* 5th ed. Oxford: Oxford University Press.

Warr, M. 2002. *Companions in Crime.* New York: Cambridge University Press.

Wood, Pter B., Betty Pfefferbaum, and Brucec J. Arneklev. 1993. "Risk-Taking and Self-Control: Social Psychological Correlates of Delinquency." *Journal of Crime and Justice* 16: 111-130.

Wright, B., R. Entner, A. Caspi, T. Moffitt, and P. Silva. 1999. "Low Self-Control, Social Bonds, and Crime: Social Causation, Social Selection, or Both?" *Criminology* 37: 479-514.

Wright, J., and F. Cullen. 2000. "Juvenile Involvement in Occupational Delinquency." *Criminology* 38: 363-396.

————. 2001. "Parental Efficacy and Delinquent Behavior: Do Control and Support Matter?" *Criminology* 39: 677-706.

Zhang, L., and S. Messner. 2000. "The Effects of Alternative Measures of Delinquent Peers on Self-Reported Delinquency." *Journal of Research in Crime and Delinquency* 37: 324-337.

Zhang, L., J. Welte, and W. Wieczorek. 2002. "Underlying Common Factors of Adolescent Problem Behaviors." *Criminal Justice and Behavior 29: 161-182.*

3

General Strain Theory: Current Status and Directions for Further Research

Robert Agnew

General strain theory (GST) states that a range of strains or stressors increase the likelihood of crime (Agnew 1992). These strains may involve the inability to achieve positively-valued goals (e.g., money, status, autonomy), the loss of positively-valued stimuli (e.g., loss of romantic partners, property), and the presentation of negatively-valued or aversive stimuli (e.g., verbal and physical abuse). These strains make people feel bad and they may cope through crime. Crime may be a method for reducing or escaping from strains (e.g., stealing the money you desire, running away from abusive parents), seeking revenge against those who inflict strains or related targets (e.g., assaulting the peers who abuse you), or alleviating the negative emotions that result from strains (e.g., through illicit drug use). Whether individuals cope with strains through crime, however, depends on their ability to engage in legal and illegal coping, the costs of crime, and their disposition for crime. These factors, in turn, are influenced by a range of variables, including coping skills and resources, conventional social supports, social control, association with delinquent peers, and exposure to situations conducive to crime.

There has been much research on GST since these core ideas were first presented in 1992, and many individuals—myself included—have suggested revisions in, and extensions of, the theory. This chapter describes the research on GST, the proposed revisions/extensions in the theory and areas where further research is needed. My discussion focuses on: a) the types of strain most likely to result in crime; b) the reasons why strains increase the likelihood of crime; c) the factors that influence or condition the effect of strains on crime; d) the consequences of criminal coping on strains and negative emotions; e) efforts to use GST to explain group differences in crime, crime across the life course, and situational variations in crime; g) the relationship between GST and other theories; and h) the policy implications of GST. I conclude by presenting what I now consider to be the core propositions of GST.

The Types of Strain Most Likely to Result in Crime

GST dramatically expanded the scope of strain theory. Until 1992, most researchers focused on one type of strain: the inability to achieve conventional success goals (although see Agnew 1984, 1985; Elliott et al. 1979; Greenberg 1977). GST stated that there are several types of goal blockage and that strain may also involve the loss of positive stimuli as well as the presentation of negative stimuli. The three broad categories of strain in GST themselves encompass hundreds of more specific strains, as evidenced by the long inventories of stressful life events, chronic stressors and life hassles used by stress researchers. More recently, GST has been expanded to include "vicarious" and "anticipated" strains (Agnew 2002). Vicarious strains refer to the strains experienced by others around the individual, such as family members and friends, while anticipated strains refer to the individual's expectation that his or her current strains will continue into the future or that new strains will be experienced (also see Eitle and Turner 2002; Maxwell 2001). *Certain* of these strains may also contribute to crime, although experienced strains should generally have a larger effect on crime than vicarious and anticipated strains.

Researchers have tried to determine whether many of these new strains are related to crime. Their results are generally encouraging and suggest that numerous strains increase the likelihood of crime. Such strains include parental rejection; discipline that is erratic, excessive, and/or harsh; child abuse and neglect; negative secondary school experience such as low grades and negative relations with teachers; work in the secondary labor market; chronic unemployment; and homelessness. Certain research in this area employs longitudinal data and controls for a broad range of variables. In some cases, this research finds that strain variables have a larger effect on crime than variables associated with the leading crime theories (e.g., Agnew 1989, 2001, 2006; Agnew et al. 1996; Agnew and White 1992; Aseltine et al. 2000; Baron 2004; Baron and Hartnagel 2002; Colvin 2000; Hagan and McCarthy 1997; Paternoster and Mazerolle 1994; Sigfusdottir et al. 2004; Warner and Fowler 2003). As a result, I now think it is safe to say that GST is firmly established as one of the major theories of crime.

At the same time, it is clear that not all strains are related to crime. For example, the inability to achieve educational and occupational success goals appear to be unrelated to crime. As a consequence, I recently tried to better describe those types of strain that are and are not related to crime (Agnew 2001). In particular, I argued that strains are most likely to result in crime when they: 1) are seen as unjust; 2) are high in magnitude; 3) are associated with low social control; and 4) create some pressure or incentive to engage in criminal coping. Drawing on these criteria, I listed several specific strains that should have relatively strong and weak effects on crime (see the conclusion for a list of those strains predicted to have strong effects on crime). This work represents a fundamental extension of GST. I originally argued that whether an individual reacts to strain in a criminal manner is largely a function of the individual's characteristics, such as coping skills and resources, social supports, social controls, and disposition for crime. I now argue that the individual's reaction to strain is a function of *both* the individual's characteristics and the characteristics of the strain that is being experienced.

These arguments, however, need to be tested. In particular, researchers should test my predictions about those strains that have relatively strong and weak effects on crime. Many of these predictions focus on strains that are seldom examined in the literature; for example, I predict that criminal victimization, peer abuse, discrimination based on ascribed characteristics, and the inability to achieve autonomy and masculinity goals will increase crime. Preliminary data from several recent studies provide some support for these predictions (e.g., Agnew 2002; Agnew and Brezina 1997; Aseltine et al. 2000; Baron 2004; Eitle 2002; Eitle and Turner 2002; Jakupcak 2003; Katz 2000; Maxwell 2001; Messerschmidt 1993; Simons et al. 2003). In particular, a few studies suggest that race- and gender-based discrimination increase the likelihood of crime. A growing body of evidence suggests that criminal victimization increases the likelihood of crime; in fact, certain data suggest that victimization may be one of the most important causes of crime. Certain types of peer abuse also appear to contribute to crime. And some data suggest the failure to achieve autonomy and masculinity goals increases at least certain types of crime. More research on the effect of specific strains on crime is needed, however.[1]

Researchers also need to better measure strains. Many tests now employ single-item measures that poorly index the nature and magnitude of strains. Data from the stress literature provide evidence for the low validity of such measures, and strain researchers should follow the lead of stress researchers by developing better strain measures (Herbert and Cohen 1996; Wethington et al. 1995; Wheaton 1996). To give one example, recent research demonstrates the importance of considering the timing of strains (a dimension of magnitude), with data suggesting the *childhood* maltreatment has little effect on *adolescent* delinquency while adolescent maltreatment and maltreatment over the life course both increase adolescent delinquency (Ireland et al. 2002; Thornberry et al. 2001). These findings reinforce my argument that recent and on-going strains are more consequential than those experienced in the past (Agnew 1992 2001).

Further, researchers should ideally measure both "objective" and "subjective" strains. Objective strains "refer to events or conditions disliked by most members of a group." Subjective strains refer to "events or conditions disliked by the people who are experiencing (or have experienced) them" (Agnew 2001: 321).

Researchers testing GST typically examine objective strains (they ask individuals whether they have experienced an event or condition assumed to be aversive; no effort is made to measure the individual's subjective reaction to the event/condition (for exceptions, see Agnew and White 1992; Landau 1997)). However, objective strains sometimes create little subjective strain and, as a consequence, they should be less likely to affect crime than subjective strains. I describe ways to measure both objective and subjective strains (Agnew 2001). Measuring both types of strain will not only allow us to better explain crime, but will also allow us to examine those factors that influence the subjective reaction to objective strains (e.g., determine why divorce creates depression in one person and joy in another, see Wheaton 1990). Understanding why objective strains like divorce, poverty, and criminal victimization differentially affect individuals is critical for the further development of GST. Among other things, it will allow researchers to better integrate GST with macro-level theories that focus on the objective strains experienced by large groups of people (e.g., feminist theories that focus on gender-based oppression, conflict theories that focus on class-based oppression).

Finally, researchers should better explore the ways in which strains work together to affect crime. Drawing on the stress literature, I argue that crime is most likely when several strains cluster together in time (Agnew 1992: 65-66). Such clustering is more likely to elicit negative emotions and overwhelm legitimate coping efforts. The measurement of such clustering however, requires that researchers pay more attention to the timing of and interaction between strains (see Hoffmann and Cerbone 1999; Ireland et al. 2004; Slocum et al. 2004). In particular, researchers should determine whether multiple strains are experienced at the same time (with a focus on those types of strains most likely to cause crime).

Much of the research suggested above will be difficult, or impossible, to carry out without collecting new data. But ultimately, such research should provide a much better idea of those types of strains most likely to cause crime.

Why Strains Increase the Likelihood of Crime

According to GST, strains lead to a range of negative emotions. Such emotions create pressure for corrective action; individuals feel bad and want to do something about it. Certain negative emotions may also reduce the ability to cope in a legal manner, reduce concern for the costs of crime, and/or increase the individual's disposition for crime. Anger, for example, reduces the ability to engage in effective problem solving, reduces awareness of and concern for the costs of crime (individuals are "consumed with rage"), creates a desire for revenge, fosters the belief that crime is justified (since the crime is done to "right a perceived wrong"), and energizes the individual for action. Anger occupies a central role in GST for these reasons and it is not surprising that the GST research has focused on this emotion. Research generally finds that strains increase anger and that anger partly mediates the effect of strains on crime, although not all studies find this and the mediating role of anger is generally greatest for crimes of violence (e.g., Agnew 1985; Aseltine et al. 2000; Bao et al. 2004; Baron 2004; Baron and Hartnagel 2002; Brezina 1998; Broidy 2001; Jang and Johnson 2003; Mazerolle et al. 2000; Mazerolle and Piquero 1997, 1998; Piquero and Sealock 2004).

While such research is supportive of GST, I believe that further research should examine negative emotions in addition to anger and take account of the distinction between emotional states and emotional traits. Further, more attention needs to be paid to additional mechanisms by which strains increase crime.

Negative Emotions in Addition to Anger

While anger is the key emotion in GST, other negative emotions may also play an important role in explaining the effect of strains on crime. A few studies have examined the effect of strains on emotions such as depression and anxiety, and their results are somewhat encouraging. Strains usually increase these emotions and these emotions *sometimes* play a role in mediating the effect of strains on crimes (Aseltine et al. 2000; Bao et al. 2004; Brezina 1996; Broidy 2001; Gibson et al. 2001; Jang and Johnson 2003; Landau 1997; Manasse 2002; Piquero and Sealock 2000, 2004; Sharp et al. 2001; Sigfusdottir et al. 2004; Simons et al. 2003). Researchers should examine the effect of strains on still other negative emotions, such as frustration, malicious envy, jealousy, hopelessness, fear, and shame (for overviews of the major emotions, see Levinson et al. 1999; Morgan and Heise 1988).

Such work should take account of the possibility that certain strains may be more relevant to some emotions than others (e.g., Bao et al. 2004; Baron 2004; Broidy 2001). For example, the inability to achieve monetary goals may create much frustration and envy, but little fear. Further, researchers should also consider the ways in which individual characteristics—like gender, personality traits, social support, and association with delinquent peers—condition the effect of strains on emotions (see Broidy 2001; Hay 2003). And researchers should take account of the possibility certain emotions or combinations of emotions are more relevant to some types of crime than others. For example, anger may be most relevant to violence, frustration and envy to property crime, and fear to illegal escape attempts like running away from home and truancy (for illustrations, see Baron 2004; Broidy and Agnew 1997; Boa et al. 2004; Hay 2003; Jang and Johnson 2003; Piquero and Sealock 2004; Sharp et al. 2001; Sigfusdottir et al. 2004). These arguments, of course, imply that particular strains may be more relevant to some types of crime than others—an argument also in need of further investigation (e.g., De Coster and Kort-Butler 2004).

Emotional States and Emotional Traits

More attention needs to be paid to the distinction between emotional states and emotional traits (see Mazerolle et al. 2003; Spielberger et al. 1995). Emotional states refer to the actual experience of an emotion while emotional traits refer to the individual's general tendency to experience certain emotions. GST predicts that strains lead to negative emotional states, like state anger. Most tests of GST, however, examine emotional traits, like trait anger. This may explain why strains only have a moderate effect on anger in certain studies since other factors have a large effect on trait anger, including biological factors and one's socialization experiences (e.g., exposure to angry models). This may also explain why anger only partly mediates the effect of strains on crime in certain studies. While individuals high in trait anger are more likely to react to strains with state anger (see Mazerolle and Piquero 1997: 330-331; Mazerolle et al. 2003), trait anger is an imperfect surrogate for state anger. A proper test of GST, then, requires an examination of emotional *states*.

A variety of methods can be used to determine whether strains lead to negative emotional states and whether such states, in turn, lead to crime. Such methods include observational studies, experimental studies, surveys where individuals are asked to report on strainful events and their reaction to them and vignette studies (see Stein and Karno 1994 for an overview of certain of these methods). Jang and Johnson (2003) examined a survey where respondents were asked about the "personal problems" (strains) they had experienced, their emotional reactions to these problems—including state anger, and "how they acted" when experiencing these problems. They found that strains had a large effect on state anger, that state anger had a large effect on deviance and that state anger mediated much of the effect of strains on deviance (also see Broidy 2001; Sigfusdottir et al. 2004). Capowich et al. (2001) employed a vignette study in which individuals were presented with descriptions of strainful events, asked about their likely emotional reaction to such events and asked about the likelihood they would respond to such events, with crime. They found the strainful events frequently resulted in state anger, state anger had a major effect on intentions to fight and state anger played a major role in mediating the effect of strains on intentions to fight (also see Mazerolle et al. 2003). Preliminary studies examining emotional *states*, then, provide much support for GST.

At the same time, it is important to note that the chronic or repeated experience of strains may lead to negative emotional *traits* and thereby influence the individual's general predisposition to crime. Bernard (1990), for example, makes this argument. He lists the many strains experienced by people who live in poor, inner-city communities and argues such strains lower the individual's threshold for "perceived wrong or injury" and increase the intensity of one's anger—thereby contributing to trait anger. There are several reasons for this, including the fact that chronic or repeated strains tax the individual's ability to cope in a legal manner, thereby increasing the likelihood that new strains will overwhelm the individual and elicit strong emotional reactions. A number of studies have examined the relationship between strains and trait anger, and they generally find that strains increase the likelihood of such anger (see above references).

Additional Reasons Why Strains Increase the Likelihood of Crime

Finally, it is important to emphasize that strains may increase crime for reasons other than their effect on negative emotional states and traits. Research on GST usually examines the direct effect of strains on crime with controls for social learning variables, control variables, and, sometimes, personality traits. But several theorists, myself included, have argued that strains may reduce social control, foster the social learning of crime, and lead to personality traits conducive to crime (Agnew 1992, 1995a, 1995b; Agnew et al. 2000, 2002; Agnew and White 1992; Colvin 2000; Elliott et al. 1979; Paternoster and Mazerolle 1994). In fact, the classic strain theories of Merton (1938), Cohen (1955) and Cloward and Ohlin (1960) make many of these points, with these theorists arguing that strains may reduce certain types of social control, foster beliefs favorable to crime, and promote association with delinquent peers.

In particular, strains may reduce each of the major types of social control. Strains frequently involve negative treatment by conventional others like parents, spouses, teachers, and employers. For example, parents may harshly discipline their children, teachers may give students low grades and treat them in a demeaning manner, spouses may get into conflicts with one another, and employers may fire employees or pay them poorly. These sorts of strains can reduce direct control by causing individuals to avoid or retreat from conventional others (e.g., family strain leads juveniles to run away from home). They can weaken attachments to conventional others and institutions (e.g., conflict with teachers reduces school attachment). They can reduce stake in conformity (e.g., school problems lead to drop out and poor jobs). And they can weaken one's acceptance of conventional values that condemn crime (e.g., monetary strain may weaken one's condemnation of theft).

Further, strains can contribute to personality traits conducive to crime. Colvin (2000: 22-24), for example, argues that the harsh, erratic discipline of parents may foster low self-control since the child fails to learn that rule-violations are consistently sanctioned in an appropriate manner. And I have argued that strains may contribute to the related traits of low constraint and negative emotionality (Agnew et al. 2002). For example, chronic or repeated strains may increase one's sensitivity to subsequent strains and the intensity of one's anger—key components of negative emotionality (note: negative emotionality is closely related to trait anger).

Strains may also foster the adoption of beliefs favorable to crime. In particular, individuals may use their strains to justify their criminal behavior. Cloward and Ohlin (1960), for example, argue that many poor individuals use their inability to achieve monetary success through legal channels to justify income-generating crimes (also see Anderson 1999). Strains may also prompt individuals to associate with criminal others who, in turn, foster the social learning of crime (see Eitle et al. 2004). As Cohen (1955) and others have argued, strained individuals sometimes form or join criminal groups in an effort to cope with their strains. Among other things, they may join criminal groups in an effort to better achieve their goals—with such goals including status, money, and autonomy (Cloward and Ohlin 1960; Cohen 1955; Moffitt 1993). Or they may join criminal groups in an effort to reduce victimization by others or escape from family problems (e.g., Miller 2001).

Strains, then, may have a large indirect effect on crime through their effect on social control, personality traits conducive to crime, beliefs favorable to crime, and association with criminal peers. Further, there is reason to believe that strains may condition the effect of social control, personality, and social learning variables on crime. Individuals who are low in control, for example, may be more likely to turn to crime when they are high in strain (see Agnew 1993).

Few researchers, however, examine such indirect (and conditioning) effects. The few studies that have been done in this area, however, generally find support for such effects (Agnew 1985, 1993; Agnew et al. 2002; Elliott et al. 1985; Hoffmann and Miller 1998; Hoffmann and Su 1997). Paternoster and Mazerolle (1994), for example, found that a measure encompassing several strains contributed to reduced social control and increased association with delinquent peers. Future studies should follow the lead of these researchers. Strain theory, in fact, has much potential for shedding light on the causes of low social control, personality traits like low self-control, criminal beliefs, and association with criminal others. This is, of course, a point that Cohen (1950) made over fifty years ago.[2]

The Factors That Condition the Effect of Strains on Crime

While strains increase the likelihood of crime, it is clear that most people do not respond to strains with crime. GST, therefore, devotes much attention to the factors that condition the effect of strains on crime. Many plausible arguments are made in this area; for example, it is claimed that levels of social control and social support condition the effect of strains on crime. The research in this area, however, has been decidedly mixed. Significant interactions are sometimes found in the research, but often are not (e.g., Agnew and White 1992; Agnew et al. 2002; Aseltine et al. 2000; Baron 2004; Baron and Hartnagel 2002; Capowich et al. 2001; Gibson et al. 2001; Hoffmann and Cerbone 1999; Hoffmann and Miller 1998; Hoffmann and Su 1997; Jang and

Johnson 2003; Mazerolle 1998; Mazerolle et al. 2000; Mazerolle and Maahs 2000; Mazerolle and Piquero 1997; Paternoster and Mazerolle 1994; Pratt and Godsey 2003). I think the primary reason for this is that methodological problems make it very difficult to detect significant interactions when working with survey data (McClelland and Judd 1993). The fact that some significant interactions have emerged from the research should, therefore, be viewed as encouraging. Especially noteworthy is the finding that personality traits, like negative emotionality and low constraint, condition the effect of strains on crime (Agnew et al. 2002); this finding paves the way for the integration between GST and the recent bio-psychological research on crime (see Walsh 2000). Also noteworthy is Hoffmann's (2003) finding that strain is more likely to lead to crime among those living in economically-deprived urban communities; this finding paves the way for an integration between GST and macro-level theories focusing on community characteristics. Researchers should, of course, continue to search for interactions keeping in mind the difficulties they face when using survey data (see Mazerolle and Maahs 2000, for further discussion).

Researchers should also examine interactions using alternative data sources like experimental studies—including studies evaluating rehabilitation and prevention programs, vignette studies, and observational studies. Most rehabilitation and prevention programs focus on individuals who are experiencing strains; for example, individuals who are failing at school or who live in high-poverty communities. Such programs then manipulate certain of the factors that condition the effect of strains on crime, like coping skills or level of social support. Evaluations of such programs may provide much information on conditioning effects. Vignette studies typically describe strainful events to respondents and then ask them to estimate the likelihood they would respond to such events with crime (e.g., Capowich et al. 2001). Researchers might select respondents who differ on key conditioning variables and determine if such differences influence their anticipated response to strains. Alternatively, researchers might manipulate key conditioning variables when constructing the vignettes (e.g., tell some respondents the probability of being sanctioned for a criminal response is 10 percent and others it is 50 percent). Observational studies may also provide information on conditioning factors. Anderson (1999), for example, found evidence that the children of "decent" families were less likely than the children of "street families" to respond to provocations with violence. There are, then, some ways around the methodological limitations of survey research, although these alternative methods sometimes have problems of their own.

The mixed evidence on conditioning effects may also stem from a tendency to examine conditioning variables in isolation from one another. For example, a researcher might examine whether problem-solving skills condition the effect of strains on crime with a range of other conditioning variables held constant. But whether problem-solving skills influence the effect of strains on crime likely depends on the level of other conditioning variables. Individuals with poor problem-solving skills may *not* respond to strains with crime if their level of social control or conventional social support is high. To illustrate, children generally have poor problem-solving skills but most do not respond to strains in a criminal manner. That is because they usually receive much social support from parents (who often cope on their behalf) and are closely supervised by parents. Given this argument, it may be best for researchers to consider the individual's *overall standing* on all of those factors that increase the likelihood of responding to strains with crime. Criminal coping should be most likely among those who score high on all or most of these factors.

Mazerolle and Maahs (2000) employed this strategy and were able to predict the likelihood of criminal coping with much accuracy. Using data from a nationally representative sample of adolescents, they computed each individuals' "total risk" for criminal coping based on the extent to which they were low in constraint or self-control, associated with delinquent peers and held beliefs favorable to crime. When they focused on a subgroup of adolescents who scored high on several measures of strain, they found that 92 percent of the adolescents at high risk for criminal coping actually engaged in crime, versus only 26 percent of the adolescents at low risk for criminal coping.

So despite the mixed results of the current research, I am confident that further research which takes account of the above suggestions will find support for the conditioning effects described by GST.

The Consequences of Criminal Coping on Strains and Negative Emotions

GST states that strained individuals sometimes cope through crime in an effort to reduce their strains or at least make themselves feel better. But not much research has focused on the effect of crime on strains and the negative emotions associated with strains. Brezina's (1996) pioneering work, however, indicates that crime may alleviate the negative emotions associated with strains. And Brezina's (2000) more recent work suggests that crime often functions as a *short-term* solution to a broad range of strains. Brezina presents data from a range of studies to support this position (also see Brezina 1999). Other data, however, suggest the *long-term* consequences of crime are often quite negative, with crime contributing to troubled relationships and poor work experiences, among other things (e.g., De Li 1999; Tanner et al. 1999). But short-term consequences of a positive nature are quite important; many offenders focus on the short-term and the positive consequences they experience from crime may be sufficient to maintain or enhance their criminal behavior (this is, of course, a core argument of social learning and rational choice theories). More research, however, is needed to verify and extend the work of Brezina—particularly work that explores the conditions under which crime is most likely to reduce strains and alleviate negative emotions (see Brezina 2000).

Using GST to Explain Group Differences in Crime Rates, Crime Over the Life Course, and Situational Variation in Crime

GST has, for the most part, been used to explain why some individuals have a greater predisposition for crime than others. The theory however, can also be used to explain group differences in crime, patterns of offending over the life course, and situational variations in crime.

Group Differences in Crime Rates

GST can help explain group differences in crime rates by arguing that there are group differences in the experience of strains conducive to crime and in the likelihood of responding to such strains with crime. This argument has been used to explain age (Agnew 1997), gender (see below), race/ethnic (Eitle and Turner 2003; Kaufmann et al., forthcoming; Simons et al. 2003), community (Agnew 1999; Brezina et al. 2001; Hoffmann 2003; Warner and Fowler 2003), and cross-national (Pratt and Godsey 2003) differences in crime. (GST has also been applied to the explanation of crime in particular groups, including street youth (e.g., Baron 2004; Hagan and McCarthy 1997), police officers (Gibson et al. 2001), Skinheads (Blazak 1999), Chinese youth (Bao et al. 2004), Filipino youth (Maxwell 2001), and adjudicated delinquents (Piquero and Sealock 2000). There has also been some discussion of how GST might be applied to white-collar offenders (Langton and Piquero 2004.) Nevertheless, much work remains to be done in these areas. Such work, however, is not without its challenges.

Several studies have applied GST to the explanation of gender differences in crime (Agnew and Brezina 1997; Broidy 2001; Broidy and Agnew 1997; Burt and Clay-Warner 2004; Hay 2003; Hoffmann and Cerbone 1999; Hoffmann and Su 1997; Piquero and Sealock 2004; Mazerolle 1998; Sigfusdottir et al. 2004). Such studies frequently find that females experience as many strains as males, although they *sometimes* find that males are more likely to cope with strains through crime. However, studies in this area typically examine a limited number of strains; they sometimes group disparate strains together, including strains predicted to be strongly and weakly related to crime; and they often employ delinquency scales biased toward minor offenses—where gender differences in offending are smallest. This is not to criticize the authors of such studies; it is difficult to find data sets that examine a broad range of strains and, until recently, I urged researchers to combine all of their strain measures into more general scales. I predict that future research will find that males are more likely than females to experience strains *conducive to crime* and to cope with such strains through *serious* crime. Further, such research will shed additional light on why males are more likely to cope with crime (see Broidy and Agnew 2004; Burt and Clay-Warner 2004). (I also believe that future research will shed additional light on the causes of female (and male) crime. Females, for example, are often subject to many strains conducive to crime, including sexual abuse, intimate violence, and the monetary strain associated with the feminization of poverty.)

It is important to note, however, that while GST can help explain group differences in crime, it cannot explain *why* groups differ in their exposure to strains conducive to crime and in those factors that condition the effect of strains on crime. For example, GST cannot explain why males and females differ in their exposure to strains conducive to crime. Such explanations however, are provided by many macro–level theories, including feminist, conflict, social disorganization, institutional anomie, subcultural deviance, and other theories (see Cullen and Agnew 2003). For example, institutional anomie theory helps explain why individuals in certain countries are more likely to experience strains conducive to crime. And subcultural deviance theories help explain why individuals in certain groups are more likely to cope with strains through crime. One major challenge for future research is to better integrate GST with such macro-level theories.

Crime Over the Life Course

GST can also explain patterns of offending over the course of the individual's life ("within-individual" differences in offending). Two major patterns have emerged from the research: the "adolescence-limited" patterning in which offending is largely limited to the adolescent years; and the "life-course persistent" pattern in which individuals offend at relatively high rates over much of their lives (see Agnew 1997). GST explains the adolescence-limited pattern by arguing that the biological and social changes associated with adolescence lead to an increase in those strains conducive to crime and in the tendency to cope with such strains through crime. For example, adolescents experience a dramatic increase in the size, diversity, and demands of their social world. This is due to such things as reduced levels of parental supervision; entrance into secondary schools—which are generally larger and more demanding than primary schools; and the development of romantic ties. As a consequence, adolescents are more likely to be treated negatively by others—since they are interacting with many more people, including many whom they do not know well, and such interactions are more demanding. GST explains life-course persistent offending primarily by arguing that some people develop personality traits early in life that lead to increased levels of strain over the life course and a tendency to respond to such strains with crime. In particular, traits like low constraint and negative emotionality are strongly influenced by biological factors and the early family environment. Individuals with these traits are likely to provoke negative reactions from others in particular situations, alter their environments in ways that increase the likelihood of negative treatment, sort themselves into environments where negative treatment is common, and perceive given environments as aversive (see Agnew 1997, 2005a, 2005b; Agnew et al. 2002; Walsh 2000). Further, such individuals are more likely to respond to such treatment with crime. These arguments are in need of testing. A few recent studies, however, suggest that levels of strain over the life course influence levels of crime over the life course (Hoffmann and Cerbone 1999; Ireland et al. 2004; Slocum et al. 2004).

Situational Variation in Crime

Finally, GST can explain the fact that crime is more likely in some types of situations than others, a fact usually explained in terms of the routine activities and rational choice perspectives. These perspectives argue that criminal acts are most likely when motivated offenders encounter attractive targets in the absence of capable guardians. GST, however, would argue that crime is also likely in those situations where individuals encounter strains of various types. Such strains may be viewed as provocations to crime, and they include physical and verbal insults and a desperate need for money. A variety of accounts suggest that such provocations play a major role in generating crime in particular situations—turning individuals into motivated offenders, turning those who provoke them into attractive targets and reducing concern for the costs of crime (e.g., Agnew 1990, 2006: 30-31; Lockwood 1997; Wright and Decker 1997).

The Relationship Between GST and Other Crime Theories

I have argued that strains may reduce social control, foster the social learning of crime, and contribute to personality traits conducive to crime. I have also argued that strain, control, social learning and personality variables may interact with one another in their effect on crime. In addition, there is good reason to believe that control, social learning and personality variables may affect strain. Such effects have been discussed in several previous works (Agnew 1993, 1995b, 1997; Agnew and White 1992; Agnew et al. 2000, 2002).

With respect to control variables, individuals who are poorly supervised by others, like parents, are more likely to experience strains. In fact, parents supervise their children primarily to protect them from harm, including those harms considered by strain theorists (see Agnew et al. 2000). Individuals who are weakly attached to others are more likely to be negatively treated by these others. And individuals with a low investment in conventional society (e.g., low grades, poor jobs) are more prone to goal blockage and other types of strain. With respect to social learning variables, individuals who closely associate with delinquent peers are more likely to experience strains. In particular, individuals in delinquent groups are more likely to abuse one another and to draw abuse from others (Colvin 2000; Schreck et al. 2004).

Further, personality traits like low self-control, low constraint and negative emotionality increase the likelihood that individuals will experience strains. Individuals with such traits are more likely to interpret objective strains and ambiguous situations as unpleasant. A consideration of personality traits, then, can shed much light on the relationship between objective and subjective strains. Individuals with such traits are more likely to provoke negative reactions from others in particular situations. They are more likely to transform their environment in ways that increase the likelihood of strain; for example, they often frustrate parents to the point that parents avoid and/or harshly discipline them. And they are more likely to sort themselves into environments where strain is common, like delinquent peer groups, bad jobs, and bad marriages (Agnew 1997, 2005a, 2005b; Agnew et al. 2002; Caspi 1998; Walsh 2000).

As is apparent, the relationship between GST and other theories is quite intimate. Strain may reduce control, foster the social learning of crime, and contribute to personality traits conducive to crime; these factors, in turn, may increase strain; and all of these factors may interact with one another in their effect on crime. If that were not enough, at a more concrete level it is often difficult to uniquely classify a variable as a strain, control, or social learning variable. For example, variables like weak parental attachment, low grades, and unemployment might be considered control variables from one perspective, but strain variables from another. I argue in certain of my work that the leading theories are distinguished from one another not so much in terms of the independent variables they examine, but rather in terms of the intervening processes said to link these independent variables to crime (Agnew 1993, 1995a). So while a control theorist argues that unemployment increases crime by reducing the individual's stake in conformity, a strain theorist argues that unemployment increases crime primarily through its effect on negative emotional states. In any event, the very close relationship between the different crime theories highlights the need to develop an integrated theory of crime, but at the same time this relationship makes it difficult to construct a parsimonious theory (unless there is parsimony in stating that everything causes everything else). I describe one approach to developing an integrated theory in a recent book (Agnew 2005a), but this is a ripe area for further work.

The Implications of GST for Controlling Crime

GST has not had much direct impact on efforts to control crime; although the theory is quite compatible with many crime control programs (see Agnew 1995c, 2005a, 2005b). GST makes two major recommendations for controlling crime. First, reduce the exposure of individuals to strains conducive to crime. This may be achieved by eliminating strains conducive to crime, altering strains so as to make them less conducive to crime, removing individuals from strains conducive to crime, equipping individuals with the traits to avoid strains conducive to crime, and altering the perceptions and goals of individuals to reduce subjective strain (see Agnew 2006). Second, GST recommends reducing the likelihood that individuals will react to strains with crime. For example, teach individuals to better manage their anger or increase their level of conventional social support.

As I have argued (1995c, 2001, 2005a, 2005b, 2006), a range of programs try to achieve these goals to varying degrees, although none are based explicitly on GST. For example, restorative justice programs are quite compatible with GST. Such programs often impose less severe sanctions on offenders and take steps to ensure that offenders perceive these sanctions as just; in particular they make offenders aware of the harm they have caused and give offenders some "voice" or say in determining the sanctions they receive. Restorative justice programs also take steps to ensure that the sanctioning process does not reduce social control or promote association with delinquent others—which may increase the likelihood of criminal coping (see Bazemore 2000; Braithwaite 2002). Such programs, then, alter a strain (official sanctions by the justice system) in ways that make it less conducive to crime. There is a need for additional research that examines the links between GST and existing crime-control strategies and explorres the ways in which GST might contribute to such strategies. GST, in particular, can help better identify those types of negative treatment and factors influencing the reaction to negative treatment that should be targeted in prevention and rehabilitation programs. GST may also suggest new strategies for controlling crime like altering the goals and perceptions of individuals in ways that reduce subjective strain. For example, we might alter the masculinity goals of individuals.

Summary

Perhaps the most fitting way to end this chapter is to draw on the work discussed above to describe the major propositions of GST as of 2006.

1. Strains refer to events and conditions that are disliked by individuals. There are three major types of strains. Individuals may: a) lose something they value; b) be treated in an aversive or negative manner by others; or c) be unable to achieve their goals. It is also useful to distinguish between "objective" and "subjective" strains. Objective strains refer to events and conditions that are disliked by most people (or at least most people in the group being examined). Subjective strains refer to events and conditions disliked by the individuals experiencing them. Individuals sometimes differ in their subjective evaluation of the same events and conditions, so there is only partial overlap between objective and subjective strains. Subjective strains should have a stronger impact on crime.

2. Those strains most likely to cause crime: a) are seen as high in magnitude; b) are seen as unjust; c) are associated with low control; and d) create some pressure or incentive to engage in criminal coping (Agnew 2001). In Western, industrialized societies, such strains likely include:

- parental rejection;
- parental supervision/discipline that is erratic, excessive, and/or harsh;
- child abuse and neglect;
- negative secondary school experiences (e.g., low grades, negative relations with teachers, the experience of school as boring and a waste of time);
- abusive peer relations (e.g., insults, threats, physical assaults);
- work in the secondary labor market (i.e., "bad jobs");
- chronic unemployment;
- the failure to achieve selected goals, including thrills/excitement, high levels of autonomy, masculine status, and the desire for much money in a short period of time;
- criminal victimization;
- residence in economically deprived communities;
- homelessness;
- experiences with prejudice and discrimination based on characteristics like race/ethnicity and gender.

Both "experienced" strains and *certain types* of vicarious and anticipated strains may result in crime, although experienced strains should have larger effects on crime (Agnew 2002).

3. Strains increase the likelihood of crime primarily through their impact on a range of negative emotional *states*. While anger is the key negative emotion in GST, particularly with respect to violent crime, other negative emotions are also important. Negative emotions create pressure for corrective action, with crime being one possible response. Individuals may engage in crime to reduce or escape from their strains, seek revenge against the source of their strains or related targets, and/or alleviate their negative emotions. Negative emotions may also reduce the ability to engage in legal coping, reduce the perceived costs of crime, and increase the disposition for crime. Different emotions may be relevant to different types of crime. For example, anger may be most conducive to violent crime, while frustration and envy may be most conducive to property crime. Further, *chronic or repeated strains* may create a predisposition for or general willingness to engage in crime by contributing to negative emotional *traits*, reducing social control, fostering beliefs favorable to crime, increasing association with delinquent peers, and contributing to traits conducive to crime, like low constraint and negative emotionality.

4. The likelihood that individuals will react to strains and negative emotions with crime depends on a range of factors that influence the individual's: a) ability to engage in legal and illegal coping; b) costs of crime; and c)

disposition for crime. Those factors that increase the likelihood of criminal coping include:

- poor conventional coping skills and resources including poor problem-solving and social skills, personality traits like negative emotionality and low constraint, low socio-economic status, and low self-efficacy;
- criminal skills and resources such as "criminal self-efficacy" and, for violent crime, large physical size and strength;
- low levels of conventional social support;
- low levels of social control, including low direct control, stake in conformity and internal control;
- association with criminal others and beliefs favorable to crime;
- exposure to situations where the costs of crime are low and the benefits are high.

5. While GST focuses on the explanation of individual differences in offending, it can also shed light on patterns of offending over the life course, group differences in crime, and situational differences in crime. Such patterns and differences can be partly explained in terms of differences in the exposure to strains conducive to crime and in the possession of factors that influence the likelihood of criminal coping. For example, gender differences in crime are partly due to the fact males are more often exposed to strains conducive to crime and are more likely to possess those traits that foster criminal coping.

6. Crime can be reduced by reducing the individual's exposure to strains conducive to crime and his or her likelihood of responding to strains with crime. Strategies for reducing the exposure to strains include: a) eliminating strains conducive to crime; b) altering strains so as to make them less conducive to crime; c) removing individuals from strains conducive to crime; d) equipping individuals with the traits and skills to avoid strains conducive to crime; and e) altering the perceptions/goals of individuals to reduce subjective strain. Strategies for reducing the likelihood that individuals will respond to strains with crime include: a) improving conventional coping skills and resources; b) increasing social support; c) increasing social control; d) reducing association with delinquent peers and criminal beliefs; and e) reducing exposure to situations conducive to crime.

These propositions remain true to the original statement of GST, but extend that statement in several important ways. Additional research will likely result in further extensions of the theory. Also, the development of the theory will likely be influenced by research in related areas, like the research on stress, justice, emotions, and psychological traits. Such research has played a pivotal role in the development of GST and it should continue to do so. For example, Agnew (2001) has discussed the ways in which the stress research can contribute to the better measurement of strain, Aseltine et al. (2000: 271) has discussed the ways in which the literature on coping can shed light on reactions to strain (also see Compas et al. 2001), and Walsh (2000) has discussed the ways in which recent bio-psychological research can strengthen GST. As GST is further refined and applied to new areas, like the explanation of group differences in crime, it should continue to solidify its position as one of the leading theories of crime and delinquency.

Notes

1. At a more specific level, researchers should examine the extent to which the effect of strains on crime depends on the perceived injustice, perceived magnitude, level of social control and the pressure/incentive for criminal coping associated with the strains. Such research will shed much light on why some strains are related to crime while others are not.
2. Researchers should also examine those factors that condition the effect of strain on these other variables. For example, Cohen (1955) and Cloward and Ohlin (1960) point out that strain does not always lead individuals to form or join gangs. They then discuss certain of the factors that condition the effect of strain on gang formation like the opportunity for strained individuals to interact with one another. Given current circumstances, it would be interesting to extend their work by examining the conditions that influence whether strained individuals form or join terrorist organizations. Media accounts suggest several types of strain, including the problems associated with globalization, contribute to terrorism. But more work is needed to explain why only a small number of individuals respond to such strains with terrorist activity.

References

Agnew, Robert. 1984 "Goal Achievement and Delinquency." *Sociology and Social Research* 68: 435-451.

———. 1985. "A Revised Strain Theory of Delinquency." *Social Forces* 64: 151-167.

———. 1989. "A Longitudinal Test of the Revised Strain Theory." *Journal of Quantitative Criminology* 5: 373-387.

———. 1990. "The Origins of Delinquent Events: An Examination of Offender Accounts." *Journal of Research in Crime and Delinquency* 27: 267-294.

———. 1992. "Foundation for a General Strain Theory of Crime and Delinquency." *Criminology* 30: 47-87.

———. 1993. "Why Do They Do It? An Examination of the Intervening Mechanisms Between 'Social Control' Variables and Delinquency." *Journal of Research of Crime and Delinquency* 30: 245-266.

———. 1995a. "Testing the Leading Crime Theories: An Alternative Strategy Focusing on Motivational Processes." *Journal of Research in Crime and Delinquency* 32: 363-398.

———. 1995b. "The Contribution of Social-Psychological Strain Theory to the Explanation of Crime and Delinquency." In Freda Adler and William S. Laufer (eds.), *The Legacy of Anomie Theory. Advances in Criminological Theory, Vol. 5.* New Brunswick, NJ: Transaction.

———. 1995c. "Controlling Delinquency: Recommendations from General Strain Theory." In Hugh Barlow (ed.), *Crime and Public Policy.* Boulder, CO: Westview.

———. 1997. "Stability and Change in Crime Over the Life Course : A Strain Theory Explanation." In Terence P. Thornberry (ed.), *Developmental Theories of Crime and Delinquency. Advances in Criminological Theory, Vol. 7.* New Brunswick: Transaction.

————. 1999. "A General Strain Theory of Community Differences in Crime Rates." *Journal of Research in Crime and Delinquency* 36: 123-155.

————. 2001. "Building on the Foundation of General Strain Theory: Specifying the Types of Strain Most Likely to Lead to Crime and Delinquency." *Journal of Research in Crime and Delinquency* 38: 319-361.

————. 2002. "Experienced, Vicarious, and Anticipated Strain: An Exploratory Study Focusing on Physical Victimization and Delinquency." *Justice Quarterly* 19: 603-632.

————. 2005a. *Why Do Criminals Offend? A General Theory of Crime and Delinquency.* Los Angeles: Roxbury.

————. 2005b. *Juvenile Delinquency: Causes and Control.* Los Angeles: Roxbury.

————. 2006. *Pressured Into Crime.* Los Angeles: Roxbury. Agnew, Robert, and Timothy Brezina. 1997. "Relational Problems with Peers, Gender, and Delinquency." *Youth and Society* 29: 84-111.

Agnew, Robert, Timothy Brezina, John Paul Wright, and Francis T. Cullen. 2002. "Strain, Personality Traits, and Delinquency: Extending General Strain Theory." *Criminology* 40: 43-72.

Agnew, Robert, Francis T. Cullen, and Velmer S. Burton, Jr. 1996. "A New Test of Classic Strain Theory." *Justice Quarterly* 13: 681-704.

Agnew, Robert, Cesar Rebellon, and Sherod Thaxton. 2000. "A General Strain Theory Approach to Families." In Greer Litton Fox and Michael L. Benson (eds.). *Families, Crime and Criminal Justice.* New York: JAI.

Agnew, Robert, and Helene Raskin White. 1992. "An Empirical Test of General Strain Theory." *Criminology* 30: 475-499.

Anderson, Elijah. 1999. *Code of the Street.* New York: W. W. Norton.

Aseltine, Robert H., Jr., Susan Gore, and Jennifer Gordon. 2000. "Life Stress, Anger and

Anxiety, and Delinquency: An Empirical Test of General Strain Theory." *Journal of Health and Social Behavior* 41: 256-275.

Bao, Wan-Ning, Ain Haas, and Yijun Pi. 2004. "Life Strain, Negative Emotions, and Delinquency: An Empirical Test of General Strain Theory." *International Journal of Offender Therapy and Comparative Criminology* 48: 281-297.

Baron, Stephen W. 2004. "General Strain, Street Youth and Crime: A Test of Agnew's Revised Theory." *Criminology* 42: 457-483.

Baron, Stephen W., and Timothy F. Hartnagel. 2002. "Street Youth and Labor Market Strain." *Journal of Criminal Justice* 30: 519-533.

Bazemore, Gordon. 2000. "Community Justice and a Vision of Collective Efficacy: The Case of Restorative Conferencing." In Julie Horney (ed.). *Policies, Processes, and Decisions of the Criminal Justice System, Criminal Justice 2000. Vol. 3.* Washington, DC: National Institute of Justice.

Bernard, Thomas J. 1990. "Angry Aggression Among the 'Truly Disadvantaged.'" *Criminology* 28: 73-96.

Blazak, Randy. 1999. "Hate in the Suburbs: The Rise of the Skinhead Counterculture." In Lisa J. McIntyre (ed.), *The Practical Skeptic: Readings in Sociology.* Mountain View, CA: Mayfield.

Braithwaite, John. 2002. *Restorative Justice and Responsive Regulation.* Oxford: Oxford University Press.

Brezina, Timothy. 1996. "Adapting to Strain: An Examination of Delinquent Coping Responses." *Journal of Research in Crime and Delinquency* 34: 39-60.

————. 1998. "Adolescent Maltreatment and Delinquency: The Question of Intervening Processes." *Journal of Research in Crime and Delinquency* 35: 71-99.

————. 1999. "Teenage Violence Toward Parents as an Adaptation to Family Strain: Evidence from a National Survey of Male Adolescents." *Youth and Society* 30: 416-444.

————. 2000. "Delinquent Problem-Solving: An Interpretative Framework for Criminological Theory and Research." *Journal of Research in Crime and Delinquency* 37: 3-30.

Brezina, Timothy, Alex R. Piquero, and Paul. Mazerolle. 2001. "Student Anger and Aggressive Behavior in School: An Initial Test of Agnew's Macro-Level Strain Theory." *Journal of Research in Crime and Delinquency* 38: 362-386.

Broidy, Lisa M. 2001. "A Test of General Strain Theory." *Criminology* 39: 9-33.

Broidy, Lisa, and Robert Agnew. 1997. "Gender and Crime: A General Strain Theory Perspective." *Journal of Research in Crime and Delinquency* 34: 275-306.

Burt, Callie Harbin, and Jody Clay-Warner. 2004. "'Not Just Rouge Males': Gender Identity in General Strain Theory." Paper presented at the annual meeting of the American Society of Criminology, Nashville, TN.

Capowich, George P., Paul. Mazerolle, and Alex R Piquero. 2001 "General Strain Theory, Situational Anger, and Social Networks: An Assessment of Conditional Influences." *Journal of Criminal Justice* 29: 445-461.

Caspi, Avshalom. 1998. "Personality Development Across the Life Course." In Nancy Eisenberg (ed.), *Handbook of Child Psychology*. New York: John Wiley & Sons.

Cloward, Richard, and Lloyd Ohlin. 1960. *Delinquency and Opportunity*. Glencoe, IL: Free Press.

Cohen, Albert K. 1955. *Delinquent Boys*. Glencoe, IL: Free Press.

Colvin, Mark. 2000. *Crime and Coercion*. New York: St. Martin's Press.

Compas, Bruce, Jennifer K. Connor-Smith, Heidi Saltzman, Alexandra Harding Thomsen, and Martha E. Wadsworth. 2001. "Coping with Stress During Childhood and Adolescence: Problems, Progress, and Potential in Theory and Research." *Psychological Bulletin* 127: 87-127.

Cullen, Francis T., and Robert Agnew. 2003. *Criminological Theory: Past to Present*. Los Angeles: Roxbury.

De Coster, Stacy, and Lisa Kort-Butler. 2004. "How General Is General Strain Theory: Assessing the Domains of Stress and Delinquency." Paper presented at the annual meeting of the American Society of Criminology, Nashville, TN.

De Li, Spencer. 1999. "Legal Sanctions and Youths' Status Achievement: A Longitudinal Study." *Justice Quarterly* 16: 377-401.

Eitle, David J. 2002. "Exploring a Source of Deviance-Producing Strain for Females: Perceived Discrimination and General Strain Theory." *Journal of Criminal Justice* 30: 429-442.

Eitle, David, Steven Gunkel, and Karen Van Gundy. 2004. "Cumulative Exposure to Stressful Life Events and Male Gang Membership." *Journal of Criminal Justice* 32: 95-111.

Eitle, David, and R. Jay Turner. 2002. "Exposure to Community Violence and Young Adult Crime: The Effects of Witnessing Violence, Traumatic Victimization, and Other Stressful Life Events." *Journal of Research in Crime and Delinquency* 39: 214-237.

————. 2003. "Stress Exposure, Race, and Young Adult Male Crime." *Sociological Quarterly* 44: 243-69.

Elliott, Delbert S., Susan Ageton, and Rachel Canter. 1979. "An Integrated Theoretical Perspective on Delinquent Behavior." *Journal of Research in Crime and Delinquency* 16: 3-27.

Elliott, Delbert S., David Huizinga, and Susan S. Ageton. 1985. *Explaining Delinquency and Drug Use*. Beverly Hills, CA: Sage.

Gibson, Chris L., Marc L. Swatt, and Jason R. Jolicoeur. 2001. "Assessing the Generality of General Strain Theory: The Relationship Among Occupational Stress Experienced by Male Police Officers and Domestic Forms of Violence." *Journal of Crime and Justice* 24: 29-57.

Greenberg, David F. 1977. "Delinquency and the Age Structure of Society." *Contemporary Crisis* 1: 189-223.

Hagan, John, and Bill McCarthy. 1997. *Mean Streets.* Cambridge: Cambridge University Press.

Hay, Carter. 2003. "Family Strain, Gender, and Delinquency." *Sociological Perspectives* 46: 107-136.

Herbert, Tracy B., and Sheldon Cohen. 1996. "Measurement Issues in Research on Psychosocial Stress." In Howard B. Kaplan (ed.), *Psychosocial Stress.* San Diego: Academic Press.

Hoffmann, John. 2003. "A Contextual Analysis of Differential Association, Social Control, and Strain Theories of Delinquency." *Social Forces* 81: 753-786..

Hoffman, John P., and Felicia G. Cerbone. 1999. "Stressful Life Events and Delinquency Escalation in Early Adolescence." *Criminology* 37: 343-374.

Hoffman, John P., and Alan S. Miller. 1998. "A Latent Variable Analysis of General Strain Theory." *Journal of Quantitative Criminology* 14: 83-110.

Hoffman, John P., and S. Susan Su. 1997. "The Conditional Effects of Stress on Delinquency and Drug Use: A Strain Theory Assessment of Sex Differences." *Journal of Research in Crime and Delinquency* 34: 46-78.

Ireland, Timothy O., John P. Hoffmann, and Craig J. Rivera. 2004. "Developmental Trajectories and General Strain Theory." Paper presented at the annual meeting of the American Society of Criminology, Nashville, TN.

Ireland, Timothy O., Carolyn A Smith, and Terence P. Thornberry. 2002. "Developmental Issues in the Impact of Child Maltreatment on Later Delinquency and Drug Use." *Criminology* 40: 359-400.

Jakupcak, Matthew. 2003. "Masculine Gender Role Stress and Men's Fear of Emotions as Predictors of Self-Reported Aggression and Violence." *Violence and Victims* 18: 533-541.

Jang, Sung Joon, and Byron R. Johnson. 2003. "Strain, Negative Emotions, and Deviant Coping Among African Americans: A Test of General Strain Theory." *Journal of Quantitative Criminology* 19: 79-105.

Kaufmann, Joanne C., Cesar Rebellon, Sherod Thaxton, and Robert Agnew. Forthcoming. "A General Strain Theory of the Race-Crime Relationship." In Paul Mazerolle and Robert Agnew (eds.), *General Strain Theory: Essential Readings.* Belmont, CA: Wadsworth.

Katz, Rebecca. 2000. "Explaining Girls' and Women's Crime and Desistance in the Context of Their Victimization Experiences." *Violence Against Women* 6: 633-660.

Landau, Simha F. 1997. "Crime Patterns and Their Relation to Subjective Social Stress and Support Indicators: The Role of Gender." *Journal of Quantitative Criminology* 13: 29-56.

Langton, Lynn, and Nicole Leeper Piquero. 2004. "Can General Strain Theory Explain White-Collar Crime? A Preliminary Investigation." Paper presented at the annual meeting of the American Society of Criminology, Nashville, TN.

Levinson, David, James J. Ponzetti, Jr., and Peter F. Jorgensen, eds. 1999. *Encyclopedia of Human Emotions.* New York: Macmillan Reference.

Lockwood, Daniel. 1997. *Violence Among Middle School and High School Students: Analysis and Implications for Prevention.* Washington, DC: National Institute of Justice.

Manasse, Michelle. 2002. "Gender, Crime, and Depression." Paper presented at the annual meeting of the American Society of Criminology, Chicago, IL.

Maxwell, Shelia Royo. 2001. "A Focus on Familial Strain: Antisocial Behavior and Delinquency in Filipino Society." *Sociological Inquiry* 71: 265-292.

Mazerolle, Paul. 1998. "Gender, General Strain, and Delinquency: An Empirical Examination." *Justice Quarterly* 15: 65-91.

Mazerolle, Paul., Velmer S. Burton, Jr., Francis T. Cullen, T. David Evans, and Gary L. Payne. 2000. "Strain, Anger, and Delinquent Adaptations: Specifying General Strain Theory." *Journal of Criminal Justice* 28: 89-101.

Mazerolle, Paul and Jeff Maahs. 2000. "General Strain and Delinquency: An Alternative Examination of Conditioning Influences." *Justice Quarterly* 17: 323-43.

Mazerolle, Paul, and Alex Piquero. 1997. "Violent Responses to Strain: An Examination of Conditioning Influences." *Violence and Victims* 12: 323-343.

Mazerolle, Paul, and Alex Piquero. 1998. "Linking Exposure to Strain with Anger: An Investigation of Deviant Adaptations." *Journal of Criminal Justice* 26: 195-211.

Mazerolle, Paul, Alex R. Piquero, and George E. Capowich. 2003. "Examining the Links Between Strain, Situational and Dispositional Anger, and Crime." *Youth and Society* 35: 131-157.

McClelland, Gary H., and Charles M. Judd. 1993. "Statistical Difficulties of Detecting Interactions and Moderator Effects." *Psychological Bulletin* 114: 376-390.

Merton, Robert K. 1938. "Social Structure and Anomie." *American Sociological Review* 3: 672-82.

Messerschmidt, James W. 1993. *Masculinities and Crime*. Lanham, MD: Rowman and Littlefield.

Miller, Jody. 2001. *One of the Guys: Girls, Gangs, and Gender*. New York: Oxford University Press.

Moffitt, Terrie E. 1993. "Life-Course-Persistent and Adolescence-Limited Antisocial Behavior: A Developmental Taxonomy." *Psychological Review* 100: 674-701.

Morgan, Rick L., and David Heise. 1988. "Structure of Emotions." *Social Psychology Quarterly* 51: 19-31.

Paternoster, Raymond, and Paul Mazerolle. 1994. "General Strain Theory and Delinquency: A Replication and Extension." *Journal of Research in Crime and Delinquency* 31: 235-263.

Piquero, Nicole Leeper, and Miriam D. Sealock. 2000. "Generalizing General Strain Theory: An Examination of an Offending Population." *Justice Quarterly* 17: 449-484.

————. 2004. "Gender and General Strain Theory: A Preliminary Test of Broidy and Agnew's Gender/GST Hypotheses," *Justice Quarterly* 21: 125-158.

Pratt, Travis C., and Timothy W. Godsey. 2003. "Social Support, Inequality, and Homicide: A Cross-National Test of an Integrated Theoretical Model." *Criminology* 41: 611-672.

Schreck, Christopher J., Bonnie S. Fisher, and J. Mitchell Miller. 2004. "The Social Context of Violent Victimization: A Study of the Delinquent Peer Effect." *Justice Quarterly* 21: 23-47.

Sharp, Susan F., Toni L. Terling-Watt, Leslie A. Atkins, Jay Trace Gilliam, and Anna Sanders. 2001. "Purging Behavior in a Sample of College Females: A Research Note on General Strain Theory." *Deviant Behavior* 22: 171-188.

Sigfusdottir, Inga-Dora, George Farkas, and Eric Silver. 2004. "The Role of Depressed Mood and Anger in the Relationship Between Family Conflict and Delinquent Behavior." *Journal of Youth and Adolescence* 33: 509-522.

Simons, Ronald L., Yi-Fu Chen, Eric A. Stewart, and Gene H. Brody. 2003. "Incidents of Discrimination and Risk for Delinquency: A Longitudinal Study of Strain Theory with an African American Sample." *Justice Quarterly* 20: 827-854.

Slocum, Lee Ann, Sally S, Simpson, and Doug Smith. 2004. "General Strain Theory and Within-Individual Change in Offending." Paper presented at the annual meeting of the American Society of Criminology, Nashville, TN.

Spielberger, C.D., E.C. Reheiser, and S.J. Sydeman. 1995. "Measuring the Experience, Expression, and Control of Anger." In H. Kassonove (ed.), *Anger Disorders: Definition, Diagnosis, and Treatment*. Washington, DC: Taylor & Francis.

Stein, Stephanie, and Mitchell Karno. 1994. "Behavioral Observation of Anger and Aggression." In Michael J. Furlong and Douglas C. Smith. (eds.), *Anger, Hostility, and Aggression*. Brandon, VT: CPPC.

Tanner, Julian, Scott Davies, and Bill O' Grady. 1999. "Whatever Happened to Yesterday's Rebels? Longitudinal Effects of Youth Delinquency on Education and Unemployment." *Social Problems* 46: 250-274.

Thornberry, Terence P., Timothy O. Ireland, and Carolyn A. Smith. 2001. "The Importance of Timing: The Varying Impact of Childhood and Adolescent Maltreatment on Multiple Problem Outcomes." *Development and Psychopathology* 13: 957-979.

Walsh, Anthony. 2000. "Behavior Genetics and Anomie/Strain Theory." *Criminology* 38: 1075-1108.

Warner, Barbara D., and Shannon K. Fowler. 2003. "Strain and Violence: Testing a General Strain Theory Model of Community Violence." *Journal of Criminal Justice* 31: 511-521.

Wethington, Elaine, George W. Brown, and Ronald Kessler, C. 1995. "Interview Measurement of Stressful Life Events." In Sheldon Cohen, Ronald C. Kessler, and Lynn Underwood Gordon (eds.), *Measuring Stress*. New York: Oxford University Press.

Wheaton, Blair. 1990. "Life Transitions, Role Histories, and Mental Health." *American Sociological Review* 55: 209-224.

————. 1996. "The Domains and Boundaries of Stress Concepts." In Howard B. Kaplan (ed.), *Psychosocial Stress*. San Diego: Academic Press.

Wright, Richard T., and Scott H. Decker. 1997. *Armed Robbers in Action*. Boston: Northeastern University Press.

Part II

Macro-Level Theories

4

The Present and Future of
Institutional-Anomie Theory

Steven F. Messner and Richard Rosenfeld

Over a decade ago, we published the first edition of *Crime and the American Dream*. Our principal objectives in writing the book were twofold (Messner and Rosenfeld 1994: iii-iv). One, we set out to offer an explanation of the empirical evidence about crime in the United States. Our point of departure was the claim of "American exceptionalism"—the view that levels and patterns of serious crime in the U.S. are distinctive when viewed in comparison with other advanced nations. Two, we were committed to applying a macro-sociological perspective to crime in American society. While the general influence of sociology on the development of criminology has been amply documented elsewhere (see, for example, Akers 1992), we were convinced that the promise of the sociological perspective for understanding crime had yet to be fully realized. The end result of our labors was a set of arguments about the interconnections between the basic features of the social organization of American society—its core cultural commitments and major social institutions—and observed levels and patterns of crime.

The original explanation of crime in the U.S. advanced in *Crime in the American Dream* has subsequently been interpreted more broadly as a macro-sociological *theory* of crime. In their widely cited article published in *Criminology* in 1995, Chamlin and Cochran christened our analytic framework and causal propositions with the felicitous label: "institutional-anomie theory." They proceeded to derive propositions from the theory and assessed these propositions using conventional regression-based techniques. The results of their analyses lent sufficient support to the hypotheses to encourage others to draw upon institutional-anomie theory to guide macro-level research on crime.

Consistent with the theme of this volume, the purpose of our chapter is to "take stock" of the current status of institutional-anomie theory (hereafter

IAT). We begin with a brief synopsis of the underlying assumptions and core propositions of IAT as it has evolved over the years, locating the theory within the anomie tradition in criminology more generally. Next, we present an analytic review of the quantitative research informed by IAT. We explicate the logic of efforts at empirical assessments and highlight the general thrust of the findings. Finally, we discuss the theoretical implications of the empirical literature, address issues that have been raised in theoretical commentary, and identify the challenges that must be confronted to enhance the theory's utility for future research on the macro-social sources of crime.

Synopsis of IAT

IAT incorporates central elements of the anomie perspective in criminology as developed by Robert K. Merton. In his classic essay "Social Structure and Anomie," Merton (1938, 1968) establishes the foundation for a sociological explanation of crime and other forms of deviant behavior by providing what might be regarded as an analytic accounting scheme. To understand crime, or for that matter virtually any form of patterned behavior at the macro-level, the analyst needs to direct attention to social organization—the prevailing culture and social structure. Merton applies his basic analytic accounting scheme to the case of the U.S.

As has been fully explicated in the literature (e.g., Bernard 1995; Messner 2004; Rosenfeld 1989), Merton's substantive thesis centers on alleged "contradictions" and "disjunctions" within the culture, and between the culture and a central feature of the social structure, the stratification system. Within American culture, Merton detects a disproportionate emphasis on the importance of realizing cultural goals, especially the goal of monetary success relative to the emphasis placed on the importance of using the legitimate means for pursuing goals. This cultural imbalance fosters *anomie*, wherein the selection of the means for social action is governed purely on the basis of considerations of technical efficiency. Merton further observes a structural strain built into the social organization of American society that derives from the combination of universal success goals and unequal access to the legitimate means for realizing success. Persons for whom access to the legitimate means is blocked are exposed to structural pressures to adapt in various ways, including the selection of technically efficient, but illegal, means to realize goals. Through these insightful and provocative arguments, Merton skillfully illustrates the utility of explaining macro-level phenomena, such as crime rates, with explicit reference to the fundamental features of the social organization of a society.

Our explanation of the interconnections between crime and social organization in the U.S. takes as its point of departure Merton's characterization of the goals-means imbalance in the culture. The disproportionate emphasis on achieving the goal of material success relative to the emphasis on the importance of using legitimate means is a defining feature of the culture: It is encapsulated in the cultural ethos of the "American Dream." Similarly, following Merton, we conceptualize anomie as a condition wherein the means of social action have been literally *de*-moralized; considerations of the legitimacy of the means are rendered subservient to assessments of their technical efficiency.

We then extend Merton's characterization of the cultural component of social organization in the U.S. by making explicit the value-foundations of the ethos of the American Dream. As noted by Parsons (1951: 107-108) in his classic treatment of the "pattern variables" of social systems, the value complex in the U.S. is an exemplar of a "universalistic achievement" pattern. People are evaluated on the basis of what they have accomplished, what they have done, rather than who they are. This evaluative standard of achievement is applied broadly: Everyone is encouraged to succeed. Moreover, American culture exhibits a distinctive type of materialism. "Money" becomes the principal sign of success. As Marco Orru (1990: 235) observes, money is the "*currency* for measuring achievement." American culture also places a particularly strong emphasis on individualism. Individual rights and entitlements are awarded priority over collective duties and obligations. In this manner, we elaborate Merton by proposing that the anomic type of culture in the U.S. that he so aptly describes rests upon a distinctive value-complex, one heavily tilted toward achievement orientation, universalism, individualism, and a pecuniary materialism.

While our approach to the cultural component of social organization follows Merton's lead rather closely, we shift attention in our analysis of social structure from the stratification system to selected institutions that bear primary responsibility for meeting the survival requirements of a society. Our analysis is based on the premise that the integration of institutions in a society or social system requires the balancing of sometimes competing "claims" of institutional roles.[1] In any given society, a particular "institutional balance of power" emerges that reflects the ways in which its members accomplish this balancing task. The distinctive feature of the institutional structure in the U.S., we propose, is that it is characterized by dominance of the economy. Non-economic roles tend to be devalued relative to economic roles; non-economic roles typically are accommodated to economic roles when conflicts emerge; and the logic and mentality of the marketplace penetrates into the non-economic realms of social life. We illustrate economic dominance in the institutional balance of power in the U.S. with reference to the interconnections among the economy, the family, the polity, and the educational system.

Finally, to apply our characterization of the form of social organization in the U.S. specifically to the explanation of crime, we incorporate strands of conventional criminological theory. A high degree of anomie in the culture implies weak internal controls. Social norms are relatively ineffective in governing behavior, thus increasing the likelihood that people will pursue their goals "by any means necessary," including criminal means. At the same time, economic dominance gives rise to enfeebled non-economic institutions. This leads to weak institutional controls—with the exception of the permissive "controls" emanating from a free-market economy—and meager institutional support which can be linked with crime via classical social disorganization theory and social support theory (Cullen 1994; Cullen and Wright 1997). As depicted schematically in Figure 4.1, the basic analytical model of social organization and crime underlying IAT thus incorporates values and norms from the culture, along with institutional interrelationships and corresponding controls and support from the social structure, to serve as the conceptual foundation for a macro-social explanation of crime

Figure 4.1
The Analytical Model of Social Organization and Crime in IAT

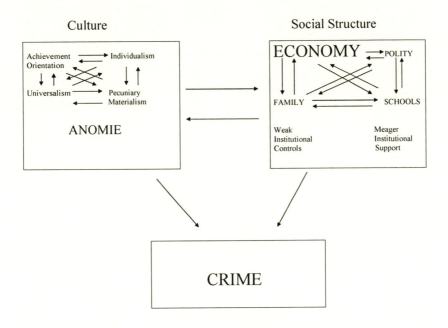

Analytic Review of Empirical Applications of IAT

IAT represents an attempt to understand the social sources of crime by applying core sociological concepts that are applicable to societies in general. Although this high level of abstraction enhances the scope of IAT, it renders empirical assessments difficult. Deriving specific causal propositions and identifying operational measures of the key concepts pose daunting challenges. Nevertheless, efforts to apply IAT in empirical analyses of crime have begun to accumulate. In our review of this literature, we restrict attention to macro-level research that has appeared in published sources[2] and include studies that integrate IAT with other theoretical perspectives if the authors themselves regard the analyses as bearing directly on IAT. Our review is organized around two overarching themes: assessment of IAT's institutional dynamics and assessment of its cultural dynamics.

Analyses of Institutional Dynamics

Researchers have confronted the challenge of applying the arguments about institutional structure and functioning advanced in IAT in several creative ways. Chamlin and Cochran (1995), in their pioneering application of IAT cited above, draw on a policy recommendation presented in *Crime and the American Dream* to deduce specific propositions to guide their research. They note the claim in *Crime and the American Dream* that changes in economic conditions are unlikely to lead to significant reductions in crime in the absence of other changes in the culture and institutional structure of society and, more specifically, changes in the institutional balance of power. Building on the logic underlying this claim, they hypothesize that the effect of conventional indicators of adverse economic conditions that have been theoretically linked to crime will exhibit *interactive* rather than main effects on crime rates, reflecting a moderating role of the institutional balance of power.

Chamlin and Cochran thus elaborate the analytical model of IAT to incorporate the interrelationships between the institutional balance of power and "outputs" of the economy. They select poverty as the output of the economy to examine and conceptualize the institutional balance of power in terms of the vitality of three non-economic institutions: the family, religion, and the polity. This enables them to translate the highly abstract analytic model of IAT into a causal model that is amenable to empirical assessment via standard regression techniques (see Figure 4.2). Using data on property crime rates for the U.S. states in 1980 and indicators of the vitality of the non-economic institutions, they find evidence consistent with theoretical expectations. The regression coefficients for the product terms representing the hypothesized interactions are statistically significant in the predicted direction.

Several subsequent studies have followed the "moderating effects" framework to investigate the institutional dynamics depicted by IAT. Piquero and Piquero (1998) set out to replicate and extend Chamlin and Cochran's research. They conduct cross-sectional analyses of crime rates for the U.S. states with more recent (1990) data. In addition, they include violent crime rates as well as property crime rates in their analyses and assess the sensitivity of the results to alternative operationalizations of key concepts.[3] The results of their analyses offer mixed support for IAT. The regression coefficients for the product terms

Figure 4.2
Chamlin and Cochran's Translation of IAT into a Casual Model

The Elaborated Analytical Model:

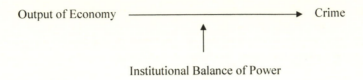

Output of Economy ──────────────────▶ Crime

Institutional Balance of Power

The Causal Model of Moderating Effects:

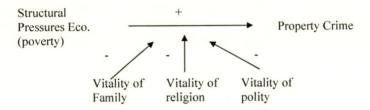

Structural
Pressures Eco.   +
(poverty)   ──────────────────▶ Property Crime

Vitality of   Vitality of   Vitality of
Family   religion   polity

are consistent with the theory in some instances, and this can be observed for both property and violence crimes but not in others. The authors accordingly caution that conclusions about IAT may be sensitive to decisions about operationalization.

Four other studies have extended the "moderating effects" framework to analyze additional institutional domains and different units of analysis. Hannon and DeFronzo (1998) draw on an integrated formulation of IAT and social support theory to hypothesize that levels of welfare assistance will moderate the effects of economic deprivation on crime rates. Using data on total, violent, and property crime rates for a sample of large metropolitan areas in the U.S. in 1990, they find that their composite index of "resource deprivation" exhibits the expected interaction effect with their welfare index: "higher levels of welfare assistance reduce the strength of the positive relationship between the size of the disadvantaged population and crime rates" (1998: 389). They interpret these results as supportive of IAT.

Stucky (2003) also focuses on subnational units within the U.S., specifically cities. He combines insights from IAT and "systemic" social disorganization theory to predict that indicators of the responsiveness of local political structures will interact with indicators of deprivation (considering "family deprivation" as well as the more commonly studied "economic deprivation") in their effects on crime. He tests these hypotheses with data on violent crime rates for a sample of cities in 1990. His results are consistent with expectations. The effects of structural indicators of deprivation are mitigated in cities with local political structures that reflect greater responsiveness to citizens.

In addition to these studies based on data for population aggregates within the U.S., two analyses using cross-national data have adopted the "moderating effects" framework in the application of IAT. Savolainen (2000) employs a measure of "decommodification," or the generosity and extensiveness of social welfare policies, as an indicator of the vitality of non-economic institutions. He hypothesizes that the effects of income inequality and ascribed economic inequality on homicide rates should be less pronounced in nations that have "tamed the market" through policies of decommodification. His analyses of two cross-national samples offer support for the hypotheses. Subsequent research by Pratt and Godsey (2003), using different operationalizations of key concepts, essentially reaffirms Savolainen's main conclusions. Pratt and Godsey observe that their indicator of social welfare policies (the percent of the nation's gross domestic product spent on health care) moderates the effect of an indicator of income inequality on homicide rates in the theoretically expected manner.

Although the bulk of the research on the institutional dynamics stipulated by IAT has followed the moderating effects strategy, two other approaches can also been discerned in the literature. In our study of "decommodification" that preceded Savolainen's work, we treat the measure of decommodification as an indicator of the balance between the polity and economy and hypothesize that it will exhibit a direct effect on homicide rates, net of controls (Messner and Rosenfeld 1997). Our analyses of a cross-national sample offer evidence consistent with this "main effects" model.[4] However, following the same logic but using data for a slightly different sample of nations, and employing a regression model with different control variables, Jensen (2002) does not replicate these findings about the effect of decommodification on homicide rates.

Batton and Jensen (2002) also examine the main effects of measures of decommodification in a time-series analysis of U.S. homicide rates for the period 1900 to 1997. Their analysis produces mixed support for IAT arguments. Although they find no significant effect of decommodification on homicide rates for the period as a whole, they do find an effect in the expected direction for the earlier subperiod 1900 to 1945. They interpret their results as suggesting that decommodification has a conditional effect on homicide that occurs under particular institutional circumstances.

Cullen et al. (2004) similarly apply IAT with a "main effects" approach but shift attention from the kinds of behaviors typically studied—violent and property crimes—to a very different dependent variable: managerial ethical reasoning. They examine the extent to which managers are willing to justify behavior that is ethically suspect. Drawing on IAT, they hypothesize that features of the institutional structure of a nation indicative of (or possibly casually related to) economic dominance will be positively associated with the tendency of managers to regard ethically suspect behavior as justified. The structural characteristics under consideration include indicators of welfare socialism, family breakdown, educational attainment and industrialization. Cullen et al. assess their hypotheses with data from a sample of 3,450 managers from 28 nations. Using the techniques of hierarchical linear modeling, they find support for three of the four hypotheses. The one unexpected finding emerges for the indicator of welfare socialism that is positively, rather than negatively, associated with managers' willingness to justify ethically suspect behaviors. The authors speculate that this finding may reflect the fact that members of the managerial classes are likely to be "net losers" under socialist policies.

A final approach to assessing the institutional dynamics of IAT in the literature assesses the possibility of "mediating" effects in the linkages among economic institutions, non-economic institutions, and crime. Maume and Lee (2003) argue that the language in *Crime and the American Dream* can be interpreted as consistent not only with the "moderating effects" model but also with a model wherein economic dominance undermines the vitality of non-economic institutions which, in turn, leads to high levels of crime in a manner suggested by classical social disorganization theory. They conceptualize family income inequality as an indictor of the dominance of the economy and estimate main and interaction effects of income inequality on homicides (disaggregated on the basis of "expressive" and "instrumental" motivation) with an array of indicators of the strength of non-economic institutions for a sample of U.S. counties circa 1990. They report that the evidence offers greater support for the mediation model than for the moderation model that has been assessed more frequently.

Analyses of Cultural Dynamics

Research on the cultural dynamics of IAT is much more limited than that on institutional dynamics. To a large extent, this reflects the difficulties in obtaining valid and reliable measures of cultural orientations for quantitative analysis. Nevertheless, a few noteworthy efforts along these lines have appeared in the literature.

The research by Cullen et al. (2004) on managerial ethical reasoning discussed above includes an indirect assessment of claims about the interconnections among basic societal values, the normative orders, and attitudes that are presumably conducive to illegal behavior. Drawing on the arguments about the value foundations of the American Dream, the authors hypothesize that strong commitments to achievement, individualism, universalism, and pecuniary materialism should be related to high rates of crime because these kinds of value commitments give rise to relatively weak social norms (2004: 413). In the absence of measures of the weakness of norms or the degree of anomie, Cullen et al. assess their hypotheses by treating anomie as an unmeasured, intervening construct. The logic of this approach is depicted in the top panel of Figure 4.3.

Cullen et al. (2004) construct measures of the specified value orientations using cross-national survey responses from a variety of sources. As in the analyses of institutional dynamics, they employ hierarchical linear modeling to estimate the effect of the nation-level indicators of values on managers' willingness to justify ethically suspect behavior, net of selected individual-level variables. The results of their analyses offer mixed support for IAT. The measures of universalism and pecuniary materialism are related to managers'

Figure 4.3
The Logic of Assessments of IAT Cultural Dynamics

Anomie as an Unmeasured Intervening Construct (Cullen et al. 2004):

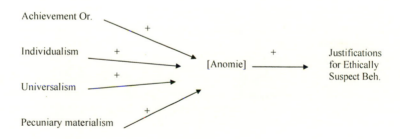

Altruism as an Unmeasured Correlate of Anomie (Chamlin and Cochran 1997):

willingness to justify ethically suspect behavior in the expected positive direction. In contrast, the indicators of achievement orientation and individualism exhibit significant negative effects on the dependent variables. The authors once again speculate that the application of IAT to the specific population under investigation—managers—may not be straightforward because of the distinctive opportunity structures that confront this population.

Chamlin and Cochran (1997) adopt a different strategy. They apply IAT to the cultural component of social organization by directing attention to a hypothesized correlate of anomie: social altruism. They suggest that communities characterized by strong commitment to altruistic values are likely to be less anomic than those with a weaker commitment to altruism (p. 207). IAT thus provides a rationale for anticipating a negative effect of measures of altruism on crime (see the bottom panel of Figure 4.3).[5] Chamlin and Cochran operationalize altruism by means of the ratio of contributions to United Way campaigns, relative to aggregate income, and assess the effect of this measure on personal and property crime rates for a sample of U.S. cities. The results reveal significant, negative effects of altruism on both types of crime rates in multivariate analyses consistent with the logic of IAT.

Finally, studies by Jensen (2002) and Cao (2004) report evidence relevant to the empirical premise of American "cultural exceptionalism" underlying IAT. Jensen compares the U.S. with other nations on items from the World Values Survey (WVS) that might be regarded as indicators of the importance accorded economic roles relative to other activities, the embracement of pecuniary success goals, and the adoption of self-interested and utilitarian standards concerning law breaking. He concludes that respondents in the U.S. are not distinctive in displaying particularly utilitarian or materialistic orientations, nor do they stand out as having attitudes of expediency toward the law.

Cao similarly use items from the WVS to make cross-national comparisons of cultural orientations, focusing specifically on "anomie." Cao creates an anomie index by combining responses to six statements that refer to the justification of criminal or deviant scenarios: claiming government benefits the person is not entitled to, avoiding a fare on public transport, cheating on a tax if given the chance, buying stolen property, accepting a bribe, and failing to report damage the person has done to a parked vehicle. Cao reports that the mean level of anomie so measured in the U.S. "is not particularly high" (p. 26) raising questions about the claim that American society is exceptionally anomic.

Summary of Findings

As our review indicates, IAT has inspired a fair amount of research over the course of a relatively short period. Table 4.1 presents a summary of the key findings that have emerged in the literature. The table is divided into two

Table 4.1
Summary of Analyses Informed by IAT

Panel A. Analyses of Institutional Dynamics

	Study	Units of Analysis	Dependent Variable(s)	Main Findings
Supportive:	Chamlin and Cochran (1995)	U. S. states	property crime	moderating effects of non-economic institutions on poverty
	Hannon and DeFronzo (1998)	U. S. metro areas	property and violent crime	moderating effects of welfare on resource deprivation
	Savolainen (2000)	45 nations	homicide	moderating effects of decommodifi-cation on economic inequality
	Pratt and Godsey (2003)	46 nations	homicide	moderating effects of social support on income inequality
	Stuckey (2003)	U. S. cities	violent crime	moderating effects of local govern-mental structures on deprivation
	Messner and Rosenfeld (1997)	45 nations	homicide	main effect of decommodification
	Maume and Lee (2003)	U. S. counties	homicide (total, instrumental, expressive)	mediating effect of noneconomic institutions for inequality, instrumental homicides
Mixed:	Piquero and Piquero (1998)	U. S. states	property and violent crime	some moderating effects on poverty but not robust across operationalizations
	Cullen et al. (2004)	3,450 managers in 28 nations	managerial ethical reasoning	support for economy, family, education; opposite effects for polity
	Batton and Jensen (2002)	U. S. (1990-1997)	homicide	support for 1900-1945 subperiod but not for 1946-1997 subperiod
Not Supportive:	Jensen (2002)	nations (Ns vary)	nonecon. inst., homicide	Opposite effects of decommodification on non-economic institutions; no effect of decommodification on homicide

Panel B. Analyses of Cultural Dynamics

Supportive:	Chamlin and Cochran (1997)	U. S. cities	property and violent crime	main effect of altruism (United Way contributions)
Mixed:	Cullen et al. (2004)	3,450 managers in 28 nations	managerial ethical reasoning	support for universalism and materialism; opposite effects for achievement orientation and individualism
Not Supportive:	Jensen (2002)	nations (Ns vary)	importance of jobs, leisure, family, religion, materialism, legal attachment	no support for American exceptionalism
	Cao (2004)	26 nations	index of anomie	no support for American exceptionalism

panels, representing analyses of institutional dynamics and cultural dynamics respectively. Within each panel studies are arranged with reference to whether the analyses on balance are generally supportive of IAT, offer mixed support, or are not supportive of IAT.

Beginning with the institutional analyses in Panel A, a simple tabulation indicates that of the eleven analyses, seven are generally supportive of IAT and three are best characterized as mixed. Only the research by Jensen fails to provide any appreciable support for IAT. An examination of the column for "main findings" in Panel A also suggests that the model of "moderating effects" has received the greatest support in institutional analyses. The robustness of the findings across units of analysis is also worth noting. Supportive evidence in the institutional analyses has been reported for samples of cities, counties, metropolitan areas, states, and nations. The evidence concerning the cultural dynamics of IAT (Panel B) is much more sparse and less favorable toward the perspective. In particular, the two studies that have directly considered claims about the distinctiveness of American culture have been non-supportive.

Implications of the Empirical Literature for Future Research

The findings from previous research suggest that future work informed by IAT needs to address both social structural and cultural issues. On the structural front, the greater support found for the "moderating effects" model suggests that we may have strayed too far from Merton's original insights about the importance of economic deprivation and inequality for understanding the social distribution of crime. The same general point is made in Bernburg's (2002) theoretical evaluation of IAT and, in a recent critique, Beeghley (2003) maintains that IAT downplays other aspects of social structure including firearm availability, illegal drug markets, and racial discrimination, as sources of the high homicide rate in the U.S. With respect to culture, Cao (2004) and Jensen (2002) question the thesis of American exceptionalism with cross-national survey data ostensibly showing that relevant cultural orientations of Americans do not differ appreciably from those of other populations or differ in ways contrary to the claims of IAT. Although neither the empirical findings, nor theoretical critiques, in our view, undermine the basic tenets of IAT, they raise important issues for future research on the relationship between crime and the social organization of advanced industrial societies.

Social Structure: Incorporating Mertonian Insights

In an insightful theoretical analysis of IAT, Bernburg (2002) argues that the theory fruitfully extends the Mertonian anomie perspective by locating the social origins of anomie in free-market economic arrangements that have been "disembedded" from non-economic institutions. Simultaneously, however, he maintains that IAT abandons the key Mertonian insight that motivations and opportunities for deviance and crime are socially structured through the stratification system. IAT pays too little attention, that is, to the "objective conditions" under which decisions to engage in, or refrain from, crime are made (Bernburg 2002: 739-740). Similarly, the contrary results in the analyses of managerial reasoning also point toward the need to take into account managers' "higher position in the stratification system" (Cullen et al. 2004). Finally, research showing that the relationship between economic deprivation and crime rates is conditioned by non-economic institutions, while certainly supportive of the general thrust of IAT, also serves as a reminder of the importance of social stratification for explaining variation in crime rates between and within societies.

We agree that both motivations and opportunities to engage in criminal activity are influenced by the degree of economic deprivation or inequality in society. Our criticism of traditional anomie theory hinges not on the emphasis it places on the system of social stratification but on the corresponding de-emphasis of other institutions. At the same time, we have not fully explicated the relationship between economic inequality and access to what we might term non-economic resources for conformity. We have, however, offered examples of such interconnections which may help point the way to more systematic research.

In the third edition of *Crime and the American Dream* (Messner and Rosenfeld 2001) we consider the connections among racial inequality, the family, and assimilation of the American Dream in producing high rates of criminal involvement among young inner-city males. Chronic joblessness, concentrated poverty, and persisting racial segregation impede family formation and increase family disruption. Both family supports and controls weaken, especially for young black men, resulting in high levels of criminal involvement (Messner and Rosenfeld, 2001: 81-83; Sampson, 1987; Wilson 1987, 1996). But the American Dream is implicated as well. Hochschild (1995) finds that African-Americans, *especially* poor African-Americans, are strongly committed to the goal of material success. We cite ethnographic research showing that inner-city teenagers, well socialized in the consumption ethos of the broader culture, bring strong consumption pressures to bear on their parents who typically lack the money to satisfy their children's desires for clothing, jewelry, electronic devices, and other status-relevant material goods. The result is conflict with parents and a "set of cynical assumptions about other people's motives in general, a first step toward the sense that one must manipulate and hustle in order to get what one desires" (Nightingale 1993: 160).

Far from denying the importance of stratification, we read such findings as revealing how access to non-economic, as well as economic, resources are differentially distributed in the U.S. Low economic status and racial exclusion disrupt the proper functioning of non-economic institutions including, but not limited to, the family thereby leaving individuals vulnerable to the full onslaught of anomic pressures emanating from the American Dream. Those pressures, in turn, further undermine the strength of non-economic institutions. Members of higher-status groups are shielded to some degree from such cultural "overexposure" by sources of non-economic control and social support that limit motivations and opportunities for crime.

Beeghley's (2003) criticism that IAT ignores the role of racial discrimination in producing high rates of crime among African-Americans is somewhat surprising in light of our discussion of the effects of economic marginality and family disruption on young inner-city males. Indeed, concentrated disadvantage in racially segregated inner-city communities is a tragic manifestation of "institutional discrimination." Even more puzzling, however, is his claim that we "avoid" the literature connecting high rates of homicide to illicit drug markets (Beeghley 2003: 94). In fact, we link recent trends in U.S. homicide rates directly to the dynamics of urban drug markets and discuss the lure of drug dealing for many inner-city young men as a classic instance of substituting illegitimate for legitimate means in the pursuit of the American Dream (Messner and Rosenfeld, 2001: 83-86). To be sure, much more remains to be said regarding the influence of racial discrimination and drug markets on crime rates, and we find Beeghley's (2003) treatment of these topics quite insightful.

Beeghley's (2003) claim that we devote little attention to the effect of firearm availability and policy on homicide rates is closer to the mark. We find much merit in explanations of high homicide rates in the U.S. that emphasize the availability of firearms and the lack of effective gun control. However, we regard these explanations as incomplete to the extent that they fail to consider *why* firearms are so abundant and so often used in violent confrontations, and *why* regulations are so lax. We chose in *Crime and the American Dream* to address those questions rather than trace the more proximate connections between firearms and interpersonal violence, a topic that has received rather extensive scholarly attention (see, e.g., Hemenway, 2004; Kleck, 1997; Zimring and Hawkins, 1997).

Firearms are very efficient tools for pursuing personal interests or settling interpersonal disputes. A culture that emphasizes the use of technically expedient means in the pursuit of goals is one that is conducive to widespread firearm availability (Messner and Rosenfeld 2001: 21-23). The absence of comprehensive firearm regulation may be related to Constitutional issues, the power of special interest groups, or a history of frontier justice, but it also reflects the anti-regulatory climate of a society dominated by a free-market economy in which all constraints on individual freedom are regarded as suspect. Our treatment of the firearm issue in *Crime and the American Dream* is admittedly cursory, but it sets forth the lines of inquiry that might be profitably pursued in future research on firearms and violence guided by IAT.

Culture: Are Americans Exceptional?

As noted in our review of the quantitative research, the aspect of IAT that has received the least support is the claim of American cultural exceptionalism. Cultural differences are not as easily observed as differences in governmental policy or economic arrangements. They must be discerned through systematic examination of cultural artifacts (books, newspapers, magazines, film, games, etc.) or ritual practices, manners, and customs. Or they can be measured in social surveys. Like most contemporary sociologists and criminologists, researchers investigating the cultural arguments in anomie and institutional anomie theory have preferred surveys.

As noted earlier, Cao (2004) and Jensen (2002) base their conclusions that Americans do not differ markedly from other populations in values, goals, and beliefs, or differ in unexpected ways, on evidence from the World Values Surveys (WVS). Cao (2004) finds that Americans are not particularly "anomic" in the sense of being able to justify rule transgressions. Jensen (2002) finds that Americans assign great importance to the family and religion and lesser importance to either work or leisure. What are we to make of such findings?

The World Values Surveys are a valuable and unique data source for studying cross-national differences in culture. However, interpretation of the exact meaning of the items is not always straightforward. Consider the item Jensen uses to capture "materialism." The exact wording is as follows:

> Here is a list of various changes in our way of life that might take place in the near future. Please tell me for each one, if it were to happen, whether you think it would be a good thing, a bad thing, or don't you mind? ... [One of the changes is] Less emphasis on money and material possessions.

Jensen interprets the percentage responding that less emphasis on money and material possession would be "a good thing" as reflecting non-materialism in society. The U.S. has the fifth highest score, which leads him to conclude that Americans do not appear to be particularly materialistic.

Upon reflection, however, the meaning of the item is inherently ambiguous. It confounds the respondent's personal evaluation of the importance of money with an assessment of the existing emphasis on money in the culture at large. One might speculate that a change toward less emphasis on money would be cited as a good thing in a highly *materialistic*, rather than a non-materialistic, society because in a *non-materialistic* society people already place little emphasis on money and, hence, there is little need for change in the direction of less emphasis on money.

The interpretation of the WVS items used by Cao to measure anomie is also open to question. Respondents are presented with the following lead in question: "Please tell me for each of the following statements whether you think it can always be justified, never be justified or something in between." Six statements are then provided that describe illegal behaviors. In essence, these items reflect the capacity of respondents to come up with justifications for illegal behavior.[6] While certainly tapping into meaningful features of culture, anomie can also be conceptualized in somewhat different ways, such as the *demoralization* of the means. According to this conceptualization, in a truly anomic society the selection of means is not governed by moral considerations at all, so there is no need to justify means. Justifiability is essentially irrelevant to social action. We thus concur with Cao (2004: 26) that the WVS allows for the measurement of anomie only according to a "narrow definition" and suggest that further inquiry into the various dimensions of the concept is warranted.

In addition, a search through the WVS reveals other items according to which the U.S. does, in fact, appear to exhibit the anticipated "American exceptionalism." Consider the question of whether competition is "good" ("It stimulates people to work hard and develop new ideas") or "harmful" ("It brings out the worst in people"). [7] Competition is a core element of the American Dream, and so we might expect that Americans would be more likely than the populations of other nations to view it as beneficial rather than harmful. In fact, a larger percentage of Americans than the populations of other advanced industrial nations rate competition as beneficial. On a scale of one to ten, with one indicating competition is "good," fully 32 percent of American respondents gave it a one, compared with 14 percent of West Germans, 9 percent of Japanese, and 18 percent of Norwegians. Only the Swiss (29 percent) and Australians (27 percent) come close to Americans in their positive view of competition among the ten advanced industrial nations included in the 1995 to 1997 WVS.

Two other WVS items ask respondents whether they favor or oppose private ownership and management of business enterprises. These items tap attitudes relevant, in the terms of IAT, to the dominance of a free market economy relative to the polity in the institutional structure of a society. One item asks whether business and industry should be managed by private owners alone, employees should participate in selecting managers, government should own businesses and appoint managers, or employees should own businesses and elect managers. The other asks respondents to rate on a scale of one to ten whether they favor greater private or government ownership of business and industry with "one" equaling greater private ownership and "ten" greater government ownership. Table 4.2 presents nationally aggregated responses for the ten advanced industrial societies in the 1995 to 1997 WVS.

Although sizable fractions of the populations of the ten nations prefer private ownership and control of business enterprises, the U.S. is first or tied for first on the two measures displayed in Table 4.2 and far exceeds the average values for the other nine nations on both measures. These results roughly mirror the history of private ownership and control of business enterprises in the ten nations. The populations of nations with strong social democratic

Table 4.2
Attitudes Toward Private Ownership and Management of Business and Industry in Ten Advanced Industrial Nations, 1995-1997

	% Favoring Owner Management	% Favoring Greater Private Ownership [a]
United States	55.3	61.4
Australia	50.3	49.4
Switzerland	43.2	60.4
Japan	39.6	23.3
Spain	37.5	25.3
Sweden	36.0	34.6
Finland	35.1	40.2
Norway	34.4	30.4
W. Germany	29.8	42.1
Britain	na	27.7
Avg. excluding US	38.2	37.0

[a] Percent selecting 1, 2, or 3 on 10-point scale (1=greater private ownership)

Source: World Values Survey, 1995-1997

parties and labor unions, or a tradition of "crony" capitalism as in Japan, tend to exhibit correspondingly weaker preferences for private ownership and control of business and a greater receptivity to government control. These nations, not surprisingly, also afford greater protections to their populations from the vicissitudes of free-market forces in the form of generous and inclusive social welfare policies. And these are not recent developments but are rooted in the historical origins of capitalism in each of the societies (Esping-Andersen 1990; Heilbroner 1991; Messner and Rosenfeld 1994: 75-78; 1997). A stronger tradition of economic individualism in the U.S. than other advanced nations, and correspondingly greater opposition to government regulation of market forces, are at the heart of the thesis of American exceptionalism (cf. Lipset 1997).

These examples, in combination with the findings of prior research, suggest that the WVS data yield mixed results for IAT. On some items American attitudes do, in fact, appear to be "exceptional" compared with those of other populations. On others, Americans are less exceptional. However, we caution against the uncritical use of survey responses as indicators of cultural differences among nations regardless of whether they appear more or less consistent with the claims of IAT.

The World Values Surveys undeniably tap important dimensions of, and orientations to, culture but survey responses alone do not constitute culture. "Culture" consists of more than the sum of individual attitudes. It is a sociological truism that culture is enacted in the attitudes and beliefs of individuals but also stands apart from individual orientations. Culture is a product of history that predates and outlasts the lifetimes of individual members of a society. Individual attitudes and beliefs *confront* culture while at the same time constituting it. The historical context, therefore, must be taken into account when interpreting survey responses on the importance of family, work, competition, private ownership, or the pursuit of material wealth. Otherwise, the analyst risks treating individual attitudes and beliefs as disembedded from the very cultural conditions he or she wishes to understand. Conducting research that is fully able to capture the subtleties of culture serves as a critically important task not only for criminologists interested in assessing claims of IAT, but those who strive to apply any comprehensive sociological theory crime.

Conclusion

Thirty years ago, in a collection of papers published in honor of Robert K. Merton, Stephen Cole (1975) traced the influence of the theory of social structure and anomie on deviance research during the period extending from the 1950s through the early 1970s. Cole examined all articles dealing with deviance that had appeared in four leading sociology journals: *American Sociological Review, American Journal of Sociology, Social Forces,* and *Social Problems.* On the basis of his analysis of the number and nature of citations to SS&A, Cole concluded that the era of great prominence for Mertonian anomie theory had passed. Cole further proposed that the declining influence of Merton's theory could not be attributed to any conclusive disconfirmation of its core claims. To the contrary, "there was certainly as much evidence in support of SS&A and derivative theories as in opposition" (1975: 212). Instead, the fate of SS&A reflected a latent function of theory, namely, to provide "puzzles for research." The reason for the declining significance of Merton's theory, Cole speculated, was that the field had simply "exhausted most of the puzzles it had provided" (p. 214).

It certainly would be an exaggeration to claim that IAT has received overwhelming empirical support to date. Our review of the literature indicates that the results of efforts to evaluate hypotheses derived from the theory have been mixed and have been more supportive in some areas (institutional dynamics) than in others (cultural dynamics). In addition, the theory is clearly incomplete in important respects. We have noted, in particular, that Mertonian insights about the social structuring of criminal incentives and opportunities have yet to be incorporated systematically and formally into the framework of IAT. Nevertheless, an appreciable body of research informed by IAT has been steadily accumulating over recent years. This suggests to us the theory has served well the key latent function of replenishing the "puzzles" that stimulate criminological research.

Two general "puzzles" for subsequent research on IAT suggested by the literature that we have reviewed in this paper are as follows:

1. How does the system of social stratification interact with other social institutions in producing high rates of crime in advanced industrial societies?
2. In what respects does the culture of American society differ from and in what respects is it similar to the cultures of other advanced societies? How are the observed cultural differences and similarities related to cross-national differences in crime rates?

The two puzzles offer general guidance to future research on the institutional and the cultural dynamics, respectively, specified in IAT. Within each of them, methodological issues emerge regarding appropriate valid and reliable measurement of key concepts. The extension of IAT to include interactions of the system of social stratification with other social institutions is likely to extend the focus on offending beyond "garden variety" street crimes to include illegal activities of the well to do. Data sources for comparative analyses of elite crimes are limited but some promising efforts have appeared in recent years, such as the creation of The Corruption Perceptions Index as a joint initiative of the University of Passau and Transparency International (http://www.icgg.org/corruption.index.html). With respect to culture, we have proposed that the measurement of cultural differences across nations should not be based on the results of surveys alone and that, when survey data are used, they must be cast in relevant historical context. That will require the use of comparative historical and anthropological methods not often employed in the study of crime but that are essential if the promise of macro-sociological approaches such as IAT is to be realized fully. We look forward to continued progress in confronting the puzzles posed by institutional-anomie theory, building on the promising work of the past decade.

Notes

1. Our approach to social institutions is informed by Parson's (1951) treatment of the functional exigencies of social systems and his AGIL (adaptation, goal attainment, integration, latent pattern maintenance) framework.
2. For a review of relevant papers presented at professional meetings but as yet unpublished see Messner (2004). Although we limit our review to macro-level studies, we note that IAT has been applied to individual-level analyses of labor market participation and youth crime. Several studies suggest that being embedded in the work role as a teenager has negative consequences (Cullen, Williams, and Wright 1997; Williams, Cullen, and Wright 1996; Wright, Cullen, Agnew, and Brezina 2001; Wright, Cullen, and Williams, 2002). These findings are consistent with the general hypothesis of IAT that those who place especially high priority on the institutional claims of the economy are likely to be exposed to particularly strong criminogenic pressures.

3.   In contrast with the earlier study by Chamlin and Cochran, Piquero and Piquero include indicators of the educational system in their analyses but do not include indicators of religion.

4.   As noted, we conceptualize "decommodification" as an indicator of the balance between the economy and polity and, thus, the main hypothesis under investigation involves the interrelationship among institutions. The estimation procedure is a "main effects" model in the sense of regression analysis, i.e., there is no product term to capture a statistical interaction.

5.   Chamlin and Cochran also draw on Braithwaite's (1989) discussion of communitarianism and Cullen's (1994) social support paradigm to develop a "synthetic" thesis about the effects of altruism on crime.

6.   This approach to the operationalization of anomie is similar to that taken by Cullen et al. (2004) in their analyses of managerial behavior. As noted, they find general support for IAT in a cross-national regression analysis, whereas Cao does not detect "American exceptionalism" for anomie so understood in the ranking of nations.

7.   This example and those below are based on data from the third wave of the WVS, conducted 1995 to 1997 (Inglehart, 2000). The results reported in the text are from WVS data compiled in the MicroCase Analysis System (Wadsworth Thomson Learning, 2004).

References

Akers, Ronald L. 1992. "Linking Sociology and Its Specialties: The Case of Criminology." *Social Forces* 71: 1-16.

Batton, Candice and Gary Jensen. 2002. "Decommodification and Homicide Rates in the 20th-Century United States." *Homicide Studies* 6: 6-38.

Beeghley, Loenard. 2003. *Homicide: A Sociological Explanation.* Lanham, MD: Roman & Littlefield.

Bernard, Thomas J. 1995. "Merton versus Hirschi: Who is Faithful to Durkheim's Heritage?" Pp. 81-90 in Freda Adler and William S. Laufer (eds.), *The Legacy of Anomie Theory.* New Brunswick, NJ: Transaction.

Bernburg, Jon Gunar. 2002. "Anomie, Social Change, and Crime: A Theoretical Examination of Institutional-Anomie Theory." *British Journal of Criminology* 42: 729-742.

Braithwaite, John. 1989. *Crime, Shame and Reintegration.* Cambridge: Cambridge University Press.

Cao, Liqun. 2004. "Is American Society More Anomic? A Test of Merton's Theory With Cross-National Data." *International Journal of Comparative and Applied Criminal Justice* 28: 17-31.

Chamlin, Mitchell B., and John K. Cochran. 1995. "Assessing Messner and Rosenfeld's Institutional Anomie Theory: A Partial Test." *Criminology* 33: 411-429.

———. 1997. "Social Altruism and Crime." *Criminology* 35: 203-228.

Cole, Stephen. 1975. "The Growth of Scientific Knowledge: Theories of Deviance as a Case Study." Pp. 175-220 in Lewis A. Coser (ed.), *The Idea of Social Structure: Papers in Honor of Robert K. Merton.* New York: Harcourt Brace Jovanovich.

Cullen, Francis T. 1994. "Social Support as an Organizing Concept for Criminology." *Justice Quarterly* 11: 527-559.

Cullen, Francis T., and John Paul Wright. 1997. "Liberating the Anomie-Strain Paradigm: Implications from Social-Support Theory." Pp. 187–206 in Nikos Passas and Robert Agnew (eds.), *The Future of Anomie Theory.* Boston: Northeastern University Press.

Cullen, Francis T., Nicolas Williams, and John Paul Wright. 1997. "Work Conditions and Juvenile Delinquency: Is Youth Employment Criminogenic?" *Criminal Justice Policy Review* 8: 119-143.

Cullen, John B., K. Praveen Parboteeah, and Martin Hoegl. 2004. "Cross-National Differences in Managers' Willingness to Justify Ethically Suspect Behaviors: A Test of Institutional Anomie Theory." *Academy of Management Journal* 47: 411-421.

Esping-Andersen, Gosta. 1990. *The Three Worlds of Welfare Capitalism.* Princeton, NJ: Princeton University Press.

Hannon, Lance, and James DeFronzo. 1998. "The Truly Disadvantage, Public Assistance, and Crime." *Social Problems* 45: 383-392.

Heilbroner, Robert. 1991. "A Pivotal Question Unanswered." *The World & I: A Chronicle of Our Changing Era* (November): 538–540.

Hemenway, David. 2004. *Private Guns, Public Health.* Ann Arbor: University of Michigan Press.

Hochschild, Jennifer. 1995. *Facing Up to the American Dream: Race, Class, and the Soul of the Nation.* Princeton, NJ: Princeton University Press.

Inglehart, Ronald. 2000. *World Values Survey, 1995-1997* [ICPSR Computer file]. Ann Arbor, MI: Institute for Social Research.

Jensen, Gary. 2002. "Institutional Anomie and Societal Variations in Crime: A Critical Appraisal." *International Journal of Sociology and Social Policy* 22: 45-74.

Kleck, Gary. 1997. *Targeting Guns: Firearms and Their Control.* New York: Aldine.

Lipset, Seymour Martin. 1997. *American Exceptionalism: A Double-Edged Sword.* New York: Norton.

Maume, Michael O. and Matthew R. Lee. 2003. "Social Institutions and Violence: A Sub-National Test of Institutional Anomie Theory." *Criminology* 41: 1137-1172.

Merton, Robert K. 1938. "Social Structure and Anomie." *American Sociological Review* 3: 672-682.

———. 1968. *Social Theory and Social Structure.* New York: Free Press.

Messner, Steven F. 2004. "An Institutional-Anomie Theory of Crime: Continuities and Elaborations in the Study of Social Structure and Anomie." *Cologne Journal of Sociology and Social Psychology* 43: 93-109.

Messner, Steven F., and Richard Rosenfeld. 1994. *Crime and the American Dream.* Belmont, CA: Wadsworth.

———. 1997. "Political Restraint of the Market and Levels of Criminal Homicide: A Cross-National Application of Institutional Anomie Theory." *Social Forces* 75: 1393-1416.

———. 2001. *Crime and the American Dream,* 3rd ed. Belmont, CA: Wadsworth.

Nightingale, Carl Husemoller. 1993. *On the Edge: A History of Poor Black Children and Their American Dreams.* New York: Basic Books.

Orru, Marco. 1987. *Anomie: History and Meanings.* Boston: Allen & Unwin.

Parsons, Talcott. 1951. *The Social System.* New York: Free Press.

Piquero, Alex, and Nicole Leeper Piquero. 1998. "On Testing Institutional Anomie Theory with Varying Specifications." *Studies on Crime and Crime Prevention* 7: 61-84.

Pratt, Travis C., and Timothy W. Godsey. 2003. "Social Support, Inequality, and Homicide: A Cross-National Test of an Integrated Theoretical Model." *Criminology* 41: 611-643.

Rosenfeld, Richard. 1989. "Robert Merton's Contributions to the Sociology of Deviance." *Sociological Inquiry* 59: 453-466.

Sampson, Robert J. 1987. "Urban Black violence: The Effect of Male Joblessness and Family Disruption." *American Journal of Sociology* 93: 348-382.

Savolainen, Jukka. 2000. "Inequality, Welfare State, and Homicide: Further Support for the Institutional Anomie Theory." *Criminology* 38: 1021-1042.

Stucky, Thomas D. 2003. "Local Politics and Violent Crime in U.S. Cities." *Criminology* 41: 1101-1135.

Wadsworth Thomson Learning. 2004. *MicroCase Analysis System*. Belmont, CA.

Williams, Nicolas, Francis T. Cullen, and John Paul Wright. 1996. "Labor Market Participation and Youth Crime: The Neglect of 'Working' In Delinquency Research." *Social Pathology* 2: 195-217.

Wilson, William Julius. 1987. *The Truly Disadvantaged: The Inner City, the Underclass, and Public Policy*. Chicago: University of Chicago Press.

———. 1996. *When Work Disappears: The World of the New Urban Poor*. New York: Knopf.

Wright, John Paul, Francis T. Cullen, Robert S. Agnew, and Timothy Brezina. 2001. "'The Root of All Evil'? An Exploratory Study of Money and Delinquent Involvement." *Justice Quarterly* 18: 239-268.

Wright, John Paul, Francis T. Cullen, Nicolas Williams. 2002. "The Embeddedness of Adolescent Employment and Participation in Delinquency: A Life-Course Perspective." *Western Criminology Review* 4: 1-19.

Zimring, Franklin E., and Gordon Hawkins. 1997. *Crime Is Not the Problem: Lethal Violence in America*. New York: Oxford University Press.

5

Collective Efficacy Theory: Lessons Learned and Directions for Future Inquiry

Robert J. Sampson

In this essay I consider the role of neighborhoods in the modern city. Despite our increasingly global and interconnected world, neighborhoods show remarkable continuities in patterns of criminal activity. Indeed, for at least a hundred years, criminological research in the ecological tradition has continually confirmed the non-random concentration of crime in certain neighborhoods, especially those characterized by poverty, the racial segregation of minority groups, and the concentration of single parent families. But why? By focusing primarily on correlates of crime at the level of community social composition—especially poverty and race—traditional neighborhood research has tended toward a risk-factor rather than an explanatory approach. The aim of this paper is to move away from community-level correlations, or markers, to a theory of the underlying *social mechanisms* theoretically at work. I conceptualize a social mechanism as a theoretically plausible (albeit typically unobservable) contextual process that accounts for or explains a given phenomena (Sorenson 1998), in this case crime rates.

I specifically "take stock" of the social-mechanistic theory of collective efficacy with which I have been associated. I begin with a brief review of its intellectual legacy and the basic ideas that animate collective efficacy theory. I then turn to a synthesis of relevant empirical literature, although I do not intend this as a comprehensive review. Fortunately, independent scholars have undertaken the task of summarizing the evidence to date through rigorous meta-analysis, leaving me the opportunity to make a case for the larger patterns and implications. After laying out the main ideas and the empirical regularities, I then turn to the future—where do we go from here? Science advances through the reasoned criticism of received knowledge and so my goal is to lay out the challenges to collective efficacy theory and, potentially, fruitful avenues of future work. Along the way I introduce key methodological issues and work in progress that I hope sharpens our theoretical approach to community level theories of crime.

From Social Disorganization to Networks

The idyllic notion of local communities as 'urban villages' characterized by dense personal networks has proven to be a durable and seductive image, one that traditional perspectives on neighborhood crime find hard to resist. A reigning image is that tight-knit neighborhoods produce safety because of their rich supply of social networks. In the classic work of the Chicago School of Urban Sociology in the early twentieth century however, it was hypothesized that density, low economic status, ethnic heterogeneity and residential instability led to the rupture of local social ties which, in turn, accounted for high rates of crime and disorder. The prototypical scholar of the Chicago School of "community lost" was Louis Wirth (1938) who analyzed modernity in terms of its deleterious effects on primary relationships.

The concept of social disorganization emerged out of the Chicago School, defined theoretically as the inability of a community to realize the common values of its residents and maintain effective social order (Shaw and McKay 1942; Kornhauser 1978). This definition came to be operationalized in systemic terms—the allegedly disorganized community was viewed as suffering from a disrupted or weakened system of friendship, kinship and acquaintanceship networks and, as a consequence, ongoing processes of socialization (Sampson and Groves 1989). More recently, the intellectual tradition of community-level research has been revitalized by the increasingly popular idea of "social capital." Although there are many definitions, social capital is typically conceptualized as a resource embodied in the social ties among persons (Putnam 2000). The connection of social disorganization to social capital theory was articulated by Bursik (1999) as follows: neighborhoods bereft of social capital, indicated primarily by depleted social networks, are less able to realize common values and maintain the social controls that foster safety. Dense social ties thus play a key role in social capital/disorganization theory.

Although social disorganization theory, in particular, has enjoyed considerable support in the literature, there are reasons to problematize both its conceptual definition and the role of social networks—especially dense personal ties—in generating low crime rates. On the former, it seems to me that social disorganization is still defined largely in terms of outcome. How do we know a neighborhood is unable to achieve social order? By social *disorder*? That, in fact, is what passes for much community disorganization and crime research in which indicators of social disorder, themselves usually comprised of some violation of law, are used to measure the cause of crime (see Sampson and Raudenbush 1999). But if the cause is defined in terms of the outcome, we really have no explanation at all. Put differently, if crime and disorder are part of the same process, with disorder and crime both the observable indicators or markers for a lack of order, we have described a matrix of risk but not independent causal mechanisms or processes.

For this reason social disorganization research has moved to the operationalization of its concepts largely in systemic terms, most notably with respect to the density of social ties (Bursik 1999; Warner and Rountree 1997; Sampson and Groves 1989). Although a necessary move away from tautology, problems remain. First, there is evidence that in some neighborhood contexts strong ties may actually impede efforts to establish social control. Wilson (1987), in particular, has argued that residents of very poor neighborhoods tend to be tightly interconnected through network ties but without necessarily producing collective resources such as social control. He reasons that ties in the inner city are excessively personalistic and parochial in nature—*socially isolated* from public resources. This is so, in part, because survival mechanisms and local support takes precedent over activities centered on the collective good (Stack 1975).

Second, networks connect do-gooders just as they connect drug dealers. In her study of a black middle-class community in Chicago, Pattillo-McCoy (1999) specifically addresses the limits of tight-knit social bonds in facilitating social control. She argues that although dense local ties do promote social cohesion, at the same time they foster the growth of networks that impede efforts to rid the neighborhood of organized drug- and gang-related crime. Venkatesh (1997) finds a similar pattern in a low-income neighborhood of Chicago. Dense social ties thus potentially have both positive *and* negative ramifications, reminding us that in a consideration of networks it is important to ask what is being connected—networks are not inherently egalitarian or prosocial in nature (see also, St. Jean 2005). This argument has a long pedigree in the urban sociological and gang literature, perhaps going back as far as William F. Whyte's *Street Corner Society* (1943).

Third, shared expectations for social control and strategic connections that yield action can be fostered in the absence of thick ties among neighbors. As Granovetter (1973) argued in his seminal essay, 'weak ties'—less intimate connections between people based on more infrequent social interaction—may be critical for establishing social resources, such as job referrals, because they integrate the community by way of bringing together otherwise disconnected subgroups. Consistent with this view, there is evidence that weak ties among neighbors, as manifested in middle-range rather than either nonexistent or intensive social interaction, are predictive of lower crime rates (Bellair 1997). Perhaps more interesting, and as elaborated below, there is emerging evidence that computer technology (e.g., neighborhood list-serves) may do for coordinating social interactions and collective action among neighborhood residents what strong personal ties allegedly did in the past (Hampton and Wellman 2003).

Finally, the reality is that in modern cities the idyllic urban village endures mainly, if only, in myth. Even if we had the time or energy, most people, including me, do not want to be friends or close with their neighbors. They certainly do not want to eat dinner with them!

Collective Efficacy

To address these challenges and new urban realities, my colleagues and I have proposed a focus on mechanisms of social organization that may be facilitated by, but do not necessarily require, strong ties or associations. This move allows us to reject the outmoded (and normative) assumption that the ideal neighborhood is characterized by dense, intimate, emotional bonds. Instead, neighborhoods are defined in ecological terms where analytic properties of social organization are allowed to vary. We have also introduced a science of studying community processes—ecometrics—that is rooted in the idea that we have to take seriously the measurement of community properties in its own right (Raudenbush and Sampson 1999).

A key form of social organization that I will focus on here is *collective efficacy*. The concept of collective efficacy unites social cohesion, the "collectivity" part of the concept, with shared expectations for control, the social action or efficacy part of the concept (Sampson et al. 1997). In other words, we combine a particular kind of social structure (cohesion, with an emphasis on working trust and mutual support) with the culturally tinged dimension of *shared expectations* for social control. Moreover, we argue that just as self efficacy is situated rather than general (one has self-efficacy relative to a particular task), a neighborhood's efficacy exists relative to specific tasks. We therefore conceive of collective efficacy as a higher-order or organizing theoretical framework that draws attention to variations in the nexus of social cohesion with shared expectations for control. Viewed another way, collective efficacy theory unites the constructs of mutual support (Cullen 1994), which largely defines cohesion, with a collective-action orientation, in this case the activation or generation of community social order.

One reason I believe cohesion and support are important is that they are fundamentally about *repeated* interactions and thereby expectations about the future. There is little reason to expect that rational agents will engage in sanctioning, or other acts of social control or support, in contexts where there is no expectation for future contact or where residents mistrust one another. The insight of collective efficacy theory is that repeated interactions may signal or generate shared norms outside the "strong tie" setting of friends and kin. Another conceptual move of collective efficacy theory is its emphasis on agency. Moving away from a focus on private ties, use of the term collective efficacy is meant to signify an emphasis on shared beliefs in a neighborhood's capability for action to achieve an intended effect, coupled with an active sense of engagement on the part of residents. Some density of social networks is essential, to be sure, especially networks rooted in social trust. But the key theoretical point is that networks have to be activated to be ultimately meaningful. Collective efficacy, therefore, helps to elevate the 'agentic' aspect of social life over a perspective centered mainly on the accumulation of stocks of social resources as found in ties and memberships (i.e., social capital). This conceptual orientation is consistent with the redefinition by Portes and Sensenbrenner (1998) of social capital in terms of "expectations for action within a collectivity."

Distinguishing between the resource potential represented by personal ties, on the one hand, and the shared expectations for action among neighbors represented by collective efficacy on the other, therefore, helps clarify the dense networks paradox: *social networks foster the conditions under which collective efficacy may flourish, but they are not sufficient for the exercise of control.* The theoretical framework I propose recognizes the transformed landscape of modern urban life, holding that while community efficacy may depend on working trust and social interaction, it does not require that my neighbor or local police officer be my friend.

Collective efficacy theory also addresses the valence of social ties and, ultimately, collective action by applying the 'non-exclusivity requirement' of a social good to judge whether neighborhood structures serve collective needs. Does consumption of a social good by one member of a community diminish the sum available to the community as a whole? I would argue that safety, clean environments, quality education for children, active maintenance of intergenerational ties, the reciprocal exchange of information and services among families, and the shared willingness to intervene on behalf of the neighborhood are capable of producing a social good that yields positive 'externalities' of benefit to all residents—especially children. As with other resources that produce positive externalities, I believe that collective efficacy is widely desired but much harder to achieve, owing, in large part, to social constraints.

Empirical Results: Taking Stock

My colleagues and I tested the theory of collective efficacy in a survey of 8,782 residents of 343 Chicago neighborhoods in 1995. Applying ecometric methods, a five-item Likert-type scale was developed to measure shared expectations about social control. Residents were asked about the likelihood that their neighbors could be counted on to take action if: (i) children were skipping school and hanging out on a street corner; (ii) children were spray-painting graffiti on a local building; (iii) children were showing disrespect to an adult; (iv) a fight broke out in front of their house; and (v) the fire station closest to home was threatened with budget cuts. Our measurement relied on vignettes because of the fundamental unobservability of the capacity for control—the act of intervention is only observed under conditions of challenge. If high collective efficacy leads to low crime, then at any given moment no intervention will be observed precisely because of the lack of need. Like Bandura's (1997) theory of self efficacy, the argument is that expectations for control will increase behavioral interventions when necessary, but the scale itself taps shared expectations for social action—in our case ranging from informal intervention to the mobilization of formal controls. The emphasis is on actions that are generated "on the ground level" rather than top down.

The "social cohesion/trust" part of the measure taps the nature of community relationships and was measured by coding whether residents agreed that "People around here are willing to help their neighbors"; "People in this neighborhood can be trusted"; "This is a close-knit neighborhood"; "People in this neighborhood generally get along with each other"; and "People in this neighborhood share the same values." As hypothesized, social cohesion and social control were strongly related across neighborhoods and, thus, combined into a summary measure of collective efficacy, yielding an aggregate-level reliability in the .80 to .85 range.

In our research we found that collective efficacy was associated with lower rates of violence, controlling for concentrated disadvantage, residential stability, immigrant concentration, and a comprehensive set of individual-level characteristics (e.g., age, sex, SES, race/ethnicity, home ownership) as well as indicators of dense personal ties and the density of local organizations (Sampson et al. 1997; Morenoff et al. 2001). Whether measured by official homicide events or violent victimization as reported by residents, neighborhoods high in collective efficacy consistently had significantly lower rates of violence. This finding held up controlling for prior neighborhood violence which was negatively associated with collective efficacy. This pattern suggests a reciprocal loop where violence depressed later collective efficacy (e.g., because of fear). Nevertheless, a two-standard deviation elevation in collective efficacy was associated with a 26 percent reduction in the expected homicide rate (1997: 922).

Another finding is that the association of disadvantage and stability with violence is reduced when collective efficacy is controlled, suggesting a potential causal pathway at the community level. This pathway is presumed to operate over time, wherein collective efficacy is undermined by the concentration of disadvantage, racial segregation, family disruption, and residential instability, which, in turn, fosters more crime (Sampson et al. 1997, 1999). Morenoff et al. (2001) also showed that the density of personal ties and organizations were associated with higher collective efficacy and, hence, lower crime, even though the former did not translate directly into lower crime rates. These findings are consistent with, although do not prove, the hypothesis that collective efficacy mediates the effect of both structural resources (e.g., afflu-ence, home ownership, organizations) and dense systemic ties on later crime.

As noted at the outset, neighborhoods are, themselves, nodes in a larger network of spatial relations. Contrary to the common assumption in criminology of analytic independence, neighborhoods are interdependent and characterized by a functional relationship between what happens at one point in space and what happens elsewhere. The idea of spatial dependence challenges the urban village model which implicitly assumes that neighborhoods represent intact social systems, functioning as islands unto themselves. Our findings support the spatial argument by establishing the independent effects of spatial proxim-ity—controlling for all measured characteristics internal to a neighborhood, collective efficacy and violence are significantly and positively linked to the collective efficacy and violence rates of surrounding neighborhoods, respec-tively (Sampson et al. 1999; Morenoff et al. 2001). This finding suggests a diffusion, or exposure-like process, whereby violence and collective efficacy are conditioned by the characteristics of spatially proximate neighborhoods, which, in turn, are conditioned by adjoining neighborhoods in a spatially linked process that ultimately characterizes the entire metropolitan system. The mechanisms of racial segregation reinforce spatial inequality, explaining why it is, that despite similar income profiles, black middle-class neighbor-hoods are at greater risk of violence than white middle-class neighborhoods (Sampson et al. 1999).

An oversimplified sketch of the major argument made to this point is shown in Figure 5.1. This model makes clear that collective efficacy theory is not merely an attempt to push the burden of social control or support onto residents, "blaming the victim" as some have claimed. Inequality in resources matters greatly for explaining the production of collective efficacy. Concentrated disadvantage and lack of home ownership, for example, predict lower levels of later collective efficacy, and, vice versa, the associations of disadvantage and housing instability with violence are significantly reduced when collec-tive efficacy is controlled (Sampson et al. 1997). These patterns are consistent with the inference that neighborhood resources influence crime and violence, in part, through the mediating role of neighborhood efficacy. The capacity to exercise control under conditions of trust is, thus, seen as the most proximate to explaining crime. Collective efficacy theory has also been extended to explain community well-being and population health, although I do not cover that here (Sampson 2003; Morenoff 2003).

In theoretical terms, Figure 5.1 posits that organizations and institutional strength represent a mechanism that can sustain capacity for social action in a way that transcends traditional personal ties (see also Tripplet et al. 2003). In other words, organizations are, at least in principle, able to foster collective efficacy, often through strategic networking of their own. Whether garbage removal, choosing the site of a fire station, school improvements or police

Figure 5.1
Main Lines of Emphasis in Collective Efficacy Theory

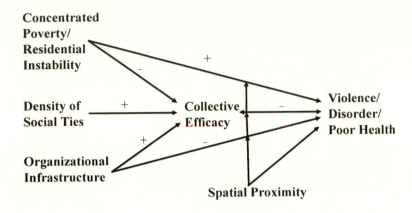

responses, a continuous stream of challenges faces modern communities, challenges that no longer can be met (if they ever were) by relying solely on individuals. Action depends on connections among organizations that are not necessarily dense, or reflective of, the structure of personal ties in a neighborhood. Our research supports this position, showing that the density of local organizations and voluntary associations predicts higher levels of collective efficacy, controlling for prior crime, poverty and the social composition of the population (Morenoff et al. 2001).

What about evidence from beyond Chicago? Rather than provide a narrative review of the evidence on collective efficacy theory that might be biased by my priors, I rely on an independent assessment. Recently, Pratt and Cullen (2005) have undertaken a painstaking review of more than 200 empirical studies from 1960 to 1999 using meta-analysis. The bottom line is that collective efficacy theory fares well with an overall correlation of -.303 with crime rates across studies (95 percent confidence interval of -.26 to -.35). By meta-analysis standards this is a robust finding; and the authors' rank collective efficacy number 4 when weighted by sample size, ahead of traditional suspects such as poverty, family disruption, and race. Although the number of studies and, hence, empirical base, is limited and, while there is considerable variability in operationalization across studies, the class of mechanisms associated with social disorganization theory and its offspring, collective efficacy theory, shows a robust association with lower crime rates (see also reviews in Sampson et al. 2002: Kubrin and Weitzer 2003).

Advances in Community-Level Theory

Despite progress that has been made in recent research, there are a number of important challenges in making inferences about the causal role of neighborhood effects in general and the social mechanism of collective efficacy in particular. In another paper I consider in more depth the methodological issues in assessing neighborhood effects, such as selection bias, when estimating contextual effects on individuals (Sampson 2005). For present purposes, I focus on what I consider fruitful new directions for a better understanding of collective efficacy theory.

Before doing so, it is important to emphasize that a theory of *crime rates*, especially one that aims to explain how neighborhoods fare as units of social control over their own public spaces in the here and now, is logically not the same enterprise as explaining how neighborhoods exert long-term or developmental effects on *individual development* and, ultimately, individual crime (Wikström and Sampson 2003). Both set of mechanisms may be at work, but one does not compel the other. For example, we may have a theory that accurately explains variation of crime event rates across neighborhoods regardless of who commits the acts (residents or otherwise), and another that accurately explains how neighborhoods influence the individual behavior of residents no matter where they are. In the latter case, neighborhoods have developmental or enduring effects (e.g., Wheaton and Clarke, 2003), in the former, situational effects. The logical separation of explanation is reinforced by considering the nature of routine activity patterns in modern cities in which residents traverse the boundaries of multiple neighborhoods during the course of a day. Urbanites occupy many different neighborhood contexts outside of home, especially when it comes to adolescents in the company of peers (Wikström and Ceccato 2004).

Interestingly, it turns out that recent research on the Chicago PHDCN data finds that collective efficacy does not, in fact, predict individual rates of self-reported violence based on the residence of the subjects (Sampson et al. 2005). It is hard to know whether this finding is partly due to the way violence was measured (self reports), but if we set that issue aside, it appears that whereas collective efficacy predicts the event rate of violence in a neighborhood, it does not necessarily predict rates of offending by neighborhood youth, the latter of which may occur anywhere in the city. Put differently, collective efficacy may be more situational than even the original theory suggested, with little "staying power" once residents are outside its purview.

Turning it Around: "Structure" as Endogenous

I now turn to the frontiers of collective efficacy theory. I consider first the rather fundamental possibility that the standard account of mediation in community-level theories of crime may simply be wrong. The standard view, one that I have advocated, is that social processes, like collective efficacy, "mediate" the effects of social structure, especially concentrated disadvantage (Sampson et al. 1997). This account is so plausible and hegemonic that no one has really challenged its logic. Yet why should collective efficacy, or any other social process, necessarily be endogenous to structure? Weber and the endogeneity of capitalism aside, the whole point of Robert Putnam's *Making Democracy Work* (1993) was to reverse the causal chain and posit social capital as the driver of economic development in Italy. Rather than see poverty as the cause of declining economic fortunes, Putnam argued that the lack of civil society was the key ingredient that held back the southern provinces of Italy (see also Banfield 1958).

A similar logic can be applied to present day America and the neighborhoods of Chicago. Areas low in trust, cooperation, and the fundamentals of collective efficacy may lead to the out-migration of those who can afford to live in more harmonious environments. As a recent mover, I can attest to the fact that real estate brokers are attuned to the cohesion of neighborhoods, a subtle, but nonetheless salient, factor that gains special currency among families with children. (It is not a coincidence that the city I chose to live in is endowed with considerable social capital and collective efficacy.) Moving beyond personal anecdotes, collective efficacy, by the terms of the theory, is expected to be correlated with the production of a number of collective goods that matter to residents, including the allocation of city services (e.g., road repair, economic development and investment). Bryk and Schneider's (2002) recent work also shows collective efficacy in the schools is a major predictor of student achievement, a point surely not lost on some parents. In short, there is reason to believe that collective efficacy is a causal factor bound up in the structural disadvantage of a community. If so, then traditional models may have gotten it backwards by controlling for disadvantage in estimating the "direct" effect of collective efficacy—under the above scenario the effect of collective efficacy *should* vanish.

There is preliminary evidence to support this position. Consider the simple prediction of future poverty from the current state of collective efficacy. Figure 5.2 demonstrates a correlation that is surprising even by social science standards—for all intents and purposes the relationship is about as strong as one could expect (R^2 = 75 percent). Areas with high collective efficacy are strongly *predictive* of where that community will end up in the stratification hierarchy. But is this just due to past poverty? The answer is no, for when we control for poverty in 1990, socioeconomic status in 1995, racial composition in 1995 *and* the violent crime rate in 1995, the direct association of collective efficacy in 1995 is strong and significant (B = -. 25, t-ratio = -4.36). The magnitude of prediction is second only to prior poverty and almost its equal.

Figure 5.2
**Turning it Around: Poverty as Predicted Outcome of Low Collective
Efficacy in Chicago Neighborhoods, 1995-2000**

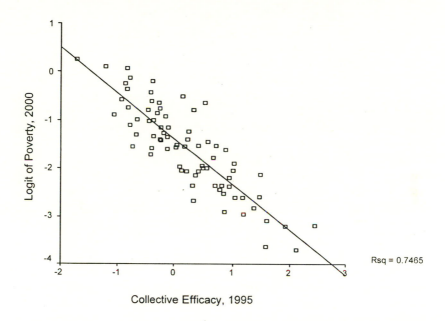

These results undermine the simplistic models that are often specified in the criminological literature. As the late Allen Liska warned us, reciprocal structural dynamics are at work in urban social systems, such that crime, itself, can be considered a path in the causal chain (see also Bellair 2000; Markowitz et al. 2001). We have already found evidence that crime and collective efficacy are reciprocally related in a self-reinforcing process (Sampson and Raudenbush 1999). Taken a step further, there is reason to argue that collective efficacy is an independent factor in the future economic trajectory of a community. If so, then structural disadvantage is, in some sense, endogenous to collective efficacy, completely the reverse of current practice. Although this hypothesis cannot be easily established, the key point for consideration is that the status of collective efficacy, as other social processes (culture), is ambiguous under the traditional model specification in criminology. Indeed, if collective efficacy has any role in the determination of prior values of structural disadvantage, then controlling that effect serves to partial out part of the causal pathway by which it leads to crime.

Discriminant Validity and the Role of Theory

A second problem, that is at once theoretical and methodological, turns on the discriminate validity of the concept of collective efficacy. Thomas Cook and his colleagues (1997) have argued that researchers of community need to pay increased attention to the "lumping" among social processes. In its simplest form, the question is whether there is just one big factor that underlies the correlations among seemingly disparate social processes. A similar point was made about the lumping among structural covariates by Land et al. (1990)—disentangling and estimating independent effects within a set of highly collinear predictors is a recipe for methodological confusion. More recently, Taylor (2002) has correctly pointed out the strong empirical overlap among many indicators of social disorganization, informal social control, and collective efficacy.

Unfortunately, resolution of this legitimate issue is not easy. The critics are right that many community concepts overlap empirically, but that does not mean they tap the same concept or that statistical methods necessarily help to resolve the problem. It is instructive to recall the debate between Bernard Lander and his critics some fifty years ago. In using factor analysis, Lander (1954) identified a concept he called anomie, which carried high loadings for home ownership, percent black, and crime, among others. As Kornhauser (1978) argued, however, Lander included in the explanatory factor (anomie) the outcome itself—crime. From Lander's perspective, the indicators could not be separated empirically (there was a lack of "discriminant validity"), but from a theoretical perspective, we would not want to say that crime is the same construct as home ownership. Rather, they are ecologically intertwined in a social process.

Fast forwarding to the present, ecological scholars are well aware that percent black typically loads on a factor defined by poverty. We can complicate this even more by adding in violent crime, reminiscent of Lander. As a simple exercise, I entered the percent poverty, unemployment, percent black and the violent crime rate in a principal components analysis for Chicago neighborhoods in 1990 and 2000. Only one factor emerged! Surely we would not want to interpret this factor as saying crime is the *same concept* as race or poverty. What the factor taps is the empirical entwinement of the multiple indicators—the factor tells us nothing about causality, sequential order, mediation or anything else of ultimate interest. The same goes for social processes. If we throw in a series of indicators from the PHDCN Community Survey, it turns out disorder loads with collective efficacy (negatively). Again, does this mean they are the *same* construct? As earlier, I would argue no—I believe disorder is a marker for low collective efficacy, like crime, but my argument derives from logic and theory, not simply from the data. All this goes to say that ecological mechanisms of allocation and segregation create groupings of variables that are difficult to interpret and even harder to study with respect to crime. No statistical method can solve what is fundamentally a theoretical issue about causal mechanisms.

Although resolution of this complex issue is surely beyond this paper, I should like to emphasize one point, however, that speaks in favor of collective efficacy theory. As I have been at pains to argue, one of the distinguishing features of collective efficacy theory is its insistence that agency and control are not redundant with dense personal ties. In point of fact, this assertion is supported despite the otherwise lumpy nature of the data when it comes to factor or principal components analysis. Specifically, indicators of control and cohesion (and yes, disorder) consistently load together on a separate factor from density of personal and friendship ties. This finding has recently been confirmed with a repeated cross-sectional replication of the 1995 Chicago Community Survey in 2002. There is also evidence that collective efficacy is highly stable over time, as is the separate construct of dense ties. Based on theory and empirical evidence, then, we have some confidence to maintain the core analytical distinction between efficacy (social action) and dense ties, all the while recognizing that there the correlations among social processes, just as among structural covariates, are high. The larger point is that neither statistical methods (e.g., LISREL) nor the correlations among social processes and structural features of the city ("the data") speak for themselves—an organizing theoretical model is needed.

Comparative Studies

A third concern I have about extant community research is its seeming disregard for the establishment of generality in causal mechanisms. The prime example is that most of our knowledge has been gained from U.S. cities and only a few of them at that. Yet nothing in the logic of collective efficacy is necessarily limited to specific cities, the United States or any country for that matter. Just how far can we push collective efficacy theory? Is it applicable in societies like France, where republican values and strong norms of state intervention, rather than individual responsibility, might conflict with the notion of neighbors intervening? Does it hold in welfare states where concentrated disadvantage is less tenacious, or in former Soviet states where public spiritedness is allegedly on the wane? Our comparative knowledge base is, unfortunately, limited—very few multi-level studies have been carried out with the explicit goal of cross-national comparison of crime rates and community social mechanisms.

An exception is found in a recent comparison of leading cities in Sweden and the U.S. Although Chicago and Stockholm vary dramatically in their social structure and levels of violence, this does not necessarily imply a difference in the processes or mechanisms that link communities and crime. In fact,

Sampson and Wikström (2004) show that rates of violence are significantly predicted by low collective efficacy in Stockholm as in Chicago. Furthermore, collective efficacy is fostered by housing stability and undermined by concentrated disadvantage—again, similarly, in both cities. These findings are rather remarkable given the vast cultural and structural differences between the countries in question. Sweden is a modern welfare state with highly planned residential communities. "Race" groups are non-existent and immigration comes primarily from Turkey and Morocco. Chicago is the quintessential American city, rank with inequality and the segregation of African Americans and with neighborhoods that are emblematic of unplanned market sorting. Immigration flows are also very different, coming primarily from Mexico rather than Europe or Africa.

That the data show an almost invariant pattern despite these differences is, thus, consistent with the general theoretical approach of this paper that emphasize neighborhood inequality in social resources and contextual conditions that foster the collective efficacy of residents and organizations. But this is only one study. The empirical application of neighborhood studies to other societal contexts is badly needed if we are to make further progress in understanding the generalizability of the link between community social mechanisms and crime rates.

Technology Mediated Efficacy

My final point of emphasis is the most speculative but it circles back to the issue raised at the outset: What produces collective efficacy if not (or besides) dense personal ties? I have offered two general hypotheses thus far that I believe are supported by the data, one in the form of structural resources (e.g., home ownership; stability, economic status) and the other in terms of the density of non-profit organizations. But this seems insufficient in the world I described at the outset, one of fleeting social ties. My speculative answer is that a partial solution may well lie in technology, although its realization will take time. My argument is that rather than undermining social organization, modern technology has the *potential* to knit together weak community ties for the purposes of building collective efficacy. We have all heard anecdotally about how the internet was effectively used to mobilize protests against the International Monetary Fund in Seattle a few years back. Internet use was also widely used in the Howard Dean campaign and on both sides of the political spectrum in the recent presidential election.

What about in the more prosaic neighborhood? Three lines of evidence suggest an interesting scenario. One, Barry Wellman and his colleagues show that, contrary to common belief, the more "wired" local residents are with respect to computer technology, the more their local contacts and involvement in community issues (Hampton and Wellman 2003; Wellman 2004). For example, compared to non-wired residents, wired residents of the Toronto community they studied recognized three times as many of their neighbors, visited 50 percent more often and more often made use of email for local contacts. Second, Keith Hampton, in an intriguing project called E-Neighbors (see http://www.i-neighbors.org/), is attempting to use technology as a means to increase community well being. Although the results are preliminary, some of the trial neighborhoods he is studying are showing positive results, such as a significant increase in the number of local social ties, more frequent communication on and offline and higher levels of community involvement. The I-Neighbors website is an attempt to apply this model to neighborhoods across the U.S. and Canada.

Third, in an on-going collaborative research project directed by Bob Putnam at Harvard, we are looking at the potential social-capital inducing effects of Meetup-Com, a technology that organizes not chat rooms in cyber or virtual space, but real meetings between people in physical spaces (see http://www.meetup.com/). From book clubs to politics to lovers of Golden Retrievers, Meetup.com brings people together in physical space to share common interests. Although many of the groups seem trivial at the outset (dog lovers, knitting, Goths), it appears that political action, in fact, generates many of the meetups. Besides, if Putnam (2000) is right and social interaction has spin-off externalities for collective action, and possible the generation of collective efficacy, then even the trivial groups should not be dismissed out of hand.

Fourth, it is now possible to imagine how the rapid spread of technology can be harnessed to improve dissemination of crime data and the mapping of "hot spots" of crime. Already some cities allow citizens to access police data and map when and where incidents of crime are occurring, almost in real time (e.g., http://12.17.79.6/ctznicam/ctznicam.asp). Although knowledge about the realities of crime's distribution and frequency might be alarming at first, such knowledge ultimately could lead to a sense of increased collective efficacy and community participation on the part of residents and, perhaps, demands that ameliorative efforts be undertaken by the appropriate authorities. After all, one of the things that research has taught us is that even in high crime areas, most areas are safe most of the time (St. Jean 2005).

It is too soon to know, of course, but rather than taking the stance of Luddites and assuming in a Wirthian manner that community automatically declines in the era of cell phones and instant messaging, these lines of evidence suggest that we need to add networks of technology to our theoretical toolkit of community social organization and collective efficacy.

Conclusion

In this paper I have "taken stock" of the theory of collective efficacy and considered four agendas that I believe are crucial to the advancement of theoretical knowledge—collective efficacy as a potential cause rather than simply mediator of structural disadvantage; discriminant validity of social-processes that constitute collective efficacy; the need for comparative studies and general theory; and role of technology in promoting collective efficacy. There are others of course, but these seem to me to cut to the core of questions that have been raised about collective efficacy. What causes it? Is collective efficacy a theoretically distinct concept? Is it doomed to be impotent in mass, modern society? What is the association with concentrated disadvantage and is it cause or consequence? Is collective efficacy merely a "Chicago" phenomenon? If this paper is any guide, progress has been made on all these fronts even though there is much work to be done. I would argue that collective efficacy does have unique theoretical value, is general in import, may be fostered under conditions of modernity and predicts not only crime but possibly community social structure itself through reciprocal, self-reinforcing processes.

In one way or another, social networks cut across all these agendas, right down to considering technology as another form of network. We live in a network society we are told, but not all networks are created equal and many lie dormant. A key mistake has been to equate the existence of networks with mechanisms of effective social control. As Arthur Stinchcombe (1989) put it in a useful analogy, just as road systems have their causal impact through the flow of traffic, so systems of links among people and organizations (and in this case, neighborhoods) have their causal impact through *what flows through them*. The problem, then, becomes obvious—through networks (whether personal, spatial, organizational or technological) flow the full spectrum of life's realities, whether criminal knowledge, friendship, or social control.

The basic theoretical position articulated in this article is that collective action for problem-solving is a crucial causal mechanism that is differentially activated under specific kinds of contextual conditions. The density of personal networks is only one, and probably not the most important, characteristic of neighborhoods that contributes to effective social action and mutual support. Attacking the agendas outlined in this paper will hopefully move us a bit closer to a better understanding of the causes and effects of collective efficacy in the modern city.

References

Bandura, Albert. 1997. *Self Efficacy: The Exercise of Control.* New York: W. H. Freeman.

Banfield, Edward. 1958. *The Moral Basis of a Backward Society.* New York: Free Press.

Bellair, Paul E. 1997. "Social Interaction and Community Crime: Examining the Importance of Neighbor Networks." *Criminology* 35: 677-703.

———. 2000. Informal Surveillance and Street Crime: A Complex Relationship. *Criminology* 38: 137-167.

Bryk, Anthony, and Barbara Schneider. 2002. *Trust in Schools: A Core Resource for Improvement.* New York: Russell Sage Foundation.

Bursik, Robert J. 1999. "The Informal Control of Crime through Neighborhood Networks." *Sociological Focus* 32: 85-97.

Cook Thomas, Shobha Shagle, and Serdar Degirmencioglu. 1997. "Capturing Social Process for Testing Mediational Models of Neighborhood Effects." Pp. 94-119 in Jeanne Brooks-Gunn, Greg Duncan and Lawrence Aber (eds.), *Neighborhood Poverty: Policy Implications in Studying Neighborhoods, Vol. 11.* New York: Russell Sage Foundation.

Cullen, Francis T. 1994. "Social Support as an Organizing Concept for Criminology: Presidential Address to the Academy of Criminal Justice Sciences." *Justice Quarterly* 11: 527-559.

Granovetter, Mark S. 1973. "The Strength of Weak Ties." *American Journal of Sociology* 78: 1360-80.

Hampton, Keith, and Barry Wellman. 2003. "Neighboring in Netville: How the Internet Supports Community and Social Capital in a Wired Suburb." *City and Community* 2: 277-311.

Kornhauser, Ruth. 1978. *Social Sources of Delinquency.* Chicago: University of Chicago Press.

Kubrin, Charis E., and Ronald Weitzer. 2003. "New Directions in Social Disorganization Theory." *Journal of Research in Crime and Delinquency* 40: 374-402.

Land, Kenneth, Patricia McCall, and Lawrence Cohen. 1990. "Structural Covariates of Homicide Rates: Are There Any Invariances Across Time and Space?" *American Journal of Sociology* 95: 922-963.

Lander, Bernard. 1954. *Toward an Understanding of Juvenile Delinquency.* New York: Columbia University Press.

Markowitz, Fred, Paul Bellair, Allen Liska, and Jianhong Liu J. 2001. "Extending Social Disorganization Theory: Modeling the Relationships between Cohesion, Disorder, and Fear." *Criminology* 39: 293-319.

Morenoff, Jeffrey D. 2003. "Neighborhood Mechanisms and the Spatial Dynamics of Birth Weight." *American Journal of Sociology* 108: 976-1017.

Morenoff, Jeffrey D, Robert J Sampson, and Stephen Raudenbush. 2001. "Neighborhood Inequality, Collective Efficacy, and the Spatial Dynamics of Homicide." *Criminology* 39: 517-60.

Pattillo-McCoy Mary. 1999. *Black Picket Fences: Privilege and Peril Among the Black Middle Class.* Chicago: University of Chicago Press.

Portes, Alejandro, and Julia Sensenbrenner. 1993. "Embeddedness and Immigration: Notes on the Social Determinants of Economic Action." *American Journal of Sociology* 98: 1320-1350.

Pratt, Travis, and Frances Cullen. 2005. "Assessing the Relative Effects of Macro-Level Predictors of Crime: A Meta-Analysis." Pp. 37 3-450 in Michael Tonny (ed.), *Crime and Justice: A Review of Research, Vol. 32.* Chicago: University of Chicago Press.

Putnam, Robert. 1993. *Making Democracy Work.* Princeton, NJ: Princeton University Press.

————. 2000. *Bowling Alone.* New York: Simon and Schuster.

Raudenbush Stephen W., and Robert J. Sampson. 1999. 'Ecometrics': Toward a Science of Assessing Ecological Settings, with Application to the Systematic Social Observation of Neighborhoods." *Sociological Methodology* 29: 1-41.

Sampson, Robert J. 2003. "The Neighborhood Context of Well Being." *Perspectives in Biology and Medicine* 46: S53-S73.

————. 2005. "How Does Community Context Matter? Social Mechanisms and the Explanation of Crime." In Per-Olof Wikström and Robert J. Sampson (eds.), *Con-*

texts and Mechanisms of Pathways in Crime. Cambridge: Cambridge University Press.

Sampson, Robert J., and W. Byron Groves. 1989. "Community Structure and Crime: Testing Social-Disorganization Theory." *American Journal of Sociology* 94: 774-802.

Sampson, Robert J., Jeffrey Morenoff, and Felton Earls. 1999. "Beyond Social Capital: Spatial Dynamics of Collective Efficacy for Children." *American Sociological Review* 64: 633-660.

Sampson, Robert J., Jeffrey D. Morenoff, and Thomas Gannon-Rowley. 2002. "Assessing Neighborhood Effects: Social Processes and New Directions in Research." *Annual Review of Sociology* 28: 443-478.

Sampson, Robert J., Jeffrey D. Morenoff, and Stephen Raudenbush. 2005. "Social Anatomy of Racial and Ethnic Disparities in Violence." *American Journal of Public Health.*

Sampson, Robert J., and Per-Olof Wikström. 2004. "The Social Order of Violence in Chicago and Stockholm Neighborhoods." Paper presented at the Conference on "Order, Conflict, and Violence," Yale University, New Haven, CT, April 30-May 2.

Sampson, Robert J., and Stephen Raudenbush. 1999. "Systematic Social Observation of Public Spaces: A New Look at Disorder in Urban Neighborhoods." *American Journal of Sociology* 105: 603-651.

Sampson, Robert J., Stephen Raudenbush, and Felton Earls. 1997. "Neighborhoods and Violent Crime: A Multilevel Study of Collective Efficacy." *Science* 277: 918-24.

Shaw, Clifford, and Henry McKay. 1942 (1969, 2nd ed.). *Juvenile Delinquency and Urban Areas.* Chicago: University of Chicago Press.

Sorensen Aage B. 1998. "Theoretical Mechanisms and the Empirical Study of Social Processes." Pp. 238-66 in Peter Hedström and Richard Swedberg (eds.), *Social Mechanisms: An Analytical Approach to Social Theory.* Cambridge: Cambridge University Press.

St. Jean, Peter. 2005. *Pockets of Crime: An Up-Close Look at Street Crime, Broken Windows and Collective Efficacy Theories.* Chicago: University of Chicago Press, forthcoming.

Stack, Carol. 1975. *All Our Kin: Strategies for Survival in a Black Community.* New York: Harper.

Stinchcombe, Arthur 1989. "An Outsider's View of Network Analyses of Power." In Robert Perrucci and Harry Potter (eds.), *Networks of Power.* New York: Aldine De Gruyter.

Taylor, Ralph 2002. "Fear of Crime, Local Social Ties, and Collective Efficacy: Maybe Masquerading Measurement, Maybe Déjà vu all Over Again." *Justice Quarterly* 19: 773-92.

Triplett, Ruth A., Randy R. Gainey, and Ivan Y. Sun. 2003. "Institutional Strength, Social Control and Neighborhood Crime Rates." *Theoretical Criminology* 7: 439-467.

Venkatesh, Sudhir Alladi. 1997. "The Social Organization of Street Gang Activity in an Urban Ghetto." *American Journal of Sociology* 103: 82-111

Warner, Barbara, and Pamela Rountree. 1997. "Local Social Ties in a Community and Crime Model: Questioning the Systemic Nature of Informal Social Control." *Social Problems* 44: 520-36.

Wellman, Barry. 2004. "Connecting Communities: On and Off-Line." *Contexts* 3: 22-28.

Wheaton, Blair, and Philippa Clarke. 2003. "Space Meets Time: Integrating Temporal and Contextual Influences on Mental Health in Early Adulthood." *American Sociological Review* 68: 680-706.

Whyte, William F. 1943. *Street Corner Society: The Social Structure of an Italian Slum.* Chicago: University of Chicago Press.

Wikström, Per-Olof, and Vania Ceccato. 2004. "Crime and Social Life: A Space-Time Budget Study." Paper presented at the Annual Meeting of the American Society of Criminology, Nashville, TN, November.

Wikström, Per-Olof, and Robert J. Sampson. 2003. "Social Mechanisms of Community Influences on Crime and Pathways in Criminality." Pp. 118-148 in Ben Lahey, Terrie Moffitt, and Avshalom Caspi (eds.), *Causes of Conduct Disorder and Serious Juvenile Delinquency.* New York: Guilford Press.

Wilson William Julius. 1987. *The Truly Disadvantaged: The Inner City, the Underclass, and Public Policy.* Chicago: University of Chicago Press.

Wirth, Louis. 1938. "Urbanism as a Way of Life." *American Journal of Sociology* 44:3-24.

6

Segregation and Race/Ethnic Inequality in Crime: New Directions

Ruth D. Peterson, Lauren J. Krivo,
and Christopher R. Browning

Crime takes place in local contexts that are highly segregated along a number of lines. Indeed, urban areas are characterized by highly uneven distributions of social groups across geographic space, most notably by race, ethnicity, and economic status (Fischer et al. 2004; Fischer 2003; Logan, Stults, and Farley 2004; Massey and Denton 1993; Wilkes and Iceland 2004). Even the most casual observer is aware of the ways in which such spatial concentrations of disadvantaged and minority populations are associated with high levels of social problems including street crime. At the same time, they see that low crime, violence, and other social ills pervade in more economically advantaged and white communities. These observations provide the starting point for our perspective on racial and ethnic inequality in crime. This approach emphasizes that segregation is a central structural force setting the stage for differences in crime across groups. Although segregation has not been ignored in previous theories and empirical analyses of crime, we argue here that its full and central role as a source of criminal inequality has been under-theorized. Thus, we propose a broad and central role for segregation that recognizes it as embedded in multiple spatial layers and as relevant to a number of social dimensions that have implications for inequality in crime.

Segregation has typically been presented as leading to crime in one of two ways: through strain or through mechanisms associated with social isolation. Logan and Messner (1987) were among the first to articulate these mechanisms. Drawing on Merton's (1938) social structure and anomie thesis and Blau and Blau's (1982) related perspective on racial inequality as a source of violence, they note:

169

racial segregation imposes a significant barrier to black upward mobility and quality of life. Place of residence locates people not only in geographical space but also in networks of social opportunities—it influences prospects for employment, for public services, for educational advancement, for appreciation in home values, and more. Residential segregation by race accordingly implies that opportunities for achievement are limited for certain groups, and it conflicts with basic American value commitments which encourage members of all groups to strive for socioeconomic success. Such a "disjuncture" between structural arrangements and fundamental cultural values, Merton argued, tends to undermine the legitimacy of social norms and thereby promotes deviant behavior (Logan and Messner 1987: 510).

From this point of view, segregation is a dimension of social inequality that results in racial and ethnic distinctions in crime by producing frustration and hostility among have-nots and, thereby, promoting criminal motivations among this group, especially racial minorities.

Also citing Merton (1938) and Blau and Blau (1982), Logan and Messner (1987) posit that racial residential segregation, coupled with the ambiguity of rules produced by high levels of anomie, undermines effective social controls and weakens the capacity of a community to defend itself from criminal victimization. This viewpoint is consonant with Massey and Denton's (1993) discussion of the links between racial segregation, concentrated poverty, and the prevalence of crime within disadvantaged communities. Wilson's (1987, 1996) social isolation perspective, while deemphasizing the contemporary significance of racial segregation as a determinant of concentrated poverty, articulates a comparable and compelling model of the consequences of extreme economic disadvantage afflicting urban African American neighborhoods. This perspective speaks directly to racial inequality in crime and other social dislocations. According to Wilson, many blacks (racial minorities) live in local areas with multiple disadvantages (including high levels of joblessness) that isolate them from mainstream society. This isolation, in turn, diminishes levels of informal and formal social control. Put simply, highly disadvantaged communities lack the monetary, social, and institutional resources to combat crime. Since white areas rarely experience such circumstances, racial differences in community contexts that result from segregation help explain black-white inequality in crime offending and victimization (see also Sampson and Wilson 1995).

Strain and social isolation arguments have generated a modest amount of research with a central focus on the segregation and crime relationship (Logan and Messner 1987; Peterson and Krivo 1993, 1999; Shihadeh and Flynn 1996; Shihadeh and Maume 1997). Logan and Messner (1987) tested the link between black-white residential segregation and violent index crimes for the *total* population in U.S. suburban rings and found that segregation increases some types of violence but not others. Despite some supportive findings, this work does not speak directly to the arguments the authors laid out. Both the strain and isolation viewpoints suggest effects of segregation for the *minority* population, while Logan and Messner's (1987) work considered only general patterns of violence. Recognizing this problem, virtually all subsequent segregation and crime studies have examined racially disaggregated rates of different types of violence (most often homicide).[1]These race-specific studies have demonstrated a sizable link between segregation and black crime (Peterson and Krivo 1993, 1999; Shihadeh and Flynn 1996; Shihadeh and Maume 1997). But collectively, they also suggest a relatively complicated picture. For example, Shihadeh and Flynn (1996) and Shihadeh and Maume (1997) show that the strength of the association between segregation and violent crime depends on how segregation is measured. Indicators that tap isolation and centralization near the core of metropolitan areas have stronger associations with black homicide and robbery than a measure of the simple uneven distribution of blacks and whites. Peterson and Krivo (1999) and Shihadeh and Maume (1997) show that segregation's effect is not necessarily direct. Rather, its impact on black killings is partially, to completely, due to the connection of segregation with either general levels or the geographic concentration of African American disadvantage.[2]

In additional studies the segregation-crime relationship is not the central issue, but this factor is included among a larger set of independent and control variables. The results of these investigations have been mixed. A number focus on black homicide and find positive significant effects of segregation (Parker and Pruitt 2000; Smith 1992), while others show no net influence (Krivo and Peterson 2000; Ousey 1999; Phillips 2002; Sampson 1985; Shihadeh and Ousey 1998). Several studies that report on segregation's influence on black homicide also examine its effect on white killings. Some of these show no effect (Krivo and Peterson 2000; Phillips 2002; Shihadeh and Ousey 1998; Smith 1992), but others exhibit relationships in directions opposite of one another (Ousey 1999; Parker and Pruitt 2000; Sampson 1985). Samspon (1985) finds that segregation increases white killings, as do Parker and Pruitt (2000) in some models. In contrast, Ousey (1999) shows that sometimes this factor is associated with lower homicide rates among whites. Thus, the role of racial residential segregation in white crime is not clear. Beyond these works, a handful of papers include segregation as part of a structural disadvantage index, thereby making it impossible to distinguish its independent effects on crime (Messner and Golden 1992; Parker 2001; Parker and Johns 2002; Parker and McCall 1999).

In brief then, the empirical evidence to date on the role of segregation in crime is limited and characterized by disparate findings, making it difficult to draw firm conclusions about segregation's contribution to inequality in crime. We argue that this situation is due to the use of overly narrow theoretical conceptualizations and empirical strategies in past work. Indeed, no one has yet articulated or explored how a wide array of crime-producing conditions (social, institutional, ecological, etc.) are embedded inequitably across geographic space in ways that are intricately connected with race and ethnicity, and, hence, with inequality in crime.

The importance of residential segregation for explaining differences in crime is tied to the fact that race and ethnicity are fundamental stratifying components of U.S. society that permeate a multitude of spatial, social and institutional arrangements across and within localities. These status dimensions determine who resides in various locations, how residents relate to one another, and how outside individual, institutional, and political actors perceive, and respond to, communities. Thus race and ethnicity are much more than simply correlated with the various crime-producing conditions reflected in segregated communities; they are a part of them. And as segregation implies, these conditions are explicitly spatial. Drawing on these general insights, below we set forth a model that integrates spatial and institutional approaches to the study of racial and ethnic inequality in crime.

A Segregation Approach

Our model of racial and ethnic differences in crime emphasizes the interconnections between race/ethnic and spatial inequality. With its roots in contemporary and historical forces, residential segregation by race and ethnicity pervades the spatial landscape of the United States with significant consequences for a range of social outcomes. However, we view segregation as operating at two distinct levels: region- or area-wide and local. Region-wide race/ethnic segregation consists of the unequal distribution of racial and ethnic groups across neighborhoods within a broad region (city, county, metropolitan area, or any other such large geographic space). This is a common macro-structural conceptualization of the property of segregation that is measured by the Index of Dissimilarity (D) which indicates the proportion of one of two segregated groups (e.g., blacks or whites, Hispanics, or whites) that would have to change their neighborhood for every residential area to have the same group proportion as in the region as a whole. While such area-wide segregation summarizes differentials in where groups live within a region, it does not take into account how homogeneous neighborhoods may cluster together, a notion that is a fundamental component of the perspective that we propose.

In contrast, local segregation refers to homophily with respect to racial, ethnic, and socioeconomic composition among neighborhoods that are linked to one another through contiguity or other physical features that spatially connect them (e.g., an urban black belt). As an example, we present a map of the race/ethnic composition and poverty rates of census tracts in Milwaukee County (Figure 6.1). This county is in the Milwaukee-Waukesha metropolitan area which has one of the highest levels of region-wide segregation in the U.S. (Index of Dissimilarity=82, Lewis Mumford Center 2004). The map shows that a large share of neighborhoods that are predominantly black (70 percent or over, see small broken lines) also have high poverty rates (30 percent or

Figure 6.1
Milwaukee County Neighborhoods by Race/Ethnic Composition and Poverty

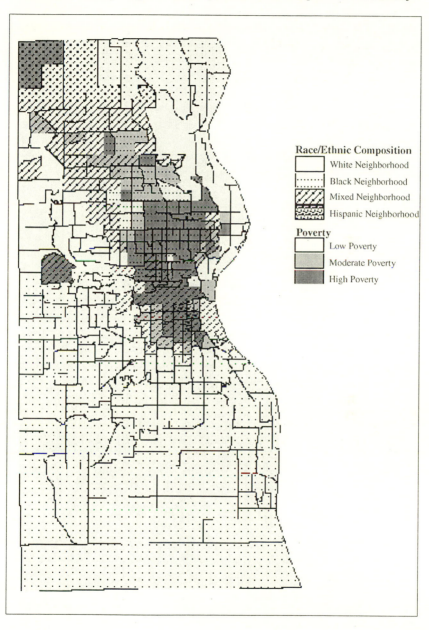

over, the darkest area). Together these areas comprise a pattern of high local segregation which is reflected in their tight clustering in space.

Fundamentally, inequalities in crime must be viewed from the lens of segregation because the separation of racial and ethnic groups across communities has significant non-neutral implications for local conditions that provide the context for crime. Indeed, neighborhood crime, and inequality across groups in crime, can be thought of as the end-products of a process set in motion by area-wide racial and ethnic residential segregation. There are three central mechanisms by which region-wide segregation's effect is forged: 1) through key internal community conditions; 2) through decisions by commercial and political actors; and, 3) through local segregation. Although these three mechanisms are overlapping and interrelated, for heuristic purposes, we discuss them separately and illustrate with diagrams how they intersect.

Area-wide Segregation and Internal Community Conditions

Figure 6.2 displays the most basic and familiar components of the model. Here, levels of region-wide residential segregation result in varying degrees of homogeneity in the racial, ethnic and immigrant composition of neighborhoods. Very high levels of segregation among some groups, particularly blacks and whites, mean that large proportions of neighborhoods are remarkably homogeneous. These white, black, Latino, and immigrant areas often vary widely in neighborhood structural conditions such as levels of disadvantage and advantage (e.g., poverty, joblessness, economic affluence, etc.), family structure, residential instability and the age/sex composition of residents that are central in affecting social control and crime facilitating processes. These, in turn, determine levels of crime.

Figure 6.2
Basic Conceptual Model: Segregation and Race/Ethnic Inequality in Crime

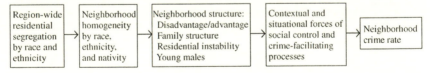

Massey and Denton (1993) described how racial segregation combines with socioeconomic stratification to produce neighborhoods that are differentially situated regarding race/ethnicity, and, consequently, structural disadvantage/advantage (Massey and Denton 1993). Very high levels of observed black-white segregation mean that these groups tend to live in separate neighborhoods with African Americans' disproportionately high levels of disadvantage (and single-parent families) being concentrated within predominantly black communities, and whites' more advantaged economic conditions and intact family structures being concentrated in heavily white areas (Krivo et al. 1998; Massey 1996; St. John 2002). Latinos experience more modest levels of segregation and, hence, are less likely to reside in homogeneous neighborhoods; thus, the concentration of disadvantage for this group is less extensive (Jargowsky 1997; Logan, Stults, and Farley 2004). Communities of color also tend to have higher rates of residential instability and a greater prevalence of young males, reflecting the social and demographic characteristics of many non-white populations.

Varying levels of disadvantage, family structure, and residential instability that are strongly connected with the racial and ethnic composition of communities are regarded as critical determinants of crime across local areas through their influence on differential social control/guardianship and crime-facilitating processes (Krivo and Peterson 1996, 2000; Peterson and Krivo 1999; Sampson, Raudenbush, and Earls 1997). Wilson (1987, 1996) points to the effects of concentrated disadvantage in diminishing social control. He notes that in extremely disadvantaged neighborhoods, there are relatively few working- and middle-class families to buffer the effects of uneven economic conditions. This impedes the ability of communities to sustain basic institutional structures and sources of formal and informal social control. Neighborhood residential instability (e.g., rapid turnover and diminished rates of homeownership) inhibits the emergence of viable social networks and weakens sentiments of attachment to local communities (Bursik and Grasmick 1993; Kasarda and Janowitz 1974). Anonymity and disengagement from the community, in turn, hinder efforts to mobilize local residents to provide informal social control of neighborhood life (Sampson et al. 1997). Social control also may be thwarted because of inadequate police protection, i.e., insufficient supply and deployment of police, failure to respond to calls from residents, or slow and irregular responses by the police. As a result, the costs associated with engaging in crime and violence are lessened and the possible deterrent effect of the law is reduced. In short, residents of extremely disadvantaged communities simply lack the financial, social, and institutional resources to prevent and fight crime effectively (Bursik and Grasmick 1993).

In terms of crime-facilitating processes, two primary mechanisms are role modeling and adaptation to impoverished and unsafe environments (Krivo and Peterson 1996). In highly disadvantaged and unstable contexts, residents more commonly witness criminal acts and are exposed to role models who do not restrain their criminal impulses. Thus, there is socialization toward engaging in criminal activity (Anderson 1990, 1999; Sampson and Wilson 1995; Skogan 1990; Wacquant 1993) which is not offset by anti-crime lessons from "old heads" who are relatively few in number and lack credibility in contemporary contexts (Anderson 1990, 1999). Crime, especially violence, is further encouraged by the need to adapt to a crime-ridden environment. In such contexts, residents most often feel the need to adopt defensive and threatening postures, including carrying weapons, to defend their lives and property. As more people adopt these postures and behaviors, the level of violence escalates (Massey 1995; Sampson and Wilson 1995).

Widespread joblessness and irregular employment likely exacerbate such role modeling and adaptive processes because many residents are idle for large parts of the day. As a consequence, they spend significant amounts of time in settings where non-conventional role modeling and defensive posturing are prevalent—local taverns, pool halls and street corners. That is, they are involved in "situations of company" and routine activities that are conducive to criminal involvement (Crutchfield 1989).

Political/Commercial Interests and Physical Characteristics of Neighborhoods

The model of criminal inequality that we propose also incorporates influences articulated in urban political economy perspectives. Figure 6.3 adds this second component to our heuristic diagram. Here, attention is directed to the significant ways in which powerful state and commercial actors make decisions about land use and levels of investment or disinvestment in local areas in response to their race/ethnic composition, the presence of immigrants, and their social and economic character (see Logan and Molotch 1987). These decisions create and reinforce significant racial, ethnic, and spatial inequalities in the physical and ecological character of local areas. Indeed, minority and poor areas are disproportionately targeted for the placement of disruptive institutions and physical structures and inadequate investments by financial institutions (Holloway and Wyly 2001; Wallace and Wallace 1998). For example, large public housing projects (and current forms of subsidized housing redevelopment) have been much more likely to be sited in disadvantaged neighborhoods and almost exclusively in black communities (Hirsch 1983; Massey and Denton 1993; Massey and Kanaiaupuni 1993). Highway and

Figure 6.3
Intermediate Conceptual Model: Segregation and Race/Ethnic Inequality in Crime

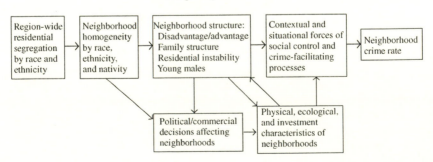

street development patterns may wall off minority communities from white areas or break them up such that different sections are disconnected (Bayor 1988). The development of sports stadiums, hospitals, colleges, and the like, often involve the seizure and leveling of residential property in economically depressed areas where residents have little capacity to resist the political and commercial interests involved (Hirsch 1983).

In addition, minority and disadvantaged communities have less access to mortgage lending and loans for property upkeep (Wyly and Holloway 1999; Holloway and Wyly 2001), and are targeted for disinvestments such as the closing of local malls, businesses, or government services (Wallace and Wallace 1998). In contrast, white and more advantaged neighborhoods tend to benefit from political and commercial decisions. The physical layout of these communities is not broken up or walled off by major thoroughfares or institutional entities, but rather is primarily comprised of occupied residential housing. White advantaged areas also profit from greater levels of investments in property and upkeep.

How do physical and ecological outcomes of political and commercial decisions lead to variation and inequality in neighborhood crime? We suggest that these characteristics help shape patterns of guardianship and the capacity of residents to engage in informal social control. They also influence levels of disadvantage and advantage by affecting differential residential mobility by class. Varying built environments reflect differences in the prevalence of "defensible space," i.e., areas amenable to guardianship (Newman 1996). Abandoned buildings and overgrown vacant lots, for instance, make for difficult-to-monitor spaces within which criminal activity may flourish (Skogan 1990). Extensive structures and patterns of land use associated with highways and rail systems in some neighborhoods also provide limited opportunities for informal control.

The physical features of an area also affect the general willingness of residents to use public space and, as such, to oversee and control public activities. Any such withdrawal weakens social networks, further limiting guardianship by residents (Skogan 1990). The placement of large-scale institutions and public projects in neighborhoods disrupts existing residentially-based informal social networks and, in doing so, attenuates neighborhood attachment, sense of territoriality, and resulting monitoring (Taylor 2001; Taylor, Gottfredson, and Brower 1984). Importantly too, acts of disinvestment, such as New York's "planned shrinkage" of firehouses during the 1970s which destroyed large segments of property in poor black and Puerto Rican areas, force individuals to move thereby severely disrupting existing community social networks and decreasing the motivation for neighborhood self-regulation (Wallace and Wallace 1998).

In addition, the attractiveness of areas to current and potential residents is affected by their physical characteristics. As a result, feedback effects are created that further reinforce differentials in disadvantage and advantage across neighborhoods. To the extent that the physical environment is blighted, replete with disruptive institutions, and broken up by various thoroughfares, individuals who have options and who can afford to leave the community will do so. Middle class and white residents are most favorably situated to make such moves. At the opposite end of the spectrum, newer and more well-kept areas with vibrant commerce, institutions, and investments are particularly attractive. The poor and minorities often lack the resources to reside in such areas, while the middle class (and whites) have much greater access. In these ways, the physical and investment characteristics of neighborhoods serve to both reinforce and exacerbate inequities in disadvantage and advantage and race/ethnic composition. As noted earlier, differentials in disadvantage are central determinants of contextual and situational forces of social control and processes that facilitate crime in local areas.

The Influence of Local Segregation

Figure 6.4 adds the final component, local segregation, and, hence, presents the full conceptual model. As the overall model of crime specifies, region-wide racial and ethnic segregation is reflected in varying levels of race and ethnic neighborhood homogeneity. However, our concept of local segregation recognizes the important fact that racially, ethnically, and economically distinct areas are generally not randomly located in space throughout a region. Rather, in many places predominantly black communities are heavily clustered together, as are white local areas, with these clusters being additionally class divided to varying degrees. Latinos are less likely to be embedded in large clusters of homogenous neighborhoods.

Figure 6.4
Full Conceptual Model: Segregation and Race/Ethnic Inequality in Crime

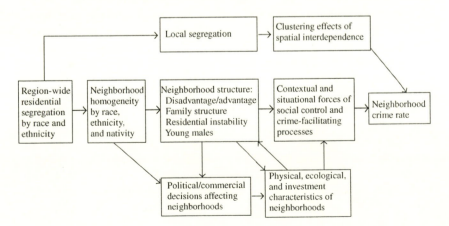

Such patterns of local segregation affect neighborhood crime through clustering effects that operate due to the varying permeability of neighborhood boundaries and the interconnections among similarly disadvantaged or advantaged communities. In locally segregated areas of disadvantage, social isolation with all of its deleterious consequences, including crime, is intensified. There is a broader area that lacks working- and middle-class families that buffer economic downturns, stable institutions that provide formal and informal social control, and political and economic connections that facilitate public social control. Further, non-employment, exposure to unconventional role models, and adaptations to criminal environments also span a wider area.

Physical characteristics also facilitate a greater porousness of boundaries in locally segregated disadvantaged areas than in other types of communities. Such areas likely have more streets leading into them and greater ease of internal circulation (e.g., fewer cul-de-sacs). Entry and exit are also enhanced by the location of disadvantaged segregated areas in older parts of the innercity that adjoin major arteries (four- as opposed to two-lane streets). Further, proximity to highway exits also increases the flow of traffic in and out of these areas (Taylor and Gottfredson 1986). Weak control of boundaries means that communities are vulnerable to spillover of crime from adjoining areas. They are also at risk from individuals who are unconstrained from entering the neighborhood to explore criminal opportunities or engage in other activities that may lead to crime. These patterns, coupled with high unemployment, likely mean a greater congregation of persons during times and in spaces conducive to crime, thus furthering the effect of local segregation.

Clustering effects in locally segregated disadvantaged areas may also come from links between young people across neighborhoods comprising a region. For example, in some cities, clusters of disadvantaged areas bring multiple local gangs into contact, potentially leading to reciprocal acts of violence across adjacent communities (Morenoff et al. 2001; Cohen and Tita 1999). Further, high school catchment areas draw on youth from multiple neighborhoods thereby connecting them together. In disadvantaged contexts with limited social control capacities, these types of connections can spread the potential for violence and youthful crime from one locale to another.

Conversely, the local segregation of advantaged racial and socioeconomic groups contributes to reduced crime levels. Communities that are ensconced in clusters of affluence and racial privilege likely have more extensive informal organizational ties to nearby neighborhoods, social networks that span larger geographic areas, and links to one another through political and economic connections that facilitate public social control, i.e., the capacity to draw resources relevant to crime-control from sources outside the neighborhood (Bursik and Grasmick 1993; Vélez 2001). Even when formal ties do not exist across areas, they may be easily generated in response to common threats to community safety. Thus, neighborhoods with well-developed social control capacities may benefit from contiguous neighborhoods through the spatial spillover of formal and informal guardianship. In this way, the effect of local segregation of advantage serves to protect these areas from crime.

Locally segregated and advantaged portions of the region also are highly insulated from the poverty and other economic sources that motivate crime. This is the case both in terms of residents' socioeconomic characteristics (e.g., high income, homeownership) and physical location and layout. Entry and exit is often extensively limited through vast cul-de-sac designs that protect communities from outsiders. Moreover, great distances from areas of disadvantage make them highly insulated from the criminal downside of urban life.

In general then, we see local segregation as helping to explain racial and ethnic inequality in crime through community interconnectedness that results from the spatial clustering of similarly disadvantaged and advantaged neighborhoods. As black-white regional segregation increases, locally segregated disadvantaged contexts are increasingly likely to be embedded in larger socially isolated areas and crime in focal neighborhoods is likely to be more pronounced. Earlier we introduced a map of race/ethnicity and poverty in census tracts in Milwaukee County (see Figure 6.1). To help illustrate our ideas about how segregation might contribute to crime and inequality in crime, we use this map along with those for two additional counties in areas with more moderate levels of segregation: Franklin County, Ohio (part of the Columbus Metropolitan Statistical Area [MSA], Figure 6.5) and Wake County, North Carolina (part of the Raleigh-Durham-Chapel Hill MSA, Figure 6.6). A comparison of the three maps suggests two noteworthy points. First, they illustrate the hypothesized association between the level of region-wide segregation and the degree of local segregation. In Milwaukee County, which is a place marked by a stark pattern of regional black-white segregation, we observe a high level of local segregation whereby African American neighborhoods with high levels of poverty are concentrated just north of downtown Milwaukee. In contrast, more advantaged white neighborhoods are concentrated in the west, south, and northeast and a large portion are located outside the city limits.

At the other extreme, Wake County, North Carolina, with a region-wide segregation level nearly forty points lower (Index of Dissimilarity=46), does not exhibit large clusters of disadvantaged racial minorities. Indeed, the disadvantaged African American local segregation pattern is limited to two small neighborhoods (small broken lines with the darkest shading) that are also close to areas with moderate or low levels of poverty (small broken lines with lighter or no shading). The remainder of blacks and Latinos are more widely dispersed in mixed neighborhoods with low poverty. In between is Franklin County, Ohio, where the level of region-wide segregation is 63 compared with 82 and 46 for Milwaukee and Wake counties, respectively. Here, we see a clustering of black neighborhoods, only a portion of which is highly impover-

Figure 6.5
Franklin County Neighborhoods by Race/Ethnic Composition and Poverty

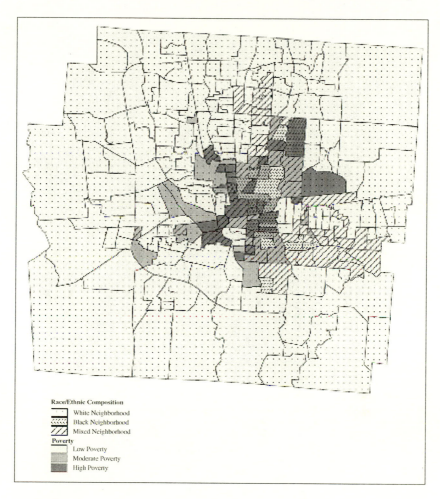

ished. Also, one of the most poverty stricken African American areas is spatially somewhat separate from the core of the heavily black portion of the city. There also are three black tracts that are low poverty (no shading and small broken lines) and geographically more distant. Similar to Milwaukee, in both Wake and Franklin counties, very large numbers of white neighborhoods are distant from concentrations of poverty and racial minorities.

Second, the patterns shown in the maps allow us to speculate about variation in crime across neighborhoods. In particular, where the local segregation of disadvantaged minorities (particularly blacks) is greatest, we would anticipate high and relatively uniform levels of neighborhood crime within minority

Figure 6.6
Wake County Neighborhoods by Race/Ethnic Composition and Poverty

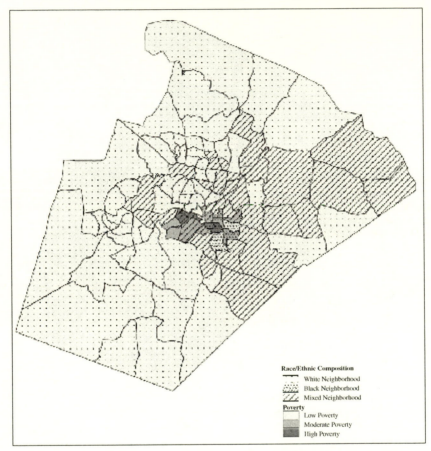

communities, including those with less poverty due to spillover and spatial interdependence. The large economically and spatially privileged white portions of the county would have rates of crimes that strongly differentiate them from the dense area of non-white and poverty populations. Thus, racial inequality in crime should be especially pronounced. The overall pattern would be different in areas with more modest local segregation of disadvantage and non-white race. Weaker clustering should produce less intense and more variable crime across areas in minority portions of the region. In turn, there should be somewhat less racial inequality in crime. For the three counties examined here, these arguments suggest that less racial differentiation in criminal offending and victimization would be found in Wake and Franklin Counties than in Milwaukee County.

An initial examination of reported index crime data for census tracts in Franklin and Milwaukee Counties shows some support for the arguments set forth above. Crime rates, especially those for violent offenses, are notably higher in predominantly African American neighborhoods within the dense area of local segregation than in black and very poor neighborhoods that are physically more separate from the black poverty belt.

Differences across geographic areas in the association between local segregation and crime might be even greater when combined with other aspects of the structural context. For example, variability in the local segregation-crime relationship may stem from regional location and the degree to which patterns of segregation have become entrenched over time. Older places in the East and Midwest developed large segregated black populations prior to World War II. The negative consequences of local segregation in such areas may be amplified by the multigenerational nature of social isolation. A comparable compounding of protection may characterize white and advantaged neighborhoods in highly segregated cities.

Conclusions and Future Directions

At the outset, we argued that a better understanding of racial and ethnic inequality in crime needs to come from incorporating multiple aspects of segregation into a broader conceptual model. We claim that segregation is critical to the understanding of criminal inequality because crime takes place within local spatial contexts that are highly differentiated by race, ethnicity, and economic status. We have proposed a model in which region-wide patterns of segregation affect criminal inequality through internal neighborhood structural conditions, political and commercial institutional arrangements, and the clustering of more or less homogeneous neighborhoods. Importantly, this viewpoint recognizes that segregation does not operate through a single spatial expression, but rather is a multi-layered structural condition which affects outcomes in significant ways at each level. Racial, ethnic, and economic segregation across areas within large regions affects the degree of neighborhood homogeneity and other structural conditions that influence crime, but it is also associated with varying amounts of spatial clustering of race/ethnically and economically similar neighborhoods (i.e., local segregation). Residents and significant outside actors respond differentially to these various layers of segregation and types of race/ethnic and economic clustering in ways that serve to create, reproduce and exacerbate inequalities in crime.

Above we described a general model but focused most heavily on observations and examples for African Americans and whites. This raises the question of the scope of application of the model we propose to a variety of diverse groups (e.g., Hispanics, Asians, and a range of immigrant populations). We suggest that the varying spatial situations, and their ramifications as articulated here, would help explain observed differences in crime patterns across a host of groups. However, we also recognize that there may be additional social and structural conditions that must be incorporated to broaden the applicability of the model. The most obvious example pertains to the variety of Latino groups. Some research has shown that crime rates in heavily disadvantaged Latino immigrant communities are lower than in similarly disadvantaged black areas (Martinez 2002, 2003; Martinez and Lee 2000). Are such differences due to the factors that we have described, or is it necessary to take into account internal and external community dynamics that are unique to immigrants?

Moving forward to address this question, and more generally the validity of our model, requires collecting data and conducting analyses that allow researchers to explore the complex interconnections across multiple spatial levels. Crime data for neighborhoods within a relatively large set of places that vary in their levels of region-wide segregation and in the types of spatial clustering of racial, ethnic, and economic groups would provide the first step for such endeavors. Unfortunately, prior work on inequality in local crime patterns has relied almost exclusively on analyses of a single or very few cities (e.g., Browning, Feinberg, and Dietz 2004; Crutchfield, Glusker, and Bridges 1999; Sampson et al. 1997; Woodredge and Thistlethwaite 2003). It is essential that research move beyond the study of just a few places if we are to come to a fuller understanding of how segregation, with all of its component manifestations, works to produce inequality in crime. Ideally too, this would include comparisons across a range of societies.

In addition, data collection efforts should include concrete information about the spatial and ecological character of areas and how such conditions connect or disconnect communities from one another, and create physical environments that make neighborhoods more vulnerable or insulated from conditions that facilitate crime. Further, to test the full model set forth here, the crime, demographic, and ecological data need to be connected with information on the social, economic, political, and institutional processes that we have argued create and recreate highly differentiated contexts for crime among racial, ethnic, and class groups. This will move the study of criminal inequality beyond considering individuals, groups, and localities as atomized, and toward research that recognizes and examines the ways in which the sources of crime are interconnected and embedded in diverse layers of our stratified social structure.

Notes

1.   Akins (2003) is the only recent study that examined the effect of segregation on total rather than racially disaggregated crimes. He studied property crime rates and showed that segregation increases burglary, larceny and motor vehicle theft, but its effect on the latter two crimes is reduced to non-significance when police strength is controlled.
2.   Messner and South (1986) and South and Felson (1990) also examined the association of segregation with robbery and rape but their analyses derived from a

different theoretical origin than either strain or social isolation. These studies tested Blau's macrostructural theory of intergroup contact and thus examined whether segregation reduces interracial but increases intraracial victimization. They found support for these hypotheses.

References

Anderson, Elijah. 1990. *Streetwise: Race, Class, and Change in an Urban Community.* Chicago: University of Chicago Press.

————. 1999. *Code of the Street: Decency, Violence, and the Moral Life of the Inner City.* New York: W.W. Norton and Company.

Bayor, Ronald H. 1988. "Roads to Racial Segregation: Atlanta in the Twentieth Century." *Journal of Urban History* 3-21.

Blau, Judith R., and Peter M. Blau. 1982. "The Cost of Inequality: Metropolitan Structure and Violent Crime." *American Sociological Review* 47: 114-129.

Browning, Christopher R., Seth L. Feinberg, and Robert Dietz. 2004. "The Paradox of Social Organization: Networks, Collective Efficacy, and Violent Crime in Urban Neighborhoods." *Social Forces* 83: 503-534.

Bursik, Robert J., and Harold G. Grasmick. 1993. "Economic Deprivation and Neighborhood Crime Rates." *Law and Society Review* 27: 263-283.

Cohen, Jacqueline, and George Tita. 1999. "Diffusion in Homicide: Exploring a General Method for Detecting Spatial Diffusion Processes." *Journal of Quantitative Criminology* 15: 451-493.

Crutchfield, Robert D. 1989. "Labor Stratification and Violent Crime." *Social Forces* 68: 489-512.

Crutchfield, Robert D., Ann Glusker, and George S. Bridges. 1999. "A Tale of Three Cities: Labor Markets and Homicide." *Sociological Focus* 32: 65-83.

Fischer, Claude S., Gretchen Stockmayer, Jon Stiles, and Michael Hout. 2004. "Distinguishing the Geographic Levels and Social Dimensions of U.S. Metropolitan Segregation, 1960-2000." *Demography* 41: 37-59.

Fischer, Mary. 2003. "The Relative Importance of Income and Race in Determining Residential Outcomes in U.S. Urban Areas, 1970-2000." *Urban Affairs Review* 38: 669-696.

Hirsch, Arnold R. 1983. *Making the Second Ghetto: Race and Housing in Chicago, 1940-1960.* New York: Cambridge University Press.

Holloway, Steven R., and Elvin K. Wyly. 2001. "'The Color of Money' Expanded: Geographically Contingent Mortgage Lending in Atlanta." *Journal of Housing Research* 12: 55-90.

Jargowsky, Paul A. 1997. *Poverty and Place: Ghettos, Barrios, and the American City.* New York: Russell Sage.

Kasarda, John D., and Morris Janowitz. 1974. "Community Attachment in Mass Society." *American Sociological Review* 39: 328-339.

Krivo, Lauren J., and Ruth D. Peterson. 1996. "Extremely Disadvantaged Neighborhoods and Urban Crime." *Social Forces* 75: 619-650.

————. 2000. "The Structural Context of Homicide: Accounting for Racial Differences in Process." *American Sociological Review* 65: 547-559.

Krivo, Lauren J., Ruth D. Peterson, Helen Rizzo, and John R. Reynolds. 1998. "Race, Segregation, and the Concentration of Disadvantage: 1980-1990." *Social Problems* 45: 61-80.

Lewis Mumford Center. 2004. *Segregation Indices-Whole Population.* http: //mumford1. dyndns.org/cen2000/WholePop/WPsort/sort_d1.html.

Logan, John R., and Steven F. Messner. 1987. "Racial Residential Segregation and Suburban Violent Crime." *Social Science Quarterly* 68: 510-527.

Logan, John R., and Harvey L. Molotch. 1987. *Urban Fortunes: The Political Economy of Place*. Berkeley: University of California Press.

Logan, John R., Brian J. Stults, and Reynolds Farley. 2004. "Segregation of Minorities in the Metropolis: Two Decades of Change." *Demography* 41: 1-22.

Martinez, Ramiro, Jr. 2002. *Latino Homicide: Immigration, Violence and Community*. New York: Routledge Press.

———. 2003. "Moving Beyond Black and White Violence: African American, Haitian, and Latino Homicides in Miami." Pp. 22-43 in Darnell F. Hawkins (ed.), *Violent Crime: Assessing Race and Ethnic Differences*. New York: Cambridge University Press.

Martinez, Ramiro, Jr., and Matthew T. Lee. 2000. "Comparing the Context of Immigrant Homicides in Miami: Haitians, Jamaicans, and Mariels." *International Migration Review* 34: 794-812.

Massey, Douglas S. 1995. "Getting Away with Murder: Segregation and Violent Crime in Urban America." *University of Pennsylvania Law Review* 143: 1203-1232.

———. 1996. "The Age of Extremes: Concentrated Affluence and Poverty in the Twenty-First Century." *Demography* 33: 395-412.

Massey, Douglas S., and Nancy A. Denton. 1993. *American Apartheid: Segregation and the Making of the Underclass*. Cambridge, MA: Harvard University Press.

Massey, Douglas S. and Shawn M. Kanaiaupuni. 1993. "Public Housing and the Concentration of Poverty." *Social Science Quarterly* 74: 109-22.

Merton, Robert K. 1938. "Social Structure and Anomie." *American Sociological Review* 3: 672-782.

Messner, Steven F., and Reid M. Golden. 1992. "Racial Inequality and Racially Disaggregated Homicide Rates: An Assessment of Alternative Theoretical Explanations." *Criminology* 30: 421-447.

Morenoff, Jeffrey D., Robert J. Sampson, and Stephen W. Raudenbush. 2001. "Neighborhood Inequality, Collective Efficacy, and the Spatial Dynamics of Urban Violence." *Criminology* 39: 517-559.

Newman, Oscar. 1996. *Creating Defensible Space*. U.S. Department of Housing and Urban Development: Office of Policy Development and Research.

Ousey, Graham C. 1999. "Homicide, Structural Factors, and the Racial Invariance Assumption." *Criminology* 37: 405-425.

Parker, Karen F. 2001. "A Move Toward Specificity: Examining Urban Disadvantage and Race-and Relationship-Specific Homicide Rates." *Journal of Quantitative Criminology* 17: 89-110.

Parker, Karen F., and Tracy Johns. 2002. "Urban Disadvantage and Types of Race-Specific Homicide: Assessing the Diversity in Family Structures in the Urban Context." *Journal of Research in Crime and Delinquency* 39: 277-303.

Parker, Karen F., and Patricia L. McCall. 1999. "Structural Conditions and Racial Homicide Patterns: A Look at the Multiple Disadvantages in Urban Areas." *Criminology* 37: 447-478.

Parker, Karen F., and Matthew V. Pruitt. 2000. "Poverty, Poverty Concentration, and Homicide." *Social Science Quarterly* 81: 555-570.

Peterson, Ruth D., and Lauren J. Krivo. 1993. "Racial Segregation and Black Urban Homicide." *Social Forces* 71: 1001-1026.

———. 1999. "Racial Segregation, the Concentration of Disadvantage, and Black and White Homicide Victimization." *Sociological Forum* 14: 495-523.

Phillips, Julie A. 2002. "White, Black, and Latino Homicide Rates: Why the Difference?" *Social Problems* 49: 349-373.

Sampson, Robert J. 1985. "Race and Criminal Violence: A Demographically Disaggregated Analysis of Urban Homicide." *Crime and Delinquency* 31: 4782.

Sampson, Robert J., Stephen W. Raudenbush, and Felton Earls. 1997. "Neighborhoods and Violent Crime: A Multilevel Study of Collective Efficacy." *Science* 277: 918-924.

Sampson, Robert J., and William Julius Wilson. 1995. "Toward a Theory of Race, Crime, and Urban Inequality." Pp. 37-54 in John Hagan and Ruth D. Peterson (eds.), *Crime and Inequality.* Stanford, CA: Stanford University Press.

Shihadeh, Edward S., and Nicole Flynn. 1996. "Segregation and Crime: The Effect of Black Social Isolation on the Rates of Black Urban Violence." *Social Forces* 74: 1325-1352.

Shihadeh, Edward S., and Michael O. Maume. 1997. "Segregation and Crime: The Relationship between Black Centralization and Urban Black Homicide." *Homicide Studies* 1: 254-280.

Shihadeh, Edward S., and Graham C. Ousey. 1998. "Industrial Restructuring and Violence: The Link between Entry-Level Jobs, Economic Deprivation, and Black and White Homicide." *Social Forces* 77: 185-206.

Skogan, Wesley G. 1990. *Disorder and Decline: Crime and the Spiral of Decay in American Neighborhoods.* Berkeley: University of California Press.

Smith, M. Dwayne. 1992. "Variations in Correlates of Race-Specific Urban Homicide Rates." *Journal of Contemporary Criminal Justice* 8: 137-149.

St. John, Craig. 2002. "The Concentration of Affluence in the United States, 1990." *Urban Affairs Review* 37: 500-520.

Taylor, Ralph B. 2001. *Breaking Away from Broken Windows: Baltimore Neighborhoods and the Nationwide Fight Against Crime, Grime, Fear, and Decline.* Boulder, CO: Westview Press.

Taylor, Ralph B., and Stephen Gottfredson. 1986. "Environmental Design, Crime, and Prevention: An Examination of Community Dynamics." Pp. 387-416 In Albert J. Reiss, Jr. and Michael Tonry (eds.), *Communities and Crime.* Chicago: University of Chicago Press.

Taylor, Ralph B., Stephen D. Gottfredson, and Sidney Brower. 1984. "Block Crime and Fear: Defensible Space, Local Social Ties, and Territorial Functioning." *Journal of Research in Crime and Delinquency* 21: 303-331.

Vélez, María. B. 2001. "The Role of Public Social Control in Urban Neighborhoods: A Multilevel Analysis of Victimization Risk." *Criminology* 39: 837-864.

Wacquant, Loic J.D. 1993. "Urban Outcasts: Stigma and Division in the Black American Ghetto and the French Urban Periphery." *International Journal of Urban and Regional Research* 17: 366-383.

Wallace, Deborah, and Roderick Wallace. 1999. *A Plague on Your Houses: How New York Was Burned Down and National Public Health Crumbled.* New York: Verso.

Wilkes, Rima, and John Iceland. 2004. "Hypersegregation in the Twenty-First Century." *Demography* 41: 23-36.

Wilson, William Julius. 1987. *The Truly Disadvantaged: The Inner City, the Underclass, and Public Policy.* Chicago: University of Chicago Press.

————. 1996. *When Work Disappears: The World of the New Urban Poor.* New York: Alfred A. Knopf.

Wooldredge, John, and Amy Thistlethwaite. 2003. "Neighborhood Structure and Race-Specific Rates of Intimate Assault." *Criminology* 41: 393-422.

Wyly, Elvin K., and Steven R. Holloway. 1999. "The *Color of Money* Revisited: Racial Lending Patterns in Atlanta's Neighborhoods." *Housing Policy Debate* 10:

Part III

Theories of Power and Peace

7

The Status of Empirical Research in Radical Criminology

*Michael J. Lynch, Herman Schwendinger,
and Julia Schwendinger*

We are pleased to participate in the important task of reviewing the state of empirical knowledge within the field of radical criminology. It is, perhaps, an historic event that radicals have been invited to represent the state of empirical knowledge within their field of research. Too often, radical criminological research and knowledge has been excluded from broader discussions of crime and criminal justice, and we gladly accept this opportunity to share the many contributions of radical criminology with a broader audience.

The research results radicals have produced provide alternative explanations of crime and justice. Given that: 1) more traditional explanations have been privileged within criminology both theoretically and empirically, and with respect to policy; 2) many of these approaches provide weak explanations of the aggregate level of crime from an empirical stand point; and 3) that crime reduction policies based on traditional theories have not provided a solution to the problem of crime, it may be time to pay greater attention to radical explanations of crime.

The empirical knowledge produced by radical criminologists is limited in volume when compared to the number of quantitative studies found within other areas of criminology. Volume aside, radicals have produced persistent empirical findings addressing a diverse array of crime and justice issues. Yet, these studies are not referenced by either critical or traditional criminologists. The designation of studies as "radical" or "critical" remains sufficient to deter mainstream readers—even those in an academic audience—from familiarizing themselves with a study's content, while the designation as "empirical" is sufficient to repel critical criminologists. This circumstance helps maintain the marginalization of radical research and limits the dissemination of knowledge produced by radical criminologists.

Despite the fact that empirical radical literature is not extensive, the findings are substantially persistent and robust enough to merit consideration. Before beginning our review, we present a few additional comments concerning the neglect of knowledge produced by radical criminology.

The Neglect of Radical Criminology

Four factors contribute to the neglect of radical research: 1) differences between mainstream and radical criminological assumptions; 2) stereotypes of radical criminology; 3) mainstream ideology; and 4) the domination of postmodern explanations within critical criminology (Russell 2002). Each factor is addressed briefly below.

The neglect of radical research is, in part, due to differing etiological assumptions employed in mainstream and radical approaches.[1] Mainstream theory favors individual level explanation while radicals examine crime relative to the structures in which individuals live. For radicals these structures—which include economic forces and conditions; class, gender and race relationships, structures, hierarchies and identities; and political and other elements of social structure—not only affect the individual's actions and *motivations*, but an individual's *opportunities* for conformity and crime, the individual's *life-course*, the range of actions that are defined and sanctioned as crime within a society, and the probability that a sanction *will be applied*.

For radicals, influential structures exist at different levels of causal priority. Tertiary or *immediate social structures*, including racial, ethnic, gender, and class identities, are consequences of primary and secondary forms of social and economic structure. Secondary or *socializing structures* contain race, ethnic, gender, and class as structures, political systems, and social structures (neighborhood characteristics, family structures, peer relations, and the organization of work and education, etc.). P*rimary structures* include the economic system and the movement of history, which are the organizing forces that define the limits and range of smaller social organizing structures.

To understand the situation of individuals requires connecting them to the social structures to which they are intimately connected (immediate structures) and, in turn, connecting those structures to socializing and primary structures. This lesson was long ago offered by Marx in his analysis of class relationships under capitalism and restated for the contemporary social theorist by C. Wright Mills (1959) in *The Sociological Imagination*. Mills argued that in order to understand contemporary social problems, the life of the individual (biography) must be contextualized by connecting it to broader social and economic forms of organization (what Mills called history). Radical criminologists employ these calls to understand the individual using theories of structured action (Messerschmidt 1997), structured choices (Lynch, Michalowski, and Groves 2000), by connecting subcultural identities and structural locations (Schwendinger and Schwendinger 1997a, b), exposing how political economic forces structure and group life courses (Lynch 1996), and by examining the fit between structuralism and subjectivity (Groves and Lynch 1990). While level of analysis issues explain a certain degree of neglect between these two approaches, this neglect also has other sources.

Too often, radical criminology is represented by a dated stereotype which states that radical criminology is: 1) "abstract" and theoretically dense; 2) has minimal relevance to describing society or the behavior of individuals; 3) unable to generate relevant crime policy; and 4) lacking empirical merit and research (for an exception, see Siegel 2002). To be sure, postmodern criminology has helped to maintain this dated and stereotypical view of radical criminology. But, radicals are not postmodernists (Russell 2002) and confusion of these critical approaches contributes to a criminological climate that justifies neglecting radical research. Minimal effort is applied to test (or when tested, using measures that are inconsistent with theoretical assumptions) radical theories of crime. Mainstream criminologists, for example, do not often include radically oriented variables in their research as control variables. While criminologists are expected to include variables that tap alternative explanations, these alternatives are restricted to mainstream explanations (e.g., control, learning, anomie, social disorganization, and life-course theories). The exclusion of radically oriented variables derails any impartial, scientific effort to discover the factors that cause or produce crime, or which affect the operation of law, regulatory agencies, or the criminal justice system.

Contrary to the antiempirical critical criminology stereotype stands the research of numerous radical criminologists, including Willem Bonger, the first radical criminologist. Although parts of *Criminality and Economic Conditions* (1916) described historical changes in capitalist societies, Bonger felt that a scientific inquiry into the causes of criminality, made possible by the collection of criminal statistics previously employed by Quetelet and other mathematicians, was a necessary element of any analysis of crime. Consequently, he delineated the social conditions prevailing among members of a particular social class (e.g., within the petty bourgeoisie, the stable working-class or among its most destitute families) and examined the impact of these conditions on crime. Bonger's work contains a variety of graphs produced by political economists, including Paul Lafargue, Marx's son-in-law.[2] From its very beginning, anchored in the empirical methods preferred by Marx, radical criminologists have maintained a commitment to employing data to analyze how political economic forces affect human behavior and to engineer appropriate social policies that would maximize human potential.

Indeed, over the past fifteen years, radical criminologists have published numerous empirical studies addressing a wide range of factors including: crime and delinquency; public health and safety; violence against women; victimization; racial bias in criminal justice processes; corporate, white collar and state crime; trends in imprisonment, policing and crime; media reporting of crime; and environmental harms, crimes and justice. This research draws on literature from economics, political science, public policy, sociology, anthropology, environmental science, geography, epidemiology, and medicine. Variables in this literature include measures of: race, class, gender, economic, and income inequality; unemployment; long cycles of economic production; the rate of surplus value; social structures of accumulation; indexes of racial concentration and dissimilarity; measures of corporate concentration and size; subcultural associations; chemical concentrations; social distance and social networks; and measures of spatial proximity. These studies also employ a variety of empirical methods and statistical procedures: ordinary least squares regression; negative binomial regression; time-series analysis; geographic dispersion and mapping; and social distance scaling techniques. This array of studies, variables and methods do not fit the old stereotype of radical criminology as abstract and empirically untestable or deficient.

It is not possible to review all of this research here. Thus, in the following sections we restrict our review of the empirical literature to topics that have been central to our research concerns: corporate and environmental crimes and harms; the factors that influence crime and justice trends; and adolescent subcultures and delinquency. In so doing, we hope to illuminate the distinctive approach that radical criminology takes to issues either ignored or treated in a narrow way by traditional criminology.

Environmental Harms and Justice

Environmental Harms

Environmental harms are, perhaps, the single most serious problem facing the world today. With the exception of nuclear or biological war that can devastate populations within moments, no other problem poses a more immediate threat to human existence. Global warming, for example, has already melted the polar ice cap sufficiently to raise sea-levels, threatening the existence of human civilizations on several small Pacific islands (Burns and Lynch 2004). Recent evidence links global warming to the accelerated extinction of numerous species of animals. In short, environmental harms can have tremendous impacts that span the face of the globe.

One of the primary concerns is the impact of exposure to hazardous waste on human health. Epidemiological, medical and geographic research illustrates the vast human costs of exposure to hazardous waste sites and hazardous waste more generally (for a criminological review, see Lynch and Stretesky 2002). Medical and epidemiological studies demonstrate that spatial proximity to hazardous waste sites is related to a host of health problems, from cancer to lung alignments (e.g., emphysema and asthma), to reproductive harms and birth defects, to kidney and urinary tract diseases, and to less publicized outcomes such as hyperactivity, learning disabilities, and IQ deficits (Colburn,

Duamoski, and Myers 1997; Davis 2002; Rodricks 1992; Liu 2001; Pueschel, Linakis, and Anderson 1996; Steingraber 1998; Wargo 1998). Exposure to the toxic substances in hazardous waste sites account for only one of the many environmental hazardous that confront modern societies.

Exposure to pesticides and other synthetic compounds and wastes, including dioxin, also pose significant human and environmental health concerns (Colburn et al. 1997). Much is known about the dangers of exposure to pesticides and synthetic chemicals (Colburn et al. 1997). Rachel Carson brought synthetic chemical harms into the national spot-light in her ground-breaking book, *Silent Spring* (1962). Since then, numerous studies have supported Carson's claim. Recent evidence suggests that synthetic chemicals act as "hormone mimics" and possess the ability to alter normal biological processes, including cell growth, which explains the synthetic chemical-cancer link (Colburn et al. 1997; Steingraber 1998). Some synthetic estrogen hormone mimics act in the womb to enhance aggressive behavior. Through a series of complicated experiments, early exposure to elevated *estrogen* (not testosterone) levels in the womb associated with synthetic chemical exposure has been clearly linked to aggression in male mice.

A host of additional studies on environmental toxins and synthetic chemicals could be reviewed. Overwhelmingly, medical and epidemiological research produced by independent scientists (i.e., scientists who do not work for or who are not supported by chemical or waste industry grants) has demonstrated the nature and extent of harms associated with synthetic chemical pollution (Lynch and Stretesky 2002). But the fact that these chemicals cause harm is not the entire story. Extending medical research findings, geographers, environmental scientists, and those involved in the environmental justice movement have established a link between patterns of exposure to toxic chemicals and community race and class characteristics. Evidence that toxic exposure patterns are class- and race-linked has become an important aspect of studying environmental harms.

Extending medical and environmental research, radical criminologists have built the case for labeling these harms as crimes and have also taken part in conducting research exposing the association between race, class and chemical crimes. Compared to the types of issues criminologists typically examine, the study of environmental toxins appears unfamiliar and even alien. Environmental toxins, however, pose an expansive form of harm that result in greater violence (measured as deaths and illnesses) than those related to street crime (Burns and Lynch 2004). Call these harms what you like—environmental crime, toxic crimes, hazardous waste crimes, corporate violence—but there is little doubt that they should be a focus of criminological research as forms of victimization that result from activities that violate regulatory and administrative laws. It is important that criminologists address these crimes for three reasons. First, these crimes are widespread and cause extensive harm. Second, studying these crimes calls attention to the behavior of powerful social actors who normally escape the gaze of criminological inspection. Third, the distribution of environmental crimes can be used to broaden discussions of a central theme in criminological research: the meaning of justice and the effort to "do justice" or remedy wrongs.

Recently, radicals have published several studies addressing the issue of hazardous waste distribution which is a central theme in the literature on distributive justice. In some cases, this research is descriptive or involves an argument detailing why these behaviors ought to be treated as any other crime and become subjects of criminological investigation. Presently, the empirical criminological literature on environmental crime is limited and greater attention to expanding empirical studies in this area is warranted.

Numerous methodologies are used to study environmental harms in three areas: 1) environmental or distributive justice approaches that map hazardous waste locations and the proximity of these sites to communities of varying racial, ethnic and class composition; 2) community spatial proximity to toxins that possess the potential to alter human behavior; and 3) assessment of fines for violation of environmental laws and the relationship between community class, race and ethnic characteristics and penalties amounts. This literature is reviewed below.

Environmental Justice

Environmental justice research examines the question of whether the racial, ethnic and class composition of a community affects the probability of exposure to toxins and hazardous waste. This question has broad social justice, public health, and, in some cases, crime related implications. Environmental justice studies have extraordinary importance to the fields of criminology and criminal justice because they tell us about the structures of justice within a society, the level of (in)justice a society is willing to tolerate and the extent of a society's commitment to equal treatment of its citizens.

Specifically, environmental justice involves the right to be free from environmental harms. Because the world is currently filled with environmental harms, environmental justice revolves around assessments of the distribution of environmental harms. Theoretically, environmental harms should be equally distributed and laws and regulations that protect communities should also be applied equally so that community race, class, and ethnic characteristics are unrelated to exposure or enforcement outcomes.

Traditionally, the environmental justice movement has often been associated with perspectives on racial discrimination. In a radical perspective, a broader view of the "justice question" is taken, and radicals hypothesize that the class, race and ethnic hierarchies and structures found in a society affect patterns of toxin exposure and enforcement of law (as will be discussed below). Given prevailing power structures and their association with race, class and ethnicity, evidence of unjust toxic waste exposure patterns is expected to be highly skewed, meaning that minorities and lower-class communities will be disproportionately exposed to toxic waste. This form of injustice is compounded by other injustices that relate to race, class and ethnicity including hierarchical divisions of power, income, wealth, and access to employment, that impact access to health care and legal remedies.

A main concern in the environmental justice literature is that exposure to hazardous waste poses quality of life concerns. For example, proximity to hazardous waste production, treatment, storage and disposal facilities impacts disease prevalence and incidence and elevates not only the likelihood of diseases such as cancers and breathing disorders, but also impacts other biological processes, such as hormonal systems, brain and CNS functions (e.g., Liu 2001). Once affected, these processes can generate a host of disorders leading to deficits in intellectual performance (IQ, learning, school performance, learning disabilities, mental retardation, elevated level of school dropouts, etc.), behavioral impairment (increased aggression, sensitivity to stimulus, low frustration tolerance, hyperactivity, diminished self-control, attention deficit disorders, impulsivity, violence, crime, antisocial behavior, etc.), and biological functions and outcomes (neurological disorders, low birth weight babies, developmental delays, etc.) that have been studied as causes of crime (Stretesky and Lynch 2001).

Environmental justice questions are typically examined using mapping techniques (e.g., GIS) and the use of cross-sectional time series data has allowed researchers to address complex time and space dependent relationships and causal processes that impinge on environmental justice issues (Stretesky and Hogan 1998). These studies have been more common within geography, sociology, and epidemiology than within criminology. The number of criminological studies are expected to expand as criminologists become more familiar with the numerous environmental hazard data sets available for analysis (for a discussion, see Burns and Lynch 2004). Currently, all known empirical studies within criminology have been undertaken by radical criminologists.

In a series of studies, Stretesky and Lynch examined the association between various measures of community race, ethnic and class characteristics and exposure to a variety of hazardous waste. These studies examine proximity to: 1) accidental chemical releases; 2) superfund sites; 3) toxic hazards defined by different Environmental Protection Agency measures that include the Toxic Release Inventory (TRI), the Biannual Reporting System data (BRS) and Comprehensive Environmental Response and Liability Information System data (CERLIS)); and 4) environmental hazards near schools. Using geographic based analysis, Stretesky and Lynch have provided evidence of several persistent findings.

1. Minorities, especially African-Americans, are much more likely to live in census tracts that are proximate to hazardous waste sites than whites (Lynch, Stretesky, and McGurrin 2001; Stretesky and Lynch 1999a, 1999b, 2003).

2. Low-income groups are more likely to live in census tracts that are closer to hazardous waste sites than high income groups. This relationship is mediated by or enhanced by the racial composition of neighborhoods (Stretesky and Lynch 1999a, 1999b, 2003).

3. The racial composition of census tracts is associated with proximity to several different indicators of hazardous waste locations (Lynch et al. 2001; Stretesky and Hogan, 1998; Stretesky and Lynch 1999a, 1999b, 2003).

4. The racial composition of schools has been shown to be related to the distance of public schools to hazardous waste sites. Specifically, the higher the percentage of African-Americans in a school, the closer that school is to a hazardous waste site (Stretesky and Lynch 2003). This finding is of particular concern because young children are more susceptible to the negative health consequences of many hazardous wastes than adults.

5. Not only are minority and low-income communities closer to hazardous waste sites, they are also more proximate to the location of chemical accidents than white communities (Stretesky and Lynch 1999a). In short, there is a predicable pattern to chemical accidents that is, in part, explained by the racial and class composition of an area.

6. Ethnicity effects, or results for Hispanic communities vary. In some cases, ethnicity effects are evident, while in others, these effects are absent. The presence of effects for Hispanic communities is more difficult to establish and may be confounded by the unique location of some Hispanic communities in rural/farming areas and by the lack of measurement of rural toxic waste problems (e.g., Stretesky, Johnston, and Arney 2003).

These findings not only speak to issues of distributive justice, but can also be used to examine crime causation.

Exposure to Behavioral Altering Toxic Hazards

The primary source of information on the effects of behavioral altering environmental toxins is the medical and epidemiological literature. Within criminology, empirical studies of chemical-altering substances have been largely limited to the study of drugs and biological processes. Environmental toxins, however, play an important role in altering behavior by disrupting CNS, hormonal and endocrine systems. In comparison to medical and epidemiological literature on behavioral toxins, criminological literature is extremely limited (on medical research, see Dietrich, Ris, Succop, Berger, and Bornschein 2001; Needleman, McFarland, Ness, Fienberg, and Tobin 2002; Needleman, Riess, Tobin, Biesecker, and Greenhouse 1996; Pihl and Ervin

1990; on criminological research, see Denno 1990; Lynch and Stretesky 2002; Stetesky and Lynch 2001, 2004).

The behavioral outcomes of exposure to toxins is not widely known. One toxin for which extensive behavioral outcome information is available is the element lead (Pb). Medically, Pb exposure impacts brain, CNS and hormonal functions and results in a host of outcomes criminologists have examined as causes of crime including: low birth-weight, attention deficit disorder, patterns of aggression, mental retardation, learning disabilities, hyperactivity, impulsivity, low frustration tolerance, low self-control, antisocial behavior, neurological dysfunction, increased rates of school failure, behavioral problems in school, poor academic achievement, dropping out, IQ deficiencies, and developmental delays (for a discussion, see Bellinger 1996).

Why would radical criminologists be interested in Pb exposure patterns? Existing research indicates Pb exposure is a function of class and race (Stretesky 2003), both in terms of hierarchies of power or in economic terms and as a result of the spatial geography of American cities (Lynch 2004). In short, the economic and racial structure of the U.S. has translated into an urban ecology that segregates classes and races. This pattern of segregation forces minorities and the lower class into physical locations more proximate to sources of Pb contamination (in terms of production, distribution, and disposal). When coupled with adverse economic conditions experienced in segregated lower-class and minority communities, Pb is capable of producing elevated levels of criminal offending. Research by Stretesky and Lynch has demonstrated a geographic relationship between lead and homicide (2001) and lead and violent and property crime rates (2004) across all U.S. census tracts (N = 3111). For example, census tracts with elevated air lead concentration have homicide rates four times the rate found in counties with the lowest levels of air lead (Stretesky and Lynch 2001).

Connecting toxin exposure to behavioral ramifications and the geography and economics of manufacturing and pollution is a recent development. The ability of radical criminology to explain the patterns of Pb's and crime's distribution has shown promise. There is, however, much more work to be done on related chemicals and their potential impact on criminal behavior. For instance, extant medical research indicates that numerous synthetic chemicals can cause aggression by altering hormonal balances and disrupting traditional masculine and feminine behavior patterns (Colburn et al. 1997; Hestein, Vrugdenhil, Slijper, Pulder, and Weisglas-Kuperus 2002). While traditional criminology has undertaken research on the relationship between hormones and crime, it has done so only at the individual level, has not taken account of more recent medical findings and has failed to address the ecological, racial and class dimensions accompanying exposure to behavioral-altering toxins.

Penalizing Polluters and Other Corporate Law Violators

Recent research by radicals has examined factors that influence Environmental Protection Agency (EPA) penalties against oil refineries (Lynch, Stretesky, and Burns 2004a, 2004b), the use of fines by the National Highway Traffic Safety Administration (NHTSA) (Burns and Lynch, 2002) and various Environmental Protection Agency responses to violations of environmental regulations (Burns and Lynch 2004). Lynch, Stretesky, and Burns (2004a) studied the effect of community race, ethnicity and income on fines levied by the EPA against oil refineries during 1998 and 1999 (N = 60) for violations of the Clean Air Act, Clean Water Act and the Resource Conservation and Recovery Act. They found that penalty amounts (in parentheses) were much lower in black ($108,563) versus white ($341,590) census tracts, and in lower-income ($259,784) versus high-income ($334,267) census tracts controlling for the effects of the seriousness of violation, the number of past violations, facility inspection history and production level, and the EPA region in which the violating refinery was situated. These results indicate that the EPA does a poor job of providing equal protection to racially and economically diverse communities.

In a related study, Lynch, Stretesky, and Burns (2004b) examined a more extensive sample of oil refinery penalties. This article addressed an important level of aggregation issue in environmental research concerning differences produced by zip codes and census tracts analysis. In comparison to census tract analyses, zip code analyses showed attenuated and non-significant community race and class effects on EPA penalties. The authors argued zip codes are small geographic units in comparison to census tracts and that it is likely that attenuated penalty effect patterns reflect the level at which fining decisions are made by the EPA.

Burns and Lynch (2002) studied the use of fines by the National Highway Traffic Safety Administration (NHTSA) to address violations of the Traffic Safety Act (TSA), the Costs Savings Act (CSA), and the Corporate Average Fuel Economy (CAFE) standard between 1970 and 1996. These Acts address three distinct issues: public safety (TSA), economic fraud (CSA) and environmental health (CAFE). Total fines meted out for violations of these acts over this period was quite large—$ 401,978,387. Average fines per violation however, were small for violation of TSA ($9,092) and CSA ($ 1,351) violations. In contrast, the average CAFE fine was $ 5,494,405. The largest number of fines were meted out under TSA (71.6 percent), while CAFE accounted for largest percentage of fine amounts (88.9 percent). Though significant financially, there were, on average, only six CAFE violations per year. CAFE fines appear to be of questionable worth as a means of altering vehicle manufacturers' behaviors and protecting the environment since the costs of these violations are easily passed on to vehicle purchasers. Consumers who purchase inefficient vehicles, particularly those in the luxury and SUV class, are the most adversely affected. In addition, despite the size of CAFE fines, they do not appear to act as a deterrent, and 88 percent of CAFE violators were repeat offenders. A significant political effect was also noted that distinguished the fining behavior of NHTSA under the Reagan administration from its behavior under other administrations. Under Reagan, NHTSA more heavily pursued CSA violators that, in contrast to CAFE and TSA, target small automobile retail businesses, particularly used car sales.

Economic Structures, Crime, and Punishment

Radical theories endeavor to explain the distribution and level of crime in society in relation to the structure and unfolding history of political-economic relations. This point is often misrepresented in traditional criminology where the structural arguments of radicals are reduced to individual level variables and measures and applied to cross-sectional studies of official crime data. Class effects typically are not supported when radical variables are measured at the individual level. This outcome is most likely due to the lack of variation in the class standing of persons charged as criminals. More appropriate tests of radical propositions would employ aggregated time-series data that include structural variables or data that span divergent justice processes which are capable of representing crimes and persons from various social classes.

Early empirical studies that support radical criminological contentions focused on: 1) the relationship between economic inequality and police functions (Jacobs 1978, 1979; Jacobs and Britt 1979; Lizotte, Mercy, and Monkkenon 1982); 2) examinations of the Rusche-Kirchheimer hypothesis concerning the relationship between economic marginalization and levels of incarceration (Box and Hale 1982; Greenberg 1977, 1980; Jankovic 1977; Laffargue and Godefroy 1989; Yeager 1979); 3) the influence of extra-legal factors on criminal sentencing and criminal processing outcomes (Lizotte 1978; Jankovic 1978); 4) economic marginalization and crime (Box and Hale 1983), and 5) crime and capital accumulation processes (Humphries and Wallace 1980).

Beginning in the late 1980s, empirical studies undertaken by radicals were extended to new economic measures, yielding research on: 1) the effects of social structures of accumulation (Carlson and Michalowski 1997; Michalowski and Carlson 1999) and long cycles of economic development (Barlow and Barlow 1995; Barlow, Barlow, and Johnson 1996; Lynch, Hogan, and Stretesky 1999) on crime, punishment, and criminal justice legislation; and 2) the impact of the extraction of surplus value on imprisonment (Lynch 1988) and crime rates (Lynch, Groves, and Lizotte 1994), and on police strength and expenditures (Nalla, Lynch, and Leiber 1997). Contemporary radical research also continued to address alternative empirical tests of the Rusche-Kirchheimer hypothesis (Chiricos and Bales 1991; Chiricos and DeLone 1992; Lessan

1991; Michalowski and Pearson 1990), the empirical validity of deterrence and the effects of rapidly expanding prison populations on crime rates (Lynch 1999), and the impact of community social structures on crime (Sampson and Groves 1989).

Over the past twenty-five years, radical criminologists have tested various hypotheses that examined the influence of macro-economic processes on trends in criminal justice processes. The results of this research have consistently indicated that a variety of criminal justice processes—legislation, policing, courts, and punishment—have been shaped by and function to control class conflict. Because class conflict is a complex phenomenon, radicals have measured its dimensions using a variety of indicators that include unemployment, marginalization, surplus value, economic inequality, long cycles, and social structures of accumulation. With the exception of unemployment—which, theoretically, is the weakest measure that can be used to represent radical criminology's assumptions—these variables have not been included in orthodox criminological studies, perhaps indicating that the orthodox view is less "scientific" and "objective" than its proponents claims.

Long cycles, social structures of accumulation (SSAs), and the extraction of surplus value serve as excellent examples of uniquely radical measures that are preferable to more simple models focusing on the relationship between unemployment and crime. Theoretically, radicals argue that trends in street crime and punishment should reflect trends in the quantity and quality of marginalization so that as economic marginalization expands, so, too, will crime and punishment. Because it is difficult to measure marginalization, early researchers had relied on measures of economic inequality and unemployment rates (see studies cited above). The results gathered from studies focusing on the association between unemployment and imprisonment, though largely favoring the radical position (see Chiricos and DeLone 1992), were inconsistent and seemed to vary with the time period under study.

One reason for this inconsistency was discovered by Michalowski and Carlson (1999), who used a time dependent analysis based on the theory of social structures of accumulation (SSAs) to assess the varying impact unemployment had on incarceration rates from 1933 through 1992. Consistent with SSA theory, Michalowski and Carlson argued that labor market conditions and state reactions to labor market conditions were not constants, but varied with the characteristics of a specific SSA. For example, when the SSA was marked by economic exploration (1933 to 1947) when investment was beginning to expand, the relationship between unemployment and incarceration was found to be positive but weak. The weak relationship for this period is due to the existence of other structural factors that attenuated the need to rely on imprisonment as a form of social control over the marginalized population (e.g., the expansion of social services, the draining off of surplus labor by WWII), and the need to maintain a population of free surplus laborers to enter the labor force and maintain a level of competition for employment that would minimize the price of labor while demand for labor expanded. Under conditions of economic consolidation (1948 to 1966) that are marked by a steady state of economic production and job growth, the relationship between unemployment and incarceration is weakest and, in the short term, may be inverted. During the period of decay (1967 to 1979), the unemployment-imprisonment relationship was strongly positive and the use of imprisonment as a form of social control over marginalized groups expanded as blue-collar jobs disappeared and racial disparities in employment accelerated. Research from this period most strongly supports the marginalization thesis and encompasses the period from which data were collected for the majority of early radical empirical studies of this relationship. The most recent SSA of exploration (1980 to 1992) features several characteristics that force the rate of incarceration and the rate of unemployment to become disassociated. In part, the lack of an unemployment effect is technical and has to do with official redefinition of how unemployment was measured. In addition, the idea of marginalization itself expanded so that it was more closely tied to racial characteristics and to crime control policies such as the "war on drugs."

In an alternative argument, Lynch (1988) pointed out that unemployment was an imprecise measure of the concept of economic marginalization and, more specifically, of the idea of surplus populations as defined by Marx. Lynch further argued that because the production of surplus populations could be tied directly to other key economic features of capitalism and because these processes—unlike the size of the surplus population—could be measured in a valid manner, it would be possible to employ these measures to test radical theories of crime and punishment. Specifically, Lynch relied on a measurement called the rate of surplus value that, following Marx's work, is defined as both an objective measure of labor's alienation and a measure of the production of surplus populations. Lynch hypothesized the rate of incarceration and the rate of surplus value should co-vary; his empirical analysis, which controlled for the effects of several traditional explanations for trends in incarceration, supported his contention.

Several others studies support these general contentions. Researchers have found, for example, that long cycles influence legislative trends so that more crime legislation—especially legislation focusing on marginal populations—is passed during phases of economic decay than in other periods (Barlow and Barlow 1995; Barlow et al. 1996; Lynch et al. 1999). Other research has shown that both crime rates (Lynch et al. 1994) and levels of police strength (Nalla et al. 1997) expand as the rate of surplus value, which measures the extent of economic marginalization, increases. Taken together, these studies support the radical position that trends in crime and punishment have economic origins and that both also are associated with economic marginalization, sometimes in rather complex ways (e.g., Michalowski and Carlson 1999).

The research reviewed above does not exhaust the array of empirical studies that radical criminologists have undertaken on these issues. Today's radicals have also assessed the biases in criminal justice processes by examining racial, ethnic and gender biases in courts, policing, and the correctional system (for a review, see Lynch and Michalowski 2005). These additional biases, which we cannot fully address due to space limitations (but, see discussion of environmental justice above), add an additional layer to the radical claim that criminal justice processes are influenced by, and, in turn, support structured inequalities.

Working Outside the Cage: Material and Cultural Structures

For a century, radical criminologists have studied criminogenic conditions at various levels. Several examples of these studies were cited previously. The current section reviews the empirical research conducted by Herman and Julia Schwendinger (1985, 1997a, 1997b) which examines how "mediating variables" complicate the straightforward relationships between economic conditions and crime discussed earlier. While radicals, like their conventional counterparts, tend to rely on analyses of official data or survey data, the Schwendingers have employed various alternative research methods to study violence and delinquency.

For instance, their work, *Rape and Inequality* (1985), drew on a Marxian study conducted by anthropologist, Karen Sacks (1979), who differentiated modes of production among four societies: the Mbuti, Lovedu, Mpondo and Baganda. Following Sacks, the Schwendingers hypothesized that the levels of violence across these societies were influenced by their modes of production. They tested this hypothesis by estimating the degree of violence reported in children's play, child rearing, gender relations, social sanctions, and relations within these societies using the *Human Area Relations Files*, a cross-cultural compendium of first-hand anthropological observations. They found that the distribution of violence in these spheres of life systematically increased as one moved from: 1) a classless society whose communal mode of production relied on hunting and gathering (Mbuti) to,; 2) a society with settled agriculture and the inter-familial exchange of cattle, controlled by elder sisters who used the cattle as dowry (Lovedu); to 3) an agrarian-market society that used cattle as commodities (Mpondo) and; to 4) a semi-feudal class society that celebrated imperial conquest (Baganda). In short, this research supported the general radical contention that a society's economic system or mode of production impacts social life, including the level and type of violence found within a society.

Beyond Modes of Production: The Economic Underpinnings of Delinquent Discourse

In addition to examining how modes of production impact levels of violence across societies, the Schwendingers also investigated how materialist theories explain levels of violence across groups within a society. This led them to develop a unique multidimensional research strategy that often yielded results that diverge from those offered by mainstream criminologists. For example, Sykes and Matza (1957) suggested that delinquents used "techniques of neutralization" that "bent the moral implications of their acts" when justifying delinquent conduct. Herman Schwendinger, however, had observed that delinquents expressed different opinions about criminal acts in private interviews compared to public interviews (when interviewed with peers or friends). He reasoned that the differences in these discourses could not be confirmed using traditional questionnaires administered by strangers in an artificial environment, and, instead, opted to employ a field experiment to assess the impact of peer presence and relationships on the moral discourse of delinquents.

To do so, the Schwendingers (1985) designed experimental sociodramas that require groups of delinquents and non-delinquents to argue about plans to commit criminal acts. The dialogues produced by this experiment refuted Sykes and Matza's contentions and, in fact, indicated that *nondelinquent groups were more likely* to neutralize guilt due to their subscription to "dominant moral norms." In contrast, the rationalizations uttered by the *delinquent* groups overwhelmingly appealed to minimizing risks or other tactical considerations. Individual gang members' responses tended to avoid humiliation, ostracism and even violence from their peers, especially their leaders, by keeping their feelings about the moral implications of their crimes hidden. Further, when associating with peers, an individual gang member's justifications for committing a crime conformed to *group* norms regardless of his/her *private* feelings.

To explain the discrepancy between public and private rhetoric, the Schwendingers (1985) adopted and extended the insights provided by Mary and Abraham May Edel's (1959) *Anthropology and Ethics*. They proposed that early in life everyone learned principles for organizing moral discourse (e.g., Commandments, the "golden rule, etc.), cultivated a "rhetoric of egoism" (i.e., "honesty because it is good policy"), and adopted an "instrumental rhetoric" that employed moral discourse to legitimize exploitative relationships (e.g., "she asked for it"). These organizing principles were socially acquired and achieve credibility because people *experience* their consequences; however, only some are internalized as "private" discourse and generalized to most situations. People, however, also engage in "mode switching" (like "code switching" which involves the shift from black English to standard English and back again)—where one mode of moral rhetoric may be used with children, with family members or among close friends, and another may be used in front of criminal court judges and at church meetings.

In the bigger picture, however, the general nature of discourses are determined by economic factors. The rhetoric of egoism, for example, is organized around equal exchange principles common in market economies. The adages cultivated by instrumental rhetoric are qualitatively different. When delinquents adopted a "hustling ethic" or contended it is advisable to "screw others before they screw you!" because the world is filled with *"Givers"* and *"Takers,"* they reflected the inequalities that are prevalent in the class structure, the corridors of power in Washington, DC and the illegal adolescent economies of local communities. Using this explanation, the Schwendingers were able to connect individual actions, to group inclinations and cultures, and to broader cultural institutions and economic structures that shaped each level of the underlying response. In this way, they were able to use empirical data to illustrate how individual responses and discourse were influenced by group dynamics and cultural and economic contexts—key themes in the radical approach to crime.

Stradom as Structure

The Schwendingers (1985) also relied on anthropological methods in a four-year study of delinquent gangs. During the first year, the evidence refuted the "delinquent subcultures" predicted by Merton's anomie theory. Consequently, Herman Schwendinger adopted a "non-reductionist" or contextual strategy that assumed the majority of delinquents were members of diffuse subcultural networks tied to the social class composition of families within school districts. This hypothesis was based on field observations conducted in middle and working class communities.

The Schwendingers argued that adolescent subcultures organized by "socialites," "street corner youth," and "intellectuals," among others (ignoring local differences in terminology), represented life styles that regularly appeared in school districts throughout the country (see also, Berger 1991). They also discovered the individual groups within subcultures were usually nested in *"stratified domains of informal groups."* They used the word "stradom" to describe these networks because the relationships were different than those associated with existing terminology (e.g., "crowds," "social circles" or "gangs"). More importantly, stradoms were, themselves, incorporated within stratified *systems* of informal relationships. *Stradom did not stand alone;* rather, stradom exist only as part of a network of relationships.

The Schwendingers found that their references to an *upper middle-class street corner* stratum and a *working-class socialite* stratum confused colleagues who habitually employed hierarchical social relationship images generated decades earlier by Warner, Hollingshead, and other structural functionalists. For example, Warner and Lunt (1942:112) asserted that "Our interview material attested to the fact all cliques fell into an interlocking vertical hierarchy which cross-cuts the entire society," while Hollingshead's (1949) argued that all peer networks were sorted into five distinct social-classes. The Schwendingers proposed that the subcultural networks they observed required a much more sophisticated theory of how *social class relations influenced the formation of peer networks.*

Traditionally, when applied to adolescent networks, the concept of social strata denoted *all-inclusive* networks that were directly determined by parental social-class status. After observing subcultures from the barrios of Los Angeles to Beverly Hills, the Schwendingers found that the economically stratified networks composed of high school groups never included the entire local high school population and a theoretically significant residual category of nonstradom formations remained. In addition, they found that informal peer groups were relatively independent, voluntaristic entities influenced by *local inequalities* that were partly (but not wholly) independent of social class relations. In fact, even though the Schwendingers recognized economic segregation of, for example, residential communities and high schools *objectively* constricted variation in friendship choices, they discovered that when adolescents with different socioeconomic statuses actually had the *latitude to choose* companions *voluntarily*, their choices were not *usually* determined directly by the economic status of their parents. Certainly, socialites were more likely to belong to families whose socioeconomic statuses were *relatively* higher than, say, families of street corner youth in the same community. But there were too many other adolescents whose friendship choices could not be predicted from family status. Indeed, numerous empirical studies supported the Schwendingers' assessment of the variation in adolescent friendship choices (for a discussion, see Schwendinger and Schwendinger 1985). In addition, the Schwendingers' field observations uncovered status anomalies such as groups of *working*-class youth emulating *socialite* life styles and upper *middle*-class groups that emulated *street corner* life styles. In other words, while social-class did not strictly determine subcultural membership, it influences the *cultural* parameters and *relative* magnitudes of the subcultures and appeared to cultivate these subcultures among youth in all classes.

In sum, stradoms are informally stratified adolescent networks with distinctive life styles, and standards of social worth that define struggles for honor. While the composition of some stradoms is influenced by economic factors, stradom networks are more akin to Max Weber's "status groups" than economic strata. Even among socialites, "money and property are not in themselves status qualifications, although they may lead to them; and the lack of property is not in itself a status disqualification, although this may be a reason for it" (Weber 1968: 306). In short, adolescent subcultures should not be hierarchically arranged merely because hegemonic-class standpoints assign the highest status to the socialites and the lowest to the street corner youth.

Nor should the values or worth of a stradom be assessed from the vantage point of a hierarchically privileged stradom (e.g., street corner groups are not worthless human beings even though this standpoint is shared by socialites).

Toward an Empirical Sociograph of Delinquency

In their effort to discover the larger contexts against which delinquency could be understood, Schwendinger and Schwendinger's (1997a, 1997b) undertook a sociographic study of informal network relationships among 3,756 individuals linked by 22,424 social ties. Sociographs, which transform empirical measures of social relationships into three dimensional network models or pictures that depict these relationships, have advantages and disadvantages. One advantage is that software applications allow the sociograph to be rotated to reveal clusters of relationships and distances between social groups. The disadvantage of this approach is that the graphs cannot be represented on a two-dimensional printed page. Thus, while the sociographs the Schwendingers employed cannot be pictured here, they can be described (interested readers can view the sociographs referred to here at:
http://web.tampabay.rr.com/hschwend detecting_fundamental_sociographs.htm
Reference to figures from this web site are inserted in the text).

Sociograph anaylsis revealed three primary dimensions that demarcate adolescent social ties as follows: 1) age (on the "X" axis); 2) gender (on the "Y" axis), and; 3) subcultural affiliation (i.e., street corner youth and surfers at one extreme and the intellectuals/brains and derogatory types on the other; on the "Z" axis). In these sociographs, *cubes* represent males while *spheres* represent females and are color coded by age as defined by school grades (7th, 8th, 9th ...12th grades). The sociograph (webpage figure 1) shows younger students on the left of the graph and the older on the right, indicating that friendships are habitually formed among adolescents of similar ages. As expected, the striking gender distribution (webpage figures 2a and 2b) indicates that boys associate with boys and girls with girls evenly. These patterns were expected from prior research.

The sociographs were also color coded to distinguish among subcultural (e.g., *preppies, socialites, elites, surfers, jocks, greasers, homeboys, shit-kickers*) and nonsubcultural (e.g., *wimps, turkeys, outsiders, neutrals, neutroms, regular guys and gals*) adolescent social-types (website figure 3). Some clear differences between these groups can be observed (website figures 4, 5a, 5b). However, the sociograph's three-dimensions contain a complex array of adolescent social types that remain hidden beneath one another. To reveal these relationships, the sociograph must be "peeled" apart. For example, when the outside "shell" of the sociograph that consists largely of nonsubcultural identities is removed (see website figure 6), subcultural identities begin to emerge when the graph is rotated, even though they are not immediately apparent (see website figures 7a, 7b, 8a, 8b, 9 and 10). That is, after removing nonsubcultural identities, and rotating the sociograph, socialite, surfer, street corner youth, and intellectual subcultures can be discerned.

The relatively greater densities of the subcultural networks found in the "middle" of the sociograph indicate that these groups are tightly bound. These identities do not arise out of thin air; they are the product of broader structural forces and have class associations. Cultural and material conditions cause the formation of subcultures and also influence the distance of these subcultures from one another. Class affiliation, for example, limits the opportunities of individuals, preordains the types of interpersonal association one will have and impacts the distribution of individuals in social space and the kinds of network ties an individual is capable of creating or joining. In a spatial sense, for instance, social classes in the U.S. are relatively isolated so that lower-class children form friendship ties with other lower-class children and so on. The limited opportunities for advancement these children experience—which begin with informal pre-school networks and which are later reinforced by truncated opportunities in formalized education—can embed lower-class children in a life course that produces little, if any, economic advancement. Strategies for dealing with these limited opportunities include adopting subcultural identities (which may be "inherited" or modified from previous generations). This is not to imply that the problem of crime or violence is the subcultures themselves. Rather, the problem is the larger material or economic conditions that produce the need for subcultural adaptations which, in turn, provide alternative systems that generate feelings of belonging and self-worth. For too long, criminologists have concentrated on subcultures as a cause of delinquency rather than seeing them as the product of broader inequalities and failures of the economic system to provide for the broad inclusion of the population. Moreover, the exclusion of the lower class can be seen in the elevated rates of suspicion of them and the enhanced mechanisms of social control that have been applied to them as a group. And, while class has a strong overall impact on the distribution of violence and delinquency, subcultures should not be overlooked and may be useful for explaining within class variations in these phenomena.

In sum, for three decades, the Schwendingers have published empirically derived findings on class, culture, and crime that contradict findings found in mainstream theories of crime. These studies have often been overlooked. Further, along with the literature reviewed in section one, these findings illustrate that: 1) propositions derived from radical criminology can be tested; 2) extant empirical research indicates that radical theories provide useful explanations of crime and justice; and 3) that the continued exclusion of radically derived explanations of crime and justice from criminology has been based on ideological rather than scientific standards.

Conclusion

Over the past decade, radical interpretations of crime and justice have matured. This maturation has several components. First, radicals expanded the theoretical scope of their endeavors by including race and gender structures along with more traditional class forms of analysis (Lynch, Michalowski, and Groves 2000). Second, theoretical maturation has also been accomplished by integrating numerous ideas from other disciplines (Barak 1998). Third, radicals have also attended to criticisms concerning empirical deficiencies and have produced a number of empirical studies that rely on a variety of methodological and statistics approaches. The evidence presented in this paper illustrated the latter point. Taken together, these observations illustrate that radical criminologists, more so than traditional criminologists, have been willing to develop and test new explanations for understanding crime and justice.

To be sure, the expansion of empirical studies by radicals has not reached the feverish pitch evident in mainstream criminology. Nevertheless, a significant number of empirically oriented radical studies have been published. Indeed, the number of such articles, and the areas examined by this research, is too diverse to adequately represent in this presentation of radical research. For example, we excluded empirical studies (including qualitative research) on news making issues and social constructionism (Aulette and Michalowski 1996; Barak 1994; Barlow, Barlow, and Chiricos 1995; Brownstein 1996; Lynch, Nalla, and Miller 1989; Lynch, Stretesky and Hammond 2000), left-realist research on working class fear of crime (Crawford, Jones, Woodhouse, and Young 1990), violence against women (DeKeseredy 1996; DeKeseredy and Kelley 1993), power-control theories of delinquency (Hagan, Gillis, and Simpson 1985, 1987) and racial bias (Patterson and Lynch 1991). While important, space limitation precluded a review of this research.

In sum, radical criminologists have produced a significant body of research that lends credence to this view. Continued neglect of this research speaks more to the penetration of ideology within criminology than to the efforts of radical criminologists who have produced this research.

Notes

1.   The theoretical neglect related to differences in causal assumptions is most assuredly a two-way street to the extent that radicals can also be criticized for neglecting empirical studies that focus attention on individuals. Radicals, however, do pay heed to some individual level research and have endeavored to incorporate at least some of this research into radical explanations of crime (Barak 1998; Groves and Lynch 1990; Lynch, Michalowski, and Groves 2000). In the radical view, the focus is on the force structures exert on the individual behavior that is of interest which are seen as unifying commonalities.

2.   Bonger's dissertation contained five foldout pages with graphs and tables that showed, for instance, how crime was affected by changes in the prices of household and manufactured goods and economic booms and busts.

3.   Assigning opposing roles created conflicts in which taken-for-granted assumptions about victimization could be challenged and openly expressed in the course of the debate. Each debate had a three-minute deadline and the antagonists were asked to come to agreement toward the end of the debate about committing the crime jointly.

References

Aulette, Judy, and Raymond J. Michalowski. 1996. "Fire in Hamlet: A Case Study in State-Corporate Crime." Pp. 171-206 in Kenneth D. Tunnell (ed.), *Political Crime*. New York: Garland.

Barak, Gregg. 1998. *Integrating Criminologies*. Boston: Allyn and Bacon.

———. ed. 1994. *Media, Process, and the Social Construction of Crime: Studies in Newsmaking Criminology*. New York: Garland.

Barlow, David E., and Melissa H. Barlow. 1995. "Federal Criminal Justice Legislation and the Post-World War II Social Structure of Accumulation in the United States." *Crime, Law and Social Change* 22: 239-267.

Barlow, David E., Melissa H. Barlow, and Theodore G. Chiricos. 1995. "Economic Conditions and Ideologies of Crime in the Media: A Content Analysis of Crime News." *Crime and Delinquency* 41: 3-19.

Barlow, David E., Melissa H. Barlow, and W. Wesley Johnson. 1996. "The Political Economy of Criminal Justice Policy: A Time Series Analysis of Economic Conditions, Crime and Federal Criminal Justice Legislation." *Justice Quarterly* 13: 223-242.

Bellinger, David. 1996. "Learning and Behavioral Sequele of Lead Poisoning." Pp. 97-116 in Siegfried M. Pueschel, James G. Linakis, and Angela C. Anderson (eds.), *Lead Poisoning in Childhood*. Baltimore: Paul H. Brookes.

Berger, Ronald. 1991. "Adolescent Subcultures, Social Type Metaphors, and Group Delinquency." In Ronald Berger (ed.), *The Sociology of Juvenile Delinquency*. Chicago: Nelson Hall.

Bonger, Willem. 1969 [1916]. *Criminality and Economic Conditions*. Boston: Little, Brown.

Box, Steven, and Chris Hale.1982. "Economic Crisis and the Rising Prisoner Population in England and Wales." *Crime and Social Justice* 17: 20-35.

———. 1983. "Liberation or Economic Marginalization? The Relationship of two Theoretical Arguments to Female Criminality in England and Wales, 1951-1980." *Criminology* 22: 473-497.

Brownstein, Henry H. 1996. *The Rise and Fall of a Violent Crime Wave: Crack Cocaine and the Social Construction of a Crime Problem*. Albany, NY: Harrow and Heston.

Burns, Ronald G. and Michael J. Lynch. 2002. "Another Fine Mess...A Preliminary Examination of the Use of Fines by the National Highway Traffic Safety Administration." *Criminal Justice Review* 27: 1-25.

———. 2004. *Environmental Crime: A Sourcebook*. New York: LFB Scholarly Publishing.

Carlson, Susan M, and Raymond J. Michalowski.1997. "Crime, Unemployment, and Social Structures of Accumulation: An Inquiry into Historical Contingency." *Justice Quarterly* 14: 209-241.

Carson, Rachel. 1962. *Silent Spring*. New York: Houghton-Mifflin.

Chiricos, Theodore G., and William D. Bales. 1991. "Unemployment and Punishment: An Empirical Assessment." *Criminology* 29: 701-724.

Chiricos, Theodore G., and Miriam A. DeLone. 1992. "Labor Surplus and Punishment: A Review and Assessment of Theory and Evidence." *Social Problems* 39: 421-446.

Colburn, Theo, Dianne Dumanoski, and John Peterson Myers. 1997. *Our Stolen Future*. New York: Plume.

Crawford, Adam., Trevor Jones, Tom Woodhouse, and Jock Young. 1990. *The Second Islington Crime Survey*. London: Middlesex Polytechnic Centre for Criminology.

Davis, Devra. 2002. *When Smoke Ran Like Water: Tales of Environmental Deception and the Battle Against Pollution*. New York: Basic Books.

DeKeseredy, Walter. 1996. "The Canadian National Survey on Women Abuse in University/College Dating Relationships." *Canadian Journal of Criminology* 38: 81-104.

DeKeseredy, Walter, and Katherine Kelly. 1993. "The Incidence and Prevalence of Women Abuse in Canadian University and College Dating Relationships." *Canadian Journal of Sociology* 18: 137-159.

Denno, Deborah. 1990. *Biology and Violence: From Birth to Adulthood*. New York: Cambridge University Press

Dietrich, K. N., M. D. Ris, P. A. Succop, U. G. Berger, and R. L. Bornschein. 2001. "Early Exposure to Lead and Juvenile Delinquency." *Neurotoxicology and Teratology* 23: 511-518.

Edel, May, and Abraham Edel. 1959. *Anthropology and Ethics*. Springfield, IL: Charles C. Thomas

Greenberg, David F. 1977. "The Dynamics of Oscillatory Punishment Processes." *Journal of Criminal Law and Criminology* 68: 643-651.

———. 1980. "Penal Sanctions in Poland: A Test of Alternative Models." *Social Problems* 28: 194-204.

Groves, W. Byron, and Michael J. Lynch. 1990. "Reconciling Structural and Subjective-Approaches to the Study of Crime." *Journal of Research in Crime and Delinquency* 27: 348-375.

Hagan, John, A. R. Gillis, and John Simpson. 1985. 'The Class Structure of Gender and Delinquency." *American Journal of Sociology* 90 6: 1151-1178.

———. 1987. "Class in the Household: A Power-Control Theory of Gender and Delinquency." *American Sociological Review* 92: 788-818.

Hestein, J., I Vrugdenhil, F. M. E. Slijper, P. G. H. Pulder, and N. Weisglas-Kuperus. 2002. "Effect of Perinatal Exposure to PCBs and Dioxins on Play Behavior in Dutch Children at School Age." *Environmental Health Perspectives* 110: A593-A-598.

Hollingshead, August B. 1949. *Elmtown's Youth: The Impact of Social Classes on Adolescents*. New York: John Wiley & Sons.

Humphries, Drew, and Don Wallace. 1980. "Capitalist Accumulation and Urban Crime, 1950-1971." *Social Problems* 20: 180-193.

Jacobs, David. 1978. "Inequality and Legal Order: An Ecological Test of the Conflict Model." *Social Problems* 25: 516-525.

———. 1979. "Inequality and Police Strength." *American Sociological Review* 44: 913-924.

Jacobs, David, and David Britt. 1979. "Inequality and Police Use of Deadly Force: An Empirical Assessment of the Conflict Hypothesis." *Social Problems* 26: 403-411.

Jankovic, Ivan. 1977. "Labor Market and Imprisonment." *Crime and Social Justice* 8: 17-31.

———. 1978. "Social Class and Criminal Sentencing." *Crime and Social Justice* 10:9-16.

Laffargue, Bernard., and Thierry. Godefroy. 1989. "Economic Cycles and Punishment: Unemployment and Imprisonment, a Time-Series Study, France, 1920-1985." *Contemporary Crises* 13: 371-404.

Lessan, Gloria. 1991. "Macro-Economic Determinants of Penal Policy: Estimating the Unemployment and Inflation Influences on Imprisonment Rate Changes in the United States, 1948-1985." *Crime, Law and Social Change* 16: 177-198.

Liu, Feng. 2001. *Environmental Justice Analysis: Theories, Methods and Practice.* Boca Raton, FL: Lewis Publishers.

Lizotte, Alan. 1978. "Extra-Legal Factors in Chicago's Criminal Courts: Testing the Conflict Model of Criminal Justice." *Social Problems* 25: 564-580.

Lizotte, Alan, James Mercy, and Eric Monkkenon. 1982. "Crime and Police Strength in an Urban Setting: Chicago, 1947-1970." Pp. 109-129 in John Hagan (ed.), *Quantitative Criminology.* Beverly Hills, CA: Sage.

Lynch, Michael J. 1988. "The Extraction of Surplus Value, Crime and Punishment: A Preliminary Empirical Analysis for the U.S." *Contemporary Crises* 12: 329-344.

———. 1996. "Race, Class, Gender and Criminology: Structured Choices and the Life Course." Pp.3-28 in Martin D. Schwartz and Dragan Milovanovic (eds.), *Gender, Race, and Class in Criminology.* Hamden, CT: Garland.

———. 1999. "Beating a Dead Horse: Is There Any Basic Empirical Evidence for a Deterrent Effect of Imprisonment?" *Crime, Law and Social Change* 31: 347-362.

———. 2004. "Towards a Radical Ecology of Urban Violence: Integrating Medical, Epidemiological, Environmental, and Criminological Research on Class, Race, Lead (Pb) and Crime." Pp. 103-120 in Margaret A. Zahn and Henry H. Brownstein (eds.), *Violence: From Theory to Research.* Cincinnati: Anderson.

Lynch, Michael J., W. Byron Groves, and Alan Lizotte. 1994. "The Rate of Surplus Value and Crime: Theoretical and Empirical Examination of Marxian Economic Theory and Criminology." *Crime, Law and Social Change* 21: 15-48.

Lynch, Michael J., Michael J. Hogan, and Paul Stretesky. 1999. "A Further Look at Long Cycles, Legislation and Crime." *Justice Quarterly* 16: 431-450.

Lynch, Michael J., Raymond J. Michalowski, and W. Byron Groves. 2000. *The New Primer in Radical Criminology: Critical Perspectives on Crime, Power and Identity.* Monsey, NY: Criminal Justice Press.

Lynch, Michael J., and Raymond J. Michalowski. 2005. *Primer in Radical Criminology,* 4th ed. Monsey, NY: Criminal Justice Press.

Lynch, Michael J., Mahesh K. Nalla, and Keith W. Miller. 1989. "Crime or Accident? The Case of Bhopal." *Journal of Research in Crime and Delinquency* 26: 7-35.

Lynch, Michael J. and Paul B. Stretesky. 2002. "Toxic Crimes: Examining Corporate Victimization of the General Public Employing Medical and Epidemiological Evidence." *Critical Criminology* 10: 153-172.

Lynch, Michael J., Paul B. Stretesky, and Ronald G. Burns. 2004a. "Slippery Business: Race, Class and Legal Determinants of Penalties Against Petroleum Refineries." *Journal of Black Studies* 34: 421-440.

———. 2004b. "Determinants of Environmental Law Violation Fines Against Oil Refineries: Race, Ethnicity, Income, and Aggregation Effects." *Society and Natural Resources* 17: 333-347

Lynch, Michael J., Paul B. Stretesky, and Paul Hammond. 2000. "Media Coverage of Chemical Crimes: Hillsborough County, Florida, 1987-1997." *British Journal of Criminology* 40: 112-126

Lynch, Michael J., Paul B. Stretesky, and Danielle McGurrin. 2001. "Toxic Crimes and Environmental Justice." Pp. 109-136 in Gary W. Potter (ed.), *Controversies in White Collar Crime.* Cincinnati: Anderson.

Messerschmidt, James W. 1997. *Crime as Structured Action: Gender, Race, Class and Crime in Criminology.* Thousand Oaks, CA: Sage.

Michalowski, Raymond J., and Susan M. Carlson. 1999. "Unemployment, Imprisonment and Social Structures of Accumulation: Historical Contingency in the Rusche-Kirchheimer Hypothesis." *Criminology* 37: 217-250.

Michalowski, Raymond J., and Michael A. Pearson. 1990. "Punishment and Social Structure at the State Level: A Cross-Sectional Comparison of 1970 and 1980. *Journal of Research in Crime and Delinquency* 27: 52-78.

Mills, C. Wright. 1959. *The Sociological Imagination.* New York: Oxford University Press.

Nalla, Mahesh, Michael J. Lynch, and Michael J. Leiber. 1997. "Determinants of Police Growth in Phoenix, Arizona, 1950-1988." *Justice Quarterly* 14: 115-144.

Needleman, Herbert. L., Christine. McFarland, Roberta. B. Ness, Stephen. E. Fienberg, and Michael. J. Tobin. 2002. "Bone Lead Levels in Adjudicated Delinquents: A Case Control Study." *Neurotoxicology and Teratology* 24: 711-717.

Needleman, Herbert L., Julie. A. Riess, Michael .J. Tobin, Gretchen. E. Biesecker, and Joel. B. Greenhouse.1996. "Bone Lead Levels and Delinquent Behavior." *Journal of the American Medical Association* 275: 363-369.

Patterson, E. Britt, and Michael J. Lynch. 1991. "Biases in Formalized Bail Processes." Pp.36-53 in Michail J. Lynch and E. Britt Patterson (eds.), *Race and Criminal Justice.* Albany, NY: Harrow and Heston.

Pihl, R. O., and F. Ervin. 1990. "Lead and Cadmium in Violent Criminals." *Psychological Reports* 66: 839-844.

Pueschel, Siegfried M., James G. Linakis, and Angela C. Anderson, eds. 1996. *Lead Poisoning in Childhood.* Baltimore: Paul H. Brookes Publishing.

Rodericks, Joseph V. 1992. *Calculated Risks: The Toxicity and Human Health Risks of Chemicals in Our Environment.* Cambridge: Cambridge University Press.

Russell, Stuart. 2002. "The Continuing Relevance of Marxism to Critical Criminology. *Critical Criminology* 11: 113-135.

Sacks, Karen. 1975. "Engels Revisited: Women, the Organization of Production and Private Property." Pp. 211-234 in Rayna R. Reiter (ed.) *Toward an Anthropology of Women.* New York: Monthly Review Press.

Sampson, Robert J., and W. Byron Groves. 1989. "Community Structure and Crime: Testing Social Disorganization Theory." *American Journal of Sociology* 94: 774-802.

Schwendinger, Herman, and Julia Schwendinger. 1985. *Adolescent Subcultures and Delinquency.* Research ed. New York: Praeger.

―――. 1997a. "When the Study of Delinquent Groups Stood Still: In Defense of a Classical Tradition." *Critical Criminology* 8: 5-38.

―――. 1997b. "Charting Subcultures at a Frontier of Knowledge." *British Journal of Sociology* 48: 71-94.

Siegel, Larry. 2001. *Criminology.* Belmont, CA: Wadsworth.

Steingraber, Sandra. 1998. *Living Downstream: A Scientist's Personal Investigation of Cancer and the Environment.* New York: Vintage.

Stretesky, Paul B. 2003. "The Distribution of Air Lead Levels across U.S. Counties: Implications for the Production of Racial Inequality." Sociological Spectrum 23: 91-118.

Stretesky, Paul B., and Michael J. Hogan. 1998. "Environmental Justice: An Analysis of Superfund Sites in Florida." *Social Problems* 45: 268-287.

Stretesky, Paul, Janis Johnston, and Jeremy Arney. 2003. "Environmental Inequity: An Analysis of Large-Scale Hog Operations in 17 States, 1982-1997." *Rural Sociology* 68: 231-252.

Stretesky, Paul B., and Michael J. Lynch. 1999a. "Environmental Justice and the Prediction of Distance to Accidental Chemical Releases in Hillsborough County, Florida." *Social Science Quarterly* 80: 830-846.

―――. 1999b. "Corporate Environmental Violence and Racism." *Crime, Law and Social Change* 30: 163-184.

————. 2001. "The Relationship Between Lead and Homicide." *Archives of Pediatric and Adolescent Medicine* 155: 579-582.

————. 2003. "Environmental Hazards and School Segregation in Hillsborough, 1987-1999." *Sociological Quarterly* 43: 553-573.

————. 2004. "The Relationship Between Lead and Crime." *Journal of Health and Social Behavior* 45: 214-229.

Sykes, Gresham M., and David Matza. 1957. "Techniques of Neutralization." *American Sociological Review* 22: 664-670.

Wargo, John. 1998. *Our Children's Toxic Legacy.* New Haven, CT: Yale University Press.

Warner, William Lloyd, and Paul S. Lunt. 1942. *The Status System of a Modern Community.* Yankee City Series, Vol. 2. New Haven, CT: Yale University Press.

Weber, Max. 1968. *Economy and Society.* Translated and edited by Guenther Roth and Claus Wittich. New York: Bedminster Press.

Yeager, Matthew G. 1979. "Unemployment and Imprisonment." *Journal of Criminal Law and Criminology* 70: 576-588.

8

The Status of Feminist Theories
in Criminology

Jody Miller and Christopher W. Mullins

In her preface to a special issue of *The Annals* on feminist theory in the social sciences, sociologist Christine Williams (2000: 9) describes academic feminism as "a general approach to understanding the status of women in society." Notwithstanding the range of feminist theoretical approaches brought to bear on the problem, she observes: "all feminist social scientists share the goals of understanding the sources of [gender] inequality and advocating changes to empower women" (Williams 2000: 9). As a consequence of these overarching goals, broader, often interdisciplinary frameworks guide feminist theories in criminology more so than most theoretical perspectives in the discipline. In the case of feminist criminology, these include theoretical frameworks on gender and gender inequality, and on intersectionality, i.e., the intersections of race, class, gender and age. Thus, what differentiates *feminist* criminology from mainstream criminological analyses that consider "women and crime" is the theoretical understanding of gender that guides our research: theories of *gender* are as much a starting point in feminist criminological analyses as are theories of *crime* (Daly 1998).

Kathleen Daly (1998: 86) observes that criminological field expansion in the study of gender—because it emanates both from traditional and feminist theoretical perspectives—has "created a somewhat incoherent theoretical field." In "taking stock" of the status of feminist theories within the discipline, we will suggest that the best feminist work—and the most promising direction for the future of feminist criminology—is that which remains critically engaged with the gendered life situations of women and men while drawing from, and enriching, its analyses from the insights of broader criminological thought (see also Simpson 2000). Moreover, we suggest that this course of action offers the best hope for the important insights of feminist scholarship to both challenge and enrich the broader enterprise of criminological theory-building.

Distinctive Features of Feminist Criminology

Feminist criminology[1] refers to that body of criminological research and theory that situates the study of crime and criminal justice within a complex understanding that the social world is systematically shaped by relations of sex and gender. Though feminist scholarship draws from diverse theoretical traditions (see Tong 1998), there are a number of central beliefs that guide feminist inquiry in criminology. In their influential paper on feminism and criminology, Daly and Chesney-Lind (1988: 504) list five aspects of feminist thought that distinguish it from traditional criminological inquiry. These include recognition that:

- Gender is not a natural fact but a complex social, historical, and cultural product; it is related to, but not simply derived from, biological sex difference and reproductive capacities.
- Gender and gender relations order social life and social institutions in fundamental ways.
- Gender relations and constructs of masculinity and femininity are not symmetrical but are based on an organizing principle of men's superiority and social and political-economic dominance over women.
- Systems of knowledge reflect men's views of the natural and social world; the production of knowledge is gendered.
- Women should be at the center of intellectual inquiry, not peripheral, invisible, or appendages to men.

In addition, contemporary feminist scholars strive to be attentive to the interlocking nature of race, class and gender oppression, recognizing that women's experiences of gender vary according to their position in racial and class hierarchies (see Daly and Maher 1998; Maher 1997; Schwartz and Milovanovic 1996; Simpson 1991).

Given this broad framework, we would like to begin by highlighting several key features that distinguish feminist theories from most theoretical perspectives in the discipline. These illustrate both the strengths and vitality of the perspective and the challenges feminist scholars face within what Dana Britton (2000: 59) aptly terms the mainstream of "hegemonic criminology." First, as noted, feminist scholarship grounds its inquiry in the examination of the meaning and nature of gender relations. As such, gender is as important to understand and theorize as crime and criminality. Specifically, feminist scholars insist that it is only with the inclusion of an understanding of gender that crime can be fully understood and theorized. It is ironic that "criminology is in possession of one of the most consistently demonstrated findings in all of the social sciences: that men are considerably more likely than women to engage in activities defined as criminal" (Britton 2000: 58), yet this emphasis on gender has resulted in the widespread misinterpretation of feminist criminology as reductionistic.[2] Such erroneous critiques persist because of the dominance of reigning paradigms and the limited range of accepted methodologies within criminology (see Williams 2000: 8). In fact, feminist scholarship challenges the simplistic notion that gender is nothing more than an individual-level independent variable to be controlled for, as our discussion here will elucidate.

Second, given the overarching goals of understanding gender inequality and advocating for change, feminist perspectives cut across a broad range of questions within criminology and criminal justice. With few exceptions, most criminological theorizing focuses attention *either* on explaining crime *or* on justice systems and processing. Feminist theories—with gender inequality as a guiding question—have been brought to bear on crime and criminal justice, as well as victimization (i.e., violence against women), work and occupations within the criminal justice system and the law.[3] Feminist activism linked to scholarly research has been particularly notable with regard to juvenile/criminal justice processing (including incarceration) and violence against women (see Britton 2000 for an overview).

There are often key substantive differences between feminist activism and mainstream criminological foci. These have led, at times, to erroneous charges of polemical bias in feminist research. In fact, the theory/praxis relationship among feminist scholars is not strikingly different in practice from the parallel reality that policy goals also drive much criminological theory and research. In general, criminological theory and research attempt to explain crime in order to offer policies to reduce it. Feminist criminology has as its goals the reduction of gender inequality, crime, and the inequitable treatment of offenders, victims, and workers emerging from the androcentric policies and practices within "gendered institutions"[4] (Acker 1990).

Third, feminist scholars must grapple with what Daly and Maher (1998: 1) refer to as an "intellectual double shift." Gender operates not just within the practices and organization of social life but also within "the discursive fields by which women (and men) are constructed or construct themselves" (1998: 4). Taken-for-granted ideologies about gender are profoundly embedded in social life and include common-sense notions of fundamental difference between women and men, coupled with the perception of maleness as the normative standard. These deeply engrained assumptions are found in: academic research and theory; the policies, practices and operation of organizations and institutions; the interpretive frameworks women and men bring to their daily lives; and even in some feminist analyses. Thus, feminist scholars face the dual challenge of examining the impact of gender and gender inequality in "real" life while simultaneously deconstructing the intertwined ideologies about gender that guide social practices (see Connell 2002; Fausto-Sterling 1992; Lorber 1994; Tavris 1992; Thorne 1993).

One arena in which the latter focus has received a great deal of attention in criminology is the interrogation of traditional theories to expose and critique the androcentric biases that have guided this work (see Campbell 1984; Smart 1976). Two overarching features of feminist critique are notable. First, much criminological theory has either ignored women—focusing exclusively or implicitly on explaining male participation in crime and defining females as unimportant or peripheral—or has ignored gender. The tendency to ignore *women* results, in part, from the fact that most serious criminal offenders are male. As a consequence, the field of criminology has been primarily concerned with understanding and explaining men's offending. Ignoring *gender* results both when theories of male crime don't seek to account for how gender structures and shapes *male* involvement in crime, and when theories assume to be generalizable—that is, theories derived from the study of men are assumed to be able to account for female crime or female offenders. Since theories derived from studies of women are not seen as generalizable, implicit in this assumption is the notion that women are a subcategory of men (see Daly 2000).

A second critique is aimed at theories that do the opposite: theories that are based on beliefs about fundamental differences between women and men—for instance, men are more rational, women more emotional; men are more aggressive, women more passive; men are instrumental, women relational. As taken-for-granted assumptions, these stereotypes about what distinguishes women from men often are reflected in criminological theory and research. It is precisely women's greater emotionality, passivity and weakness, according to these theories, which account for their involvement (or lack thereof) in crime and the nature of their criminal activities. Early theories about female crime, for example, focused on individual pathologies such as personality disorders and sexual or emotional maladjustment. This approach contrasts with theories of male crime, which have historically been much more likely to define males in relation to the broader social world around them. Because many of the gender-based assumptions that have guided criminological theories are hidden or taken-for-granted, it has taken a feminist lens to bring many of these biases to light. Moreover, while such assumptions about gender are rarely as overt in contemporary research, many recent explanations of "women and crime" continue to reproduce conventional understandings of gender difference in their search to explain gendered patterns of offending (see Miller 2002 for further discussion).

However, it is not just within criminological theory that the impact of ideologies about gender must be examined and scrutinized by feminist scholars. These interpretive frameworks—particularly cultural emphases on a psychologically-based "character dichotomy" between women and men (see Connell 2002: 40)—also guide the meanings and understandings of the individuals, groups and organizations we investigate (see Allen 1987; Britton

2003; Daly and Maher 1998; Miller and White 2003; Pierce 1999). It is through the enactment of these gendered meanings that the most persistent, yet often invisible, facets of gender inequality are reproduced. The elucidation of the relationship between ideological features of gender and gendered practice is, thus, a key facet of feminist criminology[5] but poses a significant challenge—or intellectual double shift—not faced by scholars of crime who take the categories under investigation as social facts.

A final distinguishing feature of feminist criminology is that it is best suited to the development of what Daly (1998) refers to as theories of the "middle range": those theories that seek primarily to explore how broader structural forces are realized within both particular organizational contexts and the micro-level interactions of social actors within a specific domain or area. As opposed to "grand theory," which often over-generalizes situational effects in the attempt to explain everything at once (see Mills 1959), middle range theories attempt to provide narrower, more focused explanations of situations and contexts. If a prominent goal in much of the criminological enterprise is the creation of general theories (see Agnew 1992; Gottfredson and Hirschi 1990; Hirschi 1969; Tittle 1995), feminist criminology has not been particularly successful. However, it is precisely feminist understandings of gender that require us to move beyond what broad, global explanations can provide. While our starting point is the recognition society and social life are patterned on the basis of gender, we also recognize—and empirical evidence demonstrates—that this *gender order* (Connell 2002) is complex and shifting.

Thus within feminist criminology, middle range theories most profitably start from the understanding that gender is complex, contingent and highly varied across historical context and social position. Given this recognition, advances in the field have highlighted three important problems: 1) how gendered organizations—through their structures, policies, ideologies and practices—are built on and reproduce gender hierarchies (see Britton 2003; Collier 1998; Martin 1999; McCorkel 2002; Pierce 1999); 2) how actors navigate gendered environments in an attempt to realize their personal goals and enhance their social positions (even when simultaneously reproducing inequality) (see Maher 1997; Miller 2001; Mullins and Wright 2003); and 3) how the intersections of gender with other facets of social identity and structural position—race, class, age, sexuality—create variations in the nature and effects of gender inequality (see Britton 2003; Farr 2000; Ferguson 2000; Maher 1997; Martin 1994; Simpson 1991; Steffensmeier et al. 1998; Visher 1983).

With regard to understanding offending, for instance, careful examination of the shifting nature of gendered behavioral demands, at both the structural and interactional level, provides a means to better understand the precise ways in which gender frames criminality and criminal events. Multi-level approaches: allow for the simultaneous examination of gendered ideologies and social practices; recognize and can account for variations across and within gender that result from structural positions such as race, class and age; and, thus, avoid the tendency to fall back upon easy notions of individual-level gender difference. In fact, we see recent work that addresses gender in such complex ways as among the most promising and stimulating of current trends in the field.

Theories of Gender

As with much of criminology, feminist scholarship is greatly influenced by theoretical developments within a range of social science disciplines. Sociological scholarship is most prominent among these influences. The groundbreaking works of such feminist theorists as Barrie Thorne (1993), R.W. Connell (1987, 2002), Sarah Fenstermaker and Candace West (2002), and Joan Acker (1990) have had a profound impact on recent developments within feminist criminology. In this section, we draw from these broader analyses to provide an expanded discussion of the aspects of feminist thought noted above. We use Connell's (2002) recent work as the primary framework for this discussion because he provides a comprehensive overview of gender theory and synthesizes the insights of other important feminist scholars.

Connell differentiates and draws connections between the operation of gender at the macro level (what he terms *gender order*), meso level (*gender regime*) and micro level (*gender relations*). By gender order, Connell refers to the overarching patterns of social life within society that are arranged on the basis of gender. Cutting across institutions, gender frames social organization itself. Not only does it structure life chances and opportunities, it generates and legitimates cultural norms of difference and inequality. Within criminology, macro-level structural analyses of gender and crime are perhaps the least well developed. However, several recent attempts to examine structural features of gender inequality have proven fruitful (see Bailey and Peterson 1995; Dugan et al. 1999; Peterson and Bailey 1992; Steffensmeier and Haynie 2000; Whaley 2001).

While Connell provides a broad analysis of the structures and social relations of gender, he includes a strong emphasis on the contingent and historically shifting nature of gender, gender inequality and the agency/structure nexus. As he summarizes (2002: 10):

> Gender patterns may differ strikingly from one cultural context to another, but are still "gender." Gender arrangements are reproduced socially [not biologically] by the power of structures to constrain individual action so often they appear unchanging. Yet gender arrangements are, in fact, always changing, as human practice creates new situations and as structures develop crisis tendencies.

From this account, it is clear why feminist theoretical developments are best suited for middle range analyses, even within an overarching theoretical framework that emphasizes the structural sources of gender and gender inequality. Within the gender order of any given society, gender operates at a number of levels, each of which requires examination.

Gender regimes are the patterns of gender arrangements within given institutions or organizations which usually (but don't always or entirely) correspond with the gender order (see also Acker 1990). Among feminist criminologists studying offending, gender regimes that have received particular attention include the family (see Heimer and DeCoster 1999; Hagan et al. 1985) and the streets (Miller 1986; Phoenix 2000)—including drug economies (Maher 1997; Maher and Curtis 1992), street gangs (Campbell 1984; Joe-Laidler and Hunt 1997; Miller 2001; Peterson et al. 2001; Portillos 1999) and offender networks (Mullins and Wright 2003; Steffensmeier 1983; Steffensmeier and Terry 1986). Though ample evidence exists of the gendered nature of schools (Orenstein 1994), and while criminology in general has examined the role of schooling in explaining risks for offending (Gottfredson 2001), this is an institutional arena that has received limited attention with regard to how the gendered (and raced) regimes of the school shape risks for, and patterns of, offending (but see Ferguson 2000).

Within the gender order and given gender regimes, sets of relationships emerge both across and within gender. These *gender relations* include both direct interactions between individuals as well as indirect or mediated interactions. Connell (2002: 58) identifies "four main structures in the modern system of gender relations": power relations, productive relations, emotional relations, and symbolic relations. Recognizing multiple dimensions of gender relations is key to understanding the complexity, and sometimes contradictory nature of gender relations. Power relations, for example, operate at the institutional level and, more intimately, at the discursive level, shaping our "identities and sense of…place in the world" (2002: 59). Productive relations are those that shape the gender division of labor and include production, reproduction, and consumption. Emotional relations include such aspects as romantic and sexual attachment, gender-marked emotional displays (anger and aggressiveness, compassion and nurturance, for example) and emotional labor, and are an important facet of oppression and brutality. Symbolic relations are the powerful meaning systems that exist about gender, including, as noted above, "the dichotomous gender structuring of culture" (Connell 2002: 65). These dimensions of gender relations are interwoven with one another in a complex tapestry.

To understand gender relations at the level of interaction, it is necessary to examine both the structures of relationships—that is, the enduring and expected patterns of behavior that constrain practices—as well as the agency of individuals in learning, navigating, accommodating and resisting these structures. Agency itself includes social practices and behaviors as well as the configurations of gender identity that individuals bring to these activities. In some cases the two correspond, as when individuals draw from a repertoire of behaviors in order to enact or demonstrate their gender identity (see West and Zimmerman 1987); however, the relationship between gendered social practices and gender identities is often much more complex (see Miller 2002).

One theoretical perspective developed to elucidate these facets of gender relations is the analysis of gender as situated accomplishment. From this approach, gender is "much more than a role or individual characteristic: it is a mechanism whereby situated social action contributes to the reproduction of social structure" (West and Fenstermaker 1995: 21). Specifically, these theorists argue that women and men "do gender"—or behave in gendered ways—in response to normative beliefs about femininity and masculinity. The performance of gender is a response to gendered social hierarchies and expectations but it also reproduces and reinforces them. Such actions are the "interactional scaffolding of social structure" (West and Zimmerman 1987: 147), such that the performance of gender is both an indication of, and a reproduction of, gendered (and raced, classed, generational, sexed) social hierarchies. This approach has been incorporated into feminist accounts of crime in order to explain differences in women's and men's offending. Some investigations have focused on crime as "a 'resource' for accomplishing gender" (Simpson and Elis 1995: 50; see also Messerschmidt 1993); others have examined gender as a resource for accomplishing crime (Jacobs and Miller 1998; Miller 1998); and still others have used this conceptualization to tease out the simultaneous and complex relationship between gendered structures, social practices and identities (Miller 2001; Mullins and Wright 2003; Phoenix 2000; see Miller 2002 for an overview).

Two final features of Connell's theoretical framework are noteworthy. First, he examines the important relationship of bodies to the construction of gender, focusing attention on the *social embodiment* of gender. Connell details the ways in which bodies are "both objects of social practice and agents in social practice" (2002: 47). Feminist research on the sexualization of female offenders, including the heightened emphasis on the "sexualized" bodies of female status offenders, illustrates the significance of this feature of gender[6] (see Chesney-Lind 1973; MacDonald and Chesney-Lind 2001). Feminist scholars both in, and outside of, criminology have been most attentive to the treatment of the female body, as cultural constructions of gender difference are often mapped on a male/female mind/body dichotomy (de Beauvoir 1960; Eisenstein 1988). More recently in criminology, Messerschmidt (2000, 2004) has brought more explicit theoretical attention to the role of the body in the enactment of male (as well as female) violence (see also Collier 1998).

Finally, drawing from the work of Thorne (1993) and others, Connell (2002: 82) provides a theoretical account of the *trajectories of gender formation*, including the development of *gender competence* (learning how to negotiate the gender order) and the creation of *gender projects* (characteristic strategies for handling gender relations crystallized as patterns of masculinity or femininity). This approach for understanding the development of gender identities, and the inculcation into gendered social practices, provides a more multidimensional understanding of the process of becoming gendered than traditional socialization models. Such models fail to adequately account for agency and are premised on a seamless notion of unitary sex or gender "roles" (see Thorne 1993). Moreover, recognition that gender identities and gender projects are situational, contingent, and constructed in interactions moves beyond the limitations of sex/gender role theory which often remains a conceptual underpinning in mainstream analyses of "women and crime."

These new approaches advance theoretical accounts of gender in a number of significant ways. For instance, while the concept of "sex roles" or "gender roles" assumes that "gender is logically *prior to* behavior, already settled, and can be understood as [the cause of] behavior" (Connell 1993: x), the conceptualization of gender projects emphasizes that gender is "constructed in social action...done, accomplished in the everyday actions of social life" (Connell 1993: xi). Moreover, in contrast with the notion of unitary sex or gender "roles," this more contingent approach emphasizes variations in gender identities, projects, and expectations across both situational contexts and social structural positions such as race and class. This also results in a less static and less deterministic view of social structure (see Emirbayer and Mische 1998; McNay 2000; Sewell 1992). Specifically, conceptualizing individuals' constructions of gender as actively emerging within various gender regimes or relations (at the meso and micro levels) allows for recognition of agency, but remains thoroughly grounded in the contexts of structural inequalities such as those built around relations of gender, sexuality, race, class and age. As Connell (1993: ix) notes, this approach insists that "social structure does not exist 'outside' everyday life."

Contemporary Directions in Feminist Criminology

Two questions have guided mainstream criminological examinations of gender for the last several decades: the question of generalizability and the gender ratio problem. In this section, we will briefly review and critique these approaches for theorizing "gender and crime" and will then describe more profitable developments within feminist criminology drawing from Daly's (1998) conceptual schema of *gendered pathways to lawbreaking, gendered crime,* and *gendered lives.*[7] We also highlight promising developments in the study of masculinities and crime. In keeping with our position that the best feminist research in criminology is explicitly attentive both to gender and to useful insights from broader criminological thought, we link advances within feminist criminology to trends in mainstream criminology. Though feminist theorists have been critical of traditional criminological approaches, there is, nonetheless, recognition that "many seminal ideas emerging in criminological thought can be integrated and/or elaborated in ways that can inform gendered criminological theory" (Simpson 2000). We orient our discussion to emphasize the ways in which feminist analyses challenge and enrich the criminological enterprise.

The Problem of Generalizability

For more than a century, theories developed to explain why people commit crime have actually been theories of why *men* commit crime.[8] Ironically, the gender gap in offending has long been a primary rationale for this focus (Britton 2000). In many cases, this orientation is not outwardly stated; instead theories are presumed to be "gender-neutral" and it has been taken for granted that a given theoretical approach can be applied to males or females. Given the recognition of gender as a structuring feature of society, feminists have explicitly posed the questions: "Do theories of men's crime apply to women? Can the logic of such theories be modified to include women?" (Daly and Chesney-Lind 1988: 514). If not, what alternative explanations can account for women's offending? Scholars who have attempted to test whether mainstream theories can be generalized to women have focused on such constructs as the family, social learning, delinquent peer relationships, strain and deterrence. For the most part, these studies have found mixed results (see Broidy 2001; Smith and Paternoster 1987). As Kruttschnitt (1996: 141) summarizes, "it appears the factors influencing delinquent development differ for males and females in some contexts but not others."

This lack of consistent findings is unsurprising from a feminist perspective. While mainstream theorists who include gender in their analyses often search for generalizable explanations of crime, and, thus, examine whether the same processes are at work in explaining women's and men's crime, there are several key limitations to this approach. First, they cannot account for the gender ratio of offending—that is, men's disproportionate involvement in crime.[9] Dramatic gender differences in rates of offending suggest that a general etiological process is not occurring. This is not to suggest that many of the basic factors included in such analyses are unimportant for understanding crime across gender, but to highlight that it is necessary to examine whether and how such elements influence offending across gender in the same way or with equal force.[10] Moreover, feminist scholars recognize gender as an important feature of the social organization of society and, thus, of women's and men's experiences. Theories that attempt to generalize across gender are unable to address these pivotal social forces (see Daly 1998).

For instance, much of this research takes for granted that variables or constructs have the same meaning for males and females. While such elements as learning, peer influences, social control, family attachment and supervision, individual strain and opportunity are essential in the understanding of crime for both males and females, recent work shows that, indeed, these factors have variant influence within and across gender (see Alarid et al. 2000; Broidy 2001; Burton et al. 1998; Heimer and DeCoster 1999; Katz 2000; Mears et al. 1998). Because of the gendered nature of women's and men's lives, important explanatory factors take on different meanings and have different consequences for females and males. Thus, feminists insist that while some of the theoretical concepts found in presumably "gender-neutral" theories of crime may be relevant or useful for understanding women's offending, gendered theories—i.e., those that take gender and gender stratification into account—are preferable to approaches that assume measures or constructs are gender neutral (Daly 2000; Simpson 2000). However, this does not mean that "gender difference" is the sole focus of feminist research. Instead, feminists ask the questions: when, how, and why does gender matter? Recent endeavors that examine similarities and differences within and across gender, and especially those that conceptualize gender beyond the individual level, have proven especially fruitful in understanding the causes of crime.

The Gender-Ratio of Crime

One problem with attempts to generalize theories across gender is that all of this work begs the question of why it is that women and men have vastly divergent rates of criminal offending. This is the gender-ratio problem. Scholars who address this raise the following questions: "Why are women less likely than men to be involved in crime? Conversely, why are men more crime-prone than women? What explains [these] gender differences?" (Daly and Chesney-Lind 1988: 515). These questions have led scholars to pay attention to gender differences and inequalities and to develop theories that can account for variations in women's and men's offending (see Bottcher 2001; Hagan et al. 1985; Heimer and De Coster 1999).

With men as the starting point, explanations for the gender ratio of crime are typically pursued by asking what are the factors that limit or block women's involvement in crime? But to only ask this question, again, reflects an androcentric perspective that makes men the norm upon which women deviate through their limited offending. Inverting this question, and attempting to account for why men have considerably higher rates of offending than women, raises an important set of additional queries. For instance, a key question is what is it about being male—and about masculinity specifically—that accounts for men's disproportionate levels of offending? This is a topic we return to below.

Moreover, traditional and mainstream approaches typically explain the gender gap by drawing from stereotypical notions of dichotomous gender difference and treat gender as an individual trait. More promising are approaches that treat gender as a key element of social organization (see Bottcher

2001; Heimer and DeCoster 1999). Not only does such an approach avoid the assumption of essential gender difference, but it also allows for a more complex examination of the gender gap. For instance, data on crime trends reveal that the gender gap remains more persistent for some crimes than others, fluctuates over time (Steffensmeier and Schwartz 2004) and varies by race/ethnicity, class, and age (Sommers and Baskin 1993). Thus, there is no uniform or static gender ratio of offending, leaving the differential gap across offenses an important site for inquiry.

Given that women and men live in diverse structural conditions—conditions that are especially shaped by race and class inequality—approaches that seek simply to address a uniform gender gap miss the opportunity to examine how causal factors differentially shape women's and men's offending across cross-cutting social positions. For instance, there is evidence of a link between "underclass" conditions and urban African American women's offending that does not hold explanatory power for women's offending in other contexts (see Hill and Crawford 1990). Likewise, Steffensmeier and Haynie's (2000) recent structural analysis of homicide reveals variations across gender by age.

The most promising avenues for exploring the complexities of the gender ratio of offending are those that go beyond only the reliance on "descriptive and predictive numerical analyses" (Daly 1998: 95) for theoretical development. To demonstrate, we draw from Daly's (1998) conceptual schema and examine three areas of inquiry within feminist scholarship that have resulted in a more complex examination of gender and offending:

- *Gendered Pathways to Lawbreaking*: What trajectories bring males and females to offending? What factors and social contexts facilitate entrée to (and desistance from) offending and in what ways are these gendered?
- *Gendered Crime*: What are the specific contexts and qualities of female and male offending? How are various facets of offending socially organized?
- *Gendered Lives*: How does gender organize the daily lives of females and males and how does gender structure available courses of action and identities? How do these experiences intersect with crime and criminality?

As noted earlier, the typology we draw from here provides a useful means of organizing the primary thematic aspects of feminist research, though much of the research we draw from addresses problems and questions across this categorization and also speaks to the gender ratio of offending. We also include a separate discussion of new developments in the study of masculinities and crime. While this work has been developed primarily with regard to gendered crime, it represents somewhat distinctive theoretical problems and, thus, receives separate elaboration.

Gendered Pathways to Lawbreaking

From the early 1990s, feminist scholars began carefully examining what is now commonly referred to as "gendered pathways." Emphasizing "biographical elements, life course trajectories and developmental sequences" (Daly 1998: 97), the pathways approach seeks to map the life experiences that lead women and girls to offending as well as desistence (see Daly 1992; Giordano 2002). One of the important conceptual underpinnings of this research is the recognition of the "blurred boundaries" of victimization and offending. For example, young women who run away from home to escape abuse often inadvertently enter into more dangerous and abusive situations on the streets, while their escape from abusive homes is also criminalized. As Chesney-Lind and Pasko (2004: 5) observe, girls' earlier victimization "set[s] the stage for their entry into youth homelessness, unemployment, drug use, survival sex (and sometimes prostitution), and, ultimately, other serious criminal acts."

Gilfus (1992), for example, analyzed life history interviews with incarcerated female offenders. She found that the women's childhoods and adolescence were plagued with abuse and neglect and many had run away from home in response to this. Once on the streets, an "onset of drug use, truancy and stealing" (1992: 72) followed, with a large minority entering into juvenile prostitution as a survival strategy. Illegal work was done simply to survive, but further enmeshed the young women in criminal networks. As they transitioned into adulthood, the vast majority experienced continued victimization and many developed drug habits.

While mainstream criminology has not focused on pathways approaches, developmental and life course approaches have become increasingly popular (see articles 10-12, this volume). There is also a small but growing literature within this area that expressly compares males and females (see Keenan et al. 2004; Moffitt et al. 2001; Silverthorn and Frick 1999; Tibbetts and Piquero 1999). However, similar to the problems noted earlier concerning traditional studies of female offending, these works are rarely done with specific attention to important sociological constructs related to gender. Instead, the research typically identifies and tests similar causal mechanisms across gender in the search for individual-level gender differences or similarities, rather than examining potentially gender-specific risks related to structural or situational features of gender (but see Haynie 2003).

Despite the important insights of the "blurred boundaries" approach, including its disruption of the victim/offender dichotomy, some feminist scholars have highlighted that this "'leading scenario' of women's lawbreaking" (Daly 1992: 136) needs to be broadened to recognize the diversity of women's pathways to offending. Moreover, an exclusive emphasis on victimization as the key pathway to women's offending can overlook other important facets of women's and girls' lives that put them at risk for offending, including other manifestations of gender inequality. For instance, Gaarder and Belknap's (2002) recent analysis identifies the importance of violence and victimization, but also racial and economic marginality, school experiences, structural dislocation, and drug and alcohol use in explaining girls' delinquency.

It is also the case that studies relying only on female samples cannot sufficiently specify whether and how such risks influence pathways to offending across gender. One area in which feminist pathways analyses have been applied broadly is in the study of youth gangs (Joe and Chesney-Lind 1995; Miller 2001; Moore 1991; Portillos 1999). This research is strengthened by the direct comparison of males and females, or gang and non-gang girls. Such a comparative approach provides a more definitive understanding of how gender impacts on girls' risks for offending. As with other areas of criminological inquiry, research on girls' pathways/risks for gang involvement has generally included two approaches: analyses of etiological risk factors from survey research, and qualitative analyses that focus on girls' accounts of why they joined gangs and their life contexts both prior to, and at the time of joining, gangs. Though differing in their approach, most studies include a focus on structural and neighborhood conditions, the family, and peers. In addition, feminist scholarship has focused specific attention to victimization and this is routinely found to be an important risk for gang involvement among young women (Joe and Chesney-Lind 1995; Miller 2001).

Moore's (1991) work is particularly important because of her comparative sample. She documents a myriad of family problems that contribute to the likelihood of gang involvement for young women: childhood abuse and neglect, domestic violence among adults (particularly the abuse of female caregivers), alcohol and drug addiction in the family, witnessing the arrest of family members, having a family member who is chronically ill, and experiencing a death in the family during childhood. Her conclusion, based on comparisons of male and female gang members, is young women are considerably more likely to come from families that have numerous of these problems. Likewise, Miller's (2001) comparison of gang and non-gang (but delinquent) girls highlighted the importance of cumulative risks for girls' gang involvement. Portillos' (1999) study of Chicana gang members suggests that girls are also drawn to gang involvement as a means of escaping oppressive patriarchal conditions in the home.

While much of the feminist scholarship described thus far is qualitative, and we have suggested that much quantitative research has not adequately conceptualized gender, we end this section by highlighting a study that significantly raises the bar for quantitative research on gender. Heimer and DeCoster's (1999) analysis illustrates the tremendous benefit that results from a complex conceptualization of gender. In their "The Gendering of Violent Delinquency," these scholars address two key theoretical problems of interest to feminist criminologists: *within-gender* variability in the use of violence, and variability in violence *across gender* (i.e., the gender-ratio of offending). In doing so, Heimer and DeCoster provide a theoretical model of the causes of delinquency that can address differences across and within gender as well as between-gender similarities. They accomplish this by blending insights from a traditional criminological theory—differential association theory—with feminist theory about the definitions, meanings and impact of gender.

Heimer and De Coster outline a complex theoretical model of violent delinquency based on the differentiated experiences of young women and young men that result from gender inequality. They focus specifically on the interplay between social structure and culture, and argue that different social structural positions—based on gender, race, social class—result in variations in two significant cultural processes: family controls and peer associations. With regard to family controls, Heimer and De Coster differentiate between two types of family controls which they suggest operate differently for males and females. First, *direct parental controls* include such things as supervision and coercive discipline. On the other hand, *emotional bonding* is a more *indirect* form of control that results from emotional attachment to families. Particularly as young women are taught to value interpersonal relationships to a greater extent than young men, Heimer and De Coster argue that indirect controls resulting from emotional bonds to the family are the primary controls over girls' behavior, whereas direct controls have a stronger impact on reducing boys' delinquency.

With regard to peer associations, they suggest that boys are more likely to have exposure to friends who engage in aggressive activities. This means boys are also more likely than girls to be exposed to norms favorable to violence. These two cultural processes—family control and peer associations—along with prior histories of violent behavior, influence two cultural outcomes: the extent that youths learn violent definitions (e.g., definitions of violence as an appropriate behavior) and gender definitions (traditional beliefs about the proper behavior of males and females, or of masculinity and femininity). Youths who internalize cultural values accepting of violence are more likely to engage in delinquency. However, cultural definitions of violence also run counter to traditional definitions femininity, which stress "nurturance, passivity, nonaggressiveness, and physical and emotional weakness" (Heimer and De Coster 1999: 283). Thus the attitudes and beliefs young women learn about appropriate femininity will have a direct affect on their likelihood of engaging in violence.

Through a sophisticated analysis of the National Youth Survey, Heimer and De Coster tested their theoretical model and found strong support for its ability to explain variations in girls' and boys' use of violence, as well as variations in the use of violence within gender, based on the causal pathway of social structural factors (positions tied to race, class, gender) shaping cultural processes (family controls, peer associations), shaping cultural outcomes (violent definitions, gender definitions), shaping the likelihood youths participate in violence. They (1999: 305) explain:

> In short, the conclusion of our research is violent delinquency is "gendered" in significant ways. Adolescent violence can be seen as a product of gendered experiences, gender socialization and the patriarchal system in which they emerge. Thus, consistent with feminist arguments, gender differences in violence are ultimately rooted in power differences.

Significantly, individual-level character differences across gender do not account for the gender gap in violence; instead, the intersection of gendered meanings with the contexts of family and peer interactions expose males and females to different risks for learning violent definitions and, thus, engaging in violence (see also Bottcher 2001).

Gendered Crime

Research on the gendered social organization and situational contexts of crime represents a clear growth area in feminist criminology in recent years. In fact, the analysis of situational contexts of offending has gained momentum in the discipline, both by feminist scholars and those not using feminist approaches. Among mainstream scholars, the situational turn was partially in response to the development of a conceptual distinction between the criminal event and criminality as a set of individual characteristics (see Cohen and Felson 1979; Cornish and Clarke 1986; Gottfredson and Hirschi 1990). Thus criminologists brought renewed attention to the aspects of social situations that produce criminal events, as well as the individual decision-making and opportunity structures necessary for offending. While such questions date back to Sutherland (1939), they began receiving systematic attention in the 1990s. Most mainstream work in this vein has been grounded theoretically in various opportunity theories (see Felson 1998) or within symbolic interactionist approaches (Tedeschi and Felson 1994). Some of this work has relied on qualitative data in order to produce thick descriptions of circumstances and events (see Wright and Decker 1994, 1997).

Gendered attention to organizational and situational aspects of crime emerged with Steffensmeier's (1983; Steffensmeier and Terry 1986) pioneering analyses in the 1980s of institutional sexism and gender segregation in criminal networks. As a logical evolution of feminist criminology—which sees gender as potentially omnirelevant to social behavior and recognizes the situational nature of gender accomplishment—some feminist scholars have turned attention to how situational gender expectations and gendered opportunity structures shape criminal events. This work has taken several notable directions.

First, as noted in the previous section, an important contribution of feminist criminology has been to highlight the "blurred boundaries" of victimization and offending. While this approach most typically emphasizes the experience of victimization as a background risk for subsequent involvement in crime, feminists have also analyzed victimization as a key situational factor in the foreground of offending. This is most evident in feminist analyses of women who kill their abusive spouses. These events not only involve long-term patterns of serious abuse but are often triggered by a culminating victimization incident that directly results in the woman's violence (see Richie 1996). Likewise, Lisa Maher's (1997) ethnography of a drug economy analyses one form of female offending—"viccing"—that emerges from the widespread victimization and devaluation of women. Maher's work documents the proliferation of viccing—in which women in the sex trade rob their clients—as a form of resistance against their greater vulnerability to victimization and cheapened sex markets within the drug economy. Comparing viccing with traditional forms of robbery, Maher and Curtis conclude: "The fact the act [of viccing] itself is little different to any other instrumental robbery belies the reality that the motivations undergirding it are more complex and, indeed, are intimately linked with women's collective sense of the devaluation of their bodies and their work" (1992: 246).

In addition to the emphasis on blurred boundaries, recent feminist research also suggests that there are contexts in which situational norms favorable to women's crime exist, and these are not just about avoiding or responding to victimization, but also result in economic gain, status, recognition, or emotional rewards such as the alleviation of boredom, excitement or revenge (see Miller 1998; Simpson 1991; Simpson and Elis 1995). Though key motivational factors in these instances may not be explicitly "gendered," this work, nonetheless, maintains a gendered inquiry by moving beyond individual motivation to examine how women navigate gender-stratified environments and how they accommodate and adapt to gender inequality in their commission of crime. If a goal of situational crime analysis is to examine "the decision-making process of offenders confronted with specific contexts" (Einstadter and Henry 1995: 70), this cannot be accomplished without paying attention to the gendered contexts of the decision-making process, and the ways in which "gendered status structures this participation" (Maher 1997: 13).

Still another feminist approach to the study of situational context is reflected in those studies that have utilized sociological theory on gender as situated accomplishment (West and Zimmerman 1987; West and Fenstermaker 1995). As described above, this perspective emphasizes how women and men "do gender" in response to normative beliefs about femininity and masculinity, and has been incorporated into feminist accounts of crime as a means of explaining differences in women's and men's offending (Newburn and Stanko 1994; Messerschmidt 1993; Simpson and Elis 1995). Here, for instance, violence is described as "a 'resource' for...demonstrating masculinity within a given context or situation" (Simpson and Elis 1995: 50). Though this normative emphasis has primarily been brought to bear on male offending and constructions of masculinity, feminist theorists recently have attempted to account for female crime based on the same framework but with more limited success (see Miller 2002).

Studies of situational context have also included the framing of events within meso-level (e.g., neighborhood) and macro-level (e.g., structural) contexts. Again, an eye to gender enhances our understandings. As noted, extant research highlights that social networks, especially those on the streets, are highly gender segregated (see Anderson 1999; Bourgois 1995; Maher 1997; Miller 1998, 2001; Mullins and Wright 2003; Steffensmeier 1984; Steffensmeier and Terry 1986). Moreover, concentrated disadvantage strongly shapes the nature of street social networks, which then shapes the interactions within these networks. For example, James, et al. (2004) found that residence in a low-income, disorganized community increased girls' and women's exposure to both drugs and violence, and this connection was best understood through an examination of how living in this environment shaped their social networks (see also Simpson 1991; Sommers and Baskin 1993). They note that such neighborhoods "severely restricted [women's] social networks, both because there were few choices of friends available and because the threat of violence made social activity outside the house unappealing" (2004: 1006-1007; see also McCarthy et al. 2004). In a similar vein, Rountree and Warner (1999) examine how gendered neighborhood social ties affect community crime rates. This work highlights the importance of examining gender beyond the individual level.

Drawing from these various approaches, one of the strongest contributions of situational analysis lies in its ability to examine both convergences and divergences between women's and men's offending. Much traditional work in criminology—drawing from the character dichotomy noted earlier—suggests that while male violence is instrumental, direct, and highly physical, female violence is expressive, indirect, and relational (see Hagan and Foster 2003; Steffensmeier and Allen 1996). Such interpretations embrace, rather than challenge, taken-for-granted assumptions concerning gendered behaviors. While many scholars have found notable differences between male and female offending, especially in the realm of violence, this binary analytical framework ignores variation within male and female violence. Men *do* engage in relationally-focused violence (e.g., fighting in defense of a friend or loved one; see Anderson 1999; Mullins et al. 2004) and women engage in instrumental violence (see Baskin and Sommers 1997; Miller 1998). In fact, the routine framing of women's violence as expressive often functions to discredit and undermine their more instrumental goals (see Miller and White 2003). Thus, it is through the contextual examination of violent episodes and other offending, with strong attention to situational dynamics, that similarities and differences within and across gender can be uncovered and explained.

Few studies of gendered crime have integrated the various facets outlined above (but see Maher 1997). We conclude this section with a brief overview of one such analysis in order to highlight the important potential of such a multi-faceted approach. Mullins and Wright (2003) examined the ways in which gender structures participation in residential burglary, a quintessentially group-based offense. In a quasi-replication of Miller's (1998) comparison of motivations and enactment strategies among armed robbers, they explored how gender influenced initiation into, enactment of, and potential desistance from burglary. Building on work that highlights the intense segregation and male dominance of street life social networks (Maher 1997; Steffensmeier 1983; Steffensmeier and Terry 1986) the article highlights male control of both entrée into burglary crews and access to networks for goods disposal.

Because men were "the gatekeepers to the social world of residential burglary" (Mullins and Wright 2003: 821), males were initiated into burglary crews from a broad array of associates, including male peers and relatives. In contrast, females were most often initiated into crews by a romantic connection. Moreover, while men typically held marginal roles early in their careers (e.g., lookout and get-away driver), they began undertaking more central—and more profitable—roles as they gained experience. In contrast, women's roles rarely went beyond these peripheral acts. Mullins and Wright emphasize how stereotypes about gender were "expressed, reinforced and exploited within [these] street life social networks" (2003: 813), in some cases despite contradictory evidence. It was through both gender ideologies and male access to primary resources (control of crews and access to information about suitable targets) that women were marginalized.

Mullins and Wright also uncovered a striking gender difference in hypothetical desistance from crime. When men were asked to explain why they had ceased burglaries for a period of time in their lives, or what might cause them to quit entirely, they cited the influence (real or hypothetical) of a stable relationship with a woman as the primary factor (see also Laub, Nagin and Sampson 1998). Thus, the establishment of normative ties drove their desistance. For women, the situation was the opposite. Just as relationships with criminally involved men often framed their initiation into offending, the end of that relationship also tended to signal the end of their offending. However, women's offending behaviors were not simply a product of the relationship; instead, the relationship facilitated offending by providing opportunities and access to crews. Once the tie to the network was broken, the misogyny that dominates the streets kicked in and women found it difficult to gain entrée into another crew. Moreover, Mullins and Wright found that women—but not men—expressed strong concerns about how their families would react to their offending, suggesting that "female burglars are more sensitive than males to conventional informal social control" (2003: 832; see also Heimer and De-Coster 1999).

This study demonstrates the utility of situational analyses of gender and crime. Through close attention to the nature and dynamics of criminal situations, feminist approaches such as Mullins and Wright's can uncover and elucidate in a more precise fashion how gender operates in both the foreground and background of offending events. Through the discovery of contingencies, variations in crime within and across gender, and the careful examination of the evolution of criminal events, this form of inquiry can more precisely specify dynamic relationships between gender and crime.

Masculinities and Crime

Much early feminist work in criminology correctly critiqued existing theory and research for focusing on men's and boy's crime at the expense of women and girls. Yet, as gender-focused modes of inquiry evolved within the field, the key questions scholars asked concerning female offending and offenders also pointed to the need to "gender" the criminal behavior of men. While the danger in this focus lies in a return to the pre-feminist era of placing men back at the center of inquiry (Daly 1998: 87), it is nonetheless the case that criminology has ignored the significance of gender in the study of male offending. Given men's overrepresentation as offenders, the study of masculinities and crime is an important area for feminist inquiry. Historically, the gendered nature of male offending was assumed (and normalized), but was neither explored nor theorized. Parallel with the growth in the sociological study of masculinity, recent work in feminist criminology has attempted to look at the criminal behavior of men in the context of gendered theories. This approach has enhanced our understanding of male offending.

While not framed as such, much early research in criminology reflected the salience of masculinity for understanding criminal behavior. Work such as Miller's (1958), Cohen's (1955), and Wolfgang and Ferricutti's (1968), which emphasized subcultural approaches to the study of crime, clearly linked offending, especially violence, to the notions of self comportment we would today distinctly identify as masculine. Offenders' expressions of focal concerns such as independence, toughness, and strength clearly reflect the core of Western hegemonic masculinity. Even more recent research, such as that of Anderson (1999), Shover (1996), and Wright and Decker (1994, 1997) has highlighted the powerful conceptualizations of male identity among persistent offenders. Yet this work has been done without drawing from theories of gender, to the detriment of both subcultural and feminist criminology.

Similar to the focus on intersectionality in studying women's offending, some of this research has directly examined gender identity in the context of exploring racial/ethnic identity. For example, Davidson (1974) provided one of the earliest, nuanced linkages of masculinity and violence in the ethnographic literature. Studying Chicano prisoners housed in San Quentin, he centralizes the concept of *machismo*, Latino hegemonic masculinity, as the organizing principle behind violence specifically, and the totality of the inmate experience generally. Oliver's (1994) analysis of black male street violence strongly linked violent enactment and victimization to a distinct form of urban black masculinity. Other works suggest that violence is central to the generation and maintenance of a distinctly black masculinity that arises from the unique history of racial oppression and persistent denial of access to legitimate avenues of mainstream masculinity. In contexts of concentrated disadvantage, street reputation and associated violence become central to some black men's identities (see Anderson 1999).

As part of a broader attempt to situate criminal behavior within gendered social structures, Messerschmidt's (1993, 2000) structured action theory highlights intersectionality in examining the criminal behavior of both men and women. This approach sees gender norms and definitions as a product of social structures, but it is through micro-level processes of social action/interaction that gender is (re)produced. In *Masculinities and Crime*, Messerschmidt establishes an analytical framework for understanding the intersection of masculinity and crime by indicating that "men do masculinity according to the social situation in which they find themselves" (1993: 84). Masculinity and criminality will be more intertwined in certain environments than others. In the absence of more normative and mainstream avenues to masculinity construction (e.g., work and family life), Collison (1996: 440) notes, "a masculine self identify [is] fashioned around money, consumption, toughness and respect." According to Messerschmidt, men in these social locations may view crime as a "masculine-validating resource" (1993: 83). Such processes have been used primarily to explain men's participation in violence (but see Hochstetler and Copes 2003).

Scholars have drawn on the concept of "masculinity challenges"—interactions in which one's gendered identity is questioned and a specifically gender-scripted response is provoked—to frame men's interpersonal violence. In his study of homicide, for example, Polk (1994) analyzed how masculinity guided social actors: public challenges between men produced violent events that often turned lethal. Yet the source of the challenge need not come from another man. Alder and Polk (1996) uncovered similar processes within child homicide cases, where motivation often emerged from some form of challenge to the man's authority or power. Messerschmidt (2000) also shows how responses to such challenges can be directed toward other targets. For example, boys who are pushed into subordinate masculinities by their male peers can reassert their internal claims on hegemonic masculinity through the sexual assault of girls.

Recent work has also explored the contradictions and nuances of a specifi-cally situated street masculinity in framing criminal action. Mullins et al. (2004) found that most of men's interpersonal disputes with other men were grounded in their need to build and maintain gendered reputations (see also Graham and Wells 2003). They found that gendered perceptions of appropriate and inap-propriate behavior served as triggers for—and barriers against—retaliation. Men viewed violent retaliation as a key street survival tactic, deeply rooted in their identities *as men*. However, due to more traditional attitudes held by men concerning appropriate inter-gender interactions, if they were "wronged" by a woman, the path to action was sometimes more complex. Direct use of violence against women in a street context could lead to one appearing as a "punk" (a subordinated masculinity), as it was commonly believed that men should only involve themselves in "fair fights"—something not possible since women were seen as physically and emotionally weaker. At the same time, men strongly believed that they could not ignore a slight—this too is a mark of "punkness." A number of solutions to this conundrum were revealed in the interviews, from enlisting women to carry out the retaliation, to assigning the women retaliated against temporary symbolic status as "men" and, thus, le-gitimate targets because they were engaged in male-dominated activities[11] (see also Miller and White 2003). These findings highlight the contingent nature of masculinity on the streets. The connection between masculinity and crime is not so straightforward as to produce a consistent set of action frames. Instead, multiple contingencies seem to be the rule despite the deeply embedded nature of street masculinities.

While most research on masculinities and crime focuses on violence, Hoch-stetler and Copes (2003) provide an analysis of how the situational construction of masculinity frames property crime events. Based on interviews with con-victed property offenders, they explore how masculine posturing immediately prior to the criminal event often "boxes" offenders into a position where backing out of the crime would result in a loss of masculine capital. They also suggest that such reputational maintenance is much more salient for younger than for older men. Other work has shown that gains from property crime are often spent to enhance one's status on the streets which is significantly gendered (Mullins and Wright 2003).

Future work on masculinities will be strengthened by attention to several key theoretical problems. First, contradictions and contingencies. While research calls our attention to how masculinity frames, encourages, and le-gitimates violence and other crimes, even the most criminally embedded men are not always violent. Thus, an important area for further study is how men negotiate potentially violent encounters, including the mechanisms by which they are sometimes pushed toward, and other times pulled away from, violent resolution. Second, future work should explore the overlap of pragmatic mo-tivations with motives driven by masculinity construction. This will result in careful detailing (rather than overuse of) gender ascriptions. While masculinity is deeply integrated with street identity, the potential to over-ascribe gendered meanings to violence can obscure, rather than enhance, our understandings (see Miller 2002). Embedded offenders operate on the basis of other motivations, even in the realm of reputation. For instance, Katz (1988) notes while armed robbery can serve as a profoundly violent way to "do masculinity," it also serves other purposes in the minds and lives of robbers (for instance, "kicks," resource acquisition, and revenge). A man can use such violence to build and maintain a street reputation as a "bad ass" but this is just one facet of such events.

Finally, as with feminist scholarship more broadly, the importance of the intersections of age, class, and race/ethnicity have been noted in research on masculinities and crime and warrant further research. Thus far, limited work has used comparative samples to verify the observations made in the study of specific populations. Finally, the primary aspect of feminist research that has been explicitly attentive to masculinity falls within the purview of the situational analysis of "gendered crime." To more fully understand the impact of masculinities on crime, future research should also focus attention to broader aspects of feminist analysis, namely gendered pathways to lawbreaking and gendered lives. Such analyses will provide a more comprehensive understanding of the relationship between gender and crime for men.

Gendered Lives

Daly (1998: 98) describes the concept of *gendered lives* as the examination of the "significant differences in the ways women experience society compared with men." Compared with the other aspects of feminist criminology we have described, this is perhaps the most challenging because it requires systematic attention to gender well beyond the analysis of crime. As Daly (1998: 99) notes, "rather than analyze gender as a correlate of crime, one would analyze crime as a correlate of gender." Feminist research has made important inroads in the study of pathways to offending and the gendered nature of offending, but less work has had the scope required to address gendered lives. In this section, we highlight two studies that have accomplished this goal.

Jean Bottcher's (2001) analysis of gender and delinquency focuses not on gender as individual action, but instead on the gendering of social practices. This provides a conceptualization of gender as active and dynamic, and "[m]ost critically, this approach decenters the individual, enabling us to isolate components of social practices which…include rules governing human behavior and the resources making human activity possible" (2001: 897). Based on comparative interviews with male and female siblings, Bottcher's analysis draws from Giddens' structuration theory, and "plac[es] types of activities—activities by which gender was defined—at the center of the analytic frame" (2001: 903).

Bottcher identified three broad types of social practices: making friends and having fun; relating sexually and becoming parents; and surviving hardship and finding purpose. Within these she also identified more specific gendered dimensions that were related to exposure to, and risks for, delinquency. For example, gender segregated friendship groups, boundary maintenance among male peer groups and male access to privacy and nighttime "continuously placed the high-risk males, compared with the high-risk females, at greater risk of delinquent involvement" (2001: 910). Likewise, the meanings and rules guiding sexual relationships and childcare responsibilities had similar consequences.

Notable in Bottcher's approach is that her emphasis on practices, rather than individuals, challenges the gender dichotomy often found in studies of gender and crime. She demonstrates that these gendered patterns are not universally applicable to all males or all females:

> Some male-typed social practices appear to encourage or enable delinquent activity for either sex. Conversely, some female-typed social practices appear to discourage delinquent activity for both sexes. Thus, the social practices of gender disclose social conditions and activities influencing delinquent involvement, regardless of sex (Bottcher 2001: 904).

This approach offers a promising avenue for the study of gendered lives, particularly when coupled with analyses of gendered crime and grounded in how gendered practices may be shaped by other social positions such as race, class and generation. Moreover, her study demonstrates that the broader examination of gendered lives contributes to our understanding of the gender gap in offending, as well as gendered pathways.

Lisa Maher's (1997) *Sexed Work* also provides a systematic examination of gendered lives, based on several years of ethnography and in-depth interviews with women in a street level drug economy. While focused primarily on the foreground of offending, her groundbreaking study goes beyond "gendered crime" through her complex, layered account of women's everyday lives, including their participation in the local drug market. Maher's study is particularly exemplary because of her consistent examination of the intersections of race, class and gender in shaping women's experiences and lives, and illustrates the strengths of feminist scholarship that moves beyond an exclusive emphasis on gender. Like other feminist scholars whose works we've highlighted, Maher blends feminist analysis with a traditional theoretical approach—cultural reproduction theory.

Revealing the interdependence of formal and informal economies, including the illicit drug economy, the study focuses on the impact of stratification within formal and informal market economies and the consequent truncation of women's economic opportunities. Though some (primarily non-feminist) scholars have suggested the drug trade has opened new opportunities for women, Maher's study provides compelling evidence to the contrary. Gender inequality, as she demonstrates, is institutionalized on the streets: gender segregation and stereotypes of women as unreliable and weak limit women's participation in informal economic street networks. Specifically, the study documents a rigid gender division of labor in the drug economy, shaped as well along racial lines, in which women are "clearly disadvantaged compared to their male counterparts" (1997: 54).

Describing the three spheres of income generation on the streets—drug business hustles, non-drug hustles, and sex work—Maher details the ways in which women are excluded from more lucrative opportunities and find sex work one of their few viable options for making money. Moreover, the introduction of crack cocaine into urban drug markets has further disadvantaged women by increasing competition, as well as the degradation and mistreatment women often experience on the streets. In addition, she shows how racial stratification further differentiates the opportunities and experiences of white, African American, and Latina women within street-level sex work.

Sexed Work challenges several dimensions of previous work on women's participation in drug markets—including both previous feminist studies and traditional criminological approaches. For example, it contradicts "the highly sexualized images of women crack users dominating the social science literature" (1997: 195). This sexualized imagery—of desperate women willing to do "anything" for their next hit—is part and parcel of the dominant view of drug users (and especially women) as pathological, dependent, and lacking any control over their lives. In contrast, Maher shows that women are involved in a wide array of income-generating activities within the drug economy, with occupational norms governing their activities, despite the rigid division of labor on the streets. Likewise, Maher's analysis provides a critique of feminist research that over-emphasizes women's victimization. When "women's lawbreaking is presented as symptomatic of their victimization," (1997: 200), it likewise denies women agency and continues to frame them only in terms of passivity and dependence. Instead, Maher's research displays a complex understanding of the relationship between structure and agency. As she summarizes (1997: 201):

> I have tried to strike a balance between the twin discourses of victimization and volition that inform current understandings of women's drug-related lawbreaking. While this space must be large enough to include the constraints of sexism, racism and poverty that structuring women's lives, it cannot be so big as to overwhelm the active, creative and often contradictory choices, adaptations and resistances that constitute women's criminal agencies."

Maher's work exemplifies the aspects of feminist thought highlighted at the beginning of this chapter, and its scope and depth demonstrates the benefits of a *gendered lives* approach for understanding how gender intersects with cross-cutting structural positions, and how ideologies and social practices reproduce structural inequalities.

Conclusion

Contemporary feminist criminology is rich with theoretical development and stimulating research. The fusion of gendered theories with criminological theories has advanced our understanding of the complex ways that gender intersects with crime and criminality. In this essay, we have broadly explored the major theoretical and empirical directions within feminist criminology. Along the way, we have highlighted exemplary studies and pointed toward profitable future directions. Drawing from Daly's (1998) typology, we have examined the central themes that remain current in feminist criminology, including the gender ratio question, gendered pathways, gendered crime, and gendered lives. Some of these have been particularly fruitful in recent years.

With recent qualitative work, including feminist attention to masculinities and crime, we have seen the development of an increasing number of studies highlighting situational contexts and the overall complexity of gender's relation to crime. These works have pushed the field well past dichotomous conceptualizations of gender, as is evident as well in recent quantitative analyses of gender (see Heimer and DeCoster 1999). As these works emphasize the contingent nature of gender, they compel us to envision crime similarly. Likewise, feminist pathways research has drawn scholarly attention to those experiences that lead women and girls into criminal behaviors and networks, and have also pointed toward critically needed changes in prevention and intervention programs (see Acoca 1998; Henriques and Manata-Rupert 2001). This body of research will be strengthened further with more explicit comparisons across gender. And while the last theme, gendered lives, has received the least systematic attention, it perhaps offers the most promising potential for illuminating the intertwined nature of gendered social structures, behavioral expectations, and identities with crime and criminality. All of this work will be strengthened with continued systematic attention to the intersections of gender with race, class, generation and other structuring features of society.

As we see it, feminist criminology has advanced well beyond the questions of generalizability and the gender-ratio question that guided early works. Contemporary guiding questions have opened up a scholarly space that benefits from the rich theoretical tradition and contemporary developments in criminology, without remaining bound by its often narrow and androcentric conceptualizations of gender. Remaining cognizant of advances in interdisciplinary theories of gender as we "take stock" of the current status of feminist criminology, we find a healthy field of inquiry that continues to advance our understanding of the complex relation between gender and crime. The past three decades of feminist scholarship have firmly established both the legitimacy and utility of this area of inquiry. Continuing developments, both qualitative and quantitative, promise to continue the refinement of our understanding not just of crime, but of gender as well.

Notes

*   The authors would like to thank Kathleen Daly, Candace Kruttschnitt, and Francis Cullen for their feedback on an earlier draft.

1.   Mindful of Smart's (1995) critique of the phrase, we use "feminist criminology" here as a shorthand method of referring to the enterprise of theorizing crime, law and justice from feminist perspectives.

2.   To wit, a student recently queried, "Why would you build your career around the study of one independent variable?" and a colleague complained of scholars who "list independent variables as research interests."

3.   Given the breadth of these contributions, space constraints and the specific task requested of us here, our primary focus in this chapter will be feminist approaches to theorizing crime with specific emphasis on research in the social sciences.

4.   Ironically, androcentrism is evident both in patterns of paternalistic treatment of female offenders and also in recent philosophical shifts toward equality in the treatment of male and female offenders. For instance, "get tough" policies of recent decades have resulted in what Chesney-Lind and Pollock (1995) call "equality with a vengeance" given the masculine conceptualization of "justice" in contemporary penal philosophy (see Kruttschnitt, Gartner and Miller 2000).

5.   This tension will be further illustrated below in our examination of scholarship on gender and crime. For excellent examples in other facets of feminist scholarship in the field, see Britton (2003) and McCorkel (2002).

6.   See Daly (1997), Naffine (1996) and Smart (1992 1995) for feminist socio-legal analyses of how legal discourses write sexed subjectivities onto women's bodies. These studies highlight important aspects of feminist epistemology that are beyond the scope of our discussion here.

7.   Daly's conceptual schema provides a useful means of organizing the primary thematic aspects of feminist research in criminology. We should note that as with any typology, any single study can address questions within several of these categories. In fact, we see the best work as that which simultaneously addresses multiple aspects and will make note of these overlaps where relevant.

8.   This certainly remains the case today. As illustration, a number of the articles in this volume—which synthesize the current state of leading criminological theories—make little to no reference to gender or do so in the ways problematized here.

9.   Gender is one of the strongest and most persistent known correlates with offending. Historically, this led researchers to use all-male samples. More recently, quantitative research with samples that include both genders also includes a dichotomous measure of gender in order to avoid misspecification. Unfortunately, much work does not go beyond this methodological step and thus fails to theorize gender's effects.

10.   The fallacy of gender neutrality is demonstrated by the fact that criminologists never draw from all-female samples and assume their findings are generalizable to males. Thus, the notion of gender neutrality is based on the implicit perspective of the male subject (see Daly 2000).

11.   Given extensive evidence of the widespread and visible nature of violence against women in street contexts, it is also likely that men's reluctance to discuss their use of violence against women during their interviews was related to concerns over presentation of self. Miller and White (2003) examine this phenomenon with regard to dating violence.

References

Acoca, Leslie. 1998. "Outside/Inside: The Violation of American Girls at Home, on the Streets, and in the Juvenile Justice System." *Crime and Delinquency* 44: 561-589.

Acker, Joan. 1990. "Hierarchies, Jobs, Bodies: A Theory of Gendered Organizations." *Gender and Society* 4: 139-158.

Agnew, Robert. 1992. "Foundation for a General Strain Theory of Crime and Delinquency." *Criminology* 30: 47-87.

Alder, Christine, and Kenneth Polk. 1996. "Masculinity and Child Homicide." *British Journal of Criminology* 36: 396-411.

Alarid, Leanna Fiftal, Velmer S. Burton Jr., and Francis T. Cullen. 2000. "Gender and Crime Among Felony Offenders: Assessing the Generality of Social Control and Differential Association Theories." *Journal of Research in Crime and Delinquency* 37: 171-199.

Allan, Hillary. 1987. "Rendering them Harmless: The Professional Portrayal of Women Charged with Serious Violent Crimes." In Pat Carlen and Anne Worrall (eds.), *Gender, Crime & Justice.* Maidenhead, Berkshire, UK: Open University Press.

Anderson, Elijah. 1999. *Code of the Street: Decency, Violence and the Moral Life of the Inner City.* New York: W.W. Norton.

Bailey, William C., and Ruth D. Peterson. 1995. "Gender Inequality and Violence Against Women: The Case of Murder." Pp. 174-205 in John Hagan and Ruth D. Peterson (eds.), *Crime and Inequality.* Stanford, CA: Stanford University Press.

Baskin, Deborah R. and Ira B. Sommers. 1997. *Casualties of Community Disorder: Women's Careers in Violent Crime.* New York: Westview Press.

Britton, Dana M. 2000. "Feminism in Criminology: Engendering the Outlaw." *The Annals of the American Academy of Political and Social Science* 571: 57-76.

————. 2003. *At Work in the Iron Cage: The Prison as Gendered Organization.* New York: NYU Press.

Bottcher, Jean. 2001. "Social Practices of Gender: How Gender Relates to Delinquency in the Everyday Lives of High-Risk Youths." *Criminology* 39: 893-932.

Bourgois, Philippe. 1995. *In Search of Respect: Selling Crack in El Barrio.* Cambridge: Cambridge University Press.

Broidy, Lisa. 2001. "A Test of General Strain Theory." *Criminology* 39: 9-32.

Burton, Velmer S., Francis T. Cullen, T. David Evans, Leanne Fiftal Alarid, and R. Gregory Dunaway. 1998. "Gender, Self Control, and Crime." *Journal of Research in Crime and Delinquency* 35: 123-147.

Campbell, Anne. 1984. *The Girls in the Gang.* New York: Basil Blackwell.

Chesney-Lind, Meda. 1973. "Judicial Enforcement of the Female Sex Role." *Issues in Criminology* 8: 51-71.

Chesney-Lind, Meda and Lisa Pakso. 2004. *The Female Offender,* 2nd ed. Thousand Oaks, CA: Sage.

Chesney-Lind, Meda and Joycelyn M. Pollock. 1995. "Women's prisons: Equality with a vengeance." Pp. 155-175 in Alida V. Merlo and Joycelyn M. Pollock (eds.), *Women, Law and Social Control.* Boston: Allyn and Bacon.

Cohen, Albert. 1955. *Delinquent Boys.* New York: Free Press.

Cohen, Lawrence E. and Marcus Felson. 1979. "Social Change and Crime Rate Trends: A Routine Activity Approach." *American Sociological Review* 44: 588-608.

Collier, Richard. 1998. *Masculinities, Crime and Criminology: Men, Heterosexuality, and the Criminal(ised) Other.* London: Sage Publications.

Collison, Mike. 1996. "In Search of the High Life: Drugs, Crime, Masculinities and Consumption." *British Journal of Criminology* 36: 428-444.

Connell, R.W. 1987. *Gender and Power.* Stanford, CA: Stanford University Press.

―――. 1993. "Foreword." Pp. vii-xvi in James W. Messerschmidt (ed.), *Masculinities and Crime.* Lanham, MD: Rowman & Littlefield.

―――. 2002. *Gender.* Cambridge, UK: Polity Press.

Cornish, Derek B. and Ronald V. Clarke, eds. 1986. *The Reasoning Criminal: Rational Choice Perspectives on Offending.* New York: Springer-Verlag.

Daly, Kathleen. 1992. "Women's Pathways to Felony Court: Feminist Theories of Lawbreaking and Problems of Representation." *Review of Law and Women's Studies* 2: 11-52.

―――. 1997. "Different Ways of Conceptualizing Sex/Gender in Feminist Theory and Their Implications for Criminology." *Theoretical Criminology* 1: 25-51.

―――. 1998. "Gender, Crime and Criminology." Pp. 85-108 in Michael Tonry (ed.), *The Handbook of Crime and Justice.* Oxford: Oxford University Press.

―――. 2000. "Feminist Theoretical Work in Criminology." *DivisioNews.* Newsletter of the Division of Women and Crime, American Society of Criminology, August. (http://www.ou.edu/soc/dwc/newsletter.htm).

Daly, Kathleen, and Meda Chesney-Lind. 1988. "Feminism and Criminology." *Justice Quarterly* 5: 497-538.

Daly, Kathleen, and Lisa Maher, eds. 1998. *Criminology at the Crossroads: Feminist Readings in Crime and Justice.* Oxford: Oxford University Press.

Davidson, R. Theodore. 1974. *Chicano Prisoners: The Key to San Quentin.* Prospect Heights, IL: Waveland.

De Beauvoir, Simone. 1953. *The Second Sex.* New York: Knopf.

Dugan, Laura, Daniel S. Nagin, and Richard Rosenfeld. 1999. "Explaining the Decline in Intimate Partner Homicide: The Effects of Changing Domesticity, Women's Status, and Domestic Violence Resources." *Homicide Studies* 3: 187-214.

Einstadter, Werner and Stuart Henry. 1995. *Criminological Theory: An Analysis of Its Underlying Assumptions.* Fort Worth: Harcourt Brace College Publishers.

Eisenstein, Zellah R. 1988. *The Female Body and the Law.* Berkeley: University of California Press.

Emirbayer, Mustafa, and Ann Mische. 1998. "What is Agency?" *American Journal of Sociology* 103: 962-1023.

Farr, Kathryn Ann. 2000. "Defeminizing and Dehumanizing Female Murderers: Depictions of Lesbians on Death Row" *Women and Criminal Justice* 11: 49-66.

Fausto-Sterling, Anne. 1992. *Myths of Gender: Biological Theories about Women and Men.* New York: Basic Books.

Felson, Marcus. 1998. *Crime and Everday Life,* 2nd ed. Thousand Oaks, CA: Pine Forge.

Ferguson, Ann Arnett. 2000. *Bad Boys: Public Schools in the Making of Black Masculinity.* Ann Arbor: University of Michigan Press.

Fenstermaker, Sarah, and Candace West, eds. 2002. *Doing Gender, Doing Difference: Inequality, Power, and Institutional Change.* New York: Routledge.

Gaarder, Emily and Joanne Belknap. 2002. "Tenuous Borders: Girls Transferred to Adult Court." *Criminology* 40: 481-518.

Gilfus, Mary E. 1992. "From Victims to Survivors to Offenders: Women's Routes of Entry and Immersion in to Street Crime." *Women and Criminal Justice* 4: 63-89.

Giordano, Peggy, Stephen A. Cherkovich, and Jennifer Rudolf. 2002. "Gender, Crime and Desistance: Toward a Theory of Cognitive Transformation." *American Journal of Sociology* 107: 990-1064.

Gottfredson, Denise C. 2001. *Schools and Delinquency.* Cambridge: Cambridge University Press.

Gottfredson, Michael and Travis Hirschi. 1990. *A General Theory of Crime.* Stanford, CA: Stanford University Press.

Graham, Kathryn, and Samantha Wells. 2003. "'Somebody's Gonna Get Their Head Kicked In Tonight!' Agression Among Young Males in Bars—A Question of Values?" *British Journal of Criminology* 43: 546-566.

Hagan, John, and Holly Foster. 2003. "S/He's a Rebel: Toward a Sequential Stress Theory of Delinquency and Gendered Pathways to Disadvantage in Emerging Adulthood." *Social Forces* 82: 53-86.

Hagan, John, A.R. Gillis, and John Simpson. 1985. "The Class Structure of Gender and Delinquency: Toward a Power-Control Theory of Common Delinquent Behavior." *American Journal of Sociology* 90: 1151-1178.

Haynie, Dana L. 2003. "Contexts of Risk? Explaining the Link Between Girls' Pubertal Development and their Delinquency Involvement." *Social Forces* 82: 355-397.

Heimer, Karen, and Stacy De Coster. 1999. "The Gendering of Violent Delinquency." *Criminology* 37: 277-317.

Henriques, Zelma Weston, and Norma Manatu-Rupert. 2001. "Living on the Outside: African American Women Before, During and After Imprisonment." *The Prison Journal* 81: 6-19.

Hill, Gary D., and Elizabeth M. Crawford. 1990. "Women, Race, and Crime." *Criminology* 28: 601-623.

Hirschi, Travis. 1969. *Causes of Delinquency.* Berkley: University of California Press.

Hochstetler, Andrew, and Heith Copes. 2003. "Situational Construction of Masculinity Among Male Street Thieves." *Journal of Contemporary Ethnography* 32: 279-304.

Jacobs, Bruce A., and Jody Miller. 1998. "Crack Dealing, Gender and Arrest Avoidance." *Social Problems* 45: 550-569.

Jacobs, Bruce A., Volkan Topalli, and Richard Wright. 2000. "Managing Retaliation: Drug Robbery and Informal Sanction Threats." *Criminology* 38: 171-198.

Joe, Karen A., and Meda Chesney-Lind. 1995. "'Just Every Mother's Angel': An Analysis of Gender and Ethnic Variations in Youth Gang Membership." *Gender and Society* 9: 408-430.

Joe-Laidler, Karen A., and Geoffrey Hunt. 1997. "Violence and Social Organization in Female Gangs." *Social Justice* 24: 148-169.

Katz, Jack. 1988. *Seductions of Crime: Moral and Sensual Attractions of Doing Evil.* New York: Basic Books.

Katz, Rebecca S. 2000. "Explaining Girls' and Women's Crime and Desistance in the Context of Their Victimization Experiences: A Developmental Test of Revised Strain Theory and the Life Course Perspective." *Violence Against Women* 6: 633-660.

Keenan, Kate, Magda Stouthamer-Loeber, and Rolf Loeber. 2004. "Developmental Approaches to Studying Conduct Problems in Girls." Pp. 29-46 in Debra J. Pepler, Kirsten C. Madsen, Christopher Webster and Kathryn S. Levene (eds.), *The Development and Treatment of Girlhood Aggression.* Mahwah, NJ: Lawrence Erlbaum Associates Publishers.

Kruttschnitt, Candace. 1996. "Contributions of Quantitative Methods to the Study of Gender and Crime, or Bootstrapping Our Way into the Theoretical Thicket." *Journal of Quantitative Criminology* 12: 135-161.

Kruttschnitt, Candace, Rosemary Gartner, and Amy Miller. 2000. "Doing Her Own Time? Women's Responses to Prison in the Context of the Old and the New Penology." *Criminology.* 38: 681-718.

Laub, John H., Daniel S. Nagin, and Robert J. Sampson. 1998. "Trajectories of Change in Criminal Offending: Good Marriages and the Desistance Process." *American Sociological Review* 63: 225-238.

Lorber, Judith. 1994. *Paradoxes of Gender.* New Haven, CT: Yale University Press.

MacDonald, John M., and Meda Chesney-Lind. 2001. "Gender Bias and Juvenile Justice Revisited: A Multiyear Analysis." *Crime and Delinquency* 47: 173-195.

Maher, Lisa. 1997. *Sexed Work: Gender, Race and Resistance in a Brooklyn Drug Market.* Oxford, UK: Clarendon Press.

Maher, Lisa, and Richard Curtis. 1992. "Women on the Edge: Crack Cocaine and the Changing Contexts of Street-Level Sex Work in New York City. *Crime, Law and Social Change* 18: 221-258.

Martin, Susan E.. 1994. "'Outside Within' the Station House: The Impact of Race and Gender on Black Women Police." *Social Problems* 41: 383-400.

————. 1999. "Police Force or Police Service? Gender and Emotional Labor." *Annals of the American Academy of Political and Social Science* 561: 111-126.

McCarthy, Bill, Diane Felmlee, and John Hagan. 2004. "Girl Friends are Better: Gender, Friends, and Crime Among School and Street Youth." *Criminology* 42: 805-836.

McCorkel, Jill A. 2003. "Embodied Surveillance and the Gendering of Punishment." *Journal of Contemporary Ethnography.* 32: 41-76.

McNay, Lois. 2000. *Gender and Agency: Reconfiguring the Subject in Feminist and Social Theory.* Cambridge, UK: Polity Press.

Mears, Daniel P., Matthew Ploeger, and Mark Warr. 1998. "Explaining the Gender Gap in Delinquency: Peer Influence and Moral Evaluations of Behavior." *Journal of Research in Crime and Delinquency* 35: 251-266.

Messerschmidt, James W. 1993. *Masculinities and Crime.* Lanham, MD: Rowman and Littlefield.

————. 2000. *Nine Lives: Adolescent Masculinities, The Body, and Violence.* Boulder, CO: Westview Press.

————. 2004. *Flesh and Blood: Adolescent Gender Diversity and Violence.* Lanham, MD: Rowman and Littlefield.

Miller, Eleanor. 1986. *Street Woman.* Philadelphia: Temple University Press.

Miller, Jody. 1998. "Up It Up: Gender and the Accomplishment of Street Robbery." *Criminology* 36: 37-66.

————. 2001. *One of the Guys: Girls, Gangs and Gender.* New York: Oxford University Press.

————. 2002. "The Strengths and Limits of 'Doing Gender' for Understanding Street Crime." *Theoretical Criminology* 6: 433-460.

Miller, Jody and Norman A. White. 2003. "Gender and Adolescent Relationship Violence: A Contextual Examination." *Criminology* 41: 1501-1541.

Miller, Walter. 1958. "Lower Class Culture as a Generating Milieu of Gang Delinquency." *Journal of Social Issues.* 14: 5-19.

Mills, C. Wright. 1959. *The Sociological Imagination.* New York: Oxford University Press.

Moffitt, Terrie E., Avshalom Caspi, Michael Rutter and Phil A. Silva. 2001. *Sex Differences in Antisocial Behaviour: Conduct Disorder, Delinquency, and Violence in the Dunedin Longitudinal Study.* Cambridge: Cambridge University Press.

Moore, Joan. 1991. *Going Down to the Barrio: Homeboys and Homegirls in Change.* Philadelphia: Temple University Press.

Mullins, Christopher W., and Richard Wright. 2003. "Gender, Social Networks, and Residential Burglary." *Criminology* 41: 813-840.

Mullins, Christopher W., Richard Wright, and Bruce A. Jacobs. 2004. "Gender, Streetlife and Criminal Retaliation." *Criminology* 42: 911-940.

Naffine, Ngaire. 1996. *Feminism and Criminology.* Philadelphia: Temple University Press.

Newburn, Tim, and Elizabeth Stanko. 1994. *Just Boys Doing Business? Men, Masculinities and Crime.* London: Routledge.

Oliver, William. 1994. *The Violent Social World of Black Men.* New York: Lexington Books.

Orenstein, Peggy. 1994. *School Girls: Young Women, Self Esteem and the Confidence Gap.* New York: Doubleday.

Peterson, Dana, Jody Miller, and Finn-Aagee Esbensen. 2001. "The Impact of Sex Composition on Gangs and Gang Member Delinquency." *Criminology.* 39: 411-439.

Peterson, Ruth, and William C. Bailey. 1992. "Rape and Dimensions of Gender Socioeconomic Inequality in U.S. Metropolitan Areas." *Journal of Research in Crime and Delinquency.* 29: 162-177.

Phoenix, Joanna. 2000. "Prostitute Identities: Men, Money and Violence." *British Journal of Criminology* 40: 37-55

Pierce, Jennifer L. 1999. "Emotional Labor Among Paralegals." *Annals of the American Academy of Political and Social Science* 561: 127-142.

Polk, Kenneth. 1994. "Masuclinity, Honor and Confrontational Homicide." Pp. 166-188 in Tim Newburn and Elizabeth Stanko (eds.), *Just Boys Doing Business? Men, Masculinities and Crime.* London: Routledge.

Portillos, E. 1999. "Women, Men and Gangs: The Social Construction of Gender in the Barrio. Pp. 232-244 in Meda Chesney-Lind and John Hagedorn (eds), *Female Gangs in America: Essays on Girls, Gangs and Gender.* Chicago: Lake View.

Richie, Beth E. 1996. *Compelled to Crime: The Gender Entrapment of Battered Black Women.* New York: Routledge.

Rountree, Pamela Wilcox, and Barbara Warner. 1999. "Social Ties and Crime: Is the Relationship Gendered?" *Criminology* 37: 789-814.

Schwartz, Martin D., and Dragan Milovanovic. 1996. *Race, Gender, and Class in Criminology: The Intersection.* New York: Garland Publishing.

Sewell, William H., Jr. 1992. "A Theory of Structure: Duality, Agency, and Transformation." *American Journal of Sociology* 98: 1-29.

Silverthorn, Persephanie, and Paul J. Frick. 1999. "Developmental Pathways to Antisocial Behavior: The Delayed-Onset Pathway in Girls." *Development and Psychopathology* 11:101-126.

Simpson, Sally. 1991. "Caste, Class and Violent Crime: Explaining Differences in Female Offending." *Criminology* 29: 115-135.

————. 2000. "Gendered Theory and Single Sex Research." *DivisioNews.* Newsletter of the Division of Women and Crime, American Society of Criminology, August. (http://www.ou.edu/soc/dwc/newsletter.htm).

Simpson, Sally, and Lori Elis. 1995. "Doing Gender: Sorting out the Caste and Crime Conundrum." *Criminology* 33: 47-81.

Shover, Neal. 1996. *Great Pretenders: Pursuits and Careers of Persistent Thieves.* Boulder, CO: Westview.

Smart, Carol. 1976. *Women, Crime and Criminology: A Feminist Critique.* London: Routledge & Kegan Paul.

————. 1992. "The Women of Legal Discourse." *Social and Legal Studies.* 1: 29-44.

————. 1995. *Law, Crime and Sexuality: Essays in Feminism.* London: Sage.

Smith, Douglas A., and Raymond Paternoster. 1987. "The Gender Gap in Theories of Deviance: Issues and Evidence." *Journal of Research in Crime and Delinquency* 24: 140-172.

Sommers, Ira and Deborah R. Baskin. 1993. "The Situational Context of Violent Female Offending." *Journal of Research in Crime and Delinquency* 30: 136-162.

Steffensmeier, Darrell. 1983. "Organizational Properties and Sex-Segregation in the Underworld: Building a Sociological Theory of Sex Differences in Crime." *Social Forces* 61: 1010-1032.

Steffensmeier, Darrell and Emilie Allen. 1996. "Gender and Crime: Toward a Gendered Theory of Female Offending." *Annual Review of Sociology.* 22: 459-487.

Steffensmeier, Darrell, and Dana L. Haynie. 2000. "The Structural Sources of Urban Female Violence in the United States: A Macrosocial Gender-Disagreggated Analysis of Adult and Juvenile Homicide." *Homicide Studies* 4: 107-134.

Steffensmeier, Darrell and Jennifer Schwartz. 2004. "Trends in Female Criminality: Is Crime Still a Man's World?" Pp. 95-111 in Barbara Raffel Price and Natalie J. Sokoloff (eds.), *The Criminal Justice System and Women: Offenders, Prisoners, Victims and Workers,* 3rd ed. New York: McGraw Hill.

Steffensmeier, Darrell, and Robert Terry. 1986. "Institutional Sexism in the Underworld: A View from Inside." *Sociological Inquiry* 56: 304-323.

Steffensmeier, Darrell, Jeffery Ulmer, and John Kramer. 1998. "The Interaction of Race, Gender and Age in Criminal Sentencing: The Punishment Cost of Being Young, Black and Male." *Criminology* 36: 763-797.

Sutherland, Edwin. 1939. *Criminology.* Philadelphia: Lippencott.

Tavris, Carol.1992. *The Mismeasure of Woman.* New York: Simon and Schuster.

Tedeschi J.T. and R.B. Felson. 1994. *Violence, Aggression and Coercive Actions.* Washington, DC: American Psychological Association.

Thorne, Barrie. 1993. *Gender Play: Girls and Boys in School.* New Brunswick, NJ: Rutgers University Press.

Tibbetts, Stephen, and Alex R. Piquero. 1999. "The Influence of Gender, Low Birth Weight, and Disadvantaged Environment in Predicting Early Onset of Offending: A Test of Moffitt's Interactional Hypothesis." *Criminology* 37: 843-877.

Tittle, Charles. 1995. *Control Balance: Toward a General Theory of Deviance.* Boulder, CO: Westview Press.

Tong, Rosemarie. 1998. *Feminist Thought,* 2nd ed. Boulder, CO: Westview Press.

Visher, Christy A. 1983. "Gender, Police Arrest Decisions, and Notions of Chivalry." *Criminology* 21: 5-28.

West, Candace, and Sarah Fenstermaker. 1995. "Doing Difference." *Gender and Society* 9: 8-37.

West, Candace, and Don H. Zimmerman. 1987. "Doing Gender." *Gender and Society* 1: 125-151.

Whaley, Rachel Bridges. 2001. "The Paradoxical Relationship between Gender Inequality and Rape: Toward a Refined Theory." *Gender and Society* 531-555.

Williams, Christine L. 2000. "Preface." *The Annals of the American Academy of Political and Social Science* 571: 8-13.

Wolfgang, Marvin E., and Franco Ferracuti. 1967. *The Subculture of Violence.* London: Tavistock.

Wright, Richard, and Scott Decker. 1994. *Burglars on the Job: Streetlife and Residential Break-ins.* Boston: Northeastern University Press.

——————. 1997. *Armed Robbers in Action: Stick Ups and Street Culture.* Boston: Northeastern University Press.

9

Peacemaking Criminology:
Past, Present, and Future

John Randolph Fuller and John F. Wozniak

Peacemaking Criminology is one of the newer theoretical perspectives to arrive on the criminological landscape. Like other critical investigations such as feminist criminology, postmodernist theory, and left realism, peacemaking criminology looks beyond the traditional explanations of the causes of crime residing in deviant individuals and the appropriate responses as involving deterrence, punishment, and incapacitation (Williams 2002). Peacemaking criminology can be viewed as a more holistic perspective that critiques the processes in which: the individual is subject to broad social forces that define what crime is; the criminal justice system is used as a tool of selective enforcement and punishment; and a war mentality drives the multi-billion dollar industry of (in)justice.

In this chapter, we seek to explain the origins of peacemaking criminology, assess both its theoretical logic and its empirical support, and suggest how this perspective might be integrated further into the criminal justice system as an effort to enhance humane and effective rehabilitative treatment, alternative justice processing and the establishment of safer communities where citizens are confident in the fairness and effectiveness of the justice system. We appreciate the formidable tasks we have set for our journey but we embark on it with a sense of excitement for situating peacemaking in the universe of criminological theory and humility for our limited knowledge of all the many intellectual terrains we must traverse. Nonetheless, we believe this to be an important quest given the need to reform the way society creates and responds to crime.

Thereby, the first part of this chapter observes some favorable and unfavorable reactions that have been commonly expressed about peacemaking criminology and then shows how this perspective has emerged upon the development of three major traditions. In part two, each of these major traditions of peacemaking criminology is explored.

Next, a section of this chapter is titled "The Overarching Context of Peacemaking Criminology" in order to draw attention toward how this perspective can be applied at multiple levels within society. Part four provides an outline of peacemaking criminology as a theoretical approach, including its major contributors, its link with restorative justice, and two illustrations of its theoretical frameworks.

The fifth part discusses some promising empirical support of peacemaking criminology's stance against nonviolence. Here, the general ineffectiveness of both corporal and capital punishment are viewed respectively in terms of current research. Relatedly, the effectiveness of socially supportive treatment is briefly raised as a peacemaking alternative to the latter forms of punishment. In the conclusion, an effort is made to pull together the analysis undertaken within this chapter by identifying core concepts and propositions of peacemaking criminology that might be investigated within future criminological research.

Why Peacemaking and Why Now?

Peacemaking Criminology is struggling to gain legitimacy in academic criminology and in the day-to-day activities of the criminal justice system. As a new perspective it has gained both adherents and critics. Its adherents present papers and roundtables at the annual meetings of the American Society of Criminology and the Academy of Criminal Justice Sciences. As testimony to its momentum, a roundtable session in November of 2001 drew a Saturday 8 a.m. crowd of over fifty participants where the discussion centered on peacemaking in a time of terrorism. Additionally, the vitality of peacemaking criminology can be seen in research on the attitudes of criminologists and in the coverage peacemaking receives in criminal justice textbooks. In regard to the former, it has been found within survey research that progressive criminologists tend to express hope that their teaching might help students to recognize the failures of the existing approach to crime and that there is a different way to organize social life and justice—to take a road not commonly chosen: to engage in peacemaking criminology (Wozniak 2000). Concerning the latter, an overview of recent crime-related textbooks has indicated that peacemaking criminology has not only attained increased coverage, but also become blended with other criminological approaches to criminality (Wozniak 2002b).

There are, however, dissenters who view peacemaking criminology as marginal or irrelevant. Criticisms range from asserting that peacemaking presents nothing new to criminology, to arguments that peacemaking is vague and cannot offer a blueprint of policy changes that would result in a humanistic criminal justice system. It is our contention many of the critics have not invested in the study of peacemaking criminology and find fault with it based on their misconceptions of the breath and scope of the perspective (Wozniak 2002b). It is one of our goals here to provide a clear and succinct overview of peacemaking criminology that can serve as the basis for informed criticism.

Peacemaking criminology first appeared in the literature with the publication of Harold Pepinsky and Richard Quinney's edited book *Criminology as Peacemaking* in 1991.[1] The book marks a watershed event in the lives of many criminologists (including, or maybe even especially, us), given that it brought together under a unified theme the writings and ideas of many authors who have attacked traditional criminology's claims of being objective, rational, and scientific. Much like some of the postmodern critics of the relationship between culture and crime, peacemaking criminology looks outside the narrow confines of mainstream criminal justice and makes linkages to broader intellectual traditions in an effort to expand the focus on crime and criminality.

This emphasis seems even more relevant today with the blurring of the lines between domestic law enforcement and international events brought on by the preoccupation with the war on terror. From a peacemaking perspective, the Patriot Act, Guantanamo Bay, and the scandal at the Abu Ghraib prison are all excesses of the misguided ideology of the war on crime. In order to appreciate how the peacemaking perspective addresses crime, and especially how it is pertinent to the war on terror, it is necessary to consider how it is related to what has come before. The three intellectual traditions identified by Pepinsky and Quinney are a logical place to start the task of situating peacemaking criminology in a broader context. By linking peacemaking to its religious and humanist roots, and considering how it incorporates the more recent feminist and critical traditions, we can began to understand how it promises to be a overarching theory that speaks to a wide range of criminal justice issues. Best of all, however, we will see that peacemaking criminology is connected to a more inclusive scheme that goes well beyond criminal justice and can impact on issues ranging from the interpersonal to the international and global.

Three Major Intellectual Traditions of Peacemaking Criminology

Pepinsky and Quinney's *Criminology as Peacemaking,* is a collection of original readings that are grouped according to the intellectual tradition from which they draw inspiration. These intellectual traditions are the religious and humanist, the feminist, and the critical. While not mutually exclusive (for example, many feminist criminologists also consider themselves to be critical), this organization gives the book a useful way in which to consider the many strains of intellectual endeavors that inform peacemaking criminology.

Religious and Humanist Intellectual Traditions

Criminology is grounded in the great religious and humanist thought of past centuries. Even the word penitentiary has religious connections to the concept of doing penance (Welch 2004). To ignore the religious foundations of the criminal justice system is to misunderstand the development of modern criminology. In a secular state such as the United States where the separation of church and state is a legal concern, the archeology of religious traditions in the construction of the social fabric of life is even more important to acknowledge. Peacemaking criminology does not advocate a return to religious doctrine but rather argues that in order to appreciate the history and development of our systems of social control, we need to take into account just how religion and humanist thought has been an influence in how our institutions, particularly the criminal justice system, have evolved into what they are today.

According to Braswell, Fuller, and Lozoff (2001: 11), "peacemaking criminology draws from a variety of ancient wisdom and religious traditions including Christianity, Buddhism, Hinduism, Islam, Judaism, and Native American." While each of these religions has had its share of conflict, wars and social problems, at the root of each is a teaching of peace and harmony. Without going into the various doctrinal fine points of each of these ways of knowing, we submit that there are commonalities that suggest individuals, groups, and nation-states can coexist in mutually rewarding work, trade, and leisure. While the state of peace is elusive, it is consistent with the teachings, if not always the practice, of the major religious traditions of the world.

Much the same can be said of humanist traditions. A system of ethics need not be grounded in an established religion to be a peaceful and nurturing vehicle. For example the Golden Rule that encouraging to "do unto others as you would have them do unto you," is an inherently peacemaking principle.

The reclaiming of one's soul, or the rehabilitation of one's patterns of behavior, are two sides of the same optimistic coin that says individuals change. The implications for the criminal justice system that arise from the religious and humanist traditions have been deeply embedded in the structure and function of justice for centuries. By overtly recognizing this fact, peacemaking criminology more accurately and effectively appreciates both the reasons why individuals commit crimes and how the criminal justice system responds (Braswell 1990).

Feminist Traditions

The second major intellectual tradition from which peacemaking criminology draws its inspiration is the feminist movement. There is a long and rich history of women challenging the instruments of justice that have accorded them a secondary status in the United States (Daly and Chesney-Lind 1988). Issues ranging from the right to vote, the right to own property, the right to work in numerous occupations and positions of leadership, and the right to be treated with fairness and dignity by the criminal justice system have all been hard won by the feminist movement.

There are a variety of ways in which feminism addresses the issues of crime and justice and it is beyond the scope of this chapter to trace the nuances and contributions of each. However, it is important to recognize that these major strains of feminism: liberal, Marxist, and radical, each offer substantially different critiques of the ways in which the institutions of society, and particularly for our purposes here, the criminal justice system, have treated gender as an occasion to produce differential outcomes (Moyer 2001).

What peacemaking criminology shares with the feminist perspective is the understanding that a rational, humane, and ultimately effective criminal justice system must not only treat individuals the same regardless of their gender, but also recognize that because of historical and social processes, women continue to be placed at a disadvantage. Only by challenging the inequities in the criminal justice system (as well as in other institutions) can the ingrained injustices be corrected. Peacemaking criminology regards this emphasis on social justice as a cornerstone of its philosophy in much the same way as does feminism.

Critical Traditions

The third type of intellectual tradition to which peacemaking criminology can be traced is the critical tradition. The term critical criminology is used to refer to a broad range of theories that critique the power arrangements in society, particularly those encompassing social class, race, and gender. As with the feminist intellectual tradition, we will not delineate all the various strains of critical criminology here, but rather point to some of the major themes that influence peacemaking criminology. The first critique of criminology in the critical tradition is the analysis of crime and social class presented by those steeped in Marxism. While Karl Marx actually had little to say about crime, his theories about the way the powerful used the means of production to control the working classes continues to inform criminologists (Bohm 1982; Lynch, Michalowski, and Groves 2000). Even though the manufacturing economy of mid-eighteenth century Europe is no longer the vehicle of oppression, the inequitable power arrangements of contemporary society continue to produce a working environment where getting fair compensation for one's labor and ideas is problematic. It also seems reasonable to suggest that other critical theories, such as Left Realism (DeKeseredy and Schwartz 1991) and Critical Race theory (Mann 1993), can be viewed as approaches which similarly inform peacemaking criminology in important ways.

The Overarching Context of Peacemaking Criminology

In order to fully appreciate peacemaking criminology as a perspective that can speak to the problems of crime, it is necessary to realize that it is a theory that can be applied to a number of social problems at multiple levels of inquiry

(Fuller 1998).   In fact, there is nothing about the peacemaking perspective that makes it an inherently a theory about crime as opposed to a theory about childrearing, international relations, or self-improvement. This is both strength and a weakness of the theory. First, it is a strength because it is relevant to other lines of inquiry and shares features with other well-established theories that have successfully dealt with social problems. It is also a weakness because while speaking to the broader issues of violence and social justice, peacemaking criminology does not directly address the issues of crime and criminality in quite the same manner as traditional criminological theories.

The potential for the wide-ranging impact of peacemaking criminology is reflected on the right side of Figure 9.1 where the four levels of analysis are detailed:

Figure 9.1
Peacemaking Pyramid Intrapersonal: Self Love

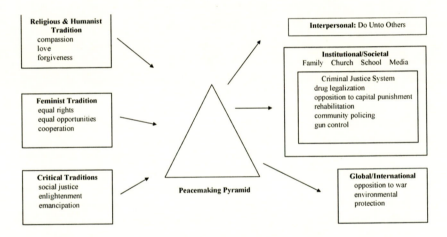

1. *Intrapersonal.* One of the foundations of peacemaking criminology is the observation that to do truly good one must incorporate a philosophy of love and compassion towards oneself. People who are personally conflicted and full of self-hate are seldom able to relate to others in positive ways. Many individuals gain serenity in their religious beliefs while others find it in other ways. Regardless of the source, a healthy self-concept can be a buffer against a number of ills, including the propensity to hurt others or steal their property. The resurgence of programs based on a religious faith is one example of how an emphasis on self-love can be incorporated into the counseling of criminal offenders.

2. *Interpersonal.* In addition to being peaceful toward oneself, peacemaking criminology advocates being fair, decent, and compassionate toward others. In order to live in civilized communities, this ability to love others, including those who disagree with you, is paramount (Boulding 2000). This is the territory of numerous psychological and sociological theories that deal with crime and peacemaking criminology sharing the concerns of communal living in complex societies.

3. *Institutional/Societal.* While the impact of crime is intensely personal, the response of society to the causes of crime is vested in the institutional. Therefore, peacemaking criminology has the most to offer at this level as it addresses the practices of the criminal justice and mental health systems. Additionally, schools, families, churches, and the media have much to benefit from if they embrace the principles of the peacemaking perspective. A book could be written on peacemaking in each of these institutions and while this task is beyond the scope of this chapter, it is, nevertheless, important to realize that the overarching perspective of peacemaking is pertinent to each. Specifically, for the criminal justice system, there are some issues that are anathemas to peacemaking. The love affair that many Americans have with firearms is a national problem that is directly addressed by peacemaking criminology. While there are legitimate uses for guns such as hunting and target shooting, the downward spiral of individuals buying guns for protection from other citizens who have bought guns for protection has resulted in a level of gun violence that other countries find appalling. There is an old saying in the theater that if a gun is presented in the first act, it goes off by the third act. In many neighborhoods and families, it often does not take that long.

Another criminal justice issue that is especially relevant to peacemaking criminology is capital punishment. The killing of offenders by the state is something that is inconsistent with the principles of peacemaking and is counterproductive to the development of trust in citizens in the fairness of the system. There are other policies that are currently being employed in the criminal justice system that peacemaking would accelerate. The efforts of community policing to re-involve law enforcement officers in the social fabric of the neighborhoods they patrol is one example. Another example of peacemaking criminology is the emphasis on rehabilitation that was, at one time, more prevalent before the war on crime perspective begin to dominate criminal justice policy (Cullen and Gilbert 1982). Finally the war on drugs has been exposed as a major failure. A more humane, rational, and effective policy toward drug use could involve an emphasis on treatment rather than punishment (see, for example, Currie 1993).

4. *Global/International.* Finally, the peacemaking perspective can be applied to international issues such as terrorism, war, the environment, and international trade. The squandering of the goodwill demonstrated toward the United States after the terrorist attacks of September 11, 2001 by the attack on

Iraq has robbed us of the moral high ground in the conversation about human rights. It is particularly applicable to peacemaking criminology because of the policies of imprisonment by the military in their prisons in Iraq, Cuba, and the United States (Strasser 2004). Human rights are particularly vulnerable during wartime and the United States has failed to set an example that is consistent with peacemaking criminology as well as international law.

An Outline of Peacemaking Criminology as a Theoretical Perspective

So far we have traced the intellectual traditions from which peacemaking criminology draws inspiration and have delineated the multiple social and theoretical contexts where it can be applied. Now it is time to specify exactly what constitutes a peacemaking perspective. Because the theory is new and evolving, and because there are many architects dedicated to its construction, it is with a sense of hesitation that we offer this outline of peacemaking criminology. As with any "work in progress," events and writings may overtake our offering, but we believe Fuller's peacemaking pyramid offers a reasonable outline of the facets of the theory as it is now understood. While some may object to the hierarchical nature of the pyramid, it is essential to understand that solutions to the problems of crime require building on the base of nonviolence. Therefore, we present Figure 9.2 as a basis for discussing peacemaking criminology.

Figure 9.2
Peacemaking Pyramid

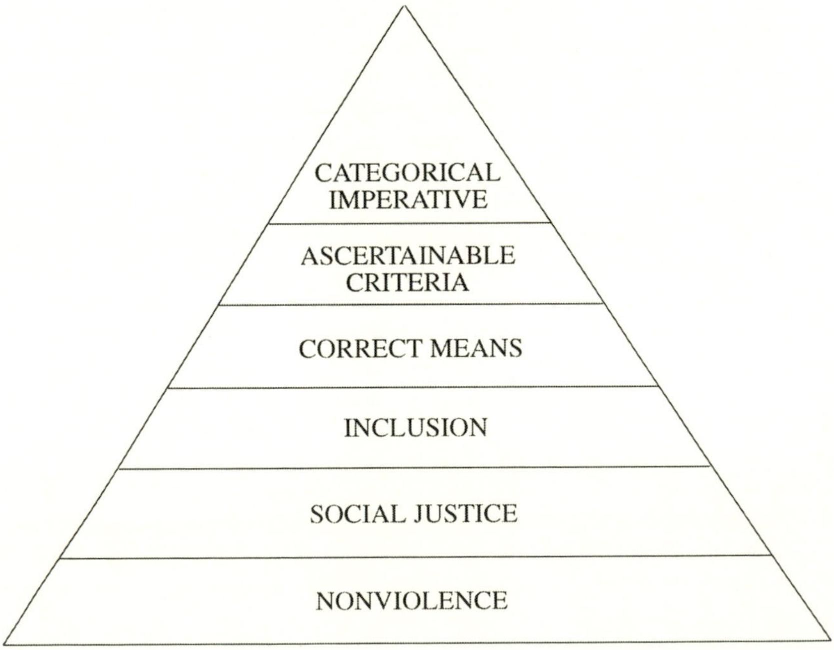

CATEGORICAL IMPERATIVE

ASCERTAINABLE CRITERIA

CORRECT MEANS

INCLUSION

SOCIAL JUSTICE

NONVIOLENCE

Some criminological theories are the product of one individual's perceptive insights and exhibit a clear and focused structure that allows for systematic discussion and testing. Other contributors to this book like Ronald Akers, John Braithwaite, and Robert Agnew are readily identified with the theories they describe. Peacemaking criminology has many architects and can be said to still be in the process of construction. As such, we can simply point to some of the criminologists who toil in the peacemaking field and look at the fruits that are coming to bear. The crop is, by no means, in on peacemaking criminology and it will be many seasons before we know for sure whether the theory will prove testable and make a continued contribution to the field. Let us now briefly examine some of the major contributors to peacemaking criminology.

Pepinsky and Quinney as Pioneers of Peacemaking Criminology

Criminologists Harold (Hal) Pepinsky and Richard Quinney (1991) were among the first to advocate for a peacemaking focus in criminology. They looked at how the criminal justice system contributes to the suffering of not only the victims of crime but also the offender and the general society. In searching for explanations for this suffering, they have drawn on the three intellectual traditions in some interesting ways. Richard Quinney has had a fascinating career as a social thinker (Martin, Mutchnick, and Austin 1990: 379-407; Quinney 2000) and is now being generally recognized as a founding father of an alternative way of approaching the field. While tracing the evolution of Quinney's thinking is beyond the scope of this chapter, it is important to note that his contributions to critical criminology are well established and that his writings on peacemaking criminology are fundamental. Specifically, Quinney (1991: 11) brings his personal involvement in Buddhism to bear in the issues of crime and suffering as he concludes:

> All of this is to say, to us as criminologists, that crime is suffering and that the ending of crime is possible only with the ending of suffering. And the ending both of suffering and of crime, which is the establishing of justice, can come only out of peace, out of a peace that is spiritually grounded in our very being. To eliminate crime—to end the construction and perpetuation of an existence that makes crime possible—requires a transformation of our human being. We as human beings must *be* peace if we are to live in a world free of crime.

Quinney's conception of peacemaking begins with this very personal reflection and moves on to the transformation of society by individuals who have embraced peace. While it may appear to be utopian by some, Quinney contends that the liberation of oneself is necessary before one can truly work to reform the criminal justice system.

In a very similar vein, Hal Pepinsky has played a key role in the spread of knowledge about peacemaking criminology. That is, in his summarizing chapter of his edited peacemaking book (with Quinney), Pepinsky (1991:300) poignantly observes that:

> The problem is not that peacemaking in criminology is new and untested; the problem is our ignorance of the vast amount that is being taught and done by peacemakers in criminology and criminal justice.

Pepinsky also has helped to spread the good word about people increasingly working to challenge a "warmaking" approach to crime within his "Peacemaking Primer" (Pepinsky 1999). Notably, while presenting information about peacemaking in respect to its basic principles and perils, Pepinsky (1999:59) maintains that:

> Peacemaking is the art and science of weaving and reweaving oneself with others into a social fabric of mutual love, respect and concern. This is one of two ways, or attitudes, with which one may enter any social interaction. The other attitude is that of working to win wars against personal enemies, those one tries to identify, isolate and subdue for the sake of one's own and one's loved ones safety. This attitude is called warmaking.

In this light, Pepinsky's slant on peacemaking coincides with Quinney's previously mentioned notion that peacemaking involves both an individual and social transformation process. For instance, Pepinsky (1999:68) contends:

> No real construction of peace depends on any single person to make it happen; and when peace breaks out, it is the concertedness of everyone's resonant and mutually accommodating actions that makes it so.

The Link of Restorative Justice to Peacemaking Criminology

Restorative justice practices are a large part of the peacemaking perspective (Braswell, Fuller, and Lozoff 2001). Some criminologists such as Mickey Braswell have argued that peacemaking criminology is the theory and restorative justice is the practice. Peacemaking criminology and restorative justice are certainly related, yet there are some differences in scope, real-world practicality, and theoretical focus. While we will touch on restorative justice in our discussion of peacemaking criminology, we will not elaborate in any detail because the topic is covered in this volume by John Braithwaite much more elaborately than we can do now. It is sufficient to say here that restorative justice shares many of the goals of peacemaking criminology. While there are many forms of restorative justice programs, they all focus on repairing the harm done by crime and re-establishing relationships between offenders and victims, and strengthening communities (Van Ness and Heetderks Strong 2002; Bazemore and Schiff 2001).

The Peacemaking Pyramid

The peacemaking pyramid has been developed in an effort to bring together all the strains and variations of a perspective that cover a wide range of ideas. To the extent it is successful in this task, it can illustrate how seemingly dissimilar or unconnected ideas can fit into a scheme that can address crime. The peacemaking pyramid is comprehensive enough to encompass all the various perspectives that have been termed peacemaking criminology. The pyramid is based on the following six concepts:

- *Nonviolence.* The most important concept embedded in peacemaking criminology is nonviolence. This does not simply mean that offenders should not commit violent crimes but additionally, that the criminal justice system, in its response to offending, should not perpetuate the violence. The war on crime metaphor is inappropriate and counterproductive to the fashioning of humane and effective responses to the problems of crime. Capital punishment, mandatory sentencing, the availability of firearms, and a host of other traditional responses to crime are in violation of the principle of nonviolence. There are a number of individuals who have advocated nonviolence as a policy including Leo Tolstoy, Mahatma Gandhi, and Dr. Martin Luther King. Critics of peacemaking criminology often contend that the principle of nonviolence is utopian and unrealistic, but those who espouse this principle are able to point to numerous examples of how nonviolence not only worked, but was the only policy that could work (Holmes 1990).
- *Social Justice.* The absence of violence does not guarantee a just world according to peacemaking criminology. Individuals like Gandhi "fought" in nonviolent ways to ensure that social justice was enhanced. Only by promoting the welfare of all, including those without power, can a society develop a long-term atmosphere of cooperation and commitment on the part of all citizens. As long as racism, sexism, and discrimination according to social class are supported by the state, the concept of social justice is violated even if the society has a high degree of nonviolence (Klein, Luxenburg, and Gunther 1991).
- *Inclusion.* One of the confusions that continues to perplex citizens is how the state takes the responsibility of a case away from the victim and offender. Nils Christie[2] likens the case to property and contends that when the state prosecutes in the name of the people, that it neglects those most intimately involved. The peacemaking principle of inclusion attempts to put the victim and the offender back into the criminal justice equation. This is best illustrated by restorative justice programs that promote reintegrative shaming, conciliation, and forgiveness. In addition to the victim and offender, others impacted by the crime are included in fashioning a solution. There entities include

family members of the victim and the offender, representatives from law enforcement, schools, and the community. The overall intention of inclusion is to enlist the support and cooperation of everyone involved in order to repair the harm done by the crime (Karp and Clear 2002).

- *Correct Means.* How does the criminal justice system arrive at its solutions to the problems of crime? The concept of correct means dictates that it must do so in an ethical and moral way. Correct means is a Gandhian term that says the means employed are as important as the result because they form a behavioral model (Erikson 1969: 198-199). The law enforcement officer who tricks a juvenile into a confession may have solved the case but, in the long run, may have set the seeds for future criminality by alienating the youth.

- *Ascertainable Criteria.* The criminal justice system is a bureaucracy that has evolved its own procedures, language, and protocols that can be extremely confusing to the uninitiated. Offenders and victims get lost in maze of overlapping jurisdictions, self-serving organizational politics, and well-meaning but confusing procedures that are required by law but often seeming to be counter-intuitive. Educational outreach programs that assist citizens in negotiating the complexities of the criminal justice system are desirable in order to assure that everyone understands the legal process. Too often criminal justice practitioners forget that most individuals have only an occasional contact with their system and are not privy to the insider language, shortcuts in procedure or already established relationships among the courtroom workgroup (Perry 2000).

- *Categorical Imperative.* Justice demands that there should be some uniformity in the outcomes as well as the process. The idea of categorical imperative belongs to Immanuel Kant who argues that decisions should be fashioned so that in subsequent cases a guiding principle can be used to ensure fairness (Kant 1995). From a peacemaking perspective, this categorical imperative suggests that like cases be treated the same regardless of social factors such as class, race and gender. However, this does not imply that the criteria on sentencing be reduced to a matrix that is exclusively weighted toward the seriousness of offense and prior record. Rather, a certain level of individualized justice is desirable in order to promote rehabilitation, healing, and restoration relationships.

The peacemaking pyramid is offered as one example of how the peacemaking perspective might be developed as a criminological theory. It is viewed as inclusive of all the propositions that might make up peacemaking criminology although all those who consider themselves peacemaking criminologists might not agree. It is, however, a starting point that can give future researchers a comprehensive overview of the perspective from which to draw testable propositions.

Another Perspective: A Circular Model of Peacemaking Criminology

A circular model of peacemaking criminology has been developed upon a survey of peacemaking authors (Wozniak 2000) and a content analysis of chapters in Pepinsky and Quinney's *Criminology as Peacemaking* reader (2002b). Space limitations do not permit an expanded discussion of this additional theoretical model of peacemaking criminology. However, several core features of this latter peacemaking model will be sketched at this time.

Figure 9.3
Circular Model of Peacemaking Criminology

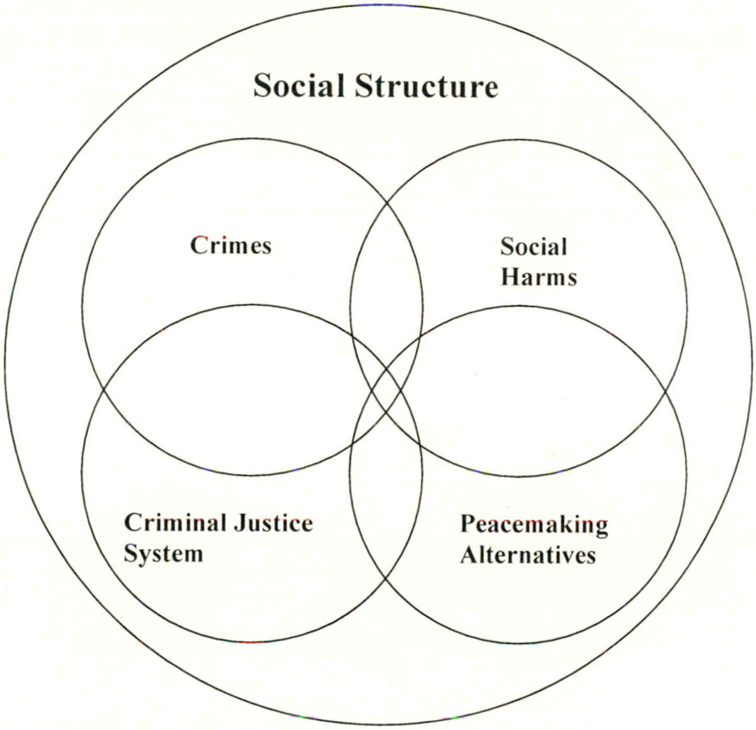

Figure 9.3, for example, depicts five key elements, within the circular model of peacemaking, which form the basis of addressing crime and its control. In a nutshell, this circular approach to peacemaking criminology "calls upon us to refuse to invest in a social ethic separating us from one another and instead to visualize all people — including those responsible for serious harms — as being connected" (Wozniak 2002b: 213). This latter theme corresponds with Quinney's (1993: 3) view of peacemaking criminology as he states: "Criminologists are encouraged to support and engage in a 'compassionate' crimi-

nology recognizing the interrelatedness of everything; that everyone is connected to each other and to their environment."

In this light, the circular model of peacemaking criminology (Wozniak 2002b: 221) focuses upon the problem of crime in these ways:

> The theory, research and policy of peacemaking criminology consists very much of a connected endeavor on the whole. By this, it is meant that peacemaking criminologists tend to examine the connections among social structure, crimes, social harms, the criminal justice system and peacemaking alternatives. In other words, peacemaking criminology research, in its strictest sense, will opt to examine how people in our present times become affected by and, in turn, affect these five basic elements within the peacemaking criminology theoretical model. Leaving out an element would lead, in a peacemaking criminology view, to an incomplete understanding of crime and how to address crime in a humane way.

Parenthetically, within the circular model of peacemaking criminology (Wozniak 2002b: 222), peacemaking criminologists endeavor to study varying types of crime in juxtaposition with diverse kinds of social harms with a goal to "transform the present criminal justice system through greater humanization of police work, court processing and correctional environment." Moreover, peacemaking criminologists opt to propose peacemaking alternatives at varying social levels (interpersonal, group, organizational, national, international, etc.) to lessen crimes/social harms. As such, like the pyramid model of peacemaking criminology, this circular model can be drawn upon to formulate testable propositions.

Promising Empirical Support of Peacemaking Criminology for Nonviolence

Is the peacemaking perspective effective at either reducing crime or in making better and more productive citizens? Is there any evidence that peacemaking is anything more than an untestable theory with lofty and unrealistic goals? These are difficult questions to answer because the peacemaking perspective has not been a recognized theory in academic criminology for very long. In fact, it is still so new the necessary groundwork has yet to be done in forming testable propositions and gathering empirical evidence. There are no programs that label themselves peacemaking that can be examined. In short, unlike other criminological theories, there is little more than direct anecdotal evidence from which to evaluate peacemaking criminology.

Complicating the fact that there is little direct evidence upon which to evaluate peacemaking criminology is the sheer range and scope of its applicability. Unlike social learning theory or differential association that look at why children become delinquent, peacemaking criminology covers the workings of the criminal justice system and can be extended to other institutions as well as different levels of analysis. Peacemaking criminology is so inclusive that it would be difficult to conclude that it actually works because of all the various issues needing examination. It is probable that parts of it are effective while other parts are sound in theory, but ineffective in the current political and social environment. With the caveat, let us attempt to answer the empirical question anyway, because it is important to the future development of the perspective.

If we cannot directly address the empirical question of the effectiveness of peacemaking criminology, we will attempt indirectly to do so. Because peacemaking criminology is founded on the principle of nonviolence, we can look at violent reactions to deviance and see how efficacious they have been. Specifically, we look next at the research that has been done on corporal and capital punishment to see if they have achieved the results that their proponents put forth.

Ineffectiveness of Corporal Punishment

Can children be taught correct behavior by being physically punished when they commit undesirable acts? This principle is so ingrained in American thought that it shocks students when it is suggested that spanking is a counter-productive practice. Students are apt to look at the professor and say, "I was spanked and I turned out ok." Students might further claim "If you don't spank your children they will run all over you." However, when presented with the empirical evidence that corporal punishment causes immense damage both physically and psychologically, students are often quick to see that violence against children is not a productive childrearing technique. While some students may want to quibble about the level and severity of violence (there is a difference between spanking and beating), the research does not make such distinctions.

We use as our authority for this discussion the book, *Beating the Devil out of Them: Corporal Punishment in American Families and its Effects On Children,* by Straus of the Family Research Lab at the University of New Hampshire. Straus' (2001) work is an indictment of corporal punishment that is grounded in research. While he is quick to point out in the introduction of the 2001 edition that there is still a dispute over the evidence on spanking, he contends that those who advocate the procedure have not actually read the evidence and are arguing from pre-existing positions rather than from data. Straus emphasizes that corporal punishment is linked to violence in the family, school, and in the street. He also argues that spanking has sexual overtones later resulting in masochistic sex. Alienation, reduced income, depression, and suicide are also related to corporal punishment.

Straus likens the hitting of children to the hitting of one's spouse. While wife beating was once not considered a social problem, it is now an ever growing research topic for criminologists to address and much of what has been found shows the criminal justice system to be unsympathetic. According to Straus, our attitudes toward the beating of children are undergoing the same change and one day it will receive the same attention from the law.

Ineffectiveness of Capital Punishment

Another issue that can shed some light on the empirical impact of peace-making criminology is capital punishment. The death penalty is used in about thirty-five states, however many of them employ it so sparingly that little can be concluded about whether it has any real influence. Those who support capital punishment use deterrence as one justification. The idea of general deterrence suggests that capital punishment prevents future murders because offenders are afraid of the ultimate punishment.

Measuring the deterrent effects of capital punishment has been a difficult proposition. There are a number of theoretical and methodological obstacles in linking executions to future murder rates. Do those who commit murder ever factor in the possibility they might later be executed? Because deterrence rests on the certainty, swiftness, and severity of the perceived punishment, capital punishment is an uncertain policy.

There is little certainty that anyone who commits murder will be the recipient of the death penalty. Only a tiny fraction of killers are executed. For anyone who might attempt to calculate the odds of receiving capital punishment, it seems like a good risk. The swiftness of the execution of the sentence is also problematic. The time span between the crime, the trial, the appeals, and the actual imposition of sentence, can typically take over a decade. While the death penalty is the most severe form of punishment available, the evidence does not show it deters offenders from killing others. Robert Bohm (2003: 114) points to one reason why capital punishment does not deter as follows:

> Most murderers, especially capital murderers, probably do not rationally calculate the consequences of their actions before they engage in them. Many murderers who end up on death row killed someone during the course of an armed robbery. Many never intended to kill but did so because of unexpected circumstances. Any who have calculated the consequences of their actions before engaging in their crimes probably did not consider that the punishment might be death. And even if would-be killers knew that execution was the possible penalty for their actions, it likely would not deter them anyway.

Bohm also identifies another problem with the death penalty that relates to its supposed deterrent effects. He reviews the issue of the brutalizing effects of capital punishment. When the state kills, it presents a model of behavior that can have far-reaching consequences. The brutalizing effects of the death penalty may actually cause more murders in a number of ways. According to Bohm (2003), this could happen because of the following:

- *Suicide-murder syndrome.* Some people are unable to commit suicide and thus murder someone in the hopes the state will execute them.
- *Executioner syndrome.* There are times when individuals believe they are doing society a service by killing undesirables.
- *Notoriety.* Some people see the intense media attention given to sensational cases and so kill in order to have their fifteen minutes of fame.

It is difficult to maintain any confidence in the deterrent effects of capital punishment when one looks at the empirical evidence. While proponents of capital punishment point to several studies that use use econometric models, these studies have been discredited on methodological matters and are not taken seriously by most criminologists.

Effectiveness of Socially Supportive Treatment

There are a number of other issues that could be examined to assess the empirical support for the peacemaking perspective but space limits our ability to go in to detail. However, much of the evidence on the importance of treatment of criminal offenders instead of punishment can be employed as support for peacemaking. Ronald Berger, Marvin Free, and Patricia Searles (2001: 435-436) argue in favor of "peacemaking alternatives to the war on crime" predicated upon primary prevention (social actions), secondary prevention (treatment of vulnerable and at-risk youths) and tertiary prevention (reducing the likelihood of recidivism through the justice system).

Notably, Elliott Currie (1998) has identified successful crime prevention approaches that have been brought about at each of these three levels (see also, Wozniak 2002a). That is, some promising social actions (primary prevention) which pertain to increasing social supports and opportunities within the labor market, can be practical initiatives for fighting violent crime. Similarly, some successful treatment programs for at-risk youth (secondary prevention) currently center upon not only providing support and guidance to vulnerable adolescents but also financing these children's intellectual and social development.[3] For Currie, fruitful tertiary prevention programs strive to reduce violence in the community through more effective police strategies that bring together police with mental health workers to work with children who have experienced violence at home or on the streets.

Furthermore, the emerging field of restorative justice that is ably covered in another chapter of this volume is pertinent to peacemaking (Sullivan and Tifft 2001). It is important to reiterate that any empirical argument concerning peacemaking criminology is indirect. Until programs and policies are developed explicitly around peacemaking principles, it is an open question as to whether the perspective actually has an impact on crime.

The Future of Peacemaking Criminology

Peacemaking criminology is a recently developed perspective that promises to influence academic and ultimately pragmatic criminal justice for some time to come. As more young criminologists, as well as criminal justice practitioners, come to see the war on crime and drugs as being counterproductive to both reducing crime and ensuring basic human rights, peacemaking criminology is likely to become a dominant theme. However, there is much to be done in developing the peacemaking perspective into a viable theory. In many ways, this will be a difficult task due to the broad scope of the perspective and the lack of programs that have tried to develop policies that concentrate on peacemaking principles. And yet, there is a backlash developing against the war on crime metaphor as evidenced by the restorative justice movement, opposition to capital punishment, dissatisfaction with drug sentencing laws, and the concerns of many about treating juvenile offenders as adults.

Figure 9.4
Core Peacemaking Criminology Variables

PERSONAL JUSTICE

- *Crime* and how it is better understood as suffering

- *Positive peace* and how to minimize human exploitation as an alternative to *negative peace* which is predicated upon applying force or deterrence upon crime and criminals

- *Social harms* and how they are inextricably linked to types of crime

- *Peacemaking* and how it is a personal, criminal justice, and social structure process

- *Responsiveness* and how to practice it

- *Dignity* and how it is preserved

- *Needs* and how to best meet them

- *Mindfulness* and how it can be more emphasized in daily lives and wide scale relations at home and with countries abroad

- *Connectedness* and how it can be more broadly valued and brought about

- *Right understanding* and how to become more aware of the limitations of actions motivated by greed, hatred, or delusion

- *Peacemaking teaching* and how to explore ways to achieve inner peace and social peace

CRIMINAL JUSTICE

- *Mainstream criminology* and how to progressively redirect how we learn about crime as well as how we deal with crime

- *Peacemaking criminology* pyramid and how to bring about its elements of *nonviolence, social justice inclusion, current means, ascertainable criteria,* and *categorical imperative*

- *Peacemaking criminology theoretical perspectives* and how they are derived from multiple influences

- *Peacemaking alternatives to criminal justice* and how they are applied at *interpersonal, group, organizational, national* and *international levels* of society

SOCIAL JUSTICE

- *Safe community* and how it is created

- *Social inequality* and how to challenge it

- *Power relations* and how to negate them

- *Social structures* and how to peacefully organize them

- *Social transformation* and how it flourishes through peaceful, personal and social structural relations

In this light, we suggest future research might attempt to examine peacemaking criminology at varying types of levels within the community and society at large. For example, Figure 9.4 provides a listing of core variables derived from the pyramid and circular models of peacemaking criminology. The results in Figure 9.4 are self-explanatory. Still, it seems useful to note that this figure organizes a set of themes that can be applied to both empirical research and actual one-on-one interactions among members of the community. It is also helpful to discern that peacemaking as an applied, empirical or theoretical approach to crime can be brought about in terms of personal, criminal and social justice. Again, while all working in this realm of emphasis might not agree with these conceptualizations, the information in Figure 9.4 nonetheless offers a vantage point to adjust future visions of peacemaking criminology.

Our work toward the development of pyramid and circular models of peacemaking criminology has further enabled the formulation of a set of peacemaking criminology propositions, which are presented in Figure 9.5. As an example, we propose as a "personal justice" type of peacemaking criminology proposition that the more responsive, mindful and connected the individual, the less

Figure 9.5
Peacemaking Criminology Propositions

PERSONAL JUSTICE

- Crimes and victimizations are more likely to decrease through the promotion of positive peace over negative peace

- Crimes and victimizations are more likely to decrease when the underlying social harms are more consistently addressed

- The more responsive, mindful, and connected the individual, the less likely a crime and victimization will be committed

- The greater the extent of dignity and right understanding for the individual, the less likely a crime and victimization will be committed

- The more likely needs are met for an individual, the less likely a crime and victimization will be committed

CRIMINAL JUSTICE

- The greater the movement toward peacemaking criminology and away from mainstream criminology/criminal justice, the lesser the crime and victimization

- The greater the movement toward achieving elements of the peacemaking pyramid, the lesser the crime and victimization

- The greater the unity of peacemaking circles, the lesser the crime and victimization

- The greater the use of peacemaking alternatives to criminal justice at varying levels, the lesser the crime and victimization

- The greater use of primary, secondary, and tertiary peacemaking prevention, the lesser the crime and victimization

SOCIAL JUSTICE

- The safer the community, the lesser the crime and victimization

- The greater the challenges made against social inequality, the lesser the crime and victimization

- The greater the negation of power relations, the lesser the crime and victimization

- The more the peacemaking perspective is utilized in the family, schools, and other institutions of society, the lesser the crime and victimization

- The more sexist, racist, paternalistic, and inhumane the economy and government, the greater the crime and victimization

- The more peaceful the social structure, the lesser the crime and victimization

- The more peaceful the social transformation of society, the lesser the

likely a crime or victimization will be committed." Likewise, as a "criminal justice" type of peacemaking criminology proposition, we purport that "the greater movement toward achieving elements of the peacemaking pyramid, the lesser the crime and victimization." In terms of a "social justice" type of peacemaking criminology proposition, we maintain that "the more the peacemaking perspective is utilized in the family, the schools and other institutions of society, the lesser the crime and victimization."

Most importantly, it is hoped our views of peacemaking criminology presented here will inspire future applications of peacemaking principles into the study of and response to crimes and victimizations. It is quite apparent that much conceptualization of peacemaking criminology variables remains to be done. We are heartened by the promising work of criminologists and crime practitioners who have contributed to the peacemaking criminology perspective on the whole.

It will take some time and another generation of criminologists before peacemaking criminology develops into a testable theory that can concretely guide criminal justice policy. In the meantime, it is enough to say that many think this is a fruitful direction in which to proceed. Even if peacemaking criminology ultimately proves ineffectual, it is a low risk perspective that ought to be examined. The first axiom of research ethics is "do no harm" and compared to the war on crime perspective that currently is in fashion, peacemaking is clearly superior.

Notes

1. It is evident, of course, these co-editors and others have produced writings addressing peacemaking criminology at an earlier time (i.e., Quinney 1988, 1989; Pepinsky 1988; see also "Peacemaking in Criminology" in Moyer 2001).
2. For further elaboration of this theme, see Christie (2000).
3. For further development of use of social support in relation to criminology, see Cullen (1994).

References

Bazemore, Gordon, and Mara Schiff, eds. 2001. *Restorative Community Justice: Repairing Harm and Transforming Communities*. Cincinnati: Anderson.

Berger, Ronald J., Marvin D. Free, Jr., and Patricia Searles. 2001. *Crime, Justice, and Society: Criminology and the Sociological Imagination*. New York: McGraw Hill.

Bohm, Robert M. 1982. "Radical Criminology: An Explication." *Criminology* 19: 565-589.

————. 2003. *Deathquest II: An Introduction to the Theory and Practice of Capital Punishment in the United States*, 2nd ed. Cincinnati: Anderson.

Boulding, Elise. 2000. *Cultures of Peace: The Hidden Side of History*. Syracuse, NY: Syracuse University Press.

Braswell, Michael C. 1990. "Peacemaking: A Missing Link in Criminology." *The Criminologist* 15: 3-5.

Braswell, Michael, John Fuller, and Bo Lozoff. 2001. *Corrections, Peacemaking, and Restorative Justice: Transforming Individuals and Institutions*. Cincinnati: Anderson.

Christie, Nils. 2000. *Crime Control as Industry: Toward Gulags Western Style*, 3rd ed. New York: Routledge.

Cullen, Francis T. 1994. "Social Support as an Organizing Concept for Criminology: Presidential Address to the Academy of Criminal Justice Sciences." *Justice Quarterly* 11: 527-559.

Cullen, Francis T., and Karen Gilbert. 1982. *Reaffirming Rehabilitation*. Cincinnati: Anderson.

Currie, Elliott. 1993. *Reckoning: Drugs, the Cities, and the American Future*. New York: Hill and Wang.

————. 1998. *Crime and Punishment in America*. New York: Henry Holt.

Daly, Kathleen, and Meda Chesney-Lind. 1988. "Feminism and Criminology." *Justice Quarterly* 5: 497-538.

DeKeseredy, Walter S., and Martin D. Schwartz. 1991. "British Left Realism on the Abuse of Women: A Critical Appraisal." Pp. 154-171 in Harold E. Pepinsky & Richard Quinney (eds.), *Criminology as Peacemaking*. Bloomington: Indiana University Press.

Erikson, Erik H. 1969. *Gandhi's Truth: On the Origins of Militant Nonviolence*. New York: Norton.

Fuller, John R. 1998. *Criminal Justice: A Peacemaking Perspective*. Boston: Allyn and Bacon.

Holmes Robert L. 1990. *Nonviolence in Theory and Practice*. Prospect Heights, IL: Waveland Press.

Kant, Immanuel. 1995. The Categorical Imperative." Pp. 45-50 in Daryl Close and Nicholas Meier (eds.), *Morality in Criminal Justice: An Introduction to Ethics*. Belmont, CA: Wadsworth.

Karp, David R., and Todd R. Clear, eds. 2002. *What Is Community Justice: Case Studies of Restorative Justice and Community Supervision*. Thousand Oaks, CA: Sage Publications.

Klein, Lloyd, Joan Luxenburg, and John Gunther. 1991. "Taking a Bite Out of Social Injustice." Pp. 280-296 in Harold E. Pepinsky and Richard Quinney (eds.), *Criminology as Peacemaking*. Bloomington: Indiana University Press.

Lynch, Michael J., Raymond Michalowski, and W. Byron Groves. 2000. *The New Primer in Radical Criminology: Critical Perspectives on Crime, Power and Identity*, 3rd ed. Monsey, NY: Criminal Justice Press.

Mann, Coramae Richey. 1993. *Unequal Justice: A Question of Color*. Bloomington: Indiana University Press.

Moyer, Imogene L. 2001. *Criminology Theories: Traditional and Nontraditional Voices and Themes*. Thousand Oaks, CA: Sage.

Martin, Randy, Robert J. Mutchnick, and W. Timothy Austin. 1990. *Criminological Thought: Pioneers Past and Present*. New York: Macmillan.

Pepinsky, Harold E. 1988. "Violence as Unresponsiveness: Toward a New Conception of Crime." *Justice Quarterly* 5: 539-563.

――――. 1991. "Peacemaking in Criminology and Criminal Justice." Pp. 299-327 in Harold E. Pepinsky and Richard Quinney (eds.), *Criminology as Peacemaking*. Bloomington: Indiana University Press.

――――. 1999. "Peacemaking Primer." Pp. 52-70 in Bruce A. Arrigo (ed.), *Social Justice/Criminal Justice: The Maturation of Critical Theory in Law, Crime, and Deviance*. Belmont, CA: West/Wadsworth.

Pepinsky, Harold E., and Richard Quinney, eds. 1991. *Criminology as Peacemaking*. Bloomington: Indiana University Press.

Perry, Barbara. 2000. "Exclusion, Inclusion, and Violence: Immigrants and Criminal Justice." Pp. 59-70 in The Criminal Justice Collective of Northern Arizona University (eds.), *Investigating Differences: Human and Cultural Relations in Criminal Justice*. Boston: Allyn and Bacon.

Quinney, Richard. 1988. "Beyond the Interpretive: The Way of Awareness." *Sociological Inquiry* 58: 101-116.

――――. 1989. The Theory and Practice of Peacemaking in the Development of Radical Criminology. *The Critical Criminologist* 1: 5.

――――. 1991. "The Way of Peace: On Crime, Suffering, and Service." Pp. 3-13 in Harold E. Pepinsky and Richard Quinney (eds.), *Criminology as Peacemaking*. Bloomington: Indiana University Press.

――――. 1993. A Life of Crime: Criminology and Public Policy as Peacemaking. *Journal of Crime and Justice* 26: 3-9.

――――. 2000. *Bearing Witness to Crime and Social Justice*. Albany: State University of New York Press.

Straus, Murray. 2001. *Beating the Devil Out of Them: Corporal Punishment In American Families and its Effects on Children*. New Brunswick, NJ: Transaction Books.

Strasser, Steven, ed. 2004. *The Abu Ghraib Investigations: The Official Reports of the Independent Panel and the Pentagon on the Shocking Prisoner Abuse in Iraq*. New York: Public Affairs.

Sullivan, Dennis, and Larry Tifft. 2001. *Restorative Justice: Healing the Foundations of our Everyday Lives*. Monsey, NY: Willow Tress Press.

Van Ness, Daniel W. and Karen Heetderks Strong. 2002. *Restoring Justice*. Cincinnati: Anderson.

Welch, Michael. 2004. *Corrections: A Critical Approach*, 2nd ed. New York: Mc-Graw Hill.

Williams, Christopher R. 2002. "Towards a Transvaluation of Criminal 'Justice': On Vengeance, Peacemaking, and Punishment." *Humanity and Society* 26: 101-116.

Wozniak, John F. 2000. The Voices of Peacemaking Criminology: Insights into a Perspective with an Eye Toward Teaching." *Contemporary Justice Review* 3: 267-289.

――――. 2002a. "Peacemaking Criminology Approaches to Crime Prevention. A Review of Successful Primary, Secondary, and Tertiary Strategies." Paper presented at the annual meeting of the American Society of Criminology, Chicago.

――――. 2002b. Toward a Theoretical Model of Peacemaking Criminology: An Essay in Honor of Richard Quinney. *Crime and Delinquency* 48: 204-231.

Part IV

Life-Course Theories

10

A Review of Research on the Taxonomy of Life-Course Persistent Versus Adolescence-Limited Antisocial Behavior

Terrie E. Moffitt

This chapter reviews ten years of research into a developmental taxonomy of antisocial behavior that proposed two primary hypothetical prototypes: life-course persistent versus adolescence-limited offenders. According to the taxonomic theory, life-course persistent offenders' antisocial behavior has its origins in the neurodevelopmental processes beginning in childhood and continuing persistently thereafter. In contrast, adolescence-limited offenders' antisocial behavior has its origins in social processes beginning in adolescence, and desists in young adulthood. According to the theory, life-course persistent antisocial individuals are few, persistent, and pathological. Adolescence-limited antisocial individuals are common, relatively transient, and near normative (Moffitt 1990, 1993, 1994, 1997, 2003).

Discussions in the literature have pointed out that if the taxonomic theory is proven accurate, then it could usefully improve classification of subject groups for research (Nagin, Farrington, and Moffitt 1995; Silverthorn and Frick 1999; Zucker, Ellis, Fitzgerald, Bingham, and Sanford 1996), focus research into antisocial personality and violence toward the most promising causal variables (Brezina 2000; Lahey, Waldman, and McBurnett 1999; Laucht 2001; Osgood 1998), and guide the timing and strategies of interventions for delinquent types (Howell and Hawkins 1998; Scott and Grisso 1997; Vermeiren 2002). Several writers have extracted implications for intervention from the taxonomy. Howell and Hawkins (1998) observed that preventing life-course persistent versus adolescence-limited antisocial behavior requires interventions that differ in both timing and target. Preventing life-course persistent lifestyles requires early childhood interventions in the family. In contrast, adolescence-limited offending ought to be prevented by treating adolescents

277

individually to counteract peer influence (instead of in groups that facilitate deviant peer influence [Dishion, McCord, and Poulin 1999]). Scott and Grisso (1997) argued compellingly that the juvenile justice system should identify adolescence-limited delinquents and give them room to reform. Surveys of juvenile court judges and forensic psychologists reveal that the offender characteristics they rely on to recommend a juvenile for transfer to adult court match the characteristics that distinguish life-course persistent delinquents (Salekin, Yff, Neumann, Liestico, and Zalot 2002). In contrast, Scott and Grisso (1997) argue that waiving life-course persistent delinquents to adult court is wrong because the cognitive deficits typical of these delinquents render them unlikely to meet legal criteria for competency to stand trial.

The taxonomy of childhood versus adolescent-onset antisocial behavior has been codified in the *DSM-IV* (American Psychiatric Association 1994), presented in many abnormal psychology and criminology textbooks and invoked in the NIMH Factsheet *Child and Adolescent Violence Research* (2000), the U.S. Surgeon General's report *Youth Violence* (2001), the World Health Organization's *World Report on Violence and Health* (2002) and the National Institutes of Health's *State-of-the-Science Consensus Statement in Preventing Violence* (2004). But is it valid?

The reader is referred to two prior publications that articulate the main hypotheses derived from this taxonomic theory. The first article published that proposed the two prototypes and their different etiologies ended with a section headed "Strategies for Research" which described predictions about epidemiology, age, social class, risk correlates, offense types, desistance from crime, abstainers from crime, and the longitudinal stability of antisocial behavior (Moffitt 1993, 694-696). The article specified which findings would disconfirm the theory. A version published elsewhere specified hypotheses about sex and race (Moffitt 1994). When these hypotheses from the taxonomy were put forward ten years ago, none of them had been tested, but since then several have been tested by us and by others. This chapter reviews the results of that research, as of summer 2004, and points out where more research is needed.

A Brief Introduction to the Two Prototypes

In a nutshell, we suggested that life-course persistent antisocial behavior originates early in life, when the difficult behavior of a high-risk young child is exacerbated by a high-risk social environment. According to the theory, the child's risk emerges from inherited or acquired neuropsychological variation, initially manifested as subtle cognitive deficits, difficult temperament or hyperactivity. The environment's risk comprises factors such as inadequate parenting, disrupted family bonds, and poverty. The environmental risk domain expands beyond the family as the child ages to include poor relations with people such as peers and teachers. Opportunities to learn prosocial skills are lost. Over the first two decades of development, transactions between the individual and the environment gradually construct a disordered personality with hallmark features of physical aggression and antisocial behavior persisting to midlife. The theory predicts that antisocial behavior will infiltrate multiple adult life domains: illegal activities, problems with employment and victimization of intimate partners and children. This infiltration diminishes the possibility of reform.

In contrast, we suggested that adolescence-limited antisocial behavior emerges alongside puberty when otherwise ordinary healthy youngsters experience psychological discomfort during the relatively role-less years between their biological maturation and their access to mature privileges and responsibilities, a period we called the "maturity gap." They experience dissatisfaction with their dependent status as a child and are impatient for what they anticipate are the privileges and rights of adulthood. While young people are in this "gap" it is virtually normative for them to find the delinquent style appealing and to mimic it as a way to demonstrate autonomy from parents, win affiliation with peers, and hasten social maturation. However, because their predelinquent development was normal, most adolescence-limited delinquents are able to desist from crime when they age into real adult roles, returning gradually to a more conventional lifestyle. This recovery may be delayed if the antisocial activities of adolescence-limited delinquents attract factors we called "snares," such as a criminal record, incarceration, addiction, or truncated education without credentials. Such snares can compromise the ability to make a successful transition to adulthood.

The Hypothesis that Life-Course Persistent Antisocial Development Emerges from Early Neuro-Developmental and Family-Adversity Risk Factors

The original hypothesis about childhood risk specified that predictors of life-course persistent antisocial behavior should include "health, gender, temperament, cognitive abilities, school achievement, personality traits, mental disorders (e.g., hyperactivity), family attachment bonds, child-rearing practices, parent and sibling deviance and socioeconomic status, but not age" (Moffitt 1993: 695).

Our own tests of this hypothesis have been carried out in the Dunedin Multidisciplinary Health and Development Study, a thirty-two-year longitudinal study of a birth cohort of 1,000 New Zealanders. A full description of the Dunedin Study and the New Zealand research setting can be found in Moffitt, Caspi, Rutter, and Silva (2001). These tests have examined childhood predictors measured between ages three and thirteen, operationalizing the two prototypes of antisocial behavior using both categorical and continuous statistical approaches. These studies showed that the life-course persistent path was differentially predicted by individual risk characteristics including undercontrolled temperament measured by observers at age three, neurologi-

[handwritten: low intellect / difficulty reading / poor memory / hyperactivity / slow heart rate]

cal abnormalities and delayed motor development at age three, low intellectual ability, reading difficulties, poor scores on neuropsychological tests of memory, hyperactivity, and slow heart rate (Jeglum-Bartusch, Lynam, Moffitt, and Silva 1997; Moffitt 1990; Moffitt and Caspi 2001; Moffitt, Lynam, and Silva 1994). The life-course persistent path was also differentially predicted by *[handwritten: Parenting Risk Factors →]* parenting risk factors including teenaged single parents, mothers with poor mental health, mothers who were observed to be harsh or neglectful, as well as by experiences of harsh and inconsistent discipline, much family conflict, many changes of primary caretaker, low family socio-economic status (SES), and rejection by peers in school. In contrast, study members on the adolescence-limited path, despite being involved in teen delinquency to the same extent as their counterparts on the life-course persistent path, tended to have backgrounds that were normative, or sometimes even better than the average Dunedin child's (Moffitt and Caspi 2001). A replication of this pattern of differential findings was reported by a study of 800 children followed from birth to age fifteen years (Brennan, Hall, Bor, Najman, and Williams 2003). An early-onset persistent antisocial group, an adolescent-onset antisocial group, and a non-antisocial group were identified. Measured "biological risks" (e.g., neuropsychological test deficits at age fifteen) and childhood "social risks" (e.g., harsh discipline, maternal hostility) and an interaction between these two risks, predicted membership in the early-onset persistent group, but membership in the adolescent-onset group was unrelated to childhood social risks or biological risks.

The aforementioned Dunedin findings about differential neurodevelopmental and family risk correlates for childhood-onset versus adolescent-onset offenders are generally in keeping with findings reported from other samples in Australia, Canada, England, Mauritius, New Zealand, Norway, Russia, Sweden, and several states within the United States. These studies operationalized the types using a variety of conceptual approaches, many different measures of antisocial behaviors, and very different statistical methods (Aguilar, Sroufe, Egeland, and Carlson 2000; Arseneault, Tremblay, Boulerice, and Saucier 2002; Brennan et al. 2003; Chung, Hill, Hawkins, Gilchrist and Nagin 2002; Dean, Brame, and Piquero 1996; Donnellan, Ge, and Wenk 2000; Fergusson, Horwood, and Nagin 2000; Kjelsberg 1999; Kratzer and Hodgins 1999; Lahey et al. 1998; Magnusson, af Klintberg, and Stattin 1994; Maughan, Pickles, Rowe, Costello, and Angold 2001; Mazerolle, Brame, Paternoster, Piquero, and Dean 2000; McCabe, Hough, Wood, and Yeh 2001; Nagin et al. 1995; Nagin and Tremblay 1999; Nagin and Tremblay 2001a; Patterson, Forgatch, Yoerger, and Stoolmiller 1998; Piquero 2001; Piquero and Brezina 2001; Raine et al. 2005; Raine, Yaralian, Reynolds, Venables, and Mednick 2002; Roeder, Lynch, and Nagin 1999; Tibbetts and Piquero 1999; Tolan and Thomas 1995; Ruchkin, Koposov, Vermeiren, and Schwab-Stone 2003; Wiesner and Capaldi 2003). Each of the above-cited studies added support for the taxonomy's construct validity by reporting differential correlates for early-onset/persistent antisocial behavior versus later-onset/temporary antisocial behavior. However, at least one research team found mixed evidence for the taxonomy (cf. Brame, Bushway, and Paternoster 1999 vs. Paternoster and Brame 1997).

Other studies, although not necessarily presented as a formal test of the two types, have reported findings consonant with our predictions about the types' differential childhood risk. For example, children's hyperactivity interacts with poor parenting skill to predict antisocial behavior that has an early onset and escalates to delinquency (Patterson, De Garmo, and Knutson 2000), an interaction that fits the hypothesized origins of the life-course persistent path. Other studies have reported that measures reflecting infant nervous-system maldevelopment interact with poor parenting and social adversity to predict aggression that is chronic from childhood to adolescence (Arseneault et al. 2002). Measures indexing infant nervous-system maldevelopment and social adversity also interact to predict early-onset violent crime (Raine, Brennan, and Mednick 1994; Raine, Brennan, Mednick, and Mednick 1996), but do not predict non-violent crime (Raine, Brennan, and Mednick 1997; Arseneault et al. 2000). Two additional findings are consistent with our prediction that infant nervous-system maldevelopment contributes to long-term life-course persisent antisocial outcomes. First, prenatal malnutrition has been found to predict adult antisocial personality disorder (Neugebauer, Hoek, and Susser 1999). Second, adults with antisocial personality disorder exhibit two nervous system abnormalities attributable to disruption of brain development in early life: enlargement of the corpus callosum assessed by structural magnetic resonance imaging and abnormal corpus callosum connective function assessed by divided visual field tests (Raine et al. 2003).

Our differential-risk prediction encountered a particular challenge from a longitudinal study of a low-SES Minneapolis sample (Aguilar et al. 2000). This research team observed that differences between their childhood-onset and adolescent-onset groups were not significant for neurocognitive and temperament measures taken prior to age three, although they found that significant differences did emerge later in childhood. The authors inferred that childhood psychosocial adversity is sufficient to account for the origins of life-course persistent antisocial behavior, which is similar to Patterson and Yoerger's (1997) thesis that unskilled parenting is sufficient to account for the early-onset antisocial type. Such exclusive socialization hypotheses are probably not defensible, in view of emerging evidence that the life-course persistent pattern of antisocial behavior appears to have substantial heritable liability (DiLalla and Gottesman 1989; Eley, Lichtenstein, and Moffitt 2003; Taylor, Iacono, and McGue 2000), a finding we revisit later in this chapter. The lack of significant early-childhood differences in the Minneapolis study may have arisen from methodological features of the study, including the unrepresentative and homogeneous nature of the sample (all high-risk, low SES families), irregular sex composition of the groups (more females than males were antisocial) or weak psychometric qualities of the infant measures (unknown predictive validity). Infant measures are known for their poor predictive validity (McCall and Carriger 1993), and thus it is possible that the failure of the infant measures to predict the life-course persistent path is part of such measures' more general failure to predict outcomes.

One study has reported that difficult temperament assessed at age five-months distinguished a group of children who showed a trajectory of high rates of physical aggression, as compared to cohort peers, across ages seventeen, thirty and forty-two months (Tremblay et al. 2004). However, until this cohort of 572 infants is followed beyond age 3.5 years, into adolescence, we cannot be confident that they represent youngsters on the life-course persistent pathway. Other studies have reported a significant relation between life-course persistent type offending and problems known to be associated with neurocognitive and temperamental difficulties in infancy: perinatal complications, minor physical anomalies and low birth weight (Arseneault et al. 2000, 2002; Kratzer and Hodgins 1999; Tibbetts and Piquero 1999; Raine et al. 1994). These studies illustrate desirable features for testing neurodevelopmental risks from the beginning of infancy for persistent antisocial behavior: large samples, representative samples, infant measures with proven predictive validity, and attention to interactions between neurodevelopmental and social adversity (Cicchetti and Walker 2003).

What research is needed? Research already documents that life-course persistent antisocial behavior has the predicted neurodevelopmental correlates in the perinatal and middle childhood periods, but the Aguilar et al. (2000) study remains the only one that has reported objective measures of infants' temperament and neurocognitive status prior to age three years, and it did not find the associations predicted by the theory. This study constitutes an important challenge that must be taken seriously, particularly as Brennan et al. (2003) also found no significant connection between temperament or vocabulary assessed in early life and early-onset persistent aggression. Clearly more research is needed to fill in the critical gap between birth and age three years. This might be accomplished by following up the antisocial outcomes of infants tested with newer neurocognitive measures having documented predictive validity, such as the infant attention-habituation paradigm (Sigman, Cohen, and Beckwith 1997).

Another feature of life-course persistent theory that needs testing is the argument that antisocial behavior becomes persistent because a child's early difficult behavior provokes harsh treatment or rejection from parents and teachers and peers which, in turn, promotes more difficult child behavior. Adoption and twin studies have documented an initial "child effect"; that is, children carrying a genetic liability to antisocial behavior provoke harsh parenting

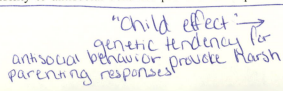

"Child effect" → genetic tendency for antisocial behavior provoke harsh parenting responses

responses from their parents (Ge et al. 1996; Jaffee et al. 2004a; O'Connor, Deater-Deckard, Fulker, Rutter, and Plomin 1998; Riggins-Caspers, Cadoret, Knutson and Langbehn 2003). Such genetically informative studies should be followed up to ascertain whether this process beginning with a 'child effect' ultimately leads to antisocial behavior that persists long term.

Is a Third Group Needed? Childhood-Limited Aggressive Children May Become Low-Level Chronic Criminal Offenders with Personality Disorders

The original theoretical taxonomy asserted that two prototypes, life-course persistent and adolescence-limited offenders, account for the preponderance of the population's antisocial behavior and, thus, warrant the lion's share of attention by theory and research. However, our analyses revealed a small group of Dunedin study males who had exhibited extreme, pervasive, and persistent antisocial behavior problems during childhood, but who surprisingly engaged in only low to moderate delinquency during adolescence from age fifteen to eighteen, not extreme enough to meet criteria for membership in the life-course persistent group (Moffitt, Caspi, Dickson, Silva, and Stanton 1996). Like the life-course persistent offenders they had extremely under-controlled temperaments as three-year-olds (Moffitt et al. 1996) and in childhood they, too, suffered family adversity, parental psychopathology and had low intelligence (unpublished analyses). The existence of a small group of boys who exhibit serious aggression in childhood, but are not notably delinquent in adolescence, has been replicated in the Pittsburgh Youth Survey, where they were called "childhood-limited" antisocial children (Raine et al. 2005). In the Pittsburgh cohort too, these boys had many risk factors, including family adversity, parental psychopathology, and severe neuropsychological deficits.

This group was a surprise to the theory, because the theory argued that an early-onset chain of cumulative interactions between aggressive children and high-risk environments will perpetuate disordered behavior. On that basis, we had predicted that "false positive subjects, who meet criteria for a stable and pervasive antisocial childhood history and yet recover (eschew delinquency) after puberty, should be extremely rare" (Moffitt 1993: 694). When we discovered this group, we optimistically labeled it the "recovery group" (Moffitt et al. 1996). Many researchers, we among them, hoped that this group would allow us to identify protective factors that can be harnessed to prevent childhood aggression from persisting and becoming more severe. However, our study of this group has revealed no protective factors.

Researchers testing for the presence of the life-course persistent and adolescence-limited types have since uncovered a third type that replicates across longitudinal studies, first identified in trajectory analyses of a British cohort (Nagin et al. 1995). This third group of offenders has been labeled "low-level chronics" because they have been found to offend persistently but at a low rate from childhood to adolescence (Fergusson et al. 2000) or from adolescence to adulthood (D'Unger, Land, McCall, and Nagin 1998; Nagin et al. 1995). Persuaded by these findings, we followed up the so-called recovery group in the Dunedin cohort at age twenty-six to see if they might fit the low-level chronic pattern as adults. We found that recovery was clearly a misnomer, as their modal offending pattern over time fit a pattern referred to by criminologists as "intermittency," in which some offenders are not convicted for a period but then reappear in the courts (Laub and Sampson 2001). This Dunedin group's long-term offending pattern closely resembles that of the low-level chronic offender.

Anticipating true recoveries from serious childhood conduct disorder to be extremely rare, the taxonomic theory had argued that teens who engage in less delinquency than predicted on the basis of their childhood conduct problems might have off-putting personal characteristics that excluded them from the social peer groups in which most delinquency happens. Consistent with this prediction, a group in the Oregon Youth Study, who showed high levels of antisocial behavior at age twelve which decreased thereafter, scored low as adolescents on a measure of involvement with pro-delinquency peers (Wiesner and Capaldi 2003). In the Dunedin cohort followed up to age twenty-six, the members of this low-level chronic group, unlike other cohort men, were often social isolates; their informants reported that they had difficulty making friends, none had married, few held jobs, and many had diagnoses of agoraphobia and/or social phobia. Almost all social phobics meet the criteria for avoidant, dependent and/or schizotypal personality disorders (Alnaes and Torgersen 1988), and we speculate that men in this group may suffer from these isolating personality disorders. As many as one-third of this group had diagnosable depression, their personality profile showed elevated neuroticism, and their informants rated them as the most depressed, anxious men in the cohort. This pattern in which formerly antisocial boys develop into depressed, anxious, socially isolated men resembles closely a finding from a British longitudinal study of males followed from ages eight to thirty-two. In that study, too, at-risk antisocial boys who became adult "false positives" (committing less crime than predicted) had few or no friends, held low-paid jobs, lived in dirty home conditions and had been described in case records as withdrawn, highly strung, obsessional, nervous, or timid (Farrington, Gallagher, Morley, St. Ledger, and West 1988).

Robins (1966) is often quoted as having said that one half of conduct-problem boys do not grow up to have antisocial personalities. Such quotations are intended to imply that early conduct problems are fully malleable and need not be a cause for pessimism. However, less often quoted is Robins's (1966) observation that conduct-problem boys who do not develop antisocial personalities generally suffer other forms of maladjustment as adults. This is an assertion of "multifinality" in the poor outcomes of at-risk children (Cicchetti and Cohen 1995). In the Dunedin birth cohort, eighty-seven boys

multifinality

had childhood conduct problems (i.e., forty-seven in the life-course persistent group and forty in the so-called recovery group). Of these eighty-seven males, only 15 percent (n = 13) seemed to have truly recovered as adults, escaping all adjustment problems measured in the study at age twenty-six. Taken together, findings from Dunedin, and the studies by Farrington and Robins, are consistent with our taxonomic theory's original assertion that childhood-onset antisocial behavior is *virtually always* a prognosticator of poor adult adjustment.

What research is needed? Several studies have detected an unexpected group, variously labeled "recoveries," "childhood-limited" or "low-level chronic offenders," depending on how long the cohort was followed. However, few studies have been able to shed any light on their personal characteristics. The characteristics revealed so far are suggestive of avoidant, dependent, schizotypal personality disorders and/or low intelligence, but these outcomes have not been directly measured in adulthood. It is important to know if this group has adult psychopathology to test the theory's assertion that serious childhood-onset antisocial behavior reliably predicts long-term maladjustment.

Is a Fourth Group Needed? Adult-Onset Antisocial Behavior

Some investigators have suggested, on the basis of examining official data sources, that significant numbers of offenders first begin to offend as adults (Eggleston and Laub 2002; Farrington, Ohlin, and Wilson 1986). This would appear to challenge our developmental taxonomy's assertion that two groups, life-course persistent and adolescence-limited, suffice to account for the majority of antisocial participation across the life course. However, the observation that many antisocial individuals are adult-onset may be an artifact of official measurement. Estimates of the age at which antisocial behavior begins depend on the source of the data. For example, in the Dunedin Study only 4 percent of boys had been convicted in court by age fifteen years, but 15 percent had been arrested by police by age fifteen, and 80 percent had self-reported the onset of illegal behaviors by age fifteen (Chapter 7 in Moffitt et al. 2001). This suggests that official data lag behind the true age of onset by a few years. Similar findings have emerged from other studies in other countries. For example, a Canadian survey showed that self-reported onset antedated conviction by about 3.5 years (Loeber and LeBlanc 1990), and a U.S. survey showed that self-reported onset of "serious" delinquency antedated the first court contact by 2.5 years and onset of "moderate" delinquency antedated the first court contact by five years (U.S. Office of Juvenile Justice and Delinquency Prevention 1998). In the Seattle Social Development cohort, the self-reported onset of crime antedated the first court referral by 2.4 years, and the study estimated that the average offender committed twenty-six crimes before his official crime record began (Farrington, Jolliffe, Hawkins, Catalano, Hill, and Kosterman 2003). These comparisons of data sources suggest that investigations relying on official data will ascertain age of onset approximately three to five years after it has happened. A three to five year lag is relevant because most studies have defined adult-onset offenders as those whose official crime records began at or after age eighteen years (Eggleston and Laub 2002).

It also is useful to note that whereas the eighteenth birthday may have demarked adulthood for young people born before 1960, the eighteenth birthday falls only midway between puberty and adulthood for contemporary generations. This shift emerged because contemporary generations are experiencing a more protracted adolescence, lasting until the mid-twenties (Arnett 2000) or even into the early thirties for the cohort born after 1970 (Ferri, Bynner and Wadsworth 2003; Furstenberg, Cook, Sampson, and Slap 2002). Although adult-onset crime begins at age eighteen in legal terms, in developmental terms for contemporary cohort samples, it begins sometime after age twenty-five.

In contrast to studies using official crime records, self-report cohort studies show that fewer than 4 percent of males commit their first criminal offense after age seventeen (Elliott, Huizinga, and Menard 1989). Self-report studies of American and European cohorts agree (Junger-Tas, Terlouw, and Klein 1994). By age eighteen virtually all of the Dunedin Study members had already engaged in some form of illegal behavior at some time, according to their self-reports (Moffitt et al. 2001). Only 9 percent of Dunedin males and 14 percent of females remained naive to all delinquency by age eighteen, and only 3 percent of males and 5 percent of females first offended as an adult, between ages eighteen and twenty-one. These findings carry an important lesson for methodology in developmental research into antisocial behavior. "Adult-onset" offenders cannot be defined for study with any certainty unless self-reported data are available to rule out juvenile onset prior to participants' first official contact with the judicial system. When self-report data are consulted, they reveal that onset of antisocial behavior after adolescence is extremely rare. This conclusion extends to serious and violent offending (Elliott 1994).

One way to ascertain whether adult-onset offenders constitute a significant group for study is to apply semi-parametric modeling techniques (Nagin 1999; Nagin and Tremblay 2001b; Roeder et al. 1999) to identify trajectories within a population-representative cohort of individuals whose behavior has been followed into adulthood. Three studies have done so. The Dunedin Study identified no adult-onset trajectory in self-reports of delinquency from ages seven to twenty-six years (Moffitt et al. in preparation). The Oregon Youth Study identified no adult-onset trajectory in self-reports of offending from ages twelve to twenty-four years (Wiesner and Capaldi 2003). The Cambridge Longitudinal Study identified no adult-onset trajectory in official crime records followed to age thirty-two for a cohort born in the 1950s (Nagin et al. 1995).

The original theoretical taxonomy asserted that two prototypes, life-course persistent and adolescence-limited offenders, can account for the preponderance of the population's antisocial behavior. After more than ten years of research, this assertion appears to be correct. Some studies of the taxonomy have reported an adult-onset group (e.g., Kratzer and Hodgins 1999). However, these studies used official crime data and, thus, most of their adult-onset offenders would probably be revealed as adolescent-onset if self-report data were available. These so-called adult-onset offenders can probably be accommodated by the adolescence-limited theory because when studied, the alleged adult-onset group has not differed from ordinary adolescent offenders (Eggleston and Laub 2002). Moreover, like adolescence-limited offenders, adult-onset offenders' crime careers tend to be brief and not serious (Farrington, Ohlin, and Wilson 1986). In our view, the existence of individuals whose official crime record begins after age eighteen does not constitute a threat to the taxonomy.

The Hypothesis that Adolescence-Limited Antisocial Behavior is Influenced by the Maturity Gap, and by Social Mimicry of Antisocial Models

The original theory asserted that "individual differences should play little or no role in the prediction of short-term adolescent offending careers. Instead, the strongest predictors of adolescence-limited offending should be peer delinquency, attitudes toward adolescence and adulthood reflecting the maturity gap [such as a desire for autonomy], cultural and historical contexts influencing adolescence, and age" (Moffitt 1993: 695).

Most research on the taxonomy to date has focused on testing hypotheses about the etiology of life-course persistent offenders. Unfortunately, adolescence-limited offenders have been relegated to the status of a contrast group and the original hypotheses about the distinct etiology of adolescent-onset offending have not captured the research imagination. This is unfortunate because adolescent-onset offenders are quite common (one-quarter of both males and females as defined in the Dunedin cohort) and their antisocial activities are not benign. They are found among adjudicated delinquents as well as in the general population (Scholte 1999). Moreover, even if adolescence-limited individuals commit fewer violent offenses than life-course persistent individuals, the size of the adolescence-limited group is much larger than the size of the life-course persistent group, and, as a result, the adolescence-limited group can be expected to account for an important share of a society's serious and violent offenses. In Dunedin, life-course persistent men (10 percent of the cohort) accounted for 53 percent of the cohort's 554 self-reported violent offenses at age twenty-six, but adolescence-limited men (26 percent of the chort) accounted for 29 percent of the cohort's violent offenses, a non-trivial amount of violence (Moffitt, Caspi, Harrington and Milne 2002).

Do adolescents find the maturity gap psychologically aversive, and does this motivate their newfound interest in delinquency? Aguilar et al. (2000) discovered that adolescent-onset delinquents experienced elevated internalizing symptoms and perceptions of stress at age sixteen, which may be consistent with the taxonomy's assertion that these adolescents experience psychological discomfort during the maturity gap. The theory suggested that this discomfort motivated adolescents to engage in antisocial behavior in order for them to seem older. In a study of the Gluecks' sample, adolescents' concerns about appearing immature increased their likelihood of delinquency (Zebrowitz, Andreoletti, Collins, Lee, and Blumenthal 1998). One interesting ethnographic study has made use of the maturity gap to explain '*kortteliralli*,' the street-racing alcohol youth culture of Finland (Vaaranen 2001). The Victoria Adolescence Project studys 452 adolescents and their parents to examine how young people negotiate the maturity gap (Galambos, Barker, and Tilton-Weaver 2003). This study identified a group of 25 percent of adolescents who exhibited a cluster of characteristics they called "pseudo-maturity." These adolescents, relative to their age cohort, were characterized by more advanced biological pubertal status, older subjective age ("I feel a lot older than my age"), elevated perceptions of self-reliance, more wishes to emulate older brothers (but not sisters), more older friends, a greater desire to be older ("I would like to look a lot older than my age"), more involvement in pop culture, and less involvement in school but more involvement with peers. This cluster was not associated with SES level. The study concluded that for a large proportion of teens, pubertal maturation brings about a poor fit between their developmental stage and their social environment, "...they are caught in the maturity gap" (Galambos et al. 2003: 262). Parent and self-reports confirmed that this pseudo-mature group of teenagers engaged in elevated rates of problem behaviors, as expected by the theory of adolescence-limited delinquency.

Do adolescence-limited teenagers want to be more like life-course persistent offenders? The theory of adolescence-limited delinquency borrowed the concept of "social mimicry" from the field of ethology to explain how adolescents might mimic the antisocial behavior of life-course persistent antisocial boys in their midst, in an effort to attain the mature status embodied in the antisocial lifestyle. New developmental research has shown that when ordinary young people age into adolescence they begin to admire good students less and to admire aggressive, antisocial peers more (Bukowski, Sippola, and Newcomb 2000; Luthar and McMahon 1996; Rodkin, Farmer, Pearl and Van Acker 2000). One sociometric study that followed 905 children from age ten to fourteen reported that the association between physical aggression and being disliked by peers dissolved during this age period; as they grew older, the teenagers came to perceive their aggressive age-mates as having higher social status and more influence (Cillessen and Mayeux 2004). Moreover, during adolescence, young people who place a high value on conforming to adults' rules become unpopular with their peers (Allen, Weissberg, and Hawkins 1989).

Our Dunedin studies documented that an increase in young teens' awareness of peers' delinquency antedates and predicts onset of their own later delinquency (Caspi, Lynam, Moffitt, and Silva 1993). We also showed that the adolescence-limited path is more strongly associated with delinquent peers, as compared against the life-course persistent path (Jeglum-Bartusch et al. 1997; Moffitt and Caspi 2001). However, one study that traced peer-affiliation trajectories concluded that peers were as influential for childhood-onset persistent offenders as for adolescent-onset offenders (LaCourse, Nagin, Tremblay, Vitaro, and Claes 2003). In contrast, others have shown that delinquent peer influences directly promote increases in delinquency, specifically among young males whose antisocial behavior onsets in adolescence (Simons, Wu, Conger, and Lorenz 1994; Vitaro, Tremblay, Kerr, Pagani, and Bukowski 1997). In contrast, these same studies suggest that among males whose antisocial behavior onsets in childhood, the direction of influence runs the other way; the child's own early antisocial behavior promotes increases at adolescence in the number of delinquent peers who selectively affiliate with him. This is consistent with our life-course persistent theory's assertion that during adolescence life-course persistent antisocial boys become "magnets" for peers who wish to learn delinquency.

The most direct test of the adolescence-limited etiological hypothesis was carried out in the Youth in Transition Survey of 2,000 males (Piquero and Brezina 2001). This study was introduced to the literature with lyrics from a song entitled "*Eighteen*" by rocker Alice Cooper that express the ennui of the maturity gap: "I'm in the middle without any plans, I'm a boy and I'm a man." The study tested the hypothesis that desires for autonomy promoted adolescent-onset offending. It found that, as predicted, the offenses committed by adolescence-limited delinquents were primarily rebellious (not physically aggressive) and that this rebellious offending was accounted for by the interaction between maturational timing and aspects of peer activities that were related to personal autonomy. However, one measure of youth autonomy in this study did not predict offending.

It is important to acknowledge that alternative accounts of late-onset delinquency have been put forward. In particular, Patterson and Yoerger (1997) outlined a learning model in which decreases in parents' monitoring and supervision when their children enter adolescence cause adolescents to begin offending. We had argued that although parents' monitoring and supervision were certainly negatively correlated with adolescent-onset delinquency, the direction of cause and effect was unclear, and our adolescence-limited theory would say that this correlation arises because teens' desires to gain autonomy via delinquency motivate them to evade their parents' supervision (Moffitt 1993: 693). A longitudinal study of 1,000 Swedish fourteen-year-olds and their parents suggested that our interpretation may be correct (Kerr and Stattin 2000). Adolescents actively controlled their parents' access to information about their activities, and teens who took part in deviant behavior limited their parents' capacity to monitor them. The study showed that parents' efforts to supervise and monitor were not very effective in controlling their teen-agers' activities, and could even backfire if teens felt controlled.

What research is needed? Clearly, there is not very much research testing whether measures of the maturity gap and social mimicry can account for adolescence-limited delinquency, so any new studies with this aim would add to our understanding. Agnew (2003) offers a cogent breakdown of maturity-gap elements that can be tested. Short-term longitudinal studies of young teens might ask if a developmental increase in attitudes rejecting childhood and favoring autonomy is correlated with a growing interest in and approval of illicit activities. Moreover, there is the curious fact that life-course persistent antisocial individuals are rejected by peers in childhood but later become more popular with peers in adolescence. The theory of social mimicry predicted this shift in popularity, but more longitudinal research following individuals' changes in social standing is needed to understand it fully. Finally, we should consult historical and anthropological work to ascertain if historical periods and cultures characterized by a clearly demarcated transition from childhood dependency to adulthood rights and responsibilities are also characterized by relatively low levels of delinquency and adolescent rebelliousness.

The Hypothesis that Abstainers from Delinquency are Rare Individuals, Who are Excluded from Normative Peer Group Activities in Adolescence

If, as the theory says, adolescence-limited delinquency is normative adaptational social behavior, then the existence of teens who abstain from delinquency requires an explanation. In other words, if ordinary teens take up delinquent behavior, then teens who eschew delinquency must be extraordinary in some way. The original theory speculated that teens committing no antisocial behavior would be rare and that they must have either structural barriers that prevent them from learning about delinquency, no maturity gap because of early access to adult roles, or personal characteristics unappealing to other teens that cause them to be excluded from teen social group activities (Moffitt 1993: 689, 695). As noted above, research has shown that during adolescence, young people who place a high value on conforming to adults' rules become unpopular with their peers (Allen et al. 1989).

We have studied male abstainers in the Dunedin cohort. Consistent with the rarity prediction, the Dunedin cohort contained only a very small group of males who avoided virtually any antisocial behavior during childhood and adolescence; abstainers were fewer than 10 percent of the cohort (Moffitt et al 1996). The very small size of this group has been confirmed in other samples. Only 13 percent of seventeen-year-olds in the National Longitudinal Survey of Youth replied that they had "never" done any of the survey's thirteen offense items (Piquero, Brezina, and Turner in press). Two longitudinal cohort studies used a theory-free method to characterize heterogeneous trajectories within repeated measures aggressive behavior: Nagin and Tremblay (1999) detected an abstainer trajectory from childhood to adolescence containing very few males, and Wiesner and Capaldi (2003) detected an abstainer trajectory from adolescence to adulthood containing even fewer males (5 percent).

The small group of Dunedin abstainers described themselves at age eighteen on personality measures as extremely over-controlled, fearful, interpersonally timid, and socially inept, and they were latecomers to sexual relationships (i.e., virgins at age eighteen). Dunedin abstainers fit the profile Shedler and Block (1990) reported for youth who abstained from drug experimentation in a historical period when it was normative: over-controlled, not curious, not active, not open to experience, socially isolated, and lacking social skills. Dunedin abstainers were unusually good students, fitting the profile of the compliant good student who during adolescence can become unpopular with peers (Allen et al. 1989; Bukowski et al. 2000). Other studies have suggested that abstention from delinquency, and substance use during adolescence, are associated with feeling socially isolated from peers (Dunford and Elliott 1984), having few friends (Farrington and West 1993) or being a loner (Tolone and Tieman 1990). Such findings prompted Shedler and Block (1990: 627) to comment that abstention is "less the result of moral fiber or successful prevention programs than the result of relative alienation from peers and a characterological over-control of needs and impulses."

Dunedin's age-twenty-six follow-up data confirmed that the teen-aged abstainers did not become so-called adult-onset offenders (Moffitt et al. 2002). Although their teenaged years had been socially awkward for them, their style became more successful in adulthood. As adults they retained their self-constrained personality, had virtually no crime or mental disorder, were likely to have settled into marriage, were delaying children (a desirable strategy for a generation needing prolonged education to succeed), were likely to be college-educated, held high-status jobs, and expressed optimism about their own futures.

Another study of abstainers from delinquency was conducted using 1,600 seventeen-year olds from the 1997 National Longitudinal Survey of Youth (Piquero, Brezina, and Turner in press). Consistent with theoretical prediction, relative to participants in delinquency, the abstainers were few in number, more closely monitored by their parents, more attached to teachers, less physically mature, reported less autonomy, dated less, and were less involved with friends who drank, smoked, tried drugs and cut classes. However, an unexpected new finding was that abstainers were not wholly friendless, but rather they reported they had prosocial peers who "go to church regularly," "plan to go to college," and "participate in volunteer work." This study also attempted to test the theory's prediction that abstainers have personalities that make them unattractive to peers, using an item called "sadness/depression" intended to assess a morose, uncheerful style unlikely to appeal to peers. However, the study found that sadness/depression was correlated with delinquent participation, not abstention. This test was ambiguous because the depression item probably did not measure the over-controlled, incurious, timid, socially inept personality style thought to preclude delinquency. Thus, this study provided some modest support for the taxonomy's view of abstainers as a minority that exists outside the social scene that creates opportunities for delinquency among the teen majority. Moreover the study suggested the provocative new finding that abstainers do have friends who are pro-social like themselves.

What research is needed? To our knowledge, our finding that abstainers are social introverts as teens remains to be confirmed or discounted by another study directly designed to test this hypothesis. Adolescent sociometric studies might ask if delinquent abstention is, indeed, correlated with unpopularity and social isolation. Further study of abstainers is critical for testing the hypothesis that adolescence-limiteds' delinquency is normative adaptational behavior by ordinary young people.

The Hypothesis that Life-Course Persistent Development is Differentially Associated in Adulthood with Serious Offending and Violence

The original theory predicted that life-course persistent offenders, as compared to adolescence-limited offenders, would engage in a wider variety of offense types, including "more of the victim-oriented offenses, such as violence and fraud" (Moffitt 1993: 695).

By the time the Dunedin cohort reached age eighteen, we reported that the life-course persistent pathway was differentially associated with conviction for violent crimes (Jeglum-Bartusch et al. 1997; Moffitt et al. 1996), while the adolescence-limited pathway was differentially associated with non-violent delinquent offenses (Jeglum-Bartusch et al. 1997). These Dunedin findings are buttressed by reports from other samples that physical aggression usually begins in childhood and seldom onsets in adolescence (e.g., Brame, Nagin, and Tremblay 2001). Moreover, we had shown that preadolescent antisocial behavior that was accompanied by neuropsychological deficits predicted greater persistence of crime and more violence up to age eighteen (Moffitt et al. 1994).

Our follow-up at age twenty-six confirmed that life-course persistent men as a group particularly differed from adolescence-limited men in the realm of violence, including violence against the women and children in their homes. This finding was corroborated with large effect sizes by data from multiple independent sources, including self-reports, informant reports, and official court conviction records (Moffitt et al. 2002). In a comparison of specific offenses, life-course persistent men tended to specialize in serious offenses (carrying a hidden weapon, assault, robbery, violating court orders), whereas adolescence-limited men specialized in non-serious offenses (theft less than

$5, public drunkenness, giving false information on application forms, pirating computer software, etc.). Life-course persistent men accounted for five times their share of the cohort's violent convictions. Thus although they were a small group (10 percent of males), they accounted for 43 percent of the cohort's officially sanctioned violent crime.

Domestic violence against women and children at home was specifically predicted to be an outcome of the life-course persistent group (Moffitt 1993). At the age twenty-six Dunedin follow-up, this group's scores were elevated on self-reported and official conviction measures of abuse toward women, both physical abuse (e.g., beating her up, throwing her bodily) and controlling abuse (e.g., stalking her, restricting her access to her friends and family). Because the Dunedin cohort has been interviewed repeatedly about illicit behaviors for many years, study members now trust the study's guarantee of confidentiality and can be asked questions about hitting children, with the expectation of valid responses. Life-course persistent men were the most likely to report that they had hit a child out of anger, not in the course of normal discipline. Our finding that life-course persistent offenders perpetrated more domestic violence was supported by the Christchurch study's finding that young adults with childhood-onset antisocial behavior engaged in significantly more violence against partners than did those with adolescent-onset antisocial behavior (Woodward, Fergusson, and Horwood 2002). Similarly, a study of New York parolees reported that those defined as life-course persistent based on a childhood-onset offense record engaged in twice as much domestic violence as parolees with an adolescent-onset offense record (Mazerolle and Maahs 2002).

In general, a large empirical literature shows that the strongest long-term predictors of violence are the same predictors implicated by our theory of life-course persistent offending: early-onset antisocial behavior, neurodevelopmental risk factors, and family risk factors (for a review, see Farrington 1998). Moreover, research comparing violent crime versus general non-violent delinquency has shown that violence is differentially predicted by birth complications (Raine et al. 1997), minor physical anomalies (Arseneault et al. 2000), difficult temperament (Henry, Caspi, Moffitt, and Silva 1996), and cognitive deficits (Piquero 2001), each of which are hypothetical risks for life-course persistent development (for a review see Raine 2002). The Christchurch study reported that people with serious childhood-onset conduct problems, compared to children without conduct problems, engaged in ten times more violent crime by age twenty-five (Fergusson, Horwood and Ridder in press). The Patterns of Care Study of 1,715 service-users aged six to seventeen years also compared childhood-onset versus adolescent-onset conduct disorder cases and reported that the childhood-onset group committed significantly more "bullying" but not more of the other physically aggressive conduct-disorder symptoms (McCabe et al. 2001). However, this study did not have an adult follow-up. Lahey and colleagues (1998) reported more physical aggression associated with adolescent-onset than with childhood-onset conduct disorder.

What research is needed? The literature makes it clear that neurodevelopmental and family risks predict violence when it is measured on a continuum, but only a few studies have compared the adult violent outcomes of *groups* defined on the basis of early versus late antisocial onset. In addition, research is needed to clarify why life-course persistent offenders are more violent. Our theory implies that verbal cognitive deficits may limit their options for handling conflict (a neuropsychological explanation), that they may have learned in their families that violence is an effective way to manage conflict (a social-cognition explanation) and that broken attachment bonds lead to alienation from their potential victims (an attachment explanation) (Moffitt 1994; Moffitt and Caspi 1995). All of these explanations specify early childhood as a critical period influencing adult violence. But which, if any, of these explanatory processes are correct? Research using designs that control for genetic transmission of a predisposition to aggression in families has now documented that experiences in the family do promote childhood-onset aggression through processes that are environmentally mediated. Environmental effects on children's aggression have now been documented for exposure to parents' domestic violence (Jaffee, Moffitt, Caspi, Taylor, and Arseneault 2002), being reared by an antisocial father (Jaffee, Moffitt, Caspi, and Taylor 2003), being reared by a depressed mother (Kim-Cohen, Moffitt, Taylor, Pawlby, and Caspi, 2005), being a recipient of maternal hostility (Caspi et al. 2004), and being a victim of child maltreatment (Jaffee, Caspi, Moffitt, and Taylor 2004b). These studies controlled for familial liability to psychopathology suggesting that the risk factors influence children through environmental experience. This information gives fresh impetus for research to uncover how these experiences are mediated via the child's thoughts and emotions to produce persistent aggression. Research is needed on mediating developmental processes because findings will point to targets for intervention.

The Hypothesis that Childhood-Onset Antisocial Behavior will Persist into Middle Adulthood, whereas Adolescent-Onset Antisocial Behavior will Desist in Young Adulthood

Inherent in the name "life-course persistent" is the assertion that the antisocial activities of these individuals will persist across the life course. Though the whole population may decrease its antisocial participation as it ages, the life-course persistent individuals should remain at the top of the heap on antisocial behaviors. Thus, the taxonomy accepts that antisocial participation declines markedly in mid-life, but, nonetheless, it expects rank-order stability, particularly on age-relevant measures of antisocial activity. To test the differential desistance prediction, it is necessary to follow a cohort's antisocial behavior from childhood to adulthood, but only a few studies have done this.

We followed up the Dunedin cohort at age twenty-six (Moffitt et al. 2002) to test hypotheses critical to this part of the theory: childhood-onset antisocial behavior, but not adolescent-onset antisocial behavior, should be associated in adulthood with antisocial personality and continued serious antisocial behavior that expands into maladjustment in work-life and victimization of partners and children (Moffitt 1993: 695). Followed to age twenty-six, the adolescent-onset delinquents at twenty-six were still engaging in elevated levels of property offending and had financial problems, but did not show a pattern of serious offending. Interestingly, the adolescent-onset delinquents self-reported problems with mental health and substance dependence but these difficulties were not corroborated by informants who knew them well. Consistent with the taxonomy's predictions, the childhood-onset delinquents at age twenty-six were the most elevated on psychopathic personality traits, mental-health problems, substance dependence, numbers of children sired, financial problems, work problems, domestic abuse of women and children and drug-related and violent crimes.

In a study of 4,000 California Youth Authority inmates followed into their thirties, significantly more early-starters than later-starters continued offending past age twenty-one, past age twenty-five and past age thirty-one. Moreover, early onset and low cognitive ability significantly predicted which inmates continued to offend past age thirty-one (Ge et al. 2001). A different study of California Youth Authority offenders looked in depth at predictors of criminal career duration among 377 parolees released on average at age twenty-four and followed for twelve years (Piquero, Brame, and Lynam 2004). This study found that criminal career duration was predicted by low tested cognitive abilities and by the interaction between childhood poverty status and cognitive ability. Similarly, a large Swedish study reported less crime in adulthood among offenders who possessed positive personal characteristics resembling the characteristics of Dunedin adolescence-limited offenders (Stattin, Romelsjo, and Stenbacka 1997).

The abovementioned findings were obtained using groups of adolescence-limited and life-course persistent males defined by applying common-sense clinical cut-offs (e.g., Moffitt et al. 1996). However, in the past decade new analytic methods have become available for ascertaining whether distinctive trajectories exist within a population of individuals whose behavior has been measured repeatedly during development (Nagin 1999; Nagin and Tremblay 2001b; Roeder et al. 1999). These new semi-parametric methods offer several advantages over the clinical-cutoffs approach. First, the methods are agnostic with respect to taxonomic theories, and, thus, results are relatively free from investigator bias. Second, the methods can search a longitudinal data set to ask whether there is, indeed, more than one developmental trajectory in it, as the taxonomy implies. Third, they can ascertain the relative goodness of fit of competing models having one, two, three, four or more trajectories, to ascertain whether the taxonomic theory has specified the right number of developmental subtypes in the population. Fourth, they generate output from the best fitting model that reveals whether its trajectories rise and fall at ages specified by the theory. Fifth, they generate output about which study participants belong to which trajectory, making it possible to ascertain whether each trajectory group approximates its population prevalence as specified by the theory. It is important to keep in mind that what researchers put into the method determines what they can get out, and, therefore, testing the taxonomy of life-course persistent and adolescence-limited antisocial behavior calls for representative samples, repeated measures taken at informative ages from childhood to adulthood, and measures of antisocial behavior that capture its heterotypic continuity across developmental periods. In these respects, the Dunedin data set, although not perfect, was pretty good fodder for the semi-parametric method.

We applied this method to counts of conduct disorder symptoms assessed (via self-, mother-, and teacher-reports) for 525 male study members at ages seven, nine, eleven, thirteen, fifteen, eighteen, twenty-one and twenty-six years (Moffitt et al. in preparation). Conduct disorder symptoms are fighting, bullying, lying, stealing, cruelty to people or animals, vandalism and disobeying rules; three such symptoms earn a formal diagnosis. The model that best fit the Dunedin data detected the following groups (See Figure 10.1). A life-course persistent group, 7 percent of the cohort, had a fairly stable high trajectory, exhibiting between four and seven antisocial symptoms at every age from seven years to twenty-six years. This group had more symptoms than any of the other groups at every age. A group whose trajectory resembled an adolescence-limited pattern began with two symptoms at age seven but increased to a peak of 4.5 symptoms at age eighteen and then decreased on a slight downward trajectory to 3.5 symptoms at age twenty-six. A recovery group, 21 percent of the cohort (similar to the "childhood-limited" or "low-level-chronic" groups described in an earlier section of this chapter), began with six symptoms at age seven, but decreased steadily with age, and had only one symptom by ages twenty-one and twenty-six. An abstainer group, 11 percent, had less than one symptom on average at every age. Two further trajectory groups were identified. The first of these took an adolescence-limited shape, but at a low level, and the second took a recovery shape, but also at a low level. For illustrative purposes in Figure 10.1 these two groups were collapsed into a consistently low group, 47 percent of the cohort, which had one to two symptoms on average at each age. Thus, the best fitting model bore a not unreasonable resemblance to the taxonomy. Differential outcomes for the trajectory groups mirrored the outcomes for the clinically defined Dunedin groups (Moffitt et al. 2002). Males on the adolescence-limited trajectory were still engaging in property offending and substance abuse, but not serious offending at age twenty-six. Males on the life-course persistent trajectory were the most elevated at age twenty-six on mental-health problems and substance dependence, numbers of children sired, financial and work problems, domestic abuse of women and children, and drug-related and violent crimes.

Figure 10.1
20-Year Trajectories of Conduct Disorder Symptoms Among 525 Dunedin Males

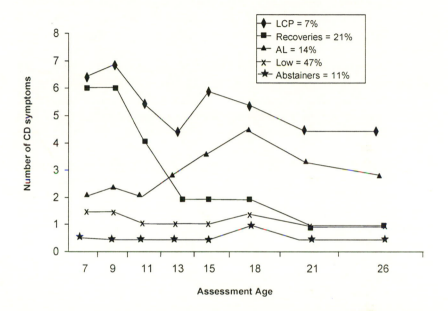

Other cohort studies have applied trajectory analysis to repeated measures of antisocial behavior from childhood to adulthood. A British longitudinal study followed official crime records for a 1950s birth cohort of 400 men to age thirty-two and detected chronic and adolescence-limited trajectories that showed the expected differential desistance (Nagin et al. 1995). Unexpectedly, offenders defined as adolescence-limited had desisted from criminal offending according to their official police records, but according to their self-reports they continued into their thirties to drink heavily and get into fights. The South Holland epidemiological study followed 2,000 Dutch children from age four to thirty years (Bongers, Koot, van der Ende, Donker, and Verhulst, under review). This study reported two trajectories of young people with high levels of externalizing problems, as assessed by the CBCL (Achenbach 1985). One trajectory was normative and distinguished by increasing truancy, alcohol and drug use, but did not markedly increase the risk of adult offending. The other trajectory was characterized by increasing oppositional behavior and hot temper, and was associated with elevated risk of serious and violent adult offending. Low trajectories were also detected.

The Rutgers Health and Human Development Project also followed its longitudinal sample into adulthood and reported a test of the taxonomy using non-parametric mixture modeling to detect trajectory groups (White, Bates, and Buyske 2001). However, this paper's figure 1, showing delinquency trajectories for the resulting groups, suggests that the group labeled "persistent" in this study was in reality adolescence-limited because this group's trajectory showed very low levels of offending at ages twelve and twenty-eight but a very pronounced adolescent offending peak at age eighteen. This sample may not have contained life-course persistent members because it was recruited via random telephone dialing with an initial 17 percent rate of refusal to the phone call and afterwards a 52 percent completion rate for enrollment in data collection. Families with life-course persistent risk characteristics are known to be difficult to engage as research participants (Farrington, Gallagher, Morley, St. Ledger, and West 1990), and, therefore, they were probably among those who did not take part in the Rutgers Study. Given the strong possibility that groups were mis-labeled in this study, it is unclear what to make of it, vis-a-vis the taxonomy.

The Oregon Youth Study applied trajectory analysis to 200 males followed from age twelve to twenty-four (Wiesner and Capaldi 2003). In addition to the abstainer trajectory and the decreasing trajectory discussed in earlier sections of this chapter, the analysis also yielded a group whose antisocial behavior was chronically at the cohort's highest level (life-course persistent?) and a group whose antisocial behavior increased somewhat from age twelve to a peak at nineteen, and then decreased from age twenty to twenty-four (adolescence-limited?). It is not clear that Weisner and Capaldi would agree with our characterization of their groups; indeed, they used different labels for them. In any case, although these two groups seemed fairly similar in late adolescence, they diverged at the study's age twenty-three to twenty-six outcome point, with the chronic group showing much higher levels of alcohol use, drug use and depression symptoms as well as more adult antisocial behavior (Wiesner, Kim and Capaldi, under review).

One clear shortcoming of the available longitudinal data base that has been used to test for the presence of life-course persistent versus adolescence-limited subtypes is that it is "right-hand censored"; in other words, study participants have generally been followed only until their twenties or thirties. What is needed is a cohort that represents the general population, and that has been followed through the age period of risk for most criminal offending, up to mid-life. Such a cohort does not yet exist. However, in the absence of the ideal representative cohort, there is one important study that warrants our focus. Sampson and Laub (2003) reported a follow-up of half of the Gluecks' sample, those who were adolescent inmates in Massachusetts in the 1940s. The authors constructed a unique data base of official criminal records for almost 500 men, covering the period from age seven years to the end of each offender's life, up to age seventy years. The study was noteworthy for collecting nationwide FBI records and for attending to artifacts in crime records arising from periods of incarceration or the offender's premature death. The authors' analyses were motivated by their skepticism about the idea of prospectively predicting a group of offenders who will account for a disproportionate amount of society's serious crime. Sampson and Laub (2003) reported two findings from the study that they believed challenge this idea. First, they found that almost all of the men in the Gluecks' sample desisted from criminal offending sooner or later. Second, they found heterogeneity in adulthood crime career patterns within the sample of adolescent inmates, and they found that this heterogeneity was not explained by measures of childhood risk.

Because the Sampson and Laub (2003) publication was represented as a challenge to the life-course persistent taxonomy, we must take a closer look at whether or not these two findings discredit the taxonomy. In so doing, it is useful to consider the nature of the sample studied by Sampson and Laub. According to the taxonomy, virtually all of the men studied would have been regarded as candidates for the life-course persistent subtype. They had been incarcerated as young adolescents as inmates in reform schools, a status reserved at that time for a very small fraction of a state's youth, those having established already by adolescence the most serious, persistent records of deviance that could not be controlled by parents or schools. It is well documented that as a group the boys had backgrounds of marked family adversity, social disadvantage, and childhood antisocial conduct. Sampson and Laub note details about the sample that fit the life-course persistent pattern, such as low mean IQ and mean first arrest at 11.9 years. Thus, this sample born in 1924 to 1932 probably comprised, relative to the much larger population of Boston males their age, a small subgroup who had started on the life-course persistent pathway.

Sampson and Laub's (2003: 577) first finding was that the men in the Gluecks' sample desisted from criminal offending sooner or later: "...aging out of crime appears to reflect a general process." Unfortunately, Sampson and Laub (2003) misrepresented the taxonomy's prediction. They set up a "straw" prediction to test: that life-course persistent offenders should carry on committing crimes at the same high rate from adolescence through old age, until their deaths. Clearly this was never implied by the taxonomy because the original publication acknowledged the population-wide process of aging out of crime and explained that the term life-course persistent antisocial behavior did not require crime per se in old age, instead "persistent" referred to the persistence of antisocial personality characteristics or antisocial behaviors within the family (Moffitt 1993: 680). The taxonomy's actual prediction was that delinquents like the Gluecks' would continue offending well beyond the age when most young men in their cohort population desisted. The study followed only reform-school boys and, thus, it could not provide comparative data on crime careers for Boston men born 1924 to 1932, but it is known that desistance from delinquency in young adulthood was the norm for cohorts such as this one which came of age in the post-war era of near-full employment. In contrast to that norm, 84 percent of the Glueck study men were arrested between ages seventeen and twenty-four, 44 percent were arrested in their forties, 23 percent were arrested in their fifties, and 12 percent were arrested in their sixties. The reform-school sample's mean crime career length was 25.6 years. It seems reasonable to believe that such remarkable statistics do not also describe the rest of the male population of Boston. Thus, the study's results seem reasonably consistent with the taxonomy's prediction that boys who begin life on the life-course persistent pathway will have unusually extended offending careers, thereby accounting for more than their share of the crime rate.

Sampson and Laub's second finding was that they found heterogeneity in adulthood crime career patterns within the Gluecks' sample. Again, the alternative hypothesis seems like a "straw man." The alternative would be that males who spent their youth and early adulthood on the life-course persistent pathway can show no variation in subsequent offending during mid-life and aging, over a span of many years. Such uniformity is implausible, and the taxonomic theory did not make such a prediction. Within the Gluecks' sample six trajectories emerged from a semi-parametric group-based modeling analysis. Thus, the men, all of whom began on the life-course persistent pathway, varied subsequently in their age at desistance from crime and in their rate of offending up to the point of their desistance. Importantly, child and family characteristics did not discriminate between these six trajectories. On the one hand, this failure of discrimination is not surprising given that the cohort members' childhood backgrounds were almost uniformly high-risk. On the other hand, this finding suggests that to the extent that different crime careers emerge during mid-life within a group of life-course persistent men, concurrent life experiences must account for the divergence. This would constitute an interesting extension to the taxonomic theory, on a topic it did not originally address: heterogeneity within life-course persistent delinquents in the ways they age out of crime.

This study by Sampson and Laub was well executed and well intentioned. The authors were concerned about practitioners who have reified the life-course persistent idea, treating it as if it describes a group having hard boundaries, made up of individual children who are easy to identify in early childhood, and who deserve radical interventions to avert their inevitable destiny as predatory criminals. The authors' concern is well-placed, and their efforts to dissuade such reification are laudable. To their credit, the authors point out that "the current bandwagon...is not consistent with the logic of Moffitt's actual argument" (pp. 576). Nonetheless, to make their points, the authors inadvertently had to misrepresent the original taxonomy as having made predictions that it did not make. Here we set the record straight. Life-course persistent delinquents do not have to be arrested for illegal crimes steadily up to age seventy, but they do have to maintain a constellation of antisocial attitudes, values, and proclivities that affects their behavior toward others. Life-course persistent delinquents do not have to all live exactly the same crime trajectory as they age out of crime; it is interesting to learn how their lives diverge. Laub and Sampson are leading the way in researching these new questions using qualitative as well as quantitative methods (Laub and Sampson 2003).

What research is needed? Overall, our theory's prediction that childhood-onset antisocial behavior persists longer into adulthood than adolescent-onset delinquency seems to be on fairly solid empirical footing. It has been known for decades that early onset of offending predicts a longer duration of crime career, and this association was recently affirmed by two careful reviews (Gendreau, Little, and Goggin 1996; Krohn, Thornberry, Rivera, and LeBlanc 2001). Nonetheless, the adolescence-limited groups in the Dunedin cohort and other cohorts continued to experience some adjustment problems as adults, and we need research to understand what accounts for this. The original taxonomy put forward the hypothesis that we should expect some adolescence-limited delinquents to recover good adult adjustment later than others, and that this age variation might be explained by "snares" such as a conviction record that harms job prospects (Moffitt 1993: 691). The idea is that engaging in even limited delinquency as a young person can diminish the probability of subsequent good outcomes, particularly if one is caught and sanctioned. Also important is the information emerging from the work of Laub and Sampson (2003) pointing to marked heterogeneity within the life-course persistent group in middle and late life, suggesting research into mid-life turning-point experiences is needed. Overall, longitudinal studies are needed that follow the life-course persistent, low-level chronic, abstainer, and adolescence-limited groups to reveal the very long-term implications of their experiences in the first two decades of life.

Conclusions

Before 1993 virtually no research compared delinquent subtypes defined on a developmental basis, but now this research strategy has become almost commonplace. Many research teams have assessed representative samples with prospective measures of antisocial behavior from childhood to adulthood, and this has enabled comparisons based on age of onset and persistence. Now that the requisite databases are available, many hypotheses derived from the original taxonomic theory are being tested. After ten years of research, what can be stated with some certainty is that the hypothesized life-course persistent antisocial individual exists, at least during the first three decades of life. Consensus about this group has emerged from all studies that have applied trajectory-detection analyses to a representative cohort sample having longitudinal repeated measures of antisocial behavior. Tremblay et al. (2004) detected a "high physical aggression" group constituting 14 percent of Canadian children followed from age seventeen months to forty-two months. Broidy et al. (2003) detected a "chronic aggressive" group constituting 3 percent to 11 percent of children followed from age six to thirteen years in six different cohorts from three countries. Maughan et al. (2001) detected a "stable high aggressive" group constituting 12 percent of North Carolina youth followed from ages nine to sixteen years. Brame et al. (2001) detected a "high chronic aggressive" group constituting 3 percent of Canadian youth followed from age six to seventeen years. Raine et al. (in press) detected a "life-course persistent path" group that constituted 13 percent of Pittsburgh youth followed from age seven to seventeen years. Fergusson et al. (2000) detected a "chronic offender" group constituting 6 percent of Christchurch youth followed from age twelve to eighteen years. Chung et al. (2002) detected a "chronic offender" group constituting 7 percent of Seattle youth followed from age thirteen to twenty-one years. Wiesner and Capaldi (2003) detected a "chronic high-level" group constituting 16 percent of Oregon youth followed from age twelve to twenty-four years. Moffitt et al. (in preparation) detected a "high-persistent" group that constituted 7 percent of Dunedin young people followed from age seven to twenty-six years. Nagin et al. (1995) detected a "high-level chronic" group that constituted 12 percent of London males followed from age ten to thirty-two years. So far as we know, no research team that has looked for a persistent antisocial group has failed to find it.

Other studies not reviewed here are now addressing how the life-course persistent versus adolescence-limited types are related to gender, race, genetic risk and adult personality outcomes. However, in this chapter, page limitations precluded reviewing those literatures. They are reviewed in Moffitt (2006). Some predictions from the taxonomy have not been tested sufficiently, including the following hypotheses: Life-course persistent antisocial individuals will be at high risk in mid-life for poor physical health, cardiovascular disease, and early disease morbidity and mortality. Adolescence-limited offenders must rely on peer support for crime, but life-course persistent offenders should be willing to offend alone (although in adolescence they serve as magnets for less expert offenders). "Snares" (such as a criminal record, incarceration, addiction or truncated education without credentials) should explain variation in the age at desistence from crime during the adult age period, particularly among adolescence-limited offenders. The two groups should react differently to turning-point opportunities: as they enter adulthood, adolescence-limited offenders should get good partners and jobs that help them to desist from crime, whereas life-course persistent offenders should selectively get undesirable partners and jobs and in turn expand their repertoire as young adults into domestic abuse and workplace crime. It is pleasing that the 1993 taxonomy has generated interest and research. Some findings have been faithful to the hypotheses originally formulated. Other findings have pointed to important revisions needed to improve the fit between the taxonomy and nature, and some findings raise serious challenges to aspects of the taxonomy. All three kinds of findings are much appreciated.

Notes

*   Preparation of this chapter was supported by grants from the U.S. National Institute of Mental Health (MH45070 and MH4941) and the British Medical Research Council (G9806489 and G0100527). Terrie Moffitt is a Royal Society-Wolfson Merit Award Holder.

This chapter updates an earlier chapter published in B. Lahey, T.E. Moffitt, and A. Caspi, (2003). *The causes of conduct disorder and serious juvenile delinquency*, New York, NY: Guilford. A longer version of this chapter, covering topics omitted here such as sex, race, genetic risk, and adult personality in relation to life-course persistent offending, will appear in T.E Moffitt (2006). Life-course persistent and adolescence-limited antisocial behavior. In D. Cicchetti and D. Cohen (Eds.). *Developmental Psychopathology 2nd Edition*. NY: Wiley.

Correspondence to t.moffitt@iop.kcl.ac.uk or T.E. Moffitt, PO80 SGDP Research Centre, Institute of Psychiatry, DeCrespigny Park, London SE5 8AF, U.K.

References

Achenbach, T.M. 1985. *Assessment and Taxonomy of Child and Adolescent Psychopathology*. Newbury Park, CA: Sage.

Agnew, R. 2003. "An Integrated Theory of the Adolescent Peak in Offending." *Youth and Society* 34: 263-299.

Aguilar, B., L.A. Sroufe, B. Egeland, and E. Carlson. 2000. "Distinguishing the Early-Onset-Persistent and Adolescent-Onset Antisocial Behavior Types: From Birth to 16 Years." *Development and Psychopathology* 12: 109-132.

Allen, J.P., R.P. Weissberg, and J.A. Hawkins. 1989. "The Relation Between Values and Social Competence in Early Adolescence." *Developmental Psychology* 25: 458-464.

Alnaes, R., and S. Torgersen. 1988. "The Relationship Between DSM-III Symptom Disorders (Axis I) and Personality Disorders (Axis II) in an Outpatient Population." *Acta Psychiatrica Scandinavica* 78: 485-492. American Psychiatric Association 1994. *Diagnostic and Statistical Manual of Mental Disorders,* 4th ed. Washington, DC: Author.

Arnett, J.J. 2000. "Emerging Adulthood: A Theory of Development from the Late Teens Through the Twenties." *American Psychologist* 55: 469-480.

Arseneault, L., R.E. Tremblay, B. Boulerice, and J.F. Saucier. 2002. "Obstetric Complications and Adolescent Violent Behaviors: Testing Two Developmental Pathways." *Child Development* 73: 496-508.

Arseneault, L., R.E. Tremblay, B. Boulerice, J.R. Seguin, and J.F. Saucier. 2000. "Minor Physical Anomalies and Family Adversity as Risk Factors for Adolescent Violent Delinquency." *American Journal of Psychiatry* 157: 917-923.

Bongers, I.L., H.M. Koot, J. Van Der Ende, A. Donke, and F.C. Verhulst. Under Review. "Predicting Delinquency in Young Adulthood from Developmental Pathways of Externalizing Behavior."

Brame, R., S. Bushway and R. Paternoster. 1999. "On the Use of Panel Research Designs and Random Effects Models to Investigate Static and Dynamic Theories of Criminal Offending." *Criminology* 37: 599-642.

Brame, R., D.S. Nagin, and R.E. Tremblay. 2001. "Developmental Trajectories of Physical Aggression from School Entry to Late Adolescence." *Journal of Child Psychology and Psychiatry* 42: 503-512.

Brennan, P.A., J. Hall, W. Bor, J.M. Najman, and G. Williams. 2003. "Integrating Biological and Social Processes in Relation to Early-Onset Persistent Aggression in Boys and Girls." *Developmental Psychology* 39: 309-323.

Brezina, T. 2000. "Delinquent Problem-Solving: An Interpretive Framework for Criminological Theory and Research." *Journal of Research in Crime and Delinquency* 37: 3-30.

Broidy, L., L.M. Broidy, D.S. Nagin, R.E. Tremblay, B. Brame, K. Dodge, D. Fergusson, J. Horwood, R. Loeber, R. Laird, D. Lynam, and T.E. Moffitt. 2003. "Developmental Trajectories of Childhood Disruptive Behaviour Disorders and Adolescent Delinquency: A Six-Sample Replication." *Developmental Psychology* 39: 222-245.

Bukowski, W.M., L.K. Sippola, and A.F. Newcomb. 2000. "Variations in Patterns of Attraction to Same-and Other-Sex Peers During Early Adolescence." *Developmental Psychology* 36: 147-154.

Caspi, A., D. Lynam, T.E. Moffitt, and P.A. Silva. 1993. "Unraveling Girls' Delinquen-cy: Biological, Dispositional, and Contextual Contributions to Adolescent Misbehavior." *Developmental Psychology* 29: 19-30.

Caspi, A., T.E. Moffitt, J. Morgan, M. Rutter, A. Taylor, L. Arseneault, L. Tully, C. Jacobs, J. Kim-Cohen, and M. Polo-Tomas. 2004. "Maternal Expressed Emotion Predicts Children's Antisocial Behavior Problems: Using MZ-Twin Differences to Identify Environmental Effects on Behavioral Development." *Developmental Psychology* 40: 149-161.

Chung, I., L.D. Hill, J.D. Hawkins, K.G. Gilchrist, and D. Nagin. 2002. "Childhood Predictors of Offense Trajectories." *Journal of Research in Crime and Delinquency* 39: 60-90.

Cicchetti, D., and D.J. Cohen. 1995. "Perspectives on Developmental Psychopathology." Pp. 3-20 in D. Cicchetti and D. Cohen (eds.), *Developmental Psychopathology, Vol. 1.* New York: Wiley.

Cicchetti, D., and E.R. Walker. 2003. *Neurobiological Mechanisms in Psychopathology.* New York: Cambridge University Press.

Cillessen, A.H.N., and L. Mayeux. 2004. "From Censure to Reinforcement: Developmental Changes in the Association between Aggression and Social Status." *Child Development* 75: 147-163.

Dean, C.W., R. Brame, and A.R. Piquero. 1996. "Criminal Propensities, Discrete Groups of Offenders, and Persistence in Crime." *Criminology* 34: 547-574.

Dilalla, L.F., and I.I. Gottesman. 1989. "Heterogeneity of Causes for Delinquency and Criminality: Lifespan Perspectives." *Development and Psychopathology* 1: 339-349.

Dishion, T.J., J. Mccord, and F. Poulin. 1999. "Iatrogenic Effects in Interventions That Aggregate High-Risk Youth." *The American Psychologist* 54: 1-10.

Donnellan, M.B., X. Ge, and E. Wenk. 2000. "Cognitive Abilities in Adolescence-Limited and Life-Course-Persistent Criminal Offenders." *Journal of Abnormal Psychology* 109: 396-402.

Dunford, F.W., and D.S. Elliott. 1984. "Identifying Career Offenders Using Self-Reported Data." *Journal of Research in Crime and Delinquency* 21: 57-86.

D'Unger, A.V., K.C. Land, P.L. McCall, and D.S. Nagin. 1998. "How Many Latent Classes of Delinquent/Criminal Careers?" *American Journal of Sociology* 103: 1593-1630.

Eggleston, E.P., and J.H. Laub. 2002. "The Onset of Adult Offending: A Neglected Dimension of the Criminal Career." *Journal of Criminal Justice* 30: 603-622.

Eley, T.C., P. Lichtenstein, and T.E. Moffitt. 2003. "A Longitudinal Analysis of the Etiology of Aggressive and Non-Aggressive Antisocial Behaviour." *Development and Psychopathology* 15: 155-168.

Elliott, D.S., 1994. "Serious Violent Offenders: Onset, Developmental Course, and Termination." *Criminology* 32: 10-21.

Elliott, D.S., D. Huizinga, and S. Menard. 1989. *Multiple Problem Youth: Delinquency, Substance Use, and Mental Health Problems.* New York: Springer-Verlag.

Farrington, D.P. 1998. "Predictors, Causes, and Correlates of Male Youth Violence." *Crime and Justice: A Review of Research* 24: 421-476.

Farrington, D.P., B. Gallagher, L. Morley, R.J. St. Ledger, and D. West. 1988. "Are There any Successful Men from Criminogenic Backgrounds?" *Psychiatry* 51: 116-130.

———. 1990. "Minimizing Attrition in Longitudinal Research." Pp. 122-147 in L.R. Bergman and D. Magnusson (eds.), *Data Quality in Longitudinal Research.* New York: Cambridge University Press.

Farrington, D.P., D. Jolliffe, J.D. Hawkins, R.F. Catalano, K.G. Hill, and R. Kosterman. 2003. "Comparing Delinquency Careers in Court Records and Self-Reports." *Criminology* 41: 933-958.

Farrington, D.P., L. Ohlin, and J.Q. Wilson. 1986. *Understanding and Controlling Crime.* New York: Springer-Verlag.

Farrington, D.P., and D.J. West. 1993. "Criminal, Penal and Life Histories of Chronic Offenders." *Criminal Behaviour and Mental Health* 3: 492-523.

Fergusson, D.M., L.J. Horwood, and D.S. Nagin. 2000. "Offending Trajectories in a New Zealand Birth Cohort." *Criminology* 38: 525-552.

Fergusson, D.M., L.J. Horwood,. and E.M. Ridder. In Press. "Show Me the Child at Seven: The Consequences of Conduct Problems in Childhood for Psychosocial Functioning in Adulthood." *Journal of Child Psychology and Psychiatry.*

Ferri, E., J. Bynner, and M. Wadsworth. 2003. *Changing Britain, Changing Lives: Three Generations at the Turn of the Century.* London: Institute of Education, University of London.

Furstenberg , Jr., F.F, T.D. Cook, R. Sampson, and G. Slap, eds. 2002. *Early Adulthood in Cross-National Perspective.* London: Sage Publications.

Galambos, N.L., E.T. Barker, and L.C. Tilton-Weaver. 2003. "Who Gets Caught in the Maturity Gap? A Study of Pseudomature, Immature, and Mature Adolescents." *International Journal of Behavioral Development* 27: 253-263.

Ge, X., R.D. Conger, R.J. Cadoret, J.M. Neiderhauser, W. Yates, E. Troughton, and M.A. Stewart. 1996. "The Developmental Interface Between Nature and Nurture: A Mutual Influence Model of Child Antisocial Behavior and Parent Behaviors." *Developmental Psychology* 32: 574-589.

Ge, X., M.B. Donnellan, and E. Wenk. 2001. "The Development of Persistent Criminal Offending in Males." *Criminal Justice and Behavior* 28: 731-755.

Gendreau, P., T. Little, and C. Goggin. 1996. "A Meta-Analysis of the Predictors of Adult Offender Recidivism: What Works!" *Criminology* 34: 575-607.

Henry, B., A. Caspi, T.E. Moffitt, and P.A. Silva. 1996. "Temperamental and Familial Predictors of Violent and Non-Violent Criminal Convictions: From Age 3 to Age 18." *Developmental Psychology* 32: 614-623.

Howell, J.C., and J.D. Hawkins. 1998. "Prevention of Youth Violence." *Crime and Justice: A Review of Research* 24: 263-316.

Jaffee, S. R., T.E. Moffitt, A. Caspi, A. Taylor, and L. Arseneault. 2002. "The Influence of Adult Domestic Violence on Children's Internalizing and Externalizing Problems: An Environmentally-Informative Twin Study." *Journal of the American Academy of Child and Adolescent Psychiatry* 41: 1095-1103.

Jaffee, S.R., A. Caspi, T.E. Moffitt, M. Polo-Tomas, T. Price, and A. Taylor. 2004a. "The Limits of Child Effects: Evidence for Genetically Mediated Child Effects on Corporal Punishment, but not on Physical Maltreatment." *Developmental Psychology* 40: 1047-1058.

Jaffee, S.R., T.E. Moffitt, A. Caspi, and A. Taylor. 2003. "Life With (or Without) Father: The Benefits of Living With Two Biological Parents Depend on the Father's Antisocial Behavior." *Child Development* 74: 109 126.

Jaffee, S.R., A. Caspi, T.E. Moffitt, and A. Taylor. 2004b. "Physical Maltreatment Victim to Antisocial Child: Evidence of an Environmentally Mediated Process." *Journal of Abnormal Psychology* 113: 44-55.

Jeglum-Bartusch, D., D. Lynam, T.E. Moffitt, and P.A. Silva. 1997. "Is Age Important? Testing General Versus Developmental Theories of Antisocial Behavior." *Criminology* 35: 13-47.

Junger-Tas, J., G. Terlouw, and M. Klein. 1994. *Delinquent Behaviour Among Young People in the Western World.* Amsterdam: Kugler Publications.

Kerr, M., and H. Stattin. 2000. "What Parents Know, How they Know It, and Several Forms of Adolescent Adjustment: Further Support for Reinterpretation of Monitoring." *Developmental Psychology* 36: 366-380.

Kim-Cohen, J., T.E. Moffitt, A. Taylor, S. Pawlby, and A. Caspi. 2005. "Maternal Depression and Child Antisocial Behavior: Nature and Nurture Effects." *Archives of General Psychiatry* 62: 173-181.

Kjelsberg, E. 1999. "Adolescent-Limited Versus Life-Course Persistent Criminal Behaviour in Adolescent Psychiatric Inpatients." *European Child and Adolescent Psychiatry* 8: 276-282.

Kratzer, L., and S. Hodgins. 1999. "A Typology of Offenders: A Test of Moffitt's Theory Among Males and Females from Childhood to Age 30." *Criminal Behaviour and Mental Health* 9: 57-73.

Krohn, M.D., T.P. Thornberry, C. Rivera, and M. Leblanc. 2001. "Later Delinquency Careers of Very Young Offenders." Pp. 67-94 in R. Loeber and D.P. Farrington (eds.), *Child Delinquents.* Thousand Oaks, CA: Sage.

Lacourse, E., D. Nagin, R.E. Tremblay, F. Vitaro, and M. Claes. 2003. "Developmental Trajectories of Boys' Delinquent Group Membership and Facilitation of Violent Behaviors During Adolescence." *Development and Psychopathology* 15: 183-197.

Lahey, B.B., R. Loeber, H.C. Quay, B. Applegate, D. Shaffer, I. Waldman, E. Hart, K. Mcburnett, P.J. Frick, P.S. Jensen, M.K. Dulcan, G. Canino, H.R. Bird. 1998. "Validity of DSM-IV Subtypes of Conduct Disorder Based on Age of Onset." *Journal of the American Academy of Child and Adolescent Psychiatry* 37: 435-442.

Lahey, B.B., I.D. Waldman, and K. Mcburnett. 1999. "The Development of Antisocial Behavior: An Integrative Causal Model." *Journal of Child Psychology and Psychiatry* 40: 669-682.

Laub, J.H., and R.J. Sampson. 2001. "Understanding Desistance from Crime." *Crime and Justice: A Review of Research* 28: 1-69.

———. 2003. *Shared Beginnings, Divergent Lives: Delinquent Boys to Age 70.* Cambridge, MA: Harvard University Press.

Laucht, M. 2001. "Antisoziales Verhalten Im Jugendalter: Entstehungsbedingungen Und Verlaufsformen." *Zeitschrift Fur Kinder-Jugendpsychiatry* 29: 297-311.

Loeber, R., and M. Leblanc. 1990. "Toward a Developmental Criminology." *Crime and Justice: A Review of Research* 7: 29-149.

Luthar, S.S., and T.J. Mcmahon. 1996. "Peer Reputation Among Inner-City Adolescents: Structure and Correlates." *Journal of Research on Adolescence* 6: 581-603.

Magnusson, D.A., B. af Klintberg, and H. Stattin. 1994. "Juvenile and Persistent Offenders: Behavioral and Physiological Characteristics." Pp. 81-91 in R.D. Kettelinus and M. Lamb (eds.), *Adolescent Problem Behaviors.* Hillsdale, NJ: Erlbaum.

Maughan, B., A. Pickles, R. Rowe, E.J. Costello, and A. Angold. 2001. "Developmental Trajectories of Aggressive and Non-Aggressive Conduct Problems." *Journal of Quantitative Criminology* 16: 199-222.

Mazerolle, P., R. Brame, R. Paternoster, A. Piquero, and C. Dean. 2000. "Onset Age, Persistence, and Offending Versatility: Comparisons Across Gender." *Criminology* 38: 1143-1172.

Mazerolle, P., and J. Maahs. 2002. *Developmental Theory and Battering Incidents: Examining the Relationship Between Discrete Offender Groups and intimate Partner Violence.* Final Report Submitted to the U.S. National Institute of Justice, U.S. Dept. of Justice.

McCabe, K.M., R. Hough, P.A. Wood, and M. Yeh. 2001. "Childhood and Adolescent Onset Conduct Disorder: A Test of the Developmental Taxonomy." *Journal of Abnormal Child Psychology* 29: 305-316.

Mccall, R.B., and M.S. Carriger. 1993. "A Meta-Analysis of Infant Habituation and Recognition Memory Performance As Predictors of Later IQ." *Child Development* 64: 57-79.

Moffitt, T.E. 1990. "Juvenile Delinquency and Attention-Deficit Disorder: Developmental Trajectories from Age Three to Fifteen." *Child Development* 61: 893-910.

———. 1993. "'Life-Course-Persistent' and 'Adolescence-Limited' Antisocial Behavior: A Developmental Taxonomy." *Psychological Review* 100: 674-701.

———. 1994. "Natural Histories of Delinquency." Pp. 3-61 in E. Weitekamp and H. J. Kerner (eds.), *Cross-National Longitudinal Research On Human Development and Criminal Behavior.* Dordrecht, the Netherlands: Kluwer Academic Press.

———. 1997. "Adolescence-Limited and Life-Course-Persistent Offending: A Complementary Pair of Developmental Theories." Pp. 11-54 in T. Thornberry (ed.), *Advances in Criminological Theory: Developmental Theories of Crime and Delinquency.* London: Transaction Press.

———. 2003. "Life-Course Persistent and Adolescence-Limited Antisocial Behaviour: A 10-Year Research Review and Research Agenda." Pp. 49-75 in B. Lahey, T.E. Moffitt, and A. Caspi (eds.), *The Causes of Conduct Disorder and Serious Juvenile Delinquency.* New York: Guilford.

———. 2006. "Life-Course Persistent and Adolescence-Limited Antisocial Behavior. In D. Cicchetti and D. Cohen (eds.), *Developmental Psychopathology,* 2nd ed. New York: Wiley.

Moffitt, T.E., L. Arseneault, A. Taylor, D. Nagin, B. Milne, and H. Harrington. In Preparation. "Life-Course Persistent and Adolescence-Limited Antisocial Trajectories Detected in 26-Year Longitudinal Study Using Theory-Agnostic Semiparametric Modeling."

Moffitt, T.E., and A. Caspi. 1995. "The Continuity of Maladaptive Behavior: From Description to Explanation in the Study of Antisocial Behavior." In D. Cicchetti and D. Cohen (eds.), *Developmental Psychopathology, Vol. 2.* New York: Wiley.

———. 2001. "Childhood Predictors Differentiate Life-Course Persistent and Adolescence-Limited Pathways, Among Males and Females." *Development and Psychopathology* 13: 355-375.

Moffitt, T.E., A. Caspi, N. Dickson, P.A. Silva, and W. Stanton. 1996. "Childhood-Onset Versus Adolescent-Onset Antisocial Conduct in Males: Natural History From Age 3 To 18." *Development and Psychopathology* 8: 399-424.

Moffitt, T.E., A. Caspi, H. Harrington, and B. Milne. 2002. "Males on the Life-Course Persistent and Adolescence-Limited Antisocial Pathways: Follow-Up at Age 26." *Development and Psychopathology* 14: 179-206.

Moffitt, T.E., A. Caspi, M. Rutter, and P.A. Silva. 2001. *Sex Differences in Antisocial Behaviour: Conduct Disorder, Delinquency, and Violence in the Dunedin Longitudinal Study*. Cambridge: Cambridge University Press.

Moffitt, T.E., D. Lynam, and P.A. Silva. 1994. "Neuropsychological Tests Predict Persistent Male Delinquency." *Criminology* 32: 101-124.

Nagin, D.S. 1999. "Analyzing Developmental Trajectories: Semi-Parametric, Group-Based Approach." *Psychological Methods* 4: 139-177.

Nagin, D.S., D.P. Farrington, and T.E. Moffitt. 1995. "Life-Course Trajectories of Different Types of Offenders." *Criminology* 33: 111-139.

Nagin, D.S., and R.E. Tremblay. 1999. "Trajectories of Boys' Physical Aggression, Opposition, and Hyperactivity on the Path to Physically Violent and Non-Violent Juvenile Delinquency." *Child Development* 70: 1181-1196.

———. 2001a. "Parental and Early Childhood Predictors of Persistent Physical Aggression in Boys from Kindergarten to High School." *Archives of General Psychiatry* 58: 389-394.

———. 2001b. "Analyzing Developmental Trajectories of Distinct but Related Behaviors: A Group-Based Method." *Psychological Medicine* 6: 18-34.

National Institutes of Health 2004. *State-of-the-Science Consensus Statement on Preventing Violence and Related Health-Risking Social Behaviors in Adolescents*. Bethesda, MD: National institutes of Health. Http://Consensus.Nih.Gov

National Institute of Mental Health. 2000. *Child and Adolescent Violence Research* (NIH Publication No. 00-4706) Bethesda, MD: National institute of Health

Neugebauer, R., H.W. Hoek, and E. Susser. 1999. "Prenatal Exposure to Wartime Famine and Development of Antisocial Personality Disorder in Early Adulthood." *Journal of the American Medical Association* 282: 455-462.

O'Connor, T.G., K. Deater-Deckard, D. Fulker, M. Rutter, and R. Plomin. 1998. "Genotype-Environment Correlations in Later Childhood and Early Adolescence: Antisocial Behavioral Problems and Coercive Parenting." *Developmental Psychology* 34: 970-981.

Osgood, D.W. 1998. "Interdisciplinary Integration: Building Criminology by Stealing From Our Friends." *The Criminologist* 23: 1-4.

Paternoster, R., and R. Brame. 1997. "Multiple Routes To Delinquency? A Test of Developmental and General Theories of Crime." *Criminology* 35: 49-84.

Patterson, G.R., D.S. Degarmo, and N. Knutson. 2000. "Hyperactive and Antisocial Behaviors: Comorbid or Two Points in the Same Process?" *Development and Psychopathology* 12: 91-106.

Patterson, G.R., M.S. Forgatch, K.L. Yoerger, and M. Stoolmiller. 1998. "Variables that Initiate and Maintain an Early Onset Trajectory for Juvenile Offending." *Development and Psychopathology* 10: 531-548.

Patterson, G.R. and K.L. Yoerger. 1997. A Developmental Model For Later-Onset Delinquency. Pp. 119-177 in R. Deinstbeir and D.W. Osgood (eds.), *Motivation and Delinquency*. Lincoln: University of Nebraska Press.

Piquero, A.R. 2001. "Testing Moffitt's Neuropsychological Variation Hypothesis for the Prediction of Life-Course Persistent Offending." *Psychology, Crime and Law* 7: 193-216.

Piquero, A.R., R. Brame, and D. Lynam. 2004. "Studying the Factors Related to Career Length." *Crime and Delinquency* 50: 412-435.

Piquero, A.R., and T. Brezina. 2001. "Testing Moffitt's Account of Adolescence-Limited Delinquency." *Criminology* 39: 353-370.

Piquero, A.R., T. Brezina., and M.G. Turner. In Press. "Testing Moffitt's Theory of Delinquency Abstinence." *Journal of Research in Crime and Delinquency.*

Raine, A., 2002. "Annotation: The Role of Prefrontal Deficits, Low Autonomic Arousal, and Early Health Factors in the Development of Antisocial and Aggressive Behaviour in Children." *Journal of Child Psychology and Psychiatry* 43: 417-434.

Raine, A., P. Brennan, and S.A. Mednick. 1994. "Birth Complications Combined with Early Maternal Rejection At Age 1 Year Predispose to Violent Crime at Age 18 Years." *Archives of General Psychiatry* 51: 984-988.

————. 1997. "Interaction Between Birth Complications and Early Maternal Rejection in Predisposing Individuals to Adult Violence: Specificity to Serious, Early-Onset Violence." *American Journal of Psychiatry* 154: 1265-1271.

Raine, A., P. Brennan, B. Mednick, and S.A. Mednick. 1996. "High Rates of Violence, Crime, Academic Problems, and Behavioral Problems in Males with Both Early Neuromotor Deficits and Unstable Family Environments." *Archives of General Psychiatry* 53: 544-549.

Raine, A., T. Lencz, K. Taylor, J.B. Hellige, S. Bihrle, L. Lacasse, M. Lee, S.S. Ishikawa, and P. Colletti. 2003. "Corpus Callosum Abnormalities in Psychopathic Antisocial Individuals." *Archives of General Psychiatry* 60: 1134-1142.

Raine, A., T.E. Moffitt, A. Caspi, R. Loeber, M. Stouthamer-Loeber, and D. Lynam. 2005. "Neurocognitive and Psychosocial Deficits in Life-Course Persistent Offenders." *Journal of Abnormal Psychology* 114: 38-41.

Raine, A., P.S. Yaralian, C. Reynolds, P.H. Venables, and S.A. Mednick. 2002. "Spatial but not Verbal Cognitive Deficits at Age 3 Years in Persistently Antisocial Individuals." *Development and Psychopathology* 14: 25-44.

Riggins-Caspers, K.M., R.J. Cadoert, J.F. Knutson, and D. Langbehn. 2003. "Biology-Environment Interaction and Evocative Biology-Environment Correlation: Contributions of Harsh Discipline and Parental Psychopathology to Problem Adolescent Behaviors." *Behavior Genetics* 33: 205-220.

Robins, L.N. 1966. *Deviant Children Grown Up.* Baltimore: Williams and Wilkins.

Rodkin, P.C., T.W. Farmer, R. Pearl, and R. Van Acker. 2000. "Heterogeneity of Popular Boys: Antisocial and Prosocial Configurations." *Developmental Psychology* 36: 14-24.

Roeder, K., K.G. Lynch, and D.S. Nagin. 1999. "Modeling Uncertainty in Latent Class Membership: A Case Study in Criminology." *Journal of the American Statistical Association* 94: 766-776.

Ruchkin, V., R. Koposov, R. Vermeiren, and M. SchwabStone. 2003. "Psychopathology and the Age of Onset of Conduct Problems in Juvenile Delinquents." *Journal of Clinical Psychiatry* 64: 913-920.

Salekin, R.T., R.M. Yff, C.S. Neumann, A.R. Leistico, and A.A. Zalot. 2002. "Juvenile Transfer to Adult Courts: A Look at the Prototypes of Dangerousness, Sophistication-Maturity, and Amenability to Treatment Through a Legal Lens." *Psychology, Public Policy and Law* 8: 373-410.

Sampson, R.J., and J.H. Laub. 2003. "Life-Course Desisters? Trajectories of Crime Among Delinquent Boys Followed to Age 70." *Criminology* 41: 555-592.

Scholte, E.M. 1999. "Factors Predicting Continued Violence into Adulthood." *Journal of Adolescence* 22: 3-20.

Scott, E.S., and T. Grisso. 1997. "The Evolution of Adolescence: A Developmental Perspective on Juvenile Justice Reform." *Journal of Criminal Law and Criminology* 88: 137-189.

Shedler, J., and J. Block. 1990. "Adolescent Drug Use and Psychological Health." *American Psychologist* 45: 612-630.

Sigman, M., S.E. Cohen, and L. Beckwith. 1997. "Why Does Infant Attention Predict Adolescent Intelligence?" *Infant Behavior and Development* 20: 133-140.

Silverthorn, P., and P.J. Frick. 1999. "Developmental Pathways to Antisocial Behavior: The Delayed-Onset Pathway in Girls." *Development and Psychopathology* 11: 101-126.

Simons, R.L., C.I. Wu, R. Conger, and F.O. Lorenz. 1994. "Two Routes to Delinquency: Differences between Early and Late Starters in the Impact of Parenting and Deviant Peers." *Criminology* 32: 247-275.

Stattin, H., A. Romelsjo, and M. Stenbacka, 1997. "Personal Resources as Modifiers of the Risk for Future Criminality." *British Journal of Criminology* 37: 198-223.

Taylor, J., W.G. Iacono, and M. Mcgue. 2000. "Evidence for a Genetic Etiology for Early-Onset Delinquency." *Journal of Abnormal Psychology* 109: 634-643.

Tibbetts, S., and A. Piquero. 1999. "The Influence of Gender, Low Birth Weight, and Disadvantaged Environment on Predicting Early Onset of Offending: A Test of Moffitt's Interactional Hypothesis." *Criminology* 37: 843-878.

Tolan, P.H. and P. Thomas. 1995. "The Implications of Age of Onset for Delinquency Risk II: Longitudinal Data." *Journal of Abnormal Child Psychology* 23: 157-181.

Tolone, W.L., and C.R. Tieman. 1990. "Drugs, Delinquency, and 'Nerds': Are Loners Deviant?" *Journal of Drug Education* 20: 153-162.

Tremblay, R.E., D.S. Nagin, J.R. Seguin, M. Zoccolillo, P.D. Zelazo, M. Boivin, D. Perusse, and C. Japel. 2004. "Physical Aggression During Early Childhood: Trajectories and Predictors." *Pediatrics* 114: E43-E50.

U.S. Office of Juvenile Justice and Delinquency Prevention. 1998. *Serious and Violent Juvenile Offenders.* Washington, DC: U.S. Department of Justice.

U.S. Surgeon General. 2001. *Youth Violence: A Report of the Surgeon General.* Http://Www.Surgeongeneral.Gov/Library/Youthviolence/.

Vaaranen, H. 2001. "The Blue-Collar Boys at Leisure: An Ethnography on Cruising Club Boys' Drinking, Driving, and Passing Time in Cars in Helsinki." *Mannsforsking* 1: 48-57.

Vermeiren, R. 2002. "Psychopathology and Delinquency in Adolescents: A Descriptive and Developmental Perspective." *Clinical Psychology Review* 583: 1-42.

Vitaro, F., R.E. Tremblay, M. Kerr, L. Pagani, and W.M. Bukowski. 1997. "Disruptiveness, Friends' Characteristics, and Delinquency in Early Adolescence: A Test of Two Competing Models of Development." *Child Development* 68: 676-689.

White, H.R., M.E. Bates, and S. Buyske. 2001. "Adolescence-Limited Versus Persistent Delinquency: Extending Moffitt's Hypothesis into Adulthood." *Journal of Abnormal Psychology* 110: 600-609.

Wiesner, M., and D.M. Capaldi. 2003. "Relations of Childhood and Adolescent Factors to Offending Trajectories of Young Men." *Journal of Research in Crime and Delinquency* 40: 231-262.

Wiesner, M., H.K. Kim, and D. Capaldi. Under Review. "Developmental Trajectories of Offending: Validation and Prediction to Young Adult Alcohol Use, Drug Use, and Depressive Symptoms."

Woodward, L.J., D.M. Fergusson, and L.J. Horwood. 2002. "Romantic Relationships of Young People With Early and Late Onset Antisocial Behavior Problems." *Journal of Abnormal Child Psychology* 30: 231-243.

World Health Organization 2002. *World Report on Violence and Health.* 1211 Geneva 27, Switzerland: Author.

Zebrowitz, L.A., C. Andreoletti, M. Collins, S.H. Lee, and J. Blumenthal. 1998. "Bright, Bad, Babyfaced Boys: Appearance Stereotypes Do Not Always Yield Self-Fulfilling Prophecy Effects." *Journal of Personality and Social Psychology* 75: 1300-1320.

Zucker, R.A., D.A. Ellis, H.E. Fitzgerald, C.R. Bingham, and K. Sanford. 1996. "Other Evidence for at Least Two Alcoholisms: II. Life-Course Variation in Antisociality and Heterogeneity of Alcoholic Outcome." *Development and Psychopathology* 8: 831-848.

11

Assessing Sampson and Laub's Life-Course Theory of Crime

John H. Laub, Robert J. Sampson, and Gary A. Sweeten

What explains the onset of criminal behavior? Are explanations of property crime different from explanations of violent crime? Why do some adolescent offenders stop offending in adulthood? Why do some offenders continue offending across different phases of the life course? These are fascinating and important questions in the study of criminal behavior. Sampson and Laub's life-course theory of crime was designed to speak to these issues as well as other important questions in the field of criminology.

According to Sampson and Laub, age-graded informal social control explains the onset of offending, continuity in offending, and changes in offending (for example, from offender to non-offender and vice versa) throughout the life course. The first presentation of this theory—*Crime in the Making: Pathways and Turning Points through Life* (1993)—focused on the role of informal social controls at distinct stages of the life course, with an explication of the processes that account for continuity and change in offending from childhood to adolescence to young adulthood. The most recent presentation of this theory—*Shared Beginnings, Divergent Lives: Delinquent Boys to Age 70* (2003)—identifies a number of factors in addition to informal social control which explain crime across the full life course, the most important of which are routine activities and human agency. According to the revised theory, social control, routine activities and human agency, both directly and in interaction, shape trajectories of offending across the entire life span.

The task of this chapter is to assess the empirical support for the central propositions in Sampson and Laub's life-course theory of crime. We first contextualize the theory by discussing its origins. We then outline and assess both the 1993 and 2003 versions of the age-graded theory of informal social control. We end our assessment by discussing the implications for future directions in the study of crime over the life course.

The Life-Course Perspective

The life-course perspective provides a broad framework for studying lives over time and has been applied to numerous domains of human behavior, including crime. The life course is defined as a pathway through the life span, involving a sequence of culturally-defined, age-graded roles and social transitions enacted throughout an individual's life (Elder 1985). Two central concepts underlie the analysis of life-course dynamics: trajectories and transitions. *Trajectories* may be described as pathways or lines of development throughout life. These long-term patterns of behavior may include work life, marriage, parenthood, or criminal behavior. *Transitions*, on the other hand, are short-term events embedded in trajectories which may include starting a new job, getting married, having a child, or being sentenced to prison (Elder 1985). Transitional events may lead to *turning points*, or changes in an individual's life-course trajectory. For example, getting married may have a significant influence on a person's life and behavior, from changing where a person lives or works to changing the number and type of friends with whom one associates. Turning points may modify trajectories in ways that cannot be predicted from earlier events.

The life-course perspective attempts to link social history and social structure to the unfolding of human lives. Elder (1985) argues that social change may be consequential in shaping the life course of individuals and age groups. The developmental impact of an historical or life event may vary depending on when they occur in a person's life. For example, those who were working adults during the Great Depression were affected differently from those who were very young at the time (see Elder 1998).

Another objective of the life-course perspective is to explain continuity and change in behavior over time by linking past events and experiences to the present. Of central concern is the extent of continuity in behavior between childhood, adolescence, and adulthood. At the same time, the life-course perspective focuses attention on turning points which can modify life trajectories in unexpected ways. To address these phenomena, individual lives are studied through time. The nature and extent of continuity and change may be one of the most complex themes of the life-course perspective as well as one of the most hotly debated and controversial issues in the social sciences.

Age-Graded Theory of Informal Social Control

"When you got nothing, you got nothing to lose."
–Bob Dylan (1965)

Synthesizing the literature on childhood antisocial behavior, adolescent delinquency, and adult crime, Sampson and Laub (1993) drew on the life-course framework to develop a theory of age-graded informal social control and crime. The unique advantage of the life-course perspective is that it brings the formative period of childhood back into the picture yet recognizes that individual behavior is mediated over time through interaction with age-graded institutions. Sampson and Laub (1993) were thus driven by the challenge to develop and test a theoretical model that would account for crime and deviance in childhood, adolescence, *and* adulthood.[1]

Their age-graded theory of informal social control integrates the life-course perspective with social control theory to meet this challenge. The organizing principle of the theory is that delinquency or crime is more likely to occur when an individual's bond to society is attenuated. This perspective differs from Hirschi's (1969) static version of social control by focusing on changing social bonds over the life course. Social ties also provide social and psychological resources that individuals may draw on as they move through life transitions. The concept of social bond echoes Toby's (1957) "stake in conformity," suggesting that the stronger an individual's social bonds, the more that person risks by engaging in criminal behavior. From this general theoretical framework Sampson and Laub (1993) propose three major themes. First, structural context is mediated in fundamental respects by informal family and school social controls, which, in turn, explain delinquency in childhood and adolescence. Second, there is strong continuity in antisocial behavior running from childhood through adulthood across a variety of life domains. Finally, informal social control in adulthood explains changes in criminal behavior over the life span, independent of prior individual differences in criminal propensity.

Structure and Process in Adolescent Delinquency

To explain the onset of delinquency, criminologists have typically embraced either structural (e.g., Shaw and McKay's [1942] social disorganization theory) or process constructs (e.g., Hirschi's [1969] social control theory). According to the age-graded theory of informal social control, this separation is a mistake. The age-graded theory joins structural and process variables, along with individual characteristics, into a single theoretical model. The theory explains onset of antisocial behavior and delinquency with both structural factors such as poverty or broken homes, and process variables such as attachment to parents or attachment to school. It proposes that structural context influences the dimensions of informal social controls, which in turn explain variations in delinquency.

The theory points to three components of informal social control in the family context: consistent discipline, monitoring, and attachment to the family. To the extent that these three link the child to the family, they inhibit delinquency. These three components of informal control can reduce delinquency through emotional bonds, or through direct control (monitoring and punishment). The school context is another important socializing institution in the prevention of delinquency and in this theory attachment to school and school performance are inversely related to delinquency.

The age-graded theory also suggests that social structural factors, such as family disruption, unemployment, residential mobility, and socioeconomic status, indirectly affect delinquency through social bonds. Previous research failed to account for the influence of social-structural context on delinquency through family life and social bonds, and the theory seeks to rectify this mistake. To illustrate, some authors have argued that socioeconomic disadvantage has potentially adverse effects on parents, such that parental difficulties are more likely to develop and good parenting is impeded (McLoyd 1990). Similarly, factors related to socioeconomic disadvantage, such as poverty and household crowding, may disrupt bonds of attachment between the child and school and may lead to educational deficiencies (Rutter and Giller 1983: 185-186). If true, one would expect poverty and disadvantage to have their effects on delinquency transmitted through parenting and education. Therefore, the age-graded theory predicts that family and social bonding will mediate the effects of structural background factors on delinquency.

Continuity between Adolescent Delinquency and Adult Offending

The age-graded theory argues that weak social bonds explain continuity in antisocial behavior across adolescence and adulthood. That is, early antisocial behavior, such as conduct disorder, delinquency, and violent temper tantrums, predicts adult antisocial behavior, such as crime and substance abuse. In addition, adolescent antisocial behavior predicts weak adult social bonds as evidenced by low educational attainment, erratic labor force participation, and poor quality marital attachment. These adult outcomes are independent of traditional sociological and psychological variables such as social class background, ethnicity, IQ, and even family and school factors known to predict the onset of delinquency.

There are numerous explanations for continuity between adolescent delinquency and adult crime and the two most popular explanations are population heterogeneity and state dependence (Nagin and Paternoster 1991). The population heterogeneity argument suggests that each individual possesses a unique and relatively stable propensity to offend which accounts for antisocial behavior in adolescence and adulthood (see, for example, Gottfredson and Hirschi 1990, or Wilson and Herrnstein 1985). On the other hand, the state dependence explanation proposes that the consequences of offending can have a criminogenic effect (see, for example, Lemert 1972 or Akers 1998). The age-graded theory emphasizes a developmental model of cumulative continuity that suggests that delinquency continues into adulthood because of its negative consequences for future life chances (Sampson and Laub 1993, 1997). For example, arrest, conviction, incarceration, and other negative life events associated with delinquency may lead to decreased opportunities, including school failure and unemployment. Delinquent activities are also likely to sever informal social bonds to school, friends, and family and jeopardize the development of adult social bonds. In this way, childhood delinquency has an indirect effect on adult criminal behavior through the weakening of social bonds. Thus, the theory proposes that crime, deviance, and informal social control are intimately linked over the life course.

Change in Offending across the Life Course

While both population heterogeneity and state dependent arguments are employed to explain continuity in offending, the age-graded theory holds that salient life events and socialization experiences in adulthood can, to some extent, counteract the influence of early life experiences. Recognizing that the concepts of continuity and change are not mutually exclusive, the theory incorporates explanations for both. In addition, the theory identifies turning points in the life course, such as marriage, work and the military, which can alter life trajectories. The age-graded theory suggests that social ties embedded in adult transitions (e.g., marital attachment, job stability) provide social capital and can change an individual's path from a delinquent trajectory to a nondelinquent one or vice versa. In other words, pathways to both crime and conformity are modified by key institutions of social control in the transition to adulthood, independent of prior differences in criminal propensity.

While this focus on change may appear inconsistent with the earlier discussion of the stability of antisocial behavior over time, evidence suggests that continuity is far from perfect. In fact, most antisocial adolescents do not become antisocial adults (Robins 1978). The fact is lives are often unpredictable and change is ever present. This theoretical framework implies that adult social ties can modify trajectories of crime despite general stability as predicted from childhood risk factors. Specifically, the theory suggests that adult social bonds have a direct negative effect on adult criminal behavior, controlling for childhood delinquency.

The age-graded theory of informal social control incorporates explanations of stability and change in criminal behavior. This theoretical framework proposes a dynamic process whereby transitions within trajectories may generate turning points in the life course. While the theory was developed in the context of reconstruction and re-analysis of the Gluecks' data, the ideas have wider appeal and are not bound by these data. This assertion and general support for the theory will be demonstrated with a discussion of the empirical literature.

Empirical Literature

The age-graded theory of informal social control contains a number of testable hypotheses that can be examined in the empirical literature. The theory proposes that bonds to family and school directly influence delinquency, and that structural factors indirectly influence delinquency through those bonds. The theory also suggests that childhood delinquency and deviance will continue into adulthood through a process of cumulative continuity, resulting in criminal behavior in adulthood and weakened adult social bonds. Finally, despite a history of delinquency, the theory predicts that those who develop strong adult social bonds will be less likely to engage in criminal or deviant behavior in adulthood. Empirical support for these propositions is derived from a number of independent sources.[2]

Explaining Childhood and Adolescent Delinquency

The theoretically-predicted relationship between social bonds to family and school and delinquent behavior in childhood is supported by a great deal of research. In a review of seventy-one studies of control theory, Kempf (1993) found that attachment to parents was the most tested and most consistently supported component of social control theory. Moreover, parenting variables continued to have a direct effect even after controlling for other predictors found to be important determinants of delinquency. Attachment to school, although less often tested, also displayed a consistent negative relationship with delinquency.

In addition to the importance of ties to family and school, the theoretical prediction of an indirect effect of structural factors also finds support in the empirical literature. A study by Larzelere and Patterson (1990) showed that the effect of socioeconomic status on delinquency is mediated entirely by parental discipline and monitoring. Confirming these findings, Wadsworth (2000) found that the effect of parental labor market position on child delinquency was mediated by parental monitoring and child attachment to family and school. Simons and colleagues (1998) found that childhood antisocial behavior increased the likelihood of adolescent delinquency because of weakened social controls. These authors also found that youths who experienced increased social bonds in adolescence had less offending despite childhood antisocial behavior.

It is evident that family relationships powerfully influence delinquency such that children are more likely to be delinquent if they are poorly monitored by, supervised by, or attached to, their parents. Overall, the empirical evidence is consistent with age-graded theory's first theoretical prediction that both structural factors and bonds to family and school predict childhood and adolescent delinquency and that the influence of structural factors is primarily mediated through social bonding.

Continuity of Antisocial Behavior into Adulthood

The second theoretical prediction, that there is continuity in delinquent and antisocial behavior from childhood to adulthood, also receives support from the empirical literature. Research spanning several decades indicates a great deal of continuity in criminal behavior over time. Robins (1978) demonstrated that childhood delinquency is almost a prerequisite for adult offending. A review of several research studies revealed substantial stability between early aggressive behavior and later criminality (Olweus 1979). Caspi and Moffitt (1995) noted that continuities in antisocial behavior have been replicated internationally (e.g., Canada, England, Finland, New Zealand, and Sweden) and with multiple methods of assessment (e.g., official records, teacher ratings, parent reports, peer nominations). More recently, Wright and colleagues (1999) found that childhood self-control predicted social bonds into adulthood, and that social bonds and adolescent delinquency predicted adult offending. The effect of childhood self-control was partially mediated by later social bonds, but both remained significant in their final model, lending support to both state dependent and population heterogeneity explanations for continuity. A later study by Wright and colleagues (2001) found that social bonds interact with self-control in affecting crime, bonds being more salient for individuals with low self-control. Cernkovich and Giordano (2001) found that prior delinquency was a stable predictor of future delinquency. They did, however, find that social bonds affected continued criminality only among youths who had not been institutionalized for offending.

Continuity in offending may be due to the negative effects of official sanctions on opportunities in adulthood. Hagan (1993) found a detrimental effect of delinquent behavior on the labor market prospects of young males, supporting the cumulative continuity hypothesis. Nagin and Waldfogel (1995) presented strong evidence indicating that conviction leads to instability in employment. Their study used panel data, allowing them to control for observed and unobserved stable between-individual differences. Bushway (1998) confirmed these findings by comparing two groups of individuals in the National Youth Survey who resembled one another in terms of job stability and offending behavior in 1983, but differed in 1986. The group that had been arrested in the interim displayed less job stability.

In general, the evidence suggests that delinquent behavior is relatively stable across stages of the life course and that antisocial behavior in childhood and adolescence predicts a wide range of troublesome outcomes in adulthood.

Change in Behavior through Adult Social Bonds

The stability of criminal behavior patterns, especially aggression, throughout the life course is one of the most consistently documented patterns found in longitudinal research. However, although studies show that antisocial behavior in children is one of the best predictors of antisocial behavior in adults, most antisocial children do not become antisocial adults. The age-graded theory suggests that this change is the result of important life events and social bonds in adulthood, particularly job stability and attachment to a spouse. There is considerable evidence for the importance of adult social bonds.

Jobs + offending

Numerous studies have found that adult bonds to work are inversely related to offending. Irwin (1970) identified finding a good job as one component leading to desistance from a criminal career. Farrington and colleagues (1986) found that individuals are more likely to commit property crimes during periods of unemployment. In an extensive account of desistance from crime, based on qualitative interviews with persistent thieves, Shover (1996) found that a good job altered or terminated criminal careers. More recently, analyzing the National Supported Work Demonstration Project, a random-assignment experiment, Uggen (2000) found that assignment to the supported work program decreased crime for those over age twenty-six.

Marriage

There has been considerable evidence with respect to marriage as a turning point as well. Irwin identified an "adequate and satisfying relationship with a woman, usually in a family context" (1970: 203), as a key component in the desistance process. Along similar lines, Shover (1996) found that developing a satisfying relationship with a woman was an important component of desistance. In a study of incarcerated offenders, Horney, Osgood, and Marshall (1995) reported that regardless of their overall level of offending, men were less likely to be involved in crime when they were living with a wife or attending school. Employing both within-individual and between-individual analyses, Farrington and West (1995) found that staying married and having children, indicators of a strong marital bond, were related to decreased offending. Separation from a spouse, on the other hand, led to increased offending.

Finally, Piquero, Brame, Mazerolle, and Haapanen (2002) employed a composite stakes in conformity measure that captured the effects of full-time employment and marriage in a high-risk sample of males. They also included in their statistical model controls for time-stable individual differences. Somewhat contrary to prior studies, they found that stakes in conformity predicted less nonviolent offending but had no effect on violent offending. In a similar study, Piquero, MacDonald, and Parker (2002) found that employment and marriage reduced crime for both white and nonwhite parolees, although common-law marriages appeared to generate crime for nonwhites compared with whites. Taken as a whole, while these findings give support to the notion that changing social bonds can induce changing offending patterns, caution is warranted about generalizability across all subgroups and all crime types.

In sum, a growing body of empirical evidence supports the empirical propositions of the age-graded theory of informal social control. These results support the theoretical explanation of the onset of delinquency as well as the dual concern of the theory with continuity and change in behavior over the life course.

Theoretical and Empirical Challenges

Although we believe the bulk of the evidence supports Sampson and Laub's (1993) age-graded life-course theory of crime, certain authors disagree with some of their theoretical propositions. Perhaps the most fundamental challenge comes from Hirschi and Gottfredson (1995) who argue that the observed continuity in behavior from childhood to adulthood is not due to cumulative continuity, a state dependent process. On the contrary, these authors suggest that childhood delinquency, adult criminal behavior, and other troublesome adult outcomes are all the result of an underlying criminogenic trait, namely low self-control (see Gottfredson and Hirschi 1990). Thus, Gottfredson and Hirschi argue that adult criminal behavior and other outcomes are the result of self-selection—that individuals choose particular events and environments consistent with their underlying level of self-control.

The age-graded theory of informal social control recognizes self-selection, but does not regard self-selection and cumulative continuity as fundamentally incompatible (see Sampson and Laub 1995). The fact that individual differences influence the choices one makes does not imply that social mechanisms emerging from these choices have no causal significance. Although delinquents may be less likely to choose stable employment and marriage, sometimes they do make these choices and when strong social ties result they are less likely to continue their criminal behavior.

Another argument in contradiction to Sampson and Laub's (1993) age-graded, life-course theory is the contention that social bonds and social capital are not the important causal mechanisms. Instead, some authors suggest that the effects of marriage and employment may be due to differential association or social learning mechanisms, i.e., reduction in exposure to delinquent peers (see Akers 1998: 351; Warr 1998; Simons et al. 2002; Wright and Cullen 2004). One of the strongest predictors of adolescent delinquency is the number of delinquent friends (Warr 2002). Though Warr (1998) established that marriage was linked with a reduction in criminal behavior, he argued that this relationship was the result of reduced interactions with peers, particularly delinquent peers, rather than strong attachment to a spouse (see also Warr 2002: 101-105). Along similar lines, while Simons and colleagues (2002) found that job attachment predicted less criminal behavior, they emphasized peer influences to explain continuity in offending across adolescence and early adulthood.

However, these studies do not provide a critical test of opposing theories, in part because they do not directly assess the varying possible social mechanisms explaining desistance from crime. In the case of marriage, a spouse may exert pressure to change his or her partner's habits regarding time spent with peers, particularly antisocial peers. In a similar fashion, peer associations may affect routine activities or opportunities for crime and deviance as well as situations involving social learning of delinquent or nondelinquent behavior. Clearly, more research is needed on the mechanisms underlying continuity and change in offending.

Revising the Age-Graded Theory of Social Control

In this section we explore the modifications to the age-graded theory of informal control as presented in *Shared Beginnings, Divergent Lives* (Laub and Sampson 2003). The motivations for this work included the study of age and crime over the full life course, unpacking the mechanisms underlying persistent offending and desistance from crime, and the integration of qualitative and quantitative data on crime. These motivations were pursued in a follow-up study of the Glueck men as they approached age seventy. Three sources of new data were collected: criminal records, death records, and life history interviews with a sample of fifty-two of the original Glueck men, stratified to ensure variability in patterns of persistence in and desistance from crime (see Laub and Sampson 2003: chapter 4). These combined data represent a roughly sixty-year window on "criminal careers," including connections to life experiences as far back as early childhood. When combined with the original Glueck archives these follow-up data represent the longest known longitudinal study in the field of criminology.

Emergent findings from analyses of these quantitative and qualitative longitudinal data led Laub and Sampson to revise the age-graded theory of informal social control. While the modified theory still maintains that social bonds explain persistence and desistance throughout the life course, independent of pre-existing factors, the theory recognizes a number of other causal factors as well. To illustrate, the revised theory suggests that criminal behavior (or lack thereof) is a result of individual actions (choice) in conjunction with situational contexts and structural influences linked to key institutions. In the modified theory, social controls, structured routine activities and purposeful human agency are the causal elements in explaining persistent offending and desistance from crime in adulthood. Weak informal social controls, minimal structured routine activities, and human agency explain persistence in criminal behavior, independent of earlier patterns of offending. On the flip side, strong informal social control, highly structured routine activities, and human agency explain desistance in adulthood, independent of a history of antisocial behavior.

The core proposition of the age-graded theory remains intact in its most recent version: levels of offending are reciprocally related to social bonds throughout the life course. The revised theory seeks to expand the understanding of informal and formal social control across the entire life course by highlighting how social bonds interact with individual choice and situational context. The modified theory notes that social bonds may interact with age and life experiences. That is, the inhibiting effect of the increased costs of offending due to potential loss of social capital may increase with age (see also Shover 1996; Graham and Bowling 1995).

Structured routine activities modify the array of behavioral choices available to an individual (see Birbeck and LaFree 1993). The modified theory contends that structured routine activities condition the effect of social controls on offending. Persistent offenders are notable in their lack of structured routine activities across the life course. On the other hand, increased structure surrounding routine activities facilitates desistance from crime regardless of prior offending trajectories.

The third factor proposed to shape offending trajectories across the life course is human agency. At first glance, the concept of human agency might seem inconsistent with the social control perspective, since a key distinction of control theories is their assumption of universal motivation to offend. That is, in the absence of constraints (social controls), individuals will offend (Hirschi 1969). However, in the revised age-graded theory a less stringent version of control theory is offered, assuming that human nature is malleable across the life course. In addition, the concept of human agency cannot be understood simply as a proxy for motivation. Rather, the concept of agency has the element of projective or transformative action within structural constraints. This goes beyond selection effects; that is, structures are in part determined by individual choices, and in turn structures constrain individual choices. Thus, the bi-directional interaction of choice and structure produces behavior that cannot be predicted from a focus on one or the other. The modified theory refers to agentic moves within structural context as "situated choice" (see Laub and Sampson 2003).

Beyond these three causal factors, the revised theory of age-graded informal social control gives theoretical expression to "random developmental noise." The theory conceives of development as the constant interaction between individuals and their environment, coupled with the factor of chance (Lewontin 2000). This implies that there will always be considerable heterogeneity in criminal offending no matter how many factors are taken into account. One implication is that prospective identification of long-term patterns of offending among delinquent children is not possible with any degree of rigor. Although distinct trajectories of criminal offending may appear in post-hoc analyses, these trajectories are not necessarily identifiable when the aim is to prospectively validate predictions of the future pathways of crime and delinquency (Sampson and Laub 2003; Laub and Sampson 2003).

Drawing heavily from detailed life-history interviews, Laub and Sampson describe the mechanisms underlying desistance from crime. The self-described turning points that the Glueck men implicated in the desistance process include: marriage, the military, reform school, and work. While acknowledging that there are multiple pathways to desistance, Laub and Sampson emphasize the general mechanisms whereby these institutions facilitate desistance. These institutional or structural turning points all involve, to varying degrees, new situations that: 1) "knife off" the past from the present; 2) provide both supervision and monitoring as well as new opportunities of social support and growth; 3) change and structure routine activities; and/or 4) provide the opportunity for identity transformation. Laub and Sampson believe that most offenders choose to desist in response to structurally-induced turning points that serve as a catalyst for sustaining long-term behavioral change. In the short term, these institutions reorder situational inducements to crime while in the long-term they enhance commitments to conformity (see Briar and Piliavin 1965).

The revised age-graded theory presents a number of theoretical claims with implications for the prediction of offending across the life course. Evidence for the significance of structured routine activities, informal social controls, and human agency, both separately and in interaction, constitutes support for the revised life-course theory of crime. The following section will assess the available empirical evidence.

Assessing the Revised Theory

In evaluating evidence for the revised age-graded theory of informal social control, readers should keep in mind its relative infancy. A full test is yet to come, as researchers operationalize key constructs and formulate critical tests of central hypotheses. Nevertheless, prior research evidence bears on the theory's hypothesized causal mechanisms, and Laub and Sampson themselves have provided some empirical support for the theory.[3] The evaluation of this theory will proceed in three sections: social controls, routine activities, and human agency.

Social Control across the Life Course

Social control theory provides the foundation upon which age-graded theory of informal social control is built. The modified life-course theory maintains this core emphasis, adding in the constructs of structured routine activities and human agency. Because the recently revised theory upholds the original theory's hypotheses regarding social control and its effects on crime, it inherits the existing empirical support for this portion of the theory. As discussed above, the available research evidence suggests that the strongest and most consistent effects on crime and delinquency flow from the social bonds derived from family, school, and work.

Routine Activities across the Life Course

The revised life-course theory maintains that situational contexts, in interaction with social control and human agency, affect offending behavior across the life course. Specifically, those with structured routine activities will be less likely to offend compared with those lacking in structured routines. There is fairly strong evidence in the literature for this hypothesis.

Osgood and colleagues (1996) reported a strong relationship between unstructured socializing and a variety of antisocial outcomes, controlling for unobserved between-individual differences with a fixed effects analysis. In open-ended life-history interviews of four individuals with high-risk profiles yet unexpectedly crime-free behavior, Haggard and colleagues (2001) found evidence for the interaction between human agency and routine activities in facilitating desistance. They noted that the decision to desist alone was not sufficient, but that stable relationships including the care of children aided in facilitating desistance.

Emphasizing cognitive transformation in the desistance process, Giordano, Cernkovich and Rudolph (2002) found that a "respectability package," combining work and marriage, led to decreased offending. This "respectability package" entails not only increased structured routine activities, but also increased informal social controls. Interviewing thirty-six-year-olds in Finland who had displayed high-risk characteristics at age eight, Rönkä and colleagues (2003) found that "resilients"—those who displayed unexpected positive outcomes—identified a changed living environment and withdrawal from non-supportive roles as important to the desistance process. Rumgay (2004) emphasized routine activities as part of a "conformist script." That is, as individuals develop new routines that are consistent with a conventional lifestyle, they are more likely to remain in a state of desistance.

Finally, Wright and Cullen (2004) found that the interaction of hours worked with their measure of prosocial coworkers was a significant predictor of reduced drug use, even in the presence of a lagged measure of drug use. This study provides suggestive evidence for the interaction of social controls and structured routine activities (number of hours worked) in predicting offending behavior.

In sum, the available evidence appears to confirm the importance of routine activities or situational contexts in modifying life-course trajectories of offending. In addition, several studies are supportive of the modified theory's emphasis on interactions between routine activities and social controls, and one study has suggested that human agency and routine activities interact to affect offending patterns.

Human Agency across the Life Course

Taking stock of the role of human agency in persistent offending as well as desistance from crime represents a challenge for criminology. There are few direct empirical tests of this construct and some researchers have noted that that retrospective reports present some difficulty in interpretation. Namely, in retrospect, individuals may reinterpret past events, attributing intentionality where none existed at the time (Farrall and Bowling 1999). In order to determine the extent of reinterpretation of past events in life-history interviews, one would prefer to compare contemporary measures of life events to recalled ones. Notwithstanding this concern, there is a small, but growing body of literature that points to the importance of personal agency, especially in interaction with social bonds and routine activities, as essential to understanding offending patterns over the life course.

Giordano and colleagues (2002) presented a symbolic-interactionist theory of cognitive transformation, which emphasized "cognitive shifts" and human agency as fundamental steps in the desistance process. Specifically, these authors argue that "a high level of individual motivation or 'up-front' commitment would seem to be required for successful and long-lasting change" (2002: 1054). While largely compatible, the revised age-graded theory of informal social control rejects the notion that cognitive transformation is necessary for desistance to occur. This highlights the important distinction between human agency and cognitive transformation. Cognitive transformation entails a change in self-identity while human agency is intentional action that may or may not be accompanied by an identity change. Emphasizing the interactive nature of human agency within structural constraints, the revised theory embraces the concept of "situated choice." Individuals may be intentional in their decisions, but their actions are subject to structural constraints.

This theme is echoed in several other studies. First, some theoretical accounts emphasize structural constraints on agentic decisions, suggesting that human agency may be constrained in ways that individuals are not aware of (see Farrall and Bowling 1999; Bottoms et al. 2004). Second, some interview-based studies find that decisions to desist alone are not sufficient to bring about desistance. The difficulty of putting into practice a decision to desist emerged as a key theme in Rex's (1999) study of sixty probationers. This theme was also found in Haggard and colleagues' (2001) interviews with formerly violent offenders.

Farrall and Bowling (1999) point out that most of the evidence supporting the importance of agency is qualitative while most of the studies supporting the importance of structure are quantitative. This highlights the difficulty in fashioning good empirical work on human agency and social structure. Most existing longitudinal data sets do not provide the researcher with the opportunity to study agency. However, with increased theoretical attention given to agency, we expect that future data collection efforts will include measures that attempt to capture human agency (see, for example, Bottoms et al. 2004).

To date, the available evidence underscores the importance of human agency in interaction with structure. It is especially encouraging that this evidence comes from studies with widely different populations: males who were incarcerated as juveniles in Boston in the 1930s and 1940s (Laub and Sampson 2003), males and females incarcerated as juveniles in Ohio in 1982 (Giordano et al. 2002, 2003), and prior violent offenders in Sweden (Haggard et al. 2001). Nevertheless, further research on the topic of human agency would be beneficial for understanding life-course trajectories of crime.

Implications for Life-Course Criminology

In Sampson and Laub's life-course theory of crime, development is conceived as the constant interaction between individuals and their environment, coupled with purposeful human agency and "random developmental noise" (Lewontin 2000: 35-36). Recognizing developmental noise implies that "The organism is determined neither by its genes nor by its environment nor even by interaction between them, but bears a significant mark of random processes" (2000: 38). The challenge is that random processes, along with purposeful human agency, are ever-present realities, making prediction of future behavior once again problematic. It further follows that long-term patterns of offending among high-risk populations cannot be divined by individual differences (for example, low verbal IQ), childhood characteristics (for example, early onset of misbehavior) or even adolescent characteristics (for example, chronic juvenile offending).

Evidence for this contention can be found in a number of works. For example, Laub, Nagin, and Sampson (1998) conducted semi-parametric trajectory analyses of offending patterns of the Glueck men through age thirty-two. These analyses, which were extended to age seventy for *Shared Beginnings, Divergent Lives*, showed that distinct patterns of offending were revealed over time, but childhood risk factors were not able to distinguish between these patterns. For the latter analysis, they constructed a high-risk group that scored on the upper 20 percent for risk factors in childhood. This group exhibited identical patterns to the rest of the sample, only at a higher level of offending over the entire time period. No matter how they divided the sample, all groups exhibited desistance from crime at different rates (see Sampson and Laub 2003 for additional evidence on this matter).

In a similar fashion, Eggleston, Laub, and Sampson (2004) examined the methodological sensitivities of the semi-parametric group-based methodology, finding considerable numbers who shifted to unexpected offending trajectories after age thirty-two. That is, when utilizing offending information up to age thirty-two, individuals were categorized in a different offending group than when data up to age seventy were included. This shows that even prediction of the adult life course past age thirty entails a considerable amount of uncertainty (see Sampson, Laub, and Eggleston 2004 for additional discussion).

Few other studies speak to this issue. In fact, most studies seek to uncover sturdy predictors of various dimensions of offending without explicit consideration of the limits of this endeavor. It is instructive to note that Laub and Sampson came to this conclusion when faced with offending data that spanned over sixty years while most researchers examine risk factors and outcomes which span a much smaller time period. For example, Wright and colleagues (1999) found that low self-control in childhood predicted disrupted social bonds and offending at age twenty-one. Piquero, Brame, and Lynam (2004) sought sturdy predictors of career length from youths released from the California Youth Authority at age eighteen and followed for an average of 12.5 years. As the follow-up time increases, chance processes as well as other non-random processes will have more time to influence outcomes, potentially confounding causal analyses as time span increases, but having little effect in short-term studies.

Researchers who ignore the influence of human agency and chance in criminal trajectories thus risk making two serious errors: reifying statistically-identified offending groups and losing sight of the humanity of individuals behind the statistics and their capacity for change. Both of these errors can lead to mistakes of greater importance in the arena of criminal justice policy. The findings reviewed here imply that neat prediction—even from adult factors—is inherently a difficult, if not impossible endeavor. Turning points and structural supports may be necessary conditions in the revised theory, but they are not sufficient. Human beings make choices to participate in crime or not, and theories of the life course have been remiss to have left agency—which is essentially human social action—largely out of the theoretical picture. Laub and Sampson (2003) have positioned human agency as a central element in understanding crime and deviance over the life course (see also Wikström 2004). To be sure, the modified age-graded, life-course theory does not provide an explicit theory of human agency replete with testable causal hypotheses. The theoretical claim is simply that agency is a crucial ingredient in causation and, thus, will be a first-order challenge for future work in life-course criminology.

Concluding Remarks

Laub and Sampson's revised theory of informal social control was developed in response to shortcomings in their original theory in explaining patterns of offending across the life course. In particular, the modified theory was an attempt to explain both sides of the coin—persistent offending and desistance from crime—across the entire life course. The revised life-course theory identifies three causal factors which affect offending patterns both directly and in interaction: social controls, routine activities and human agency. As a result, there is considerable heterogeneity in offending patterns over the long haul and this confounds efforts to identify meaningful patterns of adult offending based on childhood risk factors.

We believe the strongest support exists for the influence of social bonds over the life course, and some evidence speaks to the interaction of social control with routine activities and human agency. Employment and marriage, in particular, tend to offer opportunities to desist through both increased informal social controls and structured routine activities. Although work and marriage tend to be associated with desistance, there is little consensus in the field regarding the mechanisms by which these affect offending. There is perhaps greater consensus regarding the interplay of agency and structure in determining life outcomes. This "situated choice" emphasizes the interplay of social controls, situational contexts and human agency in producing changes in offending across the life course.

We warn against an overly deterministic understanding of human development, especially one that only focuses on childhood characteristics and experiences. In contrast, we see development as unfolding throughout the life course. The result is considerable heterogeneity in offending outcomes that confound efforts to predict adult offending trajectories based on childhood or even adolescent risk factors. As statistical techniques for grouping offending trajectories become more commonly used in the literature, we also warn against an unreflective application of these techniques (see Sampson, Laub, and Eggleston 2004 for more discussion of this point).

Overall, we believe the evidence generated to date is supportive of the central propositions of Sampson and Laub's life-course theory of crime. That said, we look forward to future studies—both quantitative and qualitative—that examine the dynamic interplay between social controls, routine activities, human agency and criminal offending across the life course. From our perspective, it is especially important to reconcile the idea of "situated choice" with a structural idea of turning points. What this means is that neither agency nor structure alone are capable of explaining the life course of crime (Wikström 2004). We believe that the field of life-course criminology would benefit from a more process-oriented, generalized account of within-individual behavioral stability and change over time.

Notes

* We thank Elaine Eggleston Doherty and Sarah Boonstoppel for their helpful comments on an earlier draft of this chapter. Direct all correspondence to John H. Laub, Department of Criminology and Criminal Justice, University of Maryland, 2220 LeFrak Hall, College Park, MD 20742-8235. Email: jlaub@crim.umd.edu

1. The theory was tested within a larger empirical project that entailed the reconstruction, analysis, and eventual follow-up of the classic original study by Sheldon and Eleanor Glueck, *Unraveling Juvenile Delinquency* (1950; see also Glueck and Glueck 1968). The details of this project have been described elsewhere (Sampson and Laub 1993; Laub and Sampson 2003).

2.   This paper reviews mainly evidence other than that produced by the authors. Nonetheless, we believe the empirical infrastructure for the age-graded theory of informal social control is contained in Sampson and Laub's (1993) analysis of the reconstructed Glueck data. These findings are not reviewed here and the reader is directed to the original book for details.

3.   Laub and Sampson present a considerable amount of both quantitative and qualitative evidence for their modified theory. These results are not reviewed here and the reader is directed to Laub and Sampson (2003) and Sampson and Laub (2003) for details.

References

Akers, Ronald L. 1998. *Social Learning and Social Structure: A General Theory of Crime and Deviance.* Boston: Northeastern University Press.

Birbeck, Christopher, and Gary LaFree. 1993. "The Situational Analysis of Crime and Deviance." *Annual Review of Sociology* 19: 113-137.

Bottoms, Anthony, Joanna Shapland, Andrew Costello, Deborah Holmes, and Grant Muir. 2004. "Towards Desistance: Theoretical Underpinnings for an Empirical Study." *The Howard Journal* 43: 368-389.

Briar, Scott, and Irving Piliavin. 1965. "Delinquency, Situational Inducements, and Commitment to Conformity." *Social Problems* 13: 35-43.

Bushway, Shawn D. 1998. "The Impact of an Arrest on the Job Stability of Young White American Men." *Journal of Research in Crime and Delinquency* 35: 454-479.

Caspi, Avshalom, and Terrie E. Moffitt. 1995. "The Continuity of Maladaptive Behavior: From Description to Understanding in the Study of Antisocial Behavior." In Dante Cicchetti and Donald J. Cohen (eds.), *Developmental Psychopathology, Vol. 2, Risk Disorder, and Adaptation.* New York: Wiley.

Cernkovich, Stephen A., and Peggy Giordano. 2001. "Stability and Change in Antisocial Behavior: The Transition from Adolescence to Early Adulthood." *Criminology* 39: 371-410.

Dylan, Bob. 1965. "Like a Rolling Stone." New York: Columbia.

Eggleston, Elaine P., John H. Laub, and Robert J. Sampson. 2004. "Methodological Sensitivities to Latent Class Analysis of Long-Term Criminal Trajectories." *Journal of Quantitative Criminology* 20: 1-26.

Elder, Glen H., Jr. 1985. "Perspectives on the Life Course." In Glen H. Elder Jr. (ed.), *Life Course Dynamics.* Ithaca, NY: Cornell University Press.

————. 1998. "The Life Course as Developmental Theory." *Child Development* 69: 1-12.

Farrall, Stephen, and Benjamin Bowling. 1999. "Structuration, Human Development and Desistance From Crime." *British Journal of Criminology* 39: 253-268.

Farrington, David P., Bernard Gallagher, Lynda Morley, Raymond J. St. Ledger, and Donald J. West. 1986. "Unemployment, School Leaving, and Crime." *British Journal of Criminology* 26: 335-356.

Farrington, David P., and Donald J. West. 1995. "Effects of Marriage, Separation, and Children on Offending by Adult Males." In Zena Smith Blau and John Hagan (eds.), *Current Perspectives on Aging and the Life Cycle: Delinquency and Disrepute in the Life Course, Vol. 4.* Greenwich, CT: JAI Press.

Giordano, Peggy C., Stephen A Cernkovich, and Donna D. Holland. 2003. "Changes in Friendship Relations Over the Life Course: Implications for Desistance from Crime." *Criminology* 41: 293-327.

Giordano, Peggy C., Stephan A. Cernkovich, and Jennifer L. Rudolph. 2002. "Gender, Crime, and Desistance: Toward a Theory of Cognitive Transformation." *American Journal of Sociology* 107: 990-1064.

Glueck, Sheldon, and Eleanor Glueck. 1950. *Unraveling Juvenile Delinquency.* New York: Commonwealth Fund.

———. 1968. *Delinquents and Nondelinquents in Perspective.* Cambridge, MA: Harvard University Press.

Gottfredson, Michael R., and Travis Hirschi. 1990. *A General Theory of Crime.* Stanford, CA: Stanford University Press.

Graham, John, and Benjamin Bowling. 1995. *Young People and Crime.* Research Study 145. London: Home Office.

Hagan, John. 1993. "The Social Embeddedness of Crime and Unemployment." *Criminology* 31: 465-491.

Haggard, Ulrika, Clara H. Gumpert, and Martin Grann. 2001. "Against All Odds: A Qualitative Follow-Up Study of High-Risk Violent Offenders Who Were Not Reconvicted." *Journal of Interpersonal Violence* 16: 1048-1065.

Hirschi, Travis. 1969. *Causes of Delinquency.* Berkeley: University of California Press.

Hirschi, Travis, and Michael D. Gottfredson. 1995. "Control Theory and the Life-Course Perspective." *Studies on Crime and Crime Prevention* 4: 131-142.

Horney, Julie, D., Wayne Osgood, and Ineke Haen Marshall. 1995. "Criminal Careers in the Short-Term: Intra-Individual Variability in Crime and Its Relation to Local Life Circumstances." *American Sociological Review* 60: 655-673.

Irwin, John. 1970. *The Felon.* Englewood Cliffs, NJ: Prentice-Hall.

Kempf, Kimberly L. 1993. "The Empirical Status of Hirschi's Control Theory." In Freda Adler and William S. Laufer (eds.), *New Directions in Criminological Theory: Advances in Criminological Theory, Vol. 4.* New Brunswick, NJ: Transaction.

Larzelere, Robert E., and Gerald R. Patterson. 1990. "Parental Management: Mediator of the Effect of Socioeconomic Status on Early Delinquency." *Criminology* 28: 301-324.

Laub, John H., Daniel S. Nagin, and Robert J. Sampson. 1998. "Trajectories of Change in Criminal Offending: Good Marriages and the Desistance Process." *American Sociological Review* 63: 225-238.

Laub, John H., and Robert J. Sampson. 2003. *Shared Beginnings, Divergent Lives: Delinquent Boys to Age 70.* Cambridge, MA: Harvard University Press.

Lemert, Edwin M. 1972. *Human Deviance, Social Problems, and Social Control,* 2nd ed. Englewood Cliffs, NJ: Prentice-Hall.

Lewontin, Richard. 2000. *The Triple Helix: Gene, Organism, and Environment.* Cambridge, MA: Harvard University Press.

McLoyd, Vonnie C. 1990. "The Impact of Economic Hardship on Black Families and Children: Psychological Distress, Parenting, and Socio-Emotional Development." *Child Development* 61: 311-346.

Nagin, Daniel S., and Raymond Paternoster. 1991. "On the Relationship of Past to Future Participation in Delinquency." *Criminology* 29: 163-189.

Nagin, Daniel S., and Joel Waldfogel. 1995. "The Effects of Criminality and Conviction on the Labor Market Status of Young British Offenders." *International Review of Law and Economics* 15: 109-126.

Olweus, Dan. 1979. "Stability of Aggressive Reaction Patterns in Males: A Review." *Psychological Bulletin* 86: 852-875.

Osgood, Wayne D., Janet K. Wilson, Patrick M. O'Malley, Jerald G. Bachman, and Lloyd D. Johnston. 1996. "Routine Activities and Individual Deviant Behavior." *American Sociological Review* 61: 635-655.

Piquero, Alex R., Robert Brame, and Donald Lynam. 2004. "Studying Criminal Career Length Through Early Adulthood Among Serious Offenders." *Crime and Delinquency* 50: 412-435.

Piquero, Alex R., Robert Brame, Paul Mazerolle, and Rudy Haapanen. 2002. "Crime in Emerging Adulthood." *Criminology* 40: 137-169.

Piquero, Alex R., John M. MacDonald, and Karen F. Parker. 2002. "Race, Local Life Circumstances, and Criminal Activity." *Social Science Quarterly* 83: 654-670.

Rex, Sue. 1999. "Desistance from Offending: Experiences of Probation." *The Howard Journal of Crminal Justice* 38: 366-383.

Robins, Lee N. 1978. "Sturdy Childhood Predictors of Adult Antisocial Behavior: Replications from Longitudinal Studies." *Psychological Medicine* 8: 611-622.

Rönkä, Anna, Sanna Oravala, and Lea Pulkkinen. 2003. "'I Met This Wife of Mine and Things Got Onto a Better Track ' Turning Points in Risk Development." *Journal of Adolescence* 25: 47-63.

Rumgay, Judith. 2004. "Scripts for Safer Survival: Pathways Out of Female Crime." *The Howard Journal of Crminal Justice* 43: 405-429.

Rutter, Michael, and Henri Giller. 1983. *Juvenile Delinquency: Trends and Perspectives.* New York: Guilford Press.

Sampson, Robert J., and John H. Laub. 1993. *Crime in the Making: Pathways and Turning Points through Life.* Cambridge, MA: Harvard University Press.

———. 1995. "Understanding Variability in Lives through Time: Contributions of Life-Course Criminology." *Studies on Crime and Crime Prevention* 4: 143-158

———. 1997. "A Life-Course Theory of Cumulative Disadvantage and the Stability of Delinquency." In Terence P. Thornberry (ed.), *Developmental Theories of Crime and Delinquency.* New Brunswick, NJ: Transaction.

———. 2003. "Life Course Desisters? Trajectories of Crime Among Delinquents Boys Followed to Age 70." *Criminology* 41: 555-592.

Sampson, Robert J., John H. Laub, and Elaine P. Eggleston. 2004. "On the Robustness and Validity of Groups." *Journal of Quantitative Criminology* 30: 37-42.

Shaw, Clifford R., and Henry McKay. 1942. *Juvenile Delinquency and Urban Areas.* Chicago: University of Chicago Press.

Shover, Neal. 1996. *Great Pretenders: Pursuits and Careers of Persistent Thieves.* Boulder, CO: Westview Press.

Simons, Ronald L., Christine Johnson, Rand D. Conger, and Glen H. Elder, Jr. 1998. "A Test of Latent Trait Versus Life-Course Perspectives on the Stability of Adolescent Antisocial Behavior." *Criminology* 36: 217-244.

Simons, Ronald L., Eric Stewart, Leslie C. Gordon, Rand D. Conger, and Glen H. Elder, Jr. 2002. "A Test of Life-Course Explanations for Stability and Change in Antisocial Behavior from Adolescence to Young Adulthood." *Criminology* 40: 401-434.

Toby, Jackson. 1957. "Social Disorganization and Stake in Conformity: Complementary   Factors in the Predatory Behavior of Hoodlums." *Journal of Criminal Law, Criminology and Police Science* 48: 12-17.

Uggen, Christopher. 2000. "Work as a Turning Point in the Life Course of Criminals: A Duration Model of Age, Employment and Recidivism." *American Sociological Review* 67: 529-546.

Wadsworth, Tim. 2000. "Labor Markets, Delinquency, and Social Control Theory: An Empirical Assessment of the Mediating Process." *Social Forces* 78: 1041-1066.

Warr, Mark. 1998. "Life-Course Transitions and Desistance From Crime." *Criminology* 36: 183-216.

———. 2002. *Companions in Crime: The Social Aspects of Criminal Conduct.* Cambridge: Cambridge University Press.

Wikström, Per-Olof. 2004. "Crime as Alternative: Towards a Cross-Level Situational Action Theory of Crime Causation." In Joan McCord (ed.), *Beyond Empiricism: Institutions and Intentions in the Study of Crime.* New Brunswick, NJ: Transaction.

Wilson, James Q., and Richard J. Herrnstein. 1985. *Crime and Human Nature.* New York: Simon and Schuster.

Wright, Bradley R. Entner, Avshalom Caspi, Terrie E. Moffitt, Richard A. Miech, and Phil A. Silva. 1999. "Low Self-Control, Social Bonds, and Crime: Social Causation, Social Selection or Both?" *Criminology* 37: 479-514.

Wright, Bradley R. Entner, Avshalom Caspi, Terrie E. Moffit, and Phil A. Silva. 2001. "The Effects of Social Ties on Crime Vary by Criminal Propensity: A Life-Course Model of Interdependence." *Criminology* 39: 321-352.

Wright, John Paul, and Francis T. Cullen. 2004. "Employment, Peers, and Life-Course Transitions." *Justice Quarterly* 21: 183-205.

12

Building Developmental and Life-Course Theories of Offending

David P. Farrington

Developmental and life-course criminology (DLC) is concerned with three main issues: the development of offending and antisocial behavior, risk and protective factors at different ages, and the effects of life events on the course of development (Farrington 2003a; 2005c). DLC is especially concerned to document and explain within-individual variations in offending throughout life, for example whether people commit more crimes during periods of unemployment than during periods of employment (Farrington et al. 1986). Within-individual variations are more relevant to causes, prevention, and treatment than are between-individual variations, for example, the demonstration that unemployed people commit more crimes than employed people (Farrington 1988). The concept of cause implies that within-individual change in a causal factor is followed by within-individual change in an outcome, and ideas of prevention and treatment require within-individual change.

The key empirical issues that need to be addressed by any DLC theory are as follows:

1. Why do people start offending?
2. How are onset sequences explained?
3. Why is there continuity in offending from adolescence to adulthood?
4. Why do people stop offending?
5. Why does prevalence peak in the teenage years?
6. Why does an early onset predict a long criminal career?
7. Why is there versatility in offending and antisocial behavior?
8. Are chronic (persistent) offenders different in degree or in kind from other offenders?
9. Why are there between-individual differences in offending?
10. Why are there within-individual differences in offending?
    (a) long-term (over life)
    (b) short-term (over time and place)

11. Why are crimes committed?
12. What are the key risk factors for onset and desistance, and how can they be explained?
13. Why does co-offending decrease from adolescence to adulthood?
14. What are the main motives and reasons for offending, and how do they change at different ages?
15. What are the effects of life events on offending?

The key theoretical issues that need to be addressed in any DLC theory are as follows:

1. What is the key construct underlying offending?
2. What factors encourage offending?
3. What factors inhibit offending?
4. Is there a learning process?
5. Is there a decision-making process?
6. What is the structure of the theory?
7. What are operational definitions of theoretical constructs?
8. What does the theory explain?
9. What does the theory not explain?
10. What findings might challenge the theory? (Can the theory be tested?)
11. Crucial tests: How much does the theory make different predictions from other DLC theories?

This chapter aims to summarize key features of eight leading DLC theories, and to compare and contrast their answers to these key empirical and theoretical questions. It is based on the detailed expositions of these theories in my edited book (Farrington 2005b). The main aim is to specify where theories make different predictions, in order to decide ultimately which elements of these theories are more or less desirable or more or less plausible. I begin with very brief summaries of the eight theories (based on Farrington 2005a). To a considerable extent, all theorists primarily attempt to explain the data that they have collected, often in major prospective longitudinal surveys. Hence, DLC theories reflect findings in DLC surveys.

Brief Summary of Theories

Lahey and Waldman

Lahey and Waldman (2005) aim to explain the development of juvenile delinquency and child conduct problems, focussing particularly on childhood and adolescence. Their theory is influenced by data collected in the Developmental Trends Study (Loeber et al. 2000). They do not address adult life events or attempt to explain desistance in the adult years, for example. They assume that it is desirable to distinguish different types of people, but they propose a continuum of developmental trajectories rather than only two categories of adolescence-limited and life-course-persistent offenders, for example.

Their key construct is antisocial propensity, which tends to persist over time and has a wide variety of behavioral manifestations, reflecting the versatility and co-morbidity of antisocial behavior. The most important factors that contribute to antisocial propensity are low cognitive ability (especially verbal ability), and three dispositional dimensions: prosociality (including sympathy and empathy), daring (uninhibited or poorly controlled), and negative emotionality (e.g., easily frustrated, bored, or annoyed). These four factors are said to have a genetic basis, and Lahey and Waldman discuss gene-environment interactions.

Moffitt

Moffitt (1993) proposes that there are two qualitatively different categories of antisocial people (differing in kind rather than in degree), namely life-course-persistent (LCP) and adolescence-limited (AL) offenders (see review in Piquero and Moffitt, 2005). As indicated by the terms, the LCPs start offending at an early age and persist beyond their twenties, while the ALs have a short criminal career largely limited to their teenage years. The LCPs commit a wide range of offenses including violence, whereas the ALs commit predominantly "rebellious" non-violent offenses. This theory aims to explain findings in the Dunedin longitudinal study (Moffitt et al., 2001).

The main factors that encourage offending by the LCPs are cognitive deficits, an under-controlled temperament, hyperactivity, poor parenting, disrupted families, teenage parents, poverty, and low SES. Genetic and biological factors, such as a low heart rate, are important. There is not much discussion of neighborhood factors, but it is proposed that the neuropsychological risk of the LCPs interacts multiplicatively with a disadvantaged environment. The theory does not propose that neuropsychological deficits and a disadvantaged environment influence an underlying construct such as antisocial propensity; rather, it suggests that neuropsychological and environmental factors are the key constructs underlying antisocial behavior.

The main factors that encourage offending by the ALs are the "maturity gap" (their inability to achieve adult rewards such as material goods during their teenage years—similar to strain theory ideas) and peer influence (especially from the LCPs). Consequently, the ALs stop offending when they enter legitimate adult roles and can achieve their desires legally. The ALs can easily stop because they have no neuropsychological deficits.

The theory assumes that there can be labelling effects of "snares" such as a criminal record, incarceration, drug or alcohol addiction, and (for girls) unwanted pregnancy, especially for the ALs. However, the observed continuity in offending over time is largely driven by the LCPs. The theory focuses mainly on the development of offenders and does not attempt to explain why offenses are committed. However, it suggests that the presence of delinquent peers is an important situational influence on ALs, and that LCPs seek out opportunities and victims.

Decision-making in criminal opportunities is supposed to be rational for the ALs (who weigh likely costs against likely benefits) but not for the LCPs (who largely follow well-learned "automatic" behavioral repertoires without thinking). However, the LCPs are mainly influenced by utilitarian motives, whereas the ALs are influenced by teenage boredom. Adult life events such as getting a job or getting married are hypothesized to be of little importance, because the LCPs are too committed to an antisocial life-style and the ALs desist naturally as they age into adult roles.

Farrington

The integrated cognitive antisocial potential (ICAP) theory of Farrington (2005d) is mainly intended to explain offending by lower class males. It integrates ideas from strain, control, social learning, differential association and labelling theories. No distinct types of offenders are proposed. The key construct underlying antisocial behavior is antisocial potential (AP) and there is continuity in offending and antisocial behavior over time because of consistency in the relative ordering of people on AP. This theory aims to explain findings in the Cambridge Study in Delinquent Development (Farrington 2003b).

Long-term and short-term influences on AP are explicitly distinguished. Long-term factors encouraging offending include impulsiveness, strain, and antisocial models, while short-term (immediate situational) influences include opportunities and victims. Long-term factors inhibiting offending include attachment and socialization (based on social learning) and life events such as getting married or moving house. The theory explicitly aims to explain both the development of offending and the commission of offenses. Situational factors, motives, and cognitive (thinking and decision-making) processes are included. The theory assumes that the consequences of offending have labelling, deterrent, or learning effects on AP.

Catalano and Hawkins

According to Catalano, Hawkins, and their colleagues (2005), the Social Development Model (SDM) integrates social control/bonding, social learning and differential association theories, but does not include strain theory postulates. Their key construct is bonding to society (or socializing agents), consisting of attachment and commitment. The key construct underlying offending is the balance between antisocial and prosocial bonding. Continuity in antisocial behavior over time depends on continuity in this balance. The main motivation that leads to offending and antisocial behavior is the hedonistic desire to seek satisfaction and follow self-interest. This is opposed by the bond to society. Offending is essentially a rational decision in which people weigh the benefits against the costs. There is no assumption about different types of offenders. This theory aims to explain findings in the Seattle Social Development Project (Hawkins et al. 2003).

There are two causal pathways, leading to antisocial or prosocial bonding. On the prosocial pathway, opportunities for prosocial interaction lead to involvement in prosocial behavior; involvement and skills for prosocial behavior lead to rewards for prosocial behavior that lead to prosocial bonding and beliefs. On the antisocial pathway, opportunities for antisocial interaction lead to involvement in antisocial behavior; involvement and skills for antisocial behavior lead to rewards for antisocial behavior which lead to antisocial bonding and beliefs. Hence, the antisocial pathway specifies factors encouraging offending and the prosocial pathway specifies factors inhibiting offending. Opportunities, involvement, skills and rewards are part of a socialization process. People learn prosocial and antisocial behavior according to socialization by families, peers, schools and communities.

The SDM specifies that demographic factors (such as age, race, gender, and social class) and biological factors (such as difficult temperament, cognitive ability, low arousal and hyperactivity) influence opportunities and skills in the socialization process. There are somewhat different models for different developmental periods (preschool, elementary school, middle school, high school, young adulthood). For example, in the first two periods interaction with prosocial or antisocial family members is the most important, while in the other two periods interaction with prosocial or antisocial peers is the most important.

The development of offending and the commission of offenses are not explicitly distinguished in the SDM. However, the theory includes prosocial and antisocial opportunities as situational factors and suggests that the perceived rewards and costs of antisocial behavior influence the decision to offend. Motives for offending (e.g., utilitarian or excitement) are included under the heading of perceived rewards and costs. Neighborhood factors, official labelling, and life events are important only insofar as they influence the key constructs of opportunities, involvement, skills, rewards, and bonding. For example, official labelling may increase involvement with antisocial people and marriage may increase prosocial opportunities and involvement.

LeBlanc

LeBlanc (1997, 2005) proposes an integrative multilayered control theory that explains the development of offending, the occurrence of criminal events, and community crime rates. The key construct underlying offending is general deviance, and LeBlanc discusses its structure and how it changes over time. According to his theory, the development of offending depends on four mechanisms of control: bonding to society (including family, school, peers, marriage and work), psychological development over time (especially away from egocentrism and towards "allocentrism"), modelling (prosocial or antisocial), and constraints (external, including socialization, and internal, including beliefs). He assumes that environmental factors (e.g., social class and neighborhood) influence bonding while biological capacity (including difficult temperament) influences psychological development. Bonding and psychological development influence modelling and constraints, which are proximate influences on general deviance and hence on offending. There is continuity in offending because the relative ordering of people on control mechanisms stays fairly consistent over time. This theory aims to explain findings in LeBlanc's longitudinal surveys of adolescents and delinquents (e.g., LeBlanc and Frechette 1989).

LeBlanc proposes that there are three types of offenders: persistent, transitory, and common. Persistent offenders are most extreme on weak bonding, egocentrism, antisocial modelling, and low constraints. Common offenders are largely influenced by opportunities, while transitory offenders are in the middle (in having moderate control and being moderately influenced by opportunities). His theory includes biological and neighborhood factors, but they are assumed to have indirect effects on offending through their effects on the constructs of bonding and psychological development. Similarly, he assumes that life events have effects via the constructs and that labelling influences external constraints. The theory includes learning processes and socialization but does not include strain theory assumptions.

LeBlanc's (1997) theory of criminal events suggests that they depend on community control (e.g., social disorganization), personal control (rational choice ideas of decision-making), self-control (impulsiveness, vulnerability to temptations), opportunities, routine activities and guardianship (e.g., physical protection). People are viewed as hedonistic, and motives (e.g., excitement or utilitarian) are considered.

Sampson and Laub

The key construct in Sampson and Laub's (2005) theory is age-graded informal social control, which means the strength of bonding to family, peers, schools and later adult social institutions such as marriages and jobs. Sampson and Laub primarily aim to explain why people do not commit offenses, on the assumption that why people want to offend is unproblematic (presumably caused by hedonistic desires) and that offending is inhibited by the strength of bonding to society. This theory is influenced by their analyses of the Glueck follow-up study of male delinquents and non-delinquents (Sampson and Laub 1993; Laub and Sampson 2003).

The strength of bonding depends on attachments to parents, schools, delinquent friends and delinquent siblings, and also on parental socialization processes such as discipline and supervision. Structural background variables (e.g., social class, ethnicity, large family size, criminal parents, disrupted families) and individual difference factors (e.g., low intelligence, difficult temperament, early conduct disorder) have indirect effects on offending through their effects on informal social control (attachment and socialization processes).

Sampson and Laub are concerned with the whole life course. They emphasize change over time rather than consistency, and the poor ability of early childhood risk factors to predict later life outcomes. They focus on the importance of later life events (adult turning points) such as joining the military, getting a stable job, and getting married in fostering desistance and "knifing off" the past from the present. They also suggest that neighborhood changes can cause changes in offending. Because of their emphasis on change and unpredictability, they deny the importance of types of offenders such as "life-course-persisters."

Sampson and Laub do not explicitly include immediate situational influences on criminal events in their theory, and believe that opportunities are not important because they are ubiquitous (Sampson and Laub 1995). However, they do suggest that having few structured routine activities is conducive to offending. They focus on why people do not offend rather than on why people offend and emphasize the importance of individual free will and purposeful choice in the decision to desist. They do not include strain theory ideas, but they propose that official labelling influences offending through its effects on job instability and unemployment. They argue that early delinquency can cause weak adult social bonds which, in turn, fail to inhibit adult offending.

Thornberry and Krohn

The interactional theory of Thornberry and Krohn (2005) particularly focuses on factors encouraging antisocial behavior at different ages. It is influenced by findings in the Rochester Youth Development Study (Thornberry et al. 2003). They do not propose types of offenders but suggest that the causes of antisocial behavior vary for children who start at different ages. At the earliest ages (birth to six), the three most important factors are neuropsychological deficit and difficult temperament (e.g., impulsiveness, negative emotionality, fearlessness, poor emotion regulation), parenting deficits (e.g., poor monitoring, low affective ties, inconsistent discipline, physical punishment), and structural adversity (e.g., poverty, unemployment, welfare dependency, disorganized neighborhood). They also suggest that structural adversity might cause poor parenting.

Neuropsychological deficits are less important for children who start anti-social behavior at older ages. At ages six to twelve, neighborhood and family factors are particularly salient, while at ages twelve to eighteen school and peer factors dominate. Thornberry and Krohn also suggest that deviant opportunities, gangs, and deviant social networks are important for onset at ages twelve to eighteen. They propose that late starters (ages eighteen to twenty-five) have cognitive deficits such as low IQ and poor school performance but that they were protected from antisocial behavior at earlier ages by a supportive family and school environment. At ages eighteen to twenty-five, they find it hard to make a successful transition to adult roles such as employment and marriage.

The most distinctive feature of this interactional theory is its emphasis on reciprocal causation. For example, it is proposed that the child's antisocial behavior elicits coercive responses from parents and rejection by peers and makes antisocial behavior more likely in the future. The theory does not postulate a single key construct underlying offending but suggests that children who start early tend to continue because of the persistence of neuropsychological and parenting deficits and structural adversity. Interestingly, Thornberry and Krohn predict that late starters (ages eighteen to twenty-five) will show more continuity over time than earlier starters (ages twelve to eighteen) because the late starters have more cognitive deficits. In an earlier exposition of the theory (Thornberry and Krohn 2001), they proposed that desistance was caused by changing social influences (e.g., stronger family bonding), protective factors (e.g., high IQ and school success), and intervention programs. Hence, they do think that criminal justice processing has an effect on future offending.

Wikström

Wikström (2005) proposes a developmental ecological action theory that aims to explain moral rule breaking. The key construct underlying offending is individual criminal propensity that depends on moral judgment and self-control. In turn, moral values influence moral judgment and executive functions influence self-control. Wikström does not propose types of offenders. The motivation to offend arises from the interaction between the individual and the setting. For example, if individual propensity is low, features of the setting (persons, objects and events) become more important. Continuity or change in offending over time depends on continuity or change in moral values, executive functions, and settings.

Situational factors are important in Wikström's theory, which aims to explain the commission of offenses as well as the development of offenders. Opportunities cause temptation, friction produces provocation, and monitoring or the risk of sanctions has a deterrent effect. The theory emphasizes perception, choice, and human agency in deciding to offend. Learning processes are included in the theory, since it is suggested that moral values are taught by instruction and observation in a socialization process and that nurturing (the promotion of cognitive skills) influences executive functions. Life events also matter, since it is proposed that starting school, getting married (etc.) can trigger changes in constructs such as moral teaching and monitoring and hence influence moral rule breaking.

Comparing the Theories

I now attempt to compare and contrast the eight DLC theories systematically on key theoretical and empirical issues. Tables 12.1-12.10 summarize some similarities and differences between the theories.

Scope of the Theory

Most of the theories aim to explain the development of offending and antisocial behavior throughout life, but Lahey/Waldman focus only on the period from birth to age nineteen, Moffitt focuses on infancy to mid-life, and Hawkins/Catalano focus on preschool to young adulthood (Table 12.1). Farrington aims to explain offending by lower-class males, but the other theories are more general. A key issue is how much DLC theories should aim to be general or specific. They all focus on Western industrialized societies and are influenced by research results in countries such as the United States, Canada, the United Kingdom, New Zealand, and Sweden.

Key Constructs and Operational Definitions

In Table 12.1, I aim to identify the key underlying construct of each theory, that is, the most important construct X in the statement "changes in antisocial behavior are related to changes in X." I also aim to identify the operational definition of this key construct, that is, the empirical variable(s) that measure it. Lahey/Waldman, Farrington, LeBlanc, and Wikström assume that there is an underlying theoretical construct of antisocial or criminal propensity and that the behavioral manifestation of offending reflects this underlying construct. Lahey/Waldman, LeBlanc, and Wikström further suggest key elements and operational definitions of this construct; for example, Wikström hypothesizes that the individual crime propensity depends on or comprises moral values and executive functions, which can be measured.

In my ICAP theory, I viewed antisocial potential (AP) as an unobservable hypothetical construct. I suggested that changes in other theoretical constructs (e.g., antisocial models) caused changes in AP, and that these kinds of theoretical hypotheses could be tested using empirical variables that measured these constructs. For example, the corresponding testable empirical

Table 12.1
Scope of Theory, Key Underlying Construct, Operational Definitions

Theory	Scope of Theory	Key Underlying Construct	Operational Definitions
Lahey Waldman	child conduct problems, adolescent delinquency (birth to age 19)	antisocial propensity	4 elements: prosociality, daring, negative emotionality, cognitive abilities
Moffitt	antisocial behavior from infancy to mid-life	AL and LCP behavior: no underlying constructs	neuropsychological risk and disadvantaged environment cause LCP; maturity gap and peer influence cause AL
Farrington	offending by lower-class males throughout life	antisocial potential	antisocial attitude?
Hawkins Catalano	antisocial behavior in preschool, elementary school, middle school, high school, young adulthood	antisocial and prosocial bonding	attachment, commitment
LeBlanc	males and females in Western industrialized societies	general deviance	covert, overt, authority conflict, and reckless behaviors
Sampson Laub	antisocial behavior across the life course	informal social control or social bonding	family/school bonds (e.g. parental attachment, discipline, school, peer factors); adult bonds (e.g. job, marriage)
Thornberry Krohn	antisocial behavior across the life course	antisocial behavior; no underlying construct	caused by psychosocial risk factors and prior antisocial behavior
Wikström	moral rule breaking	individual crime propensity	depends on moral values, executive functions

Note: AL = adolescence-limited; LCP = life-course-persistent

hypothesis would be that changes in delinquent peers caused changes in antisocial behavior. I also suggested that the commission of crimes depended partly on the level of AP of the individual and partly on environmental factors such as opportunities, victims, and peer influence. However, other researchers argued that I was using AP to explain offending and simultaneously inferring the level of AP from offending, and that this was essentially tautological. I am not totally convinced by this argument, or that it is necessary to measure AP directly, but I responded to these challenges by suggesting that antisocial attitude might be identified as an empirical measure of AP that is logically independent of antisocial behavior.

Hawkins/Catalano assume that the key influence on antisocial behavior is the balance of antisocial or prosocial bonding, and that bonding can be measured through attachment and commitment. Hence, antisocial behavior depends on two constructs, the "push" of antisocial bonding versus the "pull" of prosocial bonding. The key underlying construct for Sampson/Laub is age-graded informal social control, which refers to the strength of bonding to family, peers, schools, and, later, adult social institutions such as jobs and marriages. Antisocial behavior becomes less likely as the strength of bonding to society increases. Moffitt and Thornberry/Krohn do not suggest constructs that underlie antisocial behavior but instead propose constructs that influence antisocial behavior (listed in Table 12.1 under the heading of "Operational Definitions").

These eight theories, then, vary in how much there is an underlying construct (e.g., antisocial propensity) whose behavioral manifestation is antisocial behavior, as opposed to a slightly different construct (e.g., bonding) that influences antisocial behavior, as opposed to completely different constructs (e.g., psychosocial risk factors) that influence antisocial behavior. A key issue is: What are the advantages and disadvantages of suggesting an underlying theoretical construct such as antisocial propensity? One obvious advantage is that this approach can easily explain the versatility of antisocial behavior, since all types can be different behavioral manifestations of the same underlying construct. If no underlying construct is proposed, it seems likely that a more complex theory might be needed involving different factors influencing different types of antisocial behavior. My own view is that theories should explicitly distinguish the theoretical constructs from the empirical variables that measure them.

Factors Promoting or Inhibiting Offending

Most of the theories propose factors that promote or inhibit offending, although Sampson/Laub very much emphasize the inhibiting factors and do not think it is necessary to propose promoting factors (Table 12.2). Following Hirschi (1969), they consider that why people want to offend is unproblematic and that there is a "natural motivation to offend." However, it is rare for theories to be tested by comparing within-individual changes in promoting (or inhibiting) factors with within-individual changes in antisocial behavior. Most knowledge about promoting or inhibiting factors is based on research comparing them between individuals.

In principle, the theories can be distinguished by testing the importance of these factors as independent predictors of antisocial behavior. For example, Lahey/Waldman suggest that anxiety inhibits antisocial behavior, but most of the other theories do not. If research showed that within-individual changes in anxiety were reliably followed by within-individual changes in antisocial behavior (while controlling for other influences), this would suggest that the construct of anxiety should be included in other theories. However, in order for theories to be testable, quantitative predictions about the magnitude of effects are needed.

Table 12.2
Factors Promoting or Inhibiting Offending,
Changes in Key Constructs with Age

Theory	Factors Promoting Offending	Factors Inhibiting Offending	Changes in Key Constructs with Age
Lahey Waldman	genetics, antisocial parents, peers, schools, neighborhoods	anxiety, parental supervision, socialization	4 main trajectories: always high, always low, low to high, high to low
Moffitt	LCP: genetic, biological and social risk factors AL: peer influence, maturity gap	LCP: lack of opportunities AL: adult opportunities, personality and skills. abstainers: no maturity gap, rejected or neglected by peers	LCP develop in first 20 years then stable antisocial trait. AL increase in teens and stop in 20s
Farrington	energizing factors, antisocial models, impulsiveness	attachment, socialization, life events	antisocial potential peaks in teen years
Hawkins Catalano	antisocial opportunities, skills, involvement, rewards	prosocial opportunities, skills, involvement, rewards and bonding	different models at different ages, reflecting different developmental influences
LeBlanc	antisocial models, egocentrism, low self-control, weak social control, poor constraints	bonding to society, prosocial models, internal/external constraints, allocentrism	general deviance peaks in teen years
Sampson Laub	natural motivation to offend (hedonistic: seek pleasure, avoid pain)	direct control, informal social control, structured routine activities, strong social bonding, situated choice	routine activities, social bonds, direct control, informal social control vary with age, from family and school to marriage/job/military
Thornberry Krohn	neuropsychological deficit, parenting deficit, low SES, school problems, peer rejection, deviant networks	good temperament, strong bond to family, high SES, prosocial peers	influences change with age, e.g. decreasing parents and increasing peers in teens
Wikström	parenting causes moral values	nurturing causes executive functions, caring causes attachment	increasing independence and agency: seek out settings to fulfil desires

Note: AL = adolescence-limited; LCP = life-course-persistent

Changes in Key Constructs with Age

DLC theories should, of course, include hypotheses about how constructs change with age. Hawkins/Catalano and Thornberry/Krohn propose different theoretical models in different age ranges, but this greatly increases the complexity of their theories (Table 12.2). Most theories agree that the likelihood of offending increases to a peak in the teenage years and then decreases, and suggest that this is caused by changes in social influences (initially, a decrease in parental influence and an increase in peer influence; then, a decrease in peer influence and an increase in the influence of marriage and jobs).

Types of Offenders

One of the most contentious issues is whether chronic offenders differ in kind or in degree from other offenders (Table 12.3). Moffitt explicitly distinguishes adolescence-limited from life-course-persistent offenders, as well as "abstainers" who do not offend, and low-level offenders with mental health problems. LeBlanc distinguishes persistent, transitory, and common offenders, including quantitative predictions about their prevalence. Lahey/Waldman propose a continuum of developmental trajectories, but emphasize four main trajectories, with chronics distinguished by their trajectory of continuously high antisocial behavior. Thornberry/Krohn also adopt a trajectory approach and suggest that different factors influence onset at different ages, but they are more dubious about the link between early onset and chronic offending. The other four theories do not propose types of offenders. The key empirical questions are: What are the advantages and disadvantages of proposing types of offenders in explaining observed results? To what extent can types of offenders be proved or disproved?

Explaining the Age-Crime Curve

All DLC theories, of course, have to explain why the aggregate crime rate is highest in the teenage years (Table 12.3). However, the theories vary in the extent to which they propose that individual curves tend to be similar in shape to the aggregate curve, or the extent to which individual frequencies of offending (as opposed to prevalence) peak in the teenage years. Sampson/Laub emphasize the similarities of individual age-crime curves; they say that chronic offenders start earlier, desist later, and reach a higher offending frequency but (apart from being magnified) their age-crime curves are similar to other offenders. Moffitt and LeBlanc, on the other hand, emphasize changes in composition or prevalence, as adolescence-limited or transitory offenders join in offending in the teenage years and drop out in the twenties. Lahey/Waldman and Thornberry/Krohn propose that the aggregate curve hides groups with different offending trajectories. The other theories suggest that the aggregate curve peaks in the teenage years because both prevalence and frequency reach a peak.

Explaining Changes in Behavior with Age

DLC theories should explain why antisocial behavior changes with age (Table 12.3). Moffitt invokes the concept of heterotypic continuity for the

Table 12.3
Types of Offenders, the Age-Crime Curve, Changes in Behavior with Age

Theory	Chronics/Types of Offenders	Explaining the Age-Crime Curve	Explaining Changes in Behavior with Age
Lahey Waldman	continuum of trajectories (4 main) depending on 4 elements; chronics are always high	antisocial propensity increases up to teen years but different trajectories	interaction between 4 elements and environment, e.g. negative emotionality causes coercive parents and peer rejection
Moffitt	LCP (5-8%), AL, abstainers, low level offenders with mental health problems	AL join in with LCP in teen years	LCP: heterotypic continuity, maturation. AL: offending increases then decreases
Farrington	no types, chronics have high antisocial potential	antisocial potential peaks in teen years	changes in behavior caused by changes in situational factors
Hawkins Catalano	no types, chronics have high antisocial bonding and low prosocial bonding	peak antisocial opportunities plus high rewards and low costs of antisocial behavior in teen years	changes in bonding depend on changes in developmental opportunities, skills, involvement, rewards
LeBlanc	persistent (5%) egocentric, weak bonds, antisocial models, low constraints; transitory (45%) tenuous bonds, antisocial opportunities, medium constraints; common (45%) exploratory, depend on opportunities and constraints	persistent increase frequency in teen years, transitory and common join in	persistent have low self-control and social control; transitory have adolescent crisis; common depend on opportunities
Sampson Laub	no types of offenders can be identified prospectively	processes same for all offender groups, everyone desists but at different ages depending on social control/bonding, routine activities, situated choice	depends on changes in age-graded informal social, direct control, routine activities, situated choice
Thornberry Krohn	different factors influence onset at different ages	aggregate curve hides different trajectories, need to explain onset and desistance at all ages	changes in influencing factors and in balance of risk and protective factors
Wikström	no types, variation in individual propensity and activity field	increasing criminogenic features of activity field in adolescence (e.g. less monitoring) plus changes in moral values, executive functions, decision-making	behavioral manifestation depends on opportunities, friction, monitoring

Note: AL = adolescence-limited; LCP = life-course-persistent

life-course-persistents: behavioral manifestations of continuing antisocial tendencies change because of changes in age-related factors such as maturation, opportunities and victims. Farrington and Wikström also propose that there are age-appropriate behavioral manifestations of antisocial tendencies that largely depend on changes in situational factors. The other theories focus on changes in influencing factors.

Explaining Continuity

Lahey/Waldman and Farrington attribute the relative stability in antisocial behavior over time to relative stability in their underlying constructs of antisocial propensity or potential or, in other words, to persistent heterogeneity (see Nagin and Farrington 1992). Moffitt generally agrees for life-course persistent offenders, but also emphasizes the effect of past offending on future offending (state dependence). Sampson/Laub and Thornberry/Krohn also suggest that past offending can influence future offending (Table 12.4). Wikström agrees that there is relative stability in individual propensity but suggests that stability in contexts is more important. Hawkins/Catalano and LeBlanc attribute relative stability in antisocial behavior to relative stability in their influencing constructs. Sampson/Laub give the least emphasis to continuity in antisocial behavior, arguing that childhood antisocial behavior is not a very good predictor of adult antisocial behavior because of the importance of adult life events.

Explaining Changes in Versatility, Frequency, and Seriousness

Most theories predict that these features should peak in the teenage years, since they reflect either an underlying construct such as antisocial propensity or influencing constructs such as bonding and social control (Table 12.4). Moffitt suggests that life-course-persistent offenders tend to have constant versatility, frequency, and seriousness at least up to mid-life. Sampson/Laub predict that frequency and seriousness should peak in the teenage years because of variations in their influencing constructs (e.g., social control/bonding) but surprisingly make no predictions about versatility, suggesting that it should be constant at different ages to the extent that opportunities are constant (which seems doubtful).

Explaining Early and Adult Onset, and Onset Sequences

These DLC theories all explain early onset by reference to changes in influencing constructs such as self-control and social control (LeBlanc) and caring, nurturing, and moral teaching (Wikström). However, they tend to suggest that different constructs are differentially important (Table 12.5). As usual, Moffitt suggests different influences for life-course-persistent offenders (cognitive deficits, poor parenting, low SES) compared with adolescence-limited offenders (the maturity gap, peer influence).

Lahey/Waldman and Moffitt do not proffer explanations for adult onset, which is not included in their theories (Table 12.5). Most of the other theories suggest that the influencing factors for adult onset are similar to those for early onset; for example, Hawkins/Catalano attribute both types of onset to the

Table 12.4
Changes in Continuity, Versatility, Frequency and Seriousness with Age

Theory	Explaining Continuity vs. Age	Explaining Versatility vs. Age	Explaining Frequency/Seriousness vs. Age
Lahey Waldman	relative stability in antisocial propensity	reflects high antisocial propensity: peaks in teen years	peak in teen years because reflect high antisocial propensity
Moffitt	relative stability in LCP (e.g. antisocial attitudes), not AL. for both, offending causes more offending through snares	LCP versatile, violent. AL more specialized in vandalism, public order, substance use, theft, runaway.	LCP constant (persistent heterogeneity). AL peak in teen years (state dependence)
Farrington	relative stability in antisocial potential	high versatility reflects high antisocial potential, peaks in teen years	frequency and seriousness reflect high antisocial potential, peak in teen years
Hawkins Catalano	depends on continuity in antisocial opportunities, skills for antisocial involvement, rewards for antisocial behavior	different manifestations of bonding and opportunities, peak in teen years	depends on antisocial opportunities, peak in teen years
LeBlanc	relatively stable egocentrism, bonds, antisocial models, constraints	low self-control and social control	low self-control and social control
Sampson Laub	natural motivation and prior crime/incarceration plus lack of direct control, informal social control and structured routine activities due to weak social bonds	not addressed, expect versatility at all ages, assuming opportunities are constant	assume frequency and seriousness have same causes as prevalence, so peak in teen years
Thornberry Krohn	greater deficits cause more stability, plus reciprocal causation, e.g. delinquency causes delinquent peers and vice versa	peaks in teen years because of peer influence and adolescent search for autonomy	peaks in teen years because of peer influence and adolescent search for autonomy
Wikström	depends on individual propensity and activity field, but stability in contexts more important; high continuity if high propensity and stable activity field.	depends on changes in propensity and activity field, peaks in teen years	depends on changes in propensity and activity field, peaks in teen years

Note: AL=adolescence-limited; LCP=life-course-persistent

balance of antisocial and prosocial opportunities, skills and rewards (although they add increasing mental and physical capacities as influences on early onset). Farrington and Sampson/Laub emphasize adult life events as causes of adult onset, and Thornberry/Krohn suggest that adult onset is caused by difficulties that some people have in making the transition to adult roles. Wikström focusses on environmental inducements as explanations of adult onset.

Table 12.5
Early Onset, Adult Onset, Onset Sequences

Theory	Explaining Early Onset	Explaining Adult Onset	Explaining Onset Sequences
Lahey Waldman	increasing antisocial propensity, antisocial parents and peers	not addressed	not addressed
Moffitt	LCP: cognitive deficits, poor parenting, low SES. AL: maturity gap and peer influence (from LCP)	not expected; any adult onset cases should fit AL type	LCP show heterotypic continuity because of changes in skills and opportunities
Farrington	increasing antisocial potential caused by energizing, antisocial models, decreasing attachment to parents	increasing antisocial potential caused by strain, models, changed attachment, life events	age-appropriate behavioral manifestations depending on situational factors
Hawkins Catalano	increasing mental and physical capacities, preponderance of antisocial over prosocial opportunities, skills, rewards	increasing antisocial and decreasing prosocial opportunities, skills and rewards	age-appropriate behavioral manifestations depending on opportunities
LeBlanc	low self-control and social control	increasing antisocial models, decreasing internal constraints, weak adult bonds	general deviance has different manifestations at different ages
Sampson Laub	decreased social bonds and informal social control, reflecting attachment to parents and school	decreased informal social control, routine activities, life events	heterotypic continuity depends on changes in social bonds and informal social control
Thornberry Krohn	neuropsychological deficit, low SES, poor child-rearing, school problems, peer rejection	have deficits (e.g. low IQ) but previously protected by family and school environment; have difficulty making transition to adult job, marriage, roles	response to success in meeting age-appropriate developmental challenges
Wikström	high individual propensity, caused by poor caring, nurturing and moral teaching	caused by environmental inducements: opportunities, friction, decreased monitoring/deterrence	caused by changes in activity fields

Note: AL = adolescence-limited; LCP = life-course-persistent

The theories generally agree that onset sequences (e.g., shoplifting occurring before burglary) are age-appropriate behavioral manifestations that depend on situational factors (persistent heterogeneity). (But see later comments under the heading of "Labelling or Deterrence").

Explaining Desistance

Most theories suggest that the causes of desistance are to a large extent the opposite of the causes of onset (Table 12.6). For example, LeBlanc proposes that increasing antisocial models and decreasing internal and external constraints cause onset, whereas increasing prosocial models and increasing internal and external constraints (and maturation) cause desistance. However, Farrington and Sampson/Laub emphasize the effect of adult life events in fostering desistance. Because of their focus on adult life events, Sampson/Laub propose that desistance cannot be predicted adequately on the basis of childhood factors. Lahey/Waldman do not address the topic of desistance and Moffitt argues that life-course-persistent offenders do not desist (at least up to mid-life).

Table 12.6
Desistance, Later Life Events, Onset vs. Duration

Theory	Explaining Desistance	Effect of Later Life Events	Explaining Onset vs. Duration
Lahey Waldman	not addressed	not addressed	early onset and long duration reflect high antisocial propensity
Moffitt	AL desist when can achieve adult goals. LCP persist in crime to mid-life and show antisocial personality	marriage and jobs may help AL desist but not LCP, who get antisocial partners and jobs	reflects definition of LCP and AL
Farrington	decreased antisocial potential caused by life events	marriage, jobs, moving house cause changes in antisocial potential	early onset and a long career duration both reflect high antisocial potential
Hawkins Catalano	caused by changes in opportunities and rewards; costs of antisocial behavior increase in the 20s	important if affect constructs such as opportunities, rewards and bonding	both reflect preponderance of antisocial over prosocial opportunities, skills and rewards
LeBlanc	caused by increasing internal and external constraints, bonds, prosocial models, maturation	important if affect constructs such as models, constraints, bonding	reflects classification of persistent vs. transitory, stability of self-control and social control
Sampson Laub	caused by increased social controls, structured routine activities, and situated choice; can't predict from childhood factors	strong social bonds stemming from life events (e.g. marriage, job, military) create direct control, informal social control, structured routine activities, situated choice	onset and duration are influenced by the same factors (e.g. social control)
Thornberry Krohn	caused by increasing bonds, decreasing peer influence, turning points	attachment to partners and commitment to work have good effects	early onset reflects greater deficits: predicts longer duration but relation is modest at best
Wikström	changes in nurturing, caring, moral teaching, monitoring, activity field	important if affect constructs such as nurturing, monitoring, attachments	both reflect individual propensity and activity field

Note: AL = adolescence-limited; LCP = life-course-persistent

Effect of Later Life Events

As usual, Sampson/Laub and Moffitt differ considerably in their predictions about the importance of later life events (Table 12.6). Sampson/Laub argue that adult life events, such as getting married, getting a steady job, and joining the military, are very important in fostering desistance, because of their effects on social bonds, informal social control, structured routine activities, and situated choice. In contrast, Moffitt says that adult life events may help adolescence-limited offenders to desist but have little effect on life-course-persistent offenders, partly because they select antisocial partners and jobs. The other theories generally agree with Sampson/Laub in suggesting that adult life events can cause de-escalation or desistance to the extent that they affect key constructs such as (for Wikström) nurturing, monitoring, and attachments. Farrington proposes a more direct effect of adult life events on antisocial potential, and Lahey/Waldman do not address adult life events because of their focus on early development.

Explaining Why Onset Predicts Duration

The theories generally agree that an early onset and a long criminal career both reflect the same underlying constructs, such as antisocial propensity (Lahey/Waldman) or antisocial versus prosocial opportunities, skills, and rewards (Hawkins/Catalano). This relationship is the basis for the offender types in the Moffitt and LeBlanc theories. However, Thornberry and Krohn (2005: 185) argue that the strength of the relationship between onset and duration is "moderate at best." The theories generally focus on persistent heterogeneity (but see the later comments on "Labelling or Deterrence").

Committing Crimes, Situational Factors, Decision-Making

Most DLC theories aim to explain the development of offenders but not the commission of crimes (Table 12.7). However, explaining why crimes are committed is the central feature of Wikström's theory. He suggests that opportunities cause temptation, friction causes provocation, and monitoring causes deterrence, and that all these factors influence the decision to commit crimes. Farrington and LeBlanc also aim to explain why crimes are committed, and include situational factors and decision-making processes in their theories. Hawkins/Catalano, while not explicitly trying to explain why crimes are committed, propose that prosocial and antisocial opportunities are important and suggest that people take account of costs and rewards in deciding whether to offend. Sampson/Laub include the idea of "situated choice" and postulate that the context influences human agency, but they deny that opportunities are important because they are "ubiquitous" (Sampson and Laub 1995: 151).

Similarly, Moffitt denies that victims and opportunities influence offending, suggesting instead that life-course-persistent offenders seek out victims and opportunities and commit offenses using stored repertoires, with little deliberation.

Table 12.7
Committing Crimes, Situational Factors, Decision-Making Process

Theory	Explaining the Commission of Crimes	Situational Factors	Decision-Making Process
Lahey Waldman	not addressed	environmental factors discussed (e.g. seeking out delinquent peers) but not situational factors	not addressed
Moffitt	not addressed	LCP seek out victims and opportunities; only delinquent peers important for AL	LCP use stored repertoires, with little deliberation. AL rational
Farrington	included in theory	short-term energizing factors (drunk, bored, angry) plus victims and opportunities	cognitive processes and cost-benefit analysis
Hawkins Catalano	no specific theory of committing crimes but says they depend on antisocial opportunities	prosocial and antisocial opportunities	people take account of perceived costs and rewards in deciding to offend
LeBlanc	separate theory	crimes depend on low self-control, opportunities, routine activities, guardianship	rational choice theory
Sampson Laub	situated choice	situational/historical context influences human agency; opportunities not important because ubiquitous	situated choice
Thornberry Krohn	not addressed	not addressed	not addressed
Wikström	main feature of theory	monitoring/deterrence, opportunity/temptation and friction/ provocation are important	the decision to commit crimes involves perception of alternatives and choice

Note: AL = adolescence-limited; LCP = life-course-persistent

Co-offending and Motives

Farrington suggests that co-offending decreases within individuals from the teenage years to the twenties because of the decreasing influence of peers and older siblings (Table 12.8). However, Moffitt proposes that the aggregate decrease in co-offending with age reflects the changing composition of the offender population, as adolescence-limited offenders (who disproportionally co-offend) drop out, leaving life-course-persistent offenders (who tend to commit crimes alone). Hawkins/Catalano postulate that co-offending decreases in the twenties because of decreasing social approval for antisocial behavior (decreasing peer influence). The other theories do not attempt to explain why co-offending decreases.

Table 12.8
Co-offending, Motives, Learning Processes

Theory	Co-offending vs. age	Motives vs. age	Learning Processes
Lahey Waldman	not addressed	not addressed	socialization by parents, social learning from delinquent peers
Moffitt	LCP offend alone (or in group influencing ALs), AL in groups. co-offending decreases with age because AL drop out	LCP utilitarian, AL seek excitement. utilitarian increases with age because AL drop out	LCP: socialization AL: social learning from delinquent peers
Farrington	peaks in teen years because of peers and older siblings; within-individual change	more seeking excitement in teens because more impulsiveness and peer influence	socialization by parents, social learning from antisocial models
Hawkins Catalano	decreases in 20s because less social approval/rewards for antisocial behavior	more utilitarian after 20 because less peer approval/rewards	rewards influence prosocial or antisocial bonding
LeBlanc	not addressed, but says delinquent peers most important in teens	develops from hedonistic to utilitarian	socialization (internal constraints, bonding and models) and social learning
Sampson Laub	not addressed	not addressed	socialization
Thornberry Krohn	not addressed	not addressed	socialization and social learning
Wikström	not addressed	motivation arises from interaction between individual and setting (temptation and provocation); more important if low propensity	moral values taught by instruction, observation, attachment

Note: AL = adolescence-limited; LCP = life-course-persistent

Farrington, Hawkins/Catalano, and LeBlanc attempt to explain why motives for offending change within individuals from the teenage years to the twenties, from hedonistic/excitement-seeking to utilitarian/rational (Table 12.8). For example, Farrington suggests that there is more excitement-seeking in the teenage years because of higher levels of impulsiveness and peer influence. Again, Moffitt proposes that the aggregate decrease in excitement-seeking with age reflects the changing composition of the offender population, as adolescence-limited offenders (who are disproportionately hedonistic because of peer influence) drop out, leaving life-course-persistent offenders (who tend to be utilitarian). Wikström includes postulates about how motivation arises from situational temptations and provocations, but does not attempt to explain why it changes with age and this topic is not addressed in the other three theories.

Learning Processes

DLC theories commonly include two types of learning processes (Table 12.8). First, they suggest that children are socialized (become less antisocial) as a result of rewards and punishments received in interactions with parents (involving attachment, supervision, and discipline). Second, they suggest that children become more antisocial because they learn from delinquent peers and other antisocial models. Moffitt proposes that (poor) socialization processes are more important for life-course-persistent offenders, whereas social learning processes are more important for adolescence-limited offenders. Wikström focusses on the learning of moral values and suggests that this depends on observation, attachment and instruction.

Biological and Neighborhood Factors

The DLC theories all include family and peer influences but they differ in the degree to which they explicitly include biological or neighborhood factors (Table 12.9). Lahey/Waldman and Moffitt give most emphasis to biological factors. Lahey/Waldman propose that prosociality, daring, negative emotionality, and cognitive abilities depend on gene-environment interactions. Moffitt suggests that life-course-persistent (but not adolescence-limited) offenders are influenced by biological factors such as genetics, neuropsychological risk, and low heart rate. Thornberry/Krohn propose that neuropsychological deficit has an important influence on early onset, while Wikström postulates that individual propensity depends on executive functioning and moral values. The other four theories suggest that biological factors have indirect effects on antisocial behavior, through their effects on more central constructs such as informal social control.

Similarly, most of the theories suggest that neighborhood factors have only indirect effects on antisocial behavior (Table 12.9). Wikström emphasizes "activity fields" (the contexts in which an individual develops and acts) but says little specifically about neighborhood factors. Farrington and LeBlanc suggest that neighborhood factors influence constructs such as exposure to antisocial models and bonding to society, while Moffitt proposes that neighborhood factors influence access to delinquent peers for adolescence-limited offenders. Lahey/Waldman and Hawkins/Catalano primarily view neighborhood factors as influencing opportunities. Sampson/Laub and Thornberry/Krohn discuss the indirect effects of structural adversity but do not specifically disentangle the role of neighborhood factors.

Table 12.9

Biological Factors, Neighborhood Factors, Labelling or Deterrence

Theory	Biological Factors	Neighborhood Factors	Labelling or Deterrence
Lahey Waldman	genetic and environmental factors influence 4 elements of theory	influence how much antisocial propensity becomes delinquency	not addressed
Moffitt	LCP have neuropsychological risk, genetic factors, low heart rate (not AL)	LCP influenced by disadvantaged environment, neighborhoods influence AL access to delinquent peer models	snares (criminal record, incarceration, etc.) amplify antisocial behavior of LCP (especially) and AL; AL more deterrable as adults
Farrington	could influence constructs	bad neighborhood influences antisocial potential; moving house can be beneficial	consequences of offending influence antisocial potential by labelling/deterrence
Hawkins Catalano	constitutional factors (poor concentration, cognitive abilities, low arousal, shyness, aggression) influence constructs	neighborhood SES influences antisocial and prosocial opportunities	can have labelling effects on decreasing prosocial and increasing antisocial opportunities
LeBlanc	biological capacity and environment influences egocentrism	community control influences bonding to society, models, external constraints	labelling depends on external constraints
Sampson Laub	individual predisposition important but mediated by informal social control and local context	effect of structural background factors mediated by social control	incarceration can cause labelling and poor job stability which predicts continued offending, but incarceration can also cause deterrent effects and turning points
Thornberry Krohn	neuropsychological deficit important	structural adversity influences poor parenting	consequences of antisocial behavior can cause more antisocial behavior
Wikström	executive functions important	interaction between neighborhood setting and parenting matters	risk of sanction influences decision-making in criminal opportunities

Note: AL = adolescence-limited; LCP = life-course-persistent

Labelling or Deterrence

Several theories suggest that the labelling or individual deterrent effects of official processing can influence the future probability of offending in some kind of learning process (Table 12.9). Farrington and Sampson/Laub allow for the possibility of both labelling and individual deterrence. Hawkins/Catalano, LeBlanc, and Thornberry/Krohn suggest that labelling effects are mediated by effects on their constructs. Moffitt emphasizes the importance of labelling effects as "snares" for both adolescence-limited and life-course-persistent offenders, but says that only adolescence-limited offenders might be deterred as adults. Wikström discusses only general deterrence in suggesting that the perceived risk of receiving a sanction influences decision-making in criminal opportunities. Lahey/Waldman do not address the topic of labelling or deterrence.

To the extent that the consequences of antisocial behavior can increase the probability of future antisocial behavior, this implies state dependence rather than persistent heterogeneity (Nagin and Farrington 1992). Conclusions about why there is continuity in offending, about onset sequences and about why early onset predicts a long duration should take account of labelling postulates. In light of Table 12.9, only the Lahey/Waldman and Wikström theories could focus purely on persistent heterogeneity. The other theories include some combination of persistent heterogeneity and state dependence.

Underlying Theories

To a large extent, DLC theories are integrated theories that include postulates from earlier criminological theories such as strain, social control/bonding, social learning/differential association, socialization, labelling, and routine activities/rational choice. Table 12.10 lists whether each DLC theory includes postulates from these theories and also postulates about individual difference factors. It can be seen that every theory includes ideas about bonding and socialization, but only Moffitt and Farrington include strain theory postulates. These two theories are the most wide-ranging, including all seven types of postulates, while Hawkins/Catalano and LeBlanc include six.

Preventing Onset and Fostering Desistance

In principle, DLC theories could be tested according to their policy implications about preventing onset and fostering desistance (Table 12.10). To the extent that DLC theories are correct, parent training, skills training, increasing prosocial and decreasing antisocial opportunities/peer influence, job training, and situational prevention should be effective techniques for reducing offending. In principle, randomized experiments evaluating these techniques could throw light on the correctness of postulates in DLC theories.

Hypotheses to be Tested

In the interests of identifying which elements of DLC theories are more or less correct or more or less desirable, it is important to specify questions where different theories make different predictions that can be tested empirically. There is not space in this chapter to lay out a full research agenda of crucial tests of eight theories. However, I will try to identify some priorities. The greatest priority is to mount new longitudinal studies and/or reanalyze existing longitudinal studies to establish the degree to which within-individual

Table 12.10
Underlying Theories, Preventing Onset, Fostering Desistance

Theory	Underlying Theories	Preventing Onset	Fostering Desistance
Lahey Waldman	individual, socialization, bonding, social learning	parent training, skills training, emotion control, decrease opportunities by better adult supervision, prosocial peer influence	skills training
Moffitt	individual, socialization, strain, bonding, social learning, labelling, rational choice	AL: limit contact with delinquent peers and LCP, provide opportunities to achieve aims in teen years. LCP: early parent training, skills training, reduce early neurological dysfunction	AL: provide opportunities to achieve adult aims. LCP: minimize opportunities, increase risk
Farrington	individual, socialization, strain, bonding, social learning, labelling, rational choice	parent training, skills training	provide opportunities to achieve adult aims, job training, decrease drinking, situational prevention
Hawkins Catalano	individual, socialization, bonding, social learning, labelling, rational choice	increase prosocial and decrease antisocial opportunities, involvement, skills, rewards	increase prosocial and decrease antisocial opportunities, involvement, skills, rewards
LeBlanc	individual, socialization, bonding, social learning, labelling, rational choice	increase self-control through prosocial models, parent training, skills training, increased monitoring	increase self-control and prosocial opportunities
Sampson Laub	socialization, bonding, labelling	increase bonding to family and school (e.g. parent training)	increase bonding to community and adult social institutions (e.g. job training, provide structured routine activities)
Thornberry Krohn	individual, socialization, bonding, social learning	parent training, skills training, limit contact with delinquent peers	job training, peer-resistance training
Wikström	individual, socialization, bonding	parent training, skills training	situational prevention, decrease friction, increase deterrence

Note: AL = adolescence-limited; LCP = life-course-persistent

changes in possible causal factors are followed reliably by within-individual changes in offending, after controlling for within-individual changes in other factors. It is important to conduct studies in different cities and countries to establish how much the results are replicable.

It is easy to recommend that the scope of some existing theories should be expanded. For example, Lahey/Waldman should be expanded beyond age nineteen, Moffitt should be expanded beyond mid-life, and Farrington should be expanded beyond lower-class males. All theories should seek to explain why crimes are committed as well as why offenders develop. However, these kinds of recommendations do not lead to testable predictions. There are many predictions about factors promoting or inhibiting offending that should be tested in within-individual research. If we take seriously the finding that within-individual changes in delinquent peers do not predict within-individual changes in delinquency (Farrington et al. 2002), this would threaten the importance ascribed to delinquent peers in all theories.

The most testable theory (because of its very specific predictions) is clearly Moffitt. The first key question is:

1. Are there discrete types of offenders (e.g., adolescence-limited versus life-course-persistent) or a continuum of offenders varying in ages of onset, duration of criminal careers, and frequency and seriousness of offending? Taxometric techniques (e.g., Beauchaine 2003) could be used to address this question.

Other hypotheses to be tested are as follows:

2. How does the frequency of offending vary with age within individuals? According to Moffitt, frequency does not vary with age (up to mid-life) for life-course-persistent offenders. According to Sampson/Laub, the individual offending frequency varies with age for all offenders in the same way as the aggregate age-crime curve.
3. How does the seriousness of offending vary with age within individuals? Similar conflicting predictions can be derived from these two theories.
4. How does the versatility of offending vary with age within individuals? Again, Moffitt would suggest that versatility would not vary with age for life-course-persistent offenders, whereas most other theories (but not Sampson/Lamb) would predict that versatility should peak in the teenage years.

Some predictions contrast explanations based on changes within individuals versus changes in the composition of offenders:

5. Why does co-offending decrease from the teenage years to the twenties?
6. Why do hedonistic motives decrease, and utilitarian motives increase, from the teenage years to the twenties?

According to Moffitt, these aggregate changes are observed because adolescence-limited offenders (who co-offend, and who have hedonistic motives) drop out, whereas life-course-persistent offenders (who are more likely to commit offenses alone, and who have utilitarian motives) continue. According to Farrington and Hawkins/Catalano, there are age-related changes within individuals in co-offending and motives. Research on co-offending could also test the Moffitt prediction that adolescence-limited offenders tend to co-offend with life-course-persistent offenders, or that the latter cause the former to start offending.

Some predictions focus on the observed continuity and relative stability of offending.

7. How much does this reflect persistent heterogeneity as opposed to state dependence? All theories except Lahey/Waldman and Wikström predict that official processing will have ampliflying effects on future offending. Within-individual data are needed to test the presumed causal processes.

8. Do more antisocial people show higher stability than less antisocial people? This is a clear prediction of Moffitt and Thornberry/Krohn but not of other theories. In testing it, the key issue is how to measure stability. For example, it is obvious that more antisocial people will have a higher probability of persisting but less obvious that their rank ordering on some measure of antisocial behavior will be more consistent over time than less antisocial people. Measures of stability are also needed to address the following question:

9. How much does stability in antisocial behavior depend on stability in the context?

Wikström suggests that stability in behavior depends on stability in the context, but other theories do not.

Moffitt and Thornberry/Krohn make specific predictions about different factors influencing different ages of onset. Most of these require within-individual data on influencing factors to test. The following specific prediction from Thornberry/Krohn (but not from any other theory) particularly deserves to be tested:

10. Adult onset offenders have more deficits (e.g., low IQ) and longer criminal careers than teenage onset offenders.

Since Moffitt suggest that true adult onset is very rare, it is important also to address the following question:

11. How common is adult onset of offending in the absence of previous antisocial behavior? Moffitt and Sampson/Laub draw different conclusions about the importance of life events (such as marriage) in fostering desistance. A key question is:

12. Does marriage cause antisocial people to become less antisocial?

Moffitt suggests that marriage would have little effect in most cases, but Sampson/Laub and most other theories would answer yes to this question. Sampson/Laub also contrast the importance of life events with the importance of childhood factors, arguing that childhood factors do not predict desistance very well. It is difficult to test this prediction effectively without some more quantitative statement about the strength of the relationship. However, it would be worthwhile to address the following question:

13. How accurately do childhood factors, compared with adult life events, predict desistance?

These are some of the more important questions that are specific to developmental and life-course criminology and that might help to differentiate between these DLC theories. There are many other interesting questions that might be addressed, such as:

14. To what extent is the decision to commit a crime rational?

This question is not a distinctive feature of DLC but it would help to differentiate between the theories, since some assume that the decision is rational and others do not. Similarly, the following question is important for the future:

15. How do the different DLC theories explain gender and racial differences in the development of offending and antisocial behavior?

These 15 questions represent only a starting-point in the effort to test predictions from DLC theories. Nevertheless, it seems clear that these eight DLC theories do make different predictions that can be tested empirically. However, more within-individual data and analyses, and more prospective longitudinal surveys, are needed to address all the key features of these theories adequately. In future, I hope to expand this chapter into a full-length monograph comparing predictions from these eight DLC theories with empirical evidence gained in longitudinal surveys.

Note

*   I am very grateful to Richard Catalano, David Hawkins, Marvin Krohn, Ben Lahey, John Laub, Marc LeBlanc, Terrie Moffitt, Alex Piquero, Rob Sampson, Terry Thornberry, and Per-Olof Wikström for helpful comments on and contributions to Tables 12.1-12.10.

References

Beauchaine, T.P. 2003. "Taxometrics and Developmental Psychopathology." *Development and Psychopathology* 15: 501-527.
Catalano, R.F., J. Park, T.W. Harachi, K.P. Haggerty, R.D. Abbott, and J.D. Hawkins. 2005. "Mediating the Effects of Poverty, Gender, Individual Characteristics, and External Constraints On Antisocial Behavior: A Test of the Social Development Model and Implications for Developmental Life-Course Theory." Pp. 93-123 in D. P. Farrington (ed.), *Integrated Developmental and Life-Course Theories of Offending*. New Brunswick, NJ: Transaction Publishers.
Farrington, D.P. 1988. "Studying Changes Within Individuals: The Causes of Offending." Pp. 158-183 in M. Rutter (ed.), *Studies of Psychosocial Risk: The Power of Longitudinal Data*. Cambridge, MA: Cambridge University Press.
———. 2003a. "Developmental and Life-Course Criminology: Key Theoretical and Empirical Issues—The 2002 Sutherland Award Address." *Criminology* 41: 221-255.

————. 2003b. "Key Results From the First 40 Years of the Cambridge Study in Delinquent Development." Pp. 137-183 in T. P. Thornberry and M. D. Krohn (eds.), *Taking Stock of Delinquency: an Overview of Findings From Contemporary Longitudinal Studies*. New York: Kluwer/Plenum.

————. 2005a. "Conclusions About Developmental and Life-Course Theories." Pp. 247-256 in D. P. Farrington (ed.), *Integrated Developmental and Life-Course Theories of Offending*. New Brunswick, NJ: Transaction Publishers.

————, ed. 2005b. *Integrated Developmental and Life-Course Theories of Offending. Advances in Criminological Theory, Vol. 14*. New Brunswick, NJ: Transaction Publishers.

————. 2005c. "Introduction to Integrated Developmental and Life-Course Theories of Offending." Pp. 1-14 in D. P. Farrington (ed.), *Integrated Developmental and Life-Course Theories of Offending*. New Brunswick, NJ: Transaction Publishers.

————. 2005d. "The Integrated Cognitive Antisocial Potential (ICAP) Theory." Pp. 73-92 in D. P. Farrington (ed.), *Integrated Developmental and Life-Course Theories of Offending*. New Brunswick, NJ: Transaction Publishers.

Farrington, D.P., B. Gallagher, L. Morley, R.J. St. Ledger, and D.J. West. 1986. "Unemployment, School Leaving, and Crime." *British Journal of Criminology* 26: 335-356.

Farrington, D.P., R. Loeber, Y. Yin, and S.J. Anderson. 2002. "Are Within-Individual Causes of Delinquency the Same as Between-Individual Causes?" *Criminal Behavior and Mental Health* 12: 53-68.

Hawkins, J.D., B.H. Smith, K.G. Hill, R. Kosterman, R.F. Catalano, and R.D. Abbott. 2003. "Understanding and Preventing Crime and Violence: Findings from the Seattle Social Development Project." Pp. 225-312 in T. P. Thornberry and M. D. Krohn (eds.), *Taking Stock of Delinquency: An Overview of Findings from Contemporary Longitudinal Studies*. New York: Kluwer/Plenum.

Hirschi, T. 1969. *Causes of Delinquency*. Berkeley: University of California Press.

Lahey, B.B., and I.D. Waldman. 2005. "A Developmental Model of the Propensity to Offend During Childhood and Adolescence." Pp. 15-50 in D. P. Farrington (ed.), *Integrated Developmental and Life-Course Theories of Offending*. New Brunswick, NJ: Transaction Publishers.

Laub, J.H., and R.J. Sampson. 2003. *Shared Beginnings, Divergent Lives: Delinquent Boys to Age 70*. Cambridge, MA: Harvard University Press.

Leblanc. M. 1997. "A Generic Control Theory of the Criminal Phenomenon: The Structural and Dynamic Statements of an Integrated Multilayered Control Theory." Pp. 215-225 in T. P. Thornberry (ed.), *Developmental Theories of Crime and Delinquency*. New Brunswick, NJ: Transaction Publishers.

————. 2005. "An Integrative Personal Control Theory of Deviant Behavior: Answers to Contemporary Empirical and Theoretical Developmental Criminology Issues." Pp. 125-163 in D. P. Farrington (ed.), *Integrated Developmental and Life-Course Theories of Offending*. New Brunswick, NJ: Transaction Publishers.

Leblanc, M., and M. Frechette. 1989. *Male Criminal Activity from Childhood Through Youth*. New York: Springer-Verlag.

Loeber, R., S.M. Green, B.B. Lahey, J. Frick, and K. Mcburnett. 2000. "Findings on Disruptive Behavior Disorders from the First Decade of the Developmental Trends Study." *Clinical Child and Family Psychology Review* 3: 37-60.

Moffitt, T.E. 1993. "Life-Course Persistent and Adolescence-Limited Antisocial Behavior: A Developmental Taxonomy." *Psychological Review* 100: 674-701.

Moffitt, T.E., A. Caspi, M. Rutter, and A. Silva. 2001. *Sex Differences in Antisocial Behavior*. Cambridge: Cambridge University Press.

Nagin, D.S., and D.P. Farrington. 1992. "The Stability of Criminal Potential from Child-hood to Adulthood." *Criminology* 30: 235-260.

Piquero, A.R., and T.E. Moffitt. 2005. "Explaining the Facts of Crime: How the Developmental Taxonomy Replies to Farrington's Invitation" Pp. 51-72 in D. P. Farrington (ed.), *Integrated Developmental and Life-Course Theories of Offending*. New Brunswick, NJ: Transaction Publishers.

Sampson, R.J., and J.H. Laub. 1993. *Crime in the Making: Pathways and Turning Points through Life*. Cambridge, MA: Harvard University Press.

————. 1995. "Understanding Variability in Lives through Time: Contributions of Life-Course Criminology." *Studies on Crime and Crime Prevention* 4: 143-158.

————. 2005. "A General Age-Graded Theory of Crime: Lessons Learned and the Future of Life-Course Criminology." Pp. 165-181 in D. P. Farrington (ed.), *Integrated Developmental and Life-Course Theories of Offending*. New Brunswick, NJ: Transaction Publishers.

Thornberry, T.P., and M.D. Krohn, M. D. 2001. "The Development of Delinquency: An Interactional Perspective." Pp. 289-305 in S. O. White (ed.), *Handbook of Youth and Justice*. New York: Plenum.

————. 2005. "Applying Interactional Theory to the Explanation of Continuity and Change in Antisocial Behavior." Pp. 183-209 in D. P. Farrington (ed.), *Integrated Developmental and Life-Course Theories of Offending*. New Brunswick, NJ: Transaction Publishers.

Thornberry, T.P., A.J. Lizotte, M.D. Krohn, C.A. Smith, and K. Porter. 2003. "Causes and Consequences of Delinquency: Findings From the Rochester Youth Development Study." Pp. 11-45 in T. P. Thornberry and M. D. Krohn (eds.), *Taking Stock of Delinquency: An Overview of Findings From Contemporary Longitudinal Studies*. New York: Kluwer/Plenum.

Wikström. P-O.H. 2005. "The Social Origins of Pathways in Crime: Towards a Developmental Ecological Action Theory of Crime Involvement and Its Changes." Pp. 211-245 in D. P. Farrington (ed.), *Integrated Developmental and Life-Course Theories of Offending* . New Brunswick, NJ: Transaction Publishers.

Part V

Theories of Societal Reaction

13

The Empirical Status of Deterrence Theory: A Meta-Analysis

*Travis C. Pratt, Francis T. Cullen, Kristie R. Blevins,
Leah E. Daigle, and Tamara D. Madensen*

Rooted in the classical school of criminology and its rational choice view of human behavior (see Beccaria 1764), deterrence theory possesses two features that increase its appeal, especially outside the boundaries of academia. First, unlike many of its theoretical rivals, the deterrence approach offers an easily understood, straightforward *explanation of crime*: individuals choose to go into crime when it "pays"—that is, when the benefits outweigh the costs. People may not be perfectly rational, but they are reasonably aware of the potential costs and benefits associated with criminal acts. When faced with the prospect that a wayward act will elicit punishment, they are likely to "think twice" and be "deterred" from choosing this course of action.

Second, unlike many of its theoretical rivals, the deterrence approach offers an easily understood, straightford *solution to crime*: the choice of crime can be made less attractive by implementing policies that heighten the costs of illegal conduct—that is, laws and penalties that ensure that criminal participation "does not pay" (Nagin 1998a). It seems only a matter of "common sense" that raising the costs or likely risks of crime should involve the criminal justice system, the state's instrument for detecting the criminally wayward and inflicting punishment on them. Such crime-curbing activities may come in the form of more rigorous police practices, prosecuting offenders more efficiently, and/or legislatively increasing the severity of certain criminal sanctions (Greenberg, Kessler, and Logan 1979; Logan 1975; Wilson and Boland 1978). The central empirical claim of deterrence theory, therefore, is that these types of public efforts "matter," and that they should, independent of other social processes, have an appreciable effect on criminal behavior (Tittle 1969, 1980; Tittle and Rowe 1974).

After its initial dominance, deterrence theory was later abandoned by criminologists in favor of positivist perspectives on criminology in the early 1900s—which emphasized biological factors such as innate intelligence or genetic determinism (Goddard 1914; Lombroso-Ferrero 1911)—and, later, sociological explanations of crime such as strain, differential association, social bond, and social learning theories (see the discussion by Pratt, Maahs, and Stehr 1998). However, a renewed interest in the deterrence perspective was piqued in the late 1960s with Becker's (1968) economic perspective, which was bolstered by policy-related questions concerning the potential crime-reduction capacity of rising prison populations (Blumstein, Cohen, and Nagin 1978; Nagin 1998b).

Indeed, in addition to its role in the construction of "basic" knowledge about crime, deterrence theory has proven to be salient because of its implicit or explicit embrace by lawmakers in the United States—in part, we suspect, because it resonates with the common-sense belief that people avoid things that are painful (whether hot burners on stoves or the threat of imprisonment). Reflecting the deterrence-based doctrine of "getting tough," interventions aimed at stiffening the punishments for virtually all types of crime have predominated criminal justice policymaking over last three decades (Cullen, Pratt, Miceli, and Moon 2002). As a result of these sustained efforts to deal with crime through enhanced punishments, the United States now has more of its citizens locked up behind bars (over 2.2 million) than the entire population of Kuwait (see Pratt, forthcoming), not to mention another 4.7 million under some form of community supervision (Bureau of Justice Statistics 2001). As such, there appears to be a need—in both a basic and applied sense—to determine the *empirical* validity of the deterrence perspective.

Questions about the empirical status of deterrence theory at the macro-level have been addressed by Pratt and Cullen's (2005) meta-analysis of over 200 aggregate-level studies of crime. Their investigation revealed that many of the variables specified in macro-level tests of the deterrence perspective—such as increased police size/police per capita, arrest ratios and clearance rates, stiffer sentencing policies, and other "get tough" policies (e.g., police crackdowns, state-sanctioned executions)—were consistently among the weakest predictors of crime rates across virtually all levels of aggregation. Even so, one could argue that, as originally conceived, deterrence theory is more focused on the way *individuals* weigh or *perceive* the relative costs and benefits associated with their behavioral choices.

To that end, a considerable amount of criminologists' attention has been devoted toward examining the effects of the *perceived* certainty and severity of punishment on the likelihood of offending. Studies of the "certainty" of punishment—or respondents' estimates of the odds of apprehension for a given offense—are most common in the perceptual deterrence literature. Although mixed, the findings across studies generally indicate a moderate inverse relationship between the two variables (e.g., compare Anderson, Chiricos, and Waldo 1977; Bachman, Paternoster, and Ward 1992; Bishop 1984; Burkett and Ward 1993; Cernkovich and Giordano 1992; Decker, Wright, and Logie 1993; Fogalia 1997; Green 1989; Hollinger and Clark 1983; Horney and Marshall 1992; Kraut 1976; Lanza-Kaduce 1988; Lanza-Kaduce, Bishop, and Winner 1997; Montmarquette, Nerlove, and Forest 1985; Nagin and Paternoster 1991a; Paternoster and Piquero 1995; Piquero and Rengert 1999; Saltzman, Paternoster, Waldo, and Chiricos 1982; Sherman and Berk 1984; Simpson and Koper 1992; Smith and Gartin 1989). The results for the studies evaluating the criminogenic effects of individuals' "severity of punishment" estimates, however, are generally weaker than those assessing certainty estimates (see, e.g., Anderson et al. 1977; Decker et al. 1993; Dejong 1997; Kraut 1976; Nagin and Pogarsky 2003; Paternoster, Saltzman, Waldo, and Chiricos 1983; Smith and Paternoster 1987; Weisburd, Waring, and Chayet 1995; Williams 1985). These mixed findings are compounded by variation in how researchers measure the various "sanction threats"—from separate certainty and severity estimates, to combined indexes of the two, to even the inclusion of the potential "non-legal costs" associated with punishment (see Akers, Krohn, Lanza-Kaduce, and Radosevich 1979; Bachman et al. 1992; Bishop 1984; Evans, Cullen, Dunaway, and Burton 1995; Grasmick and Bryjak 1980; Kingsnorth 1991; Larzelere and Patterson 1990; Makkai and Braithwaite 1994; Paternoster and Iovanni 1986; Piliavin, Gartner, Thornton and Matsueda 1986; Piquero and Paternoster 1998; Tittle 1977; Tittle and Rowe 1973; Williams and Hawkins 1989). Thus, the empirical status of individual-level tests of the deterrence perspective still needs to be determined.

Accordingly, our analysis builds upon Paternoster's (1987) review of the perceptual deterrence literature. A number of important findings emerged from his review. Most notably, Paternoster (1987: 173) argued that cross-sectional studies showing an inverse effect of perceived sanctions on self-reported criminal/deviant behavior may simply reflect the "experiential effect"—that is, how experiences with crime/deviance shape individuals' perceptions of the certainty and severity of punishments, rather than vice versa (see also Apospori and Alpert 1992; Bridges and Stone 1986; Carmichael, Langton, Pendell, Reitzel, and Piquero 2005; Minor and Harry 1982; Paternoster et al. 1983; Saltzman et al. 1982). If so, then a person's perception of punishment may be, in Paternoster's (1987: 179) words, "a *consequence* rather than a cause of deviant involvement." In addition to the problem of causal ordering, Paternoster noted that when studies control for other "known" predictors of crime (e.g., social bonds, moral beliefs, and/or peer involvement in delinquency), the inverse effect of the perceived certainty and severity of punishment on crime/deviance tends to disappear.

Despite this impressive contribution to the criminological literature, much has happened in the world of deterrence theory since Paternoster's (1987)

review. Indeed, new theoretical advances have been made and the roster of
empirical tests of deterrence theory has continued to grow. As such, the purpose of the present review is to pause and to reassess what is currently known
about the empirical status of deterrence theory. In "taking stock" of deterrence
theory, our objective is twofold: first, to determine the overall magnitude—or
average "effect size"—of the relationship between deterrence variables and
crime/deviance across the body of existing literature; and, second, to examine
how support for the theory varies systematically according to how researchers
go about testing it (i.e., does studying deterrence in particular ways tend to
reveal more or less support for the theory?). In the end, we find that the effects
of the variables specified by deterrence theory on crime/deviance are, at best,
weak—especially in studies that employ more rigorous research designs. Given
this pattern of findings, we argue that the continued vitality of the deterrence
perspective will hinge on the ability of scholars to integrate it into other—perhaps more comprehensive and empirically robust—theoretical frameworks.

Theoretical Developments and Empirical Advances in Deterrence Research

The literature on deterrence theory has undergone a number of changes in
recent years. With the rise of new ways of thinking about rational decision-
making and offending, four developments have changed the way criminologists
view the deterrence perspective: (1) the effectiveness of certain situational crime
prevention strategies (Clarke 1992; Kelling and Coles 1996); (2) the recognition
of the importance of the "non-legal costs" of criminal behavior (Braithwaite
1989; Sherman 1993; Tittle 1977); (3) the integration of deterrence theory
with other criminological perspectives, such as social learning and self-control
theories (Stafford and Warr 1993; Piquero and Tibbetts 1996); and (4) how the
imposition of sanctions can actually lower individuals' perceived estimates
of getting caught in the future, known as the "resetting effect" (Pogarsky and
Piquero 2003).

Deterrence Theory and Situational Crime Prevention

Based on Cohen and Felson's (1979) early work on routine activity theory
(see also Felson 1987, 1994; Felson and Cohen 1980), advocates of situational crime prevention strategies have re-cast the rational choice/deterrence
model in a way that emphasizes the importance of structural constraints that
may limit the potential "choices" of would-be offenders. Although these
strategies vary considerably in terms of what types of crime control strategies will serve as a deterrent in any given situation—from aggressive policing
practices (Mazerolle, Kadleck, and Roehl 1998; Sampson and Cohen 1988;
cf. Eck and Maguire 2000) to a natural "distance decay" function for suitable
targets for auto theft (Potchak, McGloin, and Zgoba 2002)—all of them share

the assumption that offenders engage in, at minimum, a cursory cost-benefit analysis that results in some perceptual estimate regarding the likelihood of apprehension (Clarke 1995).

In essence, the situational crime prevention approach takes a different theoretical route from traditional deterrence theory—one that has little to say about how to reduce the level of "criminal motivation" within a given individual. Rather, this perspective simply assumes that such offenders exist, and that they are, by definition, predisposed to engage in a particular pattern of offending in the absence of some external reason not to do so. In the words of routine activity theory, when individuals are presented with opportunities (suitable targets) divorced from capable guardians (either formal or informal) that may serve as a deterrent, "crime happens." Accordingly, looking at the deterrence perspective through this lens has resulted in a rather sizeable body of empirical literature that we feel can be assessed systematically within a deterrence theory framework.

Deterrence Theory and the Importance of "Non-Legal Costs"

Contemporary rational choice theorists stick to the fundamental notion that individuals behave in a way that is expected to maximize their personal utility (Clarke and Cornish 2001)—put differently, to incur the greatest benefit at the lowest personal cost. Although Paternoster's (1987) review highlighted how the threat of formal (legal) sanctions alone exerts little influence over the "cost calculus" portion of the utility equation, recent perspectives have noted how the imposition of criminal sanctions can set into motion a series of "non-legal" costs that individuals may find to be more consequential to their lives.

In particular, the potential for shame and loss of respect associated with being caught for committing a crime plays heavily in the rational decision process (see, e.g., Braithwaite 1989)—especially for individuals who may already have strong informal social bonds to legitimate social institutions (Sherman 1993). To be sure, research has indicated that perceptions of anticipated shame may serve as a deterrent to a wide spectrum of criminal/deviant behavior (Grasmick and Bursik 1990; Grasmick, Bursik, and Arneklev 1993; Grasmick, Bursik, and Kinsey 1991; Klepper and Nagin 1989; Nagin and Paternoster 1993; Tibbetts and Myers 1999). Although scholars have noted that high levels of shame can lead to increased levels of other behavioral problems (Cook 1996; Goldberg 1991), the general consensus—at least with regard to deterrence theory—is that as the "social costs" associated with criminal behavior increase, the likelihood that individuals will engage in such behavior decreases (Bishop 1984; Paternoster and Iovanni 1986; Tittle 1977; Tittle and Rowe 1973; Williams and Hawkins 1989).

Deterrence and Theoretical Integration

Another trend that has emerged in the last decade or so is that of integrating the deterrence/rational choice perspective with other criminological theories. Two of these efforts deserve particular attention: the integration of deterrence theory with concepts derived from social learning and self-control theories.

First, Stafford and Warr (1993) presented a "reconceptualization" of deterrence theory that addressed how both direct and indirect—or what Paternoster and Piquero (1995) dubbed "personal" and "vicarious"—experiences with punishment may act as a system of social reinforcements (see Akers 1990; Bandura 1977). In particular, they argued that individuals who have offended and been caught (direct experience with punishment), or have knowledge of others who have offended and been caught (indirect experience with punishment), are less likely to offend in the future. Accordingly, either direct or indirect experience with offending and "getting away with it"—what Stafford and Warr (1993: 125) term "punishment avoidance"—acts as a negative reinforcer (i.e., the suspension of an unpleasant consequence, or punishment), which should increase the likelihood of future offending. Thus, when viewed in the context of the social learning perspective, the decision process underlying offending behavior is subject to an operant conditioning response (either a punisher or a negative reinforcer), either through personal experience or the "modeling" behavior exhibited by others, which will influence individuals' future cost/benefit analyses for engaging in crime or deviance (see also Gray, Ward, Stafford, and Menke 1985).

In a second theoretical development, Piquero and Tibbetts (1996) integrated concepts from the situational crime prevention and self-control literatures with the deterrence/rational choice perspective. Building on the work of Nagin and Paternoster (1993), their analysis revealed how individuals' perceptions of situational constraints associated with offending, such as the perceived pleasure derived from offending and perceptions of shame as well as the perceived likelihood of being sanctioned, were both shaped by the respondents' levels of self-control (see also Pogarsky 2002)—a criminogenic risk factor that has consistently been linked to criminal/deviant behavior (Pratt and Cullen 2000). Put differently, Piquero and Tibbetts's (1996) analysis indicates that perceptions of sanction threats—including individuals' evaluations of the potential "non-legal costs" of offending and getting caught—are, to a certain extent, determined by an individual's level of self-control (see also Nagin and Pogarsky 2001, 2003). More specifically, their study found that individuals with low self-control are less likely to perceive "situational shame" from offending, are more likely to derive "pleasure" from criminal behavior, and are less likely to be concerned about the threat of formal sanctions (Piquero and Tibbetts 1996: 497, 501).

In the end, what both of these theoretical revisions to deterrence theory have in common is the notion that an individual's cost/benefit analysis—the central concept of deterrence theory—is *endogenous* to a number of other factors that may (e.g., direct and/or indirect punishment experiences) or may not (self-control) have anything to do with the threat of formal sanctions for criminal behavior. These theoretical developments also point to the need to recognize how individuals' perceptions of sanction threats are embedded within a host of other personal and contextual factors. To that end, the most recent theoretical development in the literature on deterrence theory also recognizes how the consequences of the imposition of punishment can be much more complex than early deterrence theorists imagined.

Deterrence Theory and the "Resetting Effect"

The body of "shaming" research points to the growing recognition of the complex effects that criminal sanctions have on individuals' future criminal behavior (Hay 2001). Even independent of shame, however, research has emerged indicating that individuals who have been punished end up being more inclined to commit future offenses than those who have not been punished (Paternoster and Piquero 1995; Piquero and Paternoster 1998; Piquero and Pogarsky 2002). This pattern of findings is counterintuitive with deterrence theory in general, and with Paternoster's (1987) notion of the "experiential effect" in particular (see also Stafford and Warr 1993; Williams and Hawkins 1986).

One potential explanation for these findings—and one that is consistent with deterrence theory—is that as offenders continue to break the law, they increase their potential exposure to getting caught (see, e.g., Gibbs 1975). Accordingly, the positive effect of punishment on future criminal behavior may simply be an artifact of the punishment of the most "high rate" offenders, who are also likely to score rather low on the "perception of sanctions" scales. As an alternative explanation, Pogarsky and Piquero (2003: 96) draw on the notion of the "gambler's fallacy" (see also Gilovich 1983; McKenna 1993), where offenders who have been caught may "increase their bets after apprehension" under the assumption that getting caught the first time was a mere fluke. Following this logic, the offenders who believe that their experience with getting nabbed for their crimes was a low probability event will therefore "reset" their perception of sanction threats downward, "apparently believing they would have to be exceedingly unlucky to be apprehended again" (Pogarsky and Piquero 2003: 96).

In their analysis of the decision to drive drunk, Pogarsky and Piquero (2003) found partial support for the resetting hypothesis, particularly with regard to low-risk subjects. Although additional research is certainly warranted in this area, this study again points to the notion that the consequences of punishment on individuals' future decision-making are much more complex than the early deterrence theorists assumed. Indeed, the body of deterrence theory literature contains empirical studies that reveal positive, inverse, and null results with regard to crime and deviance, depending largely upon the conditions under which the punishment is imposed.

Summary

Despite the apparent simplicity of the theoretical framework offered by deterrence theory, determining its empirical validity has not been so easy. This difficulty is not due to a lack of existing tests of propositions derived from deterrence theory; it is one of the more extensively tested theories of crime. Rather, the spectrum of methodological variations that has characterized the deterrence literature since the late 1970s and 1980s has muddied the waters concerning whether, and under what conditions, variables from deterrence theory will significantly predict individuals' participation in crime. The purpose of this review, therefore, is to systematically organize what this body of literature tells us about how the threat of sanctions—whether through formal channels or through the social costs such sanctions may set in motion—are related to criminal behavior.

Research Strategy

Our current understanding of the empirical status of the major research questions in criminology in general—and of the relationship between deterrence variables and crime/deviance in particular—relies almost exclusively on narrative literature reviews (see, e.g., Akers 1997; Bursik 1988; Burton and Cullen 1992; Kempf 1993; Simpson, Piquero, and Paternoster 2002; Tibbetts and Gibson 2002; Wakschlag, Pickett, Cook, Benowitz, and Leventhal 2002). Although exceptions certainly exist (Lipsey and Derzon 1998; Loeber and Stouthamer-Loeber 1986; Paternoster 1987; Pratt and Cullen 2000, 2005; Pratt, Cullen, Blevins, Daigle, and Unnever 2002; Tittle, Villemez, and Smith 1978), narrative literature reviews still dominate the practice of "knowledge organization" in criminology (see also the discussion by Pratt 2002).

Compared to a narrative review of research literature, a meta-analysis has four potential advantages. First, it can provide for a more precise estimate (e.g., a "mean effect size estimate") of the magnitude of the relationship between certain key theoretical variables and crime/deviance across all empirical tests. Second, it affords the researcher the opportunity to test for the conditioning effects of various methodological variations on the specified relationships (e.g., when certain variables are measured differently; across different types of samples; in longitudinal versus cross-sectional research designs). Third, since coding and measurement decisions are "public," as they would be in any other original quantitative study, the meta-analysis can be replicated by other researchers. Finally, the database for a meta-analysis is cumulative; thus, as additional studies are conducted and published, they can be added to the sample of studies and the key relationships can be reassessed.

The purpose of the current study, therefore, is to move beyond the narrative review of literature approach to subject the body of empirical examinations of the relationship between variables specified by deterrence theory and crime/deviance to a meta-analysis. In so doing, two issues will be addressed. First, we will calculate the overall mean effect size of the relationship between deterrence variables and crime/deviance. The second issue concerns the degree to which the calculated mean effect size estimates differ according to methodological variations across the sample of studies. To explore this possibility, we statistically examine the potential conditioning effects of certain methodological characteristics on the deterrence-crime/deviance effect size estimates.

Methods

Sample

The sample of studies was generated in three stages, the first of which involved a literature search through a number of electronic databases through the year 2003.[1] Second, and consistent with the guidelines set forth by Petrosino (1995), prior narrative reviews of the criminological literature were examined to search for additional tests of deterrence theory. Finally, studies that did not explicitly test the deterrence perspective, but included such measures in their statistical models, were also included in the sample. Overall, the sample includes forty empirical studies, which generated a total of 200 effect size estimates.[2]

Despite our sampling procedures, one potential problem associated with the meta-analysis of empirical literature is that the decision-makers associated with academic journals (editors and reviewers) may be biased in favor of statistically significant findings (see Wolf 1986)—so much so that literature searches may not uncover every study of a particular hypothesis that has been conducted. Rosenthal (1979) refers to this as the "file drawer" problem due to the tendency of studies failing to reveal significant relationships to be stashed away in file drawers by their authors and forgotten. This omission of "null-model" studies may therefore limit the utility of meta-analyses that are conducted on published research only (as is the case here). In our analysis, if there is a file drawer bias in favor of reporting significant findings, it would mean that we overestimate the strength of a deterrent effect.

We should note that the file drawer problem also applies to narrative reviews of literature as well. The difference, however, is that meta-analysis has a method for estimating the degree to which the review may be plagued by this potential bias: a statistical estimate for the number of unmeasured studies that would have to contain a null finding to reduce the mean effect size estimates so that they are not significantly different from zero. In other words, we calculate the number of studies failing to reject the null hypothesis—referred to as the "fail-safe N"—that would be needed to reverse a conclusion that a statistically significant relationship exists.[3]

Effect Size Estimate

The effect size estimate used is a standardized correlation coefficient r. This estimate was chosen because of its ease of interpretation, and because formulae are available for converting other test statistics (e.g., F, t, chi-square) into an r (see Rosenthal 1978, 1984). Using Fisher' s r to z transformation (see Wolf 1986), the effect size estimates (r values or standardized regression coefficients from multivariate models) were converted to a $z(r)$ score. The correlation coefficients were converted to z-values because the sampling distribution of $z(r)$-scores is assumed to approach normality, whereas the sampling distribution for r is skewed for all values other than zero (Blalock 1972).[4] Normally distributed effect size estimates are necessary for: (1) the accurate determination of values of central tendency for the effect size estimates; and, for (2) unbiased tests of statistical significance (Hanushek and Jackson 1977).

Predictor Domains

The effect size estimates recorded from each study are grouped under four predictor domains that are assumed to have different effects on the likelihood that individuals will engage in crime/delinquency. These domains include measures of: the *certainty of punishment*, the *severity of punishment*, *deterrence theory composites* (or indexed scales), and *the threat of non-legal sanctions* (e.g., the potential loss of employment, spouse, respect). Tests for heterogeneity[5] were conducted within each of these predictor domains and none revealed significant heterogeneity, suggesting that grouping the effect size estimates this way was statistically appropriate.

Effect Size Weighting

Sample Size. Separate analyses were conducted on each $z(r)$ after they were weighted for sample size, according to the method recommended by Rosenthal (1984), by taking the product of the $z(r)$ value and the appropriate degrees of freedom (sample size-3) from each study. Weighting the studies on the basis of their sample sizes was done to place a greater emphasis on those studies yielding outcomes from larger samples which are assumed to be more representative of the population of interest (Rosenthal 1984; see also Blalock 1972; Hanushek and Jackson 1977).

Independence of Effect Size Estimates. Separate analyses were also conducted when the mean effect size estimates were adjusted for the potential biases associated with coding multiple effect size estimates from the same dataset (i.e., the lack of statistical independence). As noted, the sample of studies (n = 40) contributed 200 effect size estimates. This means that most of the studies contributed more than one effect size estimate for our analysis (e.g., for measuring key variables in different ways; across different subsets of the sample), and that the number of effect size estimates drawn from individual studies varied in number. We had two reasons for including multiple effect sizes from individual studies. First, and most important, selecting only one effect size estimate from each study would severely limit our ability to examine how methodological variations across the studies potentially influence the effect size estimates. Second, it would be difficult to develop a methodologically defensible decision rule for selecting one effect size estimate while ignoring others from the same study. According to Pratt and Cullen (2000: 941), selecting only one effect size estimate from these different analyses "could introduce, wittingly or unwittingly, a 'researcher' bias."

We recognize, however, that coding multiple effect size estimates from the same study can *potentially* introduce a measure of bias into the meta-analysis. To the extent that one study produces a greater number of effect size estimates than do other studies, it may disproportionately contribute to the mean effect size reported across the sample of studies in the meta-analysis. Furthermore, similar to any other dataset with a hierarchical structure, this problem may also create estimation errors in a meta-analysis by reducing the variance estimates in effect sizes across studies which may, therefore, artificially increase the likelihood that the mean effect size estimates will turn out to be significantly different from zero (see Pratt 2000).

Given these concerns, the correction we employed for this potential bias involved the serial correlation correction first discussed by Pratt and Cullen (2000). This procedure creates uncorrelated residuals for effect sizes within datasets by assigning weights to each contributing effect size estimate according to the degree to which it is statistically interdependent with the other effect size estimates from the same dataset (n = 35 independent datasets across all studies), where greater statistical interdependencies are weighted downward.

Unobserved Heterogeneity. The final weighting procedure is intended to address the problems associated with gathering effect size estimates from multivariate models. Critics contend that standardized regression coefficients from multivariate models cannot be combined because of variations in model specification across studies (Hedges and Olkin 1985). Methods have, however, been developed for modeling multivariate effect sizes (Kalaian and Raudenbush 1996; Raudenbush, Becker, and Kalaian 1988), yet such approaches assume that a full variance-covariance matrix is provided by the authors of each study, which is rarely the case. As an alternative method, we treat the variation in the effect size estimates from multivariate models as "unobserved heterogeneity"—an approach that is widely accepted in other areas of criminology and criminal justice (see, e.g., Brame, Bushway, and Paternoster 1999; Kessler and Greenberg 1981; Land and Nagin 1996; Nagin and Paternoster 1991b; Worrall and Pratt 2004)—which gives lesser weight to those effect sizes with greater unobserved heterogeneity (i.e., those that are most sensitive to differences in model specification).[6]

Methodological Control Variables

A number of methodological characteristics were coded from each study to determine the degree to which they systematically influence the effect size estimates. The first set of factors are related to the sample characteristics, including the *gender* (with separate categories for mixed, male only, and female only samples), *race* (with separate categories for racially heterogeneous, white only, black only, white and black only, and race-unclear samples), and *age composition* of the sample (with separate categories for juveniles under seventeen, young adults eighteen to twenty-five, adults over twenty-five, juvenile-adult combo, and age-unclear samples), as well as the *sampling frame* (with separate categories for general, school-non-college, school-college, incarcerated adults, non-incarcerated adult offenders, and non-incarcerated juvenile offender sampling frames) used by the authors.

The second set of methodological characteristics that were coded relate to each study's model specification and research design. These factors include whether variables from *competing theories* were controlled (as well as separate categories for each of the major criminological theories), whether the *experiential effect* was estimated, and whether the research design was *cross-sectional versus longitudinal*. We also coded for the measurement of the *dependent variable* (e.g., type of offense), and whether the measure tapped into actual behavior versus "intentions to offend" based on the vignette method.

Results

The results of our analysis are presented in two stages. First, we calculated the mean effect size estimates, in their unweighted and weighted forms, for each of the four deterrence theory predictor domains specified above (the certainty of punishment, the severity of punishment, deterrence/sanction composites, the effect of non-legal costs). In the second stage of the analysis, we explored how each of these deterrence predictors varies according to methodological variations across studies. Taken together, the purpose of our analyses is to uncover the overall "strength" and "stability" of the relationships between the variables specified by deterrence theory and crime/deviance.

Strength of Effects

Table 13.1 displays the mean effect size estimates for each of the deterrence theory predictor domains. A considerable amount of information is presented here, but three issues are of particular importance. First, regardless of whether the effect sizes are weighted or unweighted, with the exception of a few of the bivariate estimates, none of the mean effect size estimates are particularly strong. Indeed, when examining all effect sizes taken together, only the certainty estimates and the effects of non-legal sanctions are large enough to be considered substantively important (ranging from -.171 to -.334, all at p<.05)[7]—a finding noted by previous narrative reviews of the deterrence literature (see, e.g., Nagin 1998a), but indicated more precisely here. To be sure, the effects of "severity" estimates and deterrence/sanction composites, even when statistically significant, are too weak to be of substantive significance (consistently below -.10).

Second, with only a couple of exceptions, none of the weighting procedures significantly impacted the calculation of the mean effect size estimates. Only the sample size weighted mean effect sizes for the certainty estimates in the pooled (all effect size estimates included) and bivariate mean effect size estimates were affected. Thus, the calculation of the mean effect size estimates were not consistently biased upward or downward as a result of variations in sample size, statistical interdependencies, or unobserved heterogeneity across studies.

Table 13.1
Mean Effect Size Estimates, Unweighted and Weighted by Sample Size

Predictor	All Effect Size Estimates	Bivariate Effect Size Estimates	Multivariate Effect Size Estimates
Certainty (n=107)	-.171**/-.334***†	-.268**/-.705***†	-.134**/-.101**
	(-.179**)	(-.256**)	(-.149**)
	[-.209**]	[-.314**]	[-.172**]
Severity (n=47)	-.049*/-.027*	-.085**/-.072*	-.026/-.021
	(-.053*)	(-.089**)	(-.032)
	[-.060*]	[-.116*]	[-.033]
Composite (n=31)	-.032/-.045	-.009/-.036	-.069*/-.056**
	(.043)	(-.025)	(-.068**)
	[-.005]	[.009]	[-.043]
Non-legal sanctions (n=15)	-.177*/-.177*	-.580*/-.520*	-.115**/-.143**
	(-.206*)	(-.580)	(-.135**)
	[-.183*]	[-.580*]	[-.098**]

Note: Effect size estimates are presented as unweighted/sample size weighted, with serial correlation weighted estimates in parenthesis and unobserved heterogeneity weighted estimates in brackets.

* = p<.05

** = p<.01

† = significantly different from unweighted mean effect size.

Finally, Table 13.1 indicates that the mean effect size estimates for nearly all of the deterrence theory predictors are substantially reduced when moving from bivariate to multivariate models. Although the deterrence theory/sanction composite mean effect sizes are an exception (and the mean effect sizes, while at times statistically significant, are well below -.10), the certainty estimates' mean effect size is reduced by 50 percent (-.286 to -.134), the severity estimates' mean effect size is reduced by 69 percent (-.085 to -.026), and the non-legal sanctions mean effect size is reduced by 80 percent (-.580 to -.115) from the bivariate to the multivariate designs.[8] The broad trend, therefore, is consistent with Paternoster's (1987) finding that, across all studies, the effects of deterrence variables on crime/deviance are substantially reduced—even, at times, to the point of statistical insignificance—in multivariate versus bivariate models.

Stability of Effects

We assessed the stability of the effects of the deterrence theory predictors[9] (i.e., the degree to which they systematically vary according to methodological differences) according to both sample characteristics and model specification and research design. Table 13.2 displays the mean effect size estimates for

Table 13.2

Methodological Conditioning Effects for Serial Correlation Weighted Multivariate Deterrence Effect Size Estimates by Sample Characteristics

Sample characteristic	Certainty (n=78)	Severity (n=29)	Composite (12)	Non-Legal Sanctions (13)
Gender				
Mixed	-.191**	-.033	—	-.166*
Males Only	-.071*	-.016	—	-.053
Females Only	-.099	.010	—	.035
Race				
Heterogeneous	-.165*	—	-.015	-.150*
White Only	-.099	—	-.116*	
Black Only	-.036	—	—	
White and Black Only	-.160	—	—	-.160
Unclear	-.113	—	—	.017
Age				
Juveniles (<17)	-.085*	.002	—	-.133
Young Adults (18-25)	-.457**	-.148	-.039	.017
Adults (25+)	-.189**	.058	-.074*	-.119
Juvenile-Adult Combo	-.058*	-.028	.041	-.159*
Unclear	-.050	-.018*	—	—
Sampling Frame				
General	-.131*	-.008	-.079*	-.154*
School (Non-College)	-.103*	.002	—	-.133
School (College)	-.342*	-.148	—	.017
Incarcerated Adults	-.069*	—	—	—
Non-Incarcerated Adult Offenders	-.089*	-.016*	-.035	—
Non-Incarcerated Juvenile Offenders	—	—	-.039	—

* = p<.05
** = p<.01

the impact of sample characteristics on the deterrence theory mean effect size estimates. Three issues warrant particular attention.

First, when broken down by these various sample specifications, less than half of the mean effect size estimates are statistically significant (21 of 51, or 41 percent). Second, for the most part there is not much variation in the mean effect sizes across these sample specifications. The primary reason for this finding is that, with a couple of exceptions, the mean effect sizes presented in Table 13.2 are uniformly weak (31 of 51, or 61 percent, are below -.10).[10] Finally, the strongest effects are found for the certainty estimates' mean effect sizes in young adult samples (mean effect size = -.457, p<.01) and in studies using college-aged sampling frames (mean effect size = -.342, p<.05). Not surprisingly, these two methodological factors are related to one another—a condition that is common when examining the variability of effects in meta-analyses (see Lipsey 2003). Accordingly, there is no way to disentangle whether these relatively strong effects are attributable to the age of the sample or to the approach of using college student sampling frames.

Table 13.3 contains the results of our analyses of the variability of effects according to differences in model specification and research design across studies. Again, with a few exceptions, most of the mean effect size estimates broken down by methodological specification are rather weak. Forty-one percent of the effect sizes displayed in Table 13.3 fail to reach statistical significance (21 of 51) and 59 percent (30 of 51) have a mean effect size below -.10.[11]

Despite this general pattern of weak effects, the mean effect sizes for the certainty predictors are consistently the most robust (often over -.10 and as high as -.544). Nevertheless, Table 13.3 also indicates that the mean effect size of the certainty predictors is substantially reduced in multivariate models that control for variables from competing theories and/or control for the "experiential effect" (e.g., prior criminal/deviant behavior). Specifically, the mean effect size for the certainty predictors is reduced by 69 percent with the controls for competing theories[12] (-.232 to -.072), and is reduced by 62 percent with controls for the experiential effect (-.208 to -.080).

Finally, although no clear pattern emerges with regard to the time dimension component (cross-sectional versus longitudinal designs), issues associated with the dependent variable are of interest. In particular, the mean effect size estimates are generally strongest—especially for the certainty estimates—in the "other" dependent variable category. What makes this finding of substantive interest is that this category of dependent variables is comprised mostly of white-collar/organization offending measures (see, e.g., Horney and Marshall 1992; Makkai and Braithwaite 1994; Simpson and Koper 1992; Tittle 1977; Tittle and Rowe 1973; cf. Simpson and Piquero 2002).

Of additional interest is the finding that the mean effect size estimates for the severity estimates and the effect of non-legal sanctions are stronger when

Table 13.3
Methodological Conditioning Effects for Serial Correlation Weighted
Multivariate Deterrence Effect Size Estimates by Model Specification
and Research Design Characteristics

Sample characteristic	Certainty (n=78)	Severity (n=29)	Composite (12)	Non-Legal Sanctions (13)
Variables from Competing Theories Controlled?				
No	-.232**	-.033	-.061	--
Yes	-.072*	-.031	-.071*	--
Control for Experiential Effect?				
No	-.208**	-.018	-.079*	-.087
Yes	-.080*	-.048*	-.036*	-.159*
Time Dimension				
Cross-sectional	-.121*	-.037	-.069*	-.138*
Longitudinal	-.195*	-.024	-.067	-.087
Dependent Variable				
Property Crime Scale	-.144	--	--	--
Alcohol/Drug Scale	-.140	--	--	--
Specific Violent Offense	-.071*	-.070*	--	-.170
Specific Property Offense	-.053*	-.043*	--	-.190*
Specific Sexual Assault Offense	-.113*	--	--	.017
Specific Alcohol/Drug Offense	-.180*	.026	.041	-.066
General Deviance/Delinquency Scale	-.098*	.068	-.070*	-.133
Other	-.544*	-.108*	-.160*	--
Dependent Variable Method				
Self-Reported Behavioral	-.159*	-.018	--	-.127*
Official Records Behavioral	-.106*	-.052	--	--
Scenario/Vignettes	-.136	-.045*	--	-.137*

* = p<.05
** = p<.01

measured via the "vignette" method. This result again highlights how a number
of the methodological factors being assessed here are related to one another. For
example, many of the studies that employ the vignette method are conducted
on convenience samples of college students. Thus, taken together, the pattern
of results reported here indicates that support for the deterrence perspective
is most likely to be found in studies that: (1) draw on college students' self-
reported intentions to offend based vignettes/scenarios of various offenses; or
(2) those that assess white-collar/organizational offending.

Discussion

Four decades ago, Jackson Toby (1964: 332) could observe that readers of
criminology textbooks "might infer that punishment is a vestigal carryover of
a barbaric past and will disappear as humanitarianism and rationality spread."
Much has changed. Today, the criminal justice system is enmeshed in a "culture of control" (Garland 2001) that has produced a "penal harm movement"
(Clear 1994) and an unprecedented era of "harsh justice" (Whitman 2003).

Humanitarian corrections now seems like a quaint ideal in the face of an array of "get tough" policies that have made escalating sentence lengths and burgeoning prison populations enduring realities. These policies not only have strained the public treasury but also have exacted a huge human toll while having a questionable impact on public safety (Fass and Pi 2002; Pratt and Cullen, 2005; Currie, 1998; Visher 1987; cf. Bennett, DiIulio, and Walters 1996).

Of course, this "get tough" policy agenda reflects broader transformations in American society that have led to the embrace of a conservative ideology that is seeking to dismantle the welfare state and to impose individual responsibility—and, if needed, punishment—on the wayward poor (Garland 2001). Still, as a discipline, criminology either lends legitimacy to or shows the fallacies of this near-hegemonic approach to crime control. Criminology thus has a responsibility to evaluate both the impact of get tough policies and their theoretical underpinnings. In this latter regard, research on deterrence takes on special significance: it speaks to the issue of whether the premise that harsher punishments will make the choice of crime less attractive is rooted in sound criminological knowledge. In turn, it illuminates whether policies based on the logic of deterrence will, in fact, contribute to public safety. These collective efforts might be ignored, but they also have the potential to create a cumulative knowledge base that, under some circumstances, might shape public policy (Cullen 2005).

Beyond its policy implications, there is another reason to "take stock" of research on deterrence: within criminology, this paradigm has become a viable theory that is prompting theoretical refinements and controversy. Understanding the empirical status of the theory thus provides guidance on the merits of the deterrence perspective and on where future research might most profitably proceed. We should note that the current project is not the only effort to assess the research on deterrence (see, e.g., Cullen et al. 2002; Nagin 1998a, 1998b; Paternoster 1987). Nonetheless, our research has the advantage of using meta-analysis to present an up-to-date report card on the strengths and weaknesses of contemporary deterrence theory. Based on our results, we have five major conclusions.

First, the mean effect sizes of the relationships between crime/deviance and variables specified by deterrence theory are modest to negligble. Hovering typically between zero and -.20 (when all effect sizes are considered, including bivariate estimates), these effects are much weaker than those found in meta-analyses of the relationships between criminal/deviant behavior and peer effects (Andrews and Bonta 1998) and self-control (Pratt and Cullen 2000)—both of which are consistently above .20. This finding suggests that the causes of criminal conduct are multifaceted and extend far outside the limited range of deterrence theory. In turn, this reality explains why punitive crime control policies (e.g., mandatory minimum sentences) and correctional programs that rely on punishment threats (e.g., boot camps, intensive supervision probation/parole) are limited in their capacity to effect long-term behavioral change among offenders (see, e.g., Andrews, Zinger, Hoge, Bonta, Gendreau, and Cullen 1990; Cullen et al. 2002; Cullen, Wright, and Applegate 1996; Petersilia and Turner 1993).

Second, the effect sizes of the deterrence variables are substantially reduced—often to zero—in multivariate models. This trend is particularly evident for the effect size estimates produced by statistical models that control for peer effects, antisocial attitudes, and/or self-control. This finding is consistent with Paternoster's (1987) review of the perceptual deterrence literature, and points to how support for the deterrence perspective is most likely to be found in studies that are methodologically the weakest of the bunch. Taken one step further, the clear drop in predictive power of the deterrence variables from bivariate to multivariate models suggests that empirical support for the effect of formal sanctions on individuals' criminal behavior is most likely an artifact of the failure to control for other "known" predictors of crime/deviance.

Third, the deterrence theory effect sizes are sensitive to a host of methodological variations—especially as they related to sampling frame (college convenience samples versus general samples) and model specification issues (controls for competing theories and the experiential effect; vignette methods; see Table 13.4 for a summary of the results of this series of analyses). Thus, in addition to being relatively weak predictors of crime, the body of deterrence literature suggests that, even if statistically significant, the magnitude of the relationship between deterrence predictors and crime fluctuates considerably according to the methodological choices made by researchers. This problem is certainly not unique to deterrence theory. To be sure, reviews of the literature testing other criminological theories, such as strain (Burton and Cullen 1992), self-control (Pratt and Cullen 2000), and social bond (Kempf 1993) theories, also highlight how support for a theory (or certain propositions derived from a theory) varies systematically according to particular methodological differences across studies. Nevertheless, the general pattern revealed in our meta-analysis is that empirical support for deterrence theory dwindles among studies that are the most rigorous methodologically.

Fourth, the certainty of punishment estimates—one of the predictors specified by deterrence theory that garnered the most consistent support in our analysis—tends to do best when predicting "white-collar" types of offenses (e.g., fraud, tax violations, non-compliance with regulatory laws). It may therefore be useful for criminologists to start thinking about the deterrence perspective in more limited terms—perhaps as more of a "mid-range" theory, as opposed to one that seeks to explain offending generally. The construction of "general theories" is still popular in criminology. With one notable exception (Gottfredson and Hirschi 1990), however, the trend among these theories is one of "integration" (Akers 1998; Colvin 2000; Cullen 1994; Laub and

Table 13.4
Summary of Methodological Conditioning Effects for Variables Specified by Deterrence Theory

Predictor	Overall Magnitude and Variation by Effect Size Weighting	Sample Characteristics	Model Specification & Research Design
Certainty	Substantially overestimated in bivariate form; sensitive to weighting by sample size.	Varies significantly by gender (strongest in mixed samples) and much stronger in college student samples.	Effects are significantly reduced when competing theories and experiential effect are controlled; varies considerably according to the dependent variable.
Severity	Substantially overestimated in bivariate form; loses significance in multivariate designs.	Varies little by sample characteristics; effects are generally weak across all categories.	Varies little by model specification and research design characteristics; effects are generally weak across all categories.
Composite	Generally non-significant; multivariate effect sizes sensitive to unobserved heterogeneity.	Varies little by sample characteristics; effects are generally weak across all categories.	Varies little by model specification and research design characteristics; effects are generally weak across all categories.
Non-Legal Costs	Substantially overestimated in bivariate form; not sensitive to weighting procedures.	Varies significantly by gender and race (strongest in mixed gender and race samples) and from samples drawn from the general population.	Effects are stronger (although not significantly) when experiential effect is controlled and in cross-sectional designs.

Sampson 2003; Moffitt 1993; Sampson and Laub 1993; Tittle 1995) and the recognition that, for a theory to be robust enough to explain all forms of criminal and deviant behavior, it must specify a set of variables that actually predict such behavior empirically. To that end, the deterrence perspective—by itself—falls well short of being a theory that should continue to enjoy the allegiance of criminologists.

Nevertheless, as stated above, we believe that the continued vitality of deterrence theory will hinge on the ability of scholars to integrate it into other—perhaps more comprehensive—theoretical frameworks. As a first step toward that goal, our fifth and final conclusion has to do with the finding that variables indicating the threat of non-legal sanctions were among the most robust of the deterrence theory predictors. This pattern of findings illustrates the importance of linking the deterrence (or rational choice) perspective with theories that rely on other types of control mechanisms, such as self-control and informal social control (see, e.g., Nagin and Paternoster 1993; Piquero and Tibbetts 1996; Tibbetts and Herz 1996; Tibbetts and Myers 1999). On a related note, others have advocated viewing the threat of formal sanctions as having an "indirect" effect on crime and deviance, where the imposition of sanctions may set into motion the non-legal costs mentioned above (see, e.g.,

Williams and Hawkins 1986). Either way, thinking about deterrence theory in these more limited terms—and in conjunction with other theoretical frameworks—will help to yield a more complete understanding of offender decision-making.

In the end, criminologists are not particularly fond of "killing" theories—we are instead more in favor of "tweaking" them in new ways to see if they pan out in their newfangled forms. Deterrence theory is likely to persist in much the same way despite the relatively poor predictive capacity of the variables specified by the theory. What is likely to "save" the perspective, then, is continued research regarding the conditions under which the threat of formal sanctions is likely to influence individuals' behavior. To that end, scholars should continue the lines of research assessing how individual differences and situational characteristics influence certainty and severity perceptions to determine when—and for whom—deterrence "works" (Sherman 1993; see also Piquero, Gomez-Smith, and Langton 2004).

The risk with this approach, however, is that scholars may take this suggestion as advocacy for placing any variable that could conceivably influence an individual's perceptions of the potential costs and benefits of criminal behavior—virtually the whole roster of individual, social, and contextual criminogenic risk factors—under the deterrence umbrella. We see this approach as moving well beyond the boundaries of reasonable theoretical integration to one of theoretical theft. We instead view sanction threats as but one piece in a much larger theoretical puzzle predicting crime and deviance, where the bulk of the variation in such behavior is likely to be explained by variables specified by theories other than deterrence. Thus, linking deterrence with other criminological perspectives seems fruitful, and it may be the only way to keep it from ultimately being viewed by criminologists as a theory that is, for the most part, bereft of empirical validity.

Notes

*   The authors would like to thank Ross Matsueda and Alex Piquero for their helpful comments. Please address all correspondence to Travis C. Pratt, Department of Political Science/Criminal Justice at Washington State University, 801 Johnson Tower, Pullman, WA 99164-4880, tcpratt@wsu.edu.

1.   The electronic databases that were searched include Medline, PsychInfo, Ingenta, Criminal Justice Abstracts.
2.   A number of studies, which either did not include enough information to calculate an effect size estimate or used statistical models that produced information that precluded the conversion of a test statistic to a common metric, and could not be included in the sample (these include: Hirschel et al. 1992; Klepper and Nagin 1989; LeBlanc and Kaspy 1998; Lotz et al. 1978; Rankin and Wells 1990; Salem and Bowers 1970; Waldo and Chiricos 1972).
3.   This statistic, the "fail-safe N" (Rosenthal 1979; see also Wolf 1986), is calculated using a .001 (two tailed) significance level by the formula: $N = (\Sigma z\text{-scores}/3.291)^2$ N (number of contributing effect size estimates).

4. The equation for the transformation of r values to z(r) values (see Blalock 1972), which converts the sampling distribution of r to one that approaches normality is:

$$z(r) = 1.151 \log[1 + r/1-r]$$

5. The test for heterogeneity is distributed as a chi-square using the folllowing equation:

$$\chi^2 = \Sigma (zr-mzr)^2$$

where zr is each effect size estimate and mzr is the mean effect size estimate, and the degrees of freedom are k-1 where k = the number of effect size estimates being combined.

6. Expressed mathematically, we assume that the effect size estimates (zr) will vary according to both observed (O) factors—such as sample characteristics and research design (i.e., factors that can be directly measured)—and unobserved (UO) factors, such as variations in model specification that cannot be fully captured by a coding scheme in meta-analysis. Thus, the equation predicting the effect size estimates would be:

$$zr = \beta(O) + \beta(UO)$$

The weight that is created is then $1/[\beta(UO)^2]$, which effectively weights downward the effect size estimates produced in studies with greater unobserved heterogeneity across models.

7. Additional analyses also indicate that the mean effect sizes for the certainty estimates, and the bivariate estimates for the non-legal sanctions, are the only ones displayed in Table 13.1 that have a "fail-safe N" above 10.

8. These percent differences are based on the unweighted mean effect sizes. The same
general trend is revealed when comparing the various weighted mean effect sizes across the bivariate and multivariate models.

9. For this series of analyses, we used the serial correlation weighted multivariate mean effect size estimates for two reasons. First, the results presented in Table 13.1 clearly demonstrated that the deterrence theory predictors are substantially inflated in bivariate models. Thus, to give a more accurate portrait of the "true" effect size of these predictors, the multivariate effect size estimates were chosen. Second, although the serial correlation weights did not influence the mean effect size estimates presented in Table 13.1, the larger problem with the potential lack of statistical independence is that the variance estimates for the effect size estimates within the same dataset will be biased downward, thus making it artificially easier to reject the null hypothesis and to achieve statistical significance. The serial correlation weight compensates for this bias. In the end, the point behind using the serial correlation weighted multivariate effect sizes is that they represent the "best" (i.e., most accurate and unbiased) estimates produced by this body of literature.

10. Subsequent analyses also indicate that none of the mean effect size estimates displayed in Table 13.2 have fail-safe N above 10.

11. Supplemental analyses indicate that the only mean effect size displayed in Table 13.3 that had a fail-safe N above 10 was the mean certainty estimate when competing theories were not controlled.

12. Additional analyses reveal that controls for peer effects and self-control have the greatest "mediating" effect on the certainty estimates.

References

Akers, Ronald L. 1990. "Rational Choice, Deterrence, and Social Learning Theory in Criminology: The Path Not Taken." *Journal of Criminal Law and Criminology* 81: 653-676.

————. 1997. *Criminological Theories: Introduction and Evaluation*, 2nd ed. Los Angeles: Roxbury.

————. 1998. *Social Learning and Social Structure: A General Theory of Crime and Deviance*. Boston: Northeastern University Press.

Akers, Ronald L., Marvin D. Krohn, Lonn Lanza-Kaduce, and Marcia Radosevich. 1979. "Social Learning and Deviant Behavior: A Specific Test of a General Theory." *American Sociological Review* 44: 636-655.

Anderson, Linda S., Theodore G. Chiricos, and Gordon P. Waldo. 1977. "Formal and Informal Sanctions: A Comparison of Deterrent Effects." *Social Problems* 25: 103-114.

Andrews, D. A., and James Bonta. 1998. *The Psychology of Criminal Conduct*, 2nd ed. Cincinnati: Anderson.

Andrews, D. A., Ivan Zinger, Robert D. Hoge, James Bonta, Paul Gendreau, and Francis T. Cullen. 1990. "Does Correctional Treatment Work? Clinically Relevant and Psychologically Informed Meta-Analysis." *Criminology* 28: 369-404.

Apospori, Eleni, and Geoffrey P. Alpert. 1992. "The Effect of Involvement with the Criminal Justice System: A Neglected Dimension of the Relationship between Experience and Perceptions." *Justice Quarterly* 9: 379-392.

Bachman, Ronet, Raymond Paternoster, and Sally Ward. 1992. "The Rationality of Sexual Offending: Testing a Deterrence/Rational Choice Conception of Sexual Assault." *Law and Society Review* 26: 343-372.

Bandura, Albert. 1977. *Social Learning Theory*. Englewood Cliffs, NJ: Prentice-Hall.

Beccaria, Cesare. 1764 (1963). *On Crimes and Punishments*. Indianapolis: Bobbs-Merrill.

Becker, Gary S. 1968. "Crime and Punishment: An Economic Approach." *Journal of Political Economy* 76: 169-217.

Bennett, William J., John J. DiIulio, Jr., and John P Walters. 1996. *Body Count: Moral Poverty . . .and How to Win America's War Against Crime and Drugs*. New York: Simon and Schuster.

Bishop, Donna M. 1984. "Legal And Extralegal Barriers to Delinquency: A Panel Analysis." *Criminology* 22: 403-419.

Blalock, Hubert M., Jr. 1972. *Social Statistics*, 2nd ed. New York: McGraw-Hill.

Blumstein, Alfred, Jacqueline Cohen, and Daniel Nagin. 1978. *Deterrence and Incapacitation:Estimating the Effects of Criminal Sanctions on Crime Rates*. Panel on Research on Deterrent and Incapacitative Effects, National Research Council. Washington, DC: National Academy of Sciences.

Braithwaite, John. 1989. *Crime, Shame and Reintegration*. Cambridge: Cambridge University Press.

Brame, Robert, Shawn Bushway, and Raymond Paternoster. 1999. "On the Use of Panel Research Designs and Random Effects Models to Investigate Static and Dynamic Theories of Criminal Offending." *Criminology* 37: 599-640.

Bridges, George S., and James A. Stone. 1986. "Effects of Criminal Punishment on Perceived Threat of Punishment: Toward an Understanding of Specific Deterrence." *Journal of Research in Crime and Delinquency* 23: 207-294.

Bureau of Justice Statistics. 2001. *Probation and Parole Statistics*. Washington, DC: U.S. Department of Justice.

Burkett, Steven R., and David A. Ward. 1993. "A Note on Perceptual Deterrence, Religiously Based Moral Condemnation, and Social Control." *Criminology* 31: 119-135.

Bursik, Robert J., Jr. 1988. "Social Disorganization and Theories of Crime and Delinquency: Problems and Prospects." *Criminology* 26: 519-51.

Burton, Velmer S., Jr., and Francis T. Cullen. 1992. "The Empirical Status of Strain Theory." *Journal of Crime and Justice* 15 (No. 2): 1-30.

Carmichael, Stephanie, Lynn Langton, Gretchen Pendell, John D. Reitzel, and Alex R. Piquero. 2005. "Do the Experiential and Deterrent Effect Operate Differently Across Gender?" *Journal of Criminal Justice* 33: 267-276.

Cernkovich, Stephen A., and Peggy C. Giordano. 1992. "School Bonding, Age, Race, and Delinquency." *Criminology* 30: 261-291.

Clarke, Ronald V., ed. 1992. *Situational Crime Prevention: Successful Case Studies.* New York: Harrow and Heston.

———. 1995. "Situational Crime Prevention." Pp. 91-150 in Michael Tonry and David P. Farrington (eds.), *Building a Safer Society: Strategic Approaches to Crime Prevention—Crime and Justice, Vol. 19.* New York: Cambridge University Press.

Clarke, Ronald V., and Derek B. Cornish. 2001. "Rational Choice." Pp. 23-42 in Raymond Paternoster and Ronet Bachman (eds.), *Explaining Criminals and Crime: Essays in Contemporary Criminological Theory.* Los Angeles: Roxbury.

Clear, Todd R. 1994. *Harm in American Penology: Offenders, Victims, and Their Communities.* Albany: State University of New York Press.

Cohen, Lawrence E., and Marcus Felson. 1979. "Social Change and Crime Rate Trends: A Routine Activity Approach." *American Sociological Review* 44: 588-608.

Colvin, Mark. 2000. *Crime and Coercion: An Integrated Theory of Chronic Criminality.* New York: St. Martin's Press.

Cook, David R. 1996. "Empirical Studies of Shame and Guilt: The Internalized Shame Scale." Pp. 132-165 in Donald L. Nathanson (ed.), *Knowing Feeling: Affect, Script, and Psychotherapy.* New York: Norton.

Cornish, Derek B., and Ronald V. Clarke, eds. 1986. *The Reasoning Criminal: Rational Choice Perspectives on Offending.* New York: Springer-Verlag.

Cullen, Francis T. 1994. "Social Support as an Organizing Concept for Criminology: Presidential Address to the Academy of Criminal Justice Sciences." *Justice Quarterly* 11: 527-559.

———. 2005. "The Twelve People Who Saved Rehabilitation: How the Science of Criminology Made a Difference—The American Society of Criminology 2004 Presidential Address." *Criminology* 43: 1-42.

Cullen, Francis T., Travis C. Pratt, Sharon Levrant Miceli, and Melissa M. Moon. 2002. "Dangerous Liason? Rational Choice Theory as the Basis for Correctional Intervention." Pp. 279-298 in Alex R. Piquero and Stephen G. Tibbetts (eds.), *Rational Choice and Criminal Behavior: Recent Research and Future Challenges.* New York: Routledge.

Cullen, Francis T., John P. Wright, and Brandon K. Applegate. 1996. "Control in the Community: The Limits of Reform?" Pp. 69-116 in Alan T. Harland (ed.), *Choosing Correctional Options That Work: Defining the Demand and Evaluating the Supply.* Thousand Oaks, CA: Sage.

Currie, Elliott. 1998. *Crime and Punishment in America.* New York: Metropolitan Books.

Decker, Scott, Richard Wright, and Robert Logie. 1993. "Perceptual Deterrence Among Active Residential Burglars: A Research Note." *Criminology* 31: 135-147.

Dejong, Christina. 1997. "Survival Analysis and Specific Deterrence: Integrating Theoretical and Empirical Models of Recidivism." *Criminology* 35: 561-575.

Eck, John, and Edward Maguire. 2000. "Have Changes in Policing Reduced Violent Crime? An Assessment of the Evidence." Pp. 207-265 in Alfred Blumstein and Joel Wallman (eds.), *The Crime Drop in America*. New York: Cambridge University Press.

Evans, T. David, Francis.T. Cullen, R Gregory Dunaway, and Velmer S. Burton, Jr.. 1995. "Religion and Crime Reexamined: The Impact of Religion, Secular Controls, and Social Ecology on Adult Criminality." *Criminology* 33: 195-224.

Fass, Simon M., and Chung-Ron Pi. 2002. "Getting Tough on Juvenile Crime: An Analysis of Costs and Benefits." *Journal of Research in Crime and Delinquency* 39: 363-99.

Felson, Marcus. 1987. "Routine Activities and Crime Prevention in the Developing Metropolis." *Criminology* 25: 911-31.

————. 1994. *Crime and Everyday Life: Insights and Implications for Society*. Thousand Oaks, CA: Pine Forge Press.

Felson, Marcus, and Lawrence E. Cohen. 1980. "Human Ecology and Crime: A Routine Activities Approach." *Human Ecology* 8: 389-406.

Foglia, Wanda D. 1997. "Perceptual Deterrence and The Mediating Effect of Internalized Norms Among Inner-City Teenagers." *Journal of Research in Crime and Delinquency* 34: 414-442.

Garland, David. 2001. *The Culture of Control: Crime and Social Order in Contemporary Society*. Chicago: University of Chicago Press.

Gibbs, Jack P. 1975. *Crime, Punishment, and Deterrence*. New York: Elsevier.

Gilovich, Thomas. 1983. "Biased Evaluation and Persistence in Gambling." *Journal of Personality and Social Psychology* 44: 1110-1126.

Goddard, Henry Herbert. 1914. *Feeble-Mindedness*. New York: Macmillan.

Goldberg, Carl. 1991. *Understanding Shame and Healing Shame*. Northvale, NJ: Jason Aronson.

Gottfredson, Michael R., and Travis Hirschi. 1990. *The General Theory of Crime*. Stanford: CA: Stanford University Press.

Grasmick, Harold G., and George J. Bryjak. 1980. "The Deterrent Effect of Perceived Severity of Punishment." *Social Forces* 59: 471-491.

Grasmick, Harold G., and Robert J. Bursik, Jr. 1990. "Conscience, Significant Others, and Rational Choice: Extending The Deterrence Model." *Law and Society Review* 24: 837-861.

Grasmick, Harold G., Robert J. Bursik, Jr., and Bruce J. Arneklev. 1993. "Reduction in Drunk Driving as a Response to Increased Threats of Shame, Embarrassment, and Legal Sanctions." *Criminology* 31: 41-67.

Grasmick, Harold G., Robert J. Bursik, Jr., and Karyl A. Kinsey. 1991. "Shame and Embarrassment as Deterrents to Noncompliance With the Law." *Environment and Behavior* 23: 233-251.

Gray, Louis N., David A. Ward, Mark C. Stafford, and Ben A. Menke. 1985. "Observational and Experiential Effects in Probability Learning: The Case of a Deviant Behavior." *Social Psychology Quarterly* 48: 78-85.

Green, Donald E. 1989. "Past Behavior as a Measure of Actual Future Behavior: An Unresolved Issue in Perceptual Deterrence Research." *Journal of Criminal Law and Criminology* 80: 781-804.

Greenberg, David F., Ronald C. Kessler, and Charles H. Logan. 1979. "A Panel Model of Crime Rates and Arrest Rates." *American Sociological Review* 44: 843-50.

Hanushek, Eric A., and John E. Jackson. 1977. *Statistical Methods for Social Scientists*. San Diego: Academic Press.

Hay, Carter. 2001. "An Exploratory Test of Braithwaite's Reintegrative Shaming Theory." *Journal of Research in Crime and Delinquency* 38: 123-153.

Hedges, Larry V., and Ingram Olkin. 1985. *Statistical Methods for Meta-Analysis.* Orlando: Academic Press.

Hirschel, J. David, Ira W. Hutchinson, and Charles W. Dean. 1992. "The Failure of Arrest to Deter Spouse Abuse." *Journal of Research in Crime and Delinquency* 29: 7-33.

Hollinger, Richard C., and John P. Clark. 1983. "Deterrence in the Workplace: Perceived Certainty, Perceived Severity, and Employee Theft." *Social Forces* 62: 398-417.

Horney, Julie, and Ineke Haen Marshall. 1992. "Risk Perceptions Among Serious Offenders: The Role of Crime and Punishment." *Criminology* 30: 575-594.

Kalaian, Hripsime A., and Stephen W. Raudenbush. 1996. "A Multivariate Mixed Linear Model for Meta-Analysis." *Psychological Methods* 1: 227-235.

Kelling, George L., and Catherine M. Coles. 1996. *Fixing Broken Windows: Restoring Order and Reducing Crime in Our Communities.* New York: Simon and Schuster.

Kempf, Kimberly L. 1993. "The Empirical Status of Hirschi's Control Theory." Pp. 143-185 in Freda Adler and William S. Laufer (eds.), *New Directions in Criminological Theory: Advances in Criminological Theory, Vol. 4.* New Brunswick, NJ: Transaction.

Kessler, Ronald C., and Greenberg, David F. 1981. *Linear Panel Analysis: Models of Quantitative Change.* New York: Academic Press.

Kingsnorth, Rodney F. 1991. "The Gunther Special: Deterrence and the DUI Offender." *Criminal Justice and Behavior* 18: 251-266.

Klepper, Steven, and Daniel Nagin. 1989. "The Deterrent Effect of Perceived Certainty and Severity of Punishment Revisited." *Criminology* 27: 721-746.

Kraut, Robert E. 1976. "Deterrent and Definitional Influences on Shoplifting." *Social Problems* 23: 358-368.

Land, Kenneth C., and Daniel S. Nagin. 1996. "Micromodels of Criminal Careers: A Synthesis of the Criminal Careers and Life Course Approaches Via Semiparametric Mixed Poisson Regression Models, with Empirical Applications." *Journal of Quantitative Criminology* 12: 163-90.

Lanza-Kaduce, Lonn. 1988. "Perceptual Deterrence and Drinking and Driving Among College Students." *Criminology* 26: 321-341.

Lanza-Kaduce, Lonn, Donna M. Bishop, and Lawrence Winner. 1997. "Risk/Benefit Calculations, Moral Evaluations, and Alcohol Use: Exploring The Alcohol-Crime Connection." *Crime and Delinquency* 43: 222-239.

Larzelere, Robert E., and Gerald R. Patterson. 1990. "Parental Management: Mediator of the Effect of Socioeconomic Status on Early Delinquency." *Criminology* 28: 301-323.

Laub, John H., and Robert J. Sampson. 2003. *Shared Beginnings, Divergent Lives.* Cambridge, MA: Harvard University Press.

Le Blanc, Marc, and Nathalie Kaspy. 1998. "Trajectories of Delinquency and Problem Behavior: Comparison of Social and Personal Control Characteristics of Adjudicated Boys on Synchronous and Nonsynchronous Paths." *Journal of Quantitative Criminology* 14: 181-214.

Lipsey, Mark W. 2003. "Those Confounded Moderators in Meta-Analysis: Good, Bad, and Ugly." *Annals of the American Academy of Political and Social Science* 587: 69-81.

Lipsey, Mark W., and James H. Derzon. 1998. "Predictors of Violent or Serious Delinquency in Adolescence and Early Adulthood: A Synthesis of Longitudinal Research." Pp. 86-105 in Rolf Loeber and David P. Farrington (eds.), *Serious and Violent Juvenile Offenders: Risk Factors and Successful Interventions.* Thousand Oaks, CA: Sage.

Loeber, Rolf, and Magda Stouthamer-Loeber. 1986. "Family Factors as Correlates and Predictors of Juvenile Conduct Problems and Delinquency." Pp. 29-149 in Michael Tonry and Norval Morris (eds.), *Crime and Justice: An Annual Review of Research, Vol. 7.* Chicago: University of Chicago Press.

Logan, Charles H. 1975. "Arrest Rates and Deterrence." *Social Science Quarterly* 56: 376-89.

Lombroso-Ferrero, Gina 1911. *Criminal Man, According to the Classification of Cesare Lombroso*. New York: Putnam.

Lotz, Roy, Robert M. Regoli, and Philip Raymond. 1978. "Delinquency and Special Deterrence." *Criminology* 15: 539-548.

Makkai, Toni, and John Braithwaite. 1994. "The Dialectics of Corporate Deterrence." *Journal of Research in Crime and Delinquency* 31: 347-373.

Mazerolle, Lorraine Green, Collen Kadleck, and Jan Roehl. 1998. "Controlling Drug and Disorder Problems: The Role of Place Managers." *Criminology* 36: 371-404.

McKenna, Frank P. 1993. "It Won't Happen to Me: Unrealistic Optimism or Illusion of Control?" *British Journal of Psychology* 84: 39-50.

Minor, W. William, and Joseph Harry. 1982. "Deterrent and Experiential Effects in Perceptual Deterrence Research: A Replication and Extension." *Journal of Research in Crime and Delinquency* 19: 190-203.

Moffitt, Terrie E. 1993. "Adolescence-Limited and Life-Course-Persistent Antisocial Behavior: A Developmental Taxonomy." *Psychological Review* 100: 674-701.

Montmarquette, Claude, Marc Nerlove, and Paul Forest. 1985. "Deterrence and Delinquency: An Analysis of Individual Data." *Journal of Quantitative Criminology* 1: 37-58.

Nagin, Daniel S. 1998a. "Criminal Deterrence Research at the Outset of the Twenty-First Century." Pp. 1-42 in Michael Tonry (ed.), *Crime and Justice: A Review of Research, Vol. 23*. Chicago: University of Chicago Press.

———. 1998b. "Deterrence and Incapacitation." Pp. 345-68 in Michael Tonry (ed.), *The Handbook of Crime and Punishment*. New York: Oxford University Press.

Nagin, Daniel S., and Paternoster, Raymond. 1991a. "The Preventive Effects of the Perceived Risk of Arrest: Testing an Expanded Conception of Deterrence." *Criminology* 29: 561-587.

———. 1991b. "On the Relationship of Past and Future Participation in Delinquency." *Criminology* 29: 163-190.

———. 1993. "Enduring Individual Differences and Rational Choice Theories of Crime." *Law and Society Review* 27: 467-496.

Nagin, Daniel S., and Greg Pogarsky. 2001. "Integrating Celerity, Impulsivity, and Extralegal Sanction Threats into a Model of General Deterrence: Theory and Evidence." *Criminology* 39: 865-891.

———. 2003. "An Experimental Investigation of Deterrence: Cheating, Self-Serving Bias, and Impulsivity." *Criminology* 41: 167-193.

Paternoster, Raymond 1987. "The Deterrent Effect of the Perceived Certainty and Severity of Punishment: A Review of the Evidence and Issues." *Justice Quarterly* 4: 173-217.

Paternoster, Raymond, and Leeann Iovanni. 1986. "The Deterrent Effect of Perceived Severity: A Reexamination." *Social Forces* 64: 751-777.

Paternoster, Raymond, and Alex R. Piquero. 1995. "Reconceptualizing Deterrence: An Empirical Test of Personal and Vicarious Experiences." *Journal of Research in Crime and Delinquency* 32: 251-286.

Paternoster, Raymond, Linda.E. Saltzman, Gordon P. Waldo, and Theodore G. Chiricos. 1983. "Estimating Perceptual Stability and Deterrent Effects: The Role of Perceived Legal Punishment in the Inhibition of Criminal Involvement." *Journal of Criminal Law and Criminology* 74: 270-297.

Petersilia, Joan, and Susan Turner. 1993. "Intensive Probation and Parole." Pp. 281-335 in Michael Tonry (ed.), *Crime and Justice: A Review of Research, Vol. 17*. Chicago: University of Chicago Press.

Petrosino, Anthony J. 1995. "The Hunt For Randomized Experimental Reports: Document Search and Efforts For a 'What Works'? Meta-Analysis." *Journal of Crime and Justice* 18: 63-80.

Piliavin, Irving, Rosemary Gartner, Craig Thornton, and Ross L. Matsueda. 1986. "Crime, Deterrence, and Rational Choice." *American Sociological Review* 51: 101-119.

Piquero, Alex R., Zenta Gomez-Smith, and Lynn Langton. 2004. "Discerning Unfairness Where Others May Not: Low Self-Control and Unfair Sanction Perceptions." *Criminology* 42: 699-733.

Piquero, Alex R., and Raymond Paternoster. 1998. "An Application of Stafford and Warr's Reconceptualization of Deterrence to Drinking and Driving." *Journal of Research in Crime and Delinquency* 35: 3-39.

Piquero, Alex R., and Greg Pogarsky. 2002. "Beyond Stafford and Warr's Reconceptualization of Deterrence: Personal and Vicarious Experiences, Impulsivity, and Offending Behavior." *Journal of Research in Crime and Delinquency* 39: 153-186.

Piquero, Alex, and George F. Rengert. 1999. "Studying Deterrence With Active Residential Burglars." *Justice Quarterly* 16: 451-471.

Piquero, Alex R., and Stephen G. Tibbetts. 1996. "Specifying the Direct and Indirect Effects of Low Self-Control and Situational Factors in Offenders' Decision Making: Toward a More Complete Model of Rational Offending." *Justice Quarterly* 13: 481-510.

Pogarsky, Greg. 2002. "Identifying 'Deterrable' Offenders: Implications for Research on Deterrence." *Justice Quarterly* 19: 431-452.

Pogarsky, Greg, and Alex R. Piquero. 2003. "Can Punishment Encourage Offending? Investigating the 'Resetting' Effect." *Journal of Research in Crime and Delinquency* 40: 95-120.

Potchak, Marissa C., Jean Marie McGloin, and Kristen M. Zgoba. 2002. "A Spatial Analysis of Criminal Effort: Auto Theft in Newark, New Jersey." *Criminal Justice Policy Review* 13: 257-285.

Pratt, Travis C. 2000. "Random and Fixed Effects Models in Meta-Analysis in Criminal Justice and Criminology: Choosing the Appropriate Method." *Journal of Crime and Justice* 23: 65-79.

————. 2002. "Meta-analysis and its Discontents: Treatment Destruction Techniques Revisited." *Journal of Offender Rehabilitation* 35: 23-40.

————. Forthcoming. *Addicted to Incarceration: Corrections Policy and the Politics of Misinformation in the United States*. Thousand Oaks, CA: Sage.

Pratt, Travis C., and Francis T. Cullen. 2000. "The Empirical Status of Gottfredson and Hirschi's General Theory of Crime: A Meta-Analysis." *Criminology* 38: 931-964.

————. 2005. "Assessing Macro-Level Predictors and Theories of Crime: A Meta-Analysis." Pp. 373-450 in Michael Tonry (ed.), *Crime and Justice: A Review of Research, Vol. 32*. Chicago: University of Chicago Press.

Pratt, Travis C., Francis T. Cullen, Kristie R. Blevins, Leah E. Daigle, and James D. Unnever. 2002. "The Relationship of Attention Deficit Hyperactivity Disorder to Crime and Delinquency: A Meta-Analysis." *International Journal of Police Science and Management* 4: 344-360.

Pratt, Travis C., Jeffrey Maahs, and Steven D. Stehr. 1998. "The Symbolic Ownership of the Corrections 'Problem': A Framework for Understanding the Development of Corrections Policy in the United States." *The Prison Journal* 78: 451-464.

Rankin, Joseph H., and L. Edward Wells. 1990. "The Effect of Parental Attachments and Direct Controls on Delinquency." *Journal of Research in Crime and Delinquency* 27: 140-165.

Raudenbush, Stephen W., Betsy Jane Becker, and Hripsime Kalaian. 1988. "Modeling Multivariate Effect Sizes." *Psychological Bulletin* 103: 111-120.

Rosenthal, Robert. 1978. "Combining Results of Independent Studies." *Psychological Bulletin* 85: 185-193.

——. 1979. "The 'File Drawer' Problem and Tolerance for Null Results." *Psychological Bulletin* 86: 638 641.

——. 1984. *Meta-Analytic Procedures for Social Research.* Beverly Hills, CA: Sage.

Salem, Richard G., and William J. Bowers. 1970. "Severity of Formal Sanctions as a Deterrent to Deviant Behavior." *Law and Society Review* 5: 21-40.

Saltzman, Linda, Raymond Paternoster, Gordon P. Waldo, and Theodore G. Chiricos. 1982. "Deterrent and Experiential Effects: The Problem of Causal Order in Perceptual Deterrence Research." *Journal of Research in Crime and Delinquency* 19: 172-189.

Sampson, Robert J., and Jacqueline Cohen. 1988. "Deterrent Effects of the Police on Crime: A Replication and Theoretical Extension." *Law and Society Review* 22: 163-89.

Sampson, Robert J., and John H. Laub. 1993. *Crime in the Making: Pathways and Turning Points Through Life.* Cambridge, MA: Harvard University Press.

Sherman, Lawrence W. 1993. "Defiance, Deterrence, and Irrelevance: A Theory of the Criminal Sanction." *Journal of Research in Crime and Delinquency* 30: 455-473.

Sherman, Lawrence W., and Richard A. Berk. 1984. "The Specific Deterrent Effects of Arrest for Domestic Violence." *American Sociological Review* 49: 261-272.

Simpson, Sally S., and Christopher S. Koper. 1992. "Deterring Corporate Crime." *Criminology* 30: 347-375.

Simpson, Sally S., and Nicole Leeper Piquero. 2002. "Low Self-Control, Organizational Theory, and Corporate Crime." *Law and Society Review* 36: 509-548.

Simpson, Sally S., Nicole Leeper Piquero, and Raymond Paternoster. 2002. "Rationality and Corporate Offending Decisions." Pp. 25-40 in Alex R. Piquero and Stephen G. Tibbetts (eds.), *Rational Choice and Criminal Behavior: Recent Research and Future Challenges.* New York: Routledge.

Smith, Douglas A., and Patrick R. Gartin. 1989. "Specifying Specific Deterrence: The Influence of Arrest on Future Criminal Activity." *American Sociological Review* 54: 94-105.

Smith, Douglas A., and Raymond Paternoster. 1987. "The Gender Gap in Theories of Deviance: Issues and Evidence." *Journal of Research in Crime and Delinquency* 24: 140-172.

Stafford, Mark C., and Mark Warr. 1993. "A Reconceptualization of General and Specific Deterrence." *Journal of Research in Crime and Delinquency* 30: 123-135.

Tibbetts, Stephen G. 1997. "Shame and Rational Choice in Offending Decisions." *Criminal Justice and Behavior* 24: 234-255.

Tibbetts, Stephen G., and Chris L. Gibson. 2002. "Individual Propensities and Rational Decision-Making: Recent Findings and Promising Approaches." Pp. 3-24 in Alex R. Piquero and Stephen G. Tibbetts (eds.), *Rational Choice and Criminal Behavior: Recent Research and Future Challenges.* New York: Routledge.

Tibbetts, Stephen G. and Denise Herz. 1996. "Gender Differences in Factors of Social Control and Rational Choice." *Deviant Behavior* 17: 183-208.

Tibbetts, Stephen G., and David L. Myers. 1999. "Low Self-Control, Rational Choice, and Student Test Cheating." *American Journal of Criminal Justice* 23: 179-200.

Tittle, Charles R. 1969. "Crime Rates and Legal Sanctions." *Social Problems* 16: 409-423.

————. 1977. "Sanction Fear and the Maintenance of Social Order." *Social Forces* 55: 579-598.

————. 1980. *Sanctions and Social Deviance.* New York: Praeger.

————. 1995. *Control Balance: Toward a General Theory of Deviance.* Boulder, CO: Westview.

Tittle, Charles R., and Alan R. Rowe. 1973. "Moral Appeal, Sanction Threat, and Deviance: An Experimental Test." *Social Problems* 20: 488-498.

————. 1974. "Certainty of Arrest and Crime Rates: A Further Test of the Deterrence Hypothesis." *Social Forces* 52: 455-462.

Tittle, Charles R., Wayne J. Villemez, and Douglad A. Smith. 1978. "The Myth of Social Class and Criminality: an Empirical Assessment of the Empirical Evidence." *American Sociological Review* 43: 643-656.

Toby, Jackson. 1964. "Is Punishment Necessary?" *Journal of Criminal Law, Criminology, and Police Science* 55: 332-337.

Visher, Christy A. 1987. "Incapacitation and Crime Control: Does a 'Lock 'Em Up' Strategy Reduce Crime?" *Justice Quarterly* 4: 513-43.

Wakschlag Lauren S., Kate E. Pickett, Edwin Cook, Jr., Neal L. Benowitz, and Bennett L. Leventhal. 2002. "Maternal Smoking During Pregnancy and Severe Antisocial Behavior on Offspring: A Review." *American Journal of Public Health* 92: 966-974.

Waldo, Gordon P., and Theodore G. Chiricos. 1972. "Perceived Penal Sanction and Self-Reported Criminality: A Neglected Approach to Deterrence Research." *Social Problems* 19: 522-540.

Weisburd, David, Elin Waring, and Ellen Chayet. 1995. "Specific Deterrence in a Sample of Offenders Convicted of White-Collar Crimes." *Criminology* 33: 587-607.

Whitman, James Q. 2003. *Harsh Justice: Criminal Punishment and the Widening Divide between America and Europe.* New York: Oxford University Press.

Williams, Frank P. 1985. "Deterrence and Social Control: Rethinking the Relationship." *Journal of Criminal Justice* 13: 141-151.

Williams, Kirk R., and Richard Hawkins. 1986. "Perceptual Research on General Deterrence: A Critical Overview." *Law and Society Review* 20: 545-572.

————. 1989. "The Meaning of Arrest For Wife Assault." *Criminology* 27: 163-181.

Wilson, James Q., and Barbara Boland. 1978. "The Effect of the Police on Crime." *Law and Society Review* 12: 367-390.

Wolf, Fredric M. 1986. "Meta-Analysis: Quantitative Methods For Research Synthesis." *Quantitative Applications in the Social Sciences Series, Vol. 59.* Thousand Oaks, CA: Sage.

Worrall, John L., and Travis C. Pratt. 2004. "On the Consequences of Ignoring Unobserved Heterogeneity When Estimating Macro-Level Models of Crime." *Social Science Research* 33: 79-105.

14

Shame, Restorative Justice, and Crime

John Braithwaite, Eliza Ahmed, and Valerie Braithwaite

Crime, Shame and Reintegration (Braithwaite, 1989) argues that, most of the time, most people do not seek to solve problems of daily living by committing crimes—like murdering the person who is causing them the problem—because murder is simply unthinkable to them. It is not that people calculate the costs that they might be caught and punished and weigh them against the benefits of killing the person. It is that murder is right off our deliberative agenda. The theory argues that murder is constituted as unthinkable by social processes of shaming.

However, the theory also argues that some forms of shaming, called stigmatization, are counterproductive. Stigmatization means shaming where the wrongdoer is treated disrespectfully as an outcast and as a bad person. While stigmatization makes crime worse, reintegrative shaming prevents crime. Reintegrative shaming means treating the wrongdoer respectfully and empathically as a good person who has done a bad act and making special efforts to show the wrongdoer how valued they are after the wrongful act has been confronted. This means that rituals of reintegration into the community of law abiding citizens are important according to reintegrative shaming theory. Hence the advocacy of restorative justice rituals will be discussed below.

In the next section we will see that when shame does become an issue in traditional criminal justice, it tends to be stigmatizing shame—shaming penalties. We proceed to consider recent literatures on the structure of shame that assess whether there is a fit with the claims of reintegrative shaming theory. Shame acknowledgement seems to prevent wrongdoing, while displacing shame into anger seems to promote wrongdoing. While reintegrative shaming is associated with shame acknowledgement, stigmatization is related to counterproductive shame management. It is argued next that some refinement of the theory of reintegrative shaming is needed in light of this recent evidence. It often seems not enough for offenders to believe that they are a good person who has done a bad act. Often change depends on them believing that they have a self in need of repair, even as they believe they are an essentially good person. This leads to the discovery of the importance of pride management as well as shame management to emotionally intelligent justice. The final section of the essay reviews the state of the evidence on whether reintegrative shaming theory has any explanatory power.

Harris's Ethical Identity Conception of Shame-Guilt

Shame is not something moderns are comfortable about. One reason for this is that it is understood crudely, and in criminal policy, used crudely. We refer here to "shaming penalties"—such as requiring drunk drivers to put a sign on their car saying they were convicted of drunk driving (Etzioni 2001; Kahan 1996, 1997, 1998; Massaro 1997). Reintegrative shaming theory gives an account of why this should make crime worse (Braithwaite 1989). The popularizing of shaming penalties in the American law review literature and some recent court decisions was one motivation of Martha Nussbaum (2004) in writing *Hiding from Humanity: Disgust, Shame and the Law*. Nussbaum argues rather persuasively that it is an unconscionable threat to our liberty and an assault on our humanity to humiliate, to consciously set out to induce shame. She finds Braithwaite's theory mostly innocent of seeking to do this:

> Braithwaite's ideas are not only very far removed from those of Kahan and Etzioni—as he himself stresses—but also quite unconnected to traditional notions of shaming punishment, and rather part of the universe of guilt punishments. Braithwaite himself acknowledges this point, when, in recent writings, he uses the term "Shame-Guilt" in place of the simple "shame" for the emotion that (within limits) he favors, and when he describes the spectatorial emotion he seeks as a "just and loving gaze" (Nussbaum 2004: 241).

Restorative justice theorists are actually not preoccupied with either shame or guilt punishments, but with decentering punishment in regulatory institutions, while acknowledging the significant place that punishment will always have within them. The biggest implications of *Crime, Shame and Reintegration* are macro-sociological in a Durkheimian sense. They are that societies that fail to communicate the idea that rape is shameful (without creating widespread defiance among rapists) will have a lot of rape. Societies that fail to communicate the notion that environmental crime is shameful (without creating business subcultures of resistance to environmental regulation) will destroy the planet. Societies that manifest no shame in defying and manipulating international law will create catastrophes like Iraq and the unlawful treatment of prisoners characteristic of such conflicts.

The reason for the move to shame-guilt referred to in the Nussbaum quote was empirical. In Nathan Harris's (2001) factor analytic work on both court and restorative justice conference offenders in Canberra, a single Shame-Guilt factor emerged. This factor was defined by feelings of having done wrong, concern that others had been hurt, feeling ashamed of oneself and one's act, feeling anger at oneself, loss of honor among family and friends. Observed remorse was associated with this factor. Indeed this factor might have been labeled Shame-Guilt-Remorse. Shame-Guilt predicted higher empathy with victims, lower feelings of hostility and had no correlation with self-esteem or self-respect in either court or conference cases (Harris 2001).

Harris's work shows that the distinction between shame and guilt may be less important than distinctions between Shame-Guilt (the feeling we have when our ethics are in question), Embarrassment-Exposure (the feeling we have when our nakedness is exposed or some other feature of ourselves we do not want displayed) and Unresolved Shame (the feeling of refusing to acknowledge a shame that is lurking within us). Harris found Embarrassment-Exposure levels to be higher in court cases than in restorative justice conferences, while Shame-Guilt has higher levels in restorative justice conferences. The latter result was replicated by Tosouni (2004) on different RISE experiments.

Perceptions of one's actions being disapproved by others during the criminal process (perceived shaming) was found to predict Shame-Guilt, but only when the shaming was by people the offender respected very highly (implying that shaming by police, prosecutors or judges is unlikely to be effective). Furthermore, Shame-Guilt was predicted by the offender's perception that the offense was wrong. Shame-Guilt was also predicted by perceptions of having been reintegrated and perceptions of not having been stigmatized. Harris (2001) argued that Shame-Guilt should be understood as a product of social influence in which internalized values, normative expectations and social context have an effect. In contrast to Shame-Guilt, Embarrassment-Exposure and Unresolved Shame were predicted by perceptions of having been stigmatized and the belief that the offense was less wrong. This highlights the importance of distinguishing between the shame-related emotions. So does the finding that Shame-Guilt was greater in restorative justice conferences but that embarrassment-exposure was greater in court cases.

Tangney's Shame and Guilt-Proneness

These results seem to fly in the face of a remarkably sustained and coherent program of research by June Price Tangney (1990, 1991, 1992, 1993, 1995a, 1995b) and her colleagues (Tangney et al. 1992, 1995, 1996a, 1996b). These studies find a clear distinction between shame-proneness and guilt-proneness as dimensions of personality (as opposed to emotion). Shame-proneness in this research is a propensity to blame or devalue the whole self in the face of failures to deal with difficult situations. Guilt-proneness is a propensity to feel responsible for specific acts over which one has control. Shame-proneness is associated with a variety of pathologies, including criminality, while guilt-proneness is negatively associated with these pathologies. Braithwaite (1989) has argued that guilt-induction is just one form of shaming. But Tangney's research challenges this viewpoint, suggesting this was a mistake—that guilt-induction in respect of serious wrongs is desirable, while shame-induction is destructive of self and therefore of law-abiding identities.

The Tangney and Braithwaite analyses actually converge at a prescriptive level. What should be avoided are degrading or disrespectful ways of communicating disapproval of wrongdoing. But conceptually, Tangney's analysis means that Braithwaite's reintegrative shaming should really be described as reintegrative guilting—induction of guilt without shame (the same theme as in the quote from Nussbaum on p. 398). Unfortunately, this pleasant reconciliation between Braithwaite and Tangney may not work because Harris's (2001) research shows that induction of Shame-Guilt together is what happens with criminal offending.

There are various ways of thinking about these conflicting results. One is that feeling ashamed in relation to a criminal offense is a special context where guilt about the act and being ashamed as a person are hard to separate. Tangney's findings are more generalized to proneness to shame across many different problems of living (not just crime). Another is that shame-proneness as a personality trait may be a very different matter than feeling the emotion of shame.

In pursuing clarification and reconciliation with the Tangney results, Harris (2001) suspects now that he has stumbled into a more subtle ethical identity conception of Shame-Guilt, found in the writings of the philosopher, Bernard Williams (1993), that might have special explanatory and normative power with respect to crime or other serious wrongdoing. It is easiest to explain at the normative level. What we had thought we wanted offenders to feel was shame about what they had done, but not shame about themselves. Now we think this may have been a normative error. If a man rapes a child or is repeatedly convicted for serious assaults, is it enough for him to feel that he has done a bad act(s) but there is nothing wrong with him as a person? It would seem more morally satisfactory for him to feel that he has done a bad act and therefore feels he must change the kind of person he is in some important ways (while still on the whole believing he is basically a good person). That is, we do not want the rapist to believe he is an irretrievably evil person; but we do want aspects of the self to be transformed. Harris's Shame-Guilt factor seems to capture empirically the nub of this halfway house of an ethical ideal. To a considerable extent one cannot experience guilt about a criminal wrong without this spilling over into feeling ashamed of oneself as a person. So long as this does not go so far as to involve a total rejection of self, this is perhaps morally appropriate, at least for serious crimes.

A Self in Need of Repair?

In some of the cultures with the strongest traditions of restoration or healing following wrongdoing, there is an explicitness of commitment to the half-way house of Shame-Guilt. In Japanese culture, for example, apology can amount to dissociation of that evil part of the self that committed a wrong (Wagatsuma and Rossett 1986). Japanese idiom sometimes accounts for wrongdoing with possession by a "mushi" (bug or worm). Criminals are hence not acting according to their true selves; they are under attack by a mushi that can be "sealed off" enabling reintegration without enduring shame (Wagatsuma and Rossett 1986: 476).

Navajo culture is another with especially rich restorative accomplishment through its peacemaking traditions. The Navajo concept of *nayéé'* is an interesting part of this accomplishment (Coker 1999: 55). Farella (1993) explains that *nayéé'* or "monsters" are anything that gets in the way of a person enjoying their life, such as depression, obsession and jealousy. "The benefit of naming something a *nayéé'* is that the source of one's 'illness'—one's unhappiness or dysfunctionality—once named can be cured." (Coker 1999: 55). And healing ceremonies are about helping people to rid themselves of *nayéé'*.

There seems a major difference between stigmatizing cultures and cultures such as these where the vague and subjective threat to a person's integrity of self is named to make it concrete, and able to be excised. Naming to excise a bad part of self creates very different action imperatives for a society from naming to label a whole self as bad (such as naming a person a junkie, criminal or schizophrenic). The former kind of shame can be discharged with the expulsion of the *mushi* or *nayéé'*. The latter kind of stigma entrenches a master status trait like schizophrenic that dominates all other identities. We can learn from other cultures the possibility of healing a damaged part of a self that is mostly good. This is the approach to which Harris's (2001) conception of Shame-Guilt cues us. It particularly cues us to the possibility of healing a mostly positive and redeemable self because of his finding that both Shame-Guilt and reintegration are greater when cases are randomly assigned to a restorative justice process.

Maruna's Repair of the Self through Redemption Scripts

Shadd Maruna's (2001) powerful study, *Making Good: How Ex-Convicts Reform and Rebuild their Lives*, showed that even though his Liverpool sample might not have had the benefit of Japanese or Navajo cultural resources, serious offenders who went straight had to find a new way of making sense of their lives. They had to restory their life histories. They defined a new ethical identity for themselves that meant that they were able to say, looking back at their former criminal selves, that they were "not like that any more" (Maruna 2001: 7). His persistent reoffender sample, in contrast, were locked into "condemnation scripts" whereby they saw themselves as irrevocably condemned to their criminal self-story.

This suggests a restorative justice that is about "rebiographing", restorative storytelling that redefines an ethical conception of the self. Garfinkel (1956: 421-2) saw what was at issue in "making good": "the former identity stands as accidental; the new identity is the basic reality. What he is now is what, after all, he was all along." So, Maruna found systematically that desisters from crime reverted to an unspoiled identity. As with the *mushi* and *nayéé'*, desisters had restoried themselves to believe that their formerly criminal self "wasn't me." The self that did it was in William James' terms, not the I (the self-as-subject, who acts) nor the Me (the self-as-object, that is acted upon), but what Petrunik and Shearing (1988) called the It, an alien source of action (Maruna 2001: 93). Even without the cultural resource of a mushi, restorative justice might therefore help Western wrongdoers to write their "It" out of the story of their true ethical identity. Maruna (2001: 13) also concluded that "redemption rituals" as communal processes were important in this sense-making because desisting offenders often narrated the way their deviance had been decertified by important others such as family members or judges—the parent or policeman who said Johnny was now his old self. Howard Zehr (2000: 10) makes the point that whether we have victimized or been victimized, we need social support in the journey "to re-narrate our stories so that they are no longer just about shame and humiliation but ultimately about dignity and triumph."

Ahmed's Shame Acknowledgement

Eliza Ahmed (2001; Ahmed and V. Braithwaite 2004, forthcoming; Ahmed and J. Braithwaite, forthcoming, in press) finds that different ways of managing shame as an emotion can make crime or bullying worse. She builds on Braithwaite's (1989) theory in *Crime, Shame and Reintegration*. This argues that both the empirical literatures of child development and criminology are consistent with the prediction that stigmatizing shaming (stigmatization) makes crime worse, while reintegrative shaming reduces crime.

Stigmatization means shaming where the wrongdoer is treated disrespectfully as an outcast and as a bad person. Reintegrative shaming means treating the wrongdoer respectfully and empathically as a good person who has done a bad act and making special efforts to show the wrongdoer how valued they are after the wrongful act has been confronted.

Among restorative justice practitioners there has been a raging debate over whether shame and shaming are useful concepts in their work. Restorative justice is about the notion that because crime hurts, justice should heal. This is an alternative to the view that justice must be punitive—responding to hurt with hurt that is the wrongdoer's just deserts. So restorative justice is about hurt begetting healing as an alternative to hurt begetting hurt. Some restorative justice advocates argue that shame and shaming have no place in restorative justice because shaming is a kind of hurting and shame is a destructive kind of hurt that can make crime and injustice worse.

Ahmed (2001) argues that these critics are right when shaming is stigmatizing and when shame is unacknowledged. However, to acknowledge shame and discharge it and to shame acts of injustice reintegratively are both important for preventing injustice and enabling restoration. So her argument is that shame and pride are indispensable conceptual tools for understanding the effects of restorative justice. This does not mean that social movement advocates should actually use the word shame as part of their reform rhetoric; with restorative justice, as Braithwaite and Mugford (1994: 165) have suggested, responsibility and healing are likely to supply a more politically resonant and a more prudent neo-liberal discourse than shame and reintegration.

Still the analytic point is that no progressive social movement is likely to be effective without shaming and promoting the just acknowledgment of shame. Restorative justice cannot be effective without shaming needlessly punitive practices such as the death penalty and skyrocketing imprisonment rates. The social movement against Apartheid could not have been effective without shaming Apartheid and urging its architects to acknowledge their shame for the evils they perpetrated. While social movements can never change the world for the better by sweeping shameful truths under the carpet, a restorative justice argument is that they can be more effective through truth and reconciliation (through shaming that is reintegrative), than through truth and stigmatization, retribution that replaces one outcast group with another.

Any actor in any kind of practical affairs cannot but be ineffective by denying shame and eschewing the challenge of understanding its dynamics. This is especially so in debates around crime—from juvenile justice to genocide and Apartheid—where shame is so acute. Ahmed (2001) shows that failure to acknowledge shame and discharge it is in different ways a characteristic of both school bullies and victims of bullying. Healthy shame management is important to preventing bullying on both the offender side and the victim side.

Ahmed (2001) distinguished Shame Acknowledgment and Shame Displacement. Shame Acknowledgment involves the discharging of shame through accepting responsibility and trying to put things right. Shame Displacement means displacement of shame into blame and/or anger toward others. Ahmed classified school children into: those who were neither bullies nor victims of bullying, those who were both bullies and victims of bullying, those who were just bullies without being victims and those who were victims without being bullies. Self-reported non-bully/non-victims acknowledged shame and were less likely to allow shame to be displaced into emotions like anger. Bullies, in contrast, were less likely to acknowledge shame and more likely to displace shame into anger. Self-reported victims acknowledged shame without displacement, but were more likely to internalize others' rejection of them. Bully/

victims were less likely to acknowledge shame, were more likely to have self-critical thoughts and to displace their shame into anger. Bully/victims are thus jointly afflicted with the shame management problems of both bullies and victims (see Table 1).

Table 14.1
Summary Conclusions from Ahmed (2001)

Non-bully/non-victim	- Acknowledge shame - Resist displacement of shame	- Shame is discharged
Bully	- Resist shame acknowledgment - Displace shame through externalizing blame and anger	- Shame is not discharged
Victim	- Acknowledge shame - Internalize shame	- Shame is not discharged
Bully/victim	- Resist shame acknowledgment - Internalize shame - Displace shame through externalizing blame and anger	- Shame is not discharged

Put another way, the shame problems victims have, which restorative justice might address, is internalization of the idea that I am being bullied because there is something wrong with me as a person—internalization of shame. The shame problem bullies have is a failure to acknowledge shame when they have done something wrong and a tendency to externalize their shame as anger. Restorative justice needs to help them be more like non-bully/non-victims who acknowledge shame when they do something wrong, who resist externalizing or internalizing their shame, and, who, thereby, manage to discharge shame. Critics of confronting shame are rightly concerned that this could cause offenders, especially young or Indigenous offenders, to internalize shame. These data suggest, however, that this is much more of a problem for victims than for offenders. Managing the acknowledgment of unavoidable shame is more the offender problem, internalized rejection of self more the victim problem, while bully/victims suffer both.

If we translated this model beyond school bullying to post-Apartheid South Africa, we can construct Nelson Mandela as a survivor who discharged the shame of being a victim of twenty-seven years imprisonment and the shame of the violence perpetrated by his party, in the name of an armed struggle he advocated and led. While he was labeled with some justification as a "terrorist" both for what he himself did prior to his imprisonment and for what was done in his name during that imprisonment, Mandela set up a Truth and

Reconciliation Commission to acknowledge this shame and transcend it. Mandela's then wife Winnie, however, remained a bully/victim who would not fully acknowledge responsibility. P. W. Botha, the former President of South Africa, remained a non-cooperative bully during the Truth and Reconciliation Commission, refusing to acknowledge wrongdoing and externalizing blame onto the Commission, black leaders and white traitors. Many were the victims with internalized shame who were helped by the Commission to discharge it, as documented in Desmond Tutu's (1999: 107), *No Future Without Forgiveness*:

> A woman from Soweto, Thandi [had been] tortured while in detention. She was raped repeatedly. She said she survived by taking her soul and spirit out of her body and putting it in a corner of the cell in which she was being raped. She could then, disembodied in this manner, look on as they did all those awful things to her body intended to make her hate herself as they had told her would happen. She could imagine then that it was not she herself but this stranger suffering the ignominy heaped on her. She then uttered words that are filled with a deep pathos. She said with tears in her eyes that she had not yet gone back to that room to fetch her soul and that it was still sitting in the corner where she had left it.

Just as Tutu shows that many victims discharged their internalized shame through seeing clearly the evil they had suffered and forgiving it, so did many perpetrators of awful violence discharge their externalized shame by apologizing, seeking and receiving forgiveness. What Ahmed's (2001) data imply is that a nation of healed victims, bullies and bully/victims has better prospects of going forward without new cycles of violence. Thus conceived, these data are of broader import than simply to the school context. They suggest that just as Truth (acknowledgment) and Reconciliation (the alternative to shame management with anger) can heal schoolyards, they might also heal South Africa, Northern Ireland, Palestine, Rwanda, or Iraq. Apology-reparation-forgiveness sequences can give bullies and victims access to both the benefits on the victim side and on the bully side of restoration. Harris's (2001) data complements Ahmed's in that it suggests that restorative process seemed to both assist the acknowledgment and inhibit the displacement of shame. Harris also found restorative conference cases to be more reintegrative and less stigmatizing than court cases. Ahmed in turn found that stigmatizing shaming by parents was associated with self-initiated bullying on the part of their children. This is therefore another part of the case as to why the reconciliation part of the Truth and Reconciliation process ought to inhibit further cycles of bullying.

Pride Management

The work of Cooley (1922) and Scheff (1990) implies that pride and shame are together the primary social emotions. For Scheff, pride is the sign of an intact bond with other human beings, shame of a severed or threatened bond. Scheff and Retzinger (1991: 175) have been critical of the original formulation of reintegrative shaming theory in *Crime, Shame and Reintegration* for its neglect of pride and praise. Parental social approval is essential to delinquency prevention (Trasler 1972). Chapman (1985) found that young people who said that their father always "praises me when I do my work well" engage in less delinquency than those who say they are seldom or never praised. Makkai and Braithwaite (1993) found that nursing home inspectors who use praise as a strategy for improving compliance with quality of care standards do better at increasing compliance (net of the "praiseworthiness" of the home and other controls). This was true even though some of the praise was of a counter-productive sort—praising poor performance. Makkai and Braithwaite found that praise had some special advantages in regulating *collective* conduct, an important feature because so much bullying and other rule breaking is collective in practice. When collectivities are praised, all involved want to share in the credit and when individual members are praised, the collectivity claims a share of the individual praise. But when collectivities are shamed, members tend to believe that it is someone other than themselves who deserve this; when individual members are shamed, collectivities disown them.

Shaming and praise may interact with identity in opposite ways. *Crime, Shame and Reintegration* argues that shaming will be most effective when it shames the act but not the person. It may be that praise is most effective when it is directed at the identity of the whole person rather than at a specific act. So when a child shows a kindness to his sister, better to say "you are a kind brother" than "that was a kind thing you did." One reason is that just as the identity degradation of stigmatization destroys healthy identities, so the identity enhancement of praising the person builds healthy identity. A second is that praise of our whole character is a more profound form of praise than praise of a single act. Third, praise that is tied to specific acts risks counterproductivity if it is seen as an extrinsic reward, if it nurtures a calculative approach to performances that cannot be constantly monitored[1]. The evidence is that extrinsic rewards, like extrinsic punishments, induce the belief that compliance is performed only to get those rewards rather than because the behaviour is intrinsically valued (Boggiano, Barrett, Weiher, McLelland, and Lusk 1987; Lepper and Greene 1978). For example, Deci and Ryan's (1980) study found that children who were given rewards for performing a task that they had enjoyed came to enjoy it less as a result of giving it an instrumental meaning. Better to avert extrinsic calculativeness by recognizing good character at times other than those of bad performance (obviously recognition of good character should not be given at a time that is seen as a reward for bad performance!). Hence, regulating social conduct is more likely to be effective when the following principles are in play:

- Shaming of bad acts that averts shaming of the actor's character
- Praise of good character that uncouples praise from specific acts.

In this way, we achieve:

- Shaming acts but not persons that repairs identity
- Praising virtues of the person rather than just their acts that nourishes a positive identity.

Moral balance requires both processes. Hubris is the risk of unremitting praise of the person that is never balanced by shaming of specific moral failures. Shaming without praise risks a failure to develop a positive identity for the moral self.

Ahmed's (2001) data show that Tangney's (1990) beta pride-proneness scale is associated with less bullying, though its effects were much weaker than guilt-proneness and the shame management variables (Shame Acknowledgment and Shame Displacement). With bullying behavior at least, it seems not to be the case that pride is a more significant emotion than shame and guilt. Indeed one of the arresting things about Ahmed's (2001) analyses is that in the prediction of bullying, the shame-management variables feature as prominently as family, school and personality variables that have traditionally been the dominant explanatory variables in the delinquency literature. Moreover, her mediational analysis found that the effects of a number of variables—such as school hassles, liking for school, empathy, self-esteem and internal locus of control—were mediated through either one or both shame management variables. Hence, doubts that too much emphasis had been given to shame/shaming and not enough to pride/praise turned out to be misplaced in this domain.

Ahmed and J. Braithwaite's (forthcoming) study of 824 Bangladesh adults confirmed previous results in showing that a propensity to shame acknowledgment was associated with less workplace bullying, shame displacement with more bullying. In addition, humble pride (respecting self and others) correlated with lower bullying and narcissistic pride (feeling dominant and arrogant) with higher bullying. Hence, just as there is good and bad shame, there is good and bad pride (Webb 2003), where the unhealthy version of pride is vaunting pride, hubris that projects a sense of superiority over others. This form of pride renders adults more capable of acts of predation against others.

Shame acknowledgment was highly correlated with humble pride, shame displacement with narcissistic pride. Nevertheless, healthy pride management has positive effects on relationships with others over and above the positive effects of healthy shame management and constructive shame management has good effects on relationships with others over and above the effects of pride management. Ahmed and J. Braithwaite's (forthcoming) bullying results are consistent with this interpretation that shame and pride management are an emotional intelligence package that together is somewhat more than the sum of its parts. By teaching our children and employees, or perhaps more importantly by displaying in our own interactions with them, the values of humility and respect for self and others, we may be simultaneously teaching them the underlying principles of both healthy pride management and healthy shame management.

Testing the Theory of Reintegrative Shaming

Four forms of testing and elaboration of the theory of reintegrative shaming were advocated by Braithwaite (1989: 108-123)—ethnographic, historical, survey research and experimental. The most impressive experimental research has been Lawrence Sherman, Heather Strang, and Daniel Woods's (2000) Re-Integrative Shaming Experiments (RISE) on 1285 Canberra criminal offenders. To date this program has produced mixed results, with a reduction of reoffending in the violence experiment and an increase in the property experiments (Sherman 2003). Reintegrative shaming theory has been a motivating framework for only some restorative justice programs. However, the theory does specifically predict that this kind of intervention will reduce crime regardless of whether those implementing it have any discursive consciousness of the theory of reintegrative shaming. The theoretically relevant features of restorative justice are confrontation of the offender in a respectful way with the consequences of the crime (shaming without degradation), explicit efforts to avert stigmatization (e.g., opportunities to counter accusations that the offender is a bad person with testimonials from loved ones that she is a good person) and explicit commitment to ritual reintegration (e.g., maximizing opportunities for repair, restoring relationships, apology and forgiveness that are viewed as sincere).

Hence, reintegrative shaming theorists (controversially) interpret the success of experiments such as McGarrell et al.'s (2000) Indianapolis Juvenile Restorative Justice Experiment in substantially reducing reoffending as support for the theory. And they so interpret Latimer et al.'s (2001) meta analysis of thirty-two mostly non-experimental studies with control groups which found a statistically significant effect of restorative justice on reoffending. Braithwaite's (2002) own review of the literature concludes that restorative justice practice is slowly improving in the theoretically important ways and that the most recent evaluations are becoming increasingly encouraging about the efficacy of the intervention.

But RISE analyses of the impact of reintegrative shaming on outcomes have not been completed, so cynics are justified in reserving judgment on whether shaming has anything to do with productive and counterproductive outcomes. Restorative anti-bullying programs in schools, often referred to as whole school anti-bullying programs, is another area where Braithwaite (2002, p. 59-61) concludes that bullying reduction has been substantial. Ahmed's (2001; Ahmed and V. Braithwaite 2004; Ahmed and J. Braithwaite, in press; Morrison 2006) has been the only work that has explored whether reintegrative shaming effects might be crucial here.

The other kind of theoretically relevant body of largely experimental research that has continued to accumulate since 1989 has been in the tradition of Baumrind's (1967) distinction between authoritarian parenting [which Braithwaite (1989) conceptualized as parenting heavy in stigmatizing shaming], permissive parenting (reintegration without disapproval of wrongdoing) and authoritative parenting (reintegration with firm disapproval of wrongdoing—reintegrative shaming). Evidence has continued to accumulate that authoritarian parenting reduces children's self-control as well as social skills, peer acceptance, social competence, self-esteem, and school achievement (Amato 1989; Baumrind 1991; Patterson et al. 1989; Lamborn et al. 1991). Not surprisingly, children of authoritarian parents often display under-control of emotions and externalizing problems (Bugenthal, Blue, and Cruscosa 1989; Janssens 1994), narcissism (Ramsay et al. 1996) and depression (Parker 1983).

Permissive parenting (sometimes described as overindulgence or reintegration without shaming) has continued to be associated with school dropout (Rumberger et al. 1990), tobacco and alcohol use (Cohen and Rice 1997), narcissism (Watson et al. 1992) and also peer victimization (Finnegan 1995).

Authoritative parenting (sometimes conceived as inductive parenting—meaning the induction of remorse over wrongdoing by confronting bad consequences of the act through moral reasoning in which the child participates (that is, not stigmatizing, not authoritarian lecturing)) has continued to be associated with positive outcomes, including lower delinquency (Pettit et al. 1997; Wright and Cullen 2001) substance use (Cohen and Rice 1997; Sigrún and Leifur 2001) and internalizing and externalizing behaviour (Amato and Gilbreth 1999). Authoritative parenting assists internalization of behavioral standards followed by action in accordance with them (Grusec and Goodnow 1994). It is related to peer acceptance, social competence and school adjustment (Chen et al. 1997), empathy, altruism, and school achievement (Hetherington and Clingempeel 1992), self-confidence and self-esteem (Noller and Callan 1991; Shucksmith et al. 1995), concern for right and wrong, taking responsibility for one's own actions, reduced truancy and alcohol abuse (Gunnoe et al. 1999).

A multitude of qualitative observational studies of restorative justice conferences have also been important to theory elaboration (Braithwaite 2002) as well as qualitative and historical research on business regulatory enforcement in industries such as nursing homes and most notably Joseph Rees's (1994) conclusions on the use of reintegrative shaming in his analysis of the successes of the "communitarian regulation" of nuclear power plant safety in cutting poor safety outcomes to one-seventh of their former level. There have been a number of researchers like Rees that have posited reintegrative shaming, *post hoc*, as a variable that makes sense of their results (Chamlin and Cochrane 1997; Hagan and McCarthy 1997; Sampson and Laub 1993; Sherman 1992, 1993; Zhang et al. 1996). Another popular genre of research with mixed

results for the theory has involved explorations of Braithwaite's (1989) interpretation of low crime rates in Japan in terms of an alleged high ratio of reintegrative to stigmatizing shaming in that culture (Johnson 2002; Leonardsen
2002; Masters 1997)

There has been much less empirical research in the survey research tradition of theory testing than one might have expected in the sixteen years since
the book was published. The first published study by Makkai and Braithwaite
(1994) found that Australian nursing home inspectors with a reintegrative
shaming philosophy were successful in substantially improving compliance
with regulatory laws in the two years after inspections while compliance substantially worsened when inspectors had a stigmatizing philosophy. Lu's (1998,
1999) survey results were consistent with the theory in a limited ecological
comparison of different Shanghai neighbourhoods.

Two recent studies have used reintegrative shaming variables to predict
self-projected future offending (as opposed to self-reports of actual past offending). Using a telephone survey method, Tittle, Bratton and Gertz (2003)
demonstrated only very partial support of Braithwaite's theory in relation to
different kinds of misbehavior such as assault, property violations and use
of illegal drugs. The predicted reintegration effects of the theory were not
supported, but the predicted stigmatization effects were. Another self-projected future offending analysis, Tosouni (2004), produced results that were
rather the mirror image of the Tittle, Bratton and Gertz (2003) findings in
this respect. The stigmatization effect predicted by the theory was not supported. But the predicted reintegration effect was, at least in respect of cases
that went to restorative justice conferences, with this effect falling just short
of statistical significance in court cases. In both court and conference cases,
Harris's shame-guilt factor was strongly positively predictive of projected
future compliance with the law.

Recent survey-based theory testing has produced a more complex picture
with some components of reintegrative shaming reducing rule breaking and
others failing to do so. The need to break down the different elements of reintegrative shaming to see which are theoretically crucial and which are not should
be an exciting challenge to criminologists in the survey research tradition, but
mostly its complexity seems to have just scared them off. The most fundamental
challenges are that reintegration and shaming might be better viewed as independent main effects on crime rather than as a reintegrative shaming interaction
effect and that reintegration and stigmatization might not be opposite poles of
a single dimension, but orthogonal (see Harris 2001).

If, as in Harris's (2001) data, shaming, reintegration and stigmatization are
independent dimensions, the theory would predict that a "Shaming X Reintegration" interaction would be positively associated with shame or remorse
or crime while a "Shaming X Stigmatization" interaction would be negatively
associated with feeling shame. In no analysis did Harris find these interaction

effects. Shaming, reintegration and stigmatization had main effects, mostly consistent with the theory, but never significant interactions. Hay's results (2001) fit this pattern. In predicting the projected delinquency of adolescents Hay found a shaming main effect and a reintegration main effect (which washed out after controlling for interdependence, another key concept in the theory), but no "Shaming X Reintegration" interaction. Similar results were obtained by Zhang and Zhang (2000, 2004) from tests of the theory in reanalyses of two waves of the U.S. National Youth Survey. While they found main effects for parental forgiveness (reintegration) and peer disapproval (shaming) in reducing delinquency, there was no significant "Shaming X Reintegration" interaction. The bivariate correlations with delinquency of all four measures of the reintegrative shaming interactions in the two waves of data were statistically significant. However, when the significant main effects of reintegration and shaming were controlled in the multivariate model the reintegrative shaming interaction effect disappeared in both waves. Also consistent were results by Deng and Jou (2000) which found a significant effect of interdependence, past and projected shame in reducing delinquency and a significant stigmatization main effect in increasing delinquency, with no interaction effect being tested.

These results contrast with Makkai and Braithwaite's (1994) analysis of nursing home regulation where shaming and reintegration did not have significant main effects on compliance with the law, but there was a significant Shaming X Reintegration effect in the predicted direction. In this context, Braithwaite and Makkai's (1994) qualitative fieldwork suggested that a highly reintegrative regulatory encounter where there was no disapproval of failure to meet the standards was interpreted as a "tolerant and understanding" inspection which could be interpreted as regulatory capture by the industry ("permissiveness"). Compliance with the law in fact significantly worsened following such encounters. Similar low-shame contexts are suggested by normal child-rearing encounters, as in Baumrind's (1971, 1978) research, where both permissive and authoritarian parenting were found to be so ineffective compared to authoritative parenting that firmly, fairly and reintegratively confronts. Schoolyard bullying can also be interpreted in this way as a low shame context—compared to the context of being in trouble with the police. In Ahmed and J. Braithwaite's (in press) study of bullying among 1,875 Bangladesh school children there was a significant parental reintegrative shaming effect. However, in the regression analysis, while reintegrative shaming reduced bullying by 11 percent, parental forgiveness of wrongdoing (really just one of the facets of reintegration) reduced bullying by 22 percent.

The most likely interpretation of these divergent results is that in cases where criminal liability has already been admitted and a formal state ritual convened to deal with the admission, causing the interaction to be inherently shameful, both the reintegration and stigmatization scales are already measuring interactions with shaming. In nursing home regulation, school bullying or normal child rearing contexts, in contrast, there had been no criminal charges and regulatory encounters were normally very low on shame. It may be premature to revise the theory of reintegrative shaming in light of such divergent results. However it is certainly a way to reconcile them to suggest that the theory might be revised to predict shaming, reintegration and stigmatization main effects but no interaction effects in contexts heavily laden with shame and no main effects but interaction effects for these variables in contexts where limited shame is normally experienced.

Conclusion

When quantitative criminologists test the theory of reintegrative shaming, it is standard for them to lament how little it has been tested compared to other criminological theories. While empirical research on restorative justice is exploding, hardly any of it compares one theory of restorative intervention with another. We are not inclined to join the lament on this state of affairs without qualification. Because all the ethnographic research on restorative justice suggests that emotional dynamics is the key issue, more systematic ethnographic work that digs deeper into these dynamics may be the highest priority. In light of the contestation revealed in the first half of this essay on how shame and guilt should be conceptualized, much of the survey research appears crude. In some cases this measurement crudity is connected to the fact that the survey was not designed to measure the facets of reintegrative shaming theory. It is doubtful if more survey analyses based on items viewed as near enough for measuring one facet or another of the theory will advance our knowledge greatly. Survey research such as that of Harris (2001) that seriously explores the factor structure of the foundational constructs of the theory seems a higher priority. In light of the first decade of research on the theory, Braithwaite and Braithwaite (2001) attempted a preliminary revision of the theory of reintegrative shaming into a specification of thirty hypotheses worth attention. But as we learn more about how much more difficult it is for people to talk about shame—compared, say, with reporting how much they like their parents—hypotheses such as these thirty may continue to motivate research in which neither the conceptual nor the measurement issues have been troubled by deep thought.

The debate about reintegrative shaming has been individualistic and socio-logically impoverished. Commentary that warns of very real dangers of shame with offenders who have already experienced too much shame in their lives often falls into the trap of implying that there is no need for institutions of criminal justice that communicate the shamefulness of predatory crime. Without institutionalized processes, without rituals of significant cultural salience, that confront assaults on our persons and property, how are the young to learn the ancient curriculum of crimes? How are victim demands for retribution to be managed if they are not vindicated through rituals that confront why the crime was wrong? Without shaming, how can an Edwin Sutherland, or social movements against specific forms of white-collar crime such as environmental or cybercrime, constitute shamefulness in new criminal curriculums? Comparative historical research on how the shamefulness of crime is constituted, sustained and compromised in cultures and subcultures remains understudied. This is especially true at the level of macrosociological studies of whole societies, as opposed to Chicago slums, and even more true at the level of transnational epistemic communities that constitute new knowledges of transnational crimes such as terrorist financing and people smuggling.

Note

1. We are indebted for the ideas in this paragraph to a discussion John Braithwaite had with Jerry Lee, a successful U.S. businessman, who explained why he did not pay bonuses to employees as a reward for doing some specific thing well but as a kind of gift for being the dedicated kind of employee they were.

References

Ahmed, Eliza. 2001. "Shame Management: Regulating Bullying." Pp. 211-314 in E. Ahmed, E. and J. Braithwaite. Forthcoming. "Shame, Pride and Workplace Bullying." In S. Karstedt, I. Loader and H. Strang (eds.), Emotions, Crime and Justice. Oxford, UK: Hart Publishing.

Ahmed, N. Harris, J. Braithwaite, and V. Braithwaite (eds.), *Shame Management through Reintegration*. Cambridge: Cambridge University Press.

Ahmed, Eliza, and John Braithwaite. In Press. "Forgiveness, Shame, Shaming and Bullying." *Australian and New Zealand Journal of Criminology*.

———. Forthcoming. "Pride and Shame Management of Workplace Bullying." In S. Karstedt, I. Loader, and H. Strang (eds.). Oxford, UK: Hart Publishing.

Ahmed, Eliza, and Valerie Braithwaite. 2004. "'What, Me Ashamed?' Shame Management and School Bullying." *Journal of Research in Crime and Delinquency* 41: 245-269.

———. Forthcoming. "Shame Management, Forgiveness and Reconciliation: Three Key Variables in Reducing School Bullying." *Journal of Social Issues*.

Amato, Paul. 1989. "Family Processes and the Competence of Adolescence and Primary School Children." *Journal of Youth and Adolescence* 18: 39-53.

Amato, Paul, and Joan Gilbreth. 1999. "Nonresident Fathers and Children's Well-Being: A Meta-Analysis." *Journal of Marriage and the Family* 61: 557-573.

Baumrind, Diana. 1967. "Child Care Practices Anteceding Three Patterns of Preschool Behavior." *Genetic Psychology Monographs* 75: 43-88.

———. 1971. "Current Patterns of Parental Authority." *Developmental Psychology* 4: 1-103.

———. 1978. "Parental Disciplinary Patterns and Social Competence in Children." *Youth and Society* 9: 239-276.

———. 1991. "The Influence of Parenting Style on Adolescent Competence and Substance Use." *Journal of Early Adolescence* 11: 56-95.

Boggiano, A.K., M. Barrett, A.W. Weiher, G.H. Mclelland, and C.M. Lusk. 1987. "Use of the Maximal Operant Principle to Motivate Children's Intrinsic Interest." *Journal of Personality and Social Psychology* 53: 866-879.

Braithwaite, John. 1989. *Crime, Shame and Reintegration*. Cambridge: Cambridge University Press.

————. 2002. *Restorative Justice and Responsive Regulation*. Melbourne, Australia: Cambridge University Press.

Braithwaite, John, and Valerie Braithwaite. 2001. "Revising the Theory of Reintegrative Shaming." Pp. 315-330 in E. Ahmed, N. Harris, J. Braithwaite, and V. Braithwaite (eds), *Shame Management Through Reintegration*. Cambridge: Cambridge University Press.

Braithwaite, John, and Stephen Mugford. 1994. "Conditions of Successful Reintegration Ceremonies: Dealing With Juvenile Offenders." *British Journal of Criminology* 34: 139-171.

Bugental, D., J. Blue, and M. Cruscoza. 1989. "Perceived Control Over Caregiving Outcomes: Implications for Child Abuse." *Developmental Psychology* 25: 532-539.

Chamlin, Mitchell B., and John K. Cochran. 1997. "Social Altruism and Crime." *Criminology* 35: 203-28.

Chapman, W.R. 1985. "Parental Attachment to the Child and Delinquent Behavior." Paper Presented at the American Society of Criminology Meeting, San Diego.

Chen, Xinyin, Qi Dong, and Hong Zhou. 1997. "Authoritative and Authoritarian Parenting Practices and Social and School Adjustment." *International Journal of Behavioral Development* 21: 855-873.

Cohen, David, and Janet Rice. 1997. "Parenting Styles, Adolescent Substance Use, and Academic Achievement." *Journal of Drug Education* 27: 199-211.

Coker, Donna. 1999. "Enhancing Autonomy for Battered Women: Lessons From Navajo Peacemaking." *UCLA Law Review* 47: 1-111.

Cooley, Charles Horton. 1922. *Human Nature and the Social Order*. New York: Scribner's.

Deci, Edward, and Richard Ryan. 1980. "The Empirical Exploration of Intrinsic Motivational Processes." In L. Berkowitz (ed.), *Advances in Experimental Social Psychology, Vol. 13*. New York: Academic Press.

Deng, X., and S. Jou,. 2000. "Shame and the Moral Educative Effects on Deviant Behavior in Cross-Cultural Context." *Proceedings of Criminology Theory and Its Applications in the Year 2000*. National Taipei University. Taipei, Taiwan.

Etzioni, Amitai. 2001. The *Monchrome Society*. Princeton, NJ: Princeton University Press.

Farella, John R. 1993. The *Wind in A Jar*. Albuquerque: University of New Mexico Press

Finnegan, R. A. 1995. "Aggression and Victimization in the Peer Groups: Links in the Mother - Child Relationship." Poster Presented at the Biennial Meeting of the *Society For Research in Child Development*, Indianapolis, IN.

Garfinkel, Harold. 1956. "Conditions of Successful Degradation Ceremonies." *American Journal of Sociology* 61: 420-24.

Grusec, Joan, and Jacqueline Goodnow. 1994. "Impact of Parental Discipline Methods on the Child's Internalization of Values: A Reconceptualization of Current Points of View." *Developmental Psychology* 30: 4-19.

Gunnoe, Lindner, E. Marjorie, Mavis Hetherington, and David Reiss. 1999. "Paternal Religiosity, Parenting Style, and Adolescent Social Responsibility." *Journal of Early Adolescence* 19: 199-225.

Hagan, John and Bill Mccarthy. 1997. *Mean Streets: Youth Crime and Homelessness*. Cambridge: Cambridge University Press.

Harris, Nathan. 2001. "Shaming and Shame: Regulating Drink-Driving." Pp. 73-210 in E. Ahmed, N. Harris, J. Braithwaite, and V. Braithwaite (eds.), *Shame Management Through Reintegration* Cambridge: Cambridge University Press.

Hay, Carter. 2001. "An Exploratory Test of Braithwaite's Reintegrative Shaming Theory." *Journal of Research in Crime and Delinquency* 38: 132-153.

Hetherington, E. Mavis, and W. Glen Clingempeel. 1992. "Marital Transitions: A Family Systems Perspective." In *Monographs of the Society for Research in Child* Development. Chicago: University of Chicago Press.

Janssens, J. M. 1994. "Authoritarian Child Rearing, Parental Locus of Control, and the Child's Behavior Style." *International Journal of Behavioral Development* 17: 485-501.

Johnson, David T. 2002. *The Japanese Way of Justice: Prosecuting Crime in Japan.* New York: Oxford University Press.

Kahan, Dan M. 1996. "What Do Alternative Sanctions Mean?" *University of Chicago Law Review* 63: 591-653.

————. 1997. "Social Influence, Social Meaning and Deterrence." *Virginia Law Review* 83: 349-395.

————. 1998. "The Anatomy of Disgust in Criminal Law." *Michigan Law Review* 69: 1621-1657.

Lamborn, S., N. Mounts, L. Steinberg, and S. Dornbusch. 1991. "Patterns of Competence and Adjustment Among Adolescents from Authoritative, Authoritarian, Indulgent, and Neglectful Families." *Child Development* 62: 1049-1065.

Latimer, Jeff, Craig Dowden, and Danielle Muise. 2001. *The Effectiveness of Restorative Justice Practices: A Meta-Analysis.* Ottawa: Department of Justice, Canada.

Leonardsen, Dag. 2002. "The Impossible Case of Japan." *Australian and New Zealand Journal of Criminology* 35: 203-229.

Lepper, M.R., and D. Greene. 1978. *The Hidden Costs of Reward.* Hillsdale, NJ: Erlbaum.

Lu, Hong. 1998. *Community Policing-Rhetoric or Reality? The Contemporary Chinese Community-Based Policing System in Shanghai.* Ph.D. Dissertation, Arizona State University.

————. 1999. "Bang Jiao and Reintegrative Shaming in China's Urban Neighborhoods." *International Journal of Comparative and Applied Criminal Justice*, 23.

Makkai, Toni, and John Braithwaite. 1993. "Praise, Pride and Corporate Compliance." *International Journal of the Sociology of Law* 21: 73-91.

————. 1994. "Reintegrative Shaming and Regulatory Compliance." *Criminology* 32: 361-385.

Maruna, Shadd. 2001. *Making Good: How Ex-Convicts Reform and Rebuild Their Lives.* Washington, DC: American Psychological Association.

Massaro, Toni M. 1997. "The Meanings of Shame: Implications for Legal Reform." *Psychology, Public Policy and Law* 3: 645-80.

Masters, Guy. 1997. "Values For Probation, Society and Beyond." *Howard Journal of Criminal Justice* 36: 237-247.

McGarrell, Edmund F., Kathleen Olivares, Kay Crawford, and Natalie Kroovand. 2000. *Returning Justice to the Community: the Indianapolis Juvenile Restorative Justice Experiment.* Indianapolis: Hudson Institute.

Morrison, Brenda. 2006. *From Bullying to Responsible Citizenship: A Restorative Approach to Building Safe School Communities.* Sydney, Australia: FederationPress

Noller, P., and V. Callan. 1991. the *Adolescent in the Family.* New York: Chapman and Hall.

Nussbaum, Martha. 2004. *Hiding From Humanity: Disgust, Shame and the Law.* Princeton, NJ: Princeton University Press.

Parker, G. 1983. "Parental "Affectionless Control" As an Antecedent to Adult Depression." *Archives of General Psychiatry* 40: 56-60.

Patterson, G. R., B. D. Debarsyshe, and E. Ramsay. 1989. "A Developmental Perspective on Antisocial Behavior." *American Psychologist* 44: 329-335.

Petrunik, M., and C. D. Shearing. 1988. "The 'I', the 'Me' and the 'It': Moving Beyond the Meadian Conception of the Self." *Canadian Journal of Sociology* 13: 435-448.

Pettit, G. S., Bates, J. E. and Kenneth Dodge. 1997. "Supportive Parenting, Ecological Context, and Children's Adjustment: A Seven-Year Longitudinal Study." *Child Development* 68: 908-923.

Ramsey, A., Paul Watson, M. D. Biderman, and A. L. Reeves. 1996. "Self-Reported Narcissism and Perceived Parental Permissiveness and Authoritarianism." *Journal of Genetic Psychology* 157: 227-238.

Rees, Joseph. 1994. *Hostages of Each Other: The Transformation of Nuclear Safety Since Three Mile Island*. Chicago: University of Chicago Press.

Rumberger, Russell W., Rita Ghatak, Gary Poulos, Phillip L. Ritter, and Sanford M. Dornbusch. 1990. "Family Influences on Dropout Behavior in One California High School." *Sociology of Education* 63: 283-299.

Sampson, Robert J. and John H. Laub. 1993. *Crime in the Making: Pathways and Turning Points Through Life*. Cambridge, MA: Harvard University Press.

Scheff, Thomas J. 1990. "Review Essay: A New Durkheim." *American Journal of Sociology* 96: 741-746.

Scheff, Thomas J. and Suzanne Retzinger. 1991. *Emotions and Violence: Shame and Rage in Destructive Conflicts*. Lexington, MA.: Lexington Books/D. C. Heath and Company.

Sherman, Lawrence. 1992. *Policing Domestic Violence*. New York: Free Press.

———. 1993. "Defiance, Deterrence, and Irrelevance: A Theory of the Criminal Sanction." *Journal of Research in Crime and Delinquency* 30: 445-473

———. 2003. "Reason For Emotion: Reinventing Justice With Theories, Innovations, and Research." *Criminology* 41: 1-38.

Sherman, Lawrence, Heather Strang, and Daniel Woods. 2000. *Recidivism Patterns in the Canberra Reintegrative Shaming Experiments (RISE)*. Canberra: Centre for Restorative Justice, Australian National University.

Shucksmith, Janet, L. B. Hendry, and A. Glendinning. 1995. "Models of Parenting: Implications for Adolescent Well-Being Within Different Types of Family Contexts." *Journal of Adolescence* 18: 253-270.

Sigrún, Aðalbjarnardóttir, and Hafsteinsson Leifur. 2001. "Parenting Styles and Adolescent Substance Use: A Longitudinal Study." *Journal of Research on Adolesence* 11: 401-423.

Tangney, June Price. 1990. "Assessing Individual Differences in Proneness to Shame and Guilt: Development of the Self-Conscious Affect and Attribution Inventory." *Journal of Personality and Social Psychology* 59: 102-111.

———. 1991. "Moral Affect: The Good, the Bad, and the Ugly." *Journal of Personality and Social Psychology* 61: 598-607.

———. 1992. "Situational Determinants of Shame and Guilt in Young Adulthood." *Personality and Social Psychology Bulletin* 18: 199-206.

———. 1993. "Shame and Guilt." Pp. 161-180 in C.G. Costello (ed.), *Symptoms of Depression*. New York: John Wiley and Sons.

———. 1995a. "Shame and Guilt in Interpersonal Relationships." Pp. 114-139 in J..P. Tangney and K.W. Fisher (eds.), *Self-Conscious Emotions:The Psychology of Shame, Guilt, Embarrassment and Pride*. New York: Guilford Press.

———. 1995b. "Recent Advances in the Empirical Study of Shame and Guilt." *American Behavioral Scientist* 38: 1132-1145.

Tangney, June Price, S. A. Burggraf, and P. E. Wagner. 1995. "Shame-Proneness, Guilt-Proneness, and Psychological Symptoms." Pp. 343-367 in J. P. Tangney and K.W. Fischer (eds.), *Self-Conscious Emotions: The Psychology of Shame, Guilt, Embarrassment, and Pride*. New York: Guilford Press.

Tangney, June Price, D. Hill-Barlow, P. E. Wagner, D. E. Marschall, J. K. Borenstein, J. M. T. Sanftner, and R. Gramzow. 1996a. "Assessing Individual Differences in Constructive Versus Destructive Responses to Anger Across the Lifespan." *Journal of Personality and Social Psychology* 70: 780-796.

Tangney, June Price, R. S. Miller, L. Flicker, and D. H. Barlow. 1996b. "Are Shame, Guilt, and Embarrassment Distinct Emotions?" *Journal of Personality and Social Psychology* 70: 1256-1269.

Tangney, June Price, P. E. Wagner, C. Fletcher, and R. Gramzow. 1992. "Shamed Into Anger? The Relation of Shame and Guilt to Anger and Self-Reported Aggression." *Journal of Personality and Social Psychology* 62: 669-675.

Tittle, Charles R., Jason Bratton, and Marc G. Gertz. 2003. "A Test of a Micro-Level Application of Shaming Theory." *Social Problems* 50: 592-617.

Tosouni, Anastasia. 2004. "Reintegrative Shaming Among Youthful Offenders: Testing the Theory Through Secondary Data Analysis." Paper Presented at the Annual Meeting of the American Society of Criminology, Nashville, TN.

Trasler, Gordon. 1972. "The Context of Social Learning." In J.B. Mays (ed.), *Juvenile Delinquency, the Family and the Social Groups.* London: Longmans.

Tutu, Desmond. 1999. *No Future Without Forgiveness.* London: Rider.

Wagatsuma, Hiroshi, and Arthur Rosett. 1986. "The Implications of Apology: Law and Culture in Japan and the United States." *Law and Society Review* 20: 461-498.

Watson, P. J., T. Little, and M. D. Biderman. 1992. "Narcissism and Parenting Styles." *Psychoanalytic Psychology* 9: 231-244.

Webb, Tony. 2003. *Towards A Mature Shame Culture: Theoretical and Practical Tools for Personal and Social Growth.* Unpublished Ph.D. Dissertation, University of Western Sydney, Australia.

Williams, Bernard. 1993. *Shame and Necessity.* Berkeley: University of California Press.

Wright, John Paul, and Francis T. Cullen. 2001. "Parental Efficacy and Delinquent Behavior: Do Control and Support Matter?" *Criminology* 39: 677-706.

Zehr, Howard. 2000. "Journey of Belonging." Paper Presented at the Fourth International Conference on Restorative Justice. Tuebingen.

Zhang, Lening, and S. Zhang. 2000. "Reintegrative Shaming and Delinquency." Unpublished Paper. Saint Francis College, Loretto, PA.

————. 2004. "Reintegrative Shaming and Predatory Delinquency." *Journal of Research in Crime and Delinquency* 41: 433-53.

Zhang, Lening, D. Zhou, S. Messner, A. E. Liska, M. D. Krohn, J. Liu, and L. Zhou. 1996. "Crime Prevention in A Communitarian Society: Bang-Jiao and Tiao-Jie in the People's Republic of China." *Justice Quarterly* 13: 199-222.

15

The Theory of Effective Correctional Intervention: Empirical Status and Future Directions

Paul Gendreau, Paula Smith, and Sheila A. French

In 1974, the comfortable world of researchers, clinicians, and policy makers in the field of correctional treatment was shaken to its core with the publication of an article in *The Public Interest* authored by Robert Martinson (Martinson 1974). Based on an analysis of 231 treatment studies, published between 1945 and 1967, Martinson concluded that most offender programs had no appreciable effect on recidivism and that correctional practitioners were unsuccessful in engineering effective treatment strategies (Martinson 1974; see also Lipton, Martinson, and Wilks 1975). Many years later, the tenuous empirical underpinnings of Martinson's conclusions were exposed (Cullen and Gendreau 2000), but it is fair to say that in the 1970s other scholars concurred with the assessment that treatment programs were generally ineffective (e.g., Sechrest, White, and Brown 1979; Wright and Dixon 1977).

Martinson's views were so provocative because they were very much at odds with the pre-eminent correctional philosophy in North American corrections over the last century (i.e., the rehabilitative ideal). Detailed summaries of the historical roots of the rehabilitative ideal have been outlined previously (see Cullen and Gendreau 2000; Gendreau, Smith, and Goggin 2001), but for our purposes in this essay, only one citation is necessary to illustrate the passion that supporters of rehabilitation felt about their cause. At a seminal conference in Cincinnati, in 1870, Brockway (1871: 42) stated:

> If punishment, suffering and degradation are deemed deterrent, if they are the best means to reform the criminal and prevent crime, then let prison reform go backward to the pillory, the whipping-post, the gallows, the stake: to corporal violence and extermination! But if the dawn of Christianity has reached us, if we have learned the lesson that *evil is to be overcome with good* [italics in original], then let prisons and prison

systems be lighted by this law of love. Let us leave, for the present, the thought of inflicting punishment upon prisoners to satisfy the so-called justice, and turn toward the two grand divisions of our subject, the real objects of the system, vis.: *the protection of society by the prevention of crime and reformation of criminals*...(italics in original)

Brockway's position was no voice in the wilderness. The sentiments expressed by he and his peers were further refined and extended to become the raison d'être of correctional professionals and agencies for many decades (Allen 1981; Glueck and Glueck 1939, 1965; Healey 1915; Task Force on Corrections 1967; Travisono and Hawkes 1995). Even in those academic quarters historically thought to be unsympathetic to offender treatment (e.g., the discipline of criminology, see Cullen and Gendreau 2001), support could be found for rehabilitation (Cressey 1955; Sutherland 1939).

As it happened, the edifice of the rehabilitative ideal was much more fragile than anyone thought. It collapsed precipitously in the face of a number of seismic socio-political shifts that were occurring in American society in the 1960s. Space does not permit a detailed exposition of these (see Cullen and Gendreau 1989, 2000; Cullen and Gilbert 1982), but suffice it to say, Martinson's pronouncement, labeled "nothing works," became a popular cliché (Walker 1985) and was used to justify competing policies for processing offenders, such as "getting tough" on criminals (Erwin 1986; Wilks and Martinson 1976) and the justice model (e.g., Fogel 1979).

Why is the Martinson saga important for the topic at hand? Precisely because, if not for Martinson's challenge, it is likely that proponents of correctional rehabilitation might not have been sufficiently motivated to confront their complacency about the value of treatment programs (Gendreau, Smith, and Goggin 2001). Leading the way to challenge Martinson's edict was the so-called "Canadian School" of rehabilitation (Cullen 2002). Members of this group adhered to the scientist-practitioner model within their discipline of psychology. They were trained to believe the pre-eminent professional role within this model was to implement, administer and evaluate offender assessment and treatment programs. Fortunately for them, Canadian correctional and governmental jurisdictions, particularly at the federal level, were supportive of rehabilitation policies throughout the Martinson era (Gendreau, Smith, and Goggin 2001). Well versed in learning theory and related behavioral treatments, they operated under the assumption that criminal behavior, like almost all forms of social behavior, was largely learned, thereby modifiable through the application of a schedule of ethically appropriate contingent rewards and punishments. Obviously they were not impressed with the curious assumption implicit within the "nothing works" doctrine that only offenders, amongst the entire human race, were incapable of acquiring pro-social behaviors (e.g., Gendreau and Ross 1979).

They opined that it was essential that one had to carefully examine what went into the "black box" of treatment programs, or as Gendreau (1996: 118) stated:

Unlike Martinson and his followers, we believe it is not sufficient just to sum across studies or file them into general categories. The salient question is what are the principles that distinguish between effective and ineffective programs?

The initial objective was to provide "bibliotherapy for cynics" (Gendreau and Ross 1979; Ross and Gendreau 1980) by undertaking a number of literature reviews and demonstration projects (e.g., Andrews 1979, 1980; Andrews and Kiessling 1980; Andrews, Kiessling, Robinson, and Mickus 1986; Barkwell 1975; Chandler 1973; Gendreau and Andrews 1979; Gendreau and Ross 1981a, 1981b, 1983-84, 1987; Ross and Fabiano 1985; Ross and McKay 1978; Wormith 1984) which would validate the utility of offender treatment programs and lead to a practical theory of effective correctional treatment. It should be stressed that members of the "Canadian School" profited by drawing upon the substantive contributions of those few like-minded American colleagues who persisted during the hostile climate of the early Martinson era by generating treatment outcome studies (e.g., Agee 1979; Braukmann, Fixsen, Phillips, and Wolf 1975; Cullen and Gilbert 1982; Davidson and Robinson 1975; Palmer 1975; Warren 1969). The foregoing, therefore, provides the backdrop for the primary goal of this chapter.

First, in outlining the theories involved, we proceed from the general to the specific. We examine some macro level psychological and criminological theories and demonstrate how they led to a micro level theory of effective correctional programming, which is often referred to in the treatment literature as the "principles of effective correctional intervention" (Andrews 1995; Gendreau 1996; Gendreau, Cullen, and Bonta 1994).

Secondly, we address the empirical status of the principles of effective correctional intervention by examining the results of treatment outcome research. Also, we present an independent test of the principles based on a measure of program quality applied to a meta-analytic database and *in situ* programs.

Thirdly, we summarize our results and discuss the directions that theory and research in this area might take in the future.

The Principles of Effective Correctional Intervention

Theoretical Base

In presenting how theory developed in our area of concern, it is necessary to go well back in time to the onset of learning theory in psychology and how, through its evolution, it became harmonious with specific criminological theories to form the substrata that led to a theory of effective correctional intervention. In so doing, we are mindful of the fact that psychological theories per se are not the focus of other chapters in this volume, or generally when social learning theories are discussed in criminology (see Cullen, Wright, Gendreau, and Andrews 2003). A brief exposition, however, of their contribution is crucial for our purposes. There are two reasons for doing this. First, members of the "Canadian School" were all psychologists who were well-grounded in, and strongly influenced by, learning theory. Of note is that those psychologists who have generated almost all of the successful intervention programs (Davidson, Gottschalk, Gensheimer, and Mayer 1984; Gendreau, Goggin, French, and Smith in press) also shared a similar theoretical perspective. Secondly, "old" theories are not necessarily passé. If not for one of the earliest learning theories, the development of effective treatment programs many years later might have been forestalled. In addition, another learning theory was later incorporated into a criminological theory that made an important contribution to the treatment agenda. In the final analysis, our position is that our field of concern is better informed by integrating several theories from both disciplines.

Initially, the psychological theories that shaped the thinking of the early generation of psychologists were three general theories of learning in the neo-behaviorist tradition. These were Hull's (1943) need/drive reduction theory, Guthrie's (1935) law of contiguity, and Tolman's (1932) purposive behaviorism. As well, there were Skinner's (1950) views on learning. His position was not theoretical in the usual sense in which the term is used; it was purely descriptive in nature. Skinner's behaviorism became known as radical behaviorism, or operant psychology.

What was the fall-out from this era of theorizing in learning in psychology? While some cynics lamented that the golden age of learning theory had not lived up to its promises (Koch 1951), fruitful trends gradually surfaced. The dominant trend was a move towards the law of parsimony, and the integration of theories in almost all learning topics (e.g., Bowers 1973). Another welcome development was reflected in the fact that psychologists started to distance themselves from a sterile neo-behaviorism, and began advocating for a more vibrant and flexible behaviorism that embraced social learning and cognitive conceptualizations of behavior. This was an important turn of events as learning theories became more compatible with those criminological theories that had implications for changing behavior.

At the present time there are several learning theories in the social learning and cognitive domains that inform practitioners how to conceptualize and change behavior. They are: 1) modeling therapy and social skills training that focuses on observational learning, behavioral rehearsal, assertion training, and self-efficacy (see Bandura 1977); and 2) cognitive behavioral therapy that attempts to restructure irrational thoughts and beliefs (Beck 1963; Ellis 1962), or is meant to enhance coping skills by training in problem solving, self-instructions and stress inoculation (D'Zurilla and Goldfried 1971; Meichenbaum 1977). Each of these contemporary learning theories is indebted to the older generation of learning theories noted previously, particularly Tolman's[1] and, possibly even more so, Skinner's prescriptions for analyzing behavior.

From the point of view of practitioners, is it worthwhile choosing one learning theory over another? Consider the view that when all is said and done, the utility of behaviorally-oriented theoretical models may be primarily limited to pragmatics (Kanfer and Phillips 1970; Masters, Burish, Hollon, and Rimm 1987). In fact, this is what occurs in the real world of correctional treatment. Based on our contact with successful programs (e.g., conducting audits), it is rare to encounter an effective offender treatment program (e.g., family therapy, individual, group treatments, etc.) that does not draw upon an amalgam of techniques from radical behavioral, social learning, and cognitive methods to various degrees (e.g., Alexander and Parsons 1982; Gendreau 1996; Goldstein 1999; Platt and Prout 1987; see the classic treatment studies described in Ross and Gendreau 1980).

How do criminological theories contribute to the mix? Admittedly, criminological theories, for the most part, have not been enamored with "psychologizing," and indifferent to offering planned treatments. The reasons for this have been documented elsewhere (Andrews and Wormith 1989; Cullen and Gendreau 2000, 2001). There were, however, two outliers amongst the criminological theories, deterrence and differential association.[2]

Deterrence theory in criminology parallels that of punishment in learning theory. While it is based on the notion that criminal behavior can be easily suppressed (Gendreau and Ross 1981a), proponents of deterrence have ignored thousands of punishment studies in the experimental human and animal learning field, the human behavior modification literature, and the social psychology of persuasion (Gendreau 1996; Gendreau, Goggin, and Cullen 1999). If deterrence were to "work" it would have to reckon with the guidelines as to how punishment can function effectively (Azrin and Holz 1966), the different types of punishment (Church 1963), and the empirical identification of effective punishing stimuli (Matson and Di Lorenzo 1984). Instead, deterrence theory relies on vague notions of "costs" and threats, with some dosages of stigmatization and pains of imprisonments thrown in for good measure (Gendreau et al. 1999).[3] Another distinguishing feature of deterrence theory is its frequent reliance on aggregate level data which inflates effect sizes (Gendreau, Goggin, and Smith 2001). For the above reasons, and also taking into consideration the outcome literature on the effect of deterrence programs on recidivism, Cullen et al. (2003) concluded that deterrence theory has little relevance to effective correctional treatment. Indeed, there is evidence forthcoming that correctional practitioners who use deterrence strategies can increase recidivism considerably (Paparozzi and Gendreau in press).

In contrast to deterrence, differential association theory has a constructive position on correctional treatment (see Andrews 1980; Cullen et al. 2003; McGuire 2004). These authors have reinforced the view Cressey (1955: 116-118) expressed a half-century ago that differential association offered considerable promise for changing offenders' attitudes by transforming antisocial group relations into pro-social patterns of behavior. Burgess and Akers (1966) and Akers, Krohn, Lanza-Kaduce, and Radosevich (1979) took a bold step within the field of criminology and reformulated differential association within a Skinnerian radical behavior framework. In other words, the primary learning mechanism in acquiring criminal behavior is operant conditioning and, we hasten to add, given the current climate of "getting tough," the choice of operant behavior modifiers is to use positive reinforcement whenever possible.

What about other theories in the criminological mold? A quiet revolution has been underway demonstrating the utility of several of them to the rehabilitative agenda. For example, McGuire (2004) remarked that two theories, Reckless's (1967) containment theory and Sykes and Matza's (1957) neutralization theory, have useful psychological processes embedded in their theoretical constructs. The five techniques of neutralization (e.g., denial of responsibility, condemning the condemners, etc.) suggested by Sykes and Matza was a thoughtful insight. Any treatment program of consequence must ensure that anti-social attitudes such as these are the primary target for intervention.

Recently, Andrews and Bonta (2003; also see Andrews, Bonta, and Hoge 1990) have incorporated a variety of psychological and criminological theories into a comprehensive social learning theory of crime, entitled: *A Personal, Interpersonal, and Community-Reinforcement Perspective on Criminal Conduct.* They mapped out similar lines of thinking amongst several psychological and criminological theories. Focusing here on just the criminological theories, they described how differential association theory, with an emphasis on operant learning principles (see Burgess and Akers 1966), is essential to understanding how criminal behavior is internally and interpersonally mediated. As well, aspects of self-control (Gottfredson and Hirschi 1990), containment, and sub-cultural theory, rational choice theories (Piliavin, Hardyck, and Vadum 1968), and the reframing of anomie-strain theory (Agnew 1992; Menard 1995) are also meritorious contributions. We also submit social support and social bond viewpoints are worthy of note (e.g., Cullen 1994; Sampson and Laub 1993).

We are not claiming that all of the theories referenced above must receive prizes of equal value; some are obviously more central to the rehabilitation agenda than others, while yet others have more to contribute to suggesting specific treatment techniques. Nevertheless, at this juncture, we believe that taking a catholic perspective on theory is a progressive step. Key aspects of several criminological theories (see Andrews and Bonta 2003) have much in common with modern day conceptualizations of learning theory. In short, it is our contention that there are compelling reasons, given its psychological and criminological underpinnings, to support the social learning theory presented by Andrews and Bonta. The ultimate confirmation of this theory's utility rests on the fact that the "Canadian School" has used this theory as a template from which to derive a number of specific principles of effective correctional intervention. The principles that are described next represent a pragmatic "how to do it" theory as to how best to change offenders' behavior.

Theory of Effective Correctional Intervention

Before describing the principles of effective correctional intervention we define some nomenclature that may be unfamiliar to non-specialists (see Table 1, adapted from Gendreau, French, and Gionet 2004).

The principles of effective correctional intervention are outlined in the sequence we follow when conducting evaluations of the quality of treatment programs in the field using the Correctional Program Assessment Inventory (CPAI-2000, see Gendreau and Andrews 2001), which is described in more detail in a subsequent section. The empirical justification for these principles, with an emphasis on Principles 4 and 5, follows later. For the reader who wishes to explore the treatment area more thoroughly, we suggest examining some of the exemplary programs that have incorporated many of the principles described below. Recommended are the programs listed in Gendreau (1996: 119-120) and the following programs of a more recent vintage:

a) EQUIP Peer-Helping Program (Gibbs, Potter, and Goldstein 1995);
b) Functional Family Therapy Model (Alexander, Pugh, and Parsons 1998; Gordon, Graves, and Arbuthnot 1995);
c) Multisystemic Therapy (Henggeler, Schoenwald, Borduin, Rowland, and Cunningham 1998);
d) Prepare Curriculum Program (Goldstein 1999); and
e) The Rideau Prison-Based Integrated Service Delivery Model (Bourgon and Armstrong 2005).

The principles of effective correctional intervention are as follows:

1. *Organizational Culture.* The organization has a culture that is receptive to implementing new ideas and has a code of ethics. A history of responding to new initiatives and coping with problematic issues in a timely manner is evident, as is a proactive orientation to problem solving. Organizational harmony is reflected in low staff turnover, frequent in-service training, and within house sharing of information.

2. *Program Implementation/Maintenance.* The implementation of the program is based upon individual level survey data on the need for the service and a thorough review of relevant treatment literatures. Implementation occurs during a period when the organization does not face contentious issues (e.g., fiscal, staffing levels, stakeholder reluctance) that might seriously jeopardize the project.

Table 15.1
Frequently Used Terms in Correctional Treatment

Behavioral Treatment. Within the rehabilitative context, treatment is usually referred to as a planned intervention that targets aspects of an offender's attitudes, behaviors, and life circumstances that contribute to his/her criminality. Interventions are meant to increase pro-social behaviors. They do not include "get tough" strategies (e.g., increased surveillance) that are designed to suppress criminal behavior. Behavioral treatments stress that the therapeutic relationship is based upon openness, warmth, and empathy with a firm yet fair application of reinforcement contingencies. There are three general classes of behavioral treatments, the techniques of which overlap. Behavior therapists often incorporate techniques from each of the following:

- *Operant Conditioning.* Radical behavioral treatments are based on the principle of operant conditioning whereby pro-social behavior is immediately reinforced (sometimes called "contingency management") using positive reinforcers.
- *Social Learning.* Social learning programs rely extensively on modeling of appropriate behavior and then having the offender engage in repeated behavioral rehearsal to develop a sense of self-efficacy in mastering the necessary pro-social skills.
- *Cognitive Behavioral.* Cognitive behavioral techniques endeavour to change the offender's cognitions that maintain the undesirable behavior. They employ cognitive restructuring, problem solving, structured learning, reasoning, and self-control techniques

Case Management. Case management practices involve assessing an offender's risk factors and implementing the appropriate level and type of intervention warranted. Example: a high-risk offender with a particular problem with alcohol and violence would be placed in an intensive substance abuse and anger management program. Changes in risk level are assessed and the level of care revised accordingly.

Criminogenic Need. There are two types of criminal risk factors that strongly correlate with recidivism: (1) static, which are fixed (e.g., criminal history, biological factors), and (2) dynamic, which are malleable. Dynamic risk factors are also known as criminogenic needs, which represent an offender's ways of thinking and behaving that support offending behavior. Because they are amenable to change, dynamic risk factors are appropriate targets for intervention and case management. There are also needs that are non-criminogenic; that is, these factors have weak links with criminal conduct (e.g., anxiety, low self-esteem, and vague emotional/personal complaints). They are not targets for treatment.

Reinforcement. Reinforcement increases pro-social behavior so that it will be repeated in the future. Behavior therapists emphasize the use of positive reinforcement of which there are three general types: (1) tangible reinforcers, for example, money or material goods; (2) activities, e.g., sports, music, TV, shopping, socialization; and (3) social reinforcers such as, attention, approval, and praise. In contrast, punishment, which attempts to suppress behavior through the use of unpleasant or harmful consequences to antisocial behavior, is used less often used for a variety of technical and ethical reasons.

Relapse Prevention. Training clients to anticipate problem situations and rehearse and practice alternative pro-social responses to cope with difficult situations in their environment that may lead to conflicts.

Responsivity. There are two kinds of responsivity, *general* and *specific*. The former refers to behavioral treatments of the sort noted above. Specific responsivity pertains to the interaction between the style of service delivery and offender and therapist characteristics.

---

3. *Management/Staff Characteristics.* The director of the program has an advanced degree in a helping profession with several years experience working in offender treatment programs. The majority of staff involved in direct service delivery has undergraduate degrees in the helping professions and clinical experience working with offenders. Staff members are hired on the basis of relationship and skill factors that enhance the integrity of the therapeutic relationship. Staff members are expected to endorse rehabilitation and have confidence in their ability (i.e., self-efficacy) to deliver quality services.

4. *Client Risk/Need Practices: Targeting Criminogenic Needs.* Offenders are assessed on a risk instrument that has adequate predictive validities and contains a wide range of criminogenic needs. These needs are routinely reassessed over time (e.g., every three to six months) in order to target them for treatment and monitor changes in risk/need levels that will have a significant impact on case management practices.

5. *Program Characteristics: General Responsivity and High Risk.* The most effective treatment programs employ behavioral treatment modalities (general responsivity). Behavioral programs should also target the criminogenic needs of higher risk offenders (for a list of criminogenic treatment targets, see Table 2). The program manual details the discrete steps to be followed in presenting the treatment protocol. Offenders spend at least 40 percent of their program time in acquiring pro-social skills. The ratio of reinforcements to punishers is 4:1 or more, and completion criteria are explicit. Relapse prevention strategy methods are extended to offenders after completion of the initial treatment phase.

6. *Core Correctional Practice.* Program therapists engage in the following therapeutic practices:

- Anti-criminal modeling;
- Effective reinforcement and disapproval;
- Problem-solving techniques;
- Structured learning procedures for skill building;
- Effective use of authority;
- Cognitive self-change;
- Relationship practices; and
- Motivational interviewing.

7. *Inter-Agency Communication.* The agency establishes a system (i.e., advocacy, brokerage) whereby offenders are referred to other community agencies that can provide high quality services.

The Empirical Status of the Theory of Effective Correctional Intervention

The empirical revivification of rehabilitation and subsequent articulation of the principles of effective correctional intervention was accomplished in three stages. Initially, researchers conducted narrative literature reviews, in-

Table 15.2
Some Appropriate Criminogenic Need Targets for Intervention

1. Change attitudes and feelings supportive of law violations and anti-criminal role models.

2. Reduce antisocial peer associations.

3. Reduce problems associated with alcohol/drug abuse.

4. Replace the skills of lying, stealing, and aggression with pro-social alternatives.

The following are also important targets when they are linked with any of the above:

5. Increase self-control, self-management, and problem-solving skills.

6. Enhance constructive use of leisure time.

7. Improve skills in interpersonal conflict resolution.

8. Promote more positive attitudes/increase performance regarding schoolwork and the workplace.

9. Resolve emotional problems associated with intra-or extra-familial child abuse.

10. Promote family affection/communication/monitoring/problem solving.

11. Resolve deviant sexual arousal.

12. Alleviate the personal and circumstantial barriers to service (client motivation, background stressors).

cluding studies published after 1967 (the closing date of the literature search for Martinson's review) and gathered insights from the clinical experience of colleagues who had conducted successful programs. This enterprise was labeled "Bibliotherapy for Cynics" (Gendreau and Ross 1979). Later, with the advent of meta-analysis, a more precise assessment of the empirical support for the principles became available.

Bibliotherapy for Cynics

Bibliotherapy for cynics came about as a result of two initiatives. First, recall the quote from Gendreau (1996) about examining the "black box" of intervention programs to discern "what works." The idea behind the "black box" came from Palmer's (1975) response to Martinson's (1974) publication.

Palmer commented that some treatment programs worked well while others failed. Palmers' insight was reinforced by the program evaluation findings of Quay (1977). He reassessed Kassebaum, Ward, and Wilner's (1971) famous prison counseling program, oft-cited as a prime example of a methodologically rigorous evaluation proving "nothing works." Quay discovered that the program in question had a weak conceptual base, used counseling groups that were unstable, and was facilitated by unqualified, poorly trained counselors, some of whom did not believe in the efficacy of the program. Additional support for the type of problems Quay uncovered came from an examination of twenty-seven empirical investigations of applied delinquency prevention behavioral programs. Emery and Marholin (1977) found that in only 30 percent of studies were the behaviors for which delinquent youth were referred to the program identified as targets for treatment (e.g., a client referred for stealing cars was treated for tardiness). Gendreau and Ross (1979) defined this type of problem as a lack of therapeutic integrity. In other words, treatment staff were not adhering to the principles and effective therapeutic techniques that are necessary to change anti-social attitudes and behaviors.

Secondly, some of the emerging principles of effective intervention (e.g., behavioral treatments) began to be articulated in narrative reviews and various demonstration projects (Andrews 1979, 1980; Andrews and Keissling 1980; Gendreau and Ross 1979, 1987; Ross and Fabiano 1985) and, later on, via a series of meta-analyses.

Why meta-analysis? Twenty years ago, it became apparent within the psychological field that the application of narrative review techniques to research literatures was compromised by a host of methodological problems (Beaman 1991; Glass, McGaw, and Smith 1981; Rosenthal 1991). The offender intervention literature was a good case in point. This body of literature was awash in testimonials, with supporters and detractors engaged in a fruitless shouting contest fueled by a great deal of colorful invective (Gendreau and Ross 1979). The narrative reviews also lacked numerical precision, as heretofore reviewers made only tentative, vague guesses about the magnitude of the effect of intervention programs (Gendreau, Goggin, and Smith 2000). If ever a research literature was in need of "therapy," this field of study was a prime candidate. Despite opposition from some quarters, much of it in our view blatantly ethnocentric (i.e., meta-analytic conclusions favoring rehabilitation were contested as they came from outside the United States; see Logan et al. 1991), meta-analysis became the new "gold standard" for arbitrating the "what works" debate.

Meta-Analysis: What Works

At this writing, there are at least thirty-four meta-analyses of correctional treatment effectiveness whose findings have been succinctly summarized by

McGuire (2004). We will focus on key contributions from three broad and somewhat overlapping categories of meta-analyses: a) those which affirm that, overall, treatment programs reduce recidivism; b) those that nominate some general principles of "what works"; and c) those that search for more specific criteria along clinically and psychologically relevant dimensions.

Garrett (1985) and the Davidson research group (Davidson et al. 1984; also see further reports in Apter and Goldstein 1986) produced the first published meta-analyses. Their results still have currency twenty years later. Garrett (1985) accumulated 433 effect sizes from studies of 13,000 juvenile offenders and reported an average reduction of $r = .12$[4] among well-designed studies, albeit recidivism was the criterion of choice for only 43 percent of effect sizes. She identified cognitive behavioral therapies as having the highest mean effect size ($r = .22$). The results from the Davidson group were similar to those of Garrett (1985) in that behavioral interventions (i.e., positive reinforcement, token economies, behavioral contracting) proved to be the most effective. As well, the type of professional training (e.g., psychology, education) and the degree of involvement of the evaluators in the design of the intervention were also important.

The gist of these findings has repeatedly been replicated. For example, Lipsey (1992) summarized the results of a huge database of juvenile interventions (443 effect sizes). Sixty-four percent of these were positive (i.e., reduced recidivism). The average reduction in recidivism within the Lipsey (1992) sample varied from 5 percent to 9 percent depending on statistical adjustments. Lösel (1995) provided a comprehensive assessment of thirteen meta-analyses of juvenile and adult offenders published between 1985 and 1995 and found that mean effect sizes ranged from .05 to .18 with an overall mean of approximately $r = .10$. The patterns of the above results remained after controlling for the effects of factors such as subject attrition, quality of research design, length of follow-up, or study publication status (Lipsey 1999). Lösel (1995) and Lipsey (1992) also suggested that the overall treatment effect size is likely underestimated as evaluations of treatment studies often use comparison groups that received some other interventions as well.

The meta-analyses referenced above identified the most effective treatment programs as those which were cognitive behavioral in nature, had a high degree of structure, were demonstration programs rather than "real world" programs, and were delivered in the community rather than an institutional setting (Cleland, Pearson, Lipton, and Yee 1997; Izzo and Ross 1990; Lipsey 1999; Lipsey, Chapman, and Landenberger 2001; Lösel 1995; Redondo, Sanchez-Meca, and Garrido 1999).

Skeptics may counter that a 10 percent reduction in recidivism is of little practical value. Nothing could be further from the truth! Lipsey and Wilson (1993) and Rosenthal and DiMatteo (2001) have documented that many medical treatments have proven to be cost-effective when the incidence of serious illness is reduced by even small percentage magnitudes (i.e., 3 percent to 10 percent). Offender treatment programs can be highly cost-effective when even small to modest reductions in recidivism result, depending on the interval in which the intervention occurs and its attendant costs (Aos, Lieb, Mayfield, Miller, and Pennucci 2004; Cohen 2001; Welsh and Farrington 2000). Furthermore, Cohen (1998) has calculated the cost-effectiveness of saving high risk juvenile offenders and found that, during the course of a criminal career, an average high-risk youth incurs costs of $1.7 to $2.3 million.

Meta-Analysis: Clinically and Psychologically Relevant Principles

The meta-analyses described in this section broadened the search for more specific principles of clinical and psychological relevance to offender treatment. The exploration began in earnest in 1990 when Andrews et al. coded the treatment literature (154 effect sizes) along a variety of dimensions that provided the basis for the development of the principles of effective correctional intervention. This database was extended to 374 effect sizes, which is the data set that we report on (see Andrews and Bonta 2003, 310-311). We attend first to the data addressing the validity of Principles 4 and 5, arguably the most important for predicting the effectiveness of a program (Gendreau and Andrews 2001).

Principle 4 pertains to the identification of empirically validated predictors of recidivism. There are two classes of predictors: static (e.g., criminal history) and dynamic (e.g., anti-social attitudes). The latter are defined as criminogenic needs (see Table 1) and are the appropriate targets for intervention. Subsequent meta-analyses demonstrated that dynamic criminogenic needs are robust predictors of recidivism (Bonta, Law, and Hanson 1998; Gendreau, Little, and Goggin 1996; Hanson and Morton-Bourgon 2004). These meta-analyses also discovered that personality characteristics, once regarded as important treatment targets, had weak predictive validities (e.g., low self-esteem, depression, anxiety; see Gendreau et al. 1996) and should not be the primary targets for intervention. Meta-analyses of composite measures of risk have identified the Level of Supervision Inventory-Revised (LSI-R) as the most appropriate for risk assessment purposes (Gendreau et al. 1996). The inventory has generated impressive predictive validities ($r = .37$, $CI = .33$ to $.41$; Gendreau, Goggin, and Smith 2002) on a wide variety of offender samples. About half of its fifty-four items are dynamic, thus the measure is useful for measuring change, and for devising case management treatment plans.

In terms of treatment results, the 2003 meta-analysis found that treatment programs that adhered to Principle 4 reduced recidivism by 20 percent more than programs that did not. Interestingly, programs that targeted non-criminogenic needs increased recidivism by 7 percent.

Principle 5 also has sound empirical support. The most effective interventions are those that were behavioral in nature (general responsivity). Behavioral treatment programs produced 19 percent greater reductions in recidivism than non-behavioral treatment programs. Principle 5 also includes a risk principle; higher risk offenders should benefit the most from treatment. When treatment programs were subdivided solely on the basis of whether higher or lower risk samples were the targets of treatment, reductions in recidivism favored the former by 7 percent.

When treatment programs were categorized as to whether they followed *both* Principles 4 and 5 in contrast to those that did not, a 23 percent difference in recidivism was reported. When the results were broken down according to treatment site location, the corresponding reduction for community-based and residential settings was 29 percent and 19 percent, respectively. It should also be noted that Principles 4 and 5 have also been found to be applicable to a variety of corrections populations, including female offenders, minority groups, youthful offenders, mentally disordered, and sex offenders (Andrews, Dowden, and Rettinger 2001), violent offenders (Dowden and Andrews 2000), as well within distinct therapeutic domains (e.g., family interventions; see Dowden and Andrews 2003).

Before moving on to the rest of the principles of effective correctional intervention, we wish to draw attention to three other findings. First, Principles 4 and 5 apply to the special case of reducing anti-social behavior in prison (i.e., misconducts). French and Gendreau (in press) tested several of the principles of effective treatment with a sample of 105 effect sizes involving 23,000 prisoners. The results were uncannily similar to those reported in the Andrews' meta-analyses. French and Gendreau (in press) reported an overall effect of $r = .14$, with the behavioral program category recording the strongest result ($r = .26$). Among programs which targeted three to eight criminogenic needs, the effect size was $r = .29$ versus $r = .06$ for those which targeted none. Secondly, in the Andrews et al., (1990) study, programs that serviced lower risk offenders and used non-behavioral treatments (i.e., non-directive, unstructured, psychodynamic, and *milieux* therapies, or services based on threats of sanctions[5]) produced an increase in recidivism ($r = -.06$). Thirdly, Andrews and Bonta (2003) also proffered a specific responsivity principle (i.e., the matching of offender, therapist, and program characteristics). For example, offenders with lower IQs might function better in a highly structured token economy program run by staff who are effective in relating to their style of thinking (e.g., Cullen, Gendreau, Jarjoura, and Wright 1997). Few outcome studies assessing this potentially useful principle have been published to date (see Andrews and Bonta 2003, 263).

Principle 6, Core Correctional Practice[6], a treatment dimension just added to the CPAI-2000, has recently received encouraging empirical support from meta-analyses (Andrews and Bonta 2003: 311; also see French and Gendreau in press). The various therapeutic practices outlined under this principle are associated with reductions in recidivism in the range of $r = .19 - .27$ for programs that apply them versus those that do not. Dowden and Andrews (2004) have updated some of the data for Principle 6 and assessed the contribution of relapse prevention strategies to effective treatment programs (Dowden, Antonowicz, and Andrews 2003). The authors found that larger reductions in recidivism were associated with programs which help offenders to recognize the sequence of events which precipitate their criminal behavior through relapse rehearsal training for themselves and their significant others.

There is less empirical support for the four other principles of effective correctional intervention (Principles 1 to 3, and 7). The validity of Principle 1, Organizational Culture, rests, so far, on the good common sense and clinical wisdom of practitioners who have found the components of this domain to be useful. For theory to develop further in this area the general management and industrial organizational theories need to be incorporated into the offender treatment literature (e.g., Stojkovic, Klofas, and Kalinich 2002).

Principles 2 and 3 are gaining empirical momentum. There are a few primary studies (Goggin and Gendreau in press; Lowenkamp 2004; Paparozzi and Gendreau in press), as well as a meta-analysis (see next section by Nesovic 2003) in support of these two Principles.

Regarding Principle 3, Management/Staff Characteristics, support for this principle stems from the general clinical psychology literature and from the correctional treatment literature (Andrews and Bonta 2003), as well as from meta-analyses (Andrews and Bonta 2003; Andrews and Dowden in press; see also, Gendreau et al. in press). For example, Andrews and Dowden (in press) found that programs that reported attending to the selection, training, and supervision of staff produced 15 percent lower recidivism rates and those that had an involved evaluator had 19 percent lower recidivism rates than those that did not.

Similar to Principle 1, there is no data attesting to the value of Principle 7. Years ago, Gendreau and Ross (1979) commented that the lack of inter-agency co-ordination represented a serious deficit in correctional programming. In our opinion, this reality still remains the case. The potential gains in effective service delivery will be considerable if this difficult task is ever taken seriously by state, provincial, and county organizations. One possible avenue for bringing about much needed change in this regard is via accreditation of service delivery setting by external program auditors (see Goggin and Gendreau in press).

Testing the Principles

The emergence of the principles of effective correctional intervention however, was not greeted with alacrity in some academic quarters. One of the recurring objections was that rehabilitation proponents might have been magi-cally transforming spurious relationships through tautological wizardry (Logan and Gaes 1993; for a counterview, see Cullen and Applegate 1997). Despite the fact that the Andrews, Zinger, et al. (1990) meta-analysis was predicated on a theoretical framework espoused ten years previously (see Gendreau 1989), there was some merit to the challenge. As a literature review technique, meta-analysis is not foolproof. Researcher biases can affect coding decisions, where accuracy is often hampered either by the lack of information provided or inconsistent and vague reporting practices. One need only conduct a meta-analysis of the offender treatment literature to recognize the enormity of the problem.

Fortunately, another way of empirically testing the principles of effective treatment was available. The idea of codifying the principles in an assessment inventory first came about during a 1988 conference presentation on prisons in Nags Head, N.C. Doris Mackenzie, one of the few criminologists at the time who was sympathetic to rehabilitation, suggested that the first author develop an inventory of principles of "what works"; from this the CPAI-2000 was born. It has since undergone several revisions, the latest of which includes 131 items designed to measure the therapeutic integrity of a program (CPAI-2000, Gendreau and Andrews 2001). The instrument captures all of the principles elucidated by Andrews (1995), Andrews and Bonta (2003), and Gendreau (1996). The current version of the measure consists of eight domains, the first seven of which assess the quality of the intervention itself and were described previously. To date, it has been used to evaluate almost 400 offender treatment programs (Gendreau, Goggin, and Smith 2001; Lowenkamp 2004), the majority (i.e., 70 percent) of which have failed to achieve a passing grade.[7]

Two investigators have used the 1997 version of the CPAI-2000 (the earlier version of the CPAI consisted of seventy items which allowed for an assessment of Principles 2-5 and 7) to measure the predictive validity of the instrument. Since the measure represents a state-of-the-art compilation of what is known about the characteristics of effective treatment, one might expect it would predict offender treatment outcome (i.e., recidivism). If it should fail to do so, the tautological argument would have credibility.

In the first study, a meta-analysis, Nesovic (2003) gathered 173 studies from the offender treatment literature and reported a mean effect of $r = .12$ with recidivism across 266 effect sizes. Using program descriptions provided by each of the studies, Nesovic (2003) assessed their quality using the CPAI and then correlated CPAI scores with effect size for each program. Overall, the CPAI program scores correlated very well with reductions in recidivism ($r = .46$), with the domain of Principle 2 having the lowest validity ($r = .10$). In contrast, the domains of Principles 4 and 5 were among the most robust ($r = .41$ and $r = .43$, respectively). Nesovic (2003) also examined correlations between individual scale items and effect sizes. Included among the strongest individual items (i.e., $r = .25$) were: the program receives appropriate clients, offenders' dynamic risk factors are assessed, the program has a written manual, relapse prevention is practiced, staff are trained and hired based on their knowledge of effective relationship and therapeutic skills, and evaluators are involved in the program. Finally, Nesovic (2003) categorized treatment programs in terms of quality (i.e., high, medium, or low) based on their CPAI scores and reported mean effects with recidivism of $r = .20$, $r = .11$, and $r = .01$, respectively.

Lowenkamp (2004) used the CPAI to conduct thirty-eight *in situ* evaluations of the quality of Ohio-based offender treatment programs. They compared the treatment group outcomes with matched comparison groups (i.e., gender, race, actuarial risk measure score) and used reincarceration as the criterion. The overall correlation with outcome was $r = .41$. Lowenkamp (2004) found that Principles 2, 4, and 5 were the most powerful predictors of recidivism ($rs = .54, 34,$ and $.52$, respectively). He also isolated those items from the CPAI which correlated with treatment outcome and reported a mean effect size of $r = .60$.

With respect to individual items, potent correlations (i.e., $r = .25$) with outcome were reported for the following: program designer qualifications; staff trained by program director; program valued by criminal justice stakeholders and 'at large" communities; offenders' risk level and dynamic needs assessed; offenders closely monitored; offenders spend at least 40 percent of time in therapeutic activities; program and staff matched; program has external quality controls; assessment of in-program progress and community follow-up provided; and the program has ethical guidelines and defined completion criteria.

When programs were categorized as high, medium, low, or very low based on their CPAI scores, Lowenkamp (2004) reported reductions in recidivism of 22 percent, 10 percent, and 5 percent, respectively, with those rated as "very low" actually increasing recidivism by 19 percent. Lowenkamp and Latessa (2005) then extended their analysis to ninety-one offender programs in Ohio. They sorted programs on the basis of a therapeutic integrity score derived from the CPAI. There were four levels of therapeutic integrity. Programs classified as low obtained a score between 0 and 19 percent, those that were medium had a score of 20 to 39 percent, high was 40 to 59 percent, and very high was greater than 60 percent. The recidivism rates for each category were 15 percent, 2 percent, 12 percent, and 16 percent, respectively

In conclusion, the results of these investigations do not support the tautological critique of Logan and Gaes (1993), and further confirm the utility of several of the principles.

Future Directions

The sequence of events we have described in this chapter have been replicated time and again when theories have attempted to explain how well human behavior can be predicted and controlled. Theories that appeared to be unassailable were later abandoned (e.g., see footnote 1) either because of changes in the socio-political zeitgeist, the emergence of a series of incisive reviews, the results from experiments that resolved critical methodological issues, or combinations therein (Hergenhahn 2001). Our field of interest proved to be no exception however, a distinguishing feature was the rapidity with which the rehabilitative agenda collapsed. For those of us who were active in corrections in the 1970s, it felt as though only a couple of years had passed after Martinson's edict that offender rehabilitation was discredited to such an extent that it was moribund. Then it was revivified within short order. Even so, widespread acceptance of the rehabilitative model portrayed in this chapter is still tenuous. The promulgation of empirically bankrupt treatment policies founded on bad common sense and ideology is alive and well in criminal justice as well as other social service areas (Gendreau, Goggin, Cullen, and Paparozzi 2002; Hunt 1999; Latessa, Cullen, and Gendreau 2002). While, we do not expect the rehabilitative ideal to be embraced at the levels evidenced in its halcyon pre-1975 era, in our opinion, it is improbable that the dramatic shifts witnessed in years passed will be repeated. For one thing, the fact that, within the disciplines of criminology and psychology, offender rehabilitation is once again respectable is a healthy sign. Our forecast is that this state of affairs will be maintained.

We have confidence in our prediction because there is a rich historical tradition in support of effective correctional interventions. It is gratifying to witness the evolution of learning theories originating from the earliest days of learning theory in psychology (e.g., Skinner), which were reformulated into social learning theories (e.g., Bandura), that led to the growth of useful theories of behavior change in general. Rewarding too were the parallel developments occurring in criminological theories. Sutherland's theory of differential association, which subsequently incorporated Skinnerian operant conditioning principles, was a significant achievement as it spoke directly to a positive rehabilitative agenda. We also documented that other criminological theories (e.g., sub-cultural, social control) were instrumental in the development of a general social learning theory of criminal behavior (e.g., Andrews and Bonta 2003) that set the stage for the emergence of the theory of effective correctional intervention.

What is the future of theory in this field? In our way of thinking, "where the action will be" is with theories that have immediate practical implication such as effective correctional intervention. As is stands this theory has sound empirical support for several of the principles (i.e., 4-6). Reductions in recidivism in the range of 15 percent to 30 percent are comparatively large in the social sciences and medicine and are certainly cost-effective. Having said that we now resort to one of the hoariest clichés in the social sciences. More research is needed! We have just begun to scratch the surface of what needs to be investigated. To illustrate this point we draw upon two examples from Principles 4 and 5. For these two principles to reach their full potential the interpretation of risk has to be clarified. The definitions of risk used in treatment studies are highly mixed. Studies report different risk measures with variable cut-off scores, use single item definitions of risk, or use the sponsoring agency's subjective designation of risk. Within study comparisons of risk where the definition of risk remains constant are needed. Changes in offender risk must also be assessed. The benefits accruing from this research agenda are that: a) security-appropriate inmate assignment and transfer decisions; b) suitability for parole and probation/parole supervision; c) pre-treatment identification of criminogenic needs; and d) monitoring of the effectiveness of interventions, will be more accurate. Regrettably, only a handful of studies have conducted evaluations of changes in risk level (Gendreau et al. 1996; Gendreau et al. in press). Even more unfortunate is the fact that few correctional practitioners and agencies use risk measures that are amenable to measuring change (Boothby and Clements 2000; Gallagher, Somwaru, and Ben-Porath 1999). Then, there are a number of other constituents within these two principles that have been the subject of very little study (treatment dosage, Bourgon and Armstrong 2005; specific responsivity, Andrews et al. 1990)) or none at all (e.g., ratio of reinforcers to punishers).

The same concern applies to Principles 2, 3, and 6, which have appreciable potential but less empirical support, and Principles 1 and 7, which have no support whatsoever. One has to recognize that it will be years before a sizable body of outcome literature appears to determine how important these principles are to recidivism outcomes. One of the reasons is that so few practitioners and managers in corrections have the requisite management skills and clinical training to establish and conduct treatment programs of therapeutic integrity. This state of affairs may be worsening (Andrews, Dowden, and Gendreau 2002). Also, it is one thing to go about the onerous task of comparing different treatment modalities in a study (e.g., Davidson, Redner, Blakely, Mitchell, and Emshoff 1987) but it is another matter to compare different organizational/management/staff/brokerage characteristics and relate these to outcome.

The enormity of the task—adequately testing all of the fine details within the principles of effective correctional intervention—is truly daunting. The means to augment the validity of the theory of effective correctional intervention (besides generating more primary studies for meta-analysis) is through the provision of training in more academic settings so that graduates will take up positions in corrections and advocate for sound treatment policies, the accreditation of treatment sites (Gendreau et al. 2002; Goggin and Gendreau in press), and through evaluations of the quality of existing treatment programs (e.g., Latessa and Lowenkamp 2005).

Notes

* We appreciate the advice of Lisa Best, Francis Cullen, and Murray Goddard on various aspects of the manuscript. Richard Lemke assisted in the preparation of the manuscript. Further enquiries regarding this chapter and related material should be directed to Paula Smith, Division of Criminal Justice, College of Education, Criminal Justice, and Human Services, University of Cincinnati, 600 Dyer Hall, Cincinnati, OH, 45221-0389 or email paula.smith@uc.edu.

1. The fate of the three grand theories of learning is a fascinating story. Until the early 1960s, Hullian theory and the extensions of it by the legion of acolytes he inspired, the most prominent being Spence (1956), utterly dominated all other theories as evidenced by research citations in the fields of learning and motivation, abnormal and social psychology (Myers 1970; Ruja 1956). Now, one searches the fine print of contemporary learning texts to find any reference to Hull's (1943) model. In contrast, a good argument can be made that Tolman, who did not take his theory very seriously, conducted little research, and generated very few followers (see Tolman 1959), had the most long term influence. The roots of social cognitive psychology (e.g., Bandura's theory) can be traced back to Tolman (Hergenhahn 2001).

2. A case might possibly be made for sub-cultural and labeling theories (Andrews and Bonta 2003: 141-147; Gendreau 1996: 126-127) but, as far as we are aware, none of the scholars involved with these theories encouraged treatment programs with much alacrity.

3. Threats are ineffective as they don't have immediate consequences or the consequences are so far in the future they are rendered meaningless. Secondly, threats may not be perceived as punishments; instead, they may foster psychological resistance (Gendreau 1996).

4. Using Rosenthal's (1991) BESD statistic, the r-value can be taken at face value. Recidivism rates for the treatment and comparison groups are computed from a base rate of 50 percent. Thus, with a correlation of $r = .20$ between treatment and reoffending, one can conclude that the recidivism rate in the treatment group is 40 percent (50 percent *minus* 10 percent) as compared with 60 percent in the comparison group (50 percent *plus* 10 percent). Moreover, when summarizing a number of studies or in instances where recidivism base rates are > 20 percent or < 80 percent and treatment and comparison group sample sizes are within a 3:1 ratio, the r value closely approximates, or is identical to, the recidivism percentage difference between the two groups (Cullen & Gendreau, 2000; French & Gendreau, in press).

5. Given the increased popularity of intermediate sanctions involving increased surveillance (Erwin 1986), it is worth noting that later meta-analyses containing very large data sets continued to report slight negative effects on recidivism (Gendreau, Goggin, Cullen, and Andrews 2000; Smith, Goggin, and Gendreau 2002). In fact, only in the instances where intermediate sanctions offered some treatment services were reduction effects on recidivism discovered ($r \sim .10$, Gendreau, Goggin, and Fulton 2000).

6. There are some excellent treatment manuals outlining how to deliver Core Correctional Practices (e.g., Goldstein 1999; Henggeler et al. 1998; Smith, Hart, Pennington, Sanford, and Milan 1972; Stumphauzer 1986).

7. Recall Lipsey (1999) found that "real world" programs are sometimes lacking in therapeutic integrity and produce lower reductions in recidivism.

References

Agee, V. 1979. *Treatment of the Violent Incorrigible Adolescent.* Toronto: D. C. Heath.

Agnew, R. 1992. "Foundations for General Strain Theory of Crime and Delinquency." *Criminology* 30: 47-87.

Akers, R. L., M. Krohn, L. Lanza-Kaduce, and M. Radosevich. 1979. "Social Learning and Deviant Behavior." *Sociological Review* 44: 636-655.

Alexander, J., and B. Parsons. 1982. *Functional Family Therapy.* Monterey, CA: Brooks/Cole.

Alexander, J., C. Pugh, and B. Parsons. 1998. *Functional Family Therapy: Book Three in the Blueprints and Violence Prevention Series.* Boulder, CO: Center for the Study and Prevention of Violence, University of Colorado.

Allen, F. A. 1981. *The Decline of the Rehabilitative Ideal: Penal Policy and Social Purpose.* New Haven, CT: Yale University Press.

Andrews, D. A. 1979. *The Dimensions of Correctional Counseling and Supervision Process in Probation and Parole.* Toronto, Ontario Ministry of Correctional Services.

———. 1980. "Some Experimental Investigations of the Principles of Differential Association Through Deliberate Manipulations of the Structure of Service Systems." *American Sociological Review* 45: 448-462.

———. 1995. "The Psychology of Criminal Conduct and Effective Treatment." Pp. 35-62 in J. MAguire (ed.), in *What Works: Reducing Reoffending,* edited by J. McGuire, 35-62. Chichester, UK: Wiley.

Andrews, D. A., and J. Bonta. 2003. *The Psychology of Criminal Conduct,* 3rd ed. Cincinnati: Anderson.

Andrews, D. A., J. Bonta, and R. D. Hoge. 1990. "Classification for Effective Rehabilitation: Rediscovering Psychology." *Criminal Justice and Behavior* 17: 19-52.

Andrews, D. A., and C. Dowden. in press. "Managing Correctional Treatment for Reducing Recidivism: A Meta-Analytic Review of Program Integrity." *Legal and Criminological Psychology.*

Andrews, D.A., C. Dowden, and P. Gendreau. 2002. "Clinically Relevant and Psychologically Informed Approaches to Reduced Re-Offending: A Meta-Analytic Study of Human Service, Risk, Need, Responsivity, and Other Concerns in Justice Contexts." Manuscript in preparation, Carleton University.

Andrews, D. A., C. Dowden, and L. J. Rettinger. 2001. "Special Populations Within Corrections." Pp. 170-212 in J.A. Winterdyk (ed.). *Corrections in Canada,* Toronto: Prentice Hall.

Andrews, D. A., and J. J. Kiessling. 1980. "Program Structure and Effective Correctional Practices: A Summary of the CaVIC Research." Pp. 441-463 in R. R. Ross and P. Gendreau (eds.), *Effective Correctional Treatment,* Toronto: Butterworths.

Andrews, D. A., J. J. Kiessling, D. Robinson, and S. Mickus. 1986. "The Risk Principle of Case Classification: An Outcome Evaluation with Young Adult Probationers." *Canadian Journal of Criminology* 28: 377-384.

Andrews, D. A., and J. S. Wormith. 1989. "Personality and Crime: Knowledge Destruction and Construction in Criminology." *Justice Quarterly* 6: 289-309.

Andrews, D. A., I. Zinger, R. D. Hoge, J. Bonta, P. Gendreau, and F. T. Cullen. 1990. "Does Correctional Treatment Work? A Clinically-Relevant and Psychologically Informed Meta-Analysis." *Criminology* 28: 369-404.

Aos, S., R. Lieb, J. Mayfield, M. Miller, and A. Pennucci. 2004. *Benefits and Costs of Prevention and Early Intervention Programs for Youth.* Olympia: Washington State Institute for Public Policy.

Apter, S. J., and A. P. Goldstein. 1986. *Youth Violence: Program and Prospects.* New York: Pergamon Press.

Azrin, N., and W. Holz. 1966. "Punishment." Pp. 380-447 in W. Hoenig (ed.), *Operant Behavior: Areas of Research and Application*. New York: Appleton-Century-Crofts.

Bandura, A. 1977. *Social Learning Theory*. Oxford, UK: Prentice Hall.

Barkwell, L. J. 1975. "Differential Treatment of Juveniles on Probation: An Evaluative Study." *Canadian Journal of Criminology and Corrections* 18: 1-16.

Beaman, A. L. 1991. "An Empirical Comparison of Meta-Analytic and Traditional Reviews." *Personality and Social Psychology Bulletin* 1: 252-257.

Beck, A. 1963. "Thinking and Depression: I. Idiosyncratic Content and Cognitive Distortions." *Archives of General Psychiatry* 9: 324-333.

Bonta, J., M. Law, and K. Hanson. 1998. "The Prediction of Criminal and Violent Recidivism Among Mentally Disordered Offenders: A Meta-Analysis." *Psychological Bulletin* 123: 123-142.

Boothby, J. L., and C. B. Clements. 2000. "A National Survey of Correctional Psychologists." *Criminal Justice and Behavior* 27: 715-731.

Bourgon, G., and B. Armstrong. 2005. "Transferring the Principles of Effective Treatment Into a 'Real World' Setting." *Criminal Justice and Behavior* 32: 3-25.

Bowers, K. 1973. "Situationism in Psychology: An Analysis and a Critique." *Psychological Review* 80: 307-336.

Braukmann, C. J., D. L. Fixsen, E. L. Phillips, and M. W. Wolf. 1975. "Behavioural Approaches to Treatment in the Crime and Delinquency Field." *Criminology* 13: 299-331.

Brockway, Z. R. 1871. "The Ideal of a True Prison System for a State." Pp. 38-65 in E.C. Wines (ed.) *Transactions of the National Congress on Penitentiary and Reformatory Discipline*. Albany, NY: Weed, Parsons.

Burgess, R., and R. L. Akers. 1966. "A Differential Association-Reinforcement Theory of Criminal Behavior." *Social Problems* 14: 128-147.

Chandler, M. J. 1973. "Egocentrism and Antisocial Behaviour: The Assessment and Training of Social Perspective-Taking Skills." *Developmental Psychology* 9: 326-333.

Church, R. M. 1963. "The Varied Effects of Punishment on Behavior." *Psychological Review* 70: 369-402.

Cleland, C. M., F. S. Pearson, D. S. Lipton, and D. Yee. 1997, November. "Does Age Make a Difference? A Meta-Analytic Approach to Reductions in Criminal Offending for Juveniles and Adults." Paper presented at the annual meeting of the American Society of Criminology, San Diego, CA.

Cohen, M. A. 1998. "The Monetary Value of Saving a High-Risk Youth." *Journal of Quantitative Criminology* 14: 5-32.

———. 2001. "To Treat or Not to Treat? A Financial Perspective." Pp. 35-49 in C. R. Hollin (ed.), in *Handbook of Offender Assessment and Treatment*. Rexdale, Ontario, Canada: Wiley.

Cressey, D. 1955. "Changing Criminals: The Application of the Theory of Differential Association." *American Journal of Sociology* 61: 116-120.

Cullen, F. T. 1994. "Social Support as an Organizing Concept for Criminology: Presidential Address to the Academy of Criminal Justice Sciences." *Justice Quarterly* 11: 527-559.

Cullen, F. T. 2002. "Rehabilitation and Treatment Programs." Pp. 253-289 in J. Q. Wilson and J. Petersilia (eds.), in *Crime: Public Policies for Crime Control*. Oakland, CA: ICS Press.

Cullen, F. T., and B. Applegate. 1997. *Offender Rehabilitation: Effective Correctional Intervention*. Aldershot, UK: Ashgate/Dartmouth.

Cullen, F. T., and P. Gendreau. 1989. "The Effectiveness of Correctional Treatment: Reconsidering the 'Nothing Works' Debate." Pp. 23-44 in L. Goodstein and D. L. MacKenzie (eds.), in *The American Prison: Issues in Research and Policy*. New York: Plenum.

————. 2000. "Assessing Correctional Rehabilitation: Policy, Practice, and Prospects." Pp. 109-175 in J. Horney (ed.), in *National Institute of Justice Criminal Justice 2000: Changes in Decision Making and Discretion in the Criminal Justice System*. Washington, DC: Department of Justice, National Institute of Justice.

————. 2001. "From Nothing Works to What Works: Changing Professional Ideology in the 21st Century." *The Prison Journal* 81: 313-338.

Cullen, F. T., P. Gendreau, G. R. Jarjoura, and J. P. Wright. 1997. "Crime and the Bell Curve: Lessons From Intelligent Criminology." *Crime and Delinquency* 43: 387-411.

Cullen, F. T., and K. E. Gilbert. 1982. *Reaffirming Rehabilitation*. Cincinnati: Anderson.

Cullen, F. T., J. P. Wright, P. Gendreau, and D. Andrews. 2003. "What Correctional Treatment Can Tell Us About Criminological Theory: Implications for Social Learning Theory." Pp. 339-362 in R. Akers and G. Jensen (eds.), in *Social Learning Theory and the Explanation of Crime*. New Brunswick, NJ: Transaction Publishers.

Davidson, W., R. Gottschalk, L. Gensheimer, and J. Mayer. 1984. *Interventions with Juvenile Delinquents: A Meta-Analysis of Treatment Efficacy*. Washington, DC: National Institute of Juvenile Justice and Delinquency Prevention.

Davidson, W., R. Redner, C., Blakely, C., Mitchell, and J. Emshoff. 1987. "Diversion of Juvenile Offenders: An Experimental Comparison." *Journal of Consulting and Clinical Psychology* 55: 68-75.

Davidson III, W. S., and M. J. Robinson. 1975. "Community Psychology and Behaviour Modification: A Community Based Program for the Prevention of Delinquency." *Corrective and Social Psychiatry* 21: 1-12.

Dowden, C., and D. A. Andrews. 2000. "Effective Correctional Treatment and Violent Reoffending: A Meta-Analysis." *Canadian Journal of Criminology* 42: 449-467.

————. 2003. "Does Family Intervention Work for Delinquents? Results of a Meta-Analysis." *Canadian Journal of Criminology and Criminal Justice* 45: 327-342.

————. 2004. "The Importance of Staff Practice in Delivering Effective Correctional Treatment: A Meta-Analytic Review of Core Correctional Practice." *International Journal of Offender Therapy and Comparative Criminology* 48: 203-214.

Dowden, C., D. Antonowicz, and D. A. Andrews. 2003. "The Effectiveness of Relapse Prevention with Offenders: A Meta-Analysis." *International Journal of Offender Therapy and Comparative Criminology* 47: 516-528.

D'Zurilla, T., and M. Goldfried. 1971. "Problem Solving and Behavior Modification." *Journal of Abnormal Psychology* 78: 107-126.

Ellis, A. 1962. *Reason and Emotion in Psychotherapy*. Secaucus, NJ: Lyle Stuart.

Emery, R. E., and D. Marholin. 1977. "An Applied Behavior Analysis of Delinquency: The Irrelevancy of Relevant Behavior." *American Psychologist* 32: 860-873.

Erwin, B. J. 1986. "Turning Up the Heat on Probationers in Georgia." *Federal Probation* 50: 17-24.

Fogel, D. 1979. *We Are the Living Proof: The Justice Model for Corrections, 2nd ed.* Cincinnati: Anderson.

French, S. and P. Gendreau. in press. "Reducing Prison Misconducts: What Works!" *Criminal Justice and Behavior*.

Gallagher, R. W., D. P. Somwaru, and Y. S. Ben-Porath. 1999. "Current Usage of Psychological Tests in State Correctional Settings." *Corrections Compendium* 24: 1-3, 20.

Garrett, C. J. 1985. "Effects of Residential Treatment of Adjudicated Delinquents: A Meta-Analysis." *Journal of Research in Crime and Delinquency* 22: 287-308.

Gendreau, P. 1989. "Programs That Do Not Work: A Brief Comment on Brodeur and Doob." *Canadian Journal of Criminology* 31: 133-135.

————. 1996. "The Principles of Effective Intervention with Offenders." Pp. 117-130 in A. T. Harland (ed.), in *Choosing Correctional Interventions That Work: Defining the Demand and Evaluating the Supply*. Newbury Park, CA: Sage.

Gendreau, P., and D. A. Andrews. 1979. "Psychological Consultation in Correctional Agencies: Case Studies and General Issues." Pp. 177-212 in J. J. Platt and R. Wicks (eds.), in *The Psychological Consultant*. New York: Grune and Stratton.

————. 2001. *Correctional Program Assessment Inventory–2000 (CPAI-2000)*. Saint John, Canada: University of New Brunswick.

Gendreau, P., F. T. Cullen, and J. Bonta. 1994. "Intensive Rehabilitation Supervision: The Next Generation in Community Corrections?" *Federal Probation* 58: 72-78.

Gendreau, P., S. A. French, and A. Gionet. 2004. "What Works (What Doesn't Work): The Principles of Effective Correctional Treatment." *Journal of Community Corrections* 13, 4-6, 27-30.

Gendreau, P., C. Goggin, and F. Cullen. 1999. "The Effects of Prison Sentences on Recidivism." *Report to the Corrections Research and Development and Aboriginal Policy Branch (Cat. #J42-87/1999E), Solicitor General of Canada*. Ottawa: Public Works and Government Services Canada.

Gendreau, P., C. Goggin, F. T. Cullen, and D. A. Andrews. 2000. "The Effects of Community Sanctions and Incarceration on Recidivism." *Forum on Corrections Research* 12, 10-13.

Gendreau, P., C. Goggin, F. T. Cullen, and M. Paparozzi. 2002. "The Common Sense Revolution and Correctional Policy." Pp. 359-386 in J. McGuire (ed.), in *Offender Rehabilitation and Treatment: Effective Programmes and Policies to Reduce Reoffending*. Chichester: Wiley.

Gendreau, P., C. Goggin, S. French, and P. Smith. in press. "Practicing Psychology in Correctional Settings." Pp. 722-750 in A. K. Hess and I. B. Weiner (eds.), *The Handbook of Forensic Psychology*, 3rd ed Hoboken, NJ: John Wiley.

Gendreau, P., C. Goggin, and B. Fulton. 2000. "Intensive Probation in Probation and Parole Settings." Pp. 195-204 in C.R. Hollin (ed.), in *Handbook of Offender Assessment and Treatment*. Chichester, UK: Wiley.

Gendreau, P., C. Goggin, and P. Smith. 2000. "Generating Rational Correctional Policies: An Introduction to Advances in Cumulating Knowledge." *Corrections Management Quarterly* 4: 52-60.

————. 2001. "Implementation Guidelines for Correctional Programs in the "Real World." Pp. 247-268 in G. A. Bernfeld, D. P. Farrington, and A. W. Leschied (eds.), in *Offender Rehabilitation in Practice*. Chichester, UK: Wiley.

————. 2002. "Is the PCL-R Really the 'Unparalleled' Measure of Offender Risk? A Lesson in Knowledge Cumulation." *Criminal Justice and Behavior* 29, 397-426.

Gendreau, P., T. Little, and C. Goggin. 1996. "A Meta-Analysis of the Predictors of Adult Offender Recidivism: What Works!" *Criminology* 34: 575-607.

Gendreau, P., and R. R. Ross. 1979. "Effective Correctional Treatment: Bibliotherapy for Cynics." *Crime and Delinquency* 25: 463-489.

————. 1981a. "Correctional Potency: Treatment and Deterrence on Trial." Pp. 29-57 in R. Roesch and R. R. Corrado (eds.), in *Evaluation and Criminal Justice Policy*. Beverly Hills, CA: Sage.

————. 1981b. "Offender Rehabilitation: The Appeal of Success." *Federal Probation* 45: 45-48.

————. 1983-84. "Correctional Treatment: Some Recommendations for Successful Intervention." *Juvenile and Family Court* 34: 31-40.

————. 1987. "Revivification of Rehabilitation: Evidence from the 1980s." *Justice Quarterly* 4: 349-407.

Gendreau, P., P. Smith, and C. Goggin. 2001. "Treatment Programs in Corrections." Pp. 238-263 in J. Winterdyk (ed.), in *Corrections in Canada: Social Reactions to Crime.* Toronto: Prentice Hall.

Gibbs, J. C., G. B. Potter, and A. P. Goldstein. 1995. *The EQUIP Program: Teaching Youth to Think and Act Responsibly Through a Peer-Helping Approach.* Champaign, IL: Research Press.

Glass, G., B. McGaw, and M. L. Smith. 1981. *Meta-Analysis In Social Research.* Beverly Hills, CA: Sage.

Glueck, S., and E. T. Glueck. 1939/1965. *Five Hundred Career Criminals.* New York: Kraus Reprint Corporation.

Goggin, C., and P. Gendreau. in press. "The Implementation and Maintenance of Quality Services in Offender Rehabilitation Programmes." In C. R. Hollin and E. J. Palmer (eds.), *Offending Behavior Programmes: Development, Application, and Controversies.* Chichester, UK: Wiley.

Goldstein, A. 1999. *The Prepare Curriculum: Teaching Prosocial Competencies Revised.* Champaign, IL: Research Press.

Gordon, D. A., K. Graves, and J. Arbuthnot. 1995. "The Effect of Functional Family Therapy for Delinquents on Adult Criminal Behavior." *Criminal Justice and Behavior* 22: 60-73.

Gottfredson, M., and T. Hirschi. 1990. *A General Theory of Crime.* Stanford, CA: Stanford University Press.

Guthrie, E. 1935. *The Psychology of Learning.* Oxford, UK: Harper.

Hanson, R. K., and K. Morton-Bourgon. 2004. *Predictors of Sexual Recidivism: An Updated Meta-Analysis* (Report 2004-02). Ottawa: Public Safety and Emergency Preparedness Canada.

Healey, W. 1915. *The Individual Delinquent: A Textbook of Diagnosis and Prognosis for All Concerned in Understanding Offenders.* Boston: Little, Brown.

Henggeler, S., S. Schoenwald, C. Borduin, M. Rowland, and P. Cunningham. 1998. *Multisystemic Treatment of Antisocial Behavior in Children and Adolescents.* New York: Guilford Press.

Hergenhahn, B. 2001. *An Introduction to the History of Psychology,* 4th ed. Belmont, CA: Wadsworth/Thomson Learning.

Hull, C. 1943. *Principles of Behavior: An Introduction to Behavior Theory.* Oxford, UK: Appleton-Century.

Hunt, M. 1999. *The New Know-Nothings.* New Brunswick, NJ: Transaction.

Izzo, R. L., and R. R. Ross. 1990. "Meta-Analysis of Rehabilitation Programs for Juvenile Delinquents." *Criminal Justice and Behavior* 17: 134-142.

Kanfer, F., and J. Phillips. 1970. *Learning Foundations of Behavioral Therapy.* New York: Wiley.

Kassebaum, G., D. A. Ward, and D. M. Wilner. 1971. *Prison Treatment and Parole Survival: An Empirical Assessment.* New York: Wiley.

Koch, S. 1951. "Theoretical Psychology, 1950: An Overview." *Psychological Review* 58: 295-301.

Latessa, E. J., F. T. Cullen, and P. Gendreau. 2002. "Beyond Correctional Quackery: Professionalism and the Possibility of Effective Treatment." *Federal Probation* 66: 43-49.

Lipsey, M. W. 1992. "Juvenile Delinquency Treatment: A Meta-Analytic Inquiry Into the Variability of Effects." Pp. 83-127 in T. D. Cook, H. Cooper, D. S. Cordray, H. Hartmann, L. V. Hedges, R. J. Light, et al. (eds.), in *Meta-Analysis for Explanation: A Casebook.* New York: Russell Sage.

————. 1999. "Can Rehabilitative Programs Reduce the Recidivism of Juvenile Offenders? An Inquiry Into the Effectiveness of Practical Programs." *Virginia Journal of Social Policy and Law* 6: 611- 641.

Lipsey, M. W., G. L. Chapman, and N. A. Landenberger. 2001. "Cognitive-Behavioral Programs for Offenders." *Annals of the American Academy of Political and Social Science* 578: 144-157.

Lipsey, M. W., and D. B. Wilson. 1993. "The Efficacy of Psychological, Educational and Behavioral Treatment." *American Psychologist* 48: 1181-1209.

Lipton, D., R. Martinson, and J. Wilks. 1975. *The Effectiveness of Correctional Treatment: A Survey of Treatment Evaluation Studies.* New York: Praeger.

Logan, C. H., and G. Gaes. 1993. "Meta-Analysis and the Rehabilitation of Punishment." *Justice Quarterly* 10: 245-263.

Logan, C. H., G. G. Gaes, M. Harer, C. A. Innes, L. Karacki, and W. G. Saylor. 1991. *Can Meta-Analysis Save Correctional Rehabilitation?* Washington, DC: Department of Justice, Federal Bureau of Prisons.

Lösel, F. 1995. "The Efficacy of Correctional Treatment: A Review and Synthesis of Meta-Evaluations." Pp. 79-111 in J. McGuire (ed.), in *What Works: Reducing Reoffending.* Chichester, UK: Wiley.

Lowenkamp, C. T. 2004. *A Program Level Analysis of the Relationship Between Correctional Program Integrity and Treatment Effectiveness.* Unpublished Ph.D. Dissertation, University of Cincinnati.

Lowenkamp, C. T., and E. J. Latessa. 2005. *Evaluation of Ohio's CCA Funded Programs: Final Report.* Cincinnati: Division of Criminal Justice, Center for Criminal Justice Research, University of Cincinnati.

Martinson, R. 1974. "What Works? Questions and Answers About Prison Reform." *The Public Interest* 3: 22-54.

Masters, J., T. Burish, S. Hollon, and D. Rimm. 1987. *Behavior Therapy: Techniques and Empirical Findings,* 3rd ed. New York: Harcourt Brace Jovanovich.

Matson, T. M., and J. L. Di Lorenzo. 1984. *Punishment and Its Alternatives: A New Perspective for Behavior Medication.* New York: Springer.

McGuire, J. 2004. *Understanding Psychology and Crime: Perspectives on Theory and Action.* Maidenhead, UK: University Press.

Meichenbaum, D. 1977. *Cognitive-Behavior Modification: An Integrative Approach.* New York: Plenum.

Menard, S. 1995. "A Developmental Test for Mertonian Anomie Theory." *Journal of Research in Crime and Delinquency* 32: 136-174.

Myers, C. R. 1970. "Journal Citations and Scientific Eminence in Psychology." *American Psychologist* 25: 1041-1048.

Nesovic, A. 2003. "Psychometric Evaluation of the Correctional Program Assessment Inventory." *Dissertation Abstracts International* 64 (09), 4674B. (UMI No. AAT NQ83525).

Palmer, T. 1975. "Martinson Revisited." *Journal of Research in Crime and Delinquency* 12: 133-152.

Paparozzi, M., and P. Gendreau. in press. "An ISP that Worked: Service Delivery, Professional Orientation, and Organizational Supportiveness." *The Prison Journal.*

Piliavin, I., J. Hardyck, and A. Vadum. 1968. "Constraining Effects of Personal Costs on the Transgressions of Juveniles." *Journal of Personality and Social Psychology* 10: 227-231.

Platt, J., and M. Prout. 1987. "Cognitive-Behavioral Theory and Interventions for Crime and Delinquency." Pp. 477-497 in E. Morris (ed.), in *Behavioral Approaches to Crime and Delinquency: A Handbook of Applications, Research, and Concepts.* New York: Plenum.

Quay, H.C. 1977. "The Three Faces of Evaluation: What Can Be Expected to Work." *Criminal Justice and Behavior* 4: 341-354.

Reckless, W. C. 1967. *The Crime Problem.* New York: Appleton-Century-Crofts.

Redondo, S., J. Sanchez-Meca, and V. Garrido. 1999. "The Influence of Treatment Programmes on the Recidivism of Juvenile and Adult Offenders: A European Meta-Analytic Review." *Psychology, Crime and Law* 5: 251-278.

Rosenthal, R. 1991. *Meta-Analytic Procedures for Social Research.* Beverly Hills, CA: Sage.

Rosenthal, R., and M. R. DiMatteo. 2001. "Meta-Analysis: Recent Developments in Quantitative Methods for Literature Reviews." *Annual Review of Psychology* 52: 59-82.

Ross, R. R., and E. A. Fabiano. 1985. *Time to Think: A Cognitive Model of Delinquency Prevention and Offender Rehabilitation.* Johnson City, TN: Institute of Social Science and Arts.

Ross, R. R., and P. Gendreau. 1980. *Effective Correctional Treatment.* Toronto: Butterworths.

Ross, R. R., and B. McKay. 1978. "Treatment in Corrections: Requiem for a Panacea." *Canadian Journal of Criminology* 20: 279-295.

Ruja, H. 1956. "Productive Psychologists." *American Psychologist* 11: 148-149.

Sampson, R. J., and J. H. Laub. 1993. *Crime in the Making: Pathways and Turning Points Through Life.* Cambridge, MA: Harvard University Press.

Sechrest, L., S. White, and E. D. Brown. 1979. *The Rehabilitation of Criminal Offenders: Problems and Prospects.* Washington, DC: National Academy of Sciences.

Skinner, B. F. 1950. "Are Theories of Learning Necessary?" *Psychological Review* 57: 193-216.

Smith, P., C. Goggin, and P. Gendreau. 2002. "The Effects of Prison Sentences and Intermediate Sanctions on Recidivism: General Effects and Individual Differences." *A Report to the Corrections Research Branch.* Ottawa: Solicitor General of Canada.

Smith, R., L. Hart, B. Pennington, W. Sanford, and M. Milan. 1972. *An Introduction to Behavior Modification Principles.* Institute, WV: West Virginia Graduate College.

Spence, K. 1956. *Behavior Theory and Conditioning.* New Haven, CT: Yale University Press.

Stojkovic, S., J. Klofus, and D. Kalinich. 2002. *Criminal Justice Organizations: Administration and Management,* 3rd ed. Belmont, CA: Wadsworth.

Stumphauzer, J. 1986. *Helping Delinquents Change: A Treatment Manual of Social Learning Approaches.* New York: Haworth Press.

Sutherland, E. 1939. *Principles of Criminology,* 3rd ed. New York: Macmillan.

Sykes, G., and D. Matza. 1957. "Techniques of Neutralization: A Theory of Delinquency." *American Sociological Review* 22: 330-338.

Task Force on Corrections, President's Commission on Law Enforcement and Administration of Justice. 1967. *Task Force Report: Corrections.* Washington, DC: U.S. Government Printing Office.

Tolman, E. C. 1932. *Purposive Behavior in Animals and Men.* Oxford, UK: Appleton-Century.

———. 1959. "Principles of Purposive Behavior." Pp. 92-57 in S. Koch (ed.), *Psychology: A Study of a Science.* New York: McGraw-Hill.

Travisono, A. P., and A. F. Hawkes. 1995. *Building a Voice: 125 Years of History.* Washington, DC: American Correctional Association.

Walker, S. 1985. *Sense and Nonsense About Crime: A Policy Guide.* Monterey, CA: Brooks/Cole.

Warren, M. Q. 1969. "The Case for Differential Treatment of Delinquents." *Annals of the American Academy of Political and Social Science* 62: 239-258.

Welsh, B. C., and D. P. Farrington. 2000. "Correctional Intervention Programs and Cost-Benefit Analysis." *Criminal Justice and Behavior* 27: 115-133.

Wilks, J., and R. Martinson. 1976. "Is the Treatment of Criminal Offenders Really Necessary?" *Federal Probation* 40: 3-8.

Wormith, J. S. 1984. "Attitude and Behavior Change of Correctional Clientele: A Three Year Follow-Up." *Criminology* 22: 595-618.

Wright, W. F., and M. C. Dixon. 1977. "Community Prevention and Treatment of Juvenile Delinquency." *Journal of Research in Crime and Delinquency* 14: 35-67.

Contributors

Robert Agnew is Professor of Sociology at Emory University.

Eliza Ahmed is a Research Fellow in the Regulatory Institutions Network (RegNet) at the Australian National University.

Ronald L. Akers is Professor of Criminology and Sociology at the University of Florida.

Kristie R. Blevins is Assistant Professor of Criminal Justice at the University of North Carolina at Charlotte.

John Braithwaite is an Australian Research Council Federation Fellow in the Regulatory Institutions Network (RegNet) at the Australian National University.

Valerie Braithwaite is a Senior Fellow in the Regulatory in the Regulatory Institutions Network (RegNet) at the Australian National University.

Christopher R. Browning is Assistant Professor of Sociology at Ohio State University.

Francis T. Cullen is Distinguished Research Professor of Criminal Justice and Sociology at the University of Cincinnati.

Leah E. Daigle is Assistant Professor of Justice Studies at Georgia Southern University.

David P. Farrington is Professor of Psychological Criminology at Cambridge University.

Sheila A. French is a Research Associate at the Centre for Criminal Justice Studies at the University of New Brunswick at Saint John.

John Randolph Fuller is Professor of Criminology at the University of West Georgia.

Paul Gendreau is University Research Professor of Psychology and Director of the Centre for Criminal Justice Studies at the University of New Brunswick at Saint John.

Michael R. Gottfredson is Professor of Criminology, Law, and Society and of Sociology and is Executive Vice Chancellor at the University of California, Irvine.

Gary F. Jensen is Professor of Sociology and Religious Studies and Chair of the Department of Sociology at Vanderbilt University.

Lauren J. Krivo is Professor of Sociology at Ohio State University.

John H. Laub is Professor of Criminology and Criminal Justice at the University of Maryland.

Michael J. Lynch is Professor of Criminology at the University of South Florida.

Tamara D. Madensen is Assistant Professor of Criminal Justice at the University of Nevada, Las Vegas.

Steven F. Messner is Distinguished Teaching Professor of Sociology at the University at Albany, State University of New York.

Jody Miller is Associate Professor of Criminology and Criminal Justice at the University of Missouri-St. Louis.

Terrie E. Moffitt is Professor of Psychology at the University of Wisconsin Madison, and Professor of Social Behavior and Development at the Institute of Psychiatry, King's College London.

Christopher W. Mullins is Assistant Professor of Sociology and Criminology at the University of Northern Iowa.

Ruth D. Peterson is Distinguished Professor of Social and Behavioral Sciences and Director of the Criminal Justice Research Center at The Ohio State University.

Travis C. Pratt is Associate Professor of Criminal Justice at Washington State University.

Richard Rosenfeld is Professor of Criminology and Criminal Justice at the University of Missouri-St. Louis.

Robert J. Sampson is Henry Ford II Professor of Social Sciences and Chair of the Department of Sociology at Harvard University.

Herman Schwendinger is Visiting Professor of Criminology at the University of South Florida.

Julia Schwendinger is Visiting Professor of Criminology at the University of South Florida.

Paula Smith is Assistant Professor of Criminal Justice at the University of Cincinnati.

Gary A. Sweeten is Assistant Professor of Criminal Justice and Criminology at Arizona State University West.

John F. Wozniak is Professor of Sociology and Chair of the Department of Sociology and Anthropology at Western Illinois University.

John Paul Wright is Associate Professor of Criminal Justice at the University of Cincinnati.

Index

Printed in the United States
210540BV00005B/13-27/P

9 781412 808569